*Family Guides*

# MAUI

## AND LANA'I

*Making the Most of Your Family Vacation*

*by Greg & Christie Stilson*

*Special thanks to*
*Dona Early, contributing editor*

PRIMA PUBLISHING

In affiliation with Paradise Pub

**MAUI and Lana'i, A Paradise Family Guide**
Copyright © 1995 Paradise Publications, Portland, Oregon

First Edition: Dec 1984       Fourth Edition: May 1990
Second Edition: May 1986    Fifth Edition:  Oct 1992
Third Edition: May 1988      Sixth Edition:  Nov 1994

Published By Prima Publishing, Rocklin, California

Library of Congress Cataloging-in-Publication Data

Stilson, Greg H.
    Maui and Lana'i, making the most of your family vacation / Greg Stilson & Christie Stilson. -- 6th ed.
        p.   cm.
    Includes bibliographical references and index.
    ISBN 1-55958-563-3  :
    1. Maui (Hawai'i)--Guidebooks.  2. Lana'i City (Hawai'i)--Guidebooks.
    I. Stilson, Christie. II. Title.
    DU628.M3S76   1994
    919.69'2044--dc20                                    94-3640
                                                          CIP

96  97  AA  10  9  8  7  6  5  4  3  2
Printed in the United States of America

**WARNING-DISCLAIMER**

Prima Publishing in affiliation with Paradise Publications has designed this book to provide information in regard to the subject matter covered. It is sold with the understanding that the publishers and authors are not liable for the misconception or misuse of information provided. Every effort has been made to make this book as complete and as accurate as possible. The purpose of this book is to educate. The author, Prima Publishing and Paradise Publications shall have neither liability nor responsibility to any person or entity with respect to any loss, damage, or injury caused or alleged to be caused directly or indirectly by the information contained in this book. They shall also not be liable for price changes, or for the completeness or accuracy of the contents of this book.

**HOW TO ORDER**

Quantity discounts are available from the publisher, Prima Publishing, PO Box ⬛BK, Rocklin, CA  95677; telephone (916) 632-4400. On your letterhead ⬛information concerning the intended use of the books and the number of ⬛wish to purchase.

# "Maui No Ka Oi"

## (Maui is the Best)

*Dedicated to Maren and Jeffrey, two terrific travelers.*

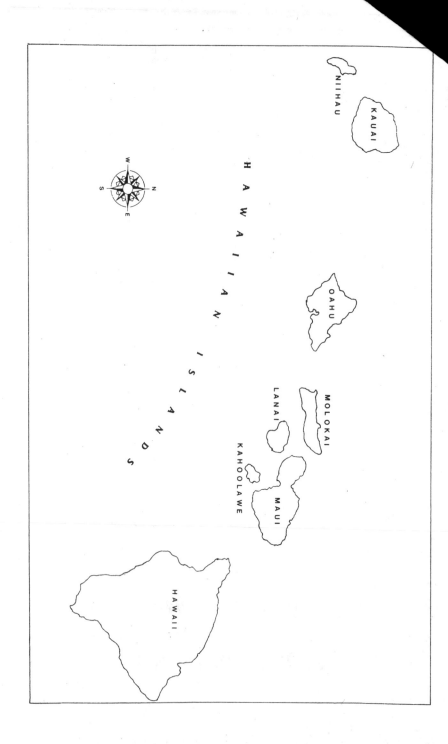

# TABLE OF CONTENTS

# V. BEACHES AND BEACH ACTIVITIES

# VI. RECREATION AND TOURS

## OCEAN ACTIVITIES

## LAND ACTIVITIES

## AIR TOURS

# VII. THE ISLAND OF LANA'I

# VIII. RECOMMENDED READING

# IX. INDEX

# X. READER RESPONSE - ORDERING INFORMATION

HIBISCUS & PALM

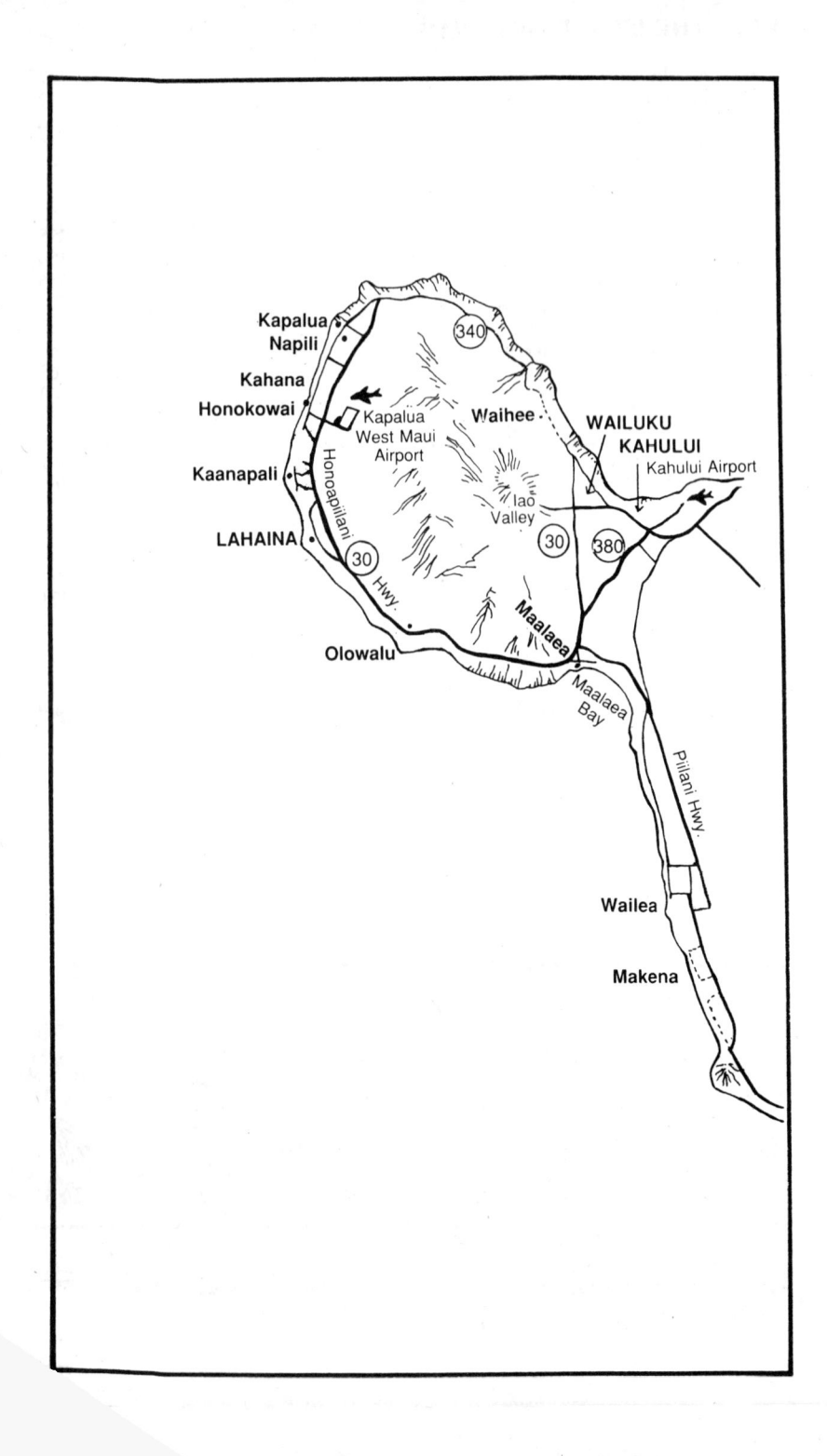

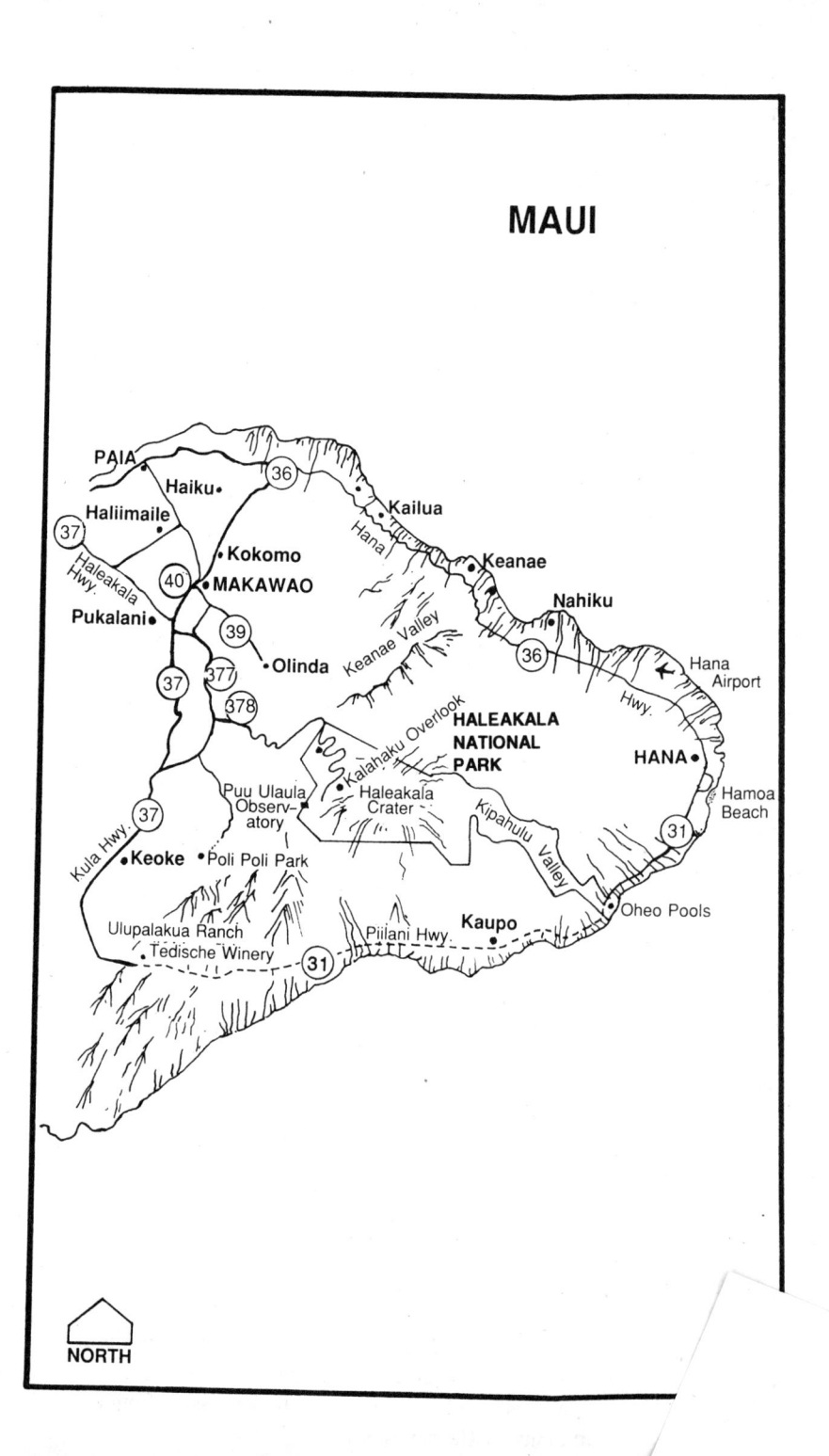

## E'Ike Mai

*I luna la, i luna*
*Na manu o ka lewa*

*I lalo la, i lalo*
*Na pua o ka honua*

*I uka la, i uka*
*Na ulu la 'au*

*I kai la, i kai*
*Na i'a o ka moana*

*Ha'ina mai ka puana*
*A he nani ke ao ne*


## Behold

Above, above
all birds in air

below, below
all earth's flowers

inland, inland
all forest trees

seaward, seaward
all ocean fish

sing out and say
again the refrain

Behold this lovely world

Excerpt from *The Echo of Our Song, Chants & Poems of the Hawaiians*. Translated and Edited by Mary K. Pukui and Alfons L. Korn. Reprinted with permission from the University of Hawaii Press.

# INTRODUCTION

Congratulations on choosing Maui as the site of your vacation. You will soon see why it has the deserved slogan, *Maui No Ka Oi* (Maui is the Best). The sun and lush tropicalness, and some of the finest accommodations, blend sublimely together to create a perfect holiday paradise - a place both magical and beautiful.

While this guide is dubbed a *Family Travel Guide* -- it is aimed for any kind of family, from a single traveler to a family reunion. It is for you the traveler who wished to be in control of his vacation plans. The perspective of this guide is that of the visitor. We continue to travel frequently to the island to update our information, discover new things, rediscover old things and to thoroughly enjoy the tropical energy and seductive charm of Maui. While first-time visitors will delight in the diversity of activities that Maui has to offer, those making a return visit can enjoy discovering new sights and adventures on this magnificent island.

The chapters on accommodations and sights, restaurants, and beaches are conveniently divided into areas with similar characteristics and indexes are provided for each chapter. This allows a better feel for, and access to, the information on the area in which you are staying, and greater confidence in exploring other areas. Remember that except for Hana, most of the areas are only a short drive and worth a day of sightseeing, beach exploring, or a meal at a fine restaurant.

Maui can be relatively inexpensive, or extravagantly expensive, depending on your preference in lodgings, activities, and eating arrangements. Therefore, we have endeavored to give complete and detailed information covering the full range of budgets. The opinions expressed are based on our personal experiences, and while the positive is emphasized, it is your right to know, in certain cases, our bad experiences. To aid in your selections, a **BEST BET** summary is included at the beginning of the General Information Chapter. Also refer to individual chapters for additional best bets and check for ★'s which identify one of our special recommendations.

Our guide is as accurate as possible at the time of publication, however, changes seem extremely rapid for an island operating on "Maui Time." Ownerships, managements, names, and menus do change frequently, as do prices. For the latest information on the island, Paradise Publications has available *THE MAUI UPDATE*, a quarterly newsletter. We invite you to receive a complimentary issue or to order a yearly subscription; see ORDERING INFORMATION at the back of this guide.

If your itinerary includes visits to the other islands, the Paradise Family Guide Series includes *Kaua'i, A Paradise Family Guide* by Dona Early and *Hawai'i: The Big Island, A Paradise Family Guide* by John Penisten. These essential travel accessories not only contain information on all the condos, hotels, restaurants, along with specific recreational activity information, but als᠎ ᠎side information that most visitors never receive, shared by an author who l loves the islands. Each of these titles also feature update newsletter DERING INFORMATION.

As this guide features pen and ink sketches, a couple of recommendations for picture books might be helpful. An inexpensive, 48-page, full-color photographic book *Maui The Romantic Island*, highlights the most memorable sights and gives you a good feel for the island. It is available through Paradise Publications; see ORDERING INFORMATION. A magnificent coffee table size publication, *Maui, On My Mind*, by Rita Ariyoshi contains outstanding photographs that depict the island at its best. The book is available at local island gift and book stores and at mainland travel bookstores.

We are confident that as you explore these islands, you too will be charmed by their magic. Keep in mind the expressive words used by Mark Twain nearly 100 years ago when he visited and fell in love with Hawaii.

> *"No alien land in all the world has any deep strong charm for me but that one, no other land could so longingly and so beseechingly haunt me, sleeping and waking, through half a lifetime, as that one has done. Other things leave me, but it abides; other things change, but it remains the same. For me its balmy airs are always blowing, its summer seas flashing in the sun; the pulsing of its surfbeat is in my ear; I can see its garlanded crags, its leaping cascades, its plumy palms drowsing by the shore, its remote summits floating like islands above the cloud wrack; I can feel the spirit of its woodland solitudes, I can hear the splash of its brooks; in my nostrils still lives the breath of flowers..."*

Although the islands have changed greatly during the century since his visits, there remains much to fall in love with. The physical beauty and seductiveness of the land remains despite what may seem rampant commercialism, and the true aloha spirit does survive.

A special mahalo to Deborah Tullis, Sally Haimo, Francine Abolofia, Jean Merrick, Lacey Fischborn, Laura Ziemer and John Stenersen for their assistance with editing, proof-reading, and their patience with the many sundry tasks which are required to put the pieces of a book together. Their support and encouragement with the preparation of this edition has been invaluable. My thanks also to all of you who have written sharing your trip experiences. (Yes! I read them all.) It is a delight to be invited to share your trip through your letters. Lastly, to Dona Early who has more stamina, energy, enthusiasm, perserverance, patience than anyone else I know! She's not only a great assistant editor, but a wonderful friend.

Aloha and happy travels to you!

*Christie*

Christie

# GENERAL INFORMATION

## *OUR PERSONAL BESTS*

BEST FOOD SPLURGE: Champagne Sunday brunch at the Prince Court (Maui Prince Resort in Makena), Sunday brunch at the Grand Dining Room of the Grand Wailea Resort & Spa, champagne Sunday brunch at Raffles' (Stouffer Wailea Beach Resort), or champagne Sunday brunch at the Sound of the Falls (Westin Maui at Kaanapali). A fabulous dinner at the Lodge at Koele on the island of Lana'i or a sumptuous seafood buffet at the Garden Restaurant at Kapalua. Dinner at the Grand Wailea's Grand Dining Room or Prince Court at the Maui Prince Resort in Makena.

BEST SUNSET AND COCKTAILS: West Maui - Kapalua Bay Lounge; South Maui - Maui Prince Resort, Molokini Lounge.

BEST SUNSET DINING VIEW: The Plantation House Restaurant at Kapalua.

BEST DINING VIEW: The Seawatch restaurant in Wailea.

BEST DAILY BREAKFAST BUFFET: Swan Court at the Hyatt Regency.

BEST LUAU VALUE: Check the Maui newspaper for advertisements listing local luaus that might be held by churches or other organizations as fund raisers. A great value and you're sure to enjoy some great food!

MOST UNUSUAL BREAKFAST BUFFET: Auntie Aloha's Breakfast Luau, at the Kaanapali Beach Hotel, is a Hawaiian buffet with eye-opening Mai Tais (at 8 am!) and entertainment for $9.95 offered Monday thru Thursday. It is a promotional and informational buffet where they also discuss activities.

BEST SALAD BAR: It is tough to find a salad bar on Maui! The Embass has a good quality one that is very basic. More interesting sele at the Royal Ocean Terrace at Kaanapali or Sunsets in Kihei

BEST SALADS: Gado Gado and Chinese Chicken Salad at Avalon restaurant in Lahaina. If you're in Mill Valley, California, check out the new Avalon restaurant!

MOST UNUSUAL SALAD: A Tiki Style salad is a signature dish at Avalon's and consists of a layered salad of mashed potatoes, eggplant, salmon, greens, mango and tomato salsa with a plum vinaigrette.

BEST AMBIANCE: Gerard's restaurant in Lahaina.

BEST DINNER VALUES: Early bird specials are offered at a number of island restaurants. There are generally more specials offered during the summer months and the price may also reflect the time of year. Some of the better early bird offerings are at the Marriott's Moana Terrace at Kaanapali and Kihei Prime Rib or Chuck's in Kihei. The Kaanapali Beach Koffee Shop has an Early Bird Prime Rib Buffet for $9.95. Also check in some of the brochures and booklets around town for dinner specials.

BEST FAMILY DINING VALUES: Koho Bar and Grill in Kahului is a good stop with plenty of selections on the menu. The Kaanapali Beach Koffee Shop is one of the best values on Kaanapali Beach. The new Peggy Sue's in Kihei has a fun, splashy atmosphere. We recommend reading the chapter on dining in Wailuku to get the most for your vacation restaurant dollar and experience some wonderful ethnic meals.

BEST FAMILY DINING EXPERIENCE, COST IS NO OBJECT: The older youth will probably insist on a trip to one of the "cool" restaurants, such as Hard Rock Cafe, Cheeseburger in Paradise or the recently opened Planet Hollywood.

BEST PIZZA: Shaka Sandwich and Pizza in Kihei. (Readers have frequently mentioned that Pizza Hut in Lahaina is great! We'll take their word for it!)

MOST LAVISH RESTAURANT ATMOSPHERE: The Sound of the Falls at the Westin and The Grand Dining Room at the Grand Wailea Resort and Spa.

MOST OUTRAGEOUS DESSERTS: The Lahaina Provision Company's Choco-holic Bar at the Hyatt Regency Maui and the artistic mastery served in dessert form at the Grand Wailea's Grand Dining Room. The Ritz-Carlton Kapalua does an excellent job on dessert fare as well.

BEST SEAFOOD RESTAURANTS: Maalaea Waterfront Restaurant, in Maalaea or Mama's Fish House in Paia. While it isn't a strictly seafood restaurant, some of the best fresh island fish we've enjoyed has been at Gerard's restaurant in Lahaina.

BEST TAKE-HOME FOOD PRODUCTS: Take Home Maui, Inc. at 121 Dickenson St., Lahaina. Ship it home or enjoy it here.

ALOHA WEAR: The traditional tourist garb is available in greatest supply at the 17,000 square foot Hilo Hattie's factory in the Lahaina Center at the Kaanapali end of Lahaina.

BEST SHOPPING: Affordable and fun - Kahului Swap Meet each Saturday, and one in Kihei too!; Touristy -Lahaina waterfront; Practical - Kaahumanu Shopping Center in Kahului; Extravagant - Any of the gift shops at the fine resorts on Maui; Odds 'n Ends - Long's Drug Store, Kahului, Lahaina and Kihei. K-mart or Woolworth's in Kahului. For the adventurous there is a Salvation Army in Kahului and Lahaina.

MOST SPECTACULAR RESORT GROUNDS: Hyatt Regency at Kaanapali and the Grand Wailea Resort & Spa in Wailea. The Westin Maui is a close second.

BEST EXCURSIONS: Most spectacular - a helicopter tour.
Most unusual - a bike trip down Haleakala or around Upcountry.
Best adventure on foot - a personalized hike with guide Ken Schmitt.
Best sailing - a day-long snorkel and picnic to Lana'i with the congenial crew of the Trilogy.

BEST BEACHES: Beautiful and safe - Kapalua Bay and Ulua Beach. Unspoiled - Oneloa (Makena) and Mokuleia (Slaughterhouse) Beaches. For kids - try Puunoa Beach near Lahaina.

BEST RECREATION AND TOURS: See beginning of Recreation & Tours chapter for ideas!

BEST MAUI GET AWAY FROM IT ALL RESORT: Hotel Hana Maui in Hana, Maui, and the Lodge at Koele or Manele Bay Resort on Lana'i.

BEST ACCOMMODATIONS DISCOUNT: Entertainment book coupon discounts continue to offer half price at several Maui hotels and condominiums. The *Entertainment book* is printed in most major cities around the country and contains coupons for dining and activities in that area. In addition, they carry discounts for accommodations in other regions of the U.S., including Hawai'i. The books are published and sold only once a year and are usually sold by non-profit organizations as fund-raisers. Check your phone book under Entertainment, Inc. There is also a Hawai'i edition which carries coupons for dining and attractions, largely for O'ahu, but the outer islands are included as well. For information contact *Entertainment Publications* at their Honolulu office at (808) 737-3252 or write them at 4211 Waialae Ave., Honolulu, HI 96816. There is a fee for these books (about $40.)

The current edition for our state (Oregon) lists several Aston properties and a few other condominiums around the island at 50% off the standard rate. Properties listed currently include Aston Kaanapali Shores, Aston Kamaole Sands, Aston Maui Kaanapali Villas, Aston Maui Park, Colony's Napili Shores, Embassy Suites Resort, Kahana Beach Condominium, Kahana Villa Maui, Kea Lani Hotel & Suites, Mahana at Kaanapali, Maui Beach Hotel, Maui Coast Hotel, Maui Eldorado Resort, Maui Hill, Maui Lu, Maui Marriott, Maui Palms, Maui Sunset, Maui Vista, Papakea Resort, Royal Lahaina Resort, Maui Hill and Paki Maui.

Restrictions are plenty, with limited times for availability and allowable only on certain categories of rooms. For example, the Aston properties are only valid January 3-31, April 1-June 30 and September 1-December 22. Others are less restrictive, disallowing only a few key weeks a year. They only offer a few rooms at these discounts, so make your travel plans well in advance to take advantage of this vacation bargain! On Maui they can be purchased through the American Lung Association or Lahaina Business and Professional Women's Association. A portion of the proceeds goes to benefit these organizations.

BEST BODY SURFING: Slaughterhouse in winter (only for experienced and strong swimmers).

BEST SURFING: Honolua Bay in winter (for experienced surfers).

BEST SNORKELING: North end - Honolua Bay in summer. Kapalua area - Kapalua Bay and Namalu Bay. Kaanapali - Black Rock at the Sheraton. Olowalu at Mile Marker 14. Wailea - Ulua Beach. Makena - Ahihi Kinau Natural Reserve. Island of Lana'i - Hulopoe Beach Park. And Molokini Crater.

BEST WINDSURFING: Hookipa Beach Park (for experienced windsurfers).

MOST UNUSUAL VISUAL ADVENTURE: The Omni-Experience Theater in Lahaina.

**BEST NIGHT SPOTS:** Lively evenings are available at the Tsunami lounge at the Grand Wailea Resort & Spa and the Blue Tropix in Lahaina. More nightlife information is listed at the conclusion of the restaurant chapter.

**BEST FLOWERS:** For best flower values visit the Kahului Swap Meet (for making your own arrangements). Leis are sometimes available here also. Check Ooka's grocery in Wailuku for fresh flowers and leis. The last Thursday of each month leis are available in front of the Baldwin Home in Lahaina from AARP. Safeway in Lahaina also has a fair selection.

**UNUSUAL GIFT IDEAS:** For the green thumb, be sure to try Dan's Green House on Prison Street in Lahaina for a Fuku-Bonsai planted on a lava rock. They are specially sprayed and sealed for either shipping or carrying home. Waikiki Aloe of Maui is located at the Lahaina Cannery Mall had has some all-island products. Homegrown Island Art at 395-A Dairy Road in Kahului (877-0399) has an interesting selection of handcrafted items. You can also order from their catalog. Maui Crafts Guild at 43 Hana Highway in Paia (579-9697) has some unusual hand-crafted, albeit expensive, gifts. Antique maps and prints make an unusual and prized gift for yourself or a family member or friend. Visit one of the Lahaina Printsellers galleries, located at the Grand Wailea, Whalers Village, Cannery Shopping Center. Chocolate Chips of Maui, "the ultimate munchie," is a combination of rich dark chocolate or milk chocolate and the original "Kitchen Cook'd" Maui potato chip. Try them frozen or use them as a scoop for ice cream (Check at Long's Drugs).

**BEST T-SHIRTS:** Our favorites are Crazy Shirts, more expensive than the run of the mill variety, but excellent quality and great designs. There is a Crazy Shirt outlet at most malls and several in Lahaina. A huge selection of inexpensive shirts are available at the T-Shirt Factory near the Kahului Airport. Sizes range from infants to XL adults and, with plenty to choose from, it is easy to mix and match styles and sizes. Also check the Kihei Swap Meet and the Kahului Swap Meet.

**BEST FREE STUFF:** *Around the island* - Free snorkeling, scuba and windsurfing instruction clinic at Ocean Activities Center at Stouffers (879-9969). Free introductory scuba instruction offered poolside at many of the major resorts. A self-guided tour of the Grand Wailea, Hyatt Regency Maui or Westin Maui Resorts. Public beaches with their free parking. Lahaina Divers has a free map of some of the most popular beach diving and snorkeling sights on Maui. It advises divers as to the special features and facilities of each beach and the suitability for diving or snorkeling. And the best news is the map is free! Stop by the new headquarters of Lahaina Divers at 143 Dickenson St. in Lahaina, or contact them at 1-800-998-3483. Maui Dive Shop in Kihei, Lahaina and Kahului offers a free snorkel guide. Also see Annual Events for more *free* activities!

*Lahaina-Kaanapali* - Friday night is "art night" in Lahaina. Stroll through the many varied Lahaina Galleries when they offer special attractions, such as an opportunity to meet the artists!

Visit Pioneer Inn now an official U.S. historic landmark. Canoe races held at Honokaoo Park. Halloween Parade in Lahaina. One of several free shuttle buses that travel between Lahaina, the Cannery and Whalers Village shops. Free admission to Wo Hing Temple in Lahaina. There are a number of free Hawaiian shows and musical entertainment around Maui. The times and days change, so please check. The Hula show at the Kapalua Shops (669-1029), currently Thursday mornings, is complimentary as is the one at Whalers Village (661-4567) performed by the Royal Lahaina Resort luau performers (currently on Tuesdays at 3 p.m., Saturdays at 12:30 p.m. and includes free poi sampling!) The Lahaina Center has hula shows Wednesday and Friday 2 pm (667-9216). Lahaina's keiki (children ages 5 - 16) perform the hula on Sundays at 1 p.m. at the Lahaina Cannery Mall (661-5304). Free Hula Show at the Kaanapali Beach Hotel, nightly at 6 pm. The Kaanapali Beach Hotel also offers complimentary Hawaiian quilting demonstrations on Mondays from 1-3 pm. Fourth of July festivities at Kaanapali Beach. Whale presentations with naturalist Phil Secretario are presented seasonally (whale season, of course!) at the Kaanapali Beach Hotel. For information call 661-0011 ext. 7145. The Whalers Village Whaling Museum at Kaanapali is free to the public. In Lahaina at the Crazy Shirts shop located on the Kaanapali end of town is a interesting display of Whaling memorabilia and a big cannon sits out behind the shop. Inside the Hobie Sports store at the Cannery shopping center is a great display of old surfing long boards. Free tour of the artwork at the Westin Maui. South Pacific Kayaks at 505 Front St. has free 4 hour bike rentals.

*Kihei-Wailea-Makena* - Sand Castle Contest in Kihei (November). Wailea Shopping Village (879-4474) features Hawaiian entertainment at no charge each Tuesday at 1:30 pm. Phone 871-6230. A string trio entertains evenings in the courtyard at the Maui Prince Resort. Free guided tour, twice weekly, of the artwork at the Grand Wailea.

*Wailuku-Waikapu-Kahului* - Visit the Iao Needle located near Wailuku. Watch windsurfing at Ho'okipa Beach on Maui's windward shore. The Maui Zoo in Wailuku. Ooka's Market in Wailuku is worth a visit just to see the many varied island foods available, from breadfruit to flying fish eggs! The Maui Tropical Plantation offers free admission to their marketplace, a charge to tour their grounds.

*Upcountry* - No charge to visit Hui No'eau Visual Arts Center in Makawao; special events may require a fee (572-6560). Visit Hot Island Glass Studio in Makawao to see glass blowing and tour their art shops. The Makawao Parade held Fourth of July weekend. Free Square Dancing in Upcountry at the Upcountry Community Center every Tuesday at 7:30 pm. Call 572-1721 for more information. Free admission to Sunrise Protea. Free tour and sampling at Tedeschi Winery.

BEST GIFT FOR FRIENDS TRAVELING TO MAUI: A copy of *MAUI, A PARADISE FAMILY GUIDE* and a subscription to the quarterly *MAUI UPDATE* newsletter!

# *HISTORY*

Far beneath the warm waters of the Pacific Ocean is the Pacific Plate, which moves constantly in a northwest direction. Each Hawaiian island was formed as it passed over a hot vent in this plate. Kaua'i, the oldest of the major islands in the Hawai'i chain was formed first and has since moved away from the plume, the source of the lava, and is no longer growing. Some of the older islands even farther to the northwest have been gradually reduced to sandbars and atolls. The Big Island is the youngest in the chain and is continuing to grow. A new island called Lo'ihi (which means "prolonged in time"), southeast of the Big Island is growing and expected to emerge from the oceanic depths in about a million years.

It was explosions of hot lava from two volcanos that created the island of Maui. Mauna Kahalawai (Ma-ow-na Ka-HA-la-why) is the oldest, creating the westerly section with the highest point (elevation 5,788 ft.) known as Pu'u Kukui (Poo'oo koo-KOO-ee). The great Haleakala (HAH-leh-AH-kuh-LAH), now the world's largest dormant volcano, created the southeastern portion of the island. (The last eruption on Maui took place about 1789 and flowed over to the Makena area.) A valley connects these two volcanic peaks, hence the source of Maui's nickname, "The Valley Isle."

The first Hawaiians came from the Marquesa and Society Islands in the central Pacific. (Findings suggest that their ancestors came from the western Pacific, perhaps as far as Madagascar.) The Polynesians left the Marquesas about the 8th century and were followed by natives from the Society Islands sometime between the 11th and 14th centuries. The Hawaiian population may well have been as high as 300,000 by the 1700's, spread throughout the chain of islands. Fish and poi were diet basics, supplemented by various fruits and occasionally meat from chickens, pigs and even dogs.

Four principal gods formed the basis of their religion until the missionaries arrived. The stone foundations of Heiaus, the ancient religious temples, can still be visited on Maui.

The islands were left undisturbed by western influence until the 1778 arrival of James Cook. He first spotted and visited Kaua'i and O'ahu and is believed to have arrived at Maui on November 25 or 26, 1778. He was later killed in a brawl on the Big Island of Hawai'i.

The major islands had a history of independent rule, with open warfare at times. On Maui, Kahului and Hana were both sites of combat between the Maui islanders and the warriors from neighboring islands.

Kamehameha the First was born on the Big Island of Hawai'i about 1758. He was the nephew of Kalaiopi, who ruled the Big Island. Following the King's death, Kalaiopi's son came to power, only to be subsequently defeated by Kamehameha in 1794. The great chieftain Kahekili was Kamehameha's greatest rival. He ruled not only Maui, but Lana'i and Moloka'i, and also had kinship with the governing

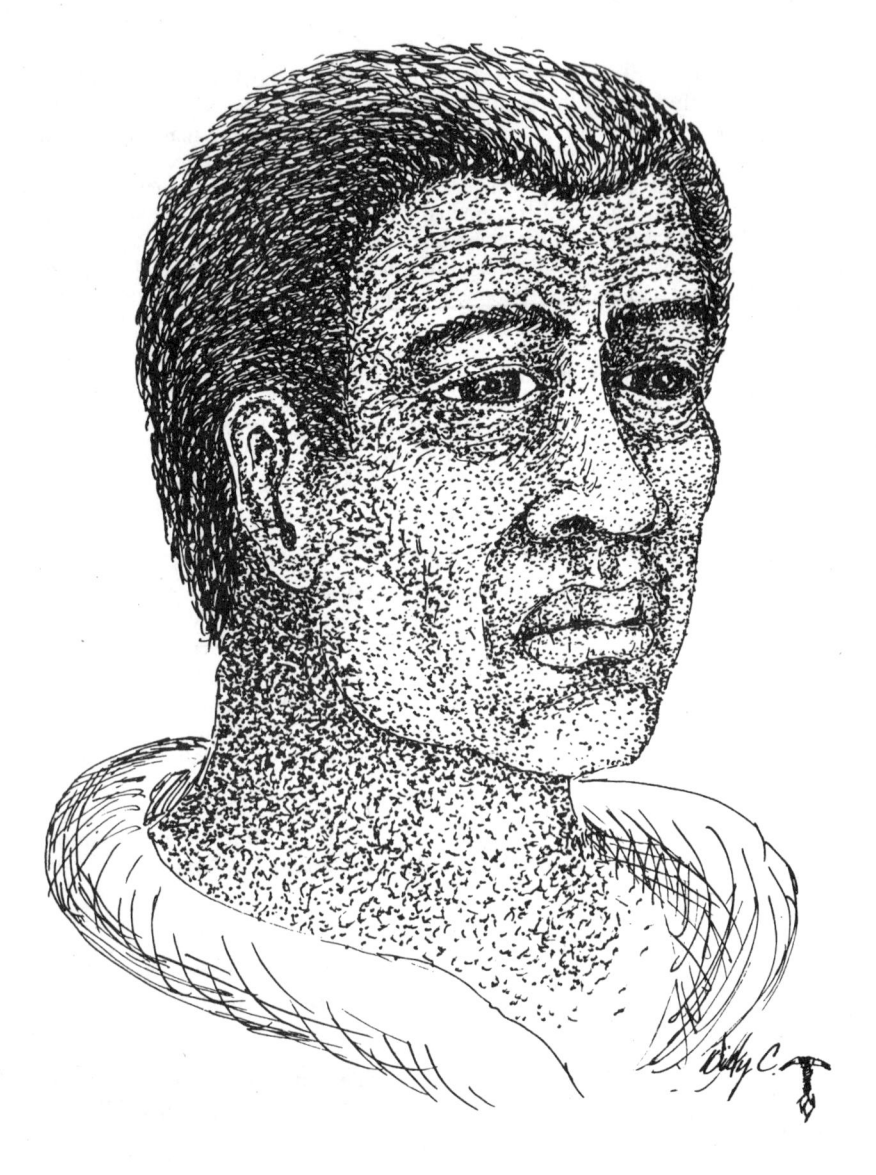

King Kamehameha the First

royalty of Oʻahu and Kauaʻi. King Kahekili died in 1794 leaving control of the island to his son. A bloody battle (more like a massacre since Kamehameha used western technology, strategy, and two English advisors) in the Iao Valley resulted in the defeat of Kahekili's son, Kalanikupule, in 1795. Kamehameha united all the islands and made Lahaina the capital of Hawaiʻi in 1802. It remained the capital until the 1840's when Honolulu became the center for government affairs. Lahaina was a popular resort for Hawaiian royalty who favored the beaches in the area. Kaahumanu, the favorite wife of Kamehameha was born in Hana, Maui, and spent much of her time there. (Quiet Hana was another popular spot for vacationing royalty.)

Liholiho, the heir of Kamehameha the Great, ruled as Kamehameha II from 1819 to 1824. Liholiho was not a strong ruler so Kaahumanu proclaimed herself prime minister during his reign. She ended many of the kapus of the old religion, thus creating a fortuitous vacuum which the soon to arrive missionaries would fill. These New England missionaries and their families arrived in Lahaina in the spring of 1823 at the invitation of Queen Keopuolani. They brought drastic changes to the island with the education of the natives both spiritually and scholastically. The first high school and printing press west of the Rockies was established at Lahainaluna. Built just outside of Lahaina, it now houses a museum, and is open to the public. Liholiho and his wife were the first Hawaiian royalty to visit the United States. When their travels continued to Europe, they succumbed to the measles while in London. Liholiho was succeeded by Kauikeaouli (the youngest son of Kamehameha the Great), who ruled under the title of Kamehameha the III from 1824 to 1854.

Beginning in 1819 and continuing for nearly 40 years, whaling ships became a frequent sight, anchored in the waters off Lahaina. The whalers hunted their prey north and south of the islands, off the Japanese coast and in the Arctic. Fifty ships were sometimes anchored off Lahaina, and during the peak year of whaling, over 400 ships visited Lahaina with an additional 167 in Honolulu's harbor. Allowing 25 to 30 seamen per ship you can quickly see the enormous number of sailors who flooded the area.

While missionaries brought their Christian beliefs, the whaling men lived under their own belief that there was "No God West of the Horn." This presented a tremendous conflict between the sailors and missionaries, with the islanders caught right in the middle. After months at sea, sailors arrived in Lahaina anxious for the grog shops and native women. It was the missionaries who put the island girls set up guidelines that forbid the native women to visit the ships in the harbor. Also horrified by the bare-breasted Hawaiian women, the missionary women quickly set about to more thoroughly clothe the native ladies. The missionary women realized that their dresses would not be appropriate for these more robust woman and using their nightwear as a guideline, fashioned garments from these by cutting the sleeves off and enlarging the armholes. The muumuu was the result, and translated means "to amputate or to cut short."

In 1832, a coral fort was erected near the Lahaina harbor following an incident with the unhappy crew of one vessel. The story goes that a captain, disgruntled when he was detained in Lahaina for enticing "base women," ordered his crew to fire shots at the homes of some Lahaina area missionaries. Although the fort was

demolished in 1854, remnants of the coral were re-excavated and a corner of the old fort reconstructed. It is located harborside by the Banyan Tree.

An interesting fact is reported in the 1846 Lahaina census. The count included 3,445 Hawaiians, 112 foreigners, 600 seamen, 155 adobe houses, 822 grass houses, 59 stone and wooden houses, as well as 528 dogs!

A combination of things brought the downfall of the whaling industry. The onset of the Civil War depleted men and ships, (one Confederate warship reportedly set 24 whaling vessels ablaze) and the growth of the petroleum industry lessened the need for whale oil. Lastly, the Arctic freezes of 1871 and 1876 resulted in many ships being crushed by the ice. Lahaina, however, continues to maintain the charm and history of those bygone whaling days. The whaling era strengthened Hawaii's ties with the United States economically and the presence of the missionaries further strengthened this bond. The last monarch was Liliuokalani, who ruled from 1891 to 1893. Hawai'i became a territory of the United States in 1900 and achieved statehood in 1959.

Sugar cane brought by the first Hawaiians was developed into a major industry on Maui. Two sons of missionaries, Henry P. Baldwin and Samuel T. Alexander, played notable roles and their construction of a water pipeline to irrigate the arid central isthmus of Maui secured the future of the sugar industry and other agricultural development on the island.

Pineapple, another major agricultural industry, has played an important role in the history of Maui. Historians believe that pineapple may have originated in Brazil and was introduced to the modern world by Christopher Columbus on return from his second visit to the Americas. When it arrived in the islands is uncertain, but Don Francisco de Paula y Marin writes, in his diary on January 21, 1813 that "This day I planted pineapples and an orange tree." The first successful report of pineapple agriculture in Hawai'i is attributed to Captain James Kidwell, an English horticulturist. He brought the smooth cayenne variety of pineapple from Jamaica and began successfully raising and harvesting the fruit on O'ahu in 1886. Since the fresh fruits perished too quickly to reach the mainland, Captain Kidwell also began the first cannery, called Hawaiian Fruit and Packing Company, which operated until 1892 when it was sold to Pearl City Fruit Company. James Dole, a young Harvard graduate, arrived on O'ahu from Boston in 1899, and by 1901 had established what has today become known as the Dole Pineapple Company.

Grove Ranch and Haleakala Ranch Company both began pineapple cultivation on Maui in 1906. Baldwin Packers began as Honolua Ranch and was owned by Henry Baldwin who started it in 1912. The Grove Ranch hired David T. Fleming as company manager and began with several acres in Haiku which soon increased to 450 acres. W. A. Clark succeeded Fleming as Grove Ranch manager and while the acreage increased, for some unknown reason the pineapples failed. For ten years the fields were leased to Japanese growers who were successful.

During these early years Haleakala Ranch Company continued to expand their acreage and to successfully produce pineapples. J. Walter Cameron arrived from Honolulu to become manager of Haleakala Ranch Company in about 1925. In 1929 the ranch division was divided from the pineapple division and the company became Haleaakala Pineapple Company. In 1932 the Company and Grove Ranch merged, forming Maui Pineapple Company Limited and thirty years later in 1962, Baldwin Packers merged with Maui Pineapple Company to form what we know today as Maui Land and Pineapple. Maui Land and Pineapple continues to raise pineapples as well as develop land into the fine resort area known as Kapalua. The company owns 29,800 acres of land and uses 7,300 acres for company operations while employing approximately 1,800 people on a year-round or seasonal basis. While competition from abroad, particularly Thailand, has been fierce, Maui Land and Pineapple has chosen to maintain their market by supplying a quality product. Maui Land and Pineapple Company is the only 100% Hawaiian producer of canned pineapple in the world.

It was about 100 years ago that the first macadamia nut trees arrived from Australia. They were intended to be an ornamental tree, since they had nuts that were extremely difficult to crack. It was not until the 1950's that the development of the trees began to take a commercial course. Today, some sugarcane fields are being converted to macadamia. It is a slow process, taking seven years for the grafted root (they do not grow from seed) to become a producing tree. While delicious, beware of their hazards: 1/2 ounce of nuts contains 100 calories!

The Kula area of Maui has become the center for many delicious fruits and vegetables as well as the unusual Protea flower, a native of South Africa. Wineries are also making a comeback with the opening of the Tedeschi Winery a few years ago. They first began producing an unusual pineapple wine. In 1984, they introduced a champagne, and in 1985, a red table wine.

Be sure to also sample the very sweet Kula onions raised in this area (these are not the same as "Maui onions" that can be grown anywhere in Maui County) and are available for shipping home. Coffee is currently being tested for commercial feasibility in Upcountry.

UPCOUNTRY PRODUCE

# MAUI'S NAMES AND PLACES

Haiku  (HAH-ee-KOO)  abrupt break
Haleakala  (HAH-leh-AH-kuh-LAH)  house of the sun

Hali'imaile  (HAH-LEE-'ee-MAH-ee-leh)  maile vines spread
Hana  (HAH-nuh)  rainy land

Honoapiilani  (HOH-noh-AH-PEE-'ee-LAH-nee) bays of Pi'ilani
Honolua  (HOH-noh-LOO-uh)  double bay

Iao  (EE-AH-oh)  cloud supreme
Kaanapali  (KAH-AH-nuh-PAH-lee)  land divided by cliffs

Kahana  (Kuh-HAH-nuh)  meaning unknown, of Tahitian origin
Kaho'olawe  (kuh-Ho-'oh-LAH-veah)  taking away by currents

Kahului  (Kah-hoo-LOO-ee)  winning
Kapalua  (KAH-puh-LOO-uh)  two borders

Kaupo  (KAH-oo-POH)  night landing
Ke'anae  (keh-'uh-NAH-eh)  the mullet

Keawakapu  (Keh-AH-vuh-KAH-poo)  sacred harbor
Kihei  (KEE-HEH-ee)  shoulder cape

Lahaina  (LAH-HAH-ee-NAH)  unmerciful sun
Lana'i  (LAH-NAH-ee)  meaning lost

Maalaea  (MAH-'uh-LAH-eh-uh)  area of red dirt
Makawao  (mah-kah-wah-oh)  forest beginning

Makena  (Mah-KEH-nuh)  abundance
Napili  (NAH-PEE-lee)  pili grass

Olowalu  (oh-loh-wah-loo)  many hills
Paia  (PAH-EE-uh)  noisy

Pukalani  (poo-kah-lah-nee)  sky opening
Ulupalakua  (OO-loo-PAH-luh-KOO-uh)  ripe breadfruit

Waianapanapa  (WAH-ee-AH-NAH-puh-NAH-puh)  glistening water
Wailea  (WAH-ee-LEH-uh)  water Lea (Lea was the canoe maker's goddess)

Wailua  (WAH-ee-LOO-uh)  two waters
Wailuku  (WAH-ee-LOO-KOO)  water of slaughter

# HAWAIIAN WORDS - MEANINGS

alii (ah-lee-ee) chief
aloha (ah-loh-hah) greetings

hale (Hah-lay) house
hana (HAHA-nah) work

Heiau (heh-ee-ah-oo) temple
kai (kye) ocean

kahuna (kah-HOO-nah) teacher, priest
Kamaaina (Kah-mah-ai-nuh) native born

kane (kah-nay) man
kapu (kah-poo) keep out

keiki (kayee-kee) child
lanai (lah-nah-ee) porch or patio

lomi lomi (loh-mee-LOH-mee) to rub or massage
luau (loo-ah-oo) feast

makai (mah-kah-ee) toward the ocean
mauka (mah-oo-kah) toward the mountain

mauna (MAU-nah) mountain
mele (MAY-leh) Hawaiian song or chant

menehune (may-nay-hoo-nee) Hawaiian dwarf or elf
moana (moh-ah-nah) ocean

nani (NAH-nee) beautiful
ono (oh-no) delicious

pali (PAH-lee) cliff, precipice
paniolo (pah-nee-ou-loh) Hawaiian cowboy

pau (pow) finished
pua (POO-ah) flower

puka (POO-ka) a hole
pupus (poo-poos) appetizers

wahine (wah-hee-nay) woman
wiki wiki (wee-kee wee-kee) hurry

# WHAT TO PACK

When traveling to paradise, you won't need too much. Comfortable shoes are important for all the sightseeing. Sandals are the norm for footwear. Dress is casual for dining. Many restaurants require men to wear sport shirts with collars, but only one or two require a tie. Clothes should be lightweight and easy care. Cotton and cotton blends are more comfortable for the tropical climate than polyesters. Shorts and bathing suits are the dress code here! A lightweight jacket with a hood or sweater is advisable for evenings and the occasional rain showers. The only need for warmer clothes is if your plans should include hiking or camping in Haleakala Crater. While it may start out warm and sunny, the weather can change very quickly in Upcountry. Even during the daytime, a sweater or light jacket is a good idea when touring Upcountry. (The cooler weather here is evidenced on the roofs of the homes where chimney stacks can be spotted.) Tennis shoes or hiking shoes are a good idea for the rougher volcanic terrain of Haleakala or hiking elsewhere as well. Sunscreens are a must. A camera, of course, needs to be tucked in. Many visitors are taking their memories home on video tape, and VHS rental units are available around the island. Binoculars are an option and may be well used if you are traveling between December and April when the whales arrive for their winter vacation. Special needs for traveling with children are discussed in the next section. Anything that you need can probably be purchased once you arrive. Don't forget to leave some extra space in those suitcases for goodies that you will want to take back home!

# TRAVELING WITH CHILDREN

Traveling with children can be an exhausting experience for parents and children alike, especially when the trip is as long as the one to Maui. There are a number of direct flights to Maui out of Seattle, San Francisco, Los Angeles, Chicago and Dallas, which saves stopping over in Honolulu. These flights are very popular and fill up well in advance.

Packing a child's goody bag for the long flight is a must. A few new activity books or toys that can be pulled out enroute can be sanity saving. Snacks (boxes of juice are a favorite with our children) can tide over the little ones at the airport or on the plane while awaiting your food/drink service. A thermos with a drinking spout works well and is handy for use during vacations. A change of clothes and a swim suit for the little ones can be tucked into your carry-on bag. (Suitcases have been known to be lost or delayed.) Another handy addition is a small nightlight as unfamiliar accommodations can be somewhat confusing for little ones during the bedtime hours. And don't forget a strong sunscreen!

Young children may have difficulty clearing their ears when landing. Many don't realize that cabins are pressurized to approximately the 6,000 foot level during flight. To help relieve the pressure of descent, have infants nurse or drink from a bottle, and older children may benefit from chewing gum. If this is a concern of yours, consult with your pediatrician about the use of a decongestant prior to descent.

**CAR SEATS:** By law, children under 4 must travel in child safety seats. While most rental agencies do have car seats for rent, you need to request them well in advance as they have a limited number. The one, and only, car seat we have rented had seen better days, and its design was only marginal for child safety. Prices run about $25 per week, $36 for two weeks or $6 per day. You may wish to bring your own with you. Several styles are permitted by the airlines for use in flight, or it may be checked as a piece of baggage.

**BABYSITTING:** Most hotels have some form of babysitting service which runs about $8 an hour. Check with your condo office as they sometimes have numbers of local sitters. As you can easily figure from the rates, spending much time away from your children can be costly. Consider the feasibility of bringing your own sitter, it may actually be less expensive, and certainly much more convenient. This has worked well for us on numerous occasions. With any of these agencies, or through your hotel, at least a 24 hour notice is requested. We suggest phoning them *as soon* as you have set up your plans. At certain times of the year, with the limited number of sitters available, it can be nearly impossible to get one. If you can plan out your entire vacation babysitting needs, it might also be possible to schedule the same sitter for each occasion.

**Babysit Services of Maui** is an independent company that will send the sitter to your hotel or condominium. Their rates are $8 per hour with a three hour minimum. $1.00 additional for each child in the family and $2.50 an hour for each additional child from another family. Contact Tony at 661-0558. We have used several of their people and found them all to be efficient and caring.

Another agency is **Kihei Keiki Babysitting Service** which charges $8 for one child, $9 for two and $1 per hour for each additional child. They provide island-wide service. Contact Darin and Angie Bernal 879-2522 or 667-7564.

Two new arrivals to the childcare referral business, which we haven't personally used are: **The Nanny Connection** which charges $10 per hour for one or two children with a three hour minimum. Extra child from the same family is an additional $1 per hour, from a different family $3 per hour per child. No travel fee, no tax. Extra charge past midnight or for holidays. PO Box 477, Puunene, Maui, HI 96784, (808) 875-4777. *Aloha Sitters* (808) 661-0298 charges $8 per hour for one child, siblings $1 each additional child, $3 each hour for non-sibling, plus $4 travel/parking fee and an additional $4 tax. PO Box 5319, Lahaina, HI 96761.

**CRIBS:** Most condos and hotels offer cribs for a rental fee that may vary from $2 to $10 per night. Companies such as Maui Rent (877-5827) charge $6 a day, $30 a week, and $42 for two weeks. For an extended stay you might consider purchasing one of the wonderful folding cribs that pack up conveniently. We tried the Fisher-Price version that weighs 20 pounds and fits into a small duffle bag. It checked easily as luggage and is very portable for car travel as well. We have heard recommendations about other types including the Snugli's carrier bed and diaper bag combo that zips easily to form a compact shoulder carryall, and the Houdini full-size playpen by Kantwent which weighs only 16 pounds and folds into a 8x8x42 inch space. Each of the units may be purchased for less than the cost of a ten-day rental fee.

**EMERGENCIES:** There are several clinics around the island which take emergencies or walk-in patients. Your condominium or hotel desk can provide you with suggestions, or check the phone book. Kaiser Permanente Medical Care Facilities are located in Wailuku (243-6000) and in Lahaina (661-7400). See the section on Helpful Information for additional numbers. Calling 911 will put you in contact with local fire, police and ambulances.

**BEACHES - POOLS:** Among the best beaches for fairly young children are the Lahaina and Puunoa beaches in Lahaina, where the water is shallow and calm. Kapalua Bay is also well protected and has fairly gentle wave action. Remember to have children well supervised and wearing floatation devices, for even the calmest beaches can have a surprise wave. Several of the island's beaches offer lifeguards, among these are the Kamaole I, II, and III beaches in Kihei. Kamaole III Park also has large open areas and playground equipment. In the Maalaea area, follow the road down past the condominiums to the public access for the beach area. A short walk down the kiawe lined beach, to the small rock jetty with the large pipe, you'll discover a seawater pool on either side that is well protected and ideal for the younger child. Another precaution on the beach that is easily neglected is the application of a good sunscreen; reapply after swimming.

A number of complexes have small shallow pools designed with the young ones in mind. These include the Marriott, Kaanapali Alii, Sands of Kahana and the Kahana Sunset. We recommend taking a life jacket or water wings (floaties). Packing a small inflatable pool for use on your lanai or courtyard may provide a cool and safe retreat for your little one. Typically Maui resorts and hotels DO NOT offer lifeguard services. Older children will be astounded by the labyrinth of pools and rivers at the Grand Wailea Resort and Spa. Non-hotel guests are invited to enjoy the pool for a day with an admission charge of $65 for adults and $50 for children. Guests of the Four Seasons Resort receive a reduced admission of $50 for adults and $35 for children.

A number of children's programs at resorts around the island are open to non-resort guests. Some of these youth programs are seasonal, offered just summer, spring and Christmas holidays. A few are available year round.

The Gemini, a 64 foot glass bottom catamaran operated by the Maui Westin, has a new program for youths ages 14-19. A Friday night sail includes pizza, music, and swimming. It departs about 5 pm. Reservation phone 661-2591.

**ENTERTAINMENT:** The 112 acre *Maui Tropical Plantation* has become one of the top visitor attractions in the state. We find it "touristy," but an interesting stop anyway. Surrounding the visitor center are acres planted in sugar cane, macadamia, guava, mango, banana, papaya, pineapple, passion fruit, star fruit, and coffee in addition to an array of flowers. There are also displays of the State's agricultural history throughout the grounds. Admission to the plantation market and restaurant are free, but there is a charge for the tram which takes visitors through the working plantation.

There are plenty of great free opportunities to enjoy Polynesian performances. See Our Personal Best Bets for this listing at the beginning of this chapter.

There is a new six-plex cinema at the Kaahumanu Center and another at the Kahului Mall. The Wharf Shopping Center in Lahaina has a tri-cinema with first run movies and a $3.50 early admission (first show of the day only, seniors are $3.50 all day). Plans are to add another set of theaters at the Lahaina Center by the end of 1994. There is also a multi-plex theater in Kihei. There are a number of video stores which rent movies and equipment. See the listing under Best Bets for other free things to do with kids!

The Napili Kai Beach Club's Sea House Restaurant has for years been involved with local performers. They offer a Friday evening dinner show where children perform Hawaiian songs and dances. The Napili Kai Foundation Dinner Show costs $25 for adults and $20 for children.

The *Maui Zoo*, located in Kahului, has free admission and while only a limited number of animals make their home here, it's a great stop-off. Bring along a picnic lunch! For more information see WHERE TO STAY - WHAT TO SEE, Wailuku & Kahului. There is also a bowling alley in Kahului.

The *Whaling Museum*, renovated and better than ever, at Whalers Village in Kaanapali is a most informative stop. Also see the Best Bets information in the front of the book for additional suggestions!

The annual *Keiki Fishing Tournament* is held sometime during July each year in Kaanapali. The large pond in the golf course is stocked with fish for the event.

In the Lahaina-Kaanapali area, the colorful *Sugar Cane Train* runs a course several times a day along Honoapiilani Highway from Kaanapali to Lahaina. Transportation can be purchased alone or in combination with one of several excursions in Lahaina. After arrival in Lahaina, you will board a red, double decker bus for the short drive to the Lahaina Harbor. (See Land Tours for additional details.) There is time for a stroll or a visit to the Baldwin missionary home before returning to the train for the trip home or combine your train excursion with a trip to the Omni-Theater.

SUGAR TRAIN

Several submarines and a number of boats offer the young and young at heart a chance to tour the underwater wonders of the Pacific without getting wet. The boats depart from Lahaina Harbor, see Water activities for more details. *Gemini Charters* offers a Kaanapali Teen Sail for 14-19 year olds. A two hour Friday evening of sailing, swimming, music and pizza. (808) 661-2591.

*Theatre Theatre Maui* is a community and youth oriented theater organization in West Maui. Adult programs are held in the spring and there are summer workshops for children and teens in the summer. For more information contact Louisa Shelton or Penny Wakida (661-1168) PO Box 12318, Lahaina, Maui, HI 96761. With the 1994 opening of the long awaited *Maui Arts & Cultural Center* in Kahului, there should be some new opportunities to enjoy some varied family entertainment. Among performance groups is the *Maui Academy of Performing Arts*. For schedule information call 244-8760. See Theater for more information.

The Embassy Suites, in Honokowai near Kaanapali, has an 18-hole *miniature golf course* on their roof-top. The only such course on the island is open 9 am to 9 pm daily, $5 for adults, $3 for guests 12 and under. 661-2000.

The local bookstores offer a wealth of wonderful *Hawaiian books* for children. There are some wonderful books with factual information designed to stimulate each child with a fundamental knowledge of Hawaii's birds, reptiles, amphibians and mammals. A number of colorful Hawaiian folk tales may be a perfect choice to take home for your children to enjoy, or as a gift.

Many restaurants offer a *Keiki* (children's) menu. There are also an assortment of Burger King's and McDonald's on the island.

Flashlights can turn the balmy Hawaiian evenings into adventures! One of the most friendly island residents is the Bufo (Boof-oh). In 1932 this frog was brought from Puerto Rico to assist with insect control in the cane fields. Today this large toad still emerges at night to feed or mate and seems to be easier to spot during the winter months, especially after rain showers. While they can be found around most condominiums, Kawiliki Park (the area behind the Luana Kai, Laule'a and several other condominium complexes with access from Waipulani Road off South Kihei Road) seems to be an especially popular gathering spot. We suggest you don't touch them, however. The secretions may cause skin irritation. We also enjoy searching for beach crabs and the African snails which have shells that may grow to a hefty five inches. The other Hawaiian creature that cannot go without mention is the gecko. They are finding their way into the suitcases of many an island visitor, in the form of tee-shirts, sunvisors and jewelry. This small lizard is a relative of the chameleon and grows to a length of three or four inches. They dine on roaches, termites, mosquitos, ants, moths and other pesky insects. While there are nearly 800 species of geckos found in warm climates around the world, there are only about five varieties found in Hawaii. The house gecko is the most commonly found, with tiny rows of spines that circle its tail, while the mourning gecko has a smooth, satiny skin and along the middle of its back it sports pale stripes and pairs of dark spots. The mourning gecko species is parthenogenic. That means that there are only females which produce fertile eggs, and no need for a mate!

stump-toed variety is distinguished by its thick flattened tail. The tree gecko enjoys the solitude of the forests, and the fox gecko, with a long snout and spines along its tail, prefers to hide around rocks or tree trunks. The first geckos may have reached Hawai'i with early voyagers from Polynesia, but the house gecko may have arrived as recently as the 1940s, along with military shipments to Hawaii. Geckos are most easily spotted at night when they seem to enjoy the warm lights outside your door. We have heard they each establish little territories where they live and breed so you will no doubt see them around the same area each night. They are very shy and will scurry off quickly. Sometimes you may find one living in your hotel or condo. They're friendly and beneficial animals and are said to bring good luck, so make them welcome. Hawai'i has no snakes!

If you headquarter your stay near the Papakea Resort in Honokowai, you might take an adventurous nighttime reef walk. If an evening low tide does not conflict with your children's bedtime, put on some old tennis shoes and grab a flashlight. (Flashlights that are waterproof or at least water resistant are recommended.) The reef comes right into shore at the southern end of Papakea where you can walk out onto it like a broad living sidewalk. Try and pick a night when the low tide is from 9 - 11 pm (tide information is available in the Maui News or call the recorded weather report) and when the sea is calm. Searching the shallow water will reveal sea wonders such as fish and eels that are out feeding. Some people looked at us strangely as we pursued this new recreation, but our little ones thought it an outstanding activity. Shoes (we recommend old sneakers) are a must as the coral is very sharp. Afterwards, be sure to thoroughly clean your shoes promptly with fresh water or they will become horribly musty smelling.

Check with your resort concierge for additional youth activities. During the summer months, Christmas holidays and Easter, many of the resort hotels offer partial or full day activities for children. Rates range from free to $55 per day. Following are a few of the programs offered by some Maui resorts. Please be sure to check with the resort to see the current status and prices for their children's programs. Be sure to call for current schedules, availability and prices.

As we mentioned previously, some of these programs are available to non-hotel or resort guests, including two in Wailea, the Kea Lani and the Maui Inter-Continental.

*Aston Kaanapali Shores Resort* features a year-round program for children ages 3 - 10 years. Camp Kaanapali is offered from 9 am - 2 pm Monday thru Friday. A $10 initial registration covers you regardless of the length of your stay and includes a camp T-shirt. Optional lunch at $6. Activities are all held on property grounds and include hula and crafts. Program available for guests only. 667-2211.

*Embassy Suites* children's program, Beach Buddies, is dedicated to perpetuating and preserving the heritage of the islands. "As a Keiki O Ka Aina Ika Pono (child of the land), let us share with you a 'Hawaiian Experience' rich in culture and tradition." Activities include hula class, lei making, coconut weaving and crafts, beach combing and aquarium time. The program is for children 4 to 10 years and operates year round Monday through Friday from 8:30 am - 2:30 pm. First-day registration fee of $15 per child, additional days are $10 and each additional child of the same family is $7. 661-2000.

**The Four Seasons Wailea** features "Kids for all Seasons," a daily complimentary program for youths age 5-12 years with year round supervised activities from 9 am-5 pm. Hawaiian songs, lei-making, hula, beach games. 874-8000.

**Grand Wailea Resort & Spa** is one of the newest properties in Wailea with an incredible 20,000 sq. foot space devoted to their youthful guests. The day camp (9 am-3 pm) is $65 including lunch, and there is an evening camp which includes. The camp area provides a computer center, soda fountain, swimming pool, video room, arts & crafts center, movie theater for children ages 6 months to 15 years. This program is available year round. Children's menus available in restaurants. Guests of the resort may accompany (and stay) with their children and enjoy the facilities of Camp Grande at no charge. 875-1234.

**Kapalua Bay Hotel and Villas** offers Camp Kapalua which includes, excursions, arts and crafts and much more. Mon.-Fri. all year to guests only. The program for 5-12 year olds runs 9 am-1 pm daily and the fee is $55. 669-5656.

**Kea Lani Hotel** offers "Keiki Lani" (Heavenly Kids) for youths aged 5 to 11 years of age. Offered year-round 9 am-3 pm includes lunch. Current charge is $15 registration fee and $10 per day per child. Activities range from face painting to sailing, picnics to hula and off-property excursions. Children's menus in the restaurant. Available to guests and non-guests.

**The Maui Inter-Continental** in Wailea offers the "Keiki's Club Gecko Program" for children age 5 and older. Cost is $35 per day and includes lunch, snacks and T-shirt. Activities include Hawaiian arts & crafts, and off-property tours. Children's menus available in restaurants. The program is open to guests and non-guests. Programs Tues., Thurs. and Sat. 9 am-3 pm. Contact 879-1922.

**Maui Westin** offers seasonal Kamp Kaanapali for 5-12 year olds. They charge $20-$40 per day and do many off-site activities including a snorkel trip on the Gemini catamaran and a trip on a submarine or the Sugar Cane Train. 667-2525.

**The Ritz Kids** is the half ($25) or full day program ($40) offered by The Ritz-Carlton Kapalua for youths ages 4-12 years. 669-6200.

**Stouffer Wailea Beach Resort** provides "Camp Wailea" for kids 5-12 years. $35 price includes admission to attractions, lunch, two snacks and craft supplies. Currently offered 7 days a week to guests only. 1-800-468-3571 or 808-879-4900.

**Wailea Golf Course** has programs twice weekly, summer only, for 6-12 year olds. The 6 week program runs two hours per session, cost is $45. 879-2966.

**Wailea Resort Company** offers junior tennis clinics and golf lessons during various weeks in the summer months, as well as tennis camps. Ages 4-13 years, the program charges a $35 registration fee and $10 each session. Some single lessons or play. 879-1958.

**The Whaler on Kaanapali Beach** provides a program during summer, Christmas and spring break sessions. Call for current information. 661-4861.

# *TRAVEL TIPS FOR THE*
# *PHYSICALLY IMPAIRED*

Make your travel plans well in advance and inform hotels and airlines when making your reservations that you are handicapped. Most facilities will be happy to accommodate. Bring along your medical records in the event of an emergency. It is recommended that you bring your own wheelchair and notify the airlines in advance that you will be transporting it. There are no battery rentals available on Maui. Other medical equipment rental information is listed below.

Additional information can be obtained from the State Commission on Persons with Disabilities, c/o State Department of Health, 54 High St., Wailuku, Maui 96793 (808-243-5441 V-TTD), or the State Commission on Persons with Disabilities, who are currently in the process of moving and have no new address, but the most recent phone number is (808-546-8121 V-TTD). They offer a book entitled *Aloha Guide to Accessibility,* currently being revised, so call for the newest edition release date and cost for mailing.

***ARRIVAL AND DEPARTURE:*** On arrival at the Kahului airport terminal, you will find the building easily accessible for mobility impaired persons. Parking areas are located in front of the main terminal for disabled persons. Restrooms with handicapped stalls (male and female) are also found in the main terminal.

***TRANSPORTATION:*** There is no public transportation on Maui and taxi service can be spendy. The only two car rental companies providing hand controls are Avis and Hertz. See the Rental Car listing for phone numbers. They need some advance notice to install the equipment. The Maui Economic Opportunity Center operates a van with an electric lift for local residents. However, visitors can make arrangements with them by calling (808) 877-7651. Wheelers Accessible Van Rentals offers van rentals with hand controls and delivery and pick up of island visitors. Phone 1-800-456-1371 or (602) 878-3540 or contact them through Over the Rainbow. Hawaii Care Van Shuttle and Tour, (Armijo, Inc.), at 85 Alo Alo Place, Lahaina, HI 96761 offers airport transports island-wide and tour services. Phone (808) 669-2300 or fax (808) 669-3811.

***ACCOMMODATIONS:*** Each of the major island hotels offer one or more handicapped rooms including bathroom entries of at least 29" to allow for wheelchairs. Due to the limited number of rooms, reservations should be made well in advance. Information on condominium accessibility is available from the Maui Commission of the Handicapped Office.

***ACTIVITIES:*** Only Hawaii Care Van Shuttle and Tour, listed above, offers wheelchair accessible touring. The Easter Seal Society of Hawai'i can provide information on recreational activities for the traveler. Among the options are wheelchair tennis or basketball, bowling and swimming. Contact them in advance of your arrival at (808) 877-4443. Wheelchair access to some of the tourist attractions may be limited. More information is in the WHAT TO DO chapter.

**MEDICAL SERVICES AND EQUIPMENT:** Maui Memorial Hospital is located in Wailuku and there are also good clinics in all areas of the island. Check the local directory. Several agencies can assist in providing personal care attendants, companions, and nursing aides while on your visit. Maui Center for Independent Living (808-242-4966) provides personal care attendants, as does Aloha International Employment Service Interim Health Care and Personnel (808-871-6373), and Medical Personnel Pool (808-877-2676).

Lahaina Pharmacy, Lahaina Shopping Center (808-661-3119) has wheelchairs, crutches, canes, and walkers with delivery by special arrangement. Gammie Home Care, located in the Kahului Commercial Center, 355 Hukilike St. #103, Kahului, HI 96732 can provide medical equipment rentals, from walking aides to bathroom accessories or wheelchairs. (808) 877-4032 or Fax (808) 877-3359. It is again recommended that you contact them well in advance of your arrival.

***Over the Rainbow Disabled Travel Service, Inc.*** is the only travel, tour and activity agency on Maui that specializes in assisting the disabled traveler. "Imagination is your limit" they report when it comes to the activities they offer. They can assist in making reservations at a condominium or hotel to fit the needs of the traveler, make airport arrangements including van accessible wheelchair lifts and arrange for personal care such as attendants, pharmacists, or interpreters. They can arrange for rental cars with hand controls, make airport arrangements including ticketing, and provide "doctors on call." Owner David McKown is a one-stop shopping connection for the disabled traveler and the Maui Representative for Wheelers Accessible Van Rentals. As for recreation, how about snorkeling, helicopter tours, bowling, golf, horseback riding, luaus, tennis (disabled opponent available), tours, jet skiing, or ocean kayaking! Wedding and honeymoon arrangements, too. The Easter Seal Society has been working with the county to make the beaches more accessible for disabled travelers. A $200,000 grant in December 1993 paved the way for work on parking lots at beaches with handicapped designations, sidewalks and curb cuts, comfort stations, picnic tables, beach showers, and an accessible pathway onto the beach. Easter Seals can also provide sand/beach wheelchairs with big inflatable rubber tires. Currently beaches that have been made accessible include Kamaole I, II and III, Hanakaoo Beach and Kanaha Beach. Contact David for updated information as improvements continue to progress. Write or call for their free brochure: 186 Mehani Circle, Kihei, Maui, HI 96753. (808) 879-5521.

# WEDDINGS - HONEYMOONS

If a Hawaiian wedding (or a renewal of vows) is in your dreams, Maui can make them all come true. While the requirements are simple, here are a few tips, based on current requirements at time of publication, for making your wedding plans run more smoothly. We advise you to double check the requirements as things change!

Both bride and groom must be over 18 years of age; birth certificates are not required, but you do need a proof of age such as a driver's license or passport. You do not need proof of citizenship or residence. If either partner has been divorced, the date, county and state of finalization for each divorce must be verbally provided to the licensing agent. If a divorce was finalized within the last

35

three months, then a decree must be provided to the licensing agent. The bride will need to have a rubella blood test and must bring proof of the screening test from her state of residence. However, the test is not required if the female has had rubella immunization, has had rubella in the past, has had sterilization, is past menopause or has other reasons for inability to conceive. A health certificate attesting to one of these reasons for not having the test is required. There is no blood test required for the groom. On Maui the test can be done at the Maui Medical Group in Lahaina or the Maui Reference Lab in Wailuku. A license must be purchased in person in the state of Hawaii. Call the Department of Health (808-243-5313) for the name of a licensing agent in the area where you will be staying. The fee is currently $16. There is no waiting period once you have the license. Check with the Chamber of Commerce in Kahului (808-871-7711) for information regarding a pastor. Many island pastors are very flexible in meeting your needs, such as an outdoor location, etc.

For copies of current requirements and forms, write in advance to the State of Hawaii, Department of Health, Marriage License Section, 1250 Punchbowl St., Honolulu, HI 96813. 808-586-4545. The Maui Visitors Bureau 808-244-3530 or 1-800-525-MAUI also can provide a copy of the requirements for weddings. Included in the information are some free public wedding locations at Hawai'i State and National Park. The Second Circuit Court is located at 2145 Main St. in Wailuku. Phone 808-244-2852. District Court Phone 808-244-2955.

Formal wear rentals for the gents in your party can be obtained from Gilbert's Formal Wear at 104 Market St. in Old Wailuku Town, 808-244-4017. Rental wedding gowns, formal dresses, and bridesmaid dresses are available through Maui Fashion Center at 341 N. Market St., Wailuku HI 96793. 808-244-3875.

If you'd like to have your food catered, here are several choices: Door Step Dining, 808-667-7001 who provide restaurant delivery service and Clambake Catering Service 808-242-5095.

Hawaii Video Memories will capture your special day on video tape. 173 Alamaha St., Suite 4, Kahului, HI 96732. 808-871-5788.

SEASIDE CHAPEL, GRAND WAILEA RESORT

A basic package costs anywhere from $300 - $400. Although each company varies the package slightly, it will probably include assistance in choosing a location and getting your marriage license, a minister and a varying assortment of extras such as champagne, limited photography, cake, leis, and a bridal garter. Video taping, witnesses, or music are usually extra.

*A Maui Wedding* 808-879-2355, 2439 S. Kihei Rd., Suite 205B, (mailing address PO Box 116, Kihei, HI 96753). Contact Jan Lyle.

*A Wedding Made in Paradise* 808-879-3444 or 1-800-453-3440 US mainland or PO Box 986, Kihei, Maui, HI 96753. Contact Alicia Bay Laurel.

*A Dream Wedding Maui Style* 129 Lahainaluna Rd. #201, Lahaina, HI 96761. 808-661-1777 or 1-800-743-2777. Tracy Flanagan, Consultant.

*Arthur's Limousine Service* 808-871-5555, 1-800-345-4667 from the US mainland or FAX 808-877-3333, 296A Alamaha St., Kahului, Maui, HI 96732.

*Beautiful Beginnings* 808-874-6444, 534 Hoala Drive, Kihei, HI 96753. Contact Sandy Barker.

*John Pierre's Photographic Studio* 808-667-7988, 129 Lahainaluna Rd., Lahaina, Maui, HI 96761.

*Royal Hawaiian Carriage Co.* 808-669-1100 has four carriages, six passengers each and eight 1,000 lb. draft type horses which pull the carriages. The company does wedding transportation to and from the ceremony and/or reception and provides pick up island-wide. They are based at The Ritz-Carlton, Kapalua. Minimum charge is $200 per hour, depending on the number of carriages. PO Box 10581, Lahaina, HI 96761.

*Royal Hawaiian Weddings* 1-800-659-1866 US or Canada or 808-875-0625, PO Box 424, Puunene, HI 96784. Andrea Thomas and Janet Renner have been putting together the ceremonies for the most special occasions since 1977. Choose from dazzling beachside sunsets, private oceanfront settings, tropical gardens, sleek yachts or remote helicopter landings. Name your dream.

*Special Services and Accommodations* 808-244-5811, 252A Awapuhi Place, Wailuku, Maui, HI 96793. Burt and Linda Freeland offer a range of wedding services in traditional or remote locations.

*Tropical Gardens of Maui* 808-244-3085, RR 1, Box 500, Wailuku, Maui, HI 96793. They provide a garden area in the Iao Valley. They can provide tables, tents, buffet tables, chairs, and flowers. Furnish your own food.

*Weddings the Maui Way* 808-877-7711, 353 Hanamau St., Suite 21, Kahului, Maui, HI 96732. Contact Beth Lovell or Richard Dickinson. Can provide wedding services in Japanese.

*The Westin Maui* 808-667-2525, Kaanapali Beach, has their own resident Director of Romance who will assist you with your wedding and honeymoon plans.

Also, the social directors of the major resorts can assist you with your wedding plans and there are a variety of locations on the grounds of these beautiful resorts to set the scene for your very special wedding.

The extraordinary Grand Wailea has constructed a seaside wedding chapel on their grounds. The picturesque white chapel features stained-glass windows, designed by artist Yvonne Cheng, that depict a royal Hawaiian wedding. Woods of red oak, teak and cherry dominate the interior which is accented by three hand-crafted chandeliers from Murano, Italy. Outside the chapel is a flower-filled garden with brass-topped gazebos. A beautiful indoor location for your wedding!

## *ESPECIALLY FOR SENIORS*

More and more businesses are beginning to offer special savings to seniors. RSVP booking agency offers special rates for seniors who book their accommodations through them. They are listed in the Rental Agents section of our accommodations chapter. Whether it is a boating activity, an airline ticket or a condominium, be sure to ask about special senior rates. And be sure to travel with identification showing your birthdate.

Check the yellow pages when you arrive on Maui for senior discount program logo. Look for a black circle with white star and in the ads.

Remember that AARP members get many travel discounts for rooms, cars and tours.

A number of airlines have special discounts for seniors. Some also have a wonderful feature which provides a discount for the traveling companion that is accompanying the senior. Coupon books for senior discounts are also available from a number of airline carriers.

## *HELPFUL INFORMATION*

***INFORMATION BOOTHS:*** Booths located at the shopping areas can provide helpful information and lots of brochures! Brochure displays are everywhere.

***MAUI VISITORS BUREAU:*** (808-871-8691), 1727 Wili Pa Loop, PO Box 580, Wailuku, Maui, HI 96793. Phone (808) 244-3530, 1-800-525-MAUI or FAX 808-244-1337.

***RADIO:*** Our favorite, KPOA 93.5 FM plays great old and new Hawaiian music, with a daily jazz program 8 pm to 1 am. Tune in and catch the local disk jockeys "talking story"! They also have a new KPOA Music and Gift Shop located at 505 Front Street. KKUA 90.7 has Hawai'i Public Radio and classical music. KDLX 94.3 has country music, KAOI on either 95.1 (or Upcountry 96.7) has contemporary rock, KMVI 98.3 has Maui's rock, KNUI 99.9 (or Upcountry 99.3) light rock/Hawaiian and KLHI 101 is adult contemporary. On the AM dial KMVI is at 550 with island music, KNUI 900 oldies and Hawaiian music and KAOI 1110 with contemporary rock.

*TELEVISION:* The Paradise Network, shown island-wide on Channel 7, is designed especially with tourists in mind. Information is provided on recreation, real estate, shopping, restaurants, history, culture and art. Maui Today, on Channel 6, is a service of Hawaiian Cable and features information, calendar of events, special programs of historical and cultural interest broadcast only in West Maui.

*PERIODICALS:* Pacific Art and Travel, This Week Maui, Maui Gold, Maui (Rent A Car) Drive Guide, Maui Island Guide, The Kaanapali Beach Guide, The Kihei/Wailea Beach Guide, The Makena Beach Guide, Lahaina Historical Guide, Real Estate Maui Style, The Maui Island Guide, Upcountry News, Haleakala Times and Maui Menus are all free publications available almost everywhere.

Most of these free publications offer lots of advertising. However, they do have coupons which will give you discounts on everything from meals to sporting activities to clothing. It may save you a bit to search through these before making your purchases.

There are also a number of newspaper-style publications which offer helpful and interesting information:

*The Maui Quick Guide* - Has some good shuttle schedules and maps. *The Maui Bulletin* - This is published newspaper-style booklet and available at no charge. *South Maui Times* - Less touristy, more local stories. *Lahaina News* - A small weekly newspaper. It contains a television guide and local news and lots of advertisements. Fee is twenty-five cents. *Maui News* - This is the local Maui newspaper, published Monday thru Friday, and is available for 35 cents. A good source of local information. *Upcountry News* - An Upcountry version of Lahaina News.

*SUN SAFETY:* The sunshine is stronger in Hawai'i than on the mainland, so a few basic guidelines will ensure that you return home with a tan, not a burn. Use a good lotion with a sunscreen, reapply after swimming and don't forget the lips! Be sure to moisturize after a day in the sun and wear a hat to protect your face.

Exercise self-control and stay out a limited time the first few days, remembering that a gradual tan will last longer. It is best to avoid being out between the hours of noon and three when it is the hottest. Be cautious of overcast days when it is very easy to become burned unknowingly. Don't forget that the ocean acts as a reflector and time spent in it equals time spent on the beach.

***FOR YOUR PROTECTION:*** Do not leave valuables in your car, even in your trunk. Many rental car companies urge you to not lock your car as vandals cause extensive and expensive damage breaking the locks. Many companies also warn not to drive on certain roads (Ulupalakua to Hana and the unpaved portion of Hwy. 34) unless you are willing to accept liability for all damages.

## *HELPFUL PHONE NUMBERS:*

EMERGENCY: Police - Ambulance - Fire . . . . . . . . . . . . . . . 911
NON-EMERGENCY POLICE:
    Lahaina . . . . . . . . . . . . . . . . . . . . . . . . . . . . . . . 661-4441
    Hana . . . . . . . . . . . . . . . . . . . . . . . . . . . . . . . . . 248-8311
    Wailuku . . . . . . . . . . . . . . . . . . . . . . . . . . . . . . . 244-6400
Poison Control . . . . . . . . . . . . . . . . . . . . . . 1-800-362-3585
Helpline (suicide & crisis center) . . . . . . . . . . . . . . . . . . 244-7407
Red Cross . . . . . . . . . . . . . . . . . . . . . . . . . . . . . . . . . 244-0051
Consumer Protection . . . . . . . . . . . . . . . . . . . . . . . . . 243-5387
Visitor Complaint Hotline (Activity Owner's Association) . 871-7947
Directory Assistance:
    Local . . . . . . . . . . . . . . . . . . . . . . . . . . . . . . . . (1) 411
    Inter-island . . . . . . . . . . . . . . . . . . . . . . . . . 1-555-1212
    Mainland . . . . . . . . . . . . . . . . . . . . 1-(area code)-555-1212
Hospital (Maui Memorial):
    Information . . . . . . . . . . . . . . . . . . . . . . . . . . 242-2036
    Emergency . . . . . . . . . . . . . . . . . . . . . . . . . . . 242-2343
Camping Permits:
    State Parks . . . . . . . . . . . . . . . . . . . . . . . . . . . 243-5354
    County Parks . . . . . . . . . . . . . . . . . . . . . . . . . . 243-7389
Maui Visitors Bureau . . . . . . . . . . . . . . . . . . . . . . . . . 871-8691
Time of Day . . . . . . . . . . . . . . . . . . . . . . . . . . . . . . . 242-0212
Information - County of Maui (Gov't info & complaint) . . 243-7866
Haleakala National Park Information (recording) . . . . . . . . 572-7749
Haleakala Park Headquarters (a real person) . . . . . . . . . . 572-9306
Haleakala Weather . . . . . . . . . . . . . . . . . . . . . . . . . . . 871-5054
Ohe'o Headquarters Ranger Station (10am-4pm) . . . . . . . . 248-7375
Carthaginian . . . . . . . . . . . . . . . . . . . . . . . . . . . . . . . 661-8527
Baldwin Home (9am-5pm) . . . . . . . . . . . . . . . . . . . . . . 661-3262
Weather:
    Maui . . . . . . . . . . . . . . . . . . . . . . . . . . . . . . . . 877-5111
    Marine (also tides, sunrises, sunsets) . . . . . . . . . . . . . 877-3477
    Recreational Area . . . . . . . . . . . . . . . . . . . . . . . . 871-5054

The Aloha pages in the front of the phone book has various hotline numbers to call for community events, entertainment, etc. While the call is free, the companies pay to be included, so information is biased.

***COSTS PER HOUR:*** Did you ever wonder what something was costing in relation to the time spent? This is what we came up with based on approximate lengths of time with average prices.

| | |
|---|---|
| $300/hr | Parasail (based on $50 for a 10 min. ride) |
| $133.00 | Maui helicopter tour (1 1/2 hour trip) |
| $ 90.00 | Round trip (straight) coach airfare LA to Maui (11 hrs.) |
| $ 75.00 | Sailboat charter (usually 4 - 8 hrs.) |
| $ 70.00 | Rolls Royce limousine service |
| $ 50.00 | Fishing boat charter (8 hrs.) |
| $ 43.00 | Dinner for two at a top restaurant (2 hrs.) |
| $ 21.40 | 18 holes of golf at a resort course ($75 greens fee - 3 1/2 hrs of play) |
| $ 20.00 | Horseback rides (up to $25 per hr.) |
| $ 17.50 | Introductory scuba dive (3 hrs.) |
| $ 16.50 | Molokini snorkel trip (4 hrs. - $66) |
| $ 15.00 | Lana'i snorkel/sail/tour (8 hrs.) |
| $ 13.75 | Haleakala bike trip (8 hrs. - $110) |
| $ 11.85 | Deep sea fishing - Shared boat (8 hrs.) |
| $ 9.38 | Hotel room ($225/day) |
| $ 7.00 | Diver certification course (36 hrs.) |
| $ 6.20 | Haleakala sunrise van tour (6 hrs.) |
| $ 6.00 | Hana van tour (10 hrs.) |
| $ 5.00 | Moderate condominium ($120/day) |
| $ 1.25 | Rental car ($30/day) |

## GETTING THERE

The best air prices can generally be arranged through a reputable travel agent who can often secure air or air with car packages at good prices by volume purchasing. Prices can vary considerably, so comparison shopping is a wise idea. All have senior citizen and companion fare discounts. The major American carriers that fly from the mainland to The Honolulu International Airport on O'ahu, Hawai'i are:

AMERICAN AIRLINES - 1-800-433-7300, In Honolulu 808-523-9376, On Maui 808-244-5522. Direct flights to Maui from San Francisco and Los Angeles.

AMERICA WEST AIRLINES - 1-800-235-9393; offers service to Honolulu through its major mainland hubs of Las Vegas and Phoenix with connecting service to over 67 cities nationwide.

CANADIAN AIRLINES INTERNATIONAL - Eighteen weekly flights from Vancouver to and from Honolulu. Then connecting inter-island carriers to Maui.

CONTINENTAL AIRLINES - 1-800-525-0280; in Honolulu, 808-836-7730. Currently flights only to Honolulu with connecting service to Maui, no direct Maui flights.

DELTA AIR LINES - 1-800-221-1212. They fly out of Atlanta, stopping in Los Angeles, then direct flights to Maui. They also have one flight direct from Dallas-Fort Worth to Honolulu.

HAWAIIAN AIRLINES - 1-800-367-5320; in Honolulu, 808-838-1555; on Maui 808-871-5132.

NORTHWEST AIRLINES - 1-800-225-2525; in Honolulu, 808-955-2255. No direct Maui flights. No Maui phone number.

PLEASANT HAWAIIAN HOLIDAYS ★ - 1-800-242-9244. We were recently informed by one of our readers that they saved over $150 per ticket (over the lowest rate quoted by another airline) using an "airfare only" package from Pleasant Hawaiian. The flight was from San Francisco direct to Maui using American Trans Air and they tell us it was as good, if not better, than the service they've had on United. They even had a separate audio channel oriented towards small children. They added that the seat configuration on the L-1011 is 3-4-3 and they recommend tall people staying away from the middle 4 seats, which seemed to have less leg room.

TWA - 1-800-221-2000.

UNITED AIRLINES - United has more flights to Hawai'i from more U.S. cities than any other airline. UAL Reservations 1-800-241-6522. Flight information 1-800-824-6100. Their Honolulu number is 808-547-2211. They have a number of direct flights to Maui from Los Angeles, Denver, Chicago, Philadelphia and San Francisco. On Maui, phone 242-7911.

The direct flights available on United, Delta, and American Airlines save time and energy by avoiding the otherwise necessary stopover on O'ahu. Travel agents schedule at least an hour and a half between arrival on O'ahu and departure for Maui to account for any delays, baggage transfers, and the time required to reach the inter-island terminal.

If you do arrive early, check with the inter-island carrier. Very often you can get an earlier flight which will arrive on Maui in time to get your car, and maybe some groceries, before returning to pick up your luggage when it arrives on your scheduled flight.

***The inter-island carriers that operate between Honolulu and Maui are:***

ALOHA AIRLINES - They fly only jets - mostly 737s. 1-800-367-5250 U.S., 1-800-663-9471 Canada. Their Honolulu number is 808-484-1111, on Maui 808-244-9071. This airline tends to have more respect for its schedule than the others. They fly 1,200 flights weekly with their fleet of 15 Boeing 737s. Also weekly charter service to Christmas Island and long range charters upon request.

ISLANDAIR - Their fleet consists of 8 - 18 passenger twin engine deHavilland Dash 6 Twin Otters (turbo-prop) aircraft. They service the Kahului, Hana and are the only airlines that currently offer service to the Kapalua West Maui Airports on Maui as well as all other islands. From Hawai'i the toll free number is 1-800-652-6541 or 1-800-323-3345 U.S., Maui 808-877-5755. Charters available.

HAWAIIAN AIRLINES - Their phone service was so awful, we couldn't even get through to verify information. Toll free 1-800-367-5320.

Most visitors arrive at the Kahului Airport, via direct or inter-island flights. The Kahului Airport has been transformed over the past few years into an attractive new passenger center. No longer do you disembark from your plane and trudge down the runway to the airport terminal, although the walk within the terminal building from the United Airlines gate to the baggage claim area is quite a distance. There is now a regular baggage claim carousel and a restaurant that even offers runway views. The Kahului Airport has emerged from the stone age with a terminal to be proud of! They have improved the parking and they have a new rental car area.

From the airport it is only a 20-30 minute drive to the Kihei-Wailea-Makena areas, but a 45 to 60 minute drive to the Kaanapali/Kapalua areas. If your destination is West Maui from O'ahu, Kaua'i, or Hawai'i, it might be more convenient to fly into the *Kapalua West Maui Airport*. The airport is serviced by IslandAir and recently, Trans Air began passenger service (1-800-634-2094) serving neighbor islands.

In addition to inter-island commuter flights, there are several options to shuttle between islands by water. *Expeditions* (661-3756) departs from Lahaina to the island of Lana'i four times daily. Cost is $50 round trip adults, $40 children (an extra trip is made on Fridays). The *Maui Princess* travels between Lahaina, Maui and Kaunakakai on Moloka'i once each day, departing at 7:30 am and returning at 5:30 pm. $50 adults, $25 children. The *Maui Princess* (661-8397) also offers cruise/drive, golf, mule ride and overnight excursions. 1-800-833-5800 from the mainland US.

One pleasant way to see the Hawaiian islands is aboard one of the *American Hawaii Cruises* ships, the *Independence* or *Constitution*. These comfortable 700-foot (800 passenger) ships provide accommodations and friendly service during the seven day sail around the islands. In 1993, American Hawaii Cruises was acquired by The Delta Queen Steamboat Co. and new plans have are being initiated. Hawaiian costumes, onboard hands-on Hawaiian museum exhibits, cabins receiving Hawaiian names, traditional Hawaiian church services, menus filled with Hawaiian specialties, tropical flowers in every room are among the changes which bring the essence of Hawaii on board. American Hawaii has recently added on board Kumus (Hawaiian teachers) to teach passengers about the culture and history of Hawaii. A Kumu's Study with historic artifacts will be developed off the central lounge. The Sports Deck Solarium, on the Independence, will be converted into top-of-the-line passenger suites. (The Fitness Center and Conference Center will be relocated.) Fully handicap-accessible suites will be created and all passenger cabins will be stripped and redecorated. Direct cellular telephone service will be available from each cabin. A major improvement includes the expansion and redesign of the Buffet on the Upper Deck. Plans call for expanding the Buffet to the embarkation decks and creating a Hawaiian-style indoor-outdoor cooking and eating area extending to the ship's fantail, part of which will be shaded by canopies. The Independence will be out of dry-dock by fall of 1994.

Also available on both ships are a number of "Theme Cruises" which range from Big Band cruises to one which combines with the island's Aloha Festival. The ships come into port at each of the major islands for a day (or in some cases two) of touring.

Wedding ceremonies can be performed aboard both of American Hawaii's ships with the purchase of a special $495 wedding package. The package includes a minister/judge fee, a Hawaiian lei and haku for the bride and matching lei or boutonniere for the group, 24 photos in an album, live Hawaiian music and an individual wedding cake for two. Anniversary couples can arrange to renew their vows in a ceremony performed by the Captain himself. See GENERAL INFORMATION chapter for information on tests and licenses.

They also offer a special six-day package which begins on Sunday, especially convenient for those folks who have mainland weddings on Saturdays and then fly to the islands the following day. These packages include a choice of spending Sunday and Monday at the Hawaii Prince in Waikiki or the Maui Prince on Maui. On Tuesday, couples meet the SS Constitution in Kahului, Maui for a four-day cruise with an overnight stay on Maui and continue their cruise by calling at the ports of Kona and Hilo on the Big Island before disembarking in Honolulu on Saturday. Anniversary and Honeymoon packages are available.

American Hawaii also offers you the option of extending your stay on land following a seven day cruise.

American Hawaii has added new shore excursions which include opportunities for passengers to discover the "hidden" Hawaii. Trips include the opportunity to relax in an authentic polynesian-style outrigger canoe as a personal tour guide paddles through tropical landscapes and by exotic wildlife or hike through a rain forest to discover a hidden waterfall.

The idea of a cruise is to give you a taste of each of the islands without the time and inconvenience of traveling by plane in-between islands. In fact, it would be impossible to see all the islands in a week in any other fashion.

The SS Constitution will be in dry dock for renovation in 1995. For additional information write American Hawai'i Cruises and Land Vacations, 550 Kearny St., San Francisco, CA 94108. Phone 1-800-765-7000 from the U.S. or Canada. In San Francisco phone (415) 392-9400.

BOUGAINVILLEA

J. BAYOT

# GETTING AROUND

*FROM THE AIRPORT:* After arriving, there are several options. Taxi cabs, because of the distances between areas, can be very costly (i.e., $48 from Kahului to Kaanapali). There are several bus/limo services available also. Arthur's Limousine Service currently quotes (below) to most resorts from the Kahului airport. The limited around-the-island public transportation that did exist has been terminated at this time with no plans to reinstate it. There are some local area shuttles. The best option may be a rental car unless your resort provides transportation. The phone number for cab service, *Alii Cab* 808-667-7800.

*Trans Hawaiian* 1-800-533-8765 U.S., 1-800-654-2282 inter-island, 808-877-7308, provides the Kahului Airport with service to Lahaina and Kaanapali. No charge for first two bags, additional charge for more. The shuttle currently departs every hour from 7 am until 6 pm. Check in by baggage claim area #3. (Call to verify current schedules and price). Service from Kahului to Lahaina-Kaanapali-Kapalua is $22 round trip. *Akina Bus Service* Ltd. offers shuttle service from the Kahului Airport to the Kihei-Wailea-Makena area every hour on the hour from 8 am until 7 pm, $12. 808-879-2828. *SpeediShuttle* offers door-to-door airport service that fits your schedule. Pick up anytime and to any location in their 7 passenger van. Especially economical for a family. Call ahead for reservations 808-875-8070.

Travel in style with one of the limousine services. Rates between them are competitive, $60 and up per hour plus tax and gratuity. Minimum 2 hours. See transportation section for a list of the limo services. Also available with some companies are chauffers as drivers for your own car.

*LOCAL TRANSPORTATION:* If you don't choose a rental car, you will find Maui offers no public transportation. There are several shuttle services that offer free fare between Lahaina and Kaanapali. The free publication, *Maui Quick Guide*, has a listing of several of the schedules. These are not part of a public system, but instead are subsidized by various business or tourism agencies.

Kapalua has a shuttle running 6:15 am to midnight between the condos and the hotel. Call the front desk to request it. Most van tours offer pickup at your hotel or condo.

In Wailea there is a shuttle that offers transportation between the hotels, restaurants and shopping. Check with the front desk or concierge at the property at which you stay.

*RENTAL CARS AND TRUCKS:* It has been said that Maui has more rental cars per mile of road than anywhere in the nation. This is not surprising when you realize that Maui has no mass transit, a population of 85,000 (1990 figures for Island of Maui), and over two million visitors per year. Recently, shuttles have been initiated to help alleviate this problem. A choice of more than 30 car rental companies offer luxury or economy and new or used models. Some are local island operators, others are nation-wide chains, but all are very competitive. The rates may vary between high and low season and the best values are during price wars, or super summer discount specials.

Given the status of public transportation on Maui, a rental car is still the best bet and sometimes the only way to get around the island and, for your dollar, a very good buy. Prices are approximated as follows: Vans $89.99, Jeeps $70-75, Mid-size $48-$55, Compacts $35-$43.

The least expensive choice is a late-model compact with stick shift and no air conditioning. Often these cars are only 2 - 3 years old and in very good condition. Also available from specialty car rental agencies are a variety of luxury cars. A Porsche or Mercedes will run $200 plus per day.

Currently there are no companies which rent camping equipment. Vans are available from a number of agencies, but camping in them is not allowed.

Many of the rental companies have booths near the main terminal building at the Kahului Airport. There is also a large courtesy phone board in the main terminal (not at the United terminal). This free phone is for those rental agencies not having an airport booth, or for regular shuttle service, so that you can call for a pick up. A pay phone is available in the United terminal. A few agencies will take your flight information when your car reservation is made and will meet you and your luggage at the airport with your car.

The policies of all the rental car agencies are basically the same. Most require a minimum age of 21 to 25 and a maximum age of 70. All feature unlimited mileage with you buying the gas ($1.65 - $1.75 per gallon). Be sure to fill up before you return your car, the rental companies charge about $2.35 per gallon to do it for you. A few require a deposit or major credit card to hold your reservation.

Insurance is an option you may wish, which can run an additional $10 a day. A few agencies will require insurance for those under age 25. Most of the car rental agencies strongly encourage you to take the additional insurance coverage. Hawai'i is a no-fault state and without the insurance, you are required to take care of all the damages before leaving the island. We suggest you check with your own insurance company before you leave to verify exactly what your policy covers. Add to the rental price a 4% sales tax and a new $2 per day highway road tax.

A few of Maui's roadways are rough and rugged. The rental agencies recommend that cars not traverse these areas (shown on the map they distribute) and that if these roads are attempted, you are responsible for any damage. Some restrict driving to Haleakala due to drivers riding the brakes.

Discounts are few and far between. You might be able to use some airline award coupons, but they are often very restrictive. If you are a member of AAA you can receive a discount on rental cars.

## RENTAL CAR LISTING:

ADVENTURES
RENT A JEEP
877-6626

ALAMO
RENT A CAR
1-800-327-9633
Kahului 871-6235
Lahaina 661-7181

ANDRES
RENT A CAR
Kahului 877-5378

ARTHUR'S
LIMOUSINE SER-
VICE
1-800-345-4667
Kahului 871-5555

ATLAS U DRIVE
1-800-367-5238
Kahului 871-2860

AVIS
1-800-331-1212
Kahului 871-7575
Kaanapali 661-4588
Kihei 879-1905

BUDGET
1-800-527-0700
Kaanapali 661-8721
Wailea 874-2831
Kahului 244-4721

DOLLAR
1-800-367-7006
Kahului 877-2731
Kaanapali 667-2651
Lahaina 661-7187
Interisland
1-800-342-7398

HERTZ
1-800-654-8200
Kahului 877-5167
Kaanapali 661-3195

ISLAND AUTO
LEASING
Kahului 877-0031

KIHEI RENT-A-
CAR
Kihei 879-7257

MAUI RENT-A-
JEEP
Kahului 877-6626

NATIONAL
1-800-227-7368
Kahului 871-8851
Kaanapali 667-9737

SEARS
contracts Budget
1-800-451-3600
Kahului 877-0916

SURF RENTS
TRUCKS
(flat beds, pick-ups)
Wailuku 244-5544

UNITED TRUCK
RENTAL
Kahului 871-9458

VIP CAR RENTAL
1-800-367-6080
Kahului 877-2054

WORD OF MOUTH
RENT A CAR
Kahului 877-2436

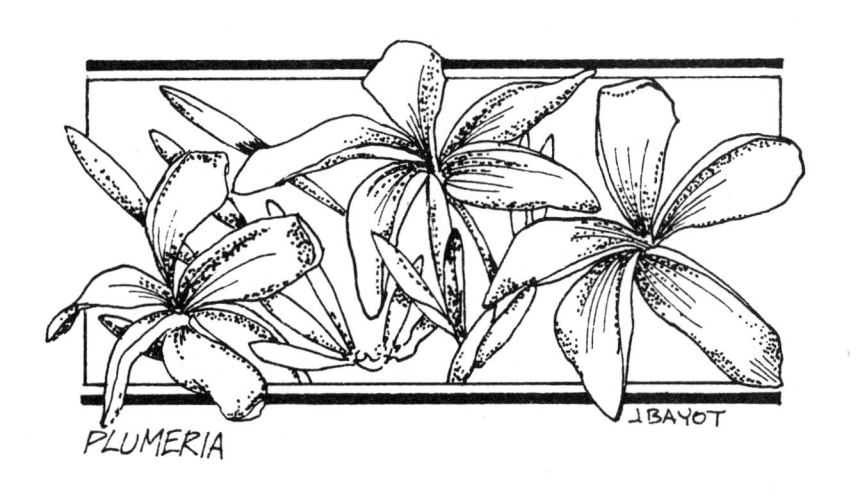

PLUMERIA

JBAYOT

# *GROCERY SHOPPING*

Grocery store prices may be one of the biggest surprises of your trip. While there are some locally grown foods and dairies, most of the products must be flown or shipped to the islands. The local folks can shop the advertisements and use the coupons, but it isn't so easy when traveling. To give you an idea of what to expect at the supermarket, here are some grocery store prices. Bread $1.65 and up, bananas .99 /lb., strained baby food 2 jars for $1, chicken $1.29 /lb., hamburger $1.99 /lb. and up, mayonnaise $1.99, Starkist Tuna $1.33, disposable diapers 12-24 count size $5.99 and up, 32 oz. ketchup $2.49, skim milk $3.79 gallon.

The three major grocery stores in Kahului are Foodland, Safeway (accepts Visa or Mastercard), and Star Market. In Lahaina you can choose between Foodland or Nagasako at the Lahaina Shopping Center, or the Safeway at the Cannery Shopping Center. In Kihei the major markets are Foodland and Star Market. These larger stores offer the same variety as your hometown store and the prices are better than at the small grocery outlets. In Hana there is Hasegawa's and the Hana Ranch Store. Long's Drug Stores carry some food items.

*Azeka's Market* (879-0611) at Azeka's Place in Kihei closed in the summer of 1994. However at the time of closure, announced they may reopen as a specialty meat and seafood market.

*The Farmers' Market* is a group of people who bring produce down from the Kula area. They set up roadside shopping, and you can't find it fresher. Their locations seem to change each time we visit. Just look for the green sandwich board signs that are set up roadside.

*Take Home Maui* (661-8067) is located just off Front Street in Lahaina and offers a selection of fruits and vegetables for shipment home. *Fresh Island Fish* (244-9633 or 242-6532) is located near the dock at Maalaea Harbor, open Mon.-Sat. 10-5. They offer a wonderful selection of fresh island fish and a cafe, open 10 am-8 pm (see restaurants). The *Nagasako Fish Market* on Lower Main Street in Wailuku have what may be the most diverse selection of fresh seafood from reef fish to live clams and crabs.

Local grocery shopping is a little more adventuresome. The largest local stores are in Wailuku and Kahului. In addition to the regular food staples they often have deli sections which feature local favorites and plate lunches. *Takamiya's* at 359 N. Market St. in Wailuku has a huge deli section with perhaps more than 50 cooked foods and salads as well as very fresh meats. *Ah Fook's* at the older Kahului Mall has a smaller deli section with plate lunches running about $3. *Ooka's* is the largest of the three. The packed parking lot and crowded aisles prove its popularity and low prices. Besides the usual sundry items, they have a fascinating and unusual array of foods. How about a tasty fresh pig ear ($1.29 lb.), pig blood ($1.99 lb.), tripe ($3.99), calf hoof or tongue. In the seafood aisle check out the Opihi ($25 lb.), cuttlefish ($13 lb.), Tobikko (Flying Fish Roe, $14.29 lb.), lomi salmon ($3.78 lb.) and whole or filets of fresh island fish like whole catfish ($3.99 lb.) or Onaga ($5.95 lb. is a great price!).

# ANNUAL MAUI EVENTS

## JANUARY/FEBRUARY
- Celebration of Whales at the Four Seasons Resorts on Maui
- Chinese New Year celebration at Ming Yuen Restaurant. A gourmet 10 course dinner is offered on several different evenings. 871-7787

## FEBRUARY
- Marine/Art Expo runs two months at the Kea Lani Resort in Wailea
- Chinese New Year champagne brunch at the Maui Inter-Continental Resort
- Professional surfing at Honolua Bay

## MARCH
- Annual Maui Marathon from Wailuku to Lahaina, sponsored by the Valley Isle Road Runners
- Annual Kukini Run along the Kahakuloa Valley Trail
- The 26th is Prince Kuhio Day, a state holiday
- Held February or March, the LPGA Women's Kemper Open at the Kaanapali Golf Course
- Maui Academy of Performing Arts Annual One Act Festival and Shakespeare Birthday Party. 244-8760.

## APRIL
- The Na Mele O Maui Festival celebrates Hawai'i's music heritage throughout the Kaanapali Resort. Children's singing only, remainder of festival in Dec.
- David Malo Day at Lahainaluna High School includes Hawaiian entertainment
- Pineapple Festival on Lana'i - a two-day annual event
- Hui No'eau Visual Arts Center, "Art Maui" - an annual juried show with works by island artists. Free admission
- East Maui Taro Festival in Hana with exhibits, demonstrations and sampling
- Budlight Triple Crown Softball Tournament - teams from Hawai'i and the mainland compete in Wailuku and Kihei
- Annual Maui Marathon, 10K Run in Iao Valley, sponsored by Valley Road Runners
- The Ritz-Carlton "Celebration of the Arts"
- Maui Agricultural Trade Show at Ulupalakua Ranch - (This event is more fun than it sounds. Held at Ulupalakua Ranch/Tedeschi Winery there is a chance to sample some creative island cooking

## MAY
- Maui Community Arts & Cultural Center presents Community Artsfest
- May Lei Day celebration in Wailea (check with the Inter-Continental Hotel for their events)
- Seabury Hall in Makawao sponsors their annual craft fair the Saturday prior to Mother's Day
- Statewide Hula Competition and Annual Lei Festival
- Annual Hard Rock Cafe World Cup of Windsurfing at Hookipa Beach Park
- On Molokai, the Molokai Ka Hula Piko, a celebration of the birth of hula on Molokai
- Tedeschi Vineyard 10K run through Upcountry Maui. Entry fee for participants
- Annual Bankoh Kayak Challenge, Molokai to Oahu, a 41 mile kayak race

## JUNE
- Kapalua Music Festival - a week of Hawaiian and classical music
- Obon Season (late June through August) - Bon Odori festivals are held at the many Buddhist temples around the island. They are announced in the local newspapers and the public is invited
- King Kamehameha Day Celebration
- Maui Upcountry Fair, Eddie Tam Center, Makawao
- Art Night Celebration & Art in the Park. A Friday/Saturday event that begins with a Friday eve street party with food, entertainment and art followed by juried arts and crafts fair under the Banyan Tree on Saturday
- Hard Rock Cafe Rock N Roll, 10K run
- Makeke Fair at the Hana Ballpark - Hawaiian music, hula, crafts, food & games

## JULY
- Annual 4th of July Rodeo & Parade in Makawao
- Fourth of July celebration at Maui Inter-Continental
- Fireworks on the Green, an Independence Day fireworks display at Kaanapali Golf Course
- Canoe races at Hookipa State Park
- Maui Jaycees Carnival at Kahului Fairground
- Annual Sausa Cup races in Lahaina, sponsored by the Lahaina Yacht Club
- Victoria to Maui Yacht Race
- Kapalua Wine Symposium culminating in the Chefs Festival, a great one day event featuring goodies from the best chefs in the best restaurants from all the islands
- Keiki Fishing Tournament at Kaanapali
- Annual Wailea Tennis Open Championship at the Wailea Tennis Club
- Friday Night is Art Night Anniversary Celebration

## AUGUST
- Run to the Sun Marathon, a grueling trek from sea level up to the 10,000 foot level of Haleakala Crater
- Maui Onion Festival at Whalers Village, Kaanapali
- The 21st is Admissions Day, a state holiday
- The "Rainbow Within You" Arts, Cultural & Environmental Festival at The Ritz-Carlton. An arts and music event includes hands-on activities & workshops
- The Molokai Ranch Rodeo, a statewide event held on the island of Moloka'i
- Maui Academy of Performing Arts annual Garden Party

## SEPTEMBER
- Maui County Rodeo in Makawao
- Aloha Festivals (events stretch into October)
- Labor Day Fishing Tournament
- The Annual Maui Writer's Conference, Labor Day Weekend at The Ritz-Carlton Kapalua
- Wailea Speed Crossing, a windsurfing regatta across the seven mile stretch of Pacific to Molokini and back. Sponsored by the Maui Inter-Continental
- "Taste of Lahaina" Food Festival at Lahaina Center. Proceeds from the festival will be donated to charity
- Haku Mele O Hana sponsored by the Hotel Hana-Maui. Traditional song, chant and dance

## OCTOBER
- Maui County Fair at the Kahului Fairgrounds
- Open Pro-Am Golf Championship
- Polo Season Begins at the Olinda Polo Field (808) 572-2790
- Parade and Halloween festivities in Lahaina
- Lahaina Coolers Historic Fun Run. A 5K run/walk with Lahaina's history with entertainment and re-enactments at each landmark. In connection with the Aloha Festival

## NOVEMBER
- Kapalua International Championship of Golf
- Queen Kaahumanu Festival at the Maui High School
- Sand Castle contest, check for current beach location in Kihei, usually held Thanksgiving weekend
- Thanksgiving weekend Santa arrives at Kaahumanu Mall
- Thanksgiving, La Hoomaikai, luau celebration at Maui Inter-Continental

## DECEMBER
- First part of December, Maui's Largest Gala Treelighting Ceremony at The Ritz-Carlton Kapalua, featuring a tree of lights to honor people around the world Proceeds benefit Maui's Ka Hale A Ke Ola Homeless Resource Center
- Kapalua/Betsy Nagelsen Pro-Am Tennis Invitational
- Christmas House at Hui Noeau, near Makawao, is a non-profit organization featuring pottery, wreaths, and other artwork
- Santa arrives by canoe at the Maui Inter-Continental Resort in Wailea

For the exact dates of many of these events, write to the Hawai'i Visitors Bureau, 2270 Kalakaua Avenue #801, Honolulu, HI 96815, and request the Hawai'i Special Events Calendar. The calendar also gives non-annual information and the contact person for each event. A more complete listing for Maui events can be obtained from the Maui Visitors Bureau, PO Box 580, Wailuku, HI 96793. Check the local papers for dates of additional events.

ANTHURIUMS

# *WEATHER*

When thinking of Hawaii, and especially Maui, one visualizes bright sunny days cooled by refreshing trade winds, and this is the weather at least 300 days a year. What about the other 65 days? Most aren't really bad - just not perfect. Although there are only two seasons, summer and winter, temperatures remain quite constant. Following are the average daily highs and lows for each month and the general weather conditions.

| | | | | | |
|---|---|---|---|---|---|
| January | 80/64 | May | 84/67 | September | 87/70 |
| Feb. | 79/64 | June | 86/69 | October | 86/69 |
| March | 80/64 | July | 86/70 | November | 83/68 |
| April | 82/66 | Aug. | 87/71 | December | 80/66 |

**Winter:** Mid October thru April, 70 - 80 degree days, 60 - 70 degree nights. Tradewinds are more erratic, vigorous to none. Kona winds are more frequent causing wide-spread cloudiness, rain showers, mugginess and even an occasional thunderstorm. 11 hours of daylight.

**Summer:** May thru mid October, 80 degree days, 70 - 80 degree nights. Tradewinds are more consistent keeping the temperatures tolerable, however, when the trades stop, the weather becomes hot and sticky. Kona winds are less frequent. 13 hours of daylight.

Summer type wear is suitable all year round. However, a warm sweater or lightweight jacket is a good idea for evenings and trips such as to Haleakala.

If you are interested in the types of weather you may encounter, or are confused by some of the terms you hear, read on. For further reference consult *Weather in Hawaiian Waters*, by Paul Haraguchi, 99 pages, available at island bookstores.

**TRADE WINDS:** Trade winds are an almost constant wind blowing from the northeast through the east and are caused by the Pacific anti-cyclone, a high pressure area. This high pressure area is well developed and remains semi-stationary in the summer causing the trades to remain steady over 90% of the time. Interruptions are much more frequent in the winter when they blow only 40 to 60% of the time. The major resort areas of South and West Maui are situated in the lee of the West Maui Mountains and Haleakala respectively. Here they are sheltered from the trades and the tremendous amount of rain (400 plus inches per year) they bring to the mountains.

**KONA WINDS:** The Kona Wind is a stormy, rain-bearing wind blowing from the southwest, or basically from the opposite direction of the trades. It brings high and rough surf to the resort side of the island - great for surfing and boogie-boarding, bad for snorkeling. These conditions are caused by low pressure areas northwest of the islands. Kona winds strong enough to cause property damage have occurred only twice since 1970. Lighter nondamaging Kona winds are much more common, occurring usually 2 - 5 times almost every winter (Nov-April).

***KONA WEATHER:*** Windless, hot and humid weather is referred to as Kona weather. The interruption of the normal trade wind pattern brings this on. The trades are replaced by light and variable winds and, although this may occur any time of the year, it is most noticeable during the summer when the weather is generally hotter and more humid, with fewer localized breezes.

***KONA LOW:*** A Kona low is a slow-moving, meandering, extensive low pressure area which forms near the islands. This causes continuous rain with thunderstorms over an extensive area and lasts for several days. November through May is the most usual time for these to occur.

***HURRICANES:*** Hawai'i is not free of hurricanes. However, most of the threatening tropical cyclones have weakened before reaching the islands, or have passed harmlessly to the west. Their effects are usually minimal, causing only high surf on the eastern and southern shores of some of the islands. At least 21 hurricanes or tropical storms have passed within 300 miles of the islands in the last 33 years, but most did little or no damage.

Hurricane Dot of 1959, Hurricane Iwa of 1982 and Hurricane Iniki in 1992 caused extensive damage. In each case, the island of Kaua'i was hit hardest, with lesser damage to southeast O'ahu and very little damage to Maui. Kaua'i has been much slower to recover from the damage caused by the September 1992 Hurricane Iniki, and more than 1 1/2 years following the devastation, there are still several major island resorts that have not yet begun restoration. Some of the difficulties in restoring real estate have been collecting on insurance and finding new companies to insurance against future natural disasters.

***TSUNAMI:*** A tsunami is an ocean wave produced by an undersea earthquake, volcanic eruption, or landslide. Tsunamis are usually generated along the coasts of South America, the Aleutian Islands, the Kamchatka Peninsula, or Japan and travel through the ocean at 400 to 500 miles an hour. It takes at least 4 1/2 hours for a tsunami to reach the Hawaiian Islands. A 24-hour Tsunami Warning System has been established in Hawai'i since 1946. When the possibility exists of a tsunami reaching Hawaiian waters, the public will be informed by the sound of the attention alert signal sirens. This particular signal is a steady one minute siren, followed by one minute of silence, repeating as long as necessary. Immediately turn on a TV or radio; all stations will carry CIV-Alert emergency information and instructions with the arrival time of the first waves. Do not take chances - false alarms are not issued. Move quickly out of low lying coastal areas that are subject to possible inundation.

The warning sirens are tested throughout the state on the first working Monday of every month at 11 am. The test lasts only a few minutes and CIV-Alert announces on all stations that the test is underway. Since 1813, there have been 112 tsunamis observed in Hawai'i with only 16 causing significant damage.

Tsunamis may also be generated by local volcanic earthquakes. In the last 100 years there have been only six, with the last one November 29, 1975, affecting the southeast coast of the island of Hawaii. The Hawaiian Civil Defense has placed earthquake sensors on all the islands and, if a violent local earthquake occurs, an urgent tsunami warning will be broadcast and the tsunami sirens will sound.

A locally generated tsunami will reach the other islands very quickly. Therefore, there may not be time for an attention alert signal to sound. Any violent earthquake that causes you to fall or hold onto something to prevent falling is an urgent warning, and you should immediately evacuate beaches and coastal low-lying areas.

For additional information on warnings and procedures in the event of a hurricane, tsunami, earthquake or flash flood, read the civil defense section located in the forward section of the Maui phone book.

*TIDES:* The average tidal range is about two feet. Tide tables are available daily in the Maui News or by calling the marine weather number, 877-3477.

*SUNRISE AND SUNSET:* In Hawaii, day length and the altitude of the noon sun above the horizon do not vary as much throughout the year as at the temperate regions because of the island's low latitude within the sub-tropics. The longest day is 13 hours 26 minutes (sunrise 5:53 am, sunset 7:18 pm) at the end of June, and the shortest day is 10 hours 50 minutes (sunrise 7:09 am and sunset 6:01 pm at the end of December). Daylight for outdoor activities without artificial lighting lasts about 45 minutes past sunset.

GINGER &
ANTHURIUMS

# WHERE TO STAY
# WHAT TO SEE

## *INTRODUCTION*

Maui has more than 16,000 hotel rooms and condominium units in vacation rental programs, with the bulk of the accommodations located in two areas. These are West Maui, a 10-mile stretch between Lahaina and Kapalua, and the South shore of East Maui, which is also about ten miles of coastline between Maalaea and Makena. On the northern side, in the Kahului/Wailuku area, as well in Upcountry Maui, accommodations are more limited. In Hana there are a number of agencies that provide homes for rent and a few condominiums. This chapter contains a list of essentially all of the condominiums that are in rental programs, as well as the island's hotels. Bed and Breakfast homes are sprinkled around the island, and we have included a few of these along with agencies that have additional listings.

***HOW TO USE THIS CHAPTER:*** For ease in locating information, the properties are first indexed alphabetically following this introduction. In both South and West Maui, the condominiums have been divided into groups that are geographically distinct and are laid out (sequentially) as you would approach them arriving from the Kahului area. These areas also seem to offer similar price ranges, building style, and beachfronts. At the beginning of each section is a description of the area, sights to see, shopping information, best bets and a sequential listing of the complexes. For each complex, we have listed the local address and/or P.O. Box and the local, fax and toll-free phone numbers. Often times the management at the property does reservations, other times not.

In many cases there are a variety of rental agents handling units in addition to the on-site management and we have listed an assortment of these. We suggest that when you determine which condo you are interested in that you call all of the agents. Be aware that while one agent may tell you they have no vacancy, another will have several. The prices we have listed are generally the lowest available (although some agents may offer lower rates but with the reduction of certain services such as maid service on check in only - that means your room is clean when you arrive - rather than daily maid service). Unfortunately, we've had at least one occasion where the cheaper rate resulted in a condo that needed not only a good cleaning, but complete renovation. On the other hand, a reputable rental agent will not let a unit fall into disrepair. We recommend ***Kihei Maui Vacations*** for their broad range of properties in South Maui, and ***Whalers Realty*** in West Maui offers moderate to expensive properties at rates lower than the posted rack rates. At the end of the accommodations chapter is an alphabetical listing of rental agents and the properties they handle. Prices can vary, sometimes greatly, from one agent to another, so we suggest again that you contact them all.

Prices are listed to aid your selection and, while these were the most current available at press time, they are subject to change without notice.

# WHERE TO STAY - WHAT TO SEE
## *Introduction*

As island vacationers ourselves, we found it important to include this feature rather than just giving you broad categories such as budget or expensive. After all, one person's "expensive" may be "budget" to someone else!

For the sake of space, we have made use of several abbreviations. The size of the condominiums are identified as studio (S BR), one bedroom (1 BR), two bedroom (2 BR) and three bedroom (3 BR). The numbers in parenthesis refers to the number of people that can occupy the unit for the price listed and that there are enough beds for a maximum number of people to occupy this unit. The description will tell you how much it will be for additional persons over two, i.e. each additional person $10/night. Some facilities consider an infant as an extra person, others will allow children free up to a specified age. The abbreviations o.f., g.v., and o.v. refer to oceanfront, gardenview and oceanview units.

The prices are listed with a slash dividing them. The first price listed is the high season rate, the second price is the low season rate. A few have a flat yearly rate so there will be only be a single price.

All listings are condominiums unless specified as a (Hotel). Condos are abundant, and the prices and facilities they offer can be quite varied. We have tried to indicate our own personal preferences by the use of a ★. We felt these were the best buys or special in some way. However, it is impossible for us to view all the units within a complex, and since condominiums are privately owned, each unit can vary in its furnishings and its condition.

**WHERE TO STAY:** As for choosing the area of the island in which to stay, we offer these suggestions. The Lahaina and Kaanapali areas offer the visitor the hub of the island's activities, but accommodations are a little more costly. The beaches are especially good at Kaanapali.

The values and choice of condos are more extensive a little beyond Kaanapali in Honokowai, Kahana (Lower Honoapiilani Hwy. area) and further at Napili. However, there are fewer restaurants here and slightly cooler temperatures. Some of the condominiums in this area, while very adequate, may be a little overdue for redecorating. While many complexes are on nice beaches, many are also on rocky shores.

Kapalua offers high class and high price condominium and hotel accommodations. Maalaea and Kihei are a half-hour drive from Lahaina and offer some attractive condo units at excellent prices and, although few are located on a beach, there are plenty of easily accessible public beach parks.

Many Maui vacationers feel that Kihei offers better weather in the winter months, and this may be true with annual rainfall only about 3" on Maui's southern shore. There are plenty of restaurants here and an even broader selection by driving the short distance to Wailuku.

The Wailea and Makena areas are just beyond Kihei and are beautifully developed resort areas. The beaches in this area are excellent for a variety of water activities However, this area is significantly more expensive than the neighboring Kihei area. The introductory section to each area offers additional information.

***HOW TO SAVE MONEY:*** Maui has two price seasons. High or "in" season and low or "off" season. Low season is generally considered to be April 15 to about December 15, and the rates are discounted at some places as much as 30%. Different resorts and condominiums may vary these dates by as much as two weeks and a few resorts are going to a flat, year round rate. Ironically, some of the best weather is during the fall when temperatures are cooler than summer and there is less rain than the winter and spring months. (See GENERAL INFORMA-TION - weather for year round temperatures).

For longer than one week, a condo unit with a kitchen can result in significant savings on your food bill. While this will give you more space than a hotel room and at a lower price, you may give up some resort amenities (shops, restaurants, maid service, etc.). There are several large grocery stores around the island with fairly competitive prices, although most things at the store will run slightly higher than on the mainland. (See GENERAL INFORMATION - Shopping.)

Money can be saved by using the following tips when choosing a place to settle. First, it is less expensive to stay during the off or low season. Second, there are some areas that are much less expensive. Although Kahului has some motel units, we can't recommend this area as a place to headquarter your stay. The weather is wetter in winter, hotter in summer, generally windier than the other side of the island, and there are few good beaches. Two renovated old hotels in Wailuku now offer serviceable, basic and affordable accommodations for the budget minded, and they should especially appeal to the windsurfing community with nearby Hookipa Beach. There are some good deals in the Maalaea and Kihei areas, and the northern area above Lahaina has some older complexes that are reasonably good values. Third, there are some pleasant condo units either across the road from the beach or on a rocky, less attractive beach. This can represent a tremen-dous savings, and there are always good beaches a short walk or drive away. Fourth, hotel rooms or condos with garden or mountain views are less costly than oceanview or oceanfront rooms. We find the mountain view, especially in Kaanapali, to be, in fact, superior. The mountains are simply gorgeous and we'd rather be on the beach than look at it!

Most condominiums offer maid service only on check-out. A few might offer it twice a week or weekly. Additional maid service may be available for an extra charge. A few condos still do not provide in-room phones or color televisions, and fewer still have no pool. (A few words of caution: condominium units within one complex can differ greatly and, if a phone is important to you, ask!) Many are adding microwaves to their kitchens. Some may also add up to $1 per in-room local call, others have no extra charge for local calls. Some units have washers and dryers in the rooms, while others do not. Most have coin-operated laundry facilities on the premises.

Travel agents will be able to book your stay in the Maui hotels and also in most condominiums. If you prefer to make your own reservation, we have listed the various contacts for each condominium and endeavored to quote the best price generally available. Rates vary between rental agents, so check all those listed for a particular condominium. We have indicated toll free 800 numbers for the U.S. when available. For additional Canadian toll free numbers, check the rental agent list at the end of this chapter. Look for an 808 area code preceding the non-toll free numbers. You might also check the classified ads in your local newspaper for owners offering their units, which may be a better bargain.

Although prices can jump, most go up only 5-10% per year. Prices listed do not include the sales tax which is over 9%.

**GENERAL POLICIES:** Condominium complexes require a deposit, usually equivalent to one or two nights stay, to secure your reservation and insure your room rate from price increases. Some charge higher deposits during winter or over Christmas holidays. Generally a 30 day notice of cancellation is needed to receive a full refund. Most require payment in full either 30 days prior to arrival or upon arrival, and many do not accept credit cards.

The usual minimum condo stay is 3 nights with some requiring one week in winter. Christmas holidays may have steeper restrictions with minimum stays as long as two weeks, payments 90 days in advance and heavy cancellation penalties. It is not uncommon to book as much as two years in advance for the Christmas season. ALL CONDOMINIUMS HAVE KITCHENS, T.V.'S, AND POOLS UNLESS OTHERWISE SPECIFIED.

Monthly and oftentimes weekly discounts are available. Room rates quoted are generally for two. Additional persons run $8 - $15 per night per person with the exception of the high class resorts and hotels where it may run as much as $25 to $35 extra. Many complexes can arrange for crib rentals. (See GENERAL INFORMATION - Traveling with Children.)

We have tried to give the lowest rates generally available, which might not be through the hotel or condo office, so check with the offices as well as the rental agents. When contacting condominium complexes by mail, be sure to address your correspondence to the attention of the manager. The managers of several complexes do not handle any reservations and we have indicated to whom you should address reservation requests. If two addresses are given, use the P.O. Box rather than street address.

# BED AND BREAKFAST

An alternative to condominiums and hotels are the Bed and Breakfast organizations. They offer homes around the island, and some very reasonable rates. *Bed & Breakfast Hawaii* is among the best known. To become a member and receive their directory, which also includes the other islands, contact: *Bed and Breakfast Hawaii*, Directory of Homes, Box 449, Kapaa, HI 96746. Another organization, *Bed and Breakfast Maui Style* can be reached at P.O. Box 886, Kihei, HI 96753 (808-879-7865) or (808-879-2352). *Go Native Hawaii* also features bed and breakfast vacations. Contact them at PO Box 13115, Lansing, MI 48901, phone (517-349-9598). Following are just a few of the Bed and Breakfast selections offered on Maui:

**Ann & Bob Babson's B & B Vacation Rentals**, 3371 Keha Drive, Kihei, Maui, HI 96753. (808) 874-1166 or toll free 1-800-824-6409. The Babson's offer four vacation rentals with panoramic Pacific Ocean views in Maui Meadows, a residential area, located above Wailea on the Southwest side of Maui. All rentals include cable TV, telephone, and washer/dryer. The main house is situated on a half acre and offers a Bougainvillea Suite (bedroom with private bath), Molokini Master Suite (Master BR with private bath & jacuzzi) or Hibiscus Hideaway Apartment (1 BR 1 BTH w/ kitchen) $65-80. 2BR 2BTH cottage w/kitchen (max 6) $95.

*Garden Gate*, PO Box 12321, Lahaina, Maui, HI 96771. (808) 661-8800, FAX (808) 667-7999. Hosts Ron & Welmoet Glover offer a Garden Studio with private deck, queen bed, queen sleeper/sofa with private bath and kitchen facilities. Their Molokai Room offers a full bed and private bath. Children accepted. Located at 67 Kaniau Road, just outside of Lahaina. Prices begins at $50 per night.

*Kula View B & B*, PO Box 322, Kula, HI 96790. (808) 878-6736. Located on two acres in the cool Upcountry region on the slopes of Haleakala. They offer private room, bath and deck with own entrance. $75 single or double occupancy. Your host, Susan Kauai, is descended from a kamaaina Hawai'i family.

*Kula Lynn Farm*, PO Box 847, Kula, HI 96789. (808) 878-6176 or FAX (808) 878-6320. Your hosts are a part of the Coon family (Trilogy cruises) and they offer several rooms on the ground floor level of their home. $75 single or double, $5 each additional person, max. 6 persons. Three night minimum.

*Old Lahaina House Bed & Breakfast*, 407 Ilikahi St., Lahaina, HI 96761. (808) 667-4663, 1-800-847-0761, FAX (808) 667-5615. Hosts John and Sherry Barbier offer a home in the historic Lahaina area. Swimming pool, Hawaiian continental breakfast. Two rooms with private bath, king size bed, air-conditioning, refrigerator at $95. Two rooms with two twin beds, air-conditioning and a shared bath at $60 per night. Prices are $10 less for singles, add $10 for each person. They are across the street from a neighborhood beach and four blocks from Lahaina Harbor.

*Pilialoha Bed & Breakfast Cottage*, 255 Kaupakalua Rd., Haiku, HI 96708. (808) 572-1440. Hosts Bill & Machiko Heyde offer a cottage with fully equipped kitchen, phone, and wash/dryer. $75 for single/double occupancy, $10 each additional person. Located in Upcountry Maui, near Makawao.

*Silver Cloud Upcountry Guest Ranch*, Old Thompson Rd., RR2 Box 201, Kula, Maui, HI 96790. (808) 878-6101. FAX (808) 878-2132. SilverCloud Ranch was originally part of the Thompson Ranch, which had its beginnings on Maui in 1902. The nine-acre ranch is located at the 2,800 ft. elevation on the slopes of Haleakala. Owners Mike and Sara Gerry have done major renovations and now offer 12 rooms, suites and cottages, each with private bathrooms and most with private lanais and entrances. The King Kamehameha and Queen Emma suites are located in the main house with a private lanai and view of the lush Upcountry. The Lana'i Cottage offers total privacy with a complete kitchen, clawfooted bathtub, woodburning stove surrounded by a lovely flower garden and lanai. The Paniolo Bunkhouse has studios that are furnished in Hawaiian motif. They offer kitchenettes and lanais. The Bunkhouse's Haleakala suite is a larger facility with a bedroom, separate living area, fireplace and complete kitchen. Room rates include breakfast and use of the main house and kitchen. No minimum stay, and discounts for seven nights or longer. Plantation Home Bedrooms with private baths $75-$95, Paniolo Bunkhouse Suites $95-$125, Lanai Cottage $135.

***Tony's Place***, 13 Kauala Rd., Lahaina, Maui, HI 96761. (808) 661-8040. Located at the corner of Kauala Rd. and Front Street. Lodging with kitchen privileges in a simply furnished home. He offers three rooms with double or twin beds, but notes "that some couples have opted to put the two twins in their room together while guesting here instead of staying elsewhere. I don't think the room is attractive that way but if they are happy, usually, so am I." Tony Mamo, a would-be writer moved from Alaska to Hawai'i in 1990 and in addition to running his guest home he works as a journeyman electrician. Complimentary Kona Coffee each morning, continental breakfast $4.50. Tax included $40 single, $50 double. Two night minimum stay.

# PRIVATE RESIDENCES

For a large family, a couple of families, or a group of friends, a vacation home rather than a condo, may be a more spacious and cost effective option. Homes are available in all areas of the island. Following are a list of agents.

***Bello Realty-Maui Beach Homes***, PO Box 1776, Kihei, Maui, HI 96753. (808-879-2598). 1-800-541-3060 U.S. & Canada. Condos and homes rented by the day, week or month. Specializing in the Kihei area.

***Elite Holidays Unlimited***, PO Box 10817, Lahaina, Maui, HI 96761. 1-800-448-9222 U.S. & Canada, (808-667-5527). Condos, family homes and luxury estates available for weekly and monthly rentals on Maui and other islands. Condos include The Whaler, Polo Beach, Kaanapali Plantation and Kapalua Bay and Golf Villas. Condo and car packages available.

***Hana Bay Vacation Rentals***, Stan Collins offers eight homes in the Hana area. Contact Hana Bay Vacation Rentals, PO Box 318, Hana, Maui, HI 96713. (808-248-7727).

***Hawaiian Apartment Leasing Enterprise***, 479 Ocean Ave., Suite B., Laguna Beach, CA 92651. 1-800-472-8449 California, 1-800-854-8843 U.S. except California, 1-800-824-8968. 150 plus homes and 90 condominium properties on all islands.

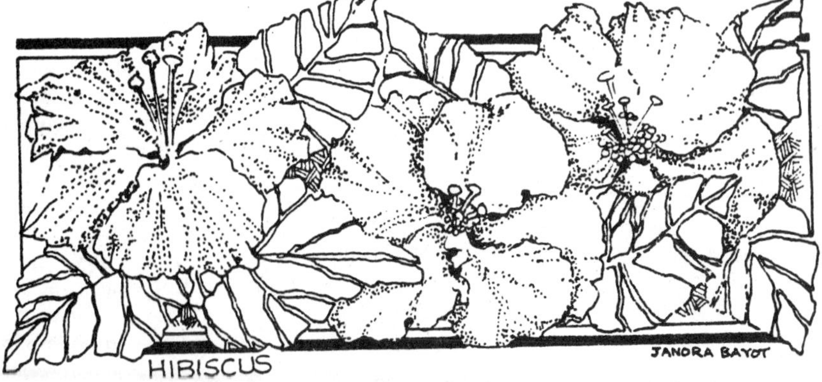

HIBISCUS

JANORA BAYOT

*Hawaiian Luxury Vacation Homes*, 1-800-982-8778, 1-808-669-1737. Luxury homes with minimum one week stay, two weeks over Christmas. Maid service available.

*Kihei Maui Vacations*, 1-800-542-6284 US, 1-800-423-8733 ext. 4000 Canada (808-879-7581). In addition to condos they offer homes and cottages in the Kihei, Wailea and Makena areas.

*Maui and All Islands*, PO Box 1089, Aldergrove, BC V0X 1A0. U.S. Mailing address PO Box 947, Lyden, WA 98264. 1-800-663-6962 from B. C. and Alberta. (604) 533-4190. Approximately 150 homes rented weekly, bi-weekly and monthly on Kaua'i and Maui.

*Maui Condo and Home Rental*, PO Box 1840, Kihei, Maui, Hi 96753. 1-800-822-3309 U.S., 1-800-822-4409 U.S. & Canada, (808-879-5445). Homes and condos rented daily, weekly and monthly in Kihei and Wailea areas.

*Vacation Locations, Hawaii*, 1-800-522-2757 or (808-874-0077). Rent homes on Maui or neighbor islands. Don't want to cook or clean? Select a home with daily maid service and a cook.

*Windsurfing West, Ltd.*, PO Box 330104, Kahului, Maui, HI 96733. 1-800-782-6105. (808-575-9228) FAX (808-575-2826). They offer South Maui condominiums available with a land package that includes a condo, car and windsurfing equipment. Lessons available.

## LONG-TERM STAYS

Almost all condo complexes and rental agents offer the long term visitor moderate to substantial discounts for stays of one month or more. Private homes can also be booked through the agents listed above.

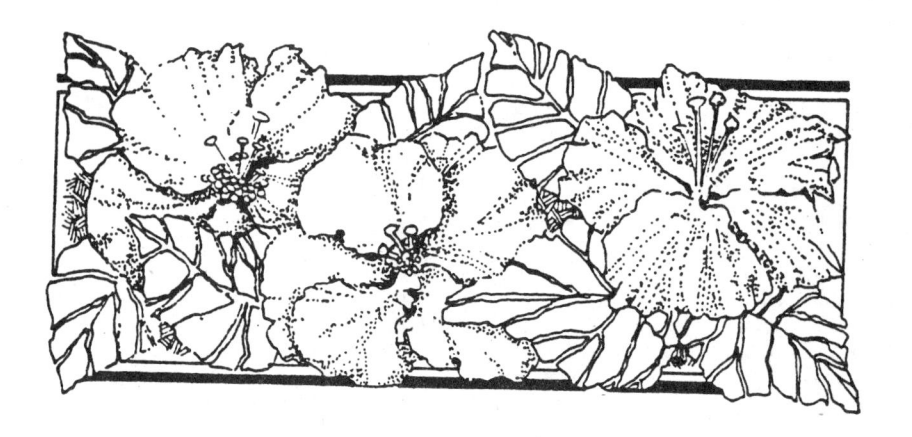

# CONDOMINIUM & HOTEL INDEX

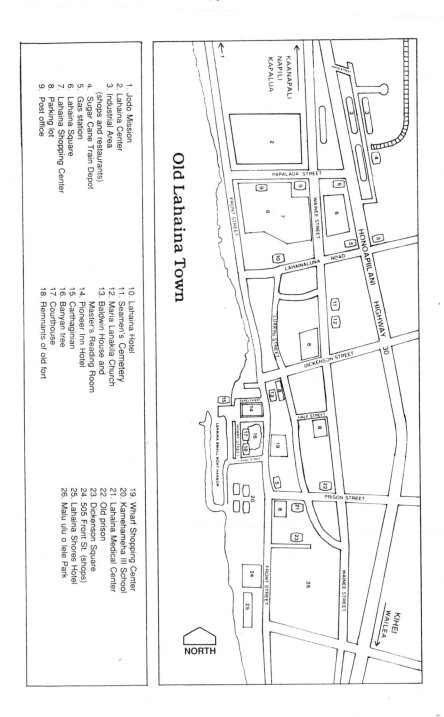

## Old Lahaina Town

1. Jodo Mission
2. Lahaina Center
3. Industrial Area
   (shops and restaurants)
4. Sugar Cane Train Depot
5. Gas station
6. Lahaina Square
7. Lahaina Shopping Center
8. Parking lot
9. Post office

10. Lahaina Hotel
11. Seamen's Cemetery
12. Maria Lanakila Church
13. Baldwin House and
    Master's Reading Room
14. Pioneer Inn Hotel
15. Carthaginian
16. Banyan tree
17. Courthouse
18. Remnants of old fort

19. Wharf Shopping Center
20. Kamehameha III School
21. Lahaina Medical Center
22. Old prison
23. Dickenson Square
24. 505 Front St. (shops)
25. Lahaina Shores Hotel
26. Malu ulu o lele Park

NORTH

# LAHAINA

## INTRODUCTION

As you leave the Kahului area on Hwy. 38, you plunge immediately into miles of sugar cane. The rugged and deeply carved valleys of the West Maui mountains are on the right, and on the left is the dormant volcano, Haleakala. Its broad base and seemingly gentle slopes belie its 11,000 foot height, and no hint of its enormous moon-like crater is discernible from below. On a clear day the mountains are so distinct and sharp edged they appear to have been cut out with giant scissors. The drive across the isthmus ends quickly as you pass Maalaea Harbor where the gently swaying sugar cane gives way to rugged sea cliffs and panoramic Pacific vistas. Across the bay is the South Maui coastline and in the distance the islands of Kaho'olawe and Lana'i. Construction of this road was to accommodate the new resort developments at Kaanapali that began in the 1960's. Traffic must have been far different on the old road which is still visible in places along the craggy cliffside. The tunnel, built in 1951, is the only one on Maui. Just beyond it are enormous metal chain blankets hanging along the rocky cliffs above the road. Termed a protective measure by some and an eyesore by others, they were installed in 1987.

As you descend from the cliffs the first glimpse of the tropical and undeveloped West Maui coastline is always a thrill. Stretching as far as the eye can see are sugar cane fields hugging the lower slopes of the mountains and a series of narrow, white sand beaches lined by kiawe trees and coconut palms. For several miles the constant stream of traffic is the only clue to the populated areas ahead. The first sign of civilization is Olowalu, a mere hamlet along the roadside and an unusual location for one of the island's best restaurants, Chez Paul. Public beaches continue to line the highway and the unobstructed view of the ocean may reward the observant with a whale sighting during the December to April humpback season.

A few homes to the left and the monolithic smoke stack of the Pioneer Mill announce your arrival to Lahaina, the now bustling tourist center of Maui. It has maintained the aura of more than a century ago when it was the whaling capitol of the world. Located about a 45 minute drive from the Kahului Airport (depending on traffic), this coastal port is noted for its Front Street, which is a several block strip of shops and restaurants along the waterfront. The Lahaina Harbor is filled with boats of varying shapes and sizes, eager to take the visitor aboard for a variety of sea excursions.

The oldest accommodation on the island, Pioneer Inn, is located here. Still popular among many a visitor, it offers a nostalgic and rustic atmosphere, and reasonable prices. Other accommodations include a luxuriously expensive condominium complex and two charming new country inns. Although several complexes are located oceanfront, the beaches in Lahaina are fronted by a close-in reef which prohibits swimming. Only Puamana has a beach suitable for swimming. If you want to be in the midst of the action on Maui, you might want to investigate staying in this area.

## WHAT TO DO AND SEE

There is much to see and do in busy Lahaina town. The word Lahaina means "merciless sun," and it does tend to become quite warm, especially in the afternoon with little relief from the tropical trade winds. Parking can be somewhat irksome. Several all day lots are located near the corner of Wainee and Dickenson (only a couple blocks off Front Street) and charge $5 for all day. One nearer to Front Street charges $7 per day. The inexpensive lots fill up early in the day. The Lahaina Shopping Center has a three hour (free) parking area, but it is always very crowded. Lahaina Center, across the street from the Lahaina Shopping Center, has pay parking, validated with purchase from one of the stores. If you don't mind a short walk, parking is available across the road from the 505 Front Street shops. (See the Lahaina map for locations of other parking areas.) On-street parking is very limited and if you are fortunate enough to find a spot, many are only for one hour. BEWARE: the police here are quite prompt and efficient at towing.

The *Lahaina Express*, a free transportation system linking the Kaanapali Beach Resort to Lahaina, is sponsored by Hilo Hattie and The Wharf Cinema Center. Two blue double-decker buses and a trolley operate daily from 8 am to 10 pm running every half hour. The two Lahaina stops will be at the entrance to Hilo Hattie at Lahaina Center, and a second at the Wharf Cinema Center.

Now that you have arrived, let's get started. Historical memorabilia abounds in Lahaina. The Lahaina Restoration Foundation has done an admirable job restoring and maintaining many historical landmarks. If you have questions, contact their office at 661-3262. The historical landmarks have all been identified by numbered markers. A free walking tour map of Lahaina can be found in a copy of the Lahaina Historical Guide. Look for free copies of this pocket-size guide on corner display racks in Lahaina town. Then enjoy your walking tour of the Baldwin House, Carthaginian, Masters Reading Room, and Wo Hing Temple.

*The Banyan Tree* is very easy to spot at the south end of Lahaina adjacent to Pioneer Inn on Front Street. Planted on April 24, 1873 by Sheriff William Owen Smith, it was to commemorate the 50th anniversary of Lahaina's first Protestant Christian Mission.

The stone ruins of *The Old Fort* can be found harborside near the Banyan Tree. The fort was constructed in the 1830's to protect the missionaries' homes from the whaling ships and the occasional cannon ball that would be shot off when the sailors were aroused. The fort was later torn down and the coral blocks reused elsewhere. A few blocks have been excavated and the corner of the fort was rebuilt as a landmark in 1964. On the corner near the Pioneer Inn is a plaque marking the site of the 1987 Lahaina Reunion Time Capsule, which contains newspapers, photos and other memorabilia.

*Pioneer Inn* is the distinguished green and white structure just north of the Banyan Tree. It was a haven for inter-island travelers during the early days of the 20th century. Built back in 1901, it managed to survive the dry years of prohibition, adding a new wing, center garden and pool area in 1966. A single restaurant operates here and accommodations are now available only in the newer structure.

The history of Pioneer Inn is an interesting one and is discussed under the accommodation information which follows. (See RESTAURANTS - Lahaina and WHERE TO STAY - Lahaina for additional information.)

The **Lahaina Courthouse** was built in 1859, at a cost of $7,000, from wood and stone taken from the palace of Kamehameha II. You'll find it near the Lahaina Harbor. The Lahaina Restoration and Preservation Foundation anticipates in the future to begin renovations to restore and convert it into a museum featuring Lahaina's plantation era, and the importance of the reign of Kamehameha III on the Hawaiian Islands. The first floor would also house an information center.

In front of Pioneer Inn is the **Lahaina Harbor**. You can stroll down and see the boats and visit stalls where a wide variety of water sports and tours can be arranged. (See RECREATION AND TOURS) *The Carthaginian,* anchored just outside the harbor, is a replica of a 19th century square rigger, typical of the ships that brought the first missionaries and whalers to these shores. The first *Carthaginian* sank on Easter Sunday, April 2, 1972. It had been built in 1921 in Denmark as a schooner and the 130 foot vessel had sailed the world as a cargo ship. She was purchased by Tucker Thompson and sailed to Hawai'i in 1964. Her original name was *Wandia*, but was rechristened *Carthaginian* in Honolulu with a bottle of passion fruit juice. The ship was used in the South Pacific for a time and later was restored to resemble a whaling vessel for the movie version of Michener's "Hawai'i." The Lahaina Restoration Foundation worked to acquire the *Carthaginian* for $75,000. The ship found a home at the Lahaina wharf, becoming an exhibit of the whaling era. On June 20, 1971 it was discovered by the ship's skipper, Don Bell, that the vessel was sinking. The ship was pumped and a large hole was patched, the cause seeming to be dry rot. It was decided the following year to tow her to Honolulu for repairs in dry dock. However, 150 yards from dock she became lodged on the reef and valiant efforts to save her were not successful. An immediate search began for a replacement and it was found in the Danish port of Soby. The ship was a 97 foot steel hulled freighter that had originally been a schooner, but had been demasted. The ship called *Komet* had been built in the shipyards in Germany in 1920 and was purchased for $20,500.

CARTHAGINIAN

An all-Lahaina crew sailed via the Panama Canal and arrived in Hawai'i in September, 1973. Volunteers set to work transforming the ship to the proud vessel it is today and it was christened *Brig Carthaginian* on April 26, 1980. Today the ship features video movies and recorded songs of humpback whales and an authentic 19th century whale boat. All items are on display below deck. The ship is open daily from 10am to 4:30pm. Admission $3 adults, seniors $2 and children free.

Whale watching is always an exciting pastime in Lahaina. The whales usually arrive in November and December to breed and calve in the warm waters off Maui for several months.There is also a number to call to report any sightings you make: WHALE WATCH HOTLINE at 879-8811. Numerous whale watching excursions are available. (See RECREATION AND TOURS.)

Adjacent to the Carthaginian is the oldest Pacific lighthouse. "It was on this site in 1840 that King Kamehameha III ordered a nine foot wooden tower built as an aid to navigation for the whaling ships. It was equipped with whale oil lamps kept burning at night by a Hawaiian caretaker who was paid $20 a year." In 1866 it increased to 26 feet in size and was again rebuilt in 1905. The present structure of concrete was dedicated in 1916. (Information from an engraved plaque placed on the lighthouse by the Lahaina Restoration Foundation.)

*The Hauola Stone* or Healing Rock can be found near the Lahaina Harbor. Look for the cluster of rocks marked with a visitors bureau warrior sign. The rock, resembling a chair, was believed to have healing properties which could be obtained by merely sitting in it with feet dangling in the surf. Here you will also find remnants of the *Brick Palace* of Kamehameha the Great. Vandals destroyed the display which once showed examples of the original mud bricks.

*The Baldwin House* is across Front Street from Pioneer Inn. Built during 1834-1835, it housed the Reverend Dwight Baldwin and his family from 1837 to 1871. Tours of the home, furnished as it was in days gone by, are given between the hours of 10 am and 4:30 pm. Adults are $3, seniors $2, no charge for children or a family rate of $5. The empty lot adjacent was once the home of Reverend William Richards, and a target of attack by cannonballs from angry sailors during the heyday of whaling. On the other side of the Baldwin Home is the Master's Reading Room. Built in 1833, it is the oldest structure on Maui. Its original purpose was to provide a place of leisure for visiting sea captains. It is not open to the public at this time.

*Hale Paahao* (The Old Prison) on Prison Street just off Wainee is only a short trek from Front Street. Upon entry you'll notice the large gate house which The Lahaina Restoration Foundation reconstructed to its original state in 1988. Nearby is a 60 year old Royal Palm, and in the courtyard an enormous 150 year old breadfruit tree. The cell block was built in 1852 to house the unruly sailors from the whaling vessels and to replace the old fort. It was reconstructed in 1959. In 1854 coral walls (the blocks taken from the old fort) were constructed. The jail was used until the 1920's when it was relocated to the basement of the Lahaina Court House next to the Harbor. While you're at Hale Paahao be sure to say hello to the jail's only tenant, George. He is a wax replica of a sailor who is reported to have had a few too many brews at Uncle Henry's Front Street Beer House back in the 1850's, then missed his ship's curfew and was tossed into jail by Sheriff William O. Smith. George will briefly converse with you by means of a taped recording. The grounds are open to the public daily, no charge.

Construction of the *Waiola Church* began in 1828 on what was then called the Wainee Church. Made of stone and large enough to accommodate 3,000 people, the church unfortunately did not survive the destructive forces of nature and man. The current structure dates from only 1953. In the neighboring cemetery you will find tombs of several notable members of Hawaiian royalty, including Queen Keopuolani, wife of Kamehameha the Great and mother of Kamehameha II and III. The church is located on Wainee and Shaw Streets. The *Maria Lanakila Church* is on the corner of Wainee and Dickenson. Built in 1928, it is a replica of the 1858 church. Next door is the Seamen's Cemetery.

*Hawaiian Experience Omni Theatre* ★ at 824 Front Street occupies what was once the site of the old Queen's Theatre. The seating for 150 persons is such that everyone gets an unobstructed view of the 180 degree screen which curves up and to the sides of the auditorium. The history of the islands is narrated as the viewer is thrilled to a bird's eye view of the remote Hawaiian leeward islands of Tern, Nihoa and Necker. Travel through the jungles and volcanoes of the major islands as well as the underwater world of the Pacific. The adults in our group found the show realistic enough to cause an occasional "seasick" sensation (especially the bike ride down Haleakala), but the kids were riveted and motionless for the 40 minute show. The film, "Hawaii: Island of the Gods," is an informative as well as entertaining show and the air-conditioned comfort is a pleasant break from the warm sidewalk shopping in Lahaina. The show is offered hourly from 10 am - 10 pm. $6.95 adults, children ages 4 - 12 $3.95, under 3 are free. Phone 661-8314.

*The Wo Hing Temple* on Front Street opened following restoration in late 1984. Built in 1912, it now houses a museum which features the influence of the Chinese population on Maui. Hours are 10 am - 4:30 pm with a $1 admission donation appreciated. The adjacent cook house has become a theater which features movies filmed by Thomas Edison during his trips to Hawai'i in 1898 and

BALDWIN HOUSE

1906. In 1993 a new Koban information booth was added near the Wo Hing Temple.

A small, but interesting **Whaling Museum** is located in the Crazy Shirts shop on Front Street. No admission is charged.

Follow Front Street towards Kaanapali to find **The Seamen's Hospital**. This structure was once a hideaway for King Kamehameha III and a gaming house for sailors of Old Lahaina. Now it houses The Paradise Television Network, a local television station.

**Hale Pa'i** is on the campus of Lahainaluna school. Founded in 1831, Lahainaluna is the oldest school and printing press west of the Rockies. You will find it located just outside of Lahaina at the top of Lahainaluna Road. The hours fluctuate depending on volunteers, so call the Lahaina Restoration office at 661-3262 for current schedule. No admission fee. Donations welcomed.

**The Lahaina Jodo Mission** is located on the Kaanapali side of Lahaina, on Ala Moana Street near the Mala Wharf. The great Buddha commemorated the 100th anniversary of the Japanese immigration to the islands which was celebrated at the mission in 1968. The grounds are open to the public, but not the buildings. The public is welcome to attend their summer O'Bon festivals, usually in late June and early July. Check the papers for dates and times.

## WHERE TO SHOP

Shopping is a prime fascination in Lahaina and it is such a major business that it breeds volatility. Shops change frequently, sometimes seemingly overnight, with a definite "trendiness" to their merchandise. It was a few years back that visitors could view artisans creating scrimshaw in numerous stores. The next few years saw the transformation to T-shirt stores. There still are plenty, but the clothing stores are diminishing in numbers. Very few of the same shops on Front Street in Lahaina when we began doing the Paradise Guide series are there today. The theme now is art, art, art, with galleries springing up on every corner. It's a wonderful opportunity to view the fine work of the many local artists with no admission charge! Original oils, watercolors, acrylics, carvings and pottery are on display, as well as fine quality lithographs.

Environmental awareness has arrived at the **Endangered Species Store** at 707 Front St. It's filled with T-shirts, collectibles, books and toys that all focus on endangered wildlife worldwide. Next door is a fun store with a novel idea that certainly makes this shop memorable from the many others that line Front Street. Step through the door of **The Gecko Store** and take a look at what is under your feet! We'll let you be surprised!

**Here are some shops that are unusual, or favorites of ours:**

**Lahaina Galleries** at 728 Front Street, plus galleries in Kaanapali and Kapalua. Begun in 1976, their art falls in the $500 - $30,000 (and up) range. The works by local artists are the most popular.

New galleries are opening constantly. Some of the larger ones are the Dolphin Gallery, David Lee Galleries, Royal Art Gallery, Galerie Lassen Maui, and The Larry Dotson Gallery. A number of "retired" movie and television stars have turned artist and you'll see the work of Tony Curtis, Red Skelton, Anthony Quinn and Buddy Epsen. Originals, numbered lithographs and poster prints by popular Hawaiian artists Peggy Hopper, Diana Hansen and others can be found in many shops as well. The best representation of local artists may be found at the Lahaina Galleries located at 728 Front St. in Lahaina and in Wailea at 370 Wailea Alanui. The Lahaina Arts Society is a non profit organization featuring work by Maui artists with locations in the Old Lahaina Courthouse, the Old Jail Gallery and the Banyan Tree Gallery, open 10 am-5 pm daily they also featur arts and craft shows on Saturday.

Friday night in Lahaina is ART NIGHT! Participating galleries feature a special event between 6 and 9 pm that might include guest artists and refreshments.

***Island Sandals*** is tucked away in a niche of the Wharf Cinema Center near the postal center at 658 Front Street, Space #125, Lahaina, Maui, HI 96761, (661-5110). Michael Mahnensmith is the proprietor and creator of custom-made sandals. He learned his craft in Santa Monica from David Webb who was making sandals for the Greek and Roman movies of the late 50's and early 60's. He rediscovered his sandal design from the sandals used 3,000 years ago by the desert warriors of Ethiopia. He developed the idea while living in Catalina in the 1960's and copyrighted it in 1978. The sandals are all leather, which is porous and keeps the feet cool and dry, with the exception of a non-skid synthetic heel.

JODO MISSION

The sandals feature a single strap which laces around the big toe, then over and under the foot, and around the heel, providing comfort and good arch support. As the sandal breaks in, the strap stretches and you simply adjust the entire strap to maintain proper fit (which makes them feel more like a shoe than a sandal). They are clever and functional. His sandals have been copied by others, but never duplicated. So beware of other sandals which appear the same, but don't offer the fit, comfort or function of Michael's! The charge is $85 for the right shoe and the left shoe is free. Charges may be slightly higher for men's sandals over size 13. Anyone who gets shoes from Island Sandals becomes an agent and is authorized to trace foot prints of others. Commissions are automatic when your sales reach the "high range." (However, you must like coconuts and bananas.) Michael stresses the importance of good footwear while on Maui, so stop in upon your arrival, or they can be ordered by sending a tracing of both feet and both big toes, including the spaces in-between (or by having an "authorized agent" do so) along with $85 to Island Sandals. Michael can also assist with leather repair of your shoes, purses, bags, or suitcases.

*Seegerpeople* at the Wharf has an interesting photographic twist. Located on the second level corner, they have on display hundreds of samples of their work. After a photographic sitting that lasts about half an hour with a dozen poses, selections are made. The prints are first adhered to a heavy plastic board, then to white plastic, after which the photographs are cut out closely around the body. This results in miniature people that can be creatively arranged and mounted on stands. They're not cheap, but they sure are fun. We enjoyed just looking at all their samples! A sitting, three mounted poses, and the stand runs about $100.

For the collector of just about anything, the *Coral Tree* at the Wharf Cinema Center needs to be penciled in on your Lahaina itinerary. The buyer, Pat Adams, has collected items from around the world and they fill shelves from the floor to ceiling of this small shop. (She adds jokingly that the smallness of the shop is because in Lahaina space is rented by the square inch per minute.) Turtles, frogs, trunk-up elephants (trunk-down elephants are bad luck) and cats are the most popular collectibles. However, if pigs or dogs or zebra are your hobby then you'll find them here! You won't find things made out of just coral either. There is black jet from England, amber from the Dominican Republic, turquoise pieces made by the Zuni Indians or bone and alabaster from Indonesia. The collector of jewelry will find this an intriguing stop as well.

A three screen movie theater is located on the upper level of the *Wharf Cinema Center* with seating capacity for330 people (special first show of the day prices are currently $3.50). The *Fun Factory* is located in the lower level with video games and prize-oriented games. The shopping center presents "Aloha Friday" - a free show each Friday at 6:30 pm. Upstairs is a also bookstore and coffee shop which offers a good selection of Hawaiian topics. *Parrots International* is a new addition to the center. A number of restaurants are found throughout the center.

*Dickenson Square* (On Dickenson St. off Front St.) bears a strong resemblance to Pioneer Inn. Kirovac's deli, hairdresser, quick stop market, Lahaina Coolers restaurant and Nautilus Center are located here.

*505 Front Street* is a short walk past the Banyan Tree. Originally developed to be a shopping center, then unsuccessfully converted into condominiums, it has now been restored into busy shops and restaurants. The *Old Lahaina Luau* is held on the beachfront and restaurants include *Hecock's, Pacific'O, Casa de Mateo* and the *Old Lahaina Cafe*. *KPOA Music and Gift Shop* has a good selection of Hawaiian CDs and tapes. Shops change here faster than we can keep track. *Scaroles Village Pizzeria* or *Juicy's Sandwich and Juice Bar* offer a respite for the hungry shopper!

*Dan's Green House* at 133 Prison Street (661-8412) has a variety of beautiful tropical birds for sale as well as an array of plants for shipping home. Their specialty is Fuku-Bonsai "Lava Rock" plants. These bonsai are well packaged to tolerate the trip home.

The *Lahaina Center* is not to be confused with the adjoining and older, more established Lahaina Shopping Center. This newer center has kept the low level, pioneer type architecture and has a paid parking area. *Hilo Hatties* has relocated here with a 17,000 square foot location. Hatties is famous around the islands for its aloha wear. The *Hard Rock Cafe* is a major attraction. Several other eateries include *La Tasca, Blue Tropix Restaurant and Night Club* and *Red Lobster*. *Liberty House* is a disappointment for us, not nearly as large as the former Kaanapali location and no toy section or books.

An area slightly removed from Lahaina's Front Street is termed the industrial area. Follow Honoapiilani Road and turn by the Pizza Hut. *The Sugar Cane Train* (661-0089) offers a nostalgic trip between Kaanapali and Lahaina. Round trip for adults is $12, children 3-12 years $6. They have several package options that combine the train ride with another Lahaina experience. The prices on the packages offer a bit of a discount if you were to price the two activities separately. The Lahaina Town Package includes a tour of the Wo Hing Temple, the Carthaginian and the Baldwin House. The Omni Theater Experience Packages includes admission to the 40-minute theater presentation. The Nautilus Package includes a trip out of the Lahaina Harbor on the semi-submersible Nautilus. Make your plans early as space is limited and sometimes the return trips are booked. The red double decker bus will transfer you from the Sugar Cane Depot to the Wharf Shopping Center and in front of Pioneer Inn. You can catch the bus back to the train depot from these same locations.

Also in the industrial area, *The Bakery* is a personal favorite for some really fine pastries and breads. *MGM, Maui Gold Manufacturing* (661-8981), not only does standard repairs, but designs outstanding jewelry pieces. They can design something to your specifications, or choose a piece from one of their many photograph books. A limited number of pieces are ready made for sale as well. *J.R.'s Music Shop* (661-0801), on the back side of The Bakery building, has a large selection of Hawaiian tapes and records as well as just about any other type of music.

Just on the Kaanapali side of Lahaina, a drive of less than a mile, is *The Lahaina Cannery Shopping Center* which opened in 1987. The original structure, built in 1920, was used as a pineapple cannery until its closure in 1963, and this new facility was built to resemble its predecessor. It's easy to spot as you leave Lahaina heading for Kaanapali. A large parking area makes for convenient access.

This enclosed air-conditioned mall is anchored by Safeway and Long's Drug Store. Within the mall are several fast food eateries, as well as sit down dining at Yum Yum Tree and Compadres restaurants. Other shops include Waldenbooks, Sir Wilfred's coffee house, jewelry, clothing and sporting goods stores. The surf board display at *Hobie Sports* is worthy of a stop.

BE FOREWARNED!!! If you have the time, do a lot of window shopping before you buy. Prices can vary significantly on some items from one store to another.

## ACCOMMODATIONS - LAHAINA

| | |
|---|---|
| Puamana | Plantation Inn |
| Lahaina Shores Beach Resort | Lahaina Hotel |
| Pioneer Inn | Lahaina Roads |
| Maui Islander Hotel | Puunoa |

**BEST BETS:** *Puamana* - A nice residential type area of two-plex and four-plex units, some oceanfront. *Lahaina Shores* - A moderately priced colonial style high rise right on the beach and within walking distance of Lahaina shops. *Plantation Inn* and *Lahaina Hotel* are both tastefully done with all the elegance of bygone days.

### PUAMANA ★
PO Box 11108, Lahaina, Maui, HI 96761. (808-667-2551) 1-800-628-6731. 228 units in a series of duplexes and four-plexes in a garden setting. This large oceanside complex resembles a residential community much more than a vacation resort. The variation in price reflects location in the complex, oceanfront to gardenview. Limited maid service. $300 deposit, weekly/monthly discounts, 3-night minimum.
*1 BR (4) $120-175 / $ 95-150*
*2 BR (6) $155-250 / $135-200*
*3 BR (6) $300-350*

### LAHAINA SHORES BEACH RESORT ★
475 Front Street, Lahaina, Maui, HI 96761. (808-661-4835 Hotel only, no reservations). Agents: Classic Resorts 1-800-628-6699, (808-667-1400).

200 oceanfront units in this 7-story building of Victorian style offer air-conditioning, lanais, full kitchens, daily maid service, and laundry facilities on each floor. The beach here is fair and the water calm due to offshore reefs, but shallow with coral. Lahaina town is only a short walk away, plus this complex neighbors the 505 Front Street which offers several restaurants and a small grocery store. Car/condo packages also available.
*SBR(2; max 3)     mtn.v.-o.f.      $105-137 /$ 95-117*
*1BR(2; max 4)     o.v.-o.f.        $147-172 /$122-147*
*PENTHOUSE(2; max 5)mtn.v.-o.f.    $192-227 /$162-182*

### PIONEER INN  (Hotel)
658 Wharf St., PO Box 243, Lahaina, Maui, HI 96764. 1-800-457-5457, FAX 1-808-667-5708, (808-661-3636). If you want rustic, this is it! The original building was constructed in 1901 as accommodations for inter-island travelers.

George Freeland a robust 300 pound, 6 ft. 5 inch Englishman, had relocated to Vancouver, Canada and become a Royal Canadian Mountie. He was sent to Hawai'i in 1900 to capture a suspect, but failing to do so, chose to make Maui his home. He formed the Pioneer Hotel Co., Ltd and sold $50 shares of stock. In October of 1901 he constructed the hotel, similar to the plantation house of the Maunalei Sugar Company on Lana'i for a total cost of $6,000. (Note: On Lana'i we heard a report that the Maunalei Plantation House was transported to Maui and became Pioneer Inn, but this was not accurate. Apparently, years ago, the Honolulu Star-Bulletin printed an article to this effect. G. Alan Freeland, son of Pioneer Inn's founder George Freeland spoke with Lawrence Gay, the owner of most of Lana'i at the turn of the century, and was told that when the construction of Pioneer Hotel was completed, the similar-designed building on the island of Lana'i was still standing.) Soon George Freeland opened the Pioneer saloon, the Pioneer Grange, the Pioneer Wholesale Liquor Company and in 1913 the Pioneer Theater. The Pioneer Theater ran silent movies to packed crowds and had stage shows and plays in the theater as well. He died on July 25, 1925, survived by his wife, a Hawaiian woman, three sons and four daughters. His eldest son, George Alan Freeland, ran the business until the early 1960's. In the late 1960's the inn was expanded and at that time the theater was torn down. A complete history of the Pioneer Inn is available along with their brochure. A guest in 1901 would have been required to adhere to the following bizarre "house rules:"

> "You must pay you rent in advance. You must not let you room go one day back. Women is not allow in you room. If you wet or burn you bed you going out. You are not allow to gamble in you room. You are not allow to give you bed to you freand. If you freand stay overnight you must see the mgr. You must leave you room at 11 am so the women can clean you room. Only on Sunday you can sleep all day. You are not allow in the down stears in the seating room or in the dinering room or in the kitchen when you are drunk. You are not allow to drink on the front porch. You must use a shirt when you come to the seating room. If you cant keep this rules please dont take the room."

PIONEER INN

With such a colorful history, Pioneer Inn remains a nostalgic Lahaina landmark. The units in the old, original building, which had shared baths and spartan furnishings, have been indefinitely closed down. Rooms available are in the Mauka Building which was added in 1966 and do have private baths, air-conditioning, and lanais. Here you are in the hub of activity in Lahaina and sounds of the music downstairs will lull you to sleep. Recently they renovated the restaurant, bar and lobby areas.
*Mauka wing: Superior $60, Deluxe $80, third person $10, child under 10 $5*

## MAUI ISLANDER HOTEL

660 Wainee Street, Lahaina, Maui, HI 96761. (808) 667-9766. 372 rooms include hotel rooms with refrigerators. Studio and 1 BR suites w/ kitchens. Located in the heart of Lahaina town, less than a 5 minute walk to the sea wall, yet far enough away to be peaceful. The back of the building borders the Honoapiilani Hwy., so there may be more traffic noise in those units - request the front units. Daily maid service, air-conditioning, laundry facilities, tennis courts, pool. Group rates available. Cribs $6 per night. Two night deposit. Room and car packages available. 1994 package rates include a rental car at a rate varying between free and $15 per day. Other free amenities with packages include dinner gift certificates.
*Room with refrigerator - no kitchen (2) $69*
*Studio with kitchen (3) $84, 1 BR (4) $96, 2 BR (6) $147*

## PLANTATION INN ★

174 Lahainaluna Rd., Lahaina, Maui, HI 96761 (808-667-9225) 1-800-433-6815, FAX 1-808-667-9293. It's wonderful to see this kind of development in Lahaina. This 18 room building has all the charm of an old inn, while all the benefits of modernization. Filled with antiques, beautiful Victorian decor, hardwood floors, and stained glass, they also offer air-conditioning, refrigerators and even VCR's. Located a block from the ocean in the heart of Lahaina, it also has a 12 foot deep tiled pool, and a spa. An added bonus is the outstanding Gerard's Restaurant, which provides guests with discounts for breakfast and dinner. Some suites include kitchens and jacuzzis. Honeymoon and car packages available.
*Room rates range from $99, $109, $129, $149, $179.*

## LAHAINA HOTEL ★ (Hotel)

127 Lahainaluna Rd., Lahaina, Maui, HI 96761. (808-661-0577), FAX (808) 667-9480, 1-800-669-3444. Rick Ralston, who also owns Crazy Shirts, undertook renovations at this ideally situated location and the transformation was dramatic. Gone are the $25 a night "rustic" units. The fully air-conditioned hotel has 13 rooms for single or double occupancy only. The hotel has been restored exactly as if it were sent into a time warp between 1860 and 1900. No details have been overlooked from the authentic antiques to the ceiling moldings. All the furnishings have come from Rick Ralston's personal collection so each room is different. The headboard/footboards are intricately carved as are the highboy dressers. Each room is unique with lush wallpaper in deep greens, burgundy, blues and golds and offers a small, but adequate private bathroom. Ten of the rooms are standard and three are larger parlour suites. Each has its own lanai complete with rocking chairs. Manager Ken Eisley emphasizes that this is a service oriented hotel with 24 hour desk service. Adjacent is the David Paul's Lahaina Grill. Parking $7 per day. Honeymoon packages. *Std. rooms with full size bed, m.v. $89, harbor view $99 - $129. Parlour suites with queen and king $129*

## LAHAINA ROADS

1403 Front St., Lahaina, Maui, HI 96761. (808-661-3166) 1-800-624-8203. Agent: Klahani Resorts 1-800-669-0795. 42 oceanview units, covered parking and elevator to upper levels. Microwaves, washer/dryer, cable TV. Maid service available for an extra charge. A very unpretentious, non-resort looking property. Additional person $10/night, 3-night minimum, two nights deposit, deposit forfeited on cancellation if unit not re-rented. Weekly and monthly discounts.
*1 BR (2,max 4) $115/95, 2 BR (4,max 6) $150/130, Penthouse (4) $200/150*

## PUUNOA BEACH ESTATES

45 Kai Pali Place, Lahaina, Maui, HI 96761. Agents: Classic Resorts (808-667-1400) 1-800-642-MAUI. Amenities include full size swimming pool, jacuzzi, his and hers sauna, and paddle tennis courts. Units include laundry rooms, lanais, master bath with jacuzzi, full bar and daily maid service. These luxury units are located on Puunoa Beach in a residential area just north of Lahaina. Beautiful and spacious air-conditioned units, convenient to restaurants and shops. The beachfront has a coral reef which makes for calm conditions for children, but swimming or snorkeling are poor due to the shallowness and coral. A full size rental car is included. Three night minimum.
*2 BR 2 bath o.f. (4) $580/550, 2 BR with loft (6) $695/580*
*3 BR o.f $730/605, 3 BR with loft (8) $800/665*


# KAANAPALI


## INTRODUCTION

The drive through Lahaina is quick (unless it's rush hour). All that is really visible are a couple of gas stations, the old mill, a few nondescript commercial buildings, and a Pizza Hut. Old Lahaina and the waterfront cannot be seen as they are a couple of large blocks off to the left. The large shopping center on the left is the Cannery, described above. As you leave Lahaina, the vista opens with a view of the Hyatt Regency and the beginning of the Kaanapali Beach Resort a mile off in the distance. The resort is beautifully framed by the West Maui mountains on the right, the peaks of Moloka'i, appearing to be another part of Maui in the background, the island of Lana'i off to the left, and of course, the ocean. The name Kaanapali means "rolling cliffs" or "land divided by cliffs" and refers to the wide, open ridges that stretch up behind the resort toward Pu'u Kukui, West Maui's highest peak. The beaches and plush resorts here are what many come to Hawai'i to find.

Kaanapali began in the early 1960's as an Amfac Development with the first hotels, the Royal Lahaina and the Sheraton, opening in late 1962 and early 1963 respectively. The Kaanapali Resort, 500 acres along three miles of prime beach-front, is reputed to be the first large-scale planned resort in the world. There are six beachfront hotels and seven condominiums which total more than 5,000 rooms and units, two golf courses, 37 tennis courts, and a shopping village.

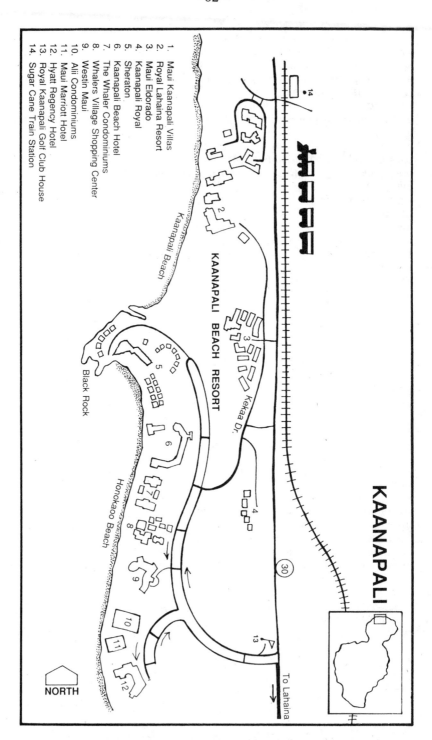

1. Maui Kaanapali Villas
2. Royal Lahaina Resort
3. Maui Eldorado
4. Kaanapali Royal
5. Sheraton
6. Kaanapali Beach Hotel
7. The Whaler Condominiums
8. Whalers Village Shopping Center
9. Westin Maui
10. Alii Condominiums
11. Maui Marriott Hotel
12. Hyatt Regency Hotel
13. Royal Kaanapali Golf Club House
14. Sugar Cane Train Station

KAANAPALI

KAANAPALI BEACH RESORT

Kaanapali Beach

Black Rock

Honokaoo Beach

Kekaa Dr.

To Lahaina

NORTH

Now that the Kaanapali Airport has been closed, there are another 700 acres available for development. Construction has been awaiting the road improvements in the Kaanapali to Lahaina area. The resort boasts the most convention space of any of the neighboring islands, with the Maui Marriott, Westin Maui and the Hyatt Regency being popular locations. All the hotels are located beachfront, although some of the condos are situated above the beach in the golf course area. All are priced in the luxury range. The wide avenues and the spaciousness of the resort's lush green and manicured grounds are most impressive. No on-street parking and careful planning have successfully given this resort a feeling of spaciousness. Nestled between a pristine white sand beach and scenic golf courses with a mountain range beyond, this may be the ideal spot for your vacation.

This may be paradise, but traffic congestion between Kaanapali and Lahaina may have reminded you more of L.A. in the past few years. Non-synchronized traffic lights, roads designed for 20 years ago, and greatly increased traffic, caused the three mile transit through Lahaina to Kaanapali (or Kaanapali to Lahaina) to consume over an hour during the afternoon rush (most other times there was only light traffic). Of deep concern to the government, residents and business interests alike, this situation was eased considerably with the recent completion of all four lanes from Kaanapali to Lahaina. The free Kaanapali to Lahaina shuttle has also somewhat eased congestion. The major bottleneck is now at the first Kaanapali entrance where the four lanes end. Getting past this point in either direction can be difficult. Hopefully, the four lanes will extend up to at least Napili or Kahana in the near future.

## WHAT TO DO AND SEE

*The Hyatt Regency* and *The Westin Maui* must be put at the top of everyone's list of things to see. Few hotels can boast that they need their own wildlife manager, but upon entry you'll see why they do. Without spoiling the surprises too much, just envision the Hyatt with palm trees growing through the lobby, peacocks strolling by, and parrots perched amid extraordinary pieces of Oriental art. The lagoon and black swans are spectacular. The pool area occupies two acres and features two swim-through waterfalls and a cavern in the middle with a swim up bar. A swinging bridge is suspended over one of the two pools and a water slide offers added thrills for hotel guests.

The newest project at Kaanapali was the renovation a number of years ago of the Westin Maui. To appreciate this property, a little background may be necessary. The Maui Surf was the original hotel with the single curved building and a large expanse of lush green lawn and two pools. The transformation has been extraordinary. The pool areas are unsurpassed, with five swimming pools on various levels fed by waterfalls and connected by two slides. There are exotic birds afloat on the lagoons which greet you upon your arrival and glide gracefully by two of the hotel's restaurants. The Oriental art collection surpasses even the Hyatt's.

Both resorts feature glamorous shopping arcades, with prices to match of course. Both developments were designed by the remarkable, champion hotel builder of Hawaii, Chris Hemmeter.

## WHERE TO SHOP

**Whalers Village Shopping Center** is located in the heart of Kaanapali. Some part or other of this center always seems to be under construction or renovation. It offers several small shops for grocery items, as well as a bounty of jewelry and clothing shops, and restaurants. A multi-level parking structure is adjacent to the mall and parking is $1 for the first two hours or fraction thereof, and 50 cents for each additional half hour, with a $10 maximum charge. Restaurants can provide validation.

"**Hale Kohola**" (House of the Whale) is a museum located on the upper level. Admission is free, but donations are welcome. They recently expanded in size and have a wonderful exhibition of the great whales with special emphasis on the Humpback Whale. The information Director gives lectures on topics from scrimshaw to the life of a sailor. Call for times at 661-5992. Private group lectures are also a possibility. Restaurants include The Rusty Harpoon, Leilani's, Hula Grill, and Chico's.

The center has a bountiful assortment of clothing stores, art galleries and jewelry stores. There is a Crazy Shirts outlet, The Sharper Image and Walden's has a very good bookstore here with an excellent selection of Hawaiian literature. The mall is a pleasant place for an evening stroll and shop browsing, before or after dinner, followed by a seaside walk back to your accommodations on the paved beachfront sidewalk.

## ACCOMMODATIONS - KAANAPALI

| | |
|---|---|
| Hyatt Regency | Royal Lahaina Resort |
| Maui Marriott | Maui Kaanapali Villas |
| Kaanapali Alii | Kaanapali Plantation |
| Westin Maui | International Colony Club |
| The Whaler | Maui Eldorado |
| Kaanapali Beach Hotel | Kaanapali Royal |
| Sheraton | |

**BEST BETS: Hyatt Regency Maui** - An elegant and exotic setting with a wonderful selection of great restaurants. **Maui Marriott** - Beautiful grounds with a nice pool area and attractively decorated rooms. **Westin Maui** - A gorgeous resort and a pool aficionados paradise. **Kaanapali Alii** - One of only three condominiums that are oceanfront. Luxurious, expensive and spacious. (Our choice to purchase a unit with future lottery winnings!). **Royal Lahaina Resort** - A beautiful property on sandy Kaanapali Beach. **The Whaler** - Condominiums on the heart of Honokaoo Beach adjacent to the Whalers Village Shopping Center.

NOTE: Some resort hotels have begun charging guests a daily parking fee.

### HYATT REGENCY ★ (Hotel)
200 Nohea Kai Drive, Lahaina, Maui, HI 96761. (808-661-1234) 1-800-223-1234. This magnificent complex is located on 18 beachfront acres and offers 815 rooms and suites. The beach is beautiful, but has a steep drop off. Adjoining Hanokaoo

Beach Park offers a gentler slope into deeper water. The pool area is an impressive feature, covering two acres and resembling a contemporary adventure that Robinson Crusoe could only have dreamt. The pool is divided by a large cavern that can be reached on either side by swimming beneath a waterfall. Once inside there is a swim up bar! One side of the pool is spanned by a large swinging rope bridge. Stand on the bridge and enjoy viewing guests whizzing into the water via the long waterslide.

Penguins, jewel-toned koi, parrots, peacocks and flamingos around the grounds require full time game keepers. The lobby is a blend of beautiful pieces of oriental art and paths that lead to the grounds. Originally there had been a huge tree, the focal point of the lobby, however, it quite unexpectedly toppled over one night. Part of the base remains and has become a popular parrot walk. The birds are apparently so at home here that one exotic pair surprisingly gave birth, a rarity for this species in captivity! Non-guests should definitely visit the Hyatt for a self guided tour of the grounds, the art, the elegant shops and for an opportunity to enjoy one of this resort's fine restaurants. It's worth coming here just to look around! Restaurants include Swan Court, Spats, Lahaina Provision Company, Mozzarella's Tiki Cafe, and Pavilion. Parking additional $5 per day.
*Terrace rooms $240, golf/mtn.v. $300, o.f. $330-360*
*Suites: Ocean $600, Deluxe $900, Regency $1,400, Presidential $3,000*

The Regency Club consists of certain floors that feature special services, including continental breakfast, evening cocktails and appetizers, and complimentary health club access. Room rates are based on single/double occupancy (for additional persons 13 years or older $25 charge per night/Regency Club level $45 charge per night). 3 adults or 2 adults 2 children maximum per room.
*Regency Club (mtn.v.) $400, (o.f.) $430*

## MAUI MARRIOTT ★ (Hotel)
100 Nohea Kai Drive, Lahaina, Maui, HI 96761. (800-228-9290) 1-808-667-1200. This 720 room complex has a large, open lobby in the middle featuring an array of fine shops. Although not as exotic as its neighbor the Hyatt, this is still a very attractive, upscale property. The pool area is large and a keiki (children's) wading pool is a welcome addition for families. On site restaurants are Nikko's Steak House, Lokelani's, Moana Terrace and the Kau Kau Bar. Inquire regarding their current package plans, one package now available offers $179 for a mtn. view room with a car. For Modified American Plan (MAP) breakfast and dinner add $67 per person, Full American Plan (FAP) for all three meals is $90 per person. *Mtn.-golf view $195, mtn.-o.v. $220, o.v. $245, deluxe o.v. $280.* Additional persons add $25. They recently began charging an additional $7 per day parking.

## KAANAPALI ALII ★
50 Nohea Kai Dr., Lahaina, Maui, HI 96761. 1-800-367-6090. Agents: Classic Resorts 1-800-642-MAUI or FAX (808) 661-0147, Whalers Realty 1-800-367-5632, Hawaiian Apt. Leasing 1-800-854-8843, 1-800-472-8449 CA, Hawaiiana Resorts 1-800-367-7040. All 264 units are very spacious and beautifully furnished, with air-conditioning, microwaves, washer/dryer, and daily maid service. Other amenities include security entrances and covered parking. The 1-bedroom units have a den, which actually makes them equivalent to a 2-bedroom. Three lighted tennis courts, pool (also a children's pool), and exercise room. No restaurants on

the property, but shops and restaurants are within easy walking distance. A very elegant, high-class and quiet property with a very cordial staff and concierge department. They charge for local phone calls from room, as do most hotels. 3-night min., extra person $15/night. The following rates are thru Whalers Realty.

*1 BR (2) partial ocean $170-190; o.v. $195-230*
*2 BR (4) partial ocean $270-310; o.v. $335-375*

## WESTIN MAUI ★ (Hotel)

2365 Kaanapali Parkway, Lahaina, Maui, HI 96761. (808-667-2525). Westin Central Reservations 1-800-228-3000. Under the direction of Chris Hemmeter, champion hotel builder in Hawaii, this gorgeous resort offers 761 deluxe rooms, including 28 suites. The Westin Maui has an ocean tower of 11 stories with 556 guest rooms and a beach tower with 206 guest rooms and suites. Guest rooms are provided for those with disabilities as well as non-smoking floors. The rooms have been designed in comfortable hues of muted peach and beige. The top two floors of the new tower, house the Royal Beach Club, which offers guests complimentary continental breakfast buffet, afternoon cocktails, evening cocktails and hors d'oeuvres, and a private concierge. Complimentary shuttle service to the Royal Lahaina Tennis Ranch, the largest tennis facility on Kaanapali with 11 tennis courts and 6 courts lit for night play. Conference and banquet facilities are available as well as an array of gift, art, and fashion shops. The focal point of this resort is the 55,000 square foot aquatic playground, complete with meandering streams, 15 - 20 foot waterfalls, and a 25,000 square foot pool area featuring five free-form pools, two waterslides and a swim-up Jacuzzi hidden away in a grotto. The pool areas are spacious and well arranged. Eight restaurants and lounges overlook the ocean, waterfalls and pools. The hotel exercise room includes complete exercise and weight rooms, with sauna and whirlpool. Tour the grounds with a guide to learn more about the Westin's family of birds and their tropical surroundings. This resort's 2.5 million art collection could put a museum to shame and each piece was carefully selected and placed personally by Chris Hemmeter. Numerous nooks with comfortable chairs and art work provide intimate conversation areas. Parents may appreciate the resort's Keiki Camp which offers activities and care for children during vacation (Thanksgiving, Xmas, Easter and Summer) periods. Cost is $20-$40 per day. For those planning a wedding on Maui, the Westin has their own Director of Romance to assist you with your wedding or honeymoon plans. On property restaurants include Sound of the Falls, The Villa Restaurant, cook's at the Beach and Sen Ju Sushi Bar.

Rates are based on single or double occupancy. Third person add $25, to Royal Beach Club add $45 (maximum 3 persons to a room). Family Plan offers no extra charge for children 18 or under sharing the same room as parents. A 25% discount is available for additional rooms occupied. Complimentary valet parking.

*Terrace $210, garden view $245, golf-mtn. view $285, oceanview $315*
*Deluxe ocean view $345, Royal Beach Club $375-395, Suites $500-$2,000*

## THE WHALER ★

2481 Kaanapali Parkway, Lahaina, Maui, HI 96761. (808-661-4861) Managed by Village Resorts 1-800-367-7052. Agents: Whalers Realty 1-800-367-5632, Kaanapali Vacations 1-800-822-4252, Hawaiian Apt. Leasing 1-800-854-8843 (U.S. except California), 1-800-472-8449 Calif., RSVP 1-800-663-1118.

Choice location in the heart of Kaanapali next to the Whalers Village Shopping Center and on an excellent beach front. A large pool area is beachfront and they provide an excellent children's program during the summer. Underground parking. $200 deposit, 2-night minimum except over holidays, balance on check-in. 2-week refund notice. Garden view studios begin with Whalers Realty begin at $135.

*S BR 1 bath (2) o.v. $185/170, g.v.   $170/155        Cribs $12/night*
*1 BR 1 bath (4) o.v. $245/230, g.v.   $210/200        Rollaway beds $15/night*
*1 BR 2 bath (4) o.v. $260/250, g.v.   $220/210,   o.f. $310/295*
*2 BR 2 bath (6) o.v. $345/330,   o.f.   $415/390*

## KAANAPALI BEACH HOTEL  (Hotel)

2525 Kaanapali Pkwy, Lahaina, Maui, HI 96761 (808-661-0011) Reservations: Outrigger Hotels 1-800-462-6262.

The planned closure for complete renovation in 1993 never happened, however, they did completely renovate the 93-room Moloka'i Wing. The wing has been refurbished in an airy, plantation-period decor. Painted in shades of sand and plantation green, the rooms are decorated with heirloom-style wicker furniture, artwork and Hawaiian quilt designed bedspreads. In-rooms safes and coffee makers were added to all 430 of the hotel's rooms.

Located on Kaanapali beach near Black Rock and Whalers Village Shops, this hotel has been welcoming guests since it opened in 1964. No doubt the best hotel value on Kaanapali Beach. Air-conditioning. Tennis available at nearby Royal Lahaina. Try their whale-shaped swimming pool! Restaurants on site include the Kaanapali Beach Hotel Koffee Shop and the Tiki Terrace Restaurant. A great location, but not a "posh" resort. The hotel could use a bit more freshening up, but then it would also be reflected in the prices! A good value and, this is Maui's most Hawaiian hotel where the staff are actually instructed in Hawaiiana. *Std. $119-135, courtyard $145-155, partial o.v. $160-170, o.v.$175, o.f. $195-230. Suites $180 - $525. Crib no charge. Roll-away bed $15 per night, additional person $20 per night. Children under 17 free when sharing room with parents using existing bedding. Special package rates include rental car or golf.*

## SHERATON HOTEL  (Hotel)

2605 Kaanapali Parkway. (808-661-0031) 1-800-325-3535. This 494 unit hotel winds around the side of Black Rock and was one of the first completed in Kaanapali. There are also six-unit cottages on the grounds. In April 1994 the resort announced their planned $130 million renovation and re-development would begin in January 1995 and will continue for two years during which time the hotel will remained closed. The architectural and landscape design is expected to reflect a Hawaiian seaside village with emphasis on water and ocean activities with an enhanced landscape. Upon completion, the room count will increase to 510 rooms and include 30 family rooms (rooms larger than regular rooms) and 16 suites. The property is expected to close beginning December 31, 1994 through November 1996. But as sometimes happens, plans might change, so we always recommend a phone call. We hope when they reopen that they re-establish the dramatic nightly cliff dive! We'll keep you updated as to their status in our quarterly Maui newsletter. The beachfront here is excellent for snorkeling and everyone comes here to enjoy the nearly tame fish. The only problem is finding a place to park!

### ROYAL LAHAINA RESORT ★

2780 Kekaa Drive, Lahaina, Maui, HI 96761. (808-661-3611) 1-800-44-ROYAL. 540 units located on excellent Kaanapali Beach just north of Black Rock. Located on 27 tropical acres, all cottage suites have kitchens and are situated around the lush, spacious grounds. A mini-shopping mall is conveniently located on the property. Ten tennis courts, three swimming pools. Restaurants on the property include Royal Ocean Terrace (which features a very good Sunday Brunch) and Beachcomber's. Made in the Shade is a poolside restaurant and the Royal Scoop is an ice cream and sandwich shop. Nightly luaus in the luau gardens. Children under 17 sharing parents room in existing beds are free. Three swimming pools.

Our brief stay in one of the bungalow/cottages that are scattered around the grounds was a relaxing one. It offered an opportunity for the kids to run around the grassy area that stretched beyond our patio. There, they made fast friends with a very friendly rabbit that they named Lettuce. This rabbit definitely had friends, since he was the most robust, hearty and all around enormous rabbit we'd ever seen. We inquired with the General Manager who was aware of this unusual resort resident. Apparently he had been a pet that an employee had let loose and that they had plans to round him up. However, the rabbit has received much admiration from resort guests as the GM noted that many have reported that they look forward to visiting with Mr. Rabbit on return visits. (My kids included.)

We also toured one of the newly decorated suites and it was fabulous! Located on the upper floors of the tower building it was tastefully appointed with pieces of furniture custom made to be replicas of pieces used by the Hawaiian royalty that compliments the spectacular oceanview. The Royal Lahaina offers some wonderful values and with a location on one of Maui's best beaches, it is a vacation oasis.

*Std. $145, superior $180, dlx. $195, dlx. o.f. $245*
*Garden cottage $235, oceanfront cottages $295, Suites $660-$1,500*
*1 BR g.v. condominium $265, 2 BR $375, 2 BR $450.*
*1 & 2 BR oceanfront cottages $375 - $1,000*

### MAUI KAANAPALI VILLAS

2805 Honoapiilani Hwy., Lahaina, HI 96761 (808-667-7791). Agents: Aston 1-800-221-2558, Whalers Realty 1-800-367-5632, Hawaiian Apt. Leasing 1-800-854-8843 (U.S. except CA.), 1-800-472-8449 CA, Kaanapali Vacation Rentals 1-800-822-4252, 1-800-423-8733 ext. 515 Canada, RSVP 1-800-663-1118. Located on fabulous, sandy Kaanapali Beach, this was once a part of the Royal Lahaina Resort, and before that the Hilton, prior to being converted into condos.The units are all air-conditioned and have kitchen facilities (except the hotel rooms). Three swimming pools, beach concessions, store nearby. Walking distance to Whalers Village shops an restaurants and adjacent to the Royal Kaanapali Golf Course.
*Room (2) $115-125/105-115, Studio w/kitchen (2) $135-150/125-140,*
*1 BR (4) $160-210/150-200, 2 BR 2 Bth (6) $220-240/195-230, Extra person $10*

### KAANAPALI PLANTATION

150 Puukolii Rd., (PO Box 845) Lahaina, Maui, HI 96761. No rental units available at this time from on-site management. 62-unit one, two and three bedroom units in a garden setting overlooking golf course and ocean.

## INTERNATIONAL COLONY CLUB

2750 Kalapu Dr., Lahaina, Maui, HI 96761 (808-661-4070) 1-800-526-6284. 44 low-rise single family cottages on 10 lush acres, across Honoapiilani Hwy. from the beach. Lanais, most have washer/dryers and coin-op laundry on site. Limited maid service. Two heated swimming pools. It is a bit of a walk to the beach. 4-day minimum low season, 7 day minimum high. NO CREDIT CARDS.

*1 BR (2) $115, 2 BR (2) $125, 3 BR (3) $145   Extra persons over age 6, $10/nite*

## MAUI ELDORADO

2661 Kekaa Drive, Lahaina, HI 96761. (808-661-0021) 1-800-367-2967, Canada 1-800-663-1118. Agents: Hawaiian Apt. Leasing 1-800-472-8449 CA, 1-800-854-8843 U.S. except CA, Kaanapali Vacations 1-800-822-4252, 1-800-667-9559, Marc Resorts 1-800-535-0085. 204 air-conditioned units located on golf course. Private lanais with free HBO and Disney cable TV. Daily maid service. Three pools. Free shuttle to cabana on nearby beachfront.

*Hotel Room g.v. (1-2) $119*
*S BR (1-2) g.v. $149, o.v. $179*   *Extra persons $15*
*1 BR (1-4) g.v. $185, o.v. $219*   *5-day minimum, weekly/monthly discounts.*
*2 BR (1-6) g.v. $255, o.v. $295*   *Rollaways $15 and cribs $5 day*

## KAANAPALI ROYAL ★

2560 Kekaa Dr., Lahaina, Maui, HI 96761. (808-661-8687) Agents: Outrigger Hotels Hawaii 1-800-OUTRIGGER, Hawaiiana Resorts 1-800-367-7040, Whalers Realty 1-800-367-5632, Hawaiian Apt. Leasing 1-800-472-8449 CA,1-800-854-8843 U.S. except CA, RSVP 1-800-663-1118. These very spacious condos, 1,600 - 2,000 sq. ft., offer air-conditioning and lanais and are situated on the 16th fairway of the Kaanapali golf course overlooking the Kaanapali resort and Pacific Ocean. Daily maid service. Washer/dryers. Note that while all units have two bedrooms, they may be rented as a one bedroom based on space availability. One bedroom reservations may be wait listed outside of 30 days of arrival. No minimum stay, except Christmas holiday. One night deposit.

*1 BR (2,max 4) garden or golf view $165/150, o.v. or dlx golf view $185/165*
*2 BR (2,max 6) garden or golf view $190/175, o.v. or dlx golf view $220/195*

GINGER

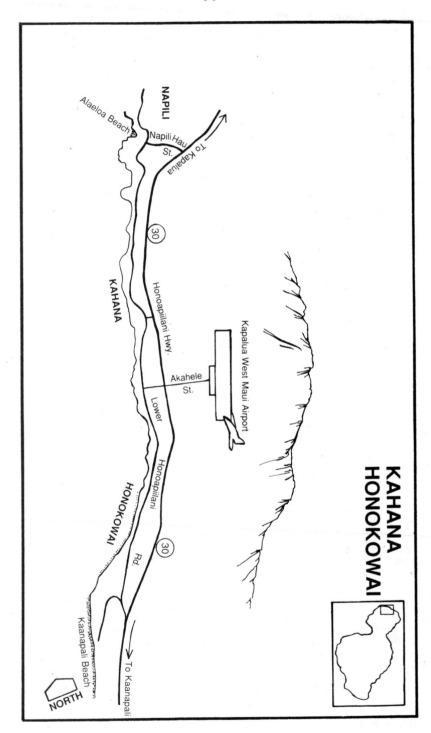

# HONOKOWAI

## INTRODUCTION

As you leave the Kaanapali Resort there is a stretch of yet undeveloped beach-front on the left still planted with sugar cane. This was the site of the old Kaanapali Airport. Resorts will be stretched along this beach within the next few years. Ahead, four large condo complexes signal the beginning of Honokowai, which stretches north along Lower Honoapiilani Highway. Accommodations are a mix of high and low-rise, some new, but most older. The beachfront is narrow and many complexes have retaining walls. A close-in reef fronts the beach and comes into shore at Papakea and at Honokowai Park. Between the reef and beach is generally shallow water unsuitable for swimming or other water activities. The only wide beach and break in the reef for swimming and snorkeling is at the Kaanapali Shores and Embassy Suites. In late 1987, several condominiums made a major investment in saving the beachfront by building a seawall beneath the sand to prevent winter erosion and it appears to have been successful. A number of the condominiums are perched on rocky bluffs with no sandy beach.

Many people return year after year to this quiet area, away from the bustle of Lahaina and Kaanapali and where prices are in the moderate range. A couple of small grocery stores are nearby. For dining out there is the Beach Club restaurant at the Kaanapali Shores and The Embassy Suites offers three restaurant choices.

The condominiums are individually owned for the most part, and the quality and care of each (or lack of) is reflected by the owner. Perhaps it is the shape of the sloping ridges of Mauna Kahalawai that cause this area to be slightly cooler and cloudier with more frequent rain showers in the afternoon than at neighboring Kaanapali.

## ACCOMMODATIONS - HONOKOWAI

| | | |
|---|---|---|
| Mahana Resort | Hale Kai | Hale Ono Loa |
| Maui Kai | Pikake | Lokelani |
| Embassy Suites | Hale Maui | Hale Mahina |
| Kaanapali Shores | Apt. Hotel | Beach Resort |
| Papakea | Nohonani | Hoyochi Nikko |
| Maui Sands | Kulankane | Kuleana |
| Paki Maui | Makani Sands | Polynesian Shores |
| Honokowai East | Kaleialoha | Mahinahina Beach |
| Maui Parkshores | Hale Royale | Mahina Surf |
| Honokowai Rsrt. Apts. | Hono Koa | Noelani |

**BEST BETS:** *Kaanapali Shores* - A high-rise surrounded by lovely grounds on the best beach in the area. *Papakea* - A low-rise complex with attractive grounds and pool. *Embassy Suites Resort Hotel* - A mix between a condo and a hotel, spacious rooms and breakfast is included, a good sandy beach.

## MAHANA

110 Kaanapali Shores Place, Lahaina, Maui, HI 96761. (808-661-8751) Agents: Aston 1-800-922-7866, Whaler's Realty 1-800-367-5632, RSVP 1-800-663-1118, Hawaiian Apt. Leasing 1-800-854-8843 in U.S. except CA, 1-800-472-8449 CA.

All units oceanfront. Two twelve-story towers with two tennis courts, heated pool, central air-conditioning, saunas, elevators, small pool area. Located on narrow beachfront with offshore coral reef precluding swimming and snorkeling. A better swimming area is 100 yards up the beach. This is a rather drab looking condominium on the outside, the pool sits out on a slab of cement without much in the way of atmosphere, but we've been told by those who return here year after year that it is just right. The earlier problems with beach erosion seems to have been remedied.

*S BR 1 bath (1-2) $130-160/105-135*          *3-night minimum*
*1 BR 1 bath (1-4) $165-195/140-170*
*2 BR 2 bath (1-6) $240-170/270-300*

## MAUI KAI

106 Kaanapali Shores Pl., Lahaina, Maui, HI 96761. (808-661-0002) 1-800-367-5635. Agents: Blue Sky Tours 1-800-678-2787, Condo Network 1-800-321-2525, Paradise Resorts 1-800-367-2644, Kumulani 1-800-367-2954.

A single ten-story building with 79 units. 2-night deposit, 2-night minimum. Units offer central air-conditioning, private lanais, full equipped kitchens. Property amenities include swimming pool, jacuzzi, laundry facilities, free parking. Some studio units may be available. Weekly/monthly discounts.
*1 BR (2) $80/70; 2 BR (4) $90-110/80*

## EMBASSY SUITES RESORT ★

104 Kaanapali Shores Place, Lahaina, Maui, HI 96761. (808-661-2000). 1-800-462-6284 U.S., 1-800-458-5848 Canada. On 7 1/2 acres this pink pyramid structure with a three-story blue waterfall cascading down the side can't be missed. A new concept in resorts on Maui, it blends the best of condo and resort living together. The pool (which is now heated) area is large and tropical with plenty of room for lounge chairs. In the past there was problems here with beach erosion, but they seem to have remedied it with erosion control measures. The lobby is open air and their glass enclosed elevators will whisk you up with a view! Atop of the resort, families can now enjoy their miniature golf course, open daily 9 am-9 pm, price is $5 per person, $2.50 for youths under 12 years.

Each one bedroom suite is a spacious 840 sq. ft, two bedroom suites are 1,200 sq. ft. Each features lanais with ocean or terrace views. Master bedrooms are equipped with a remote control 29" television and an large adjoining master bath with soaking tub. The living room, decorated in comfortable hues of blue and beige contains a massive 35" television, stereo receiver, VCR player and cassette player. Living rooms have a sofa that makes into a double bed. A dining area with a small kitchenette is equipped with a microwave, small refrigerator and sink. Toaster ovens, hot plates and ironing equipment available upon request. One phone in the living room and another in the bedroom have two lines which connect to a personal answering machine for your own recorded message.

Their two presidential suites are 2,100 sq. ft. and offer two bedrooms, two full baths and a larger kitchen. One features an Oriental theme, the other is decorated with a contemporary California flare. (Room rates include complimentary breakfasts and daily two-hour Manager's cocktail reception.) North Beach Grille for fine dining, Ohana Grill for more casual breakfast, lunch, dinner and snacks and the Deli Planet has deli sandwiches and sundries. Their children's program, Beach Buddies, is dedicated to perpetuating and preserving the heritage of the islands. "As a Keiki O Ka Aina Ika Pono (child of the land), let us share with you a 'Hawaiian Experience' rich in culture and tradition." Activities include hula class, lei making, coconut weaving and crafts, beach combing and aquarium time. The program is designed for children 4 to 10 years and operates year round Monday through Friday from 8:30 am - 2:30 pm. First-day registration fee of $15 per child, additional days are $10; additional child of the same family is $7.
*1 BR terrace view $225, mtn.v. $260, o.v. or o.v. dlx $300 o.f. $350*
*2 BR suite $475, Presidential Suite $1,200*

## KAANAPALI SHORES ★
100 Kaanapali Shores Place, Lahaina, Maui, HI 96761, (808-667-2211). Agents: Aston 1-800-922-7866, Whaler's Realty 1-800-367-5632, RSVP Reservations 1-800-663-1118. 463 units, all offer telephones, free tennis, daily maid service, and air-conditioning. Nicely landscaped grounds and a wide beach with an area of coral reef cleared for swimming and snorkeling. This is the only resort on north Kaanapali Beach that offers a good swimming area. Putting green, jacuzzi and the Beach Club Restaurant located in the pool area.

They offer Camp Kaanapali, a year-round children's program. Costs for the 9 a.m. - 2 p.m. Mon.-Fri. program is $10 for initial registration, which includes T-shirt and optional at a nominal fee are lunch at $6 per day, excursions and other special activities designed for kids three to eight years.
*Hotel Room w/ refrigerator $119/109*
*S BR (1-2) g.v. $159/129, o.v. $179/149*
*1 BR (1-4) g.v. $189/159, o.v. $209/179, family suite (1-6) $219/189*
*2 BR (1-6) g.v. $249/209, o.v. $279/249, o.f. $350/295*

## PAPAKEA ★
3543 L. Honoapiilani, Lahaina, Maui, HI 96761. (808-669-4848) 1-800-367-5037. Agents: Maui Resort Mgt. 1-800-367-5037, Whaler's Realty 1-800-367-5632, RSVP 1-800-663-1118, Hawaiian Apt. 1-800-472-8449 CA, 1-800-854-8843 U.S. except CA., Maui Network 1-800-367-5221, More Hawaii 1-800-967-6687. 364 units in five four-story buildings. Two pools, two jacuzzi's, two saunas, tennis courts, putting green, washer/dryers, and BBQ area. A seawall was installed in an effort to prevent further beach erosion. The shallow water is great for children due to a protective reef 10-30 yards offshore, but poor for swimming or snorkeling. A better beach is down in front of the Kaanapali Shores. One of the nicer grounds for a condominium complex with lush landscaping and pool areas. A comfortable, and quiet property that we recommend especially for families. No smoking units available. Crib or roll-away $6/day. Christmas holiday 14-day minimum with no refunds after October 1. 7-day refund notice, $250-$300 deposit. Cribs available.
*S BR (2) partial o.v. $134/119, o.f. $144/129*     *Weekly/monthly discounts*
*1 BR (4) partial o.v. $154/139, o.f. $174/159*
*2 BR (6) partial o.v. $189/174, o.f. $219/204*

### MAUI SANDS

3559 L. Honoapiilani, Lahaina, Maui, HI 96761. (808-669-9007) Maui Resort Management 1-800-367-5037. All 76 units have air-conditioning and kitchens. Limited maid service. Microwaves, coin-op laundry facility, rollaway & cribs available $9 night. A very friendly atmosphere where old friends have been gathering each year since it was built in the mid-sixties. A large central laundry facility is available and a large pool area with barbecues. Large boulders line the beach. A good family facility. Extra persons $9/night. 15% monthly discounts.

*1 BR (2,max 4) std. $ 80/68, g.v. $105/ 85, o.f. $135/115*
*2 BR (2,max 6) std. $100/81, g.v. $130/108, o.f. $160/135*

### PAKI MAUI

3615 L. Honoapiilani, Lahaina, Maui, HI 96761. (808-669-8235) Agents: Marc Resorts Group, 1-800-535-0085. This complex surrounds a garden and waterfall. No air-conditioning. Daily maid service.

| | |
|---|---|
| *S BR (1-2) o.f.  $139* | *2-nite deposit* |
| *1 BR (1-4) g.v.  $139  o.f. $159* | *cribs $5/nite* |
| *2 BR (1-6) o.f.  $199-219* | *children under 2 free* |

### HONOKOWAI EAST

3660 L. Honoapiilani Hwy., Lahaina, Maui, HI 96761 (808-669-8355) 51 units, mostly studios, in a 4-story building. Long term property.

### MAUI PARK

3626 L. Honoapiilani Hwy., Lahaina, Maui, HI 96761. (808-669-6622) Agents: Aston 1-800-922-7866, RSVP Reservations 1-800-663-1118, Maui Condominiums 1-800-663-6962. Located across the road from Honokowai Beach Park which lacks a sandy shoreline. A quiet area of West Maui with nearby grocery store. All units have complete kitchen. Coin-op laundry facility. Originally built as residential apartments they offer phones, and daily maid service. Because of its original intention, this property does resemble a residential area more than a vacation resort. All units are garden view. Cribs $6, rollaways $10.

*S BR (1-2) $89/79,  1 BR (1-4) $109/99,  2 BR (6) $149/139*

## HONOKOWAI PALMS RESORT
3666 L. Honoapiilani, Lahaina, Maui, HI 96761. (808-669-6130) Agent: Klahani 1-800-669-MAUI. 30 units across road from Honokowai Beachfront Park. Built of cement blocks this property lacks a great deal of ambience as a vacation retreat. Perhaps for the budget conscious it would be suitable, but it is a very basic, functional complex. *1 BR (2,max 4) $65, 2 BR (2,max 6) $70. Extra person $6.*

## HALE KAI
3691 L. Honoapiilani Hwy., Lahaina, Maui, HI 96761. (808-669-6333) 1-800-446-7307 U.S. and Canada. FAX (808) 669-7474. 40 units in a two-story building. The units do have lanais, kitchens, and a pool, but the beach is somewhat rocky. A simple and quiet property. 3-night minimum except Christmas. $250 refundable with 45 day notice. Minimum 3 nights. 10% monthly discounts - additional discounts may be given at individual owner's discretion.
*1 BR (2) $90 & up, 2 BR (4) $120 & up - Extra persons over 3 years $10/night*

## PIKAKE
3701 L. Honoapiilani, Lahaina, Maui, HI 96761. (808-669-6086) 1-800-446-3054. A low-rise, two-story, Polynesian style building with only twelve apartments completed in 1966. Private lanais open to the green lawn or balconies, with a beach protected by sea wall. Central laundry area. Light housekeeping provided after two week's stay. 3-night deposit, 3-night minimum, extra persons $10/night. NO CREDIT CARDS. *1 BR (2,max 4) $70, 2 BR (4,max 6) $85*

## HALE MAUI APARTMENT HOTEL
PO Box 516, Lahaina, Maui, HI 96761. (808-669-6312). Limited maid service. Coin-operated washer/dryer. BBQ. Weekly and monthly discounts. 3-day minimum, 7-day during Christmas. NO CREDIT CARDS.
*1 BR (2, max 5) $65-95*          *Extra persons $10/night*

## NOHONANI
3723 L. Honoapiilani, Lahaina, Maui, HI 96761. (808-669-8208) 1-800-822-7368. Agent: Klahani 1-800-669-0795. Two 4-story buildings containing 22 oceanfront two-bedroom units and 5 one-bedroom units. Complex has large pool, telephones, and is one block to grocery store. Extra persons $15/night. $200 deposit with 60-day refund notice, 4-day minimum stay. Weekly/monthly discounts. NO CREDIT CARDS. *1 BR (1-2) $110/92, 2 BR (1-4) $125/110*

## KULAKANE
3741 L. Honoapiilani (PO Box 5236), Lahaina, Maui, HI 96761. (808-669-6119) 1-800-367-6088. 42 oceanfront units with fully equipped kitchen, laundry facilities on premise. Lanais overlook ocean but no sandy beach. $10 extra person. 3 night minimum low season, 5 night high season. $150 deposit. 10% monthly discounts. *1 BR 1 bath (1-2) $90-95, 2 BR 2 bath (1-4) $135*

## MAKANI SANDS
3765 L. Honoapiilani Hwy., Lahaina, Maui, HI 96761. (808-669-8223). 30 units in a four-story building. Dishwashers, washer/dryers, elevator. Oceanfront with small sandy beach. Weekly maid service. Deposits vary, weekly/monthly discounts, 3-night minimum, extra persons $10/night.
*1 BR (2) $85, 2 BR (4) $120, 3 BR (6) $140*

## KALEIALOHA

3785 L. Honoapiilani, Lahaina, Maui, HI 96761. (808-669-8197) 1-800-222-8688. 67 units in a 4-story building. 3-night minimum. Deposit equal to three nights stay, $7.50 extra persons over age 2. Refundable if cancelled 45 days prior to arrival. Washer/dryers. Weekly discounts. 3 night minimum. Credit cards accepted. *Studio (1-2) mtn.v. $75, 1 BR (1-4) o.v. superior $85, deluxe $95*

## HALE ROYALE

3788 L. Honoapiilani, Lahaina, Maui, HI 96761. (808-669-5230). No short term rental units available at this time.

## HONO KOA

3801 L. Honoapiilani, Lahaina, Maui, HI 96761. (808-669-0979) This property is no longer vacation rental, time share only. 28 units in one four-story building. Washer/dryer, dishwasher, microwave, BBQ. Pool with jacuzzi.

## HALE ONO LOA ★

3823 L. Honoapiilani, Lahaina, Maui, HI 96761. (808-669-6362) Agents: More Hawaii 1-800-967-6687 U.S. & Canada, Klahani 1-800-669-MAUI (U.S. & Canada), Maui Accommodations 1-800-252-MAUI (U.S.) 67 oceanfront and oceanview units. Maid service extra charge. Beachfront is rocky. The units we toured were roomy and nicely furnished with spacious lanais. The grounds and pool area were pleasant and well groomed. A good choice for a quiet retreat. Grocery store nearby.
*1 BR 1 bath (4) garden or ocean view $75-85*
*2 BR 2 bath (6) g.v. $150(840/wk), o.v. 160(920), o.f. $170(1,000/wk)*

## LOKELANI

3833 L. Honoapiilani, Lahaina, Maui, HI 96761. (808-669-8110) 1-800-367-2976. Three 3-story 12 unit buildings with beachfront or oceanviews. The 1-BR units are on beach level with lanai, 2-BR units are townhouses with bedrooms upstairs and lanais on both levels. Units feature washer/dryers and dishwashers. Weekly discount, 3-night minimum low season, 7-night high season, extra persons $8, $25 cancellation fee. Three night deposit, balance due two weeks prior to arrival. *1 BR (1-2) $95/85, 2 BR (townhouses) (1-4) $125/110*

## HALE MAHINA BEACH RESORT

3875 L. Honoapiilani, Lahaina, Maui, HI 96761. (808-669-8441) 1-800-367-8047 ext. 441. Agents: Maui Network 1-800-367-5221, Kaanapali Vacation Rentals 1-800-822-4252. Hale Mahina means "House of the Pale Moon" and offers 52 units in two, four-story buildings and one two-story building featuring lanais, ceiling fans, microwaves, washer/dryer. BBQ area, jacuzzi. Extra persons $10/night. 3-day minimum, deposit within two weeks of reservations, balance on arrival. *1 BR (1-2) $115/100, 2 BR (1-4) $135/120*

## HOYOCHI NIKKO

3901 L. Honoapiilani, Lahaina, Maui, HI 96761. (808-669-8343) 1-800-487-6002. Agents: Klahani 1-800-669-MAUI (U.S. & Canada). 18 one-bedroom oceanview units (on a rocky beachfront) in two-story building bearing an oriental motif. Underground parking, "Long Boy" twin beds, some with queens, half size washer and dryers in units. Maid service on check-out only. $300 deposit with 30-day refund notice low season, 60-day high season. Prepayment required. NO CREDIT CARDS through property. Agent Klahani will take MC or Visa. *1 BR $90 - extra persons $10/night*

### KULEANA
3959 L. Honoapiilani, Lahaina, Maui, HI 96761. (808-669-8080) U.S. Mainland or Canada 1-800-367-5633. 118 1-bedroom units with queen size sofa bed in living room. Large pool with plenty of lounge chair room and tennis court. A short walk to sandy beaches. Weekly/monthly discounts. 3 night minimum stay. Extra persons $7.50. Children under 2 free. Cribs $4/night, rollaways $6. 3-night deposit refundable with 14 day notice. *1 BR o.v. $85/80, o.f. 95/90*

### POLYNESIAN SHORES
3975 L. Honoapiilani, Lahaina, Maui, HI 96761. (808-669-6065) 1-800-433-6284, from Canada toll free 1-800-488-2179. 52 units on a rocky shore but nice grounds with deck overlooking the ocean. Additional persons $10 each. 10% monthly discount. 60 days cancellation notice for refund. $300 deposit, 3-day minimum.
*1 BR 1 bath (2) $90-100/80-90, 2 BR 2 bath (4) $100-110 / $90-100 3 BR 3 bath (6) $163/155*

### MAHINAHINA BEACH
4007 L. Honoapiilani, Lahaina, Maui, HI 96761. Units only through owners.

### MAHINA SURF
4057 L. Honoapiilani, Lahaina, Maui, HI 96761 (808-669-6068) 1-800-367-6086, FAX (808) 669-4534. 56 one-bedroom and one-bedroom with loft units. Dishwashers, maid service available at hourly charge. Located on rocky shore, the nearest sandy beach is a short drive to Kahana. Large lawn area around pool offers plenty of room for lounging. $300 deposit, 4-week refund notice.
*1 BR 1 bath (2,max 4) $110/95      Extra persons $8/nite including children*
*2 BR 1 bath $125/110,  2 bath $130/125   Weekly/monthly discounts*

### NOELANI
4095 L. Honoapiilani, Lahaina, Maui, HI 96761. (808-669-8375) 1-800-367-6030. Agent: Condominium Connection 1-800-423-2976. 50 oceanfront units in one 4-story building and two 2-story structures. Kitchens with dishwashers and washer/dryers only in 1, 2, and 3-bedroom units. Three bedroom units feature a sunken livingroom as do the two bedroom units on the third floor. Complex has two pools and maid service mid-week. Located on a rocky shore, nearest sandy beach is short drive to Kahana. Weekly/monthly discounts. Extra person $7.50 day. 3 day minimum low season/7 day high season. AAA approved. 7th night free during low season.
*S BR 1 bath (1-2) $ 87-97, 1 BR 1 bath (1-2) $110      3-night deposit*
*2 BR 2 bath (1-2) $140,    3 BR 3 bath (1-6) $170      2-wk refund notice*

# *KAHANA*

## INTRODUCTION

To the north of Honokowai, and about seven miles north of Lahaina is a prominent island of high-rise condos with a handful of two-story complexes strung along the coast in its lee. This is Kahana. The beach adjacent to the high-rises is fairly wide, but tapers off quickly after this point. Several of the larger complexes offer very nice grounds and spacious living quarters with more resort type activities than in Honokowai. The prices are lower than Kaanapali, but higher than Honokowai. In the past we have reported a continuing problem in the Honokowai to Kapalua areas with algae. The algae bloom seems to come and go, causing problems to a greater or lesser degree for reasons unknown. State officials continue their investigation but a cause or reason for this condition has not yet been determined. Of late, the problem seems to have improved. The algae doesn't appear to be any health risk, but an annoyance for swimming and snorkeling.

## WHERE TO SHOP

There are in the lower level of the Kahana Manor as well as Kahana Gateway. Shops include gift and dive shops, a gas station and Whaler's General Store, beauty salon, children's fashion store, a laundry, McDonald's, Nicolinas and Roy's Kahana Bar & Grill and newer additions are Ludwig's and Fish and Games Sports Bar.

## ACCOMMODATIONS - KAHANA

| | | |
|---|---|---|
| Kahana Beach Resort | Valley Isle Resort | Kahana Reef |
| Kahana Villa | Royal Kahana | Kahana Outrigger |
| Kahana Falls | Hololani | Kahana Village |
| Sands of Kahana | Pohailaini/Maui Kalani | Kahana Sunset |

**BEST BETS: *Sands of Kahana*** - Spacious units on a nice white sand beach.
***Kahana Sunset*** - Low-rise condos surrounding a secluded cove and beach.

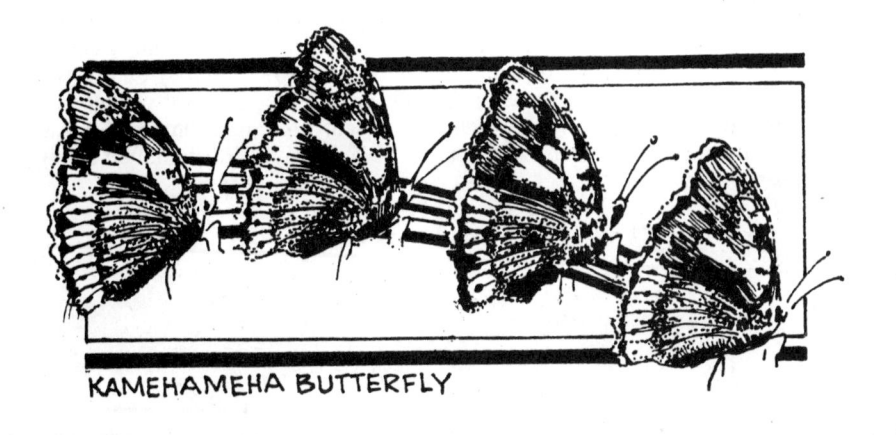

KAMEHAMEHA BUTTERFLY

## KAHANA BEACH RESORT

4221 L. Honoapiilani, Lahaina, Maui, HI 96761. (808-669-8611) Agent: Pleasant Hawaiian Holidays (package tours only) 1-800-242-9244. All units offer oceanview. The studios sleep up to four and have kitchenettes. The 1 BR units have kitchens, 2 lanais, living room with queen-size loveseat sleeper, bedroom with 2 king beds, 2 full-size baths, dressing room, and will accommodate 7. Coin-op laundry on premises. Nice, white sandy beach fronting complex.

## KAHANA VILLA

4242 L. Honoapiilani, Lahaina, Maui, HI 96761. (808-669-5613) Agents: Marc Resorts Group 1-800-535-0085, RSVP 1-800-663-1118. Across the road from the beach. Units have microwaves, washer/dryers, telephones. Daily maid service. Sauna, tennis courts, store, restaurants. Cribs $5, rollaway $15.
*Studio $115, 1 BR 1 bath g.v.(1-4) $125,  o.v. $150,  o.v. deluxe $159*
*2 BR 2 bath g.v. (1-6) $159,  o.v. $195,  o.v. deluxe $205*

## KAHANA FALLS

4260 Lower Honoapiilani Hwy., Lahaina, Maui, HI 96761. 1-800-635-MAUI, (808) 669-1050. FAX (808) 669-1848. 36 2-bedroom 2-bath (which can convert to a studio plus one bedroom unit) and 24 1-bedroom units (which can be divided to form a hotel room and one bedroom unit). The units are furnished with washer and dryer (except hotel unit), cable television, air-conditioning, telephones, whirlpool tub, VCR player. Children's pool, five waterfalls, sand-bottom swimming pool, on-site activities, fitness center. This is a vacation ownership resort, meaning people can purchase time shares. However, they currently are also operating as a hotel/condo. Children under 12 free. Rollaway or crib $8. Deposit. Check out time 9 a.m., check in 4 p.m.
*1 BR 2 bath (1-4) $120,  Hotel unit with 1 bath (1-2) $60*
*2 BR 2 bath (1-4) $160,  Studio with 1 bath $90*

## SANDS OF KAHANA ★

4299 L. Honoapiilani, Lahaina, Maui, HI 96761. Agents: Village Resorts 1-800-367-7052, (808-669-0400), Hawaiian Apt. Leasing 1-800-854-8843 (1-800-472-8449 CA), RSVP 1-800-663-1118, Whaler's Realty 1-800-367-5632.

96 units on Kahana Beach. Underground parking. If you're looking to be a little away from the hustle of Lahaina/Kaanapali, with quarters large enough for a big family, and luxuries such as microwaves and full-size washer/dryers then this may be just what you seek. Located on a sandy beachfront and only a couple miles from Kaanapali, it is also less than a mile from the West Maui Airport. Four 8-story buildings surround a central restaurant and a dual pool area.

Sands of Kahana is family oriented from the size of their rooms to their children's playground and summer programs. Spacious 1, 2 or 3 bedroom units have enormous kitchens and beautifully appointed living rooms. Moloka'i is beautifully framed in the large picture windows of the oceanview units, or select among the slightly less expensive garden view units. There was plenty of fun in the sun here with a beachside volleyball court filled each afternoon, and the large three foot deep children's pool was popular as was another larger and deeper pool with jacuzzi, three tennis courts and a putting green.

Most complexes restrict the use of snorkel gear or flotation equipment in the pool, however, here it is allowed to the delight of the children. A small children's play area offers diversion while parents make use of several garden area charcoal barbecues. The summer children's program is very reasonable and invites children between the ages of 5 and 12 to participate in activities. Across the street is a full size grocery store and several restaurants are within walking distance. Cribs $10 per night/$60 per week, rollaway $15 per night.

*1 BR 1 bath o.v. (4) $215/175, o.f. $250/205, courtyard $185/155*
*2 BR 1 bath o.v. (6) $265/235, o.f. $310/280, courtyard $250/205*
*3 BR 2 bath o.v. (8) $325/300, o.f. $355/330, courtyard $310/280*

## VALLEY ISLE RESORT
4327 L. Honoapiilani, Lahaina, Maui, HI 96761. (808-669-5511) Agents: Rainbow Reservations 1-800-367-6092, Hawaiian Apartment Leasing 1-800-854-8843 US except CA). Partial air-conditioning. Located on Kahana Beach. On site restaurant and grocery store. Payment in full 30 days prior to arrival. Weekly maid service.

*S BR 1 bath (2) o.f. $ 85/ 65*     *Extra persons $10, under 3 free*
*1 BR 1 bath (2) o.v. $ 95/ 75,  o.f. $ 95-105 / $80-90*
*2 BR 2 bath (4) o.v. $115/100,  o.f. $130/120*

## ROYAL KAHANA
4365 L. Honoapiilani, Lahaina, Maui, HI 96761. (808-669-5911) 1-800-447-7783, FAX (808) 669-5950. Agents: Hawaiiana Resorts 1-800-367-7040, Hawaiian Apartment Leasing 1-800-854-8843 US except CA). 12 story high-rise complex built in 1975 with 236 oceanview units on Kahana Beach. Underground parking and air-conditioning. Daily maid service. A nice pool area with sauna. Tennis courts. Units have full kitchens and microwaves. Nearby grocery stores, restaurants and shops. Rollaway/cribs $6/per day.

*1 BR 1 bath (1-2) o.v. $124/97,  Studio (1-3) o.v. $100/85    2-night deposit*
*2 BR 2 bath (1-6) o.v.-o.f. $170-195/150-175         15-day refund notice*

## HOLOLANI
4401 L. Honoapiilani, Lahaina, Maui, HI 96761. (808-669-8021) 1-800-367-5032, 1-800-423-8733 ext. 318 Canada. Agent: Rainbow Reservations 1-800-367-6092. 27 oceanfront units on sandy, reef protected beach. Covered parking. Grocery store. 7-day/3-day minimum. $250 deposit, full payment 60/30 days prior to arrival. Children under 5 free. NO CREDIT CARDS. Extra persons $10/night.

*1 and 2 BR 2 bath (2,max 6) $125-165 / $110-130*

## POHAILANI  (MAUI KAILANI)
4435 L. Honoapiilani, Lahaina, Maui, HI 96761 (808-669-6994) FAX (808) 669-4046. Agent: Hawaii Kailani 206-676-1434. Maui Kailani is the rental portion of the Pohailani. The Maui Kailani offers a mixture of two-bedroom and studio apartments. The larger units are situated around eight park-like acres, while the studio units sit directly on the beach. Walking distance to restaurants and grocery stores. Swimming pool, tennis courts, laundry facilities. T.V. cable and T.V. rental are available for each unit, but cannot be requested prior to arrival. Full kitchens in both studio and two bedroom units. Twice weekly maid service. Extra person $5 day. Monthly rates available. Deposit varies.

*S BR o.f. (2, max 3) $75, 2 BR g.v. (2, max 5) $75. Weekly rates $455 for either*

## KAHANA REEF ★
4471 L. Honoapiilani, Lahaina, Maui, HI 96761. (808-669-6491) 1-800-253-3773 FAX (808) 669-2192. 88 well-kept units. Limited number of oceanfront studios available. Laundry facilities on premises. 15% monthly discounts. Maid service daily except Sunday. NO CREDIT CARDS. Room and car packages available. $200 deposit, extra persons $8/night. A good value. *Studio $100/95, 1 BR 1 bath (2,max 5) $110/100, 2 BR $200/174.*

## KAHANA OUTRIGGER
4521 L. Honoapiilani, Lahaina, Maui, HI 96761. (808-669-6550) 1-800-852-4262. Agent: Rainbow Reservations 1-800-367-6092. Sixteen spacious 3-bedroom oceanview condo suites in low-rise complex on a narrow sandy beachfront. Units have microwaves and washer/dryers and are appointed with lots of Italian tile. These are rented as a vacation "home" and no on-property service provided. *3 BR 2 bath (6) $195/165, 3 BR 3 bath (6) $215/180. Extra person $10.*

## KAHANA VILLAGE ★
4531 L. Honoapiilani, Lahaina, Maui, HI 96761. (808-669-5111) 1-800-824-3065. Agents: Kumulani 1-800-367-2954, RSVP 1-800-663-1118. Attractive townhouse units. Second level units are 1,200 sq.ft.; ground level 3-bedroom units have 1,700 sq.ft. with a wet bar, sunken tub in master bath, Jenn-aire ranges, microwaves, lanais, and washer/dryers. They now offer a heated pool, newly re-landscaped grounds and many newly upgraded units. Nice but narrow beach offering good swimming. 5-day minimum. Bi-weekly maid service. NO CREDIT CARDS. $300 deposit, balance due prior to arrival. Monthly discounts. Additional person $20. *2 BR o.v. $180/150, o.f. $220/180, 3 BR o.v. $230/190, o.f. $280/230*

## KAHANA SUNSET ★
PO Box 10219, Lahaina, Maui, HI 96761. (808-669-8011) 1-800-669-1488, FAX (808) 669-9170. Agents: RSVP 1-800-663-1118, Whaler's Realty 1-800-367-5632, Hawaiian Apartment Leasing 1-800-854-8843 US except CA).

Ninety units on a beautiful and secluded white sand beach. Units have very large lanais, telephones, and washer/dryers. Each unit has its own lanai, but they adjoin one another, adding to the friendly atmosphere of this complex. One of the very few resorts with a heated pool and heated children's pool, BBQ. You can drive up right to your door on most of the two bedroom units making unloading easy (and with a family heavy into suitcases that can be a real back saver). Extra persons $8/night including infants, 10% monthly discounts. The Kahana Sunset offers condo/car packages also. Kahana Sunset Rates, room only:
*1 BR 1 bath (2) o.v. $150, 2 BR 2 bath (2) o.v. $185, o.f. $235*

Following rates for Kahana Sunset are thru Whaler's Realty, 1-800-367-5632.
*1 BR 1 bath (2) o.v. $115-125, 2 BR 2 bath (2) o.v. $150-160, o.f. $185-200*

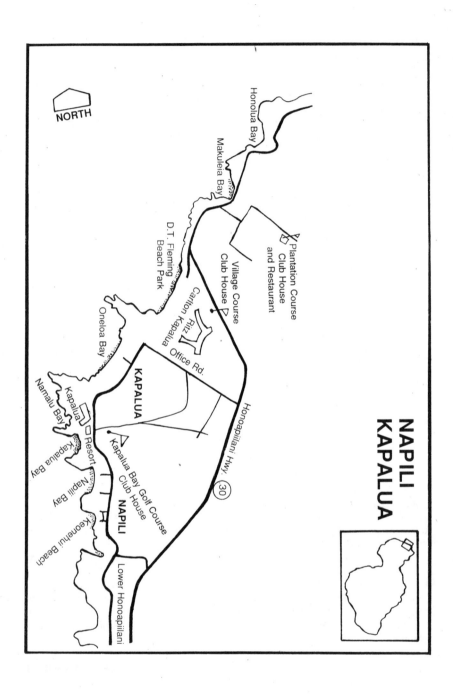

# NAPILI

## INTRODUCTION

This area's focal point is the beautiful Napili Bay with good swimming, snorkeling and boogie boarding, and it even has tide pools for children to explore. The condominium units here are low-rise, with prices mostly in the moderate range, and are clustered tightly around the bay. A number are located right on the beach, others a short walk away. The quality of the units varies considerably, but generally a better location on the bay and better facilities demand a higher price. The complexes are small, most under 50 units, and all but one has a pool. At the nearby Napili Plaza Shopping Center you'll find a full-size grocery store, restaurants and shops.

### *WHERE TO SHOP*
Napili Plaza may be within walking distance, depending on the location of your condominium. It includes Subway Sandwiches, Stanfield's West Maui Floral, Maui Tacos, The Coffee Store, Valley Isle Dry Cleaners, First Hawaiian Bank, Napili Market and Koho Grill and Bar.

## ACCOMMODATIONS - NAPILI

Honokeana Cove      Napili Bay
Napili Ridge      Napili Sunset
Coconut Inn      Hale Napili
Napili Point      Napili Village Suites
Napili Shores      Mauian
Napili Surf      The Kahili Maui
                     Napili Kai Beach Club

**BEST BETS:** *Napili Sunset* - Centered right on the edge of Napili Bay, rooms are well kept. *Napili Kai Beach Club* - A quiet facility on the edge of Napili Bay. Large grounds and a restaurant are on site. Resort activities are offered.

### HONOKEANA COVE
5255 L. Honoapiilani, Lahaina, Maui, HI 96761. (808-669-6441) 1-800-237-4948. Agent: Klahani Resort 1-800-669-0795.

38 oceanview units on Honokeana Cove near Napili Bay. Attractive grounds. 3-night minimum, 3-night deposit (except Christmas). NO CREDIT CARDS.
*1 BR 1 bath (2) $ 95, 1 BR 2 bath (2) $105*
*2 BR 2 bath (4,max 4) $135, 3 BR 2 bath (6,max 6) $155, Townhouse (4) $150*
*Weekly/monthly discounts, extra persons (all ages) $10-$15/nite*

### NAPILI RIDGE
Hui Rd. "F," Lahaina, Maui, HI 96761. (808-669-6911) 44 studios and 88 one-bedroom units in 11 two-story buildings. Pool, BBQ. Short walk to nearby Napili Market, bus stop and beach. Long term stays only, no vacation rentals.

### COCONUT INN
Hui Rd. "F," PO Box 10517, Napili, Maui, HI 96761. (808-669-5712) 40 units in two-story retreat about 1/4 mile above Napili Bay. Long term residents only.

### NAPILI POINT
5295 L. Honoapiilani, Lahaina, Maui, HI 96761. (808-669-5611) 1-800-669-6252. Agent: Hawaiian Apartment Leasing 1-800-854-8843 US except CA) Located on rocky beach, but next door to beautiful Napili Bay. Units have washer/dryer, direct dial phones, daily maid service. Two pools. In some suites the second bedroom is loft-style.
*1 BR 1 bath (4) o.v. $164/134, o.f. $174-184 / $144-154*
*2 BR 2 bath (6) o.v. $195/170, o.f. $205-225 / $180-190*

### NAPILI SHORES
5315 L. Honoapiilani, Lahaina, Maui, HI 96761. (808-669-8061) FAX (808) 669-5047. Agents: Colony Resorts 1-800-367-6046, Hawaiian Apt. Leasing 1-800-854-8843, RSVP 1-800-663-1118.

152 units on Napili Bay. Rooms offer lanais and the one-bedroom units have dishwashers. Laundry facilities on premises as well as two pools, adult hot tub, croquet, and BBQ area. Restaurant, cocktail lounge and grocery store on property. Extra persons $15/night, no minimum stay, daily maid service. Studios have one queen and one twin bed. Crib $8, rollaway $15/per day.
*S BR (2,max 3) g.v. $135/125, o.v. $165/150, o.f. $185/165*
*1 BR (2,max 4) g.v. $175/160, o.v. $190/175*

### NAPILI SURF
50 Napili Place, Lahaina, Maui, HI 96761. (808) 669-8002. 1-800-541-0638. FAX (808-669-8004). 53 units on Napili Bay. Two pools, BBQ, shuffleboard, lanais, daily maid service, and laundry facilities. Extra persons $15/night, 12% monthly discount, $300 deposit, 14-day refund notice, 5-night minimum except 10-day during Christmas, NO CREDIT CARDS.
*S BR (2,max 3) g.v. $99/95, o.v. $125/115, 1 BR (2,max 5) $165-175/155-165*

### NAPILI BAY RESORT
33 Hui Drive, Lahaina Maui, HI 96761. (808-669-6044). Agents: Whalers Realty 1-800-367-5632, Hawaiian Apt. Leasing 1-800-854-8843 (1-800-472-8449 CA).

This older complex on Napili Bay is neat, clean and affordably priced. Studio apartments offer 1 queen & 2 single beds, lanais, kitchens, daily maid service. Coin-op laundromat with public phones. Extra persons $8/night, children under 12 free. 3-night minimum, 2-night deposit, 7-day refund notice, weekly and monthly discounts. *Studio (2,max 4) g.v. $75-95, partial o.v. $100-125*

## NAPILI SUNSET ★

46 Hui Rd., Lahaina, Maui, HI 96761. (808-669-8083) 1-800-447-9229 U.S.A. 1-800-223-4611 Canada, FAX (808) 669-2730. Forty-one units located on Napili Bay. Daily maid service. These units have great oceanviews and are well maintained. A very friendly atmosphere. Kitchens have microwaves. Deposits vary. 15 day notice for full refund. 10% monthly discount. 3-day minimum. *Studio (2) g.v. $85/65, 1 BR 1 bath (2) o.f. $159/129, 2 BR 2 bath (4) o.f. $249/199*

## HALE NAPILI

65 Hui Rd., Napili, Maui, HI 96761. (808-669-6184) 1-800-245-2266, FAX (808) 665-0066. 18 units oceanfront on Napili Bay. Lanais. Daily maid service except Sunday. Ceiling fans, microwaves, laundry facilities on property. No pool. 3-night minimum. Extra persons $8/night, $225 deposit, 30-day refund notice, monthly discounts, NO CREDIT CARDS. *Studio (2) g.v. $75, o.f. $100, 1 BR (2) o.f. $120*

## NAPILI VILLAGE SUITES

5425 Honoapiilani, Lahaina, Maui, HI 96761. (808-669-6228) 1-800-336-2185, FAX (808-669-6229) U.S. & Canada. All rooms have king or queen size beds, daily maid service. Free laundry facilities on premises. Located a short walk from Napili Bay. Extra persons $8/night, 3-night deposit. Deposits $200-$250, 14 day refund notice. *Studio (2) $89/79*

## MAUIAN

5441 Honoapiilani, Lahaina, Maui, HI 96761. (808-669-6205) 1-800-367-5034, FAX (808-669-0129). Studio apartments on Napili Bay. Kitchen plus microwave, one queen and two twin day beds. BBQ area. Two public phones on property, one courtesy reservations phone. Television only in recreation center. Daily maid service. 3-day minimum, 3-night deposit, 14-day refund notice. 5% two week, 12% monthly discounts. Rental crib $8/night. Extra person $9 night, 4th person $6. They are continuing to offer their flexible rate calculation. This is a sliding scale room rate based upon occupancy. The rates quoted when reservation is made are guaranteed. The discount can be up to 30% off, so be sure to inquire when you call! Many of their guests have been returning to vacation at this quiet corner of Napili for 30 years or more. *Studio garden $116/100, o.v. $124/110, o.f. $142/129.*

LAYSAN ALBATROSS

**THE KAHILI MAUI**

5500 Honoapiilani Hwy., Lahaina, HI 96761. (808) 669-5636, 1-800-SUNSETS. Thirty studio and one-bedroom units available, some with golf course view of Kapalua's 18th hole, others garden/pool view. Spa and pool/jacuzzi, BBQ's, maid service, washer/dryer. Weekly discounts.

*Studio/1 bath 99/79; 1 BR/2 bath 130/110        Crib $10, rollaway $15*

**NAPILI KAI BEACH CLUB ★**

5900 Honoapiilani, Lahaina, Maui, HI 96761. (808-669-6271) 1-800-367-5030, Canada 1-800-263-8183. Units feature lanais, kitchenettes, telephones, and washer/dryer facilities. Complimentary tennis equipment, beach equipment, croquet, putters, and snorkel gear. Daily coffee and tea party in Beach Club. Sea House Restaurant located on grounds. 2 tennis courts, 4 pools, very large jacuzzi. The grounds are extensive and the area very quiet. A relaxed and friendly atmosphere, a great beach, and a wide variety of activities may tempt you to spend most of your time enjoying this very personable and complete resort. Approximately 30 new luxury units with an oriental motif have been added in what used to be the large lawn area. 2-night deposit. 14-day refund notice. NO CREDIT CARDS.

*S BR (2) luxury g.v. no kitchen $155, with kitchen $175, suites $290-435*
*S BR deluxe o.v. $80-195, suites $210-400, dlx. o.f. $195, suites $235-275*
*S BR luxury o.v. no kitchen $185, with kitchen $205, suites $350-505*
*S BR luxury o.f. $220-240, suites $275-450*
*Suites 2-4 persons, S BR 1-2 persons. Extra person $15. Package rates available.*

# KAPALUA

## INTRODUCTION

The modern day history of Kapalua dates back to 1836 when the Baldwin family of New England settled on the island of Maui as missionaries. By the late 1800s, the property that is now Kapalua was part of Honolua Ranch, complete with Hereford herds, taro patches, fishing boats and fields of red coffee bean bushes. At the turn of the century, H.P. Baldwin (the great-grandfather of Colin Cameron) acquired the Honolua Ranch. D.T. Fleming, whose name today signifies one of Kapalua's three beaches, served as plantation manager. Kapalua became a bustling enclave in the island, with a working ranch that supplied pork and beef to the port of Lahaina.

In the years that followed, Kapalua's acres of grassy slopes were transformed into geometric patterns of silver-blue pineapple fields and the first crop of this fruit was harvested in 1914. Today Maui Land & Pineapple Company Inc. is ranked as the largest producer of private-label pineapple and pineapple juice in the world.

In the 1970's a new master plan for Kapalua began to take place when Colin Cameron chose 750 acres of his family's 23,000 acre pineapple plantation for the development of this up-scale resort. The result is the Kapalua Bay Hotel and Villas which opened in 1979 and the surrounding resort area which includes a residential community, golf courses, and The Ritz-Carlton Kapalua resort.

The mood reflected at the Kapalua Bay Hotel is serene. Their philosophy of quality of food and service in a resort setting offers the ultimate in privacy and luxury living. The grounds are spacious with manicured lawns and an oasis of waterfalls and gardens and a butterfly-shaped pool located nearer the beachfront. More than 400 condominium units are located in the Ridge, Golf and Bay Villas, of which about 125 are available for rent. There are three 18-hole championship golf courses, a tennis garden, a shopping area with a myriad of boutiques and a deli/restaurant. The newest Ritz-Carlton Kapalua, has maintained the high standards of this area with their outstanding new resort hotel which opened in October 1992. There are several excellent restaurants in the area from which to choose. Kapalua Bay is a small cove of pristine white sand, nestled at the edge of a coconut palm grove. It has been named among the top beaches in the world. The protected bay offers good snorkeling and a safe swimming area for all ages. This area of Maui tends to be slightly wetter than in neighboring Lahaina, and the winds can and do pick up in the afternoon.

## WHAT TO SEE AND DO

Kapalua, "arms embracing the sea," is the most north-western development on Maui. The logo for Kapalua is the butterfly, and with a close look you can see the body of the butterfly is a pineapple. One might enjoy a stop at the elegant Kapalua Bay Hotel. The lobby bar is ideally situated for evening refreshment, music, and sunset viewing. The resort has a small shopping mall located just outside the Kapalua Bay Hotel and there are shops at The Ritz-Carlton Kapalua.

The road beyond Kapalua is paved and in excellent condition, (about 1 1/2 hrs. Napili to Wailuku) and offers some magnificent shoreline views. Slaughterhouse Beach is only a couple of miles beyond Kapalua and you may find it interesting to watch the body surfers challenge the winter waves. Just beyond is Honolua Bay where winter swells make excellent board surfing conditions. A good viewing point is along the roadside on the cliffs beyond the bay. Continuing on, you may notice small piles of rocks. This is graffiti Maui style. They began appearing a few years ago and these mini-monuments have been sprouting up ever since. There are some wonderful hiking areas here as well. One terrain resembles a moonscape, while another is windswept peninsula with a symbolic rock circle formation. See RECREATION & TOURS "hiking" for more details. You can follow the road around west Maui to Wailuku, although don't go if you are in a hurry. It is a slow and scenic drive and many parts of the road are windy with room enough for only one car. On occasion, parts of the road have been washed away, closing it. Some rental car companies may restrict your travel on this route.

Kapalua is home to a number of outstanding annual events. The Kapalua Tennis Jr. Vet/Sr. Championship is held each May. In June both the Kapalua Music Festival and Kapalua Wine Symposium are held at the Kapalua Bay Hotel. The Kapalua Open Tennis Tournament is in September and the Kapalua Betsey Nagelson Tennis is held the end of November and/or the first part of December. The nationally televised Kapalua International is held in November and top PGA golfers try their skills on Kapalua's Plantation Course. The Ritz-Carlton sponsors some wonderful events. The Maui Writers Conference is held over the Labor Day Weekend in September, in late March and early April they hold the Celebration of the Arts and throughout the year they host an Artists-in-Residence program.

## WHERE TO SHOP

The Kapalua Shops, an entirely covered mall, offers a showcase of treasures. Here you will find *The Kapalua Logo Shop* (669-4172) where everything from men's and women's resort wear to glassware display the Kapalua butterfly logo. The newest shop, *Kapalua Kids,* features fashions for infants through boys and girls size 7 (669-0033). *The Market Cafe* (669-4888) has fresh pastries, wines, gourmet items to go, or enjoy breakfast, lunch, or dinner at their restaurant.

## ACCOMMODATIONS - KAPALUA

Kapalua Bay Hotel & Villas          The Ritz-Carlton
Kapalua Bay and Golf Villas       The Ridge
Ironwoods

***BEST BETS:*** *The Kapalua Bay Hotel & Villas* - This resort offers quiet elegance, top service, great food with all the amenities. Any of the condominium units in this area would be excellent, however, they are not all located within easy walking distance of the beach. A shuttle service is available. The condominiums at Kapalua offer spacious living and complete kitchen facilities. Rental information for the Kapalua Villas is in three different sections, and there are a number of rental agents. The Kapalua Hotel handles rentals of these luxurious condominiums. Also see the listing below for "Kapalua Bay Villas" and "Ridge Villas" for other rental management companies. *The Ritz-Carlton Kapalua*, which opened in October 1992, is an outstanding resort.

### KAPALUA BAY HOTEL & THE KAPALUA VILLAS ★
One Bay Drive, Kapalua, Maui, HI 96761. (808-669-5656) 1-800-367-8000. 194 hotel rooms plus villa condominiums. Rooms have service bars and refrigerators, no kitchens. All rooms have air-conditioning with decor in warm neutral shades of taupe, rose and muted terra cotta. Five-star restaurants include The Bay Club and The Garden. A cafe is available in the Kapalua Shops, located adjacent to the hotel. Lovely grounds, excellent beach and breathtaking bay. The resort includes The Bay Course and The Village Course, two 18-hole championship golf courses designed by Arnold Palmer, and the newly opened Plantation Course. A tennis garden with 10-plexipave courts, 4 lighted are available for guest use.

THE RITZ-CARLTON                    KAPALUA, MAUI

The new pool is butterfly-shaped, located near the ocean. And as the sun sets Hawaiian musicians and dancers entertain near poolside. The expanse of lawn gives way to lush tropical foliage, waterfalls, pools and gardens. This is elegance on a more sophisticated scale than the glitter and glitz of the Kaanapali resorts. Other amenities include coffee and tea service from 6:30-10:30 am in the Lobby Terrace and afternoon tea is also served their daily from 3-5 pm.

Children 14 or younger free if sharing room with parent. Extra persons $35 high season, $25 low season. Cribs available at no charge. 3-night's deposit high season, one low season. 14-day refund notice. Modified American Plan is available at $65 per person.

*G.v. $225-270, o.v. $310-360, o.f. $425*
*Parlor Suite $610-710, 1 BR suite $760-960, 2 BR suite $1,060-1,260*

*Villa rates:*
*Bay-o.f. 1 BR $385, 2 BR $485; o.v. 1 BR $325, 2 BR $425;*
*Ridge-o.v. 1 BR $200, 2 BR $250; Golf Fairway View 1 BR $185 2 BR $235*
*Third day maid service on Ridge and Golf villas. Extra person ad $35.*

### THE RITZ-CARLTON, KAPALUA ★
One Ritz Carlton Drive, Kapalua, Maui, HI 96761. (808) 669-6200. The 550 room oceanfront resort opened in the fall of 1992 at D. T. Fleming Beach and follows in the same quality and high standards set for all of Kapalua. A Hawaiian motif with a plantation feel features native stonework throughout hotel. Accommodations include 320 Kings, 172 doubles, 58 executive suites and 2 Ritz-Carlton suites.

Amenities include twice daily made service, in-room terry robes, complimentary in-room safe, multilingual staff, babysitting, full service beauty salon. Ten tennis courts plus a 10,000 sq. ft., three level swimming pool are among the amenities. Restaurants include The Grill restaurant and Sunset Lounge, the Terrace Restaurant, the Banyan Tree Poolside restaurant. See the Kapalua chapter on restaurants for further information.

*The Ritz-Carlton* is certainly another jewel for West Maui. We had the opportunity to spend a couple of days enjoying the property and experiencing a Club Floor for the first time. These special floors, available at many of the finer properties on Maui, have added security. A special key was required in the elevator to reach your floor. A special Club dining room offered snacks almost continually. The continental breakfast was more than one would expect with some wonderful cereals, pastries, freshly squeezed juices and fresh fruits. The mid-day snack included sandwiches, and fresh vegetables or fruits. The early evening hours provided appetizers and wine or mix your own drinks. After dinner (which we missed because we were either too tired, too late or too full) was chocolates and cordials. There were also cold drinks and hot coffee available all day. The lounge/dining room was elegant, yet homey and the balconies provided entertaining views of golfers playing the course. The kids really enjoyed running down for a snack whenever they felt like it. In fact, they seldom were hungry at mealtimes and probably could have survived for weeks on the goodies served on the Club Floor. While it is more expensive, judging by the number of people in the lounge, it certainly appears to be a popular option and we can see why! This is the way to be pampered in paradise! The guest rooms are spacious and beautifully appointed.

The Ritz-Kids program is a half or full-day program that is distinctly Hawaiian. Geared for ages 4-12 years, counselors teach hula, basket weaving, jewelry-making with shells and other arts and crafts, along with T-shirt painting, tennis and board games. A full-day program is $40 and includes lunch and a gift from the hotel. The half-day program is $25.

*Garden Mt. $285, partial o.v. $325, o.v. $400, o.f. $455, The Ritz-Carlton Club $495 1 BR executive suite $625, 1 BR executive Club Suite $750, 1 BR o.f. suite $900 The Ritz-Carlton Suite $2,500, The Ritz-Carlton Club Suite $2,800*

## KAPALUA BAY VILLAS ★
500 Office Road, Kapalua, Maui, HI 96761, Kapalua, Maui, HI 96761. (808) 669-8088, 1-800-545-0018 U.S. and Canada. AGENTS: Kapalua Vacation Rentals (808) 669-4144, 1-800-326-6775, Kapalua Hotel (808) 669-0244, 1-800-367-8000, Hawaiian Apt. Leasing 1-800-854-8843 (1-800-472-8449 in California, 1-800-824-8968 in Canada). Whaler's Realty handles golf villas only (808) 661-8777, 1-800-367-5632, Ridge Rentals handles only Ridge villas (808) 669-9696, 1-800-326-6284 in U.S. and Canada. Agents: Kapalua Hotel 1-800-367-8000, Whaler's Realty (golf villas only) 1-800-367-5632, Hawaiian Apt. Leasing 1-800-854-8843 (1-800-472-8449 CA). There are over 400 units in the villages and each is spacious and beautifully appointed. Wonderful units for several couples or a larger family. They feel much more like a home than a condominium. Units include kitchens, washer/dryers, and daily maid service. Several pools and tennis courts. Extra persons $35 per night. 3-night deposit high season, 2-night low season. The Kapalua Hotel which is among the rental agents which handles the property, currently has gone to a flat year round rate, no discounts for low season. However, Kapalua Villas (808) 545-0018 are the company we have dealt with and they do have discounts for low season. The following prices are a mix of the high and low prices we surveyed from several different agents for high season. Differences in prices are also reflected by location and view. A little calling may be worth your while. We'd suggest starting with a call to Kapalua Villas.
*1 BR (4, max 6) fairway v. $175-275,  o.v. $225-315,  o.f. $250-375*
*2 BR (4, max 6) fairway v. $225-375,  o.v. $250-415,  o.f. $375-475*

## THE RIDGE ★
Agents: Kapalua Hotel 1-800-367-8000, Ridge Rentals 1-800-326-6284 U.S. & Canada, Kumulani 1-800-367-2954. Part of the Kapalua condominiums, these are also well appointed but slightly less expensive. With its location above the hotel in the golf course area it is quite a walk to the beach. However, if you book through the Kapalua Hotel, you have the use of the Kapalua pool, grounds, shuttle service etc., which does not apply if you rent through other agencies. 5-day minimum, $100 deposit, 14-day notice of cancellation between 12/15 and 4/15, other dates 48 hours. Maid service only on check-in. NO CREDIT CARDS.
*1 BR 2 bath o.v. $185/115,  2 BR 2 bath o.v. $265/175   (prices-Ridge Rentals)*

## IRONWOODS
Beautiful and very expensive oceanview homes. Currently no rentals available.

# MAALAEA

## INTRODUCTION

Maalaea to many is just a signpost enroute to Kaanapali, or a harbor for the departure of a tour boat. However, Maalaea (which means "area of red dirt") is the most affordable and centrally located area of the island. A short 10 minutes from Kahului, 30 minutes from Lahaina and 15 minutes from Wailea makes it easy to see all of the island while headquartered here. You can hop into the car for a beach trip in either direction. Even better is the mere six-mile jaunt to Kahului/Wailuku for some of Maui's best and most affordable eateries. This quiet and relaxing area is a popular living area for local residents. Seven of the ten condominium complexes are located on a sea wall on or near the harbor of Maalaea, while the other three are on one end of the three mile long Maalaea Bay beach. The two end complexes, Maalaea Mermaid and the Maalaea Yacht Marina are actually within the harbor.

The ocean and beach conditions are best just past the last condo, the Makani A Kai. There is less turbidity providing fair snorkeling at times, good swimming and even two small swimming areas protected by a reef. These are found on either side of the small rock jetty with the old pipe. This length of beach is owned by the government and is undeveloped, providing an excellent opportunity for beach walkers who can saunter all the way down to Kihei. The condominium complexes are small and low-rise with moderate prices and no resort activities. The vistas from many of the lanais are magnificent, with a view of the harbor activity and the entire eastern coastline from Kihei to Makena, including majestic Haleakala, as well as Molokini, Ka'aholawe and Lana'i. The view is especially pleasing at night and absolutely stunning when a full moon shimmers its light across the bay and through the palm trees with the lights of Upcountry, Kihei and Wailea as a backdrop. No other part of the island offers such a tranquil setting. Another plus are the almost constant trade winds which provide non air-conditioned cooling as opposed to the sometimes scorching stillness of the Lahaina area. Summer in Maalaea is time for surfing. Summer swells coming into the bay reportedly create the fastest right-breaking rideable waves in the world and are sometimes referred to as "the freight train." The local kids are out riding from dawn to dusk. Winter brings calmer seas with fair snorkeling over the offshore reef. The calm conditions, undisturbed by parasailing and jet-skiing, also entice the Humpback whales into the shallow waters close to shore.

Local eating options are limited. One nice restaurant, The Waterfront, at the Milowai condominiums is excellent! In addition to sandwiches at the Maalaea Mermaid market, a limited number of snacks are available at the Maalaea store. Casual seafood lunch and dinners are served Monday through Saturday at the Island Fish Market. Buzz's Wharf sits at the end of the Harbor and is open for lunch, dinner and cocktails.

Under development is the new Maalaea Fishing Village. Plans call for a shopping center about as large as the Lahaina Cannery. The two-story design is reported to incorporate a local Hawaiian theme with lots of small shops and vendors selling fresh produce and island crafts. Five or six restaurants are being figured into the

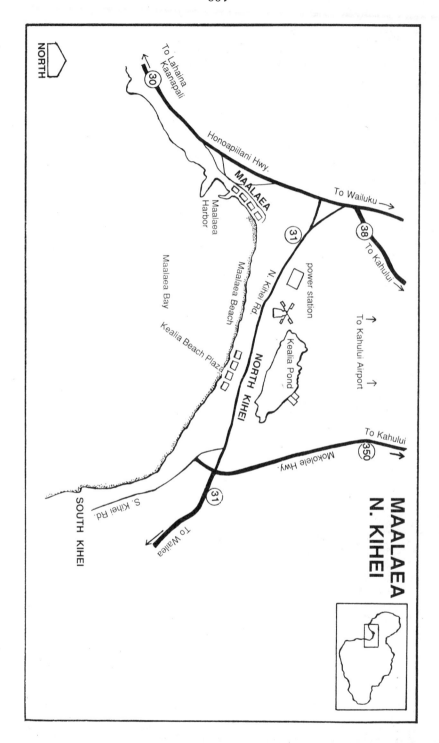

preliminary reports. There is also mention that the Maui Historical Society is reportedly considering a museum and museum shop. It will be located across from the harbor near the old fishing shrine. All in all, Maalaea is a quiet and convenient choice. It is not for those seeking the hub of activity or convenient fine dining, but for the independent and quiet traveler. Undecided about where to stay? Maybe you should try Maalaea!

## WHAT TO DO AND SEE

The Maalaea Harbor area is a scenic port from which a number of boats depart for snorkeling, fishing and whale watching. Also in this area is Buzz's Wharf Restaurant, open for dinner. Fresh Island Fish Company, a seafood market is open Monday thru Saturday 10 am-5 pm. In 1994 Maalaea Harbor is under consideration as a site for a new *aquarium project* by Coral World International, Inc. Plans for the proposed Maui Ocean Center would include an 18 acre site where the aquarium would be part of a new shopping center.

## ACCOMMODATIONS - MAALAEA

| | |
|---|---|
| Maalaea Mermaid | Island Sands |
| Maalaea Yacht Marina | Maalaea Banyans |
| Milowai | Kana'I A Nalu |
| Maalaea Kai | Hono Kai |
| Lauloa | Makana A Kai |

*BEST BETS: Kana'i A Nalu* - Attractive complex with all two-bedroom units on a sandy beachfront, affordably priced. *Lauloa* - Well designed units oceanfront on the seawall. *Makani A Kai* - Located on a sandy beachfront, two bedroom units are townhouse style. Note: the mailing address for the Maalaea Village condos DOES list the town as Wailuku.

### MAALAEA MERMAID
20 Haouli St., Wailuku, HI  96793. No rental information available. Located within the Maalaea Seawall. Small market on the ground floor.

GINGER

## MAALAEA YACHT MARINA

30 Hauoli St., Wailuku, Maui, HI 96793. (808-244-7012). Agents: Maalaea Bay Rentals 1-800-367-6084, Kihei Maui Vacations 1-800-542-6284, Hawaiian Apt. Leasing 1-800-854-8843 (1-800-472-8449 CA).

All units are oceanfront, a beach is nearby. The units we viewed were pleasant with a wonderful view of the boats from most units, and the added plus of having security elevators and stairways. Many of the units have no air-conditioning and laundry facilities are located in a laundry room on each floor. A postage stamp size grassy area in front and a small, but adequate pool.
*1 BR (2) $80/70, 2 BR (4) $90-110/80*

## MILOWAI

50 Hauoli St., Wailuku, Maui, HI 96793. Agents: Kihei Maui Vacations 1-800-542-6284, Maalaea Bay Rentals 1-800-367-6084.

One of the larger complexes in Maalaea with a restaurant on location, The Waterfront. This complex has a large pool area, with a BBQ along the seawall. The corner units are a very roomy 1,200 square feet with windows off the master bedrooms. Depending on condo location in the building, the views are of the Maalaea harbor or the open ocean. The one bedroom units have a lanai off the living room and a bedroom in the back. Washer/dryer. Weekly/monthly discounts.
*1 BR (2) $80/70, 2 BR (4) $90-110/80*

## MAALAEA KAI

70 Hauoli St., Wailuku, Maui, HI 96793. (244-7012). Agents: Maalaea Bay Rentals 1-800-367-6084, Kihei Maui Vacations 1-800-542-6284. 70 oceanfront units. Laundry facilities, putting green, BBQ, and elevator to upper levels. Located on the harbor wall, the rooms were standard and quite satisfactory. Some do not have washer and dryers in the rooms. There is a pool area and large pleasant grounds in front along the harbor wall. A few blocks walk down to a sandy beach. Monthly discounts. *1 BR (2) $80/70, 2 BR (4) $90-110/80*

## LAULOA ★

100 Hauoli Street, Wailuku, Maui, HI 96793. (808-242-6575). Agent: Maalaea Bay Rentals 1-800-367-6084.

Forty-seven 2-bedroom, 2-bath units of 1,100 sq. ft. One of the Lauloa's best features is their floor plan. The living room and master bedroom are on the front of the building with a long connecting lanai and sliding glass patio doors which offer unobstructed ocean views. A sliding shoji screen separates the living room from the bedroom. Each morning from the bed you have but only to open your eyes to see the palm trees swaying and a panoramic ocean view. The second bedroom is in the back of the unit. These two bedroom units are spacious (only two bedroom units are currently available in the rental program) and are in fair to good condition (depending on the owner). Each has a washer/dryer in the unit. The pool area and grounds are along the seawall. With a stairway in the sea wall, there often are local fishermen throwing nets and lines into the ocean. $200 deposit. 5-night minimum. Maid service extra charge. Monthly discounts.
*2 BR 2 bath (4) $80-110/70-80*

## ISLAND SANDS

150 Hauoli St., Wailuku, Maui, HI 96793. Island Sands Resort Rentals 1-800-826-7816, (808) 244-0848, FAX (808) 244-5639. Eighty-four units in a 6-story building. One of Maalaea's larger complexes located along the seawall. Offers a Maui shaped pool, a grassy lawn area, BBQ. Many of these units also have a lanai off the master bedroom, however, the lanais have a concrete piece in the middle of each railing which somewhat limits the view while sitting or laying in bed. Washer/dryers, and air-conditioning. Elevators. Extra person $7.50/night. Weekly and monthly discounts. 4-night minimum, $200 deposit with 15-day refund notice. Children under 3 free. NO CREDIT CARDS.
*Studio (2) $75/55, 1 BR 1 Bath (2) $90-95/70-75, 2 BR 2 Bath (4) $110/90*

## MAALAEA BANYANS

190 Hauoli St., Wailuku, Maui, HI 96793. (808-242-5668). Agents: Maalaea Bay Rentals 1-800-367-6084, Oihana 1-800-367-5234, Real Hawaii 1-800-967-6687, Maui Condo & Home 1-800-822-4409. Seventy-six oceanview units with lanai and washer/dryer. Weekly/monthly discounts. Oceanfront on rocky shore, short walk to beach. Pool area, jacuzzi, BBQ's. Extra persons $10/night. 7-night minimum. NO CREDIT CARDS. *1 BR (2) $80/70, 2 BR (4) $90-110/80*

## KANA'I A NALU ★

250 Hauoli Street, Wailuku, Maui, HI 96793. Agents: Maalaea Bay Rentals 1-800-367-6084, Oihana 1-800-367-5234. 80 units with washer/dryers in four buildings with elevators. No maid service. This is the first of the three condominiums along a sandy beachfront. Its name means "parting of the sea, surf or wave." The complex is V-shaped with a pool area in the middle. Nicely landscaped grounds, a decent beach and only a short walk along the beach to the best swimming and playing area. Overall one of the best values in the Maalaea area. One of the places we keep coming back to! 5-day minimum, $200 deposit, 30-day refund notice. Weekly discounts. Have you wondered where the authors of this guide stay? If we aren't moving around the island, sampling different properties, you'll find us catching our breathe here, and enjoying the sunny shores and gentle breezes of Maalaea. *2 BR (4) o.v. $110-135/$80-100, o.f. $130-165/$100-125*

## HONO KAI

280 Hauoli St., Wailuku, Maui, HI 96793. (244-7012) Agent: Maalaea Bay Rentals 1-800-367-6084. Forty-six units located on the beach. Choice of garden view, oceanview or oceanfront. Laundry facilities, BBQ, pool. This is one of three properties managed by Maalaea Bay Rentals and according to the agent this property is the "chevrolet" model. This complex is on the beach and bears attention for the budget conscious traveler, but don't expect any frills.
*1 BR $70-95/$60-75, 2 BR $77-88/$105-115, 3 BR $130/93*

## MAKANI A KAI

300 Hauoli St., Wailuku, Maui, HI 96793. Agent: Maalaea Bay Rentals 1-800-367-6084. These deluxe o.f. or o.v. units are on the beach. Laundry room on property, pool, BBQ. This is the last property along the beach in Maalaea. Beyond this is a long stretch of sandy beach along undeveloped state land and about a four mile jaunt down to North Kihei. Great for you beach walkers! The two bedroom units are townhouse style.
*1 BR $95-125 / $70-90, 2 BR $130-165 / $80-125     5-day minimum stay*

# NORTH KIHEI

## INTRODUCTION

North Kihei is 15 minutes from the Kahului Airport and located at the entrance to South Kihei. The condominiums here stretch along a gentle sloping white sand beach. The small Kealia Shopping Center is located between the Kihei Sands and Nani Kai Hale. Another small shopping area is found at the Sugar Beach Condominiums. Several snack shop restaurants can be found along Kihei Road in this area. A little to the south down Kihei Road are additional restaurants, grocery stores and large shopping areas.

Along with Maalaea, this is one of our favorite places to stay because of the good units, central but quiet location, nice beach, cooling breezes and certainly some of the island's best vacation buys.

## ACCOMMODATIONS - NORTH KIHEI

| | |
|---|---|
| Kealia | Kihei Kai |
| Sugar Beach | Maalaea Surf |
| Kihei Sands | Kihei Beach Resort |
| Nani Kai Hale | |

**BEST BETS:** *Kealia* and *Maalaea Surf.*

### KEALIA ★
191 N. Kihei Rd., Kihei, Maui, HI 96753. (808-879-9159) 1-800-367-5222. Fifty-one air-conditioned units with lanais, washer/dryers, and dishwashers. Maid service on request. The one bedroom units are a little small, but overall a good value. Well maintained and quiet resort with a wonderful sandy beach. Shops nearby. Extra person $10. 10% monthly discount. $125 deposit, $10 cancellation fee. 100% payment required 30 days prior to arrival. 7-day minimum winter, 4-day in summer. NO CREDIT CARDS. *Studio (2) $70/55, 1 BR o.v. (2) $90/75, 1 BR o.f. (2) $100/$85. Limited number of 2 BR units available.*

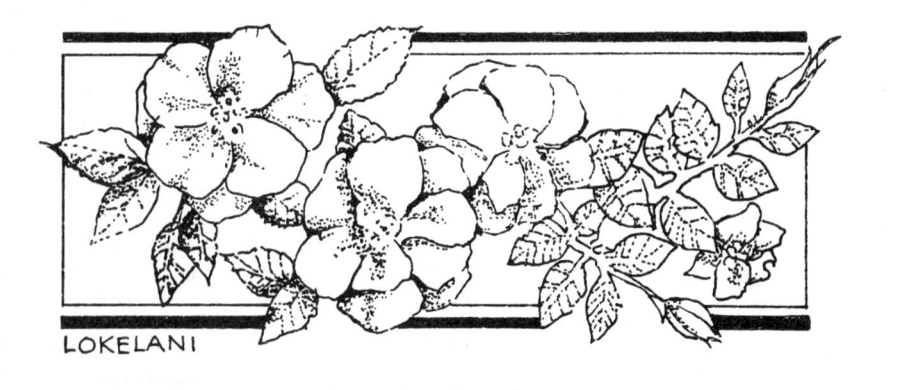

LOKELANI

### SUGAR BEACH RESORT
145 N. Kihei Rd. Kihei, Maui, HI 96753. (808-879-7765). Agents: Condo Rental HI 1-800-367-5242, Hawaiian Apt. Leasing 1-800-854-8843 (1-800-472-8449 CA), Maui Condos 1-800-663-6962 Canada, RSVP 1-800-663-1118, More Hawaii 1-800-967-6687. 215 units in several six-story buildings with elevators. Air-conditioning. Jacuzzi, putting green, gas BBQ grills. Sandwich shop and quick shop market on location. A nice pool area and located on an excellent swimming beach. *1 BR g.v. $95/75, o.f. $105/85, 2 BR o.v. $175/130*

### KIHEI SANDS
115 N. Kihei Rd., Kihei, Maui, HI 96753. (808-879-2624) Thirty oceanfront air-conditioned units, kitchens include microwaves. Shops and restaurant nearby. 7-night minimum high season/4-day minimum low season, $100 deposit with 20% cancellation fee. 50% of balance due 30 days prior to arrival, balance on arrival. No maid service or room phone. Coin laundry area. NO CREDIT CARDS. Extra persons $6/night. *1 BR (2) $90-115 / $69-90, 2 BR (4) $108-138 / $80-103*

### NANI KAI HALE ★
73 N. Kihei Rd., Kihei, Maui, HI 96753. (808-879-9120) 1-800-367-6032. Agents: Maui Condo & Home 1-800-822-4409, Hawaiian Apt. Leasing 1-800-854-8843 (1-800-472-8449 CA) . 46 units in a six-story building. Under building parking, laundry on each floor, elevator. No maid service, no room phones. Patio and BBQ's by beach. Lanais have ocean and mountain views. Prices based on 7-day/3-day minimum stay. $100 deposit. Monthly discounts. Children under 5 years no charge. Extra person $10 per night. *S BR w/o kitchen (2) $ 65/50; 1 BR 2 bath (2) o.v. $ 80/65, o.f. $125/ 90; 2 BR 2 bath (2) o.v. $125/90, o.f. $150/130*

### KIHEI KAI
61 N. Kihei Rd., Kihei, Maui, HI 96753. (808-879-2357) 1-800-735-2357. Twenty-four units in a two-story beachfront building. Recreation area and laundry room. Units have air-conditioning or ceiling fans. BBQ. On seven-mile stretch of sandy beach, near windsurfing, grocery stores. A very good value. Minimum 7-days winter, 4-days summer. $100 deposit ($200 deposit for 2 weeks or longer.) Full payment upon arrival. NO CREDIT CARDS. Extra persons $5/night. Weekly discounts. *1 BR (2,max 4) $80-95 / $65-80*

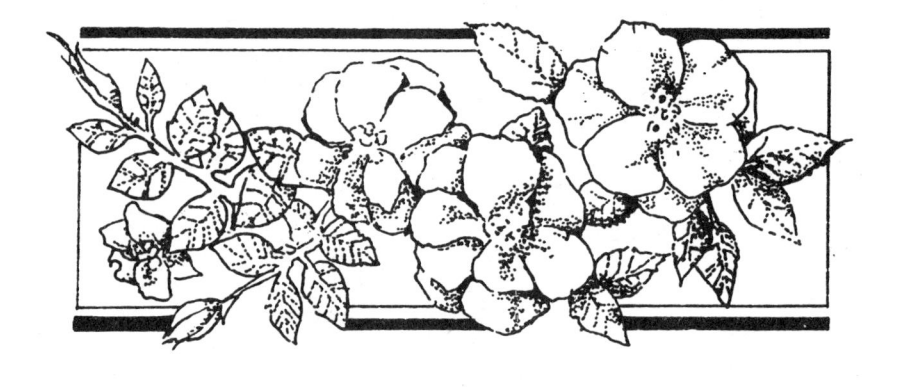

### KIHEI BEACH RESORT
36 S. Kihei Rd., Kihei, Maui, HI 96753. (808-879-2744) 1-800-367-6034. Agents: Maui Network 1-800-367-5221, Maui Condo & Home 1-800-822-4409, Maui Condo 1-800-663-6962 Canada. 54 beachfront units with oceanview, microwaves, phones. Resort offers central air-conditioning, recreation area, elevator, maid service. Minimum 3 nights. Extra person $10/night. Weekly and monthly discounts. *1 BR (2,max 4) $120/105, 2 BR (4,max 6) $155/135*

### MAALAEA SURF ★
12 S. Kihei Rd., Kihei, Maui, HI 96753. (808-879-1267) 1-800-423-7953. Sixty oceanview units in 8 two-story oceanfront buildings. These townhouse units have air-conditioning and microwaves. Daily maid service, except Sundays and holidays. Two pools, two tennis courts, shuffleboard. Laundry facilities in each building.

Very attractive and quiet low-rise complex on a great beach. In this price range, these spacious and attractive units, along with five acres of beautiful grounds, are impressive and hard to beat. Extra persons $8/night. NO CREDIT CARDS. $200-300 deposit. High season balance due 30 days prior to arrival, low season on arrival. 60-day refund notice with $10 cancellation fee during high season, 30-day notice low season.
*1 BR 1 bath (2,max 4) $160/145, 2 BR 2 bath (4,max 6) $220/190*

# SOUTH KIHEI

## INTRODUCTION

South Kihei began its growth after that of West Maui, but unfortunately with no planned system of development. The result is a six-mile stretch of coastline littered with more than 50 properties, nearly all condominiums, with some 2,400 units in rental programs. Few complexes are actually on a good beach. However, many are across Kihei Road from one of the Kamaole Beach Parks. A variety of beautiful beaches are just a few minutes drive away.

The drive from Maalaea to Kihei is but a few miles. There is a mix of sugar cane which blends into the mudflats of Maalaea on your right and a rather indistinguishable flatland on your left. The area on your left can best be seen from an aerial perspective. It is the enormous Kealia pond which recently became Hawai'i's second-largest national wildlife refuge. The federal government paid $6.9 million for ownership of the 437 acre pond and another 263 acres were donated as a federal wildlife easement by Alexander & Baldwin. Among the endangered species currently making their home in the pond are the Hawaiian coot and Hawaiian stilt.

This section of East Maui has a much different feel than West Maui or Lahaina. There are no large resorts with exotically landscaped grounds, very few units on prime beachfront, and more competition among the complexes making this area a good value for your vacation dollar. (And a good location for extended stays.) Kihei always seemed to operate at a quieter and more leisurely pace than that of Kaanapali and Lahaina, but the last couple of years has seen a significant upsurge of development, not of condos, but of shopping complexes. Sadly, in 1994 what was beginning of shopping in Kihei, the Azeka Market closed its doors. Progress has pushed out a Kihei institution.

Even parts of South Kihei Rd. have been repaved and regular curbs installed. These changes indicate the increasing tourist activity along with a corresponding loss of Kihei's once laid-back charm. Restaurant selections have expanded as well, giving visitors many options for dining, other than their condominium kitchens. Most needs can be filled locally at one of several large grocery stores or the growing number of small shopping centers. Kahului, Wailuku, Wailea and Lahaina remain an easy drive for additional shopping and dining out.

## WHAT TO DO AND SEE

The only historical landmark is a totem pole near the Maui Lu Resort which commemorates the site where Captain Vancouver landed.

## WHERE TO SHOP

Every corner of Kihei is sprouting a new shopping mall. The complexes all seem to have quick markets, video stores and a T-shirt shop. The following are now complete.

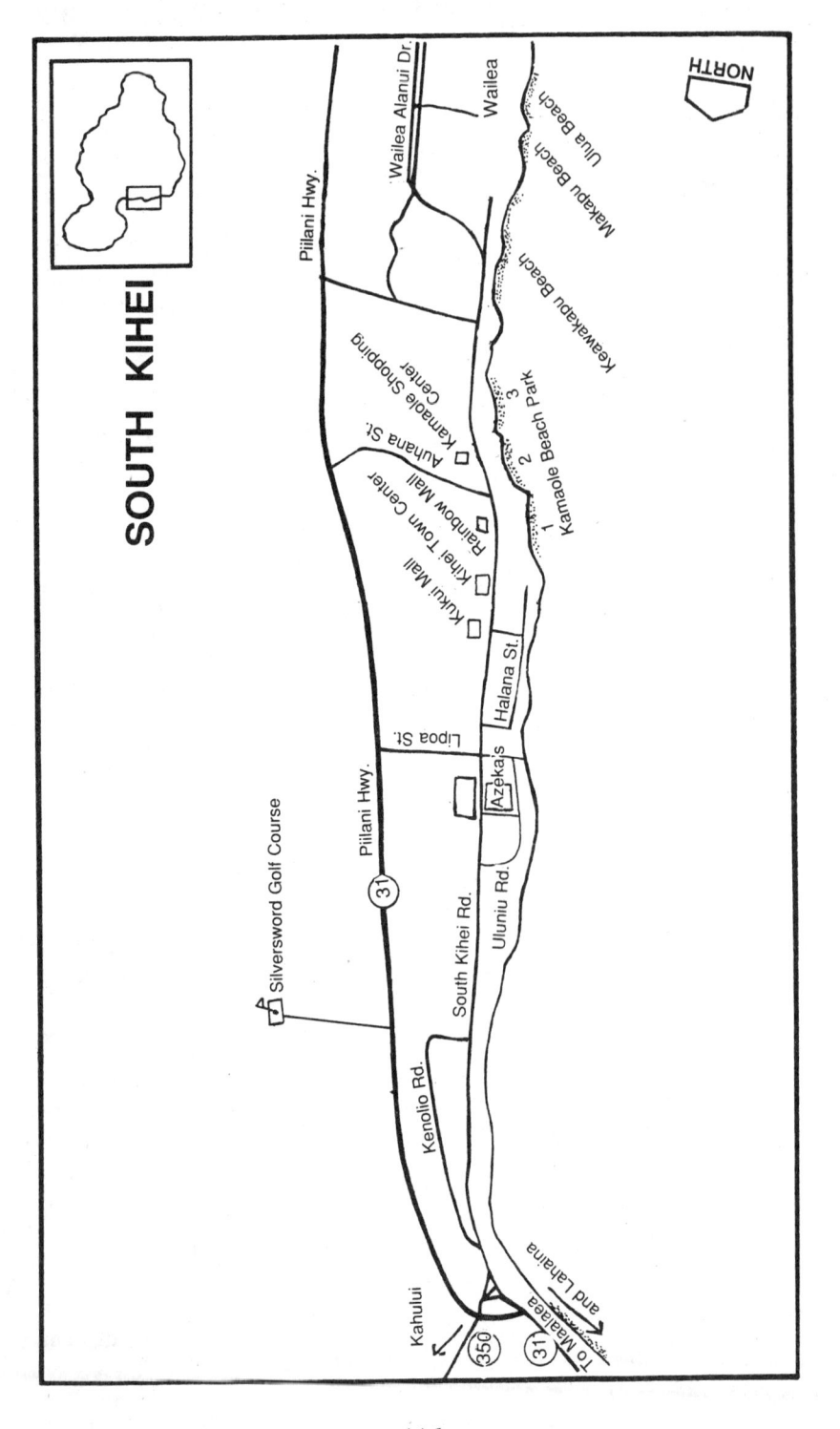

## SOUTH KIHEI

NORTH

Piilani Hwy.

Wailea Alanui Dr.

Wailea

Ulua Beach

Makapu Beach

Keawakapu Beach

Kamaole Shopping Center

Auhana St.

Kamaole Beach Park

1  2  3

Kihei Town Center

Rainbow Mall

Kukui Mall

Halana St.

Lipoa St.

Azeka's

Silversword Golf Course

Piilani Hwy.

31

South Kihei Rd.

Uluniu Rd.

Kenolio Rd.

Kahului

350

31

To Maalaea
and Lahaina

Traveling down Kihei Road the first center is **Azeka's** and across the street the new **Azeka Place II**. *Azeka's Market*, which is where Kihei began, closed in September, 1994. They hope to reopen as a specialty meat and seafood store. The mom & pop store which was opened by Bill Azeka in 1950, cited that they can't compete with the new chain stores. They announced the snack shop will also be closing, and no plans on its future. The *International House of Pancakes, Royal Thai Cuisine* and *Pizza Hut* are among the restaurants here as well as *Ben Franklin, Crazy Shirts* and assorted tourist shops which vary each year. *Liberty House* relocated to a much larger facility in the Azeka Place II and the good news is they have their discount store here as well! You'll find great buys of out-of-season or one of a kind items! A *Long's Drug Store* is a welcome addition along with eateries including *The Coffee Store, Stella Blues* and *Peggy Sue's*. *McDonald's* has a new building and relocated across the street from Azeka's II.

The **Lipoa Shopping Center** is a block down Lipoa Street and offers a medical center and pharmacy, a cycle and sport shop, *Sweet Cream's*, and *Henry's Bar and Grill*.

Just past the Kapulanikai condominiums, the **Kukui Mall**, at 1819 S. Kihei Rd., gets our vote for the most attractive mall. This large complex is done in a Spanish style of architecture with a wide assortment of shops. The multi-plex theater offers a good selection of first run movies. *Subway Sandwich* shop is a handy stop for lunch enroute to one of Wailea's fine beaches or stop by *Pair O Dice Pizza*. **Summer Palace** is an all-you-get eat Asian buffet. For a cool treat there's *I Can't Believe It's Yogurt*. A *Waldenbooks* is a welcome addition for visitors and residents alike, with a great selection of books on just about any subject (and hopefully our Paradise guides!) and several clothing shops. One bathing suit shop sells two piece suits as separates, a great idea for those of us with mis-matched figures!

Just beyond is **The Kihei Town Center** which offers a selection of shops including sporting goods, novelty, pharmacy, grocery, and clothing. The restaurants here are *Chuck's* and *Joe's Place*. The best shave ice in town and a MUST STOP for all visitors is here at *Tobi's* and next door at *Kihei Caffe* you can get a generous meal for a reasonable price.

RED CRESTED CARDINAL

117

The next few shopping areas run almost together. The *Dolphin Plaza,* 2395 S. Kihei Rd., across from Kamaole I Beach is one of the smaller new shopping centers. Here you'll find *The New York Deli, Pizza Fresh, Baskin Robbins Ice Cream,* the *Kihei Bakery* and a video store.

Between the Dolphin Plaza and Rainbow Mall is the *Kamaole Beach Center,* 2411 S. Kihei Rd. *The Sports Page Grill and Bar* is the focal point here with a yogurt place and pizza restaurant rounding out the center.

*The Rainbow Mall* is a small center also located on the mauka side (towards the mountain) of South Kihei Road offering an ice cream shop, *Chum's* restaurant which offers local style plate lunches. *The Thai Chef* opened in August 1994.

*Kamaole Shopping Center* is one of the larger new malls and offers several restaurant selections, including *C&R Cantina, Denny's,* the *Canton Chef* and *Erik's Seafood Broiler.*

The last shopping center in Kihei, across from Kamaole III Beach, is the *Nani Kai Center. La Bahia, Kihei Prime Rib & Seafood* and *The Greek Bistro* restaurants make up this complex.

## ACCOMMODATIONS - SOUTH KIHEI

| | | |
|---|---|---|
| Nona Lani | Kihei Garden | Kihei Alii Kai |
| Kihei Holiday | Hale Kai O Kihei | Royal Mauian |
| Wailana Sands | Maui Sun | Kamaole Nalu |
| Resort Isana | Waiohuli Beach | Hale Pau Hana |
| Pualani | Kihei Beachfront | Kihei Kai Nani |
| Sunseeker Resort | Kapulanikai | Kihei Akahi |
| Maui Lu Resort | Island Surf | Maui Banyan |
| Kihei Bay Vista | Kihei Park Shores | Haleakala Shores |
| Kihei Bay Surf | Shores of Maui | Maui Parkshore |
| Menehune Shores | Punahoa | Kamaole Sands |
| Kihei Resort | Kalama Terrace | Hale Kamaole |
| Koa Lagoon | Beach Club Apts. | Maui Kamaole |
| Koa Resort | Lihi Kai Cottages | Maui Hill |
| Kauhale Makai | Maui Vista | Kihei Surfside |
| Leinaala | Kamoa Views | Mana Kai Maui |
| Luana Kai | Kamaole One | Surf and Sand |
| Maui Schooner | Maui Coast Hotel | Hale Hui Kai |
| Maui Sunset | Kamaole Beach | |
| Leilani Kai | Royale | |

*BEST BETS: Maui Hill* - Situated on a hillside across the road from the ocean, some units have excellent ocean views. The three-bedroom units here are roomy and a good value for large families. *Haleakala Shores* - Across from Kamaole III Beach Park. *Mana Kai Maui* - One of Kihei's larger resorts, and one of only a few located on a very good beach.

### NONA LANI

455 S. Kihei Rd., (PO Box 655) Kihei, Maui, HI 96753. (808-879-2497). Eight individual cottages with kitchens, color TV, queen bed plus 2 day beds, full bath with tub and shower, and lanais. Large grounds, public phone, two BBQ's, and laundry facilities. Located across the road from sandy beach. Extra person $7 night. Full payment 30 days prior to arrival. Cancellation penalty. NO CREDIT CARDS. *1 BR (2) $65; $420 weekly*

### KIHEI HOLIDAY

483 S. Kihei Rd., Kihei, Maui, HI 96753. (808-879-9228) Agents: Kihei Maui Vacations 1-800-542-6284, Hawaiian Apt. Leasing 1-800-854-8843 (1-800-472-8449 CA), RSVP 1-800-662-1118. Units are across the street from the beach and have lanais with garden views. Pool area jacuzzi and BBQ's. $100 deposit, full payment 30 days prior to arrival. Maid service on request. NO CREDIT CARDS. *1 BR $90/75,  2 BR (4) $110/85*

### WAILANA SANDS

25 Wailana Place, Kihei, Maui, HI 96753. 10 units, overlook courtyard and pool area, in a two-story structure. Quiet area on a dead end road one block from the beach. No rental rates available.

### PUALANI TOWNHOUSES

15 Wailana Place, Kihei, Maui, HI. Agent: Kihei Maui Vacations 1-800-542-6284. *1 BR $85/70*

### RESORT ISANA

515 S. Kihei Road, Kihei, Maui, HI 96753 (808) 879-7800, 1-800-633-3833. One of Kihei's newer properties, these 51-one-bedroom units are decorated in muted beige and blues and complete down to an electric rice cooker and china dishes. A spacious pool area is the focal point of the central courtyard. Located across the road from the beach. Washer/dryer, cable TV., maid service. Extra person $15. *1 BR (1-3) $120,  2BR (1-5) $160     Weekly and monthly rates available*

### SUNSEEKER RESORT

551 S. Kihei Rd. (PO Box 276) Kihei, Maui, HI 96753. (808-879-1261) 1-800-532-MAUI, FAX (808) 874-3877. Six units including studios with kitchenettes, one and two bedrooms with kitchens. Monthly discounts available. No room phones, no pool. Across street from beach. Popular area for windsurfing. Minimum stay in studio or 1 BR is 3 days and in two bedroom 7 day. $150 deposit. NO CREDIT CARDS. Milt & Eileen Preston are the Owner/Managers. *S BR $55/50,  1 BR $65/60,  2 BR (4) $90/85   Extra person $6*

### MAUI LU RESORT

575 S. Kihei Rd., Kihei, Maui, HI 96753. (808-879-5881) Agent: Aston 1-800-922-7866. 180 units on 26 acres. Pool is shaped like the island of Maui. Many of the hotel rooms are set back from South Kihei Road and the oceanfront units are not on a sandy beachfront. One of the first resorts in the Kihei area and unusual with its spacious grounds. Extra persons $12, under 18 no charge. *Hotel rooms (2) gv, ov, of $89-150/$79-140*

## KIHEI BAY VISTA

679 S. Kihei Rd., Kihei, Maui, HI 96753. (879-75811), 1-800-367-7040 U.S., 1-800-423-8733 ext. 159 Canada. Agents: Outrigger Hotels Hawaii 1-800-OUTRIG-GER., Hawaiian Apt. Leasing 1-800-854-8843 (1-800-472-8449 CA), Maui condos 1-800-663-6962 Canada. Built in 1989 this complex offers pool, spa, jacuzzi, putting green, air-conditioning, washer/dryer, lanais and full kitchens. A short walk across the road to the Kamaole I Beach. Overlooking Kalepolepo Beach. *1 BR g.v. and o.v. units $95-110 / $85-100*

## KIHEI BAY SURF

715 S. Kihei Rd. (Manager Apt. 110), Kihei, Maui, HI 96753. (808-879-7650) Agents: Kihei Maui Vac. 1-800-542-6284, Island Discount Rentals 1-808-879-1466, Hawaiian Apt. Leasing 1-800-854-8843. 118 studio units in 7 two-story buildings. Pool area jacuzzi, recreation area, gas BBQ's, laundry area, tennis. Across road from Kamaole I Beach. Phones. Weekly discounts. *Studios $70/60*

## MENEHUNE SHORES

760 Kihei Rd., Kihei, Maui, HI 96753. (808-879-1508) Agents: Menehune Reservations, PO Box 1327, Kihei, Maui, HI 96753. (808) 879-3428. Kihei Kona Rentals 1-808-879-5828, Kihei Maui Vacations 1-800-542-62824, RSVP 1-800-663-1118, Menehune Reservations 1-800-558-9117 U.S., Maui Network 1-808-572-9555. 115 units with dishwashers, washer/dryers and lanais in a 6-story building. Recreation room, roof gardens with whale-watching platform, and shuffleboard. The ocean area in front of this condominium property is the last remnant of one of Maui's early fish ponds. These ponds, where fish were raised and harvested, were created by the early Hawaiians all around the islands. Extra persons $7.50/night, $200 deposit. Five day minimum stay. $25 cancellation charge. NO CREDIT CARDS.
*1 BR 1 bath (2) $ 90/ 75, 1 BR 2 bath (2) $110/88.50*
*2 BR 2 bath (2) $120/100, 3 BR 2 bath (6) $150/140*

## KIHEI RESORT

777 S. Kihei Rd., Kihei, Maui, HI 96753. Agents: Kihei Maui Vacations 1-800-542-6284, RSVP 1-800-663-1118, Maui Condo 1-800-663-6962 Canada, Rainbow Rentals 1-800-451-5366, Hawaiian Apt. Leasing 1-800-854-8843. Sixty-four units, two-story building, located across the street from the ocean, BBQ's, pool area jacuzzi. NO CREDIT CARDS.
*1 BR (2) $ 85/70  7-nite minimum, $100 deposit, 10-day refund notice*
*2 BR (4) $105/90  Extra persons $7/night, 10% monthly discount*

## KOA LAGOON

800 S. Kihei Rd., Kihei, Maui, HI 96753. (808-879-3002) 1-800-367-8030. FAX (808) 874-0429. 42 oceanview units in one 6-story building. Washer/dryers. Pool area pavilion, BBQ's. Located on a small sandy beach that is often plagued by seaweed which washes ashore from the offshore coral reef. This stretch of Kihei is very popular with windsurfers. Extra person $10 additional. $250 deposit, full payment 45 days prior to arrival. 45-day cancellation notice. 14-day minimum stay during Christmas holiday. $30 fee for less than 5 nights stay low season. Superior units $10 night more. NO CREDIT CARDS.
*1 BR 1 bath (2,max 4) $110/80, 2 BR 2 bath (4,max 6) $130/100*

## KOA RESORT

811 S. Kihei Rd., Kihei, Maui, HI 96753. (808-879-1161) 1-800-877-1314 FAX (808) 879-4001. 54 units (2,030 sq.ft.) on spacious 5 1/2-acre grounds in 2 five-story buildings across road from beach. 2 tennis courts, spa, jacuzzi, putting green. Units have washer/dryers. 10% monthly discount. Brochure indicates prices include 3% cash discount. Extra persons $10/day, children under 2 free. Five night minimum. $100 deposit. *1 BR 1 bath (2,max 4) $100/85, 2 BR 1 bath (4,max 4) $120/ 100,2 bath (4,max 6) $130/110, 3 BR 2 bath (6,max 8) $155/135, 3 bath (6,max 8) $180/160*

## KAUHALE MAKAI (Village by the Sea)

930-938 S. Kihei Rd. Kihei, Maui, HI 96753. (808-879-8888). Agents: Oihana 1-800-367-5234, Kihei Maui Vac. 1-800-542-6284, Kumulani 1-800-367-2954, RSVP 1-800-663-1118, Rainbow Rentals 1-800-451-5366, Maui Condos & Homes 1-808-879-5445, Island Discount Rentals 1-808-879-1466, VIP 1-808-879-5504. 169 air-conditioned units in 2 six-floor buildings with phones. Complex features putting green, gas BBQ's, children's pool, sauna, laundry center. The beach here is usually strewn with coral rubble and seaweed. $5 additional person. 5-night minimum. *Studio (2) $75/60, 1 BR (2) $105/90, 2 BR (4) $135/110*

## LUANA KAI ★

940 S. Kihei Rd., Kihei, Maui, HI 96753. (808-879-1268), 1-800-669-1127, FAX (808) 879-1455. Agents: Hawaiian Island Resorts 1-800-367-7042, Kihei Maui Vacations 1-800-542-6284, Rainbow Rentals 1-800-451-5366, More Hawaii 1-800-967-6687. 113 units on 8 acres with washer/dryers are located adjacent to a large oceanfront park with public tennis courts. The beach, however, is almost always covered with coral rubble and seaweed. The grounds are nicely landscaped and include a putting green, BBQ area, pool area sauna and jacuzzi. Towel service mid-week, linen service weekly. Children under 12 free. Extra person $10. 7-night minimum holiday, 2-night minimum high season. *1 BR (2) g.v./o.v. $130-145/105-120, 2 BR (6) o.v. $150-175/125-150, 3 BR (8) g.v. $225/175. Rates from resort include an economy car for one or two bedroom and a mid-size car for three bedroom. Upgrades to larger cars available.*

HAWAIIAN STILT

121

## MAUI SCHOONER RESORTS

980 S Kihei Rd, Kihei, Maui HI 96753. (808-879-5247) Reservations 1-800-877-7976 weekdays during business hours. Completed in 1984, these 58 units have been tastefully decorated in mauves and blues and have washer/dryer, microwave, phones and maid service twice weekly. Only one building has an elevator to the upper floors. Fronting these condos is a public park with 4 tennis courts and a beach (that is seasonally strewn with coral rubble). The on-site pool area is pleasant, plus they offer a separate men's and women's saunas, wet bar area, and hot tub. Now a time share resort, but offering rentals as well.
*1 BR (4) $107/ 620 weekly, 2 BR (6) $128/ 750 weekly*

## LANAKILA

992 S. Kihei Rd., Kihei, Maui, HI 96753. No vacation rentals, long term only.

## LEINAALA

998 S Kihei Rd, Kihei, Maui, HI 96753. (808-879-2235) 1-800-334-3305 U.S. & Canada. 24 one and two bedroom units in a 4-story building. Tennis courts at adjoining park. Pool, cable color TV. Oceanview. This property is fronted by a large grassy park which stretches out to the ocean. The beach is usually covered with coral rubble and much better beach activities would be enjoyed a short drive down to one of the Kamaole Beach Parks in Kihei. Weekly/monthly discounts. $200 deposit with 30-day refund notice. NO CREDIT CARDS. Extra persons $10 night. 4 night minimum.
*Studio/no view (2) $65, 1 BR (2) $85/75, 2 BR (4) $110/100*

## WAIPUILANI

1002 S. Kihei Rd., Kihei, Maui, HI 96753. (808-879-1465). 42 units in three 3-story buildings. No vacation rentals. Only long term.

## MAUI SUNSET

1032 S. Kihei, Rd., Kihei, Maui, HI 96753. (808-879-0674) Reservation Assistance 1-800-843-5880. Agents: Kihei Maui Vac. 1-800-542-6284, Kumulani 1-800-367-2954, Maui Network 1-800-367-4221, Hawaiian Apt. Leasing 1-800-854-8843 (1-800-472-8449 CA), RSVP 1-800-663-1118, Maui Condo & Home 1-800-822-4409. 225 air-conditioned units in 2 multi-story buildings. Tennis courts, pitch and putt golf green, and sauna. Large pool, exercise facility, barbecues. Located on beach park with tennis courts, however, this beach is generally covered with seaweed and coral rubble. Extra persons $7/night. *1 BR $105/85, 2 BR $145/110, Some 3 BR $185/155*

## LEILANI KAI

1226 Uluniu St., (PO Box 296) Kihei, Maui, HI 96753. (808-879-2606). Eight garden apartments with lanais. $200 deposit. Extra person $7.50. Full payment 30 days prior to arrival. 3-day minimum stay. NO CREDIT CARDS. Monthly discounts.
*Studio (2) $75/60, 1 BR (2) $100/75, 1 BR dlx (4) $115/85, 2 BR (4) $125/90*

## KIHEI GARDEN ESTATES

1299 Uluniu St., Kihei, Maui, HI 96753. (808-879-6123), 1-800-827-2786. Agents: Kihei Maui Vacations 1-800-542-6284. 84 units in eight 2-story buildings. Jacuzzi, BBQ's. Across road and short walk to beaches. Monthly discounts. $100 deposit, full payment 30 days prior to arrival. NO CREDIT CARDS. Rates for 4-6 nights. Weekly discounts. *1 BR (2,max 4) $90-100/ 75, 2 BR (4,max 6) $110/85*

## HALE KAI O KIHEI

PO Box 809, 1310 Uluniu Rd., Kihei, Maui, HI 96753. (808-879-2757). 59-oceanfront units with lanais in 3-story building. Sandy beachfront. Shuffleboard, putting green, BBQ's, laundry, recreation area. Maid service on request for extra charge. Extra person $10/night. 10% monthly discount. $200 deposit. 60-day/30-day cancellation notice (less $20 handling fee). NO CREDIT CARDS. Daily rates upon request. *1 BR (2) $5660/455 weekly, 2 BR 2 bath (4) $835/625 weekly*

## MAUI SUN     (Hotel)

175 East Lipoa, Kihei, Maui HI (808) 874-9000 or 1-800-762-5348 from Hawaii, Mainland or Canada. 229-rooms with tropical grounds, located several blocks from the beach, has a large pool and whirlpool spa, koi ponds, waterfalls. Two connecting six-story buildings feature rooms with an interconnecting system allowing them to join together for a larger family. Each room is air-conditioned with private lanai. The Frangipani restaurant is located on the property. Extra person $10. Coin-op washer/dryer. Non-smoking rooms available.
*Mountain view rooms with one king or 2 queen $79, garden view $89, partial ocean $99, 2 BR family unit $120**, 1 BR Suite m.v. $135*, 2 BR Deluxe Suite g.v. $150**, 2 BR suite partial o.v. $160**, Presidential suite $350. **5 & 6 person free in existing beds * 3 & 4 person free with existing beds.*

## WAIOHULI BEACH HALE

49 West Lipoa St., Kihei, Maui, HI 96753. (Rental Manager: 1-800-WBH-MAUI or (808 875-7729). Agents: Pali Kai 1-808-879-8550, Paradise Realty 1-808-874-8074. 52 units in four 2-story buildings. Large pool, gas BBQs. Located on beachfront that is poor for swimming or snorkeling, often covered with coral rubble and seaweed. Spacious park-like lawn area around pool. *1 BR (2) $95/70 (625/450 wk); 2 BR (4) $115/100 ($800/700 wk) Premier units slightly higher.*

## KIHEI BEACHFRONT RESORT

Located at end of Lipoa St. Agent: Maui Condos & Homes 1-808-879-5445. Eight oceanview 2-bedroom units with washer/dryers, microwaves, dishwashers, and air-conditioning in a single 2-story building. Large lawn area fronting units. Lanais on upper level. No elevator. Pool area jacuzzi. Five night minimum stay or cleaning fee required. $200 deposit. $10 additional person. Weekly, monthly discounts. *2 BR o.v./g.v. $130/95, 2 BR o.f. (4) $165/130*

## KAPULANIKAI APTS

73 Kapu Place, PO Box 716, Kihei, Maui, HI 96753. Agent: Bello Realty 1-800-541-3060. 12 units are oceanview with private lanais or open terraces. Beachfront is poor for swimming or snorkeling. Grassy lawn area in front. BBQ's, laundry facilities, pay phone on property. *1 BR 1 bath $80/65*

## ISLAND SURF

1993 S. Kihei Rd., Kihei, Maui, HI 96753. Agent: Kumulani 1-800-367-2954. This property is turning many of its units into commercial offices and shops on the first three floors which really detracts from a resort-like setting, although the economy of the place may attract some. Located across the road from the popular

Kamaole I Beach Park. $100 deposit. Five day minimum. Extra persons $8.
*Hotel rooms $50/$40, 1 BR $80/70, 2 BR $100/85*

**KIHEI PARK SHORES**   (No rental information available)

**SHORES OF MAUI**
2075 S. Kihei Rd., Kihei, Maui, HI 96753. (808-879-9140) 1-800-367-8002. 50-unit two-level complex in garden setting offers BBQ's, tennis courts, and spa. Located across the street from a rocky shoreline and 1½ blocks north of Kamaole I Beach Park. $100 deposit, 30-day cancellation notice, full payment 30 days prior to arrival. Extra persons $8/night, monthly discounts. 3-day minimum (Christmas holiday 1-week minimum). Monthly discounts. CREDIT CARDS ACCEPTED IF ARRIVAL DATE WITHIN 60 DAYS OF RESERVATION DATE. *1 BR $90/65, 2 BR $115/90*

**PUNAHOA**
2142 Iliili Rd., Kihei, Maui, HI 96753. (808-879-2720) 1-800-564-2720. 15-oceanview units with large lanais, telephones. No pool. Elevator, laundry facilities, beaches nearby. NO CREDIT CARDS. $400/200 deposit, 60-day refund notice. Extra persons $12/night, under age 2 free. Weekly/monthly discounts. 5-day minimum or pay $50 service charge.
*Studio (2) $81/62,   1 BR (2,max 4) $106-109/79-82,   2 BR (2,max 6) $87-110 / $120-140*

**KALAMA TERRACE**   (No rental information available)

**BEACH CLUB APARTMENTS**
2173 Iliili Rd., Kihei Maui, HI 96753, (808) 874-6474.   Long term rentals only.

**LIHI KAI COTTAGES**
2121 Iliili Rd., Kihei, Maui, HI 96753. (808-879-2335) 1-800-544-4524. Nine beach cottages are 1 BR 1 bath with kitchen and lanai. Self-service laundromat. Next to Kamaole I Beach. $100 deposit, 3-day minimum, 60/30 day refund notice. Maid service at additional fee. NO CREDIT CARDS. *1 BR (2) $59/54*

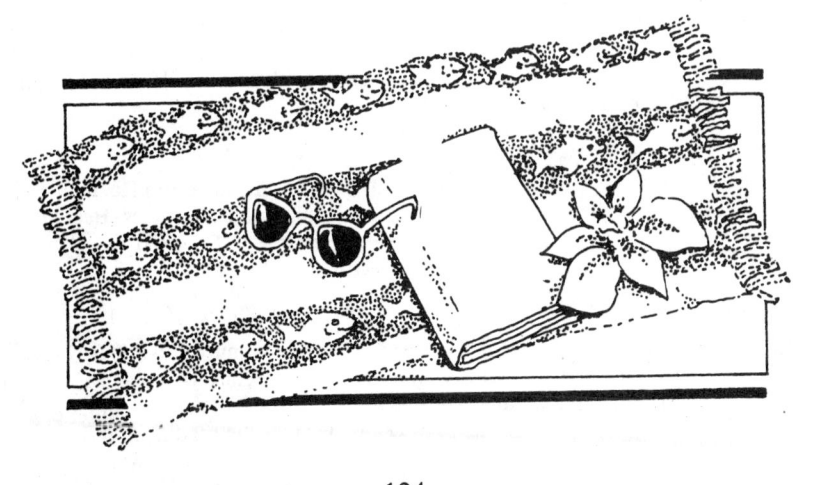

## MAUI VISTA

2191 S. Kihei Rd., Kihei, Maui, HI 96753. (808-879-7966) 1-800-367-8047 ext.330. Agents: Aston 1-800-922-7866, Oihana 1-800-367-5234 (Oihana rates: 1 BD $80/70; 2 BD $100/90), Kihei Maui Vac. 1-800-542-6284, RSVP 1-800-663-1118, Maui Condo & Home 1-800-822-4409.

280 units in three 4-story buildings, across from the beach. Some units have airconditioning, some have washer/dryers. All have kitchens with dishwashers. The 2-bedroom units are fourth floor townhouses. Some oceanview units. 6 tennis courts, 3 pools, BBQ's. We had some problem with sound carrying from a neighboring unit, but overall, a good value. Extra person $12. *Studio $88/90-95/79-85, 1 BR 1 Bath (2,max 4) $105-120/95-110, 2 BR 2 Bath (2,max 6) $145-160/125-140.*

## PACIFIC SHORES

2219 S. Kihei Rd. (808-874-3461). Residential and long term rentals only.

## KAMOA VIEWS

2124 Awihi Place. (808-879-5335). Long term rentals only.

## KAMAOLE ONE

2230 S. Kihei Rd., Kihei, Maui, HI 96753. (808-879-4811 or 808-879-2449) FAX 808-874-3744. 2-story building. Twelve units. No elevators or pool, covered parking. Beachfront. Nice location on Kamaole One Beach. Telephones, microwaves, washer/dryers, air-conditioning, ceiling fans and cable TV. $200 deposit. NO CREDIT CARDS. *2 BR ground or second floor $160-170/140-150.*

## MAUI COAST HOTEL   (Hotel)

2259 S. Kihei Rd., Kihei, Maui, HI 96753. (808) 874-MAUI, FAX (808) 875-4731. Reservations: 1-800-426-0670. Operated by West Coast Hotels they opened in February 1993 and offers 264 guestrooms, 216 sleeping rooms and 114 of them suites. The hotel offers a pool area, two outdoor whirlpools, nearby Kamaole Bar & Grill Restaurant, tennis courts (2-night lit) and complimentary laundry facilities.

The *Maui Coast Hotel* is a great concept, a more affordable hotel with some condominium conveniences. The in-room refrigerator was stocked with a couple of complimentary cans of juice daily and there was a coffee maker with the fixings. Located across the road from the Kihei Beach Parks, the pool area was pleasant and an international mix of people seemed to being staying at the property during our visit. We heard Chinese and Italian both being spoken at the pool. As a new property, we inquired as to how some of the other guests had discovered this hotel. One group was a large company group an they had needed a large cluster of rooms, wanted hotel amenities but weren't interested in the $300 mega-resort rates. Another couple were staying two nights at the hotel before they moved to another mega-resort in Wailea that couldn't accommodate them upon their arrival. Another advantage is for the short term island visitor. Many of the condominiums have a four day or even a week minimum stay. The standard room we had was a little crowded with one king bed and the two kids on a sofa bed. No frills, but nicely appointed.
*Standard (3) $109-120, Alcove Suite (4) $139-149, Deluxe 1 BR suite (4) $165-180, 2 BR suite (6) $225-250.*

## KAMAOLE BEACH ROYALE

2385 S. Kihei Rd.,(PO Box 370) Kihei, Maui, HI 96753. (808-879-3131) 1-800-421-3661, FAX (808) 879-9163. 64 units with washer/dryers and single or double lanais in a single 7-story building across from Kamaole I Beach. Recreation area, elevator, roof garden. 10% monthly discount, 5-day minimum, $200 deposit, balance due 30 days prior to arrival. $25 service charge. NO CREDIT CARDS. Management notes that all units have been recently upgraded.

*1 BR 1 bath (2) $ 90/65          Extra person $10 per night*
*2 BR 2 bath (2) $100-105 / $75-80*
*3 BR 3 bath (2) $110/85*

## KIHEI ALII KAI

2387 S. Kihei Rd., Kihei, Maui, HI 96753. (808-879-6770) Agents: Leisure Properties (PO Box 985, Kihei, 96753) )1-800-888-MAUI, Kihei Maui Vacations 1-800-542-6284, RSVP 1-800-663-1118, Rainbow Rentals 1-800-451-5366. 127 units in four buildings. All units have washer/dryers. No maid service. Complex features pool, jacuzzi, sauna, two tennis courts, BBQ. Across road and up street from beach. Nearby restaurants and shops. Extra persons $7/night. $100 deposit, 3 night minimum. Full payment 30 days prior to arrival.

*1 BR (2) $90/65,  2 BR (4) $105-115 / $80-90,  3 BR (6) $130/110*

## ROYAL MAUIAN

2430 S. Kihei Rd., Kihei, Maui, HI 96753. (808-879-1263) 1-800-367-8009, FAX 808-367-8009. 107 units with lanai, washer/dryer, in a 6-story building. Complex has shuffleboard, carpeted roof garden, and is next to the pleasant Kamaole II Beach Park. $15 extra person, 5-night minimum, $350 deposit with $50 cancellation fee. Maid service twice weekly. Following are high season rates.

*1 BR 1 bath or 2 bath (2) $137*
*2 BR 2 bath (2) $150-165,  3 BR (4) $220*
*Side wing two bedroom, two bath units are $120*

## KAMAOLE NALU

2450 S. Kihei Rd., Kihei, Maui, HI 96753 (808-879-1006) 1-800-767-1497. FAX (808) 879-8693. Thirty-six 2-bedroom, 2-bath units with large lanai, dishwasher, and washer/dryer in a 6-story building. Located between Kamaole I and II Beach Parks with all units offering oceanview. Weekly maid service during high season. $12 extra person. 3-day minimum. NO CREDIT CARDS. $200/100 deposit with $25 cancellation fee. Summer specials offered.

*2 BR 2 bath (2) o.v. $130/95, o.f. $140/105*

## HALE PAU HANA

2480 S. Kihei Rd., Kihei, Maui, HI 96753. (808-879-2715) 1-800-367-6036, FAX (808) 875-0238. Agent: Maui Condo & Home 1-800-822-4409. Seventy-eight oceanview units in four buildings. Laundry area, elevator. Located on Kamaole II Beach. NO CREDIT CARDS. Weekly and monthly discounts. Extra person $10-15. $250 deposit. $50 cancellation fee. Three seasons, lowest is April 15-Sept. 30, mid-season Oct. 1-Dec.14, high season Dec. 15-April 14.

*1 BR (2,max 4) $150-160/$115-125/$95-105; 1 BR 2 bath (2,max 4) $200/170/150*

## KIHEI KAI NANI
2495 S. Kihei Rd., Kihei, Maui, HI 96753. (Front desk: 808-879-1430), reservations 1-800-473-1493. Agents: Kihei Maui Vacations 1-800-542-6284, Hawaiian Apt. Leasing 1-800-854-8843. 180 one-bedroom units with lanai or balcony in a 2 and 3-story structure. This complex is one of the older ones along Kihei Rd. Laundry room and recreation center. Across from Kamaole II Beach. $7 extra person. Senior discount 10% low season. 4-night minimum, $100 deposit, balance due 30 days prior to arrival. NO CREDIT CARDS thru front desk reservations.
*1 BR (2) ($80/65)*

## MAUI BANYAN
2575 S. Kihei Rd. Agents: Outrigger Hotels Hawaii 1-800-OUTRIGGER, Kihei Maui Vacations 1-800-542-6284, Hawaiiana Resorts 1-800-367-7040, Kumulani 1-800-879-9272. Overlooking Kamaole II Beach Park, these suites feature kitchens, washer/dryer, lanai, air-conditioning, cable TV and telephone. Facilities include tennis court, pool and jacuzzi, BBQ. Hotel rooms have no kitchens or telephones. Daily maid service.
*Hotel Room (1-2) g.v. $90/75, partial o.v. $95/80*
*1 BR (max. 4) g.v. $125/110, partial o.v. $135/120, o.v. $145/130*
*2 BR (max. 6) g.v. $165/150, partial o.v. $175/160, o.v. $190/175*
*3 BR (Max. 8) g.v. $200/185, partial o.v. $215/205*

## KIHEI AKAHI
2531 S. Kihei Rd., Kihei, Maui, HI 96753. (808-879-1881) Agents: Maui Condo & Home Realty (808-879-5445), Oihana 1-800-367-5234, Maui Condominiums 1-800-367-5242, CANADA 1-800-663-2101, Kihei Maui Vac. 1-800-542-6284, RSVP 1-800-663-1118. 240 units with washer and dryers. 2 pools, tennis court, BBQ's. Across from Kamaole II Beach Park. $5 per night discount after 6 nites. 10% monthly discount. Extra person $12. 4-day minimum, $125 deposit, full payment 30 days prior to arrival. NO CREDIT CARDS. *Studio (2) $75/65, 1 BR 1 bath (2) $95/80, 2 BR 2 bath (4) $120/$95*

## HALEAKALA SHORES ★
2619 S. Kihei Rd., Kihei, Maui, HI 96753. (808-879-1218) 1-800-367-8047 ext. 119, 1-800-423-8733 ext. 119 Canada. Seventy-six, 2-BR units in two four story buildings. Located across the road from Kamaole III Beach. Maid service available for additional charge. Washer/dryers. Covered parking. A good value! Winter season seven night minimum, $200 deposit except Christmas season which requires a two week minimum with non-refundable full payment in advance. Summer season five night minimum, $100 deposit, 5% weekly discount. NO CREDIT CARDS. *2 BR (1-4) $115/85*

## MAUI PARKSHORE
2653 S. Kihei Rd., Kihei, Maui, HI 96753. (808-879-1600. Agent: Oihana Properties 1-808-244-7685. Sixty-four, 2-bedroom, 2-bath oceanview condos with washer/dryers, and lanais in a 4-story building (elevator) across from Kamaole III Beach. Pool area sauna. 10% monthly discount. $150 deposit, payment in full 30 days prior to arrival. 4 night minimum. NO CREDIT CARDS. Extra person $10 per night. *2 BR 2 bath (4) $100/80*

## KAMAOLE SANDS

2695 S. Kihei Rd., Kihei, Maui, HI 96753. (808-879-0666) Agents: Aston Resorts 1-800-922-7866, Kihei Maui Vacations 1-800-542-6284, Hawaiian Apt. Leasing 1-800-854-8843 (1-800-472-8449 CA), Kumulani 1-800-367-2954, Maui Condo & Home 1-800-822-4409. 440 units in 10 four-story buildings. Includes daily maid service. 4 tennis courts, wading pool, 2 jacuzzi's and BBQ's. Located on 15 acres across the road from Kamaole III Beach. In 1992 they completed a $1.2 million renovation of their suites. Check to see when they are offering their Kamp Kamaole, a seasonal program for 8-12 year olds, and is free of charge for registered guests.
*Hotel room w/refrigerator $199/109, Studio w/ kitchen $159-179/$129-149, 1 BR 2 bath (1-4) $125-160/110-135, 2 BR 2 bath (1-6) $170-225/155-205, 3 BR 3 bath (1-7) $250-275/240-250*

## HALE KAMAOLE

2737 S. Kihei Rd., Kihei, Maui, HI 96753. (808-879-2698) 1-800-367-2970. Agents: Kumulani 1-800-367-2954, Maui Condo & Home 1-800-822-4409. 188 units in 5 buildings (2 & 3-story, no elevator) across road from Kamaole III Beach. Laundry building, BBQ's, 2 pools, tennis courts. Some units have washer and dryers. Courtesy phone at office. One time cleaning fee for stays less than 5 nights. $100 deposit per week, balance due 30-60 days before arrival. 3 night minimum stay. Monthly discounts. NO CREDIT CARDS. Extra person $8. *1 BR (2) $99/67, 2 BR 2 bath (4) $129/87*

## MAUI KAMAOLE

2777 S. Kihei Rd., Kihei, Maui, HI 96743. (879-7668). Agents: Kihei Maui Vacations 1-800-542-6284, Maui Condo & Home Realty 1-800-367-5242, Pali Kai 1-808-879-8550. The newest development on South Kihei Rd. is on a bluff overlooking the ocean and across the street and a short walk down to Kamaole III Beach Park or Keawakapu Beach. 1 BR units are 1,000 - 1,300 sq.ft. and 2 BR units are 1,300 -1,600 sq.ft. Some have oceanviews. This is a four phase development that will eventually have 316 residential units on 23 acres. They are low-rise, four-plex buildings grouped into 13 clusters, each named after Hawaiian flora. Phase One is nearing completion, and Phase Two will include a pool, spa and pavilion. Phase four will add a second pool and two tennis courts.
*1 BR $130/100, 2 BR $160/130*

## MAUI HILL ★
2881 S. Kihei Rd., Kihei, Maui, HI 96753. (808-879-6321) Agents: Aston Hotels 1-800-922-7866, Kumulani 1-800-367-2954, RSVP 1-800-663-1118. 140 attractively furnished units with washer/dryers, air-conditioning, microwaves, dishwashers, and large lanais. Daily maid service. There are 12 buildings with a Spanish flair clustered on a hillside above the Keawakapu Beach area. There is a moderate walk down and across the road to the beach. Upper units have oceanviews. The 3-bedroom units are very spacious. Large pool and tennis courts.
*1 BR (1-4) $165/135, 2 BR (1-6) $185/155, 3 BR 3 bath (1-8) $275/245*

## KIHEI SURFSIDE
2936 S. Kihei Rd., Kihei, Maui, HI 96753. (808-879-1488) 1-800-367-5240. Agents: Kihei Maui Vacations 1-800-542-6284. Maui Condo & Home 1-800-822-4409. 83 units on rocky shore with tidepools, a short walk to Keawakapu Beach. Large grassy area and good view. Coin-op laundry on premise. No maid service. Extra persons $10. Children free during summer. 3-night minimum, 3-day deposit, 14-day cancellation notice. Monthly discount. This property has a three rate system. Summer, fall and winter are each priced at a slightly different rate.
*1 BR 1 bath (2) $125/80-94, 1 BR 1½ bath (2) $135/88-105,*
*2 BR 2 bath (4) $160/130*

## MANA KAI ★
2960 S. Kihei Rd., Kihei, Maui, HI 96753. (808-879-1561) 1-800-525-2025 (FAX 808-874-5042). Agents: Kumulani 1-800-367-2954, Maui Condos 1-800-663-6962. 132 rooms in an 8-story building. The studio units have a room with an adjoining bath. The 1-bedroom units have a kitchen and the 2-bedroom units are actually the hotel unit and a 1-bedroom combined, each having separate entry doors. Complex has laundry facilities on each floor, an oceanfront pool, and a restaurant off the lobby. Daily maid service. The Mana Kai is nestled at the end of Keawakapu Beach, and offers a majestic view of the blue Pacific, the 10,000 foot high Haleakala and Upcountry Maui. It is the only major facility in Kihei on a prime beachfront location. Keawakapu Beach is not only very nice, but generally very under used. 1-night deposit, balance due 30-60 days in advance of arrival. 14-day cancellation notice. The rates include a late model car with unlimited mileage. Car user must be 21 years of age.
*S BR 1 bath (2) $ 95/ 90, includes breakfast & car (no kitchen)*
*1 BR 1 bath (2) $175/155, includes car*
*2 BR 1 bath (2) $195/175, includes car*

## WAILEA OCEANFRONT HOTEL   (Hotel)
2980 S. Kihei Rd., Kihei, Maui, HI 96753. (808-879-7744) Hawaiian Pacific Resorts 1-800-367-5004. 88 units on Keaweakapu Beach. They were unable to show us units following their renovation. No pool, located on Keaweakapu Beach, but only the front unit has an oceanview. Several two-story buildings, no lanais.
*Standard $85 (3), Superior $90 (2), Deluxe $100 (2), 1 BR $160 (5)*

## HALE HUI KAI
2994 S. Kihei Rd. Kihei, Maui, HI 96753. On-site property rental agent (808-879-1219) - NO CREDIT CARDS, NO PERSONAL CHECKS. Oceanfront on Keawakapu Beach. 5-night minimum, $200 deposit. Extra person $15-20.
*2 BR 2 bath o.v. $135/115, side o.v. $115/90*

# WAILEA

## INTRODUCTION

Wailea is a well planned and well manicured resort on 1,500 acres just south of Kihei developed by Alexander and Baldwin. In addition to a selection of outstanding luxury resorts and condominiums, there are a fine selection of championship golf courses, a large tennis center and a shopping center. The spacious and uncluttered layout is impressive, as are its series of lovely beaches.

There is a shoreline paved trail that travels between the Kea Lani up to the Grand Wailea, making it a wonderful option for a stroll, day or night.

Besides visiting resorts and beaches, there isn't much to do. There is a small shopping center which will satisfy most basic needs. Tuesdays at 1:30 pm they feature a free Hawaiian show in the central courtyard of the Wailea Shopping Center that is quite good. Bring a towel or mat to sit on. You can pick up a cold drink, an ice cream cone or a sandwich to enjoy during the show.

The first two resort hotels were the 550-room Maui Inter-Continental Resort which opened in 1976, and the 350-room Stouffer Wailea Beach Resort which opened in 1978. During the past couple of years this area has been the hub of development on Maui. The Palms at Wailea is located at Wailea's entrance. The Four Seasons Hotel opened in the spring of 1990 and was followed by the September 1991 opening of the neighboring, 812 room Grand Wailea Resort & Spa, which originally opened as a Hyatt. Kea Lani, an all-suites resort, opened in November of 1992 with 450 rooms and 37 oceanfront villas on Polo Beach. The Diamond Resort, a private, primarily Japanese guest hotel, is located in the foothills above Wailea. The Wailea condominium villages are divided into four locations: two are beachfront, while two are adjacent to the golf course. The newest of these villages is the Grand Champion Villas which opened in 1989. The Polo Beach condominiums are located adjacent to Wailea resorts on Makena Road. An exclusive property, Wailea Point, has no vacation rentals.

PARROTS

## WHAT TO SEE AND DO

The lovely Wailea beaches are actually well-planned and nicely maintained public parks with excellent access, off-street parking and all but one have restrooms and rinse-off showers. Ulua Beach is our personal favorite. The Stouffer Wailea Beach Resort also offers lovely grounds you might want to enjoy.

## WHERE TO SHOP

Wailea Shopping Center is located at the southern end of Wailea. It offers a small pantry market, a mall of shops, and a restaurant. Each of the Wailea resorts also has an assortment of gift shops.

## ACCOMMODATIONS - WAILEA

The Palms at Wailea
Wailea Villas:
   Ekolu Village
   Ekahi Village
   Elua Village
   Grand Champion Villas
Stouffer Wailea Beach Resort

Maui Inter-Continental Resort
   Diamond Resorts
Wailea Point
Grand Wailea Resort & Spa
Four Seasons
Kea Lani
Polo Beach Club

**BEST BETS:** It's hard to go wrong in wonderful Wailea. Affordable accommodations are not what the visitor will find here, but there are a variety of excellent condominiums and hotels among which to choose. Each is different, each is lovely and in fact there is not one property that we would not recommend. The choice is up to the personal preference of the guest. Here is a quick synopsis of each.

*Wailea Villas* - Our choice among the four areas would be the Elua Village. These are more expensive, of course, but beach aficionados will love having Ulua Beach at their front door.

*Maui Inter-Continental Resort* - A top notch resort hotel featuring a tropical flavor with lovely spacious grounds, excellent restaurants, and two great beaches. They recently completed a major renovation which involved a convention center and a magnificent new lobby and central stairway. An added plus here is their special children's program and room rates for kids.

*Stouffer Wailea Beach Resort* - This complex is smaller, and more intimate -- as resorts go -- it has lush, tropical grounds, and it is fronted by one of the island's finest beaches.

The *Grand Wailea Resort and Spa* - This is an enormous resort, but also enormous fun! The pools are incredible, but if you prefer the ocean, there is excellent Wailea Beach. There is something to do for everyone in the family. Just walking the grounds and touring the $40 million art collection could fill up a day!

*Four Seasons Resort* - This resort is purely and simply elegant. From it's white porte cochere you enter a tranquil and serene environ. Simply sit by the pool or enjoy a day on the beach. No need to go further!

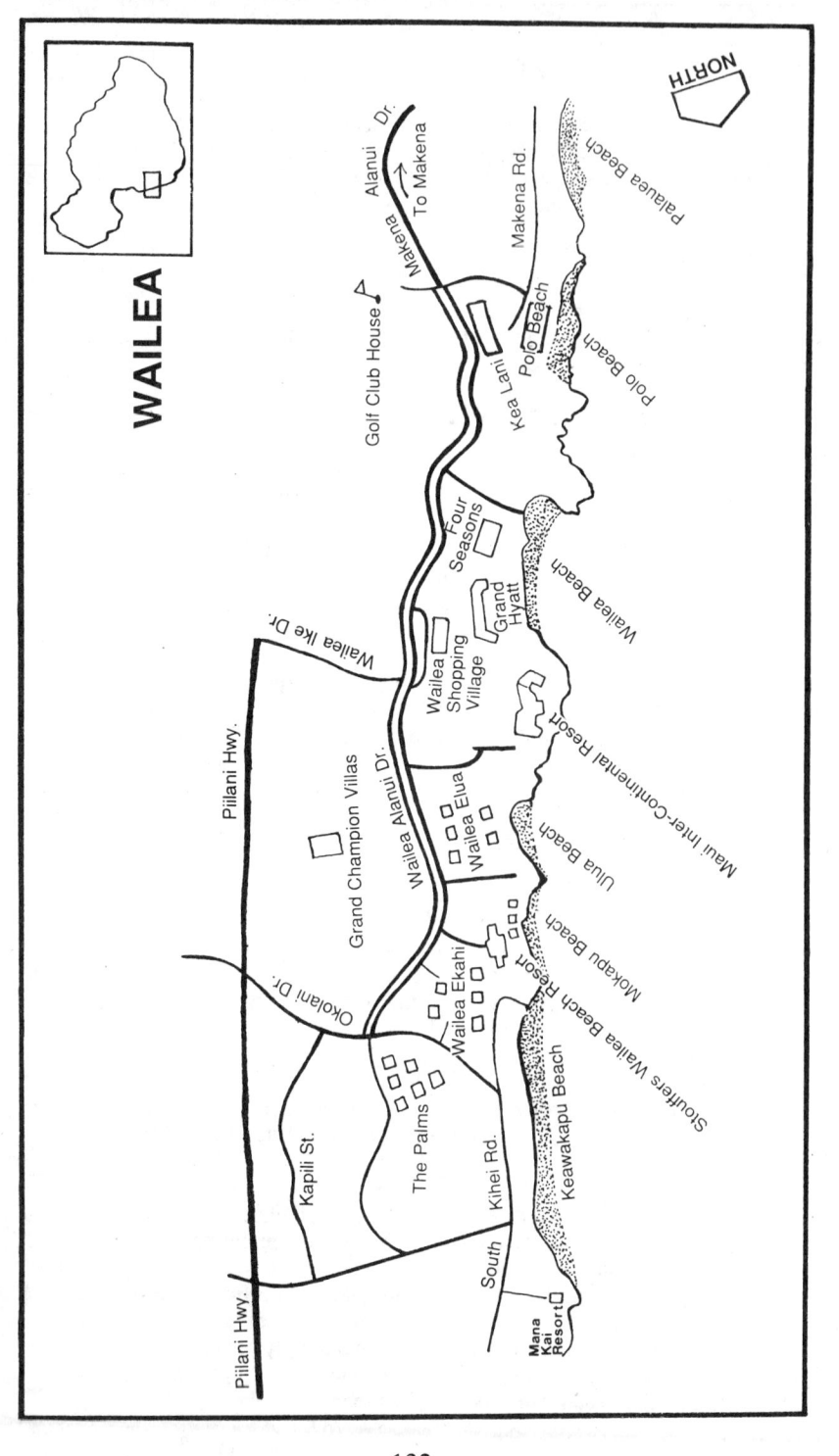

WAILEA

NORTH

Alanui Dr.
Makena
To Makena
Makena Rd.
Kea Lani
Golf Club House
Polo Beach
Polo Beach
Palauea Beach

Four Seasons
Grand Hyatt
Wailea Beach

Wailea Ike Dr.
Wailea Shopping Village
Maui Inter-Continental Resort

Piilani Hwy.
Grand Champion Villas
Wailea Alanui Dr.
Wailea Elua
Ulua Beach

Okolani Dr.
Wailea Ekahi
Mokapu Beach

Kapili St.
The Palms
Wailea Beach Resort
Stouffer's Wailea Beach Resort
Keawakapu Beach

South Kihei Rd.

Mana Kai Resort

Piilani Hwy.

The **Kea Lani** - This is an all-suites resort, a blend of the best of resorts and the comforts of a condominium, all on Polo Beach. Want to really indulge? Then how about one of their private oceanfront villas with private swimming pool?

*Polo Beach* - Luxury condominium units with easy access to two small but good beaches.

### THE PALMS AT WAILEA
3200 Wailea Alanui Drive, Wailea, Maui, HI 96753 (808) 879-5800. Agents: Outrigger Hotels Hawaii 1-800-OUTRIGGER Hawaiiana Resorts 1-800-367-7040, Maui Condo & Home 1-800-822-4409 (Rates: $130/95). Luxury units located with oceanviews in Wailea. One and two bedroom condominiums on a bluff overlooking the Wailea area with view of the islands of Kaho'olawe and Lana'i. Each unit features air-conditioning, washer/dryer. Guests have use of the recreation center which includes a pool and jacuzzi. As part of the Wailea destination, this property offers access to the two Wailea golf courses and tennis complex. Daily maid service.
*1 BR g.v. (4) $150/140, o.v. $165/155; 2 BR (6) $185/175, o.v. $205/195*

### WAILEA VILLAS
3750 Wailea Alanui, Wailea Maui, HI 96753. (808-879-1595) 1-800-367-5246. Agents: Destination Resorts Wailea (808-879-1595) 1-800-367-5246, Kumulani (only Ekahi condos) 1-800-367-2954. Some agents may have a limited number of units for slightly better prices than those quoted below. The price range reflects location in the complex. Children under 16 free in parent's room.

EKOLU VILLAGE - Located near the tennis center and the Wailea golf course.
*1 BR (2) $160/135, 2BR (4) $200/160*

EKAHI VILLAGE - On the hillside above the south end of Keawakapu Beach, some units are right above the beach.
*S BR (2) $140/120, 1 BR (2) $170-190/140-160, 2 BR (4) $275/225*

ELUA VILLAGE - Located on Ulua Beach, one of the best in the area. We would recommend these units.
*1 BR (2) g.v.-o.v. $195-230/165-200, o.f. $300/250*
*2 BR (4) g.v.-o.v. $275-315/225-270, o.f. $400/340*
*3 BR (6) g.v. only $375/300, o.f. $500/440*

GRAND CHAMPION VILLAS - Located at 155 Wailea Iki Place, Wailea, HI 96754. The fourth and newest of the Wailea Villas, this is a sportsman's dream, located between Wailea's Blue Golf Course and the "Wimbledon West" Tennis Center. Agent: Destination Resorts 1-800-367-5246, Maui Network 1-800-367-5221, Kihei Maui Vacations 1-800-541-6284. 188 luxury condominium units on 12 lush acres with garden view, golf view or oceanview units. Daily maid service, grocery delivery service, concierge service. Golf, tennis and/or car packages available. *1 BR (2) $140-160/120-135, 2 BR (4) $180-200/150-160*

### STOUFFER WAILEA BEACH RESORT ★ (Hotel)

3550 Wailea Alanui, Wailea, Maui, HI 96753. (808-879-4900) 1-800-992-4532, FAX (808-874-5370). 347 units including 12 suites. This luxury resort covers 15.5 acres above beautiful Mokapu Beach. Each guest room is 500 sq.ft. and offers a refrigerator, individual air-conditioner, a stocked mini-bar, and private lanai. The rooms have been recently redecorated in soothing rose, ash and blue tones. An assortment of daily guest activities are available as well as a year round children's program called Camp Wailea. The Mokapu Beach Club is a separate beachfront building with 26 units that feature open beamed ceilings and rich koa wood furnishings, plus a small swimming pool. The resort's restaurants are the Maui Onion, a pool-side gazebo; Palm Court, serving international buffets in an open air atmosphere; Raffles', an award-winning gourmet restaurant and Hana Gion, serving authentic Japanese cuisine. The Sunset Terrace, located in the lobby area, offers an excellent vantage point for a beautiful sunset and nightly entertainment 5:30 pm- 8:30 pm. The beach offers excellent swimming. The best snorkeling is just a very short walk over to the adjoining Ulua Beach. The grounds are a beautiful tropical jungle with a very attractive pool area which was recently expanded to include additional lounging areas and more jacuzzi pools. They also offer several "breakation" options. These include a combination of room and car, room and golf or honeymoon options.

*Deluxe mountainside & oceanside rooms $255 - $295, Deluxe oceanview rooms $350, Mokapu Beach Club, beachfront $465, Makai 1 & 2 BR suites $650-975, Alii Suite $1,600, Aloha suite $2,000.*

### MAUI INTER-CONTINENTAL RESORT ★ (Hotel)

3700 Wailea Alanui, Kihei, Maui, HI 96753. (808-879-1922), FAX (808-874-8331), 1-800-367-2960. The porte cochere greets your arrival with a grand entry and ocean view. Beautiful koa rockers tempt guests to sit, relax and enjoy the tranquil, gorgeous view. Just beyond, the new main stairway descends down and past a lily pond (a popular wedding site) to the new central pool area.

MAUI INTER-CONTINENTAL

The new oceanview, 34,000 sq. ft. conference pavilion is a topped with a rooftop observatory. Take the elevator or walk up for a panoramic view and an perfect vantage point for whale watching. The renovations blend in so well that it is hard to remember it ever being any other way. The design is unpretentious, old Hawaiian and classic. The artwork is subtle. Chests from Japan, huge stone mochi bowls, spirit houses from Thailand, roof finials from New Guinea, and calabashes from the Big Island.

Located on 22 acres they have 1/2 mile of oceanfront property and access to two great beaches, Ulua and Wailea. There are three pools, a seven-story tower and six low-rise buildings. The wonderful layout of this resort allows 80% of all guest rooms to have an ocean view and the grounds are spacious and sprawling. No "packing them in" feel here! The main pool area has two pools. One deeper and one a 4 1/2 foot depth all over. There is also a pint-size slide into a small pool that is perfect for the pint size members in your family. Nothing exotic or fancy, just plain good water fun. A separate pool in the luau area is often uncrowded. The units located nearest the beach afford wonderful private ocean views.

The restaurants in this lovely resort include poolside Sun Spot, Hula Moons and the Lana'i Terrace. There is also a Sunday brunch and seasonal Aloha Mele Luncheon offered in the Makani Room.

This resort takes a special look at family travel and offers a special family rate where a room is provided at a 50% discount for children if you book another room at standard rack rate. Another plus for the family pocketbook is that kids are offered a special menu with all items priced $6 and under at all the Hula Moons and the Lana'i Terrace. An excellent children's day and evening program offered year round called Keiki's Club Gecko. Laundry facilities are coin-op and located in several areas on property. The resort offers many complimentary daily activities as well as one of Maui's best luaus. Pau Hana from 5:30 - 8 p.m. with live entertainment. A number of exciting annual events are sponsored by the resort. Golf, tennis and honeymoon package plans also available. *G.v. $179, m.v. $199, o.v. $219, o.f. $249, deluxe $289*

**DIAMOND RESORTS OF JAPAN (Hotel)**
555 Kaukahi St., Wailea, Maui, HI 96753. (874-0500) This private resort, an extension of the Diamond Resort Corporation which manages a chain of 20 resorts throughout Japan, is located on 14.5 acres just above the Wailea Golf Course. The spa facility which includes a men's and women's daiyokujo (traditional Japanese bath), a waterfall to gently massage your neck and shoulders as well as a soothing Finlandia sauna is one of the resort's highlights. Recently, Diamond Resort has implemented the Diamond Spa Club program. Membership in the club provides the opportunity to experience the luxurious spa and spend a peaceful night in one of the exclusive hotel rooms. For rates and more information, contact a Spa Club representative.

It is a beautiful and interesting resort and the panoramic view from the lobby is dramatic! The artwork is primarily large tapestries which mimic the work of Van Gogh. The restaurants are open to the public and the Sunset Bar offers freshly made $1 sushi, complimentary pupus, happy hour drinks and live entertainment plus a fabulous sunset view.

Their three dining facilities are Satoru, Le Gunji, both fine dining restaurants, and Island Terrace which serves "nutritionally balanced cuisine." See the RESTAURANTS, Wailea section, for descriptions.

### WAILEA POINT
4000 Wailea Alanui, Wailea, Maui, HI 96753. 136 luxurious oceanview and oceanfront condominiums arranged in four-plexes which are laid out in a residential plan on 26-oceanfront acres. Privacy is maintained by a gate guard at the entrance. Unfortunately, no rental properties available here!

### GRAND WAILEA RESORT & SPA ★
3850 Wailea Alanui Drive, Wailea, Maui, HI 96753 (808) 875-1234, Reservations only 1-800-888-6100. The Grand opened their 767 room resort in September 1991 (originally it was a Hyatt Property) at a cost of $600 million with an additional $30 million in fine artwork. They are no longer working with Hyatt and are now actively promoting their outstanding spa facilities. Quite frankly when we first heard the concepts planned for this new mega-resort we were concerned it would be another Kaua'i Lagoons, or take on aspects of Orlando or Anaheim. Wrong! The resort is a bit over-whelming, but it is tasteful, innovative and truly spectacular. Beautifully appointed with great attention to detail make it is a must-see, even if you aren't lucky enough to stay! In fact, make at least two trips... a second at night to enjoy dinner and tour the grounds when they are alight like a fairy land.

The sea remains the theme throughout the resort. Guests are greeted by a huge waterfall flowing down from Mt. Haleakala as they arrive. Look closely for the Hawaiian sea spirits which are hidden amid this interesting aquatic cascade. Each of the many Hawaiian sculptures has a legend or history -- King Kamehameha stands out near the entry and was created by Herb Kane, a noted specialist on Polynesian culture and history. He also created many of the mermaids, dancers and fisherman found by the resort's lagoons and streams. Inside the resort you'll find Hena, the mother of the demigod Maui. In the open air walkway of the Molokini Wing. There are 18 bronzes around the grounds that were sculpted by world-famous artist Fernard Leger. Jan Fisher sculpted ten life-size pieces for the

GRAND WAILEA RESORT & SPA

resort including the maidens bathing and the Fisher's two-trios of hula dancers at the entry of the atrium. Be sure to take note of the beautiful relief painted on the walls of the Grand Dining Room. The murals were painted by Doug Riseborough and depict his version of the legend of the demi-God Maui. In the center of the dining room is a sculpture done by Shige Yamada, entitled "Maui Captures the Sun." Just outside the dining room is a small stage with a fabulous Hawaiian mosaic. The resort offers a complimentary art tour twice weekly led by an island art expert. The center courtyard is called the Botero Gallery. These sculptures seem to be getting the most discussion - both good and bad! Fernando Botero is a contemporary artist from Colombia and his work is "oversized." The huge Hawaiian woman reclining on her stomach (smoking a cigarette in the buff) weighs 600 pounds and is appraised at $2 million. If you're on the upper levels, be sure to look down to see her from another.... uh, interesting, perspective!

Over $20 million was spent on the waterfalls, streams, rapids, slides, reflecting pools, swimming pools, river pool, scuba pool, salt water lagoon and spa features. This is one of the most high-tech aquatic systems in the state. Strikingly beautiful, the formal reflecting pool leads you to the sweaping Wailea Beach. Beyond this pool is a formal swimming Hibscus pool made of Mexican glass tile with gold leaf. This adults only pool is lined with wide Mediterannean-style cabanas. The "action pool" (The Wailea Canyon Activity Pool) is a million gallon, 23,500 square foot pool with five large, free-form pools at various levels beginning at a height of 40 feet and dropping to sea level. Painted tiles depicting turtles & tropical fish in varying shades of green and blue line the bottom and sides, while huge rocks and landscape features line the pools. At one end of the pool is an incredible waterslide, a 225 foot twisting ride that drops three stories. The "jungle pool," another part of the Wailea Canyon Activity pool, offers a rope swing. The pools are connected by a 220 foot river which carries swimmers at varying current speeds, ranging from white water rapids to a lazy cruise. Along the way are hidden grottoes, whirlpools and saunas, six slides, six waterfalls and a bumpy white water rapids that has been created by the use of special acquatic devices. At the bottom of the river is a one-of-a-kind water elevator which lifts the swimmers back up to the top again. Below the rocky waterfall is the scuba pool which gets prospective divers in the mood with an underwater mural featuring a coral reef, and sea life made of tiles. Streams and pools also meander through elaborate gardens in Hawaiian and Japanese themes throughout the resort. It takes 50,000 gallons of water a minute to sustain their aquatic system. The pool may be used by non-resort guests for a daily fee of $65 for adults and $50 for children. A reduced rate for guests staying at the neighboring Four Seasons Resort run $50 adults and $35 for children.

Spa Grande is Hawai'i's largest spa, and spans 50,000 square feet in the atrium wing of the resort. It is designed with Italian marble, original artwork, Venetian chandeliers and inlaid gold. It provides a blend of European, Japanese and American spa philosophies. The spa's central concept is based on a longevity program which allows guests to enjoy fitness, beauty and health treatments as well as working out a regimen that will continue once their vacation has ended. An in-house physician works with guests, providing medical and fitness evaluations. Hawaiian therapies include a ti leaf wrap, limu (seawood) bath and a lomi lomi massage. The "Terme Wailea" is a 30-minute circuit on the spa's "wet" level which begins with a loofah scrub, followed by a trip to the Roman tub for a cool dip followed by a choice of specialty baths. The masso, thermo and hydrotherapy treatments are available in 42 individual rooms. Also available are a sonic relaxation room, cascading waterfall massage, authentic furo soaking tubs and white and black sand body treatments. An aerobics studio, weight room, cardiovascular room, racquetball and squash court (the only ones on Maui), a full-service beauty salon, and game room are among the many spa options.

The Tsunami Nightclub (what a great name!) offers 8,000 square feet of high tech lounge with black marble. Five restaurants give guests plenty of choices. Kincha features very authentic and expensive Japanese cuisine and is set amid a beautiful Japanese Garden. The Grand Dining Room Maui, situated 60 feet above sea level, offers a panoramic view of the Pacific, the gardens and Molokini Island from inside or on a lovely outdoor eating veranda. They serve an outstanding Sunday brunch. Cafe Kula features healthy family style foods. Humuhumunukunuku (Humuhumu) for short is named for the Hawaiian state fish. It sits surrounded by a saltwater lagoon filled with tropical fish. It is definitely worth a stop just to see this restaurant which serves Pacific Rim/seafood cuisine. Bistro Molokini serves California and Italian items and the Volcano Bar provides light dining and snacks. There is also a swim up bar. The food & beverage department has created an interesting assortment of original drinks. A Reeses peanut butter smoothie may be just the thing for sipping around the pool, or a liliokoi and orange juice splashed with champagne the ideal before dinner drink.

Now the rooms! There are 787 oceanfront rooms each 650 square feet and 53 suites. The Presidential suite (5,500 sq. ft.) is priced at a mere $8,000 per night and features what is lovingly referred to as a Imelda Marcos shoe closet, a private sauna, a room-sized shower with ocean view in one bathroom and a black marble and teak soaking tub in the other. Lots of marble is used throughout all the rooms with subtle marblized wallpapers in earthen hues. The resort was designed so that each room would provide an ocean view.

This may be the one resort that your kids will INSIST you come back to again and again. After you visit the kids' camp you will, at least momentarily, wish you could pass for a 10 or 11 year old. The 20,000 square foot Camp Grande operates year round as well as older kids. A huge area is designed with crafts complete with pottery kiln. Adjacent is a kid's dining dream, resembling a 1950's style soda fountain. An outdoor area offers a toddler-size whale-shaped pool, cushy soft grass-like play yard and playground equipment. Another room houses the computer center, another the video arcade and yet another has a Hawaiian version of F.A.O Schwartz that will ensure that your kids may not be glad to see you upon pickup time. The price is $65 per day (9 a.m. - 3 p.m.) for children ages three years (and potty-trained) to fifteen years of age and includes lunch, with an evening schedule including dinner. Package rates are available. Babysitters may be arranged through the children's program. Parents are invited to bring and supervise their own children at Camp Grande at no charge.

The 38,000 sq. ft. ballroom is a convention planner's dream, with concealed projection screens, specialized audio equipment, the works! The ballroom also has three huge, beautiful and unique artworks in gold and silver leaf which depict the story of Pele the fire goddess and her two sisters. Don't neglect a look up at the 29,000 pound Venetian glass chandelier imported from Italy.

We were frankly rather pleasantly surprised by the interesting blend of mega resort glitz and Hawaiian themes tempered with outstanding craftsmanship. It seems to work. There is actually a great deal of fine craftsmanship (notice the twisted ohia wood rails that line the pathways) and we especially like the attention to the Hawaiiana aspects. The resort is visually very stimulating and each time you stroll the grounds you're sure to see something new. The chapel, set in the middle of the grounds, however, leaves us a bit puzzled. Looking as though it were snatched from Reno and transplanted to the beach in Wailea, we wonder why anyone would choose to be married inside, where the view of the ocean is obscured by stained glass, when there are so many more beautiful sites around the hotel grounds or on the beach. However, you should still inspect the Chapel. The woodwork and stained glass windows are absolutely beautiful, and take note the chandeliers, priced at $100,000 each!

All in all, if you're seeking a resort vacation, you'll find it all here. Not everyone wants the activity of a resort, but this one certainly has something for everyone.

*Terrace $350, oceanview $425, deluxe ocean $475, 1 BR suites $950-$1,600, 2 BR $1,400-$2,000. In the Napua Tower (an exclusive 100 rooms) Napua Club $550, Napua Suite $1,300-1,800, Napual Royal $2,500-3,000, Grand Suite $8,000*

## THE FOUR SEASONS RESORT WAILEA ★

3900 Wailea Alanui, Wailea, Maui, HI 96753. (808-874-8000) (National reservations 1-800-332-3442). 380 over-sized guest rooms (600 sq. ft) on eight floors encompassing 15 beachfront acres on the beautiful white sand Wailea Beach. A full service resort featuring two pools, (one large, one smaller lava pool) and a jacuzzi on each end of the main pool, one of which is set aside for children only. The layout of the grand pool provides shelter from the afternoon breezes. In addition there are two tennis courts at the resort, croquet lawn, health spa, beauty salon, three restaurants and two lounges. The public areas are spacious, open and ocean oriented. A very different atmosphere from other Maui resorts, the blue tiled roof and creamy colored building create a very classical atmosphere. Even the grounds, although a profusion of colors with many varied Hawaiian flora, are more structured in design with a vague resemblance to a Mediterranean villa. The focus of the resort is water. Throughout the resort's gardens and courtyards are an array of attractive formal and natural pools, ponds, waterfalls and fountains.

Their guest policy features real aloha spirit, with no charge for use of the tennis courts or health spa and complimentary snorkel gear, smash or volleyball equipment. Guest services, which distinguish the Four Seasons from other properties, include their early arrival/late departure program. These guests have their luggage checked and are escorted to the Health Club where a private locker is supplied for personal items. The resort makes available for these guests an array of casual clothing from work-out gear to jogging suits or swim wear. Another unusual amenity is provided periodically to pool and beachside sunbathers who are offered a refreshing iced towel, ice water or Evian mist. For the meeting planner, the Four Seasons features a 7,000 square foot ballroom, two banquet rooms and five conference areas situated adjacent to a 3,000 square foot hospitality suite. The suite offers a large living room, two bedrooms, another living space designed for private meetings, kitchen, and a 1,000 square foot lanai.

Our stay at the **Four Seasons Resort** climaxed one of our island vacations and proved to be the highlight of our entire trip. It was restful and elegant. The pool was nothing exotic or elaborate, but it didn't make it any less enjoyable for our children. A "children's only" hot tub allowed the second adult hot tub to be a peaceful respite. There are plenty of cabanas around the pool area and on the beach to enjoy the day, while staying out of the sun. Pool and beach staff are on their toes providing prompt attention for guests in setting up their lounge chairs with towels and providing chilled lemon towels or spritzers to cool the face. A poolside restaurant (with espresso) and bar make it easy to spend the entire day without leaving your lounge chair. The chilled coffee drinks are wonderful and there are plenty to choose from. The snorkeling is best out to the left near the rocky shoreline, but go early in the day. Like clockwork, about noon the wind picks up and the water clarity rapidly deteriorates. Another plus for the Wailea area is the walkway that spans along the shoreline between resorts. It is a pleasant walk over to the neighboring southern resort, the Kea Lani, and the Grand Wailea, to the north, is definitely worth a stroll (go during the day and again at night for a very different experience). The Four Seasons is truly geared for the family. A full-time, year around children's program is complimentary to hotel guests. Milk and cookies are delivered to the room for those young guests upon arrival. Sylvester Stallone, a guest of the hotel during our visit, made a couple of poolside appearances.

Amenities for guests on the club floor* include a private lounge, 24 hr. concierge, complimentary breakfast, afternoon tea, evening cocktails and after dinner liqueurs. Numerous special package offers include a room and car, golf, romance and family packages. (Note: The Golf package offers play at the exclusive new private Waikapu course.) Complimentary, year-round "Kids for All Seasons" program designed for hotel guests aged 5 - 12 years. Restaurants include the Cabana Cafe, Pacific Grill and Seasons.

Package programs currently available include a Bed & Breakfast package, Golf for Two, Room & Car, Family, Romance for all Seasons or Romantic Interlude.

*Partial o.v. $340, o.v. $420 (club floor $520), Four Seasons executive suites o.v. $625 (club floor $725)*
*O.v. & o.f. one bedroom suites $675-$2,300, 2 bedroom suites $1,200-$5,200*
*\*Club floor plans available for additional $100 per night*
*Third adult in room $75 night, club floors $100 per night*
*Under age 18 complimentary when sharing same room with parents, except on club floor, add $50 per night per child ages 5 - 17. Adjoining children's room is available for $200 when parents pay standard room rate, except on club floors.*

## KEA LANI ★
4100 Wailea Alanui Drive, Wailea, HI 96753. (808) 875-4100 1-800-882-4100. 413 suites plus 37 2 & 3 BR oceanfront villas. Designed after Las Hadas in Manzanillo, the name means "White Heavens." Its Mediterranean-style architecture received many mixed reviews when it opened several years ago. It seems to us that perhaps this might be the home of a Sultan with a dramatic style set on 22 acres and a bit out of place in Wailea. However, the tropical lushness has grown and softened the look of the resort. You enter a drive lined with Norfolk pines and beyond the porte cochere there is a large open lobby area with a fountain

covered by nine domes. Decorations are in Hawaiian florals, with mosaic tile ceilings and floors. There are 413 spacious (840 sq. ft.) one-bedroom suites, each with a private balcony. Views are garden, partial ocean, and ocean, and deluxe ocean view. Each has a sunken marble tub, an enormous walk-in shower, king or two double beds, two closets, decorated in hues of cream and white. A cotton kimono is provided for guests. The living room features a state of the art compact and laser disc system, 27 inch television and video cassette player. Fresh ground coffee and coffee maker is provided daily in the suite and a mini-kitchen offers a microwave, a small sink, and mini-bar. An iron and ironing board will also be available in each room. The exercise room is complimentary for guests. The "Caffe Ciao" offers deli and bakery foods, pasta, pizza and an espresso bar. Polo Beach Grille & Bar has an outdoor setting under a canopy of coconut palm trees and serves kiawe grilled meats, seafood, salads, specialty ice creams and tropical drinks. The Kea Lani Restaurant offers casual meals all day with indoor and outdoor seating overlooking the formal pool. The 22,000 sq. ft. pool area is be a series of pools connected together. The upper level pool adjoins a swim up pool bar.

In addition to the suites, there are also 37 townhouse style villas, 24 are two bedroom and 13 are three bedroom, which overlook Polo Beach. An 1,800 sq. ft. two-bedroom villa runs $895-995 a night, and a 2,100 sq. ft three-bedroom unit runs $1,095-1,195. A little spendy, but it would be easy to feel at home here! Each has a private lanai, huge walk-in closets, full size kitchen and washer and dryer, and are decorated in very muted mauves. Each has a generous living room and eating area. If you don't want to make that walk to the beach, you can just meander out onto your lanai and take a dip in your private swimming pool. That's right. Each villa has its own pool!

For a small fee the resort offers "Keiki Lani" (Heavenly Kids) for youths aged 5 to 11 years of age. Offered year round 9 a.m. until 3 p.m. includes lunch. Activities range from face painting to sailing, picnics to hula and off-property excursions. Children's menus available in the restaurant. Honeymoon, wedding, family, and sporting packages are available. *1 BR suite garden m.v. (4) 255, partial o.v. $310, o.v. $360, 1 BR suite deluxe, o.v. $425, 2 BR suite $585, 2 BR villa (1-6 persons) $795-895, 3 BR villa (1-8) $1,095-1,195*

KEA LANI

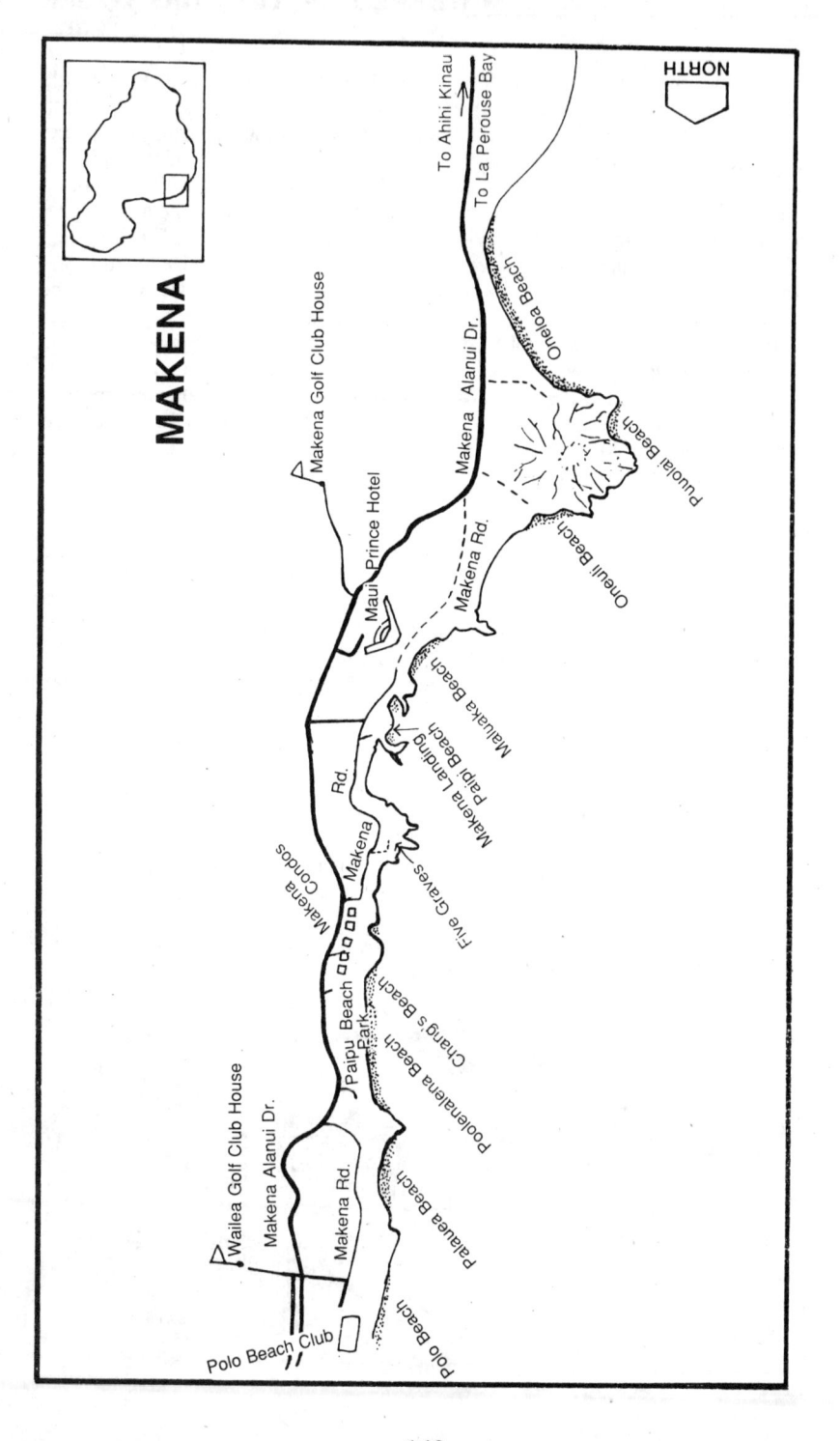

MAKENA

NORTH

To Ahihi Kinau
To La Perouse Bay

Makena Golf Club House
Maui Prince Hotel
Makena Alanui Dr.
Makena Rd.
Oneloa Beach
Puuolai Beach
Oneuli Beach

Maluaka Beach
Makena Landing
Paipi Beach
Five Graves

Makena Rd.
Makena Condos
Paipu Beach
Poolenalena Beach
Chang's Beach
Palauea Beach

Wailea Golf Club House
Makena Alanui Dr.
Makena Rd.
Polo Beach Club
Polo Beach

142

**POLO BEACH CLUB ★**
20 Makena Rd., Wailea, Maui, HI 96753. (808-879-8847) Agents: Destination Resorts 1-800-367-5246 is the on-site rental agent, Hawaiian Apt. Leasing 1-800-854-8843 (1-800-472-8449 CA), Island Dreamscape 1-800-367-8047 ext. 216 U.S.

71 apartments in a single 8-story building located on Polo Beach. The units are luxurious and spacious. Underground parking, pool area jacuzzi. This once very secluded area is soon to be "discovered." Is located next to the Kea Lani Resort. Additional persons (over 4) $20 each. Three night minimum.
*1 BR (2) o.f. $275-325 / $200-240, 2 BR 2 bath (max 6) o.f. $275-325 / $225-275*

# MAKENA

## INTRODUCTION

The area just south of Wailea is Makena, and one of the newer resort developments on Maui. The project began with the completion of an 18-hole golf course in 1981. The Makena Surf condominium project opened in 1984. The Japanese conglomerate, Seibu, has a magnificent new resort, the Maui Prince Hotel, located at Maluaka Beach. Also in this area are several beaches with public access. They include Oneloa, Puuolai, Poolenalena, Palauea and Maluaka beaches. Since the area is not fully developed the end results remain to be seen.

## WHAT TO DO AND SEE

Here are the last really gorgeous and undeveloped recreational beaches on Maui. Consequently, development in this area has met with a great deal of ongoing controversy. The paved road (Makena Alanui) runs from Wailea past the Makena Surf and Maui Prince Hotel, exiting onto the Old Makena Rd. near the entrances to Oneuli (Black Sand) Beach and Oneloa (Big Makena)-Puuolai (Little Makena) Beaches.

Past Ahihi Kinau Natural Reserve on Old Makena Rd. you will traverse the last major lava flow on Maui, which still looks pretty fresh after some 250 years and continues to La Perouse Bay. (See BEACHES)

Hiking beyond La Perouse affords some great ocean vistas. You'll see trails made by local residents in their four wheel drive vehicles, and fishermen's trails leading to volcanic promontories overlooking the ocean. You may even spot the fishing pole holders which have been securely attached to the lava boulders. The Hoapili Trail begins just past La Perouse Bay and is referred to as the King's Highway. It is believed that at one time the early Hawaiians made use of a trail that circled the entire island and this may be the remnants of that ancient route. The state Forestry and Wildlife Division and volunteers worked together recently putting in place stone barricades to keep the four wheel drive vehicles and motorcycles from destroying any more of the trail.

## ACCOMMODATIONS - MAKENA

**BEST BETS:** *The Maui Prince Hotel* and *Makena Surf* - Both are first class, luxury accommodations on beautiful beaches.

### MAKENA SURF ★

96 Makena Alanui Rd., Makena, Maui, HI 96753, Destination Resorts 1-800-367-5146, Hawaiian Apt. Leasing 1-800-854-8843, Kihei Maui Vacations 1-800-541-6284. Located 2 miles past Wailea. All units are oceanfront and more or less surround Paipu (Chang's) Beach. These very spacious and attractive condos feature central air-conditioning, fully equipped kitchens, washers and dryers, wet bar, whirlpool spa in the master bath, telephones and daily maid service. Two pools, and four tennis courts are set in landscaped grounds. Three historic sites found on location have been preserved.

*1 BR (2) $250-325 / $200-275*   *Prices listed are 2 or 3 nights*
*2 BR (2) $300-375 / $240-315*   *Discounts for 4 nights or longer*
*3 BR (4) $450 / $395*   *Extra person $15/night*

### MAUI PRINCE ★

5400 Makena Alanui, Makena, Maui, HI 96753. (808-874-1111) Reservations: 1-800-321-6284. In sharp contrast to the ostentatious atmosphere of some of the Kaanapali resorts, the Maui Prince radiates understated elegance. Its simplicity in color and design, with an Oriental theme, provides a tranquil setting and allows the beauty of Maui to be reflected. The central courtyard is the focal point of the resort with a lovely traditional water garden complete with a cool cascading waterfall and ponds filled with gleaming koi. The rooms are tastefully appointed in cool neutral hues and equipped with the comfort of the guests in mind. The units have two telephones and a small refrigerator. Terry robes are available for use during the guest's stay. A 24-hour full room service add to the conveniences.

There is plenty of room for lounging around two circular swimming pools or in a few steps you can be on Maluaka (Nau Paka) Beach with its luxuriously deep, fine white sand and good snorkeling, swimming and wave playing.

The resort is comprised of 1,800 acres including two championship golf courses. The first 18-holes were built in 1981, they were divided and each half was combined with nine new holes to create the North and South Courses. The South Course opened in August 1993 and the North Course on November 23, 1993. The courses were designed by Robert Trent Jones, Jr.

Restaurants include Prince Court serving Hawaiian Regional dishes (and one of the island's best Sunday brunches), al fresco dining in Cafe Kiowai and the Japanese restaurant and sushi bar at Hakone. The Prince Kids Program is offered year round each morning 9 am. until noon. It is a complimentary program for kids ages 4 to 12. Every child receives a logo frisbee, sun visor and water squeeze bottle. Activities are run by the pool staff and include arts and crafts, swimming, nature hikes.
*Partial o.v. $220, o.v. $270, o.v. prime $310, o.f. $360, Suites $420-820*
*No charge for third person using existing beds.*

# WAILUKU AND KAHULUI

## INTRODUCTION

The twin towns of Wailuku and Kahului are located on the northern, windward side of the island. Wailuku is the county seat of Maui and Kahului houses not only the largest residential population on the island, but also the main airport terminal and deep-water harbor. There are three motel-type accommodations around Kahului Harbor, and while the rates are economical, and the location is somewhat central to all parts of the island, we cannot recommend staying in this area for other than a quick stopover that requires easy airport access. This side of the island is generally more windy, overcast and cooler with few good beaches. Except for the avid windsurfer, we feel there is little reason to headquarter your stay in this area; however, there are good reasons to linger and explore.

## WHAT TO DO AND SEE

Kahului has a very colorful history, beginning with the arrival of King Kamehameha I in the 1790's from the big island of Hawai'i. The meaning of Kahului is "winning" and may have had its origins in the battle which ensued between Kamehameha and the Maui chieftain. The shoreline of Kahului Bay began its development in 1863 with the construction of a warehouse by Thomas Hogan. By 1879 a landing at the bay was necessary to keep up with the growing sugar cane industry. Two years later, in 1881 the Kahului Railroad Company had begun. The city of Kahului grew rapidly until 1900 when it was purposely burned down to destroy the spreading of a bubonic plague outbreak. The reconstruction of Kahului created a full-scale commercial harbor, which was bombed along with Pearl Harbor on December 7, 1941. After World War II, a housing boom began with the development of reasonably priced homes to house the increasing number of people moving to the island. The expansion has continued ever since.

Wailuku is the county seat of Maui and has been the center of government since 1930. It is now, slowly, experiencing a rebirth. It is often overlooked by visitors who miss out on some wonderful local restaurants and limited, but interesting, shopping.

*Market Street* in Old Wailuku Town is alive with the atmosphere of Old Hawai'i. The area, rich in history, was built on the site of ancient Heiaus and witnessed decisive Hawaiian battles. Later the area hosted the likes of Mark Twain and Robert Redford. It is no wonder that such an area should re-emerge in the modern day with shops of a cultural nature. One-of-a-kind items can be found here, gathered from around the world and eras gone by. Such is the case with Old Wailuku Town and the cluster of interesting shops on the upper end of Market Street in an area known as Antique Row.

Set against the lush backdrop of the Iao Valley and the West Maui Mountains, Antique Row is a small area offering a quaint alternative to the hustle-bustle vacation centers of Lahaina and Kihei. Surrounding this area is a multitude of wonderful and inexpensive ethnic restaurants. So don't limit your excursion to the few shops on the corner of Market and Main streets.

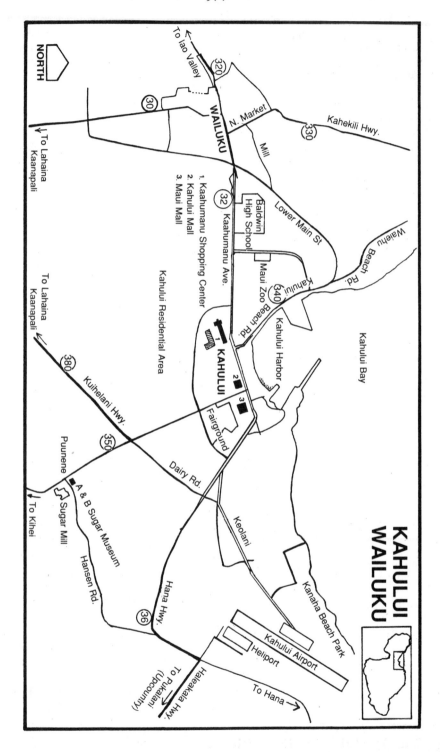

**Emura's** at 49 Market Street has consistently proven to be the spot for the best buys of eel skin items from wallets and purses, to shoes and attaches. Pay cash and get an extra discount!

The once Takata Market, a thriving butcher shop and grocery store in the 30's, is now home to **Memory Lane** (antique store) and **Traders of the Lost Art** (158 Market St.) Operated by Tye Hartall, Traders of the Lost Art features a variety of native carvings and primitive ritual art, which he brings back regularly from the secluded Sepik River area of Papua in New Guinea. Next door was the B. Hotta General Store and residence, which now houses an art gallery. **Alii Antiques** is across the street.

**Kaahumanu Church**, Maui's oldest remaining church was built in 1837 at High and Main Streets in Wailuku.

Hale Hoikeike in Wailuku houses the **Maui Historical Society** and is known as the **Bailey House** (circa 1834). To reach it, follow the signs to Iao Valley and you will see the historical landmark sign on the left side of the road. It's open daily from 9 am - 3:30 pm, and a small admission is charged. Here you will find the Bailey Gallery, (once a dining room for the female seminary that was located at this site), with paintings of Edward Bailey done during the 19th century. His work depicts many aspects of Hawaiian life during earlier days. Also on display are early Hawaiian artifacts and memorabilia from the missionary days. The staff is extremely knowledgeable and friendly.

They also have for sale an array of Hawaiian history, art, craft and photographic books, all available at prices LESS than other Maui bookstores. Originally, the Royal Historical Society was established in 1841, but it was not reactivated as the Maui Historical Society until 1956. The museum was dedicated on July 6, 1957, then closed for restoration on December 31, 1973 and reopened on July 13, 1975. Of special interest are the impressive 20 inch thick walls that are made of plaster using a special missionary recipe which included goat hair as one ingredient. The thick walls provided the inhabitants with a natural means of air conditioning.

KAAHUMANU CHURCH

The *Maui Jinsha Mission* is located at 472 Lipo Street, Wailuku. One of the few remaining old Shinto Shrines in the state of Hawai'i, this mission was placed on the National Register of Historic Places in 1978.

The *Halekii and Pihana State Monuments* are among Maui's most interesting early Hawaiian historical sites. Both are of considerable size and situated on the top of a sand dune. These temples were very important structures for the island's early Alii. Their exact age is unknown, although one resource reported that they were used from 1765 to 1895. The Halekii monument is in better condition as a result of some reconstruction done on it in 1958. Follow Waiehu Beach Road across a bridge, then turn left onto Kuhio Place and again on Hea Place. Look for and follow the Hawai'i Visitors Bureau markers. Some say the Pihana Heiau (temple) was built by the menehunes (Hawai'i's little people), others believe by the Maui chiefton, Kahekili.

The *Iao Valley* is a short drive beyond Hale Hoikeike. Within the valley is an awesome volcanic ridge that rises 2,250 feet and is known as the Iao Needle. A little known fact is that this interesting natural phenomena is not a monolithic formation, but rather what you are viewing is the end of a large, thin ridge. A helicopter view will give you an entirely different perspective! Parking facilities are available and there are a number of hiking trails. A recent addition is the *Tropical Gardens of Maui*. This botanical garden features the largest selection of exotic orchids in the Hawaiian islands. For a small fee you can stroll the grounds where they grow, and visit their gift shop filled with tropical flowers and Maui made products. Plants can be shipped home. Snack bar and picnic tables available. Phone 244-3085.

The *Heritage Garden - Kepaniwai Park* is an exhibit of pavilions and gardens which pay tribute to the culture of the Hawaiians, Portuguese, Filipinos, Koreans, Japanese and Chinese. Picnic tables and BBQ's available for public use. Located on Iao Valley Rd. Free admission, open daily. Public swimming pool for children is open daily from 9 am - noon and again from 1 until 4:30. Also a popular site for weddings and other functions, it is available for rent from the Maui Parks Dept. A deposit is required and the Wailuku permit office (1580 Kaahumanu Ave., Wailuku, Maui (808) 243-7389) can provide the necessary forms.

Just outside Wailuku on Hwy. 30, between Wailuku and Maalaea, is Waikapu, home of the *Maui Tropical Plantation*. This visitor exhibit has become one of the top ten most heavily visited in the state of Hawai'i. The fifty acres, which opened in 1984, have been planted with sugar cane, bananas, guava and other island produce. A ten acre visitor center includes exhibits, a marketplace, nursery and restaurant. There is no admission for entry into the marketplace or the restaurant. However, there is an $8 charge for admission for the narrated tram ride around the fields. The tram ride, which departs every half hour, includes several stops for samples of fresh fruit. The plantation is open seven days a week from 9 a.m. until 5 p.m. (244-7643). Several nights a week the Maui Tropical Plantation features a Hawaiian Country Barbecue and dinner show featuring Buddy Fo and his Hawaiian Country Band. For reservations or more information call 242-8605.

*Baldwin Beach* - See the section on BEACHES for Baldwin Beach and others in the area.

*The Maui Zoological and Botanical Gardens* are open 9-4 daily with FREE admission. Go up Kaahumanu to Kanaloa Street and turn by the Wailuku War Memorial Center. The zoo is on the right hand side. This is a zoo Maui style, with a few pygmy donkeys, sheep, goats, monkeys, Galapagos turtles, birds and picnic tables.

*The Kanaha Wildlife Sanctuary* is off Route 32, near the Kahului Airport, and was once a royal fish pond. Now a lookout is located here for those interested in viewing the stilt and other birds which inhabit the area.

A popular Saturday morning stop for local residents and visitors alike is *The Swap Meet* ★(877-3100) held at grounds around the Christ the King Church, next door to the Post Office off Pu'unene Hwy. 35. You'll find us referring to this event for various reasons throughout this guide. For a fifty-cent admission (children free) you will find an assortment of vendors selling local fruits and vegetables, new and used clothing, household items and many of the same souvenir type items found at higher prices in resort gift shops. Here you can pick up some fantastic tropical flowers and for only a few dollars lavishly decorate your condo during your stay. Protea are seasonally available here too for a fraction of the cost elsewhere. This is also the only place to get true spoonmeat coconuts. These are fairly immature coconuts with deliciously mild and soft (to very soft) meat and filled with sweet coconut milk. We stock up on a week's supply at a time. Another "must purchase" are some of the goodies from the Four Sisters Bakery! Free parking. Hours are 8 am - noon.

The *Alexander and Baldwin Sugar Museum* ★ is located at 3957 Hansen Road, in Puuene. Puuene is on Highway 35 between Kahului and Kihei. The tall stacks of the working mill are easily spotted. The museum is housed in a 1902 plantation home that was once occupied by the sugar mill's superintendent. Memorabilia include the strong-box of Samuel Thomas Alexander and an actual working scale

model of a sugar mill. The displays are well done and are very informative. Monday thru Friday 9:30 am- 4 pm. Admission charge: $2 adult visitors, $1 adult Maui residents. Visiting students 6-17 years $1. Maui students 6-17, 50 cents. Children under 6 are free. Call 871-8058.

## WHERE TO SHOP

There are three large shopping centers in Kahului, all on Kaahumanu Avenue. The *Maui Mall* is only a two-minute drive from the airport. It offers Woolworth's and Star Market and Safeway across the street. This Long's Drugs is great for picking up sundry items and souvenier items as well. They also have a variety of small shops and restaurants. The older, local style *Kahului Shopping Center* is lined with Monkey pod trees and is filled with local residents playing cards. Check out Ah Fook's grocery for their bentos. The largest shopping center is *Kaahumanu Center,* recently expanded more than doubling in size and adding a new second level and a food court with a nautical theme. Three major department stores, Penny's, Sears and Liberty House, anchor this mall with the island's largest selection of clothing and gift shops in between. A new addition to the mall is a Disney Store with an entirely new concept and the first of its kind in the nation. A new six-plex cinema operated by Consolidated Theater is a another new feature of the mall.

If you don't have accommodations with a kitchen, you might want to pick up a styrofoam type ice chest at one of these centers and stock it with juices, lunch meats and what not to enjoy in your hotel room and for use on beach trips or drives to Hana and Haleakala. (Check with your hotel regarding small in-room refrigerators.) Kmart opened in 1993 at the intersection of Dairy Road and the Hana Hwy and look for Costco coming soon!

Alexander & Baldwin Properties have plans to bring the mainland phenomenon known as a factory outlet mall to Maui. The proposed 110,000 square foot *Triangle Square Factory Stores* will be located near Kmart in Kahului and feature a plantation theme. Space for a total of 40 stores to be developed in two phases is planned. Completion of phase one is expected by the beginning of 1995.

Wailuku has no large shopping centers, but a cluster of shops down their Main Street makes for interesting strolling.

## ACCOMMODATIONS - WAILUKU

### BANANA BUNGALOW II
310 North Market Street, Wailuku (808) 244-6880, 1-800-8-HOSTEL. Previously the old Happy Valley Inn and Valley Isle Lodge. They describe their accommodations as an international budget hotel and hostel, with clean and comfortable accommodations with a social atmosphere attracting budget travelers, wind-surfers and international backpackers. Rooms are equipped with closet, chair, mirror and night stand. Bathrooms are shared.

The lounge offers a cable TV, refrigerator and pay phone. Laundry facilities on property. Free beach or airport shuttle, complimentary coffee and tea. They do take Visa, Mastercard and American Express.
*Shared room (sleeps 3-4) $15 per person*
*Single room with double bed $31.95*
*Double room with two twins or one queen bed $38.95*

### NORTHSHORE INN
2080 Vineyard St., Wailuku (808) 242-8999. This hotel offers fifty beds that are used as shared accommodations, with each room sleeping four or six persons. There are several private rooms available for one or two persons.

Each room has a ceiling fan and a small refrigerator, some rooms have air-conditioners. The bathrooms are shared by all. A kitchen is available for use by everyone and a TV lounge area offers a VCR. There is a locked storage area for the guests' windsurfing equipment, and a washer and dryer is on the premise. Shuttle trips are provided to and from the airport.

Owner Katie Moore has been on Maui about 10 years and operating this hotel for half of that time. The Inn features an informal, international atmosphere with windsurfers and budget backpackers from around the world staying as guests. Their motto is "Fun is Number 1 - come as guests, leave as friends." The garden in the back of the building is gone, but there are still plenty of great ethnic restaurants up and down the street. Reservations accepted. Weekly discounts.
*Shared rooms (sleep 4-6) $14.95 per night, single $29.95, double $39.95*

## ACCOMMODATIONS - KAHULUI

One advantage to choosing this area for headquarters is its proximity to the Kahului Airport and its somewhat central location to all other parts of the island. The motels are clustered together on the Kahului Harbor.

### MAUI PALMS    (Hotel)
(808-877-0051) Agent: Hawaiian Pacific 1-800-367-5004. Also located on Kaahumanu Avenue. This property is a 103 unit low-rise hotel with Polynesian decor. Restaurant on premises. They offer free airport pickup.
*Room rates (3) $67-80/57-70*

151

**MAUI BEACH HOTEL     (Hotel)**
(808-877-0051) 170 Kaahumanu Avenue, Kahului, Maui, HI 96732. Agent:
Hawaiian Pacific 1-800-367-5004. Renovated in 1991, this two story, 152 room
hotel is located oceanfront on Kahului Bay. All rooms have air-conditioning, TV,
some balconies. Complimentary airport shuttle service.
*Room rates (3-4) $85-120/$75-110*

**MAUI SEASIDE     (Hotel)**
1-800-367-7000 U.S., 1-800-654-7020 Canada, FAX (808) 922-0052. The older
Maui Hukilau has been combined with the much newer Maui Seaside to form one
property called the Maui Seaside. You might want to inquire when booking here
about which of the buildings you will be in. The management, Sand and Seaside
Hotels, tell us that all of their properties have been recently renovated and refurbished like new. Vi's Restaurant is right next door. Add $10-15 per day for car.
*Room rates (2) $85-110/$75-100. Extra person $12. Children 17 and under free.*

# UPCOUNTRY and onward to HALEAKALA

## INTRODUCTION

The Western slopes of Haleakala are generally known as Upcountry and consist
of several communities including Makawao and Pukalani. The higher altitude,
cooler temperatures and increased rainfall make it an ideal location for produce
farming. A few fireplace chimneys can be spotted in this region where the nights
can get rather chilly. Accommodations are limited to two small lodges in Kula and
a few cabins which are available with the park service for overnight use while
hiking in the Haleakala Wilderness Area. (It is actually not a crater, rather an
erosional valley.) *Refer to the Maui map at the beginning of the guidebook for the
highways and roads discussed in this section.*

## WHAT TO DO AND SEE

Enroute to Upcountry is Pukalani, meaning "opening to the sky," and it is the last
stop for gas on the way to Haleakala. There are also several places to enjoy a
hearty meal. (See RESTAURANTS.)

*Haleakala* means "house of the sun" and is claimed to be the largest dormant
volcano in the world. The volcano is truly awesome and it is easy to see why the
old Hawaiians considered it sacred and the center of the earth's spiritual power.
There is a $4 per car charge for admission to the park; U.S. residents age 62 and
older enter free.

The most direct route is to follow Hwy. 37 from Kahului then left onto Hwy. 377
above Pukalani and then left again onto Hwy. 378 for the last 10 miles. While
only about 40 miles from Kahului, the last part of the trip is very slow. There are
numerous switchbacks and bicycle tours doing the 38-mile downhill coast. Two
hours should be allowed to reach the summit.

Sunrise at the summit is a popular and memorable experience, but plan your arrival accordingly. Many visitors have missed this spectacular event by only minutes. The Maui News, the local daily, prints sunrise and sunset times. The park offers a recording of general weather information and viewing conditions which can be reached by calling 572-7749. The park headquarters number is 572-9306.

Be sure you have packed a sweater as the summit temperature can be 30 degrees cooler than the coast and snow is a winter possibility. Mid-morning from May to October generally offers the clearest viewing. However, fog can cause very limited visibility and a call may save you a trip.

At the park headquarters, you can obtain hiking and camping information and permits. Day-hike permits are not required. The first stop is Park Headquarters. Here you can see the rare silversword which takes up to 20 years to mature, then blooms once in July or August, only to wither and die in the fall. Keep your eye out for the many nene geese which inhabit the volcano.

Exhibits on Haleakala history and geology are in the Haleakala Visitors Center located at an elevation of 9,745 feet. It is open daily from sunrise - 3 pm (hours may vary). A short distance by road will bring you to the Summit Building located on the volcano rim. This glassed-in vantage point (the Puu Ulaula outlook) is the best for sunrise and is the highest point on Maui.

The rangers give morning talks here at 9:30, 10:30 and 11:30. The view, on a good day, is nothing short of awesome. The inside of the volcano is seven miles long, two miles wide, and 3,000 feet deep. A closer look is available by foot or horseback (see RECREATION AND TOURS - Horseback riding). A 2 1/2 hour hike down Sliding Sands Trail into the Haleakala Volcano is offered by the park service regularly. Check bulletin boards for schedules. They depart from the House of the Sun Visitor Center. A hike featuring native Hawaiian birds and plants is scheduled regularly. Again, check with the ranger headquarters 572-9306 to verify trips, dates and times.

The park service maintains 30 miles of well-marked trails, three cabins and two campgrounds. All are accessible only by trail. The three cabins are Holua, Kapalaoa and Paliku, all located within the Haleakala Wilderness Area. The closest cabin is about seven miles away from the observatory. Arrangements for these cabins need to be made 90 days in advance and selection is made 60 days prior to the dates requested by a lottery-type drawing. For more information, write: Superintendent, Haleakala National Park, PO Box 369, Makawao, Maui, HI 96768. Rates are currently being revised, but are a minimal charge per person. A deposit is required to hold reservations. Maximum cabin occupancy is 12. For current rates call (808) 572-9306.

Short walks might include the three-fourth mile Halemauu Trail to the volcano rim, one-tenth mile to Leleiwi Overlook, or two-tenth mile on the White Hill Trail to the top of White Hill. Caution: the thin air and steep inclines may be especially tiring. (See RECREATION AND TOURS - Hiking.)

*Haleakala Observatories* can be seen beyond the visitor center, but it is not open to the public. It houses a solar and lunar observatory operated by the University of Hawaii, television relay stations, and a Department of Defense satellite station.

To get a better visual idea of Haleakala, see back of the book for ordering information on the full-color pictorial book on Haleakala.

**If time allows, there is more of Upcountry to be seen!**

The Kula area offers rich volcanic soil and commercial farmers harvest a variety of fruits and vegetables. Grapes, apples, pineapples, lettuce, artichokes, tomatoes and, of course, Maui onions are only a few. It can be reached by retracking Hwy. 378 to the Upper Kula Road where you turn left. The protea, a recent floral immigrant from South Africa, has created a profitable business.

*The Kula Botanical Gardens* (878-1715) charges an admission of $3 for adults, and children 50 cents, open 9 am - 4 pm.

The *Maui Enchanting Gardens*, on Hwy. 37 in Kula, charges $3.50 for adults, $1.50 for children for a self guided botanical tour.

The *Sunrise Protea Farm* (878-2119) in Kula has a small, but diverse, variety of protea growing adjacent to their market and flower stand for shipment home. Dried assortments begin at about $25. Picnic tables available and no charge for just looking!

Be sure and stop in Keoke at *Grandma's Coffee House*. This wonderfully cozy, two year old restaurant is the place for some freshly made, Maui grown coffee, hot out of the oven cinnamon rolls or a light lunch. See Upcountry restaurants for more information.

TEDESCHI WINERY

*Poli Poli State Park* is high on the slopes of Haleakala, above Kula at an elevation of 6,200 feet. Continue on Hwy. 377 past Kula and turn left on Waipoli Rd. If you end up on Hwy. 37, you've gone too far. The sign indicating Poli Poli is currently missing, so you could also look for a sign indicating someone's home, it reads WALKER. It's another 10 miles to the park over a road which deteriorates to deep ruts and is often muddy. A 4-wheel drive is really a necessity for this road during wet weather. The park offers miles of trails, a picnic area, restrooms, running water, a small redwood forest and great views. A cabin, which sleeps up to 10, is available through the Division of Parks, PO Box 537, Makawao, Maui, HI 96768. For more information see the "Hiking" section in the RECREATION AND TOURS chapter.

Approximately 9 miles past the Kula Botanical Gardens on Hwy. 37 is the Ulupalakua Ranch. *The Tedeschi Vineyards* (878-6058), part of the 30,000 acre ranch, made its debut in 1974. The tasting room is located at the Ranch in the old jail and provides samples of their pineapple, champagne and red table wines. Free daily guided tours are offered between 10 am and 5 pm. The tour begins at the Tasting Room, then continues to view the presses used to separate the juice from the grapes, the large fermenting tanks, and the corking and the labelling rooms.

If you continue on past the ranch on Hwy. 37 it's another very long 35 miles to Hana with nothing but beautiful scenery. Don't let the distance fool you. It is a good 3-hour trip (each way), at least, over some fairly rough sections of road, which are not approved for standard rental cars. During recent years this road has been closed often to through traffic due to severe washouts. Check with the county to see if it is currently passable.

If you're not continuing on, we suggest you turn around and head back to Pukalani and Makawao. Unfortunately, the Ulupalakua Road down to Wailea has been closed due to a dispute between the Ranch and the county. It is hoped that this or some other access between Upcountry and the Kihei/Wailea area will soon be developed.

On the way down you can go by way of Makawao, the colorful "cowboy" town, and then on to Paia or Halemaile. Both have several good restaurants. (See RESTAURANTS - Upcountry).

## WHERE TO SHOP

The town of Makawao offers a western flavor with a scattering of shops down its main street, a few restaurants and numerous grocery stores. We recommend the *Komoda Store* for its popular bakery, but get there early! The Pukalani Shopping Center has a grocery store, and some small shops and restaurants. A number of good restaurants will allow for a diverse selection of dining options.

*Viewpoints Gallery*, 3620 Baldwin (572-5979) is a fine co-operative gallery featuring local artists and a clustering of interesting gift shops -- a must see in Makawao.

## WHAT TO SEE AND DO

The *Hui Noeau Visual Arts Center* may at first seem a little out of place, located at 2841 Baldwin Avenue, down the road from Makawao. However, there could not be a more beautiful and tranquil setting than at this estate, called Kaluanui, which was built in 1917 by famous Honolulu architect C.W. Dickey for Harry and Ethel Baldwin. The house was occupied until the mid-1950's and in 1976 Colin Cameron (grandson of Ethel Baldwin) granted Hui Noeau the use of Kaluanui as a Visual Arts Center.

Near the entrance to the nine acre estate are the remains of one of Maui's earliest sugar mills. It utilized mule power and was the first Hawaiian sugar mill to use a centrifuge to separate sugar crystals. What were once stables and tack rooms are now ceramic studios.

A gift shop is open year round and the first part of December they have a special Christmas boutique. Daily 9 am - 1 pm. 572-6560. Fourth of July weekend is wild and wonderful in Makawao. Festivities include a morning parade through town and several days of rodeo events. Check the local paper for details.

## ACCOMMODATIONS - UPCOUNTRY

Accommodations are limited in Upcountry. Five and one-half miles past Pukalani is the Kula Lodge. See listings at beginning of Accommodations section for information on Upcountry bed & breakfast facilities.

### KULA LODGE
RR 1, Box 475, Kula, Maui, HI 96790 (808-878-1535) 1-800-233-1535. FAX (808) 878-2518. Five rustic chalet-like cabins located at the 3200 foot elevation. Restaurant on the property. Full advance deposit required. $25 cancellation fee.
*Chalet 1 & 2 $150 (queen bed, fireplace, lanai, stairs to loft with 2 twin beds)*
*Chalet 3 & 4 & 5 $120 (queen bed, ladder to loft with two futons)*
*Chalet 5 $100 (single story with double bed and studio couch)*
*An additional amount of $30 will be charged for more than two guests*

MAKAWAO

### KULA SANDALWOODS
There is supposed to be a reopening of the restaurant and the cabins at the old Silversword. Judging by the response we received on inquiry, and their uncooperative and uninterested attitude in supplying us with information, their outlook is bleak. They may or may not be operating their restaurant. They requested not to be included rather than sending us any menus or information.

# HANA

## INTRODUCTION

If you do not plan an extended stay in Hana, you might consider at least an overnight stop at one of the facilities to break up the long drive to this isolated east coast of Maui. (Insider's secret! Hana can best be enjoyed before and after the throngs of visitors who daily make this drive, so plan a stay in Hana of several days or at least overnight!)

Here is a different Maui from the sunny, dry resort areas on the leeward coast. The windward coast here is turbulent with magnificent coastal views, rain forests, and mountain waterfalls creating wonderful pools for swimming. However, DO NOT drink the water from these streams and falls. The water has a high bacteria count caused from the pigs which live in the jungle-like forests above. The beaches along the Hana Hwy. are unsafe for swimming.

The trip to Hana by car from Kahului will take at least three hours, one way, and plan on plenty of time to make some stops, enjoy these waterfalls up close and experience this unique coastline.

Accommodations vary from hotel/condo to campgrounds and homes at a variety of price ranges. The 7,000 acre Hotel Hana Ranch has achieved their goal of creating an "elegant ranch atmosphere." Several moderately priced condominiums and inexpensive cottages are also available.

Waianapanapa State Park, just outside Hana, has camping facilities and cabins. (See the Camping section for more information.) Ohe'o also has a tent camping area; bring your own drinking water.

Hana offers a quiet retreat and an atmosphere of peace (seemingly undisturbed by the constant flow of tourist cars and vans) that has lured many a prominent personality to these quiet shores. Restaurant choices are extremely limited. The diversity between eating at Tutu's at Hana Bay and the fine dining of the Hotel Hana Maui is quite striking!

Shopping is restricted to the Hasegawa General Store, the Hana Ranch Store or a few shops at the Hana Hotel. The original Hasegawa store burned down a few years back, and they reopened in another location. It is almost as wonderful and cluttered as the old version.

## WHAT TO SEE AND DO

### PAIA - ALONG THE ROAD TO HANA

If you'd like a self-guided, yet narrated tour, consider renting one of the "Best of Maui" cassette tours. The $25 charge includes a tape player, Hana Highway guidebook, blossoms of Hawai'i guide book, tropical flower identification card, detailed route map and sometimes a special premium offer of a free T-shirt! The tape allows you to drive at your own pace while listening to information on the legends and history of the islands. You pick up the tape and player on Dairy Road just off Puunene Ave. For information or reservations phone 871-1555.

A little beyond Wailuku, and along the highway which leads to Hana, is the small town of Paia. The name Paia translated means "noisy," however, the origin of this name is unclear. This quaint town is reminiscent of the early sugar cane era when Henry Baldwin located his first sugar plantation in this area. The wooden buildings are now filled with antiques, art and other gift shops to attract the passing tourist. (See RESTAURANTS for more information.)

The advent of windsurfing has caused a rebirth in this small charming town and a number of new restaurants have recently appeared over the last few years with more to come.

The *Maui Crafts Guild*, a group of local artisans own and operate this store. Pottery, koa furniture, weaving, wall sculptures, wood serving pieces, prints and basketry are featured: very lovely, but expensive, hand-crafted items. *Things from the Past* is housed in a former automotive garage and is easy to spot on the Hana Hwy. with its friendly Hawaiian Santa out front. It provides a conglomeration of items that will be of interest to just about anyone.

Accommodations in Paia are a little scarce. There may be some bed & breakfast options and there has been talk of a lodging in the town of Paia, but that is still in the discussion stages.

*KUAU COVE RENTALS* - 799 Poho Place, Paia, Maui, HI 96779. (808) 579-9400. FAX (808) 579-8594. Color TV, BBQ, Washer/dryer, VCR and stereo. 20% discount at Mama's Fish House. *1 BR $60, 2 BR $125*

### HANA

Anyone who endures the three-hour (at least) drive to Hana deserves to sport the "I survived the Road to Hana" T-shirts which are sold locally. While it may be true that it is easy to fall in love with Hana, getting there is quite a different story. The drive to Hana is not for everyone, although many guide books claim otherwise. It is not for people who are prone to motion sickness, those who don't like a lot of scenery, those who are in a hurry to get somewhere or those who don't love long drives. However, it is a trip filled with waterfalls and lush tropical jungles (which flourish in the 340-inch average annual rainfall). Maps are deceiving. It appears you could make the 53-mile journey much faster than three hours but there are 617 (usually hairpin) curves and 56 miniature bridges along this narrow road. And believe it or not, each of these bridges has its own Hawaiian name! Even with recent repaving, most cars travel in the middle of the road, making each turn a possibly exciting experience, especially at night.

The Hana Hwy. was originally built in 1927 with pick and shovel, which may account for its narrowness, to provide a link between Hana and Kahului. There can also be delays on the road up to two hours if the road is being worked on. In days gone by when heavy rains caused washouts, it is said that people would literally climb the mud barricades and swap cars, then resume their journey. Despite all this, 300-500 people traverse this road daily, and it is the supply route for all deliveries to Hana and the small settlements along the way.

Now, if we haven't dissuaded you and you still want to see spectacular undeveloped scenery, plan to spend the whole day (or even better, stop overnight) in Hana. If you are driving, be sure to leave as early in the morning as possible. You don't want to be making a return trip on this road in the dark. Be sure to get gas; the last stations before Hana are in Kahului or Paia. With the exception of an occasional fruit stand, there is no place to eat and only limited stops for drinking water. Be sure you pack your own food and drink. Picnic's in Paia is a popular stop for a picnic lunch. For something a little more unusual try packing along some local style foods or a bento (box lunch). Takimaya's grocery story on Lower Market St. has an unbelievable assortment of cooked, pre-packaged food made fresh daily, including fried calamari, tako poki (raw octopus), kalbi ribs, baked yams, and much, much more. Packing some rain gear and a warm sweater or sweatshirt is a precaution against the sometimes cooler weather and rain showers. Don't forget your camera, but remember not to leave it in your car unattended.

We also might recommend that if you drive, select a car with an automatic transmission (or else be prepared for constant shifting). Another choice is to try one of the small van tours which go to Hana and leave the driving to them. Check to see whether the tours are operating their vans around the other side of the island. This will depend on the road conditions. It is also a road not recommended for rental cars. The scenery on this dry side is strikingly different from the northern coast rain forests. Good tour guides will also be able to point out the sights of interest along the way that are easy to miss! The only other alternative is to by-pass the Hana Highway by flying into Hana's small airport.

There are two good resources you might also consider taking along on your drive. Stop at the small booth on Dairy Road, across from the Shell service station. For about $25 you can rent a cassette player and narrated tape to follow along on your trip. *Maui's Hana Highway*, by Angela Kay Kepler, runs about $5.95 at local bookstores and it's eighty information-filled pages include plenty of full color photos of the area -- especially good for identifying the flora and fauna.

*Ho'okipa*, about two miles past Paia, is thought by some to offer the world's best windsurfing. There won't be much activity here in the morning, but if you are heading back past here in mid to late afternoon when the winds pick up, you are sure to see numerous windsurfers challenging wind and wave. These waves are enough to challenge the most experienced surfers and are not for the novice except as a spectator sport. You'll note that on the left are the windsurfers while the waves on the right are enjoyed by the surfers! A number of covered pavilions offer shaded viewing and the beach, while not recommended for swimming, does have some tidepools (of varying size depending on the tidal conditions) for children to enjoy a refreshing splash. This beach is also a popular fishing area for local residents and you may see some folks along the banks casting in their lines.

159

The next area you will pass through is **Haiku**, which translated means "abrupt break." It is not unusual to experience some overcast, rainy weather here. During 1989 this area had more rainy days than not! Enjoy the smooth wider highway here; the Hana Highway awaits you just ahead!

Two miles from the point where Hana Highway intersects Route 400 look for a small roadside trail marker by the Hoolawa Bridge. This area, known as **Twin Falls**, offers a pleasant spot for swimming. The first pool has two waterfalls, but by hiking a little farther, two more pools of crystal clear water created by waterfalls can be easily reached. Remember, don't drink the stream water! Mosquitos can be prolific so pack bug spray.

There are no safe beaches along this route for swimming, so for a cool dip, take advantage of one of the fresh water swimming holes provided.

*Waikamoi Ridge* - This picnic area and nature trail is about 1/2 mile past roadside marker #9 and has no restrooms or drinking water. This area is noted for its stands of majestic bamboo, and you are sure to see wild ginger and huge ferns.

*Puohkamoa Falls* - Located near roadside Marker #11 is an area to pull off the road with parking only for a couple of cars. This small picnic area offers one covered (in the event of one of the frequent windward coast rain showers) table. A short tunnel trail through lush foliage leads to a swimming hole beneath the waterfall.

*Kaumahina State Park* - Just past roadside marker #12 you'll find this lovely park. This area overlooks the spectacular Honomanu Gulch, the rugged Maui coastline and in the distance a view of the Ke'anae Peninsula. Believe it or not this is about the half-way point to Hana, and a good opportunity to make use of the toilet facilities.

*The YMCA's Camp Ke'anae* - Offers overnight accommodations for men and women (housed separately). The rate is $8 a night. Arrival is requested between 4 pm and 6 pm. Bring your own food and sleeping bag. Phone (808) 248-8355. Reservations and information number is (808) 242-9007.

Just past Camp Ke'anae is the *Ke'anae Arboretum*. This free botanical garden is managed by the Department of Land and Natural Resources and is home to a myriad of tropical plants. A number of the plants have been labeled for your assistance in identification.

The *Ke'anae Peninsula* was formed by a massive outpouring centuries ago from Haleakala. Today it is an agricultural area with taro the principal crop. The taro root is cooked and mashed and the result is a bland, pinkish brown paste called poi. Poi was a staple in the diets of early Hawaiians and is still a popular local food product which can be sampled at luaus or purchased at local groceries. Alone, the taste has been described as resembling wallpaper paste, (if you've ever tried wallpaper paste) but it is meant to be eaten with other foods, such askalua pig. It is a taste that sometimes needs time to acquire. We understand island grandmothers sending fresh poi to the mainland for their young grandchildren.

It is said to be extremely healthy, full of minerals and well tolerated by young stomachs. You'll see the fields filled with water and taro in varying stages of development. The Ke'anae Congregational Church, or *The Miracle Church*, in Wailua is a historical landmark with a fascinating history. In the mid-1800's the community was lacking in building material for their church. Quite suddenly a huge storm hit and, by some miracle, deposited a load of coral onto the beach. The crushed coral church walls are still standing today.

*The Shell Shop* - Turn left at the Coral Miracle Church sign. The shop is located across the street from the church. Since 1974 local divers have been creating original shell jewelry from the limpet shell. The jewelry is sold exclusively at this location.

*Wailua Lookout* - Located just past Wailua on the roadside, look carefully for a turnoff. Park and follow the tunnel made by the hau plants, up the steps to the Lookout. The trek up is worth the excellent view.

The *waterfalls* are spectacular along the road, but consider what they are like from the air! We had no idea of the vastness of this tropical forest until we experienced it from a bird's eye view. Almost every waterfall and pool are preceded by another waterfall and pool above it, and above it there are yet others. The slice of this green wonderland seen from the winding Hana highway is just a small piece of the rugged wilderness above.

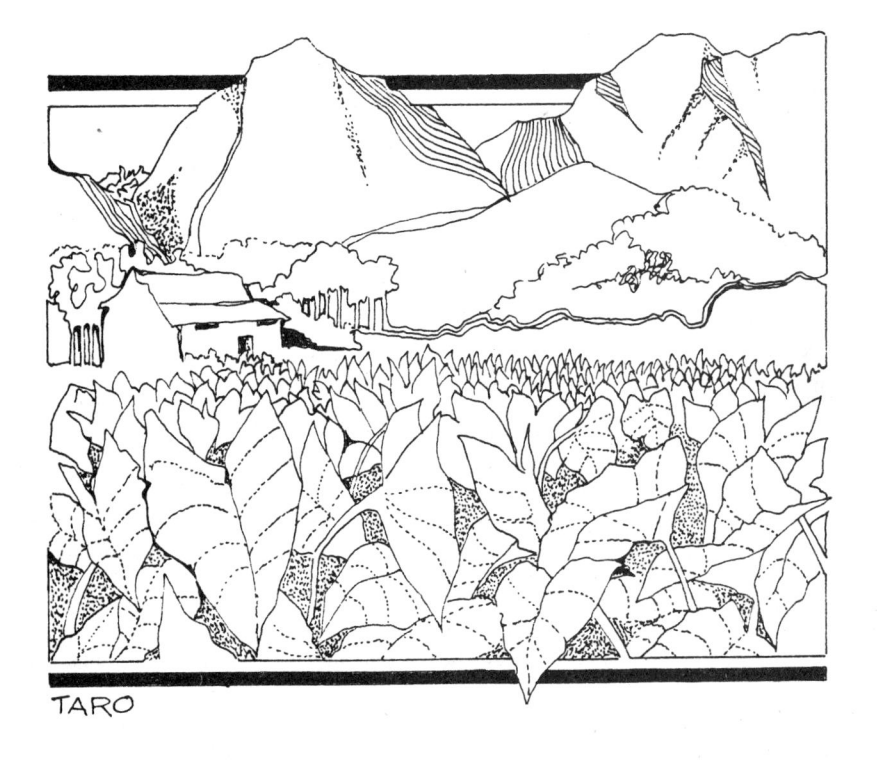

TARO

***Puaa Kaa State Park*** - Fourteen miles before Hana, this park has two waterfalls and pools that are roadside. This picture-perfect little park is a favorite stop for a picnic lunch. The waterfalls and large pool have combined with this lush tropical locale to make you feel sure a menehune must be lurking nearby. Restrooms and drinking water are available here too. Keep your eye out for mongoose. They have been "trained" by some of the van tour guides to make an appearance for a handout at some of these wayside stations. The best place to get a look at them is usually near the garbage cans. Toss a little snack and see if anyone is home.

With a little effort a sharp observer can spot the open ditches and dams along the roadside. These are the ***Spreckles Ditches*** built over 100 years ago to supply water for the young sugar cane industry. These ditches continue to provide the island with an important part of its supply of water.

***Waianapanapa*** (pronounced WHY-A-NAHPA-NAHPA) ***State Park*** is four miles before Hana and covers an area of 120 acres. Translated it is said to mean "glistening water." This area offers a number of historical sites, ancient heiaus (temples) and early cemeteries. You can spot one of the many stone walls used by the early Hawaiians for property boundaries, animal enclosures and also as home foundations. It is noted for its unusual black sand beach made of small smooth volcanic pebbles. The ocean here is not safe for swimming, but there is plenty of exploring! Don some mosquito repellent, tennis shoes are a good idea, and follow the well marked trails to the Waianapanapa Caves. The trail is lined with thick vines, a signal left by the early Hawaiians that this area was kapu (off limits). The huge lava tubes have created pools of cold, clear water. An ancient cave legend tells of a beautiful Hawaiian princess named Popoalaea who fled from Kakae, her cruel husband. She hid in the caves, but was discovered and killed. At certain times of the year the waters turn red. Some say it is a reminder of the beautiful slain princess, while others explain that it is the infestation of thousands of tiny red shrimp. Another three mile trail along the coast follows part of the ancient King's Hwy. which, in the days of the early Hawaiians, may have extended around the entire island. Several ancient heiaus can be found in this area. Another portion of the ancient highway can be found on the southern coastline past La Perouse Bay. Camping is allowed and there are rustic cabins available for rent (See ACCOMMODATIONS - "Hana," which follows).

***The Helani Gardens*** (248-8274) is a self-guided botanical tour by foot or car through some very dense vegetation. Created by Howard Cooper, it opened in 1970 after thirty years of development. The lower area consists of five acres with manicured grounds and a tropical pool filled with jewel-colored koi. The upper sixty five acres are a maze of one-lane dirt roads through an abundant jungle of amazing and enormous flowering trees and shrubs. Wild plants from around the world are raised here and you'll see plenty of gigantic versions of your own house and garden plants from back home. Keep a sharp eye out for the large treehouse built by the Cooper grandchildren. This is really quite an enjoyable adventure, and one usually overlooked by those in a hurry to or from Hana and Ohe'o. Take your time and explore this unusual attraction. Admission $2 for adults, $1 children 6-16. Located about one mile before Hana. Picnic areas and restrooms available.

The last curve of the road will put you at **Hana's Gardenland**. There is no charge to browse through their flower displays and they thoughtfully provide picnic tables and a restroom. The plants sold here include the rare and beautiful and are available for shipping anywhere.

A turn onto 'Ula'ino Road and another 1 1/2 miles over a rugged road will put you at the entrance to **Kahanua Gardens**. This is the site of the Pi'ilanihale Heiau, the largest ancient temple platform in the islands. Admission donation is $5, hours of operation are currently Tuesday to Saturday 10 am - 2 pm.

Now, back in the car for a drive into downtown Hana, but don't blink, or you might miss it. **Hana Cultural Center** (248-8622) opened in August of 1983. It contains a collection of relics of Hana's past in the old courthouse building and a small new museum. Open Monday through Sunday 10 am - 4 pm. Located near Hana Bay, watch for signs.

**Hana Bay** has been the site of many historical events. It was a retreat for Hawaiian royalty as well as an important military point from which Maui warriors attacked the island of Hawaii, and then were in turn attacked. This is also the birthplace of Ka'ahumanu (1768), Kamehameha's favorite wife. (See BEACHES for more information.)

The climate on this end of Maui is cooler and wetter, creating an ideal environment for agricultural development. The Ka'eleku Sugar Company established itself in Hana in 1860. Cattle raising, also a prominent industry during the 20th century, continues today. You can still view the paniolos (Hawaiian cowboys) at work at nearby Hana Ranch. There are 3,200 head of cattle which graze on 3,300 acres of land. Every three days the cattle are moved to fresh pastures. Our family was thrilled when a paniolo flagged us to stop on the road outside Hana, while a herd of cattle surrounded our car enroute to fresher pastures.

HELANI GARDENS

Hana has little to offer in the way of shopping. However, the **Hasegawa General Store** offers a little bit of everything. It has been operated since 1910, meeting the needs of visitors and local residents alike. Several years ago the original structure was burned down, but they reopened in the old Hana Theatre location. Hours are Monday thru Saturday 8 am - 5:30 pm and Sunday 9 am - 5:30 pm. This store has even been immortalized in song. You may even run into one of the celebrities who come to the area for vacation. The Hana Ranch Store is open daily and the Hana Resort has a gift shop and boutique. The oldest building in town, built in 1830, currently houses the laundry facility for the Hana Hotel.

## SOME LOCAL HANA INFORMATION:

**St. Mary's Church** (248-8030) Sat. Mass 6 pm, Sun. 9 am
**Wananalua Protestant Church** (248-8040) Built in 1838. Services 10 am Sundays
**Hana Ranch Store** (248-8261) 7:00 am-7 pm daily
**Hasegawa General Store** (248-8231) 8 am-5:30 pm, Mon.-Sat., Sun. 9 am-3:30
**Hana Medical Center** (248-8294) Emergencies 24 hours. Mon.-Fri. 8 am-noon
        and 2 pm-5 pm. Sat. 8 am-noon. Closed Sunday.
**Bank of Hawaii** (248-8015) Mon.-Thur. 3-4:30 pm and Fri. 3-6 pm
**Library** (248-7714) Tues.-Fri. 8-5 pm, Mon. 8-8 pm
**Post Office** (248-8258) 8 am-4:30 pm, Mon.-Fri.

On **Lyon's Hill** stands a 30 foot tall lava-rock cross in memory of Paul Fagan. It was built by two Japanese brothers from Kahului in 1960. Although the access road is chained, the front desk of the Hotel Hana will provide a key. The short trip to the top will reward the visitor with a spectacular panoramic view of Hana Bay and the open pasture land of the Hana Ranch. About a quarter of a mile up toward the cross you'll find the beginning of a jogging/walking trail that follows the track of the old narrow-gauge railroad once used on the plantation. The path runs for about 2 1/2 miles.

**Kaihalulu Beach** (Red Sand Beach) is located in a small cove on the other side of Kauiki Hill from Hana Bay and is accessible by a narrow, crumbly trail more suited to mountain goats than people. The trail descends into a lovely cove bordered by high cliffs and is almost enclosed by a natural lava barrier seaward. For more details see BEACHES.

**Hamoa Beach** - This gorgeous beach has been very attractively landscaped and developed by the Hotel Hana Maui in a way that adds to the surrounding lushness. The long sandy beach is in a very tropical setting and surrounded by a low sea cliff. As you leave Hana toward Ohe'o Gulch look for the sign 1½ miles past the Hasegawa store that says "Koki Park - Hamoa Beach - Hamoa Village." Follow the road, you can't miss it.

You quickly pass fields of grazing world-famous Maui beef and re-enter the tropical jungle once more. Numerous waterfalls cascade along the roadside and after ten curvy, bumpy miles on a very narrow two-lane road, and a 45-60 minute drive, you arrive at one of the reasons for this trip, the Kipahulu Valley and **Haleakala National Park**. The Kipahulu Ranger Station offers cultural demonstrations, talks, and guided walks. For more information call 248-7375.

Looking for the Seven Sacred Pools? They don't exist! The National Park Service notes that the term "Seven Sacred Pools" has been misused for this area for almost 50 years. The name was first promoted in 1946 by the social director of a newly developed hotel in Hana to attract visitors to the area. At 'Ohe'o Stream there are actually more than 24 large and many small pools along the 1 mile length of the gulch, so even the term "Seven Pools" is misleading and inaccurate. One may properly refer to the area as Kipahulu or Haleakala National Park - Kipahulu. 'Ohe'o is simply the name of the area where the Pipiwai Stream enters the ocean. When the Kipahulu District was acquired by Haleakala National Park in 1969, park rangers interviewed native Hawaiians born and raised in the area to document its history. Without exception all local residents claimed that none of the pools was ever considered sacred. In public hearings in 1974 and 1975, local people strongly expressed that original Hawaiian names be used in place of romantic English terms. Highway signs were changed in 1977 and in 1982 the incorrect labels were removed by the U.S. Geological Survey from its maps.

Waterfalls cascade beneath the narrow bridge (a great place for a photo) flowing over the blue-grey lava to create these lovely lower pools. The pools you see below the bridge are just a few of the more than 20 that have been formed as the water of this stream rushes to the ocean. When not in flood stage, the pools are safe for swimming so pack your suit, but no diving is allowed. Swimming off the black sand beach is very dangerous and many drownings and near-drownings have occurred here.

The best time to enjoy the park may be in late afternoon, when the day visitors have returned to their cars for the drive home. (This is another good reason to make Hana an overnight trip.) The bluff above the beach offers a magnificent view of the ocean and cliffs, so have your camera ready.

This area is of historical significance and signs warn visitors not to remove any rocks. A pleasant hike will take you to the upper falls. The falls at **Makahiku** is 184 feet high and is a fairly easy half mile hike that passes through a forest. **Waimoku Falls** is another mile and a half. Three to four hours should be allowed for this hike which traverses the stream and through a bamboo forest. Heavy rains far above in the mountains can result in flash floods. Avoid swimming in these upper streams or crossing the stream in high water. Check with the park rangers who keep advised as to possible flooding conditions. Also check with the park service (248-7375) to see when the free ranger-guided hikes are available. Cultural demonstrations are given daily; check the bulletin boards for schedules.

Camping at Kipahulu is available at no charge. Be advised there is no drinking water. Bottled water may be available for a minimal cost at the ranger station, but we suggest you arrive with your own supply.

One interesting fact about Kipahulu is that many of the marine animals have evolved from saltwater origins. Others continue to make the transition between the ocean's salty environment and the fresh water of the Palikea stream. One of the most unusual is the rare oopu which breeds in the upper stream, migrates to the ocean for its youth and then returns to the stream to mature. After a glimpse of the many waterfalls, this appears to be a most remarkable feat. The ingenious oopu actually climb the falls by using its lower front fins as a suction cup to hold onto the steep rock walls which form the falls. Using its tail to propel itself, the oopu travels slowly upstream.

The upper **Kipahulu Valley** is a sight visitors will never see. Under the jurisdiction of the park service, it is one of the last fragments of the native rain forests. The native plants in the islands have been destroyed by the more aggressive plants brought by the early Hawaiians and visitors in the centuries which followed. Some rare species, such as the green silversword, grow only in this restricted area.

Two miles further on is the **Charles Lindbergh grave**, located in the small cemetery of the 1850 **Kipahulu Hawaiian Church**. He chose this site only a year prior to his death in 1974, after living in the area for a number of years. However, he never envisioned the huge numbers of visitors that would come to Hana to enjoy the scenery and visit his gravesite. Please respect the sanctity of this area.

It is sometimes possible to travel the back road from Hana thru Upcountry and back to Kahului. This is Maui's desert region and it is a vivid contrast to the lush windward environs. While very parched, this route presents a hazard which can take visitors unaware. Flash floods in the mountains above, which are most likely November to March, can send walls of water down the mountain, quickly washing out a bridge or overflowing the road. The road is sometimes closed for months due to serious washouts. Check with the county to see the current status of this route. Car rental agencies post warnings that travel is not advised on this route for standard cars and that renters are responsible for all damage.

If this route is passable consider stopping at **The Kaupo General Store**. It has been operating for years and is open based upon the whim of the management. Take note of the many rock walls. This area supported a large native Hawaiian population and these walls served as boundaries as well as retaining walls for livestock, primarily pigs. The walls are centuries old and unfortunately have suffered from visitor vandalism and destruction by the range cattle. Cattle are now the principle area residents.

COMMON 'AMAKIHI

As you enter Upcountry and civilization once more, look for the *Tedeschi Winery*. Located at the Ulupalakua Ranch it offers tasting daily from 9 am-4 pm. They began in 1974 and produced only a pineapple wine until 1983 when they harvested their first grapes. They also offer a champagne and a red table wine. On the way back down you might stop at *The Maui Botanical Gardens* which feature a close up look at the unusual protea flowers. Admission is charged. (See Upcountry for more information.)

## ACCOMMODATIONS - HANA

| | |
|---|---|
| Aloha Cottages | Waianapanapa State Park |
| Hana Alii Holidays | |
| Hana Bay Vacation Rentals | YMCA Camp Ke'anae |
| Hana Plantation Houses | |
| Sheraton Hotel Hana Maui | Heavenly Hana Inn |

### ALOHA COTTAGES
PO Box 205, Hana, Maui, HI 96713 (808-248-8420). Six simple, clean two bedroom cottages with electric kitchens and microwaves. (Some units with oceanview). TVs in 3 units only. Daily maid service provided. No telephones, phone booths nearby. All balance must be paid on arrival by cash or traveler's cheques. NO CREDIT CARDS. $60-80 double per night. $10-$20 per night for each additional person.

### HANA ALII HOLIDAYS VACATION RENTALS ★
PO Box 536, Hana, Maui, HI, (800) 548-0478 or (808) 248-7742. They have a number of home and condominium rentals. The Hana Kai Condominiums are oceanfront one bedroom and studio units overlooking Hana Bay, kitchens, daily maid service. Rates start at $60 per night. Deluxe one bedroom ocean front condo sleeps 4 $185. $10 for late check in - after 5 pm.

Also available are several cottages, hillside homes and oceanfront locations. The Popolana Liilii is a tropical one bedroom cottage, with pullout queen size sofa in the living room. Washer/dryer. $95. Ainhau is a custom built home in the Waikaloa district of Hana with views of the Bay and Haleakala. This solar-run cottage has a fully equipped kitchen and satellite TV. $150. The Hamoa Hale Kai is a two-bedroom ocean view home within walking distance of Hamoa Beach. Sleeps six. $100 per night for 2, additional persons $10. Others $90-$145.

### HANA BAY VACATION RENTALS ★
Stan Collins, PO Box 318 Hana, Maui, HI 96713 (808-248-7727) 1-800-651-7970. As an alternative to condominium and hotel living you might be interested in one of eight private homes available in and around Hana. They offer fully equipped one, two or three bedroom homes with ocean or bay views. Prices range from $65 for the Kauiki Cabin to $150/night for a newly constructed Philippine Koa and Mahogany hand crafted duplex located 50 yards from Hana Bay. Payment in full in advance for 7 days or less, please include a SASE w/ 9.43% tax added. Stay 7 nights pay for 6! There is a 10% cancellation fee. Rates are $20 higher November 15th - March 30 and June 1 - August 30.

## HANA PLANTATION HOUSES ★

Blair Shurtleff is once again running this operation and continuing to improve and add to the number of rental properties. Current rental options include: The Plantation House, a one bedroom cedar plantation style home with vaulted ceiling, jacuzzi tub/shower, two covered lanais, runs $140. The Hale Kipa, House of Hospitality, is located in the town of Hana, a short walk to Hana Bay. This two story plantation style house is located on grounds that include a private spa. Hale Kipa has two separate accommodations, each with its own entrance. The upstairs is a split level that sleeps four with one bedroom, one bath, kitchen, private sundeck, while the downstairs sleeps two. Upstairs rents for $135, downstairs for $100. Their Waikoaloa Beach House is a mile from the town of Hana and this solar-powered home accommodates up to four guests. There is also a separate sleeping structure with outdoor private bath/shower facility that is adjacent to the main house that will accommodate two guests. The "annex" rents for $35, the Beach House for $160. Rates are for single or double occupancy, each additional person is $10 per night.

Full payment is required in advance. They have several condos on Moloka'i, too! For information on their Maui or Moloka'i accommodations contact them at PO Box 249, Hana, Maui, HI 96713. 1-800-228-HANA.

## SHERATON HOTEL HANA-MAUI ★

PO Box 8, Hana, Maui, HI 96713 (808-248-8211) 1-800-321-HANA. FAX (808) 248-7202. Discounts on extended stays. Special honeymoon package is available. *Garden accommodations $305, Garden Jr. suites $365, Garden 1 BR suites $525 Sea Ranch Cottage $425, Sea Ranch Cottage 1 BR Suites $795*

This is the most secluded Maui resort, and a Hana landmark that has been called an island on an island. Five plantations were consolidated when Paul Fagan saw that the end of the sugar industry in Hana was close at hand. There had been 5,000 residents in Hana in 1941, and only 500 remained when he began the hotel and cattle ranch which rejuvenated Hana.

Approximately 1/3 of Hana's population of over 1,000 are employed in some fashion by the hotel, ranch or flower nursery. Hotel Hana Ranch opened for public use in 1947 and was later renamed Hotel Hana Maui.

The 97-room hotel resembles a small neighborhood with the single story units scattered about the grounds. The rooms are simple but elegant with hardwood floors and tiled bathrooms with deep tubs. The resort prides itself on the fact that it has no televisions or room air-conditioning. Newer additions are the 47 sea ranch cottages located oceanview at Kaihalulu Bay. These resemble the early plantation style houses. These cottages include oceanview and the majority offer spas on the lanais.

The Wellness & Fitness Retreat is five days and four nights at $1570 per couple, $2200 including meals. It offers a complimentary upgrade to Garden Jr. Suite or sea ranch cottage, hiking excursions and nature walks, exercise classes, one 1-hour massage or one 1 1/2 hour facial, and specially planned healthy cuisine menu. Resort guests can also join the complimentary aquacize, breakfast walks or the exercise classes and hiking excursions for a small fee.

*The Historic Plantation House* has been restored to its original elegance. Built in 1928, the 4,000 square foot building was the home of August Unna, Hana's first plantation owner. The surrounding four acres are filled with beautiful plants and trees that are more than 100 years old. The Plantation House is available as a guest home and offers two bedrooms and baths, a large living room with fireplace, dining room, library, bar and complete kitchen. To provide the latest technology for private business gatherings and meetings, it has been equipped with electronic data transmission equipment and audio-visual equipment that includes a large screen closed circuit television system. An adjacent pavilion and covered deck area add outdoor meeting areas. The site is also the location of the Hotel Hana Maui's weekly Manager's cocktail party.

Activities include a weekly luau, many trails for hiking or horseback riding, or cookouts at Hamoa beach. A shuttle provides convenient transportation for the three mile trip to beautiful Hamoa Beach with private facilities for hotel guests. Tours are also available to Ohe'o Stream. Two swimming pools are located on the hotel grounds. They also offer a dining room as well as an informal family dining restaurant. (Restaurant dining and the weekly luau are available to non-hotel guests on a space available basis. Call for reservations.) Children's activities and overnight sitters are available. A bar with a large fireplace and an open deck with a quiet lounge adjoining invite guests to enjoy a peaceful atmosphere for conversation or reading. The restaurant has a 35-foot ceiling with skylight, hardwood floors and a deck opening to a magnificent oceanview and excellent food. The library contains rare volumes of early Hawaiiana as well as popular novels. There is also a small boutique with resort fashions and jewelry in addition to a beauty salon. The "golf adventure" is three holes in the midst of the resort. The Club Room has a television, and evening lectures are sometimes given here. A more peaceful and beautiful setting is difficult to imagine.

## WAIANAPANAPA STATE PARK
54 S. High Street, First Floor, Wailuku, Maui, HI 96793. (808-243-5354) The State Park Department offers cabins that sleep up to six people. The units have electric lights and hot water, showers and toilet facilities. There is a living room and one bedroom with two bunks in the bedroom and two singles in the living-room. Completely furnished with bedding, bath towels, dish cloth, cooking and eating utensils. Electric range (no oven) and refrigerator. No pets are allowed and bring your own soap!

A five-day maximum stay is the rule and guests are required to clean their units before departure, leaving soiled linens. A 50% deposit is required for reservations and they are booked way ahead (6 months to one year). Children are considered those ages 11 and under, adults are counted as being 12 years and above. A pro-rated list of rates will be sent to you by the Parks Department on request.

The beach is unsafe for swimming. However, there are some interesting trails, pools, and lava tubes. The beach is not sand, but actually very small, smooth black pebbles. Mosquito repellent is recommended, even for a short walk through the pool area. Six persons maximum. Following are a few sample prices.

*1 adult-$10/day, 2 adults-$14, 4 adults-$24, 6 adults-$30*
*1 adult 1 child-$10.50, 2 adults 2 children-$18, 2 adults 4 children-$20*

### YMCA CAMP KE'ANAE
In Ke'anae. (808-248-8355) Bring your own sleeping bag and food. Separate facilities for men and women. Accommodations are dormitory style. *$8 a night.* Reservation number (808) 242-9007.

### HEAVENLY HANA INN
PO Box 790, Hana, Maui, HI 96713. (808-248-8442) 4 units in a Japanese-style inn. New owners have recently done some major renovations. Each two bedroom suite has a Japanese style bath, a lanai and a private entrance. The inn is entirely non-smoking. No personal checks or charge cards. Room rates effective in 1994: 1 or 2 persons $175; 3 persons $205; 4 persons $235. Additional person add $30. Tax not included in prices. Payment in full must be received 10 days prior to reservation and according to the brochure, it must be paid by money order or cashier's check.

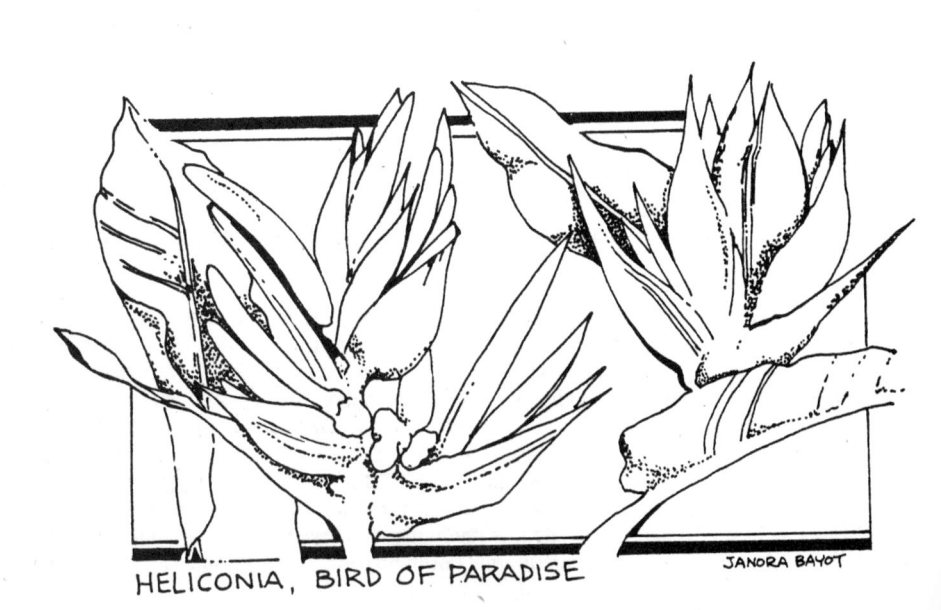

HELICONIA, BIRD OF PARADISE

JANORA BAYOT

# BOOKING AGENTS

**ASTON HOTELS & RESORTS**
2255 Kuhio Avenue
Honolulu, HI 96815
1-808-931-1400  1-800-321-2558
From Canada 1-800-445-6633

Kaanapali Villas     Maui Vista
The Mahana           Kaanapali Shores
Maui Hill            Maui Lu Resort
Kamaole Sands        Maui Park

**BELLO REALTY**
PO Box 1776
Kihei, Maui, HI  96753
1-800-541-3060
(808) 879-3328

Homes and Condos

**CLASSIC RESORTS**
50 Nohea Kai Drive
Lahaina, Maui, HI  96761
1-800-642-6284 (808-667-1400)
From Canada call collect

Kaanapali Alii
Lahaina Shores
Puunoa

**COLONY RESORTS**
32 Merchant St.
Honolulu, HI 96813
1-808-523-0411  1-800-777-1700

Napili Shores

**CONDOMINIUM
RENTALS HAWAII**
362 Huku Lii Place, #204
Kihei, Maui, HI 96753
1-808-879-2778  1-800-367-5242
Canada: 1-800-663-2101

Sugar Beach
Hale Pau Hana
Maui Kamaole
Hale Kamaole
Kihei Akahi

**DESTINATION RESORTS ★**
3750 Wailea Alanui
Wailea, Maui, HI 96753
1-800-367-5246  1-808-879-1595

Grand Champions
Makena Surf
Polo Beach Club
Wailea Condominiums

**HANA PLANTATION HOUSES**
PO Box 249
Hana, Maui, HI  96713
1-800-228-HANA
(808) 248-7049
Rental houses on Moloka'i and in Hana, Maui.

**HAWAIIAN APT. LEASING**
479 Ocean Avenue, Suite B
Laguna Beach, CA  92651
1-800-472-8449 CA
1-800-854-8843 U.S. except CA
1-800-824-8968 Canada

Kaanapali Alii        Menehune Shores
Kaanapali Royal       Mahana
Kaanapali Shores      Makena Surf
Kamaole Sands         Maui Sunset
Kapalua Villas        Maui Eldorado
Kihei Bay Surf        Napili Shores
Kihei Bay Vista       Papakea
Hale Mahina           Polo Beach Club
Kahana Sunset         Sugar Beach
Royal Kahana          The Whaler
Valley Isle           Kaanapali Villas
Maui Banyans          The Palms
Kauhale Makai         Napili Point
Kihei Akai            Kihei Resort

**HANA BAY
VACATION RENTALS ★**
PO Box 318
Hana, Maui, HI 96713
1-808-248-7727
Stan Collins has a great alternative to condo vacationing. Choose one of his Hana cottages or homes.

## HAWAIIAN PACIFIC RESORTS
1150 South King St.
Honolulu, HI 96882
1-800-367-5004
FAX 1-800-477-2329

Maui Beach    Wailea Oceanfront
Maui Palms

## HAWAIIANA RESORTS INC.
1270 Ala Moana Blvd.
Honolulu, HI 96814
1-800-367-7040 U.S. Mainland
1-800-877-7311
1-800-232-2520 inter-island

Kaanapali Royal
Kihei Bay Vista
Maui Banyan
Maui Kaanapali Villas
Palms at Wailea
Royal Kahana

## KAANAPALI VACATION
**RENTALS** PO Box 384900
Waikoloa, Hawai'i 96738
1-800-822-4252
1-808-667-9559 US & Mainland
Hale Mahina    Maui Eldorado
Kaanapali Royal    Sands of Kahana
Kuleana    The Whaler
Maui Kaanapali Villas
4-Bedroom home at Napili

## KIHEI MAUI VACATIONS ★
PO Box 1055
Kihei, Maui, HI 96753
1-808-879-7581 1-800-542-6284 U.S.
1-800-423-8733 Ext. 4000 Canada

Maalaea Yacht Marina
Kauhale Makai    Maalaea Kai
Maui Kamaole    Kamaole Sands
Grand Champions    Kihei Holiday
Maui Banyans    Kihei Kai Nani
Maui Sunset    Luana Kai
Pualani    Makena Surf
Kihei Resort    Kihei Akahi
Menehune Shores    Milowai
Kihei Alii Kai    Maui Vista

Kihei Bay Surf    Homes-Cottages
Kihei Garden Estates (good range of
South Maui properties-extra charge
for cleaning if stay less than 4 nights)

## KLAHANI
PO Box 11108
Lahaina, Maui, HI 96761
1-800-669-MAUI (U.S. & Canada)
FAX 1-808-661-5875

Hoyochi Nikko
Hale Ono Loa
Honokeana Cove
Lahaina Roads
Nohonani

## KUMULANI
PO Box 1190, Kihei, Maui, HI 96753
1-800-367-2954 U.S. & Canada
1-808-879-9272

Island Surf
Maui Sunset
Maui Banyans
Kamaole Sands
Kauhale Makai
Mana Kai Maui
Wailea Villas
Maui Sun

## MAALAEA BAY RENTALS ★
RR 1 Box 389
Wailuku, Maui, HI 96793
1-808-244-5627 1-800-367-6084

Hono Kai    Maalaea Kai
Kanai A Nalu    Makani A Kai
Maalaea Banyans Milowai
Maalaea Yacht Marina Lauloa

## MARC RESORTS HAWAII
2155 Kalakaua Ave., 7th floor
Honolulu, HI 96815
1-800-535-0085 (808) 922-9700
FAX (808) 922-2421
Kahana Villa    Maui Eldorado
Paki Maui    The Kahili

Also properties on O'ahu, Kaua'i,
Moloka'i and The Big Island.

## MAUI CONDOMINIUMS
PO Box 1089
ALDERGROVE, BC,
CANADA V0X 1A0
1-800-663-6962 Canada

| | |
|---|---|
| Aston Maui Park | Mahana |
| Hale Kamaole | Maui Islander |
| Hono Koa | Kamaole Sands |
| Island Sands | Napili Bay |
| Kihei Akahi | Paki Maui |
| Kihei Bay Surf | Papakea |
| Kihei Garden Estates | |
| Kihei Holiday | Royal Kahana |
| Kihei Kai Nani | Sugar Beach |
| Maui Palms Hotel | |
| Maui Kaanapali Villas | |
| Valley Isle Resort | |
| Village By the Sea | |
| Whaler | |

## MAUI CONDO & HOME
PO Box 1840
Kihei, Maui, HI 96753
1-800-822-3309
(808) 879-5445

Homes & Condos
Primarily Kihei/Wailea

## MAUI NETWORK LTD.
PO Box 1077
Makawao, Maui, HI 96768
1-800-367-5221 U.S. Mainland
1-808-572-9555 Canada

| | |
|---|---|
| Grand Champions | Kuleana |
| Hale Mahina | Maui Sunset |
| Kihei Beach Resort | |
| Kihei Baysurf | Papakea |

## MORE HAWAII FOR LESS
5324 Kester Ave. Suite 4
Van Nuys, CA 91411
1-800-967-6687 U.S. & Canada
1-808-986-7420

| | |
|---|---|
| Hale Ono Loa | Papakea |
| Luana Kai | Sugar Beach |
| Maalaea Banyans | |

## OIHANA PROPERTY MANAGEMENT
840 Alua
Wailuku, Maui, HI 96793
1-808-244-7684 or 1-808-244-7491
1-800-367-5234 U.S. & Canada

| | |
|---|---|
| Island Sands | Leinaala |
| Kamoa Views | Maalaea Banyans |
| Kana'I A Nalu | Maui Parkshore |
| Kauhale Makai | Maui Vista |
| Kealia | Paki Maui |
| Kihei Akahai | Puuamana |

## OUTRIGGER HOTELS HAWAII
2335 Kalakaua Ave.
Honolulu, HI 96715-2941
1-800-462-6262
FAX 1-800-456-4329

Kaanapali Beach Hotel
Kaanapali Royal
Kihei Bay Vista
Maui Banyan
The Palms at Wailea

## OVER THE RAINBOW, INC.
186 Mehani Circle
Kihei, Maui, HI 96753
(808) 879-5521

Specializes in assisting the disabled traveler with any physical limitations. Booking accommodations, tours, personal care.

## PALI KAI ★
1993 S. Kihei Rd.
Kihei, Maui, HI 96753
1-808-875-4927, 1-800-544-6050,
FAX (808) 879-2790

Bookings for many condos. This company has replaced Gentle Island Holidays. We haven't dealt with them, so let us know if you do!

### PLEASANT HAWAIIAN HOLIDAYS
2404 Townsgate Rd.
Westlake Village, CA 91361
1-800-242-9244 U.S. Mainland & HI
Bookings are for package plans of 7 to 14 nights on one or more islands and includes airfare and rental car.

### RSVP
1575 W. Georgia St., 3rd Floor
Vancouver, BC Canada V6G 2V3
1-800-663-1118 U.S. and Canada

Following is a partial list of properties. Ask about specials they may have for free rental cars, senior rates etc.

| | |
|---|---|
| Kaanapali Royal | Maui Hill |
| Kaanapali Shores | Maui Park |
| Kahana Sunset | Maui Sunset |
| Kahana Villa | Maui Vista |
| Kahana Village | Menehune Shores |
| Kauhale Makai | Napili Shores |
| Kihei Akahi | Paki Maui |
| Kihei Alii Kai | Papakea |
| Kihei Holiday | Sands of Kahana |
| Kihei Resort | Sugar Beach |
| Mahana | The Whaler |
| Maui Kaanapali Villas | |

### RAINBOW RENTALS CONDOMINIUM MANAGEMENT
PO Box 1893, Kihei, Maui, HI 96753
1-800-451-5366 U.S. Mainland
1-808-874-0233

| | |
|---|---|
| Kauhale Makai | Luana Kai |
| Kealia | Maalaea Surf |
| Kihei Alii Kai | Sugar Beach |
| Kihei Resort | |

### RAINBOW RESERVATIONS INC.
PO Box 11453
Lahaina, Maui, HI 96761-6453
1-800-367-6092 U.S. & Canada
1-808-669-5550

| | |
|---|---|
| Hololani Resort | Kuleana |
| Kahana Outrigger | Valley Isle |

### RIDGE REALTY RENTALS ★
10 Hoohui Rd. Suite 301
Kahana, HI 96761
1-800-326-6284 U.S. & Canada
1-808-669-9696

The Ridge (Kapalua)

### VILLAGE RESORTS
2481 Kaanapali Hwy.
1-808-661-4861
FAX 1-808-661-8315

The Whaler
Sands of Kahana
Papakea

### WHALER'S REALTY ★
Whaler's Village, Suite A-3
2435 Kaanapali Parkway
Lahaina, Maui, HI 96761
1-800-367-5632 U.S.
1-808-661-8777

| | |
|---|---|
| Kaanapali Alii | Kahana Sunset |
| Kaanapali Royal | Kapalua Golf |
| Kaanapali Plantation | Mahana |
| Kaanapali Shores | Papakea |
| Kaanapali Villas | The Whaler |
| Sands of Kahana | |

(They offer high quality condos at fair prices)

### WINDSURFING WEST
1-800-782-6105
(808) 572-5601
FAX (808) 871-4624

Vacation packages include car, windsurfing equipment and condo at one of several properties or homes. Windsurfing lessons available.

# RESTAURANTS

## INTRODUCTION

Whether it's a teriburger at a local cafe or a romantic evening spent dining next to a swan lagoon, Maui offers something for everyone. We're confident that you will enjoy exploring Maui's diverse dining options as much as we have!

The majority of restaurants in the Maalaea to Makena, and Lahaina to Kapalua areas have been included, and for the adventurer or budget conscious traveler, take special note of the wonderful local dining opportunities in Kahului and Wailuku.

Needless to say, we haven't been able to eat every meal served at every restaurant on Maui, but we do discuss with a great many people their experiences in order to get varied opinions. Within weeks prior to this revision hitting the presses, nearly a dozen restaurants suddenly disappeared and reappeared with new owners, names and menus. Kihei has a number of new restaurants that brings it much closer to the types of dining options you find in Lahaina. A Pacific Cafe in Kihei has an outstanding reputation at their Kaua'i location and the new Five Palms Grille shows promise. We look forward to hearing your comments on these newcomers, as well as your experiences with some of the old favorites. (See READER RESPONSE.)

Following this introduction, the restaurants are first indexed alphabetically and then also by food type. The restaurants are then divided by geographical area, separated by price range, and listed alphabetically in those price ranges. These are: "INEXPENSIVE" under $10, "MODERATE" $10 to $20, and "EXPENSIVE" $20 and above. As a means of comparison, we have taken an average meal (usually dinner), excluding tax, alcoholic beverages and desserts, for one person at that restaurant. The prices listed were accurate at time of publication, but we cannot be responsible for any price increases. For quick reference, the type of food served at the restaurant described is indicated in *Italic* type next to the restaurant name. Sample menu offerings are also included as a helpful guide. An important postscript here is the rapidity with which some island restaurants open and close, change names and raise prices. Our quarterly newsletter, THE MAUI UPDATE, will keep you abreast of these changes.

There are numerous fast food/chain restaurants, such as Subway Sandwiches, McDonald's and Pizza Hut, and we have included some of the popular ones that are in key locations, but by no means all of them. Among those not listed include KFC, Taco Bell, Wendy's, Dairy Queen, Arby's, Jack in the Box and Little Caesar. You're on your own for these!

Dinner cruises are covered in the Recreation and Tour section of this book.

Our favorite restaurants are generally either a real bargain for the price, or serve a very high quality meal, and are indicated by a ★.

# BEST BETS

## TOP RESTAURANTS

Our criteria for a top restaurant are excellence of food preparation and presentation, a pleasing atmosphere, and service that anticipates or responds promptly to one's needs. While the following exemplify these criteria, they are also all "deep pocket" restaurants, so expect to spend $70 - $100 or more for your meal, wine and gratuity for two. Generally, anything you have will be excellent. Remember, even the best restaurants may have an "off" night, but these are seldom. Also, chefs and management do change, rendering what you may have found to be excellent on one occasion quite different the next. However, the following have proven to be consistent through the years. Enjoy your meal, enjoy being a little bit spoiled, and remember those muumuus are great for covering up all those calories!!

David Paul's Lahaina Grill
Grand Dining Room, Grand Wailea Resort & Spa
Hakone, Maui Prince Hotel
Koele Lodge - Island of Lana'i
Prince Court, Maui Prince Hotel
Raffles, Stouffer Wailea Beach Resort
Sound of the Falls, Westin Maui Resort
Spats Trattoria, Hyatt Regency at Kaanapali
Swan Court, Hyatt Regency at Kaanapali
The Grill, Ritz-Carlton, Kapalua

## TOP RESTAURANTS IN A MORE CASUAL ATMOSPHERE

While some of these restaurants are slightly less expensive, it is still easy to spend $60 or more for dinner for two. They serve a superior meal in a less formal atmosphere.

A Pacific Cafe, Kihei
Avalon, Lahaina
Haliimaile General Store, Haliimaile
Kapalua's Garden Restaurant, Kapalua Resort Hotel
Kapalua Grill and Bar, Kapalua
Longhi's, Lahaina
Mama's Fish House, Paia
Nicolina, Kahana
Plantation House, Kapalua
Roy's Kahana Bar & Grill, Kahana
SeaWatch, Wailea
The Villa, Westin Maui
Waterfront, Maalaea

## RESTAURANTS WITH THE BEST VIEW

Plantation House Restaurant at Kapalua
Grand Dining Room at Grand Hyatt Wailea
SeaWatch, Wailea

## LA CUISINE FRANCAISE

Maui's French restaurants fall in the "champagne" price range. Both *Gerard's* in Lahaina and *Chez Paul* in Olowalu offer outstanding fare, although the atmosphere at Gerard's is one of our favorites.

## BEST SEAFOOD / BEST SEAFOOD BUFFET

Among the best seafood restaurants are: *Mama's Fish House* in Paia, *Gerard's* in Lahaina (though not a seafood restaurant, their fresh fish is outstanding), and *Waterfront* Restaurant in Maalaea. The *Villa Restaurant* at the Westin Maui has one of the most extensive selections of fresh fish on the menu each evening. A soon-to-open restaurant in Kahana, *Fish and Games Sports Grill* has plans for a fresh oyster bar and combined with their fresh seafood market, may also offer a very good selection of fresh fish. A number of excellent sushi bars are available around the island.

All of the top restaurants have wonderful seafood, but an All-You-Can-Eat is a seafood lover's dream come true! A number of seafood buffets are available around the island: *The Moana Terrace* at the Maui Marriott has a Saturday seafood buffet that may not be as elaborate as the others, priced at $19.95. The Westin Maui offers a seafood buffet nightly at their *Villa Terrace*. Served outside it is a casual clambake-style setting at $23.95. The Kapalua Bay Resort was one of the first to offer a seafood buffet in their *Garden Restaurant* ★, and now have added to it a Vintner dinner as well at $24.95. Arrive between 5:30 and 6 pm for an early bird savings of only $20.95. The Ritz-Carlton offers a good seafood buffet at their *Terrace Restaurant* for $26. The Maui Inter-Continental has a seafood buffet with four rotating menus at their *Lanai Terrace* ★ each Friday for $23.95. *Sandalwood*, the only non-hotel to offer a seafood buffet, features a "Fresh Fish Station," "Steamer Station" and "Caesar Salad Station" emphasizing quality over quantity for $22.50. *Palm Court* at the Stouffer Wailea Beach features a $35 seafood buffet each Friday.

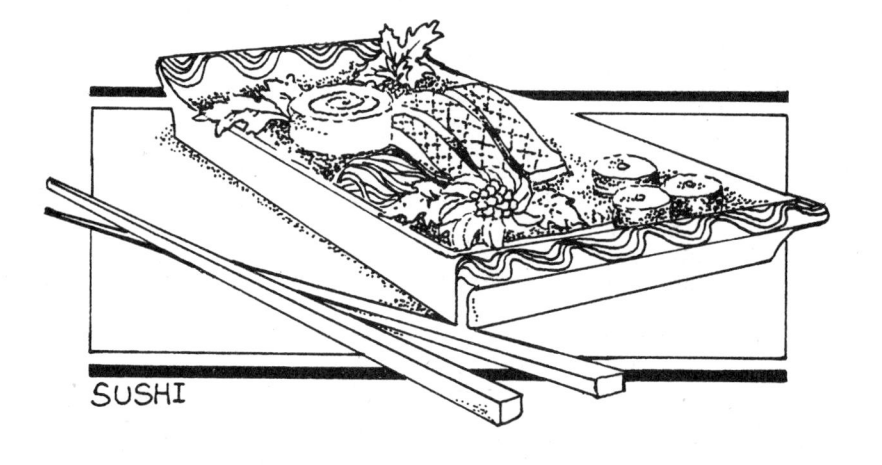

SUSHI

## BEST BREAKFAST / BRUNCH BUFFETS

Buffets are a good way to enjoy a great meal with a wide selection of food at a moderate price. And you may not have to eat for the next two days! The best Sunday brunches are *Prince Court* at the Maui Prince Resort in Makena and the *Grand Dining Room* at the Grand Wailea Resort & Spa. In West Maui, Kapalua's *Garden Restaurant* at the Kapalua Bay Resort has a wonderful brunch, as does the Westin Maui's *Sound of the Falls*. The best value for a Sunday brunch goes to the Kaanapali Beach Hotel's *Tiki Terrace* and adjoining Plantation Room.

### Daily breakfast buffets:

In South Maui, the *Grand Wailea* has an outstanding daily breakfast buffet for $18 adult, $9 children. *Lana'i Terrace* at the Maui Inter-Continental Resort offers a daily breakfast buffet for $14.95 adults, children half price, daily continental breakfast buffet is $9.50. *The Frangipani Restaurant* (Maui Sun) serves a buffet 6:30 am-10:30 am. Adults or children $8.25, children under 6 are free. 875-9000.

In West Maui the *Swan Court* ★ features a lovely breakfast buffet daily, 7 am - 11:30 am, and until 12:30 pm on Sundays. Adults are $14.95, children $12.95. The elegant atmosphere and macadamia nut pancakes earns this one a star. The best value for a daily breakfast buffet is the *Royal Ocean Terrace* at the Royal Lahaina Resort for $11.50. The *Pool Terrace* at the Kapalua Bay Hotel offers a daily breakfast buffet $14.95 adults, $9.95 children.

### The following are available on Sunday only unless otherwise noted:

*LAHAINA/KAANAPALI/KAPALUA: Old Lahaina Cafe*, 505 Front St. in Lahaina serves Sunday brunch (not buffet) 8 am-3:30 pm. 661-3303. *Compadres Bar and Grill* ★ features a Sunday Champagne Brunch 10 am-2 pm. Adults $11.95, kids 11 and under $4.95. This all you can eat buffet offers fresh chile rellenos, a taco bar, fresh pork carnitas, Mexican style eggs Benedict, and other Mexican specialties. Desserts include fruit salad, Mexican flan, bunuews and hot desserts such as bananas la bamba. A newcomer to the brunch scene, this one is a winner! *Reilly's* in Kaanapali features a Sunday Brunch, but it is not a buffet. *Royal Ocean Terrace* (Royal Lahaina Resort) provides one of the best values for a Sunday brunch buffet. Not an exotic or highly gourmet selection, but good fare at $19.95 for adults, $9.95 for children and Hawaiian musical entertainment. 661-3611. *Sound of the Falls* ★ (Westin Maui, Kaanapali) serves an elegant Sunday champagne brunch in a beautiful atmosphere. Some people come just for the sushi bar! 9 am-2 pm, $19.75. *Swan Court* ★ (Hyatt Regency, Kaanapali) features a lovely breakfast buffet daily, including Sunday, in an elegant atmosphere. 6:30-11:30 am, until 1:30 pm on Sunday $13.50. *The Garden Restaurant* ★ (Kapalua Bay Hotel) features an artistic presentation and unusual variety of gourmet specialties in an open-air setting for Sunday brunch buffet 9:30 am-1:30 pm, $24.95 adults, children $16.95.

*WAILEA: The Grand Dining Room* ★ (Grand Wailea) offers Sunday brunch at $38 and features a sample of Hawaiian regional cuisine. Selections include ham with mango chutney, Hawaiian bread sweet rolls, starfruit (fresh off the trees on the property), local gourmet Hawaiian dishes made with natural ingredients, such as jicama salad, kim chee, Oriental cole slaw, or lomi lomi salmon. Remember to save room for dessert! Save room for desserts like guava mousse! 875-1234.

**WAILEA:** *Lana'i Terrace* (Maui Inter-Continental Resort) has a fine Sunday Champagne buffet brunch in a casual setting. 10 am-2 pm $28 adults, under age 12 are $14. *Palm Court* (Stouffer Wailea Beach Resort) has a daily champagne breakfast buffet for $15.75. Under age 12 $8. 879-4900. Palm Court ★ has a taste extravaganza for their champagne Sunday brunch buffet. You may see some dishes here that you've never sampled before. Prices and times vary. 879-4900.

**MAKENA:** *Prince Court* ★ (Maui Prince Hotel, Makena) features a spectacular display of over 160 food choices at the Sunday Champagne buffet brunch, each arranged as a work of art. Each tastes as good as they look! 9:30 am-1:30 pm, $29.95, under 12 $23, under age 5 are free.

**UPCOUNTRY:** *Haliimaile General Store* in Upcountry has a great Sunday brunch menu (not a buffet).

**WAIKAPU:** *Sandalwood* in Waikapu has a Sunday brunch $18.95 for their cold buffet plus hot cooked entree. $13.95 for cold buffet only.

**BEST DINNER BUFFETS**
*Moana Terrace* ★ at the Maui Marriott has for years offered among the best dinner values. Their buffets are no exception. Their Friday night prime rib buffet is still only $9.95, their Saturday evening seafood buffet is $19.95 adults.

*Royal Ocean Terrace* at the Royal Lahaina Resort is a great dining value. International themes change nightly. Priced at $17.50 adults, $8.75 children 5 - 12 years, and under age 5 are free. 661-3611

Wednesday evening is an Italian buffet at *The Ritz-Carlton*, Kapalua. Also in Kapalua, at the Kapalua Hotel is Saturday evening Paniolo Dinner buffet ★ for only $16.95.

*Frangipani Restaurant* at the Maui Sun Hotel in Kihei offers Friday and Saturday prime rib buffet $16.95 adults, $12.95 kids.

*Lana'i Terrace* at the Maui Inter-Continental offers nightly theme buffets. Prices vary.

*The Maui Lu Long House* has one of the most reasonable evening buffets, Tuesday, Thursday and Saturday, $9.95 for adults and $5.95 for kids features a rotating menu with three entrees nightly.

*Palm Court* (Stouffer Wailea Beach Resort) serves a dinner buffet three nights weekly, prime rib $29 (Tuesday), Italian $26 (Wednesday) and Seafood $34 (Friday). The priciest of the island buffets.

*Sandalwood* in Waikapu, in addition to their Friday night seafood buffet served 5:30-8:30 they offer a Saturday night all-you-can-eat prime rib buffet for $18.50 per person, children under age 12 are charged $1 per year.

The *Summer Palace* is a new addition to Kihei featuring an Asian mix on their evening buffet table. Open for lunch $7.95, dinner $16.95 daily.

# RESTAURANTS

*Best Bets*

## BEST SALADS
The winners are the Chinese chicken and gado gado salads, both available at *Avalon* restaurant in Lahaina, 667-5559, or if you're in Northern California, visit their new location in Mill Valley. Best salad bar is at *Sunsets* in Kihei which offers homemade breads and soups along with a good selection of salad items.

## TOP "LOCAL" RESTAURANTS (Kahului/Wailuku)
We have delighted in exploring the many small, family-owned "local" restaurants in Kahului, and especially in Wailuku. The food in these establishments is not only plentiful and well prepared, but also very inexpensive. The service is often better and friendlier than at many of the resort establishments.

Aki's Hawaiian Food and Bar  (Hawaiian) 244-8122
Bangkok (Thai) 579-8979
Bangkok Royalty (Thai buffet) 871-5151
Fujiya's (Japanese) 244-0206
Mama Ding's (Puerto Rican) 877-5796
Mel's Lunch To You (Local Style) (242-8271)
Saeng's Thai Cuisine (Thai) 244-1567
Sam Sato's (Japanese/noodles) 244-7124
Siam Thai (Thai) 244-3817
Tasty Crust (Home style) 244-0845
Tokyo Tei (Japanese) 242-9630
Touch of Saigon (Vietnamese) 244-7845

## BEST PIZZA
One of our personal favorites is *Shaka Pizza and Sandwich* in Kihei, a New York subway style pizza that was wonderful and very cheesey. Some readers continue to rave about the *Pizza Hut* in Lahaina, so we'll pass the advice along to you!

## BEST SANDWICHES
Dona's favorite is the Peking Duck sandwich at *Longhi's* in Lahaina! *Juicy's* at 505 Front Street has excellent and healthy sandwich selections. Try the lobster salad sandwich at the *Pacific Grill*, Four Seasons Resort.

## BEST HAMBURGER WITH A VIEW
Best hamburger with a view goes to *Cheeseburger in Paradise*. *Kimo's* in Lahaina is another best bet with a view. Neither are inexpensive!

## BEST HAWAIIAN
*Aki's*, (244-8122) located on Market Street in Wailuku, is small, quaint, and very inexpensive, or sample Hawaiian fare at *Takimaya's* store in Wailuku. In West Maui check out the *Old Lahaina Cafe* (661-3303) at 505 Front St. Also check into the section on luaus.

## GOOD AND CHEAP
Some restaurants continue to offer a discounted meal for early diners. Hours vary with the restaurant, but usually begin between 5 and 5:30 pm and ends 6-6:30 pm. Generally, the meals are almost the same ones that you would pay more for an hour later, but you are limited in your selections. The following are ones that

we recommend. Some are good values, others are mediocre fare. Call to verify if they still have a discount and their hours.

Benihana 667-2244
China Boat, Kahana 669-5089
Erik's Kahana Keyes 669-8071
Erik's Seafood Grotto 669-4806
Friday Night Seafood Buffet at the Garden Restaurant in Kapalua ★ 879-1954
Kea Lani 875-4100
Kihei Prime Rib and Seafood House, Kihei ★ 879-1954
La Tasca ★ 661-5700
Lahaina Fish Company (Also two for one coupons in drive guides) 661-3472
Old Lahaina Cafe ★ 661-3303
Moana Terrace, Maui Marriott Kaanapali ★ 667-1200
Moose McGillycuddy's, Lahaina 667-7758
Nikko Japanese Steak House at Maui Marriott ★ 667-1200
Orient Express, Napili 669-8077
Rusty Harpoon, Whaler's Village, Kaanapali ★ 661-3123
Sea House at Napili Kai 669-1500
Sunsets on the Beach ★ 874-5787

No early bird specials, but *The Koffee Shop* at the Kaanapali Beach Hotel has a $9.95 all-you-can-eat prime rib dinner buffet, a breakfast or lunch for $5.95 and an afternoon deli buffet with make-your-own sandwiches along with salads, soups and desserts for $4.95.

## BEST FAST "LOCAL STYLE" FOODS
*Juicy's* at 505 Front Street, in Lahaina, has good 'n fast healthy sandwiches. *Sushiya's* in Lahaina on Prison Street offers very inexpensive local plate lunches.

## BEST SHAVE ICE
"Shave ice" had almost disappeared on Maui, but a few places have revived it. Shaved ice, however, should not, in our opinion, be confused with a "snow cone." Both are cold and sweet, but a shave ice should be fine bits of ice crystals. Lappert's, with two locations in Lahaina, serves what they call a "shaved ice," but we thought it should have been called a snow cone! They aren't the REAL thing.

Fortunately, there are a few better options. *Tobi's Shave Ice* ★ in Kihei offers a small, friendly atmosphere where Tobi (or her mother or brother) will take your order for a real kine shaved ice. Open Tue.-Sat. 11 am-9 pm, Sunday and Monday 11 am-6 pm. 1913 South Kihei Rd., 879-7294.

We're also told that W & F Washerette Snack Bar at 125 S. Wakea in Kahului has shaved ice. Ashley's Yogurt at Kahana Gateway claims they do, but we haven't sampled it. Sally's Sweets at Suda's Kihei Store reportedly also has shaved ice, 61 S. Kihei Rd., 875-4633.

## MOST OUTRAGEOUS DESSERT
The *Lahaina Provision Company's* Chocoholic Bar at the Hyatt Regency Kaanapali is a chocolate lover's dream come true. This dessert buffet features soft, self-serve vanilla and chocolate ice cream and an array of toppings. Hot fudge, hot

milk chocolate sauce, or hot caramel, strawberries, bananas, shredded coconut, M
& M's, fresh fruits, granola, nuts, lady fingers, and they've added some candy
bars, cookies, mousse and even chocolate truffles. You can make the trip through
as many times as you or your waistline can tolerate. Served 6-11 pm, $7.95 a la
carte, or $5.95 with dinner.

## BEST BAKERIES
*The Bakery*, in Lahaina, 991 Limahana Place, 667-9062, is a good early morning
stop that will ensure you the best selection of their wonderful French pastries.
Cheese and luncheon meats are also available. The atmosphere isn't quite as fresh
as it could be, however.

In central Maui, don't miss a stop at the *Home Made Bakery* ★ on Lower Main
Street (244-7015). Their bread pudding is fantastic.

And be sure to stop at the *Four Sisters Bakery* ★ at Vineyard St. at Hinano in
Wailuku. Melen, Mila, Beth and Bobbie arrived from the Philippines a dozen
years or so ago. Their father had operated a Spanish Bakery in Manila for 15
years before moving the family to Maui. Not a large selection, but the items are
delicious and different. One sweet bread is filled with cinnamon pudding, a
sponge cake with a thin layer of butter in the middle of two moist pieces. The
butter rolls are very good and the Spanish sweet and cinnamon rolls delicious.
They sell their items only at this location and at the Swap Meet each Saturday
morning. Hours are Monday thru Friday 4 am until 8 pm.

*Pikake Bakery and Cafe* ★ has taken the island by storm. With a clean fresh
atmosphere, they have a location in Kihei in the Kihei Industrial Area and one in
Lahaina at 505 Front Street.

*Komoda Store and Bakery* in Makawao is famous for their cream puffs throughout
the state and beyond. Arrive past noon and you'll likely not get any! (572-7261)

*The Maui Bake Shop* features fancy pastries and cakes and is operated by Jose and
Claire Fujii Krall. Jose was previously the executive pastry chef at the Maui
Prince Hotel in Makena. Located at 2092 Vineyard, 242-0064.

## BEST VEGETARIAN
*The Vegan* restaurant in Paia has probably the largest vegetarian menu. *Pupule
Cafe* located at 318 N. Market Street in Wailuku, opened in March 1994 and
specializes in vegetarian dishes and sandwiches, but does offer some meat dishes
as well. Hours are 7 am-10 pm daily, breakfast served until 11 am. Owners are
Mark and Jana Folger. *Juicy's* at 505 Front Street in Lahaina has a good selection
of vegetarian sandwiches and daily specials as well as freshly squeezed fruit and
vegetable juices. *Crossroads Caffe* in Makawao offers vegetarian cuisine.

**BEST LUAU** (See luau section which follows)
West Maui - Old Lahaina Luau
South Maui - Maui-Intercontinental and Grand Wailea Resort and Spa
Most authentic - Old Lahaina Luau

NOTE: Poolside snack bars are not included in the index.

## ALPHABETICAL INDEX

# FOOD TYPE INDEX

**BAKERIES**
The Bakery . . . . . . . . . . . . . 199
Caffe Ciao . . . . . . . . . . . . . 242
Four Sisters . . . . . . . . . . 182,252
Home Made . . . . . . . . . 182,252
The Maui Bake & Bagel . . . . . 256
Pikake (Lahaina) . . . . . . . . . . 203
Pikake (Kihei) . . . . . . . . . . . 234

**BRUNCH**
Frangipani . . . . . . . . . . . . . . 237
The Garden (Kapalua) . . . . . . 228
Grand Wailea Dining Room . . 245
Haliimaile . . . . . . . . . . . . . . 265
Lanai Terrace . . . . . . . . . . . . 244
Moana Terrace . . . . . . . . . . . 218
Old Lahaina Cafe . . . . . . . . . 210
Palm Court . . . . . . . . . . . . . 248
Sound of the Falls . . . . . . . . 221
Swan Court . . . . . . . . . . . . . 222

**CHINESE, VIETNAMESE**
**PHILIPPINE AND THAI**
A Touch of Saigon . . . . . . . 252
Bangkok Cuisine . . . . . . . . . 266
Bangkok Royalty . . . . . . . . . 253
Beachcombers . . . . . . . . . . . 216
Canton Chef . . . . . . . . . . . . 237
China Boat . . . . . . . . . . . . . 225
China Express . . . . . . . . . . . 253
Fu Wah . . . . . . . . . . . . . . 262
Golden Palace . . . . . . . . . . . 201
Harborfront . . . . . . . . . . . . 208
Ming Yuen, Kahului . . . . . . 261
Orient Express . . . . . . . . . . . 226
Panda Express . . . . . . . . 233,258
Red Dragon Chinese . . . . . . 261
Roy's Kahana Bar & Grill . . . 229
Royal Thai Cuisine . . . . . . . 234
Saeng's Thai . . . . . . . . 204,261
Seoul Kal Bi . . . . . . . . . . . . 259
Song's Oriental Kitchen . . . . 205
Summer Palace . . . . . . . . . . 236
Thai Chef, Lahaina . . . . . . . 211
Thai Chef, Kihei . . . . . . . . . 234
Tin Ying . . . . . . . . . . . . . . 260

**CONTINENTAL**
Bay Club . . . . . . . . . . . . . 228
The Garden Restaurant . . . . . 228
Kapalua Grill and Bar . . . . . 226
Longhi's . . . . . . . . . . . . . . 214
Raffles' . . . . . . . . . . . . . . 249
Sound of the Falls . . . . . . . . 221
Swan Court . . . . . . . . . . . . 222

**DESSERTS**
Grand Wailea Dining Room . . 245
Kapalua Grill and Bar . . . . . 226
Lahaina Provision Company . . 220
Longhi's . . . . . . . . . . . . . . 214

**FAMILY DINING**
Compadres . . . . . . . . . . . . 207
Cheeseburger in Paradise . . . . 200
Chris's Smokehouse . . . . . . . 207
Chucks . . . . . . . . . . . . . . . 237
Chum's . . . . . . . . . . . . . 231,253
Denny's . . . . . . . . . . . . 200,231
IHOP . . . . . . . . . . . . . 232,255
Kaanapali Beach Koffee Shop . 215
Kimo's . . . . . . . . . . . . . . . 208
Koho Grill and Bar . . . . . 226,255
Leilani's . . . . . . . . . . . . . . 217
Moana Terrace . . . . . . . . . . . 218
Peggy Sue's . . . . . . . . . . . . 233
Planet Hollywood . . . . . . . . . 204
Red Lobster . . . . . . . . . . . . 210
Royal Ocean Terrace . . . . . . . 218
Sandcastle . . . . . . . . . . . . . . 244
Sizzler . . . . . . . . . . . . . . . . 259
Summer Palace . . . . . . . . . . 236

**FRENCH**
Chez Paul . . . . . . . . . . . . . . 212
Gerard's . . . . . . . . . . . . . . . 213

**GERMAN - SWISS**
Wolfgang's Bistro Garden . . . . 262
Wunderbar . . . . . . . . . . . . . 268

# CATERING

## A TABLE FOR TWO

Owner/chef Paul Alkire offers catering service from his set menu, or request an item. He also can accommodate most dietary requirements, low fat, low sodium, heart healthy. From appetizers to desserts. 878-1350.

## AMILIO'S

Catering for Beach parties, business lunches or cocktail parties. Phone 661-8551 or FAX 661-4721. Free delivery all menu items.

## AN ABSOLUTE AFFAIR

Offers catering from 2 - 2,000 people for all occasions. 667-7154 or FAX 667-7155.

## CLAMBAKE HAWAIIAN STYLE, INC.

A full catering service providing breakfast, brunch, lunch, dinner and cocktail parties. Lite lunches $7 - $14 per person, barbecues, combination dinners $17 - $22 include seafood, steak and chicken selections. Theme parties are also available and include a sushi bar, pasta bar, oyster bar, Thai chicken bar, or baron of beef. Pupu (appetizer parties) that serve 25 people run $176 - $310. The meals are cooked on location in their self-contained steam cookers and grill. All seafood is cooked Hawaiian style with ti leaf. They require minimal space for cooking and cleaning, which can be done indoors or outdoors. Their prices include paper products, utensils, buffet service, set up and clean up. Available seven days a week. No delivery charge for a minimum of 20 people. Children's prices available. Bartender service available by the hour. RR 1 Box 52, Wailuku, Maui, HI 96793. (242-5095)

## DANI'S CATERING

If you've never been to the Takamiya Market, you're missing a culinary experience. Dani's is the kitchen for Takamiya's market and they specialize in American, Japanese, Hawaiian and even some Filipino foods. Catered parties have a 20-person minimum. They also provide Central Maui delivery at no charge. Set menus range from $10.75 to $11.25 per person and include warmers, plates, napkins, chopsticks. Takamiya's Market has been in business now for 48 years and the catering operation has been around for 10 of those! Takamiya is at 359 N. Market, Wailuku. (242-6652)

## DOOR STEP DINING, INC.

While not really a catering service, it is a Restaurant Delivery Service. Since we don't really have a category for that, we'll blend it in here! They are currently serving West Maui, with plans to expand to Kihei. They have arrangements with a number of restaurants. You can order from one or more than one restaurant. Delivery charge is $5 per restaurant, regardless of the size of the order. Each additional restaurant fee is $2. Minimum food order is $10. Payments in cash, travelers check and major credit cards and they say average delivery time is 45-60 minutes. Advance orders are welcome. Hours for lunch are 10:30 am-2 pm and dinner 5-9 pm. 667-7001.

Many island restaurants will be happy to provide catering service.

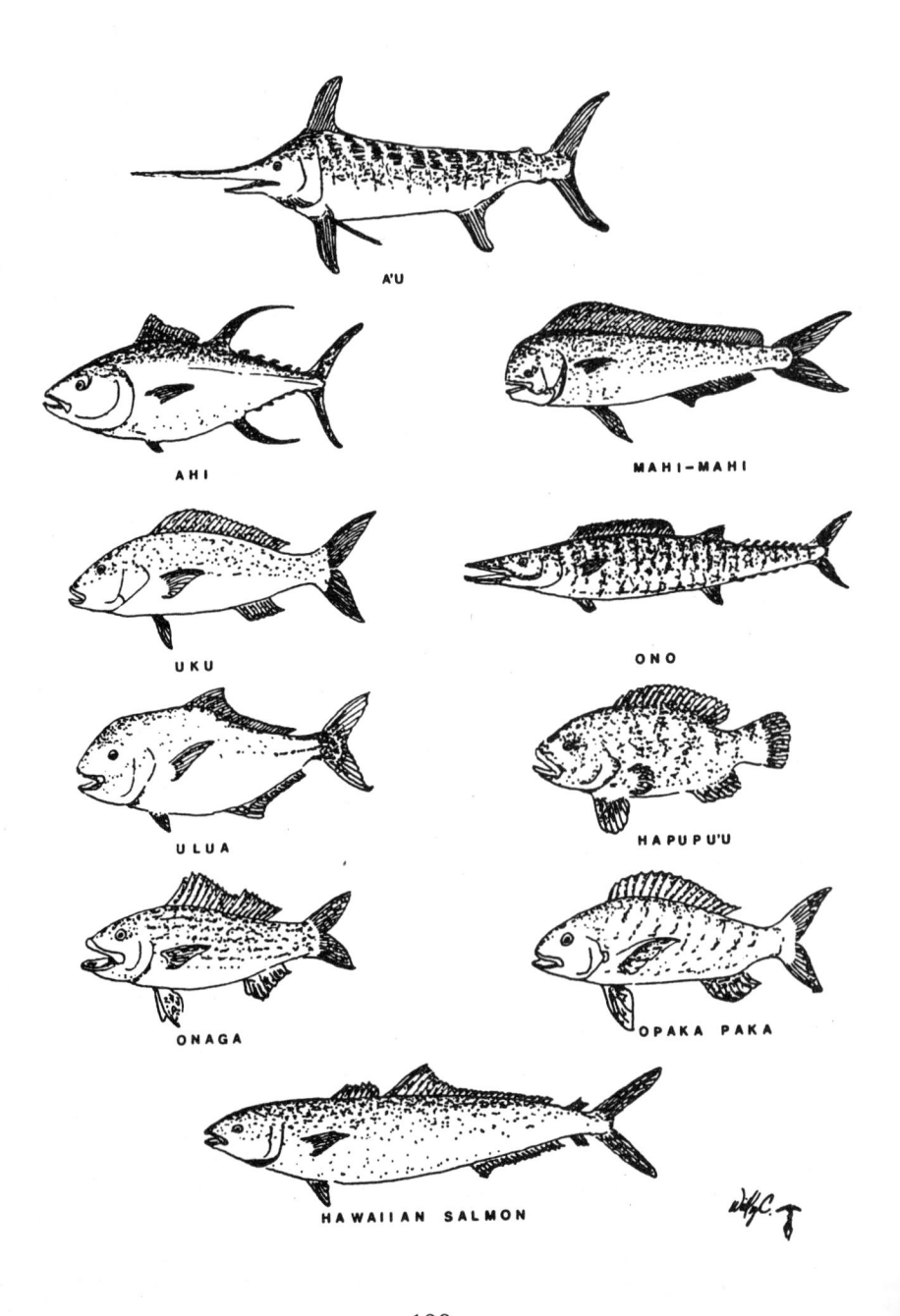

A'U

AHI

MAHI—MAHI

UKU

ONO

ULUA

HAPUPU'U

ONAGA

OPAKA PAKA

HAWAIIAN SALMON

190

# A FEW WORDS ABOUT FISH

Whether cooking fish at your condominium or eating out, the names of the island fish can be confusing. While local shore fishermen catch shallow water fish such as Goatfish or Papio for their dinner table, commercial fishermen angle for two types. The steakfish are caught by trolling in deep waters and include Ahi, Ono, and Mahi. They sometimes provide a healthy struggle before being landed. The more delicate bottom fish include Opakapaka and Onaga which are caught with lines dropped as deep as 1,500 feet to ledges or shelves off Maui's west shoreline. Here is a little background on the fish you might find on your dinner plate.

A'U - The broadbill swordfish averages 250 lbs. in Hawaiian waters. Hard to locate, difficult to hook, and a challenge to land. Considered a steakfish.

AHI - The yellow fin tuna (Allison tuna) is caught in deep waters off the Kaua'i coast. The pinkish red meat is firm yet flaky. This fish is popular for sashimi. They weigh between 60 and 280 pounds.

ALBACORE - This smaller version of the Ahi averages 40 - 50 pounds and is lighter in both texture and color.

AKU - This is the blue fin tuna.

EHU - Orange snapper

HAPU - Hawaiian sea bass

KAMAKAMAKA - Island catfish, very tasty, but a little difficult to find.

LEHI - The Silver Mouth is a member of the snapper family with a stronger flavor than Onaga or Opakapaka and a texture resembling Mahi.

MAHI - Although called the dolphin fish, this is no relation to Flipper or his friends. Caught while trolling and weighing 10-65 lbs. this is a seasonal fish which causes it to command a high price when fresh. *Beware*, while excellent fresh, it is often served in restaurants having arrived from the Philippines frozen and is far less pleasing. A clue as to whether fresh or frozen may be the price tag. If it runs less than $10 it is probably the frozen variety. Fresh Mahi will run $16 - $20 a dinner. This fish has excellent white meat that is moist and light. It is very good sauteed.

MU'U - We tried this mild white fish at the Makawao Steak House and were told there is no common name for this fish. We've never seen it served elsewhere in restaurants.

ONAGA (ULA) - Caught in holes that are 1,000 feet or deeper, this red snapper has an attractive hot pink exterior with tender, juicy, white meat inside.

ONO - Also known as Wahoo. ONO means "very good." A member of the Barracuda family, its white meat is firm and more steaklike. It is caught at depths of 25-100 fathoms while trolling and weighs 15 to 65 pounds.

'OPAE - Shrimp

OPAKAPAKA - Otherwise known as pink snapper and one of our favorites. The meat is very light and flaky with a delicate flavor.

PAPIO - A baby Ulua which is caught in shallow waters and weighs 5-25 lbs.

UKU - The meat of this grey snapper is light, firm and white with a texture that varies with size. It is very popular with local residents. This fish is caught off Kaua'i, usually in the deep Paka Holes.

ULUA - Also known as Pompano, this fish is firm and flaky with steaklike, textured white meat. It is caught by trolling, bottom fishing, or speared by divers and weighs between 15 and 110 pounds.

# LUAUS AND DINNER SHOWS

For a local luau, check the Maui News. You may be fortunate to find one of the area churches or schools sponsoring a fund-raising luau. The public is welcome and the prices are usually half that of the commercial ventures. You'll see wonderful spontaneous, local entertainment.

Most of the luaus are large, with an average of 400 - 600 guests, with one of the smallest being the Old Lahaina Luau with only 280. Most serve traditional Hawaiian foods. The entertainment ranges from splashy broadway-style productions to a country barbecue, or a more authentic Hawaiian dance and song. In general there are a few standard things to be expected at most luaus. These are shell leis, photos (usually done for an extra fee), an imu ceremony, playing the Hawaiian wedding song, kalua pig, poi, and haupia (coconut pudding). Upon arrival there may or may not be some waiting in line before it's your turn to be greeted with a shell lei and a snapshot of your group (available for purchase after the show). The exception is the Grand Wailea which includes a flower lei and a free photo.

It is very difficult to judge these luaus due to their diversity. While one reader raves about a particular show, another reader will announce their disappointment with the same event. Read carefully the information provided keeping in mind that the performers do come and go. Luau prices run $42 - $58 for adults, most have youth prices discounted by about half.

### OVERALL BEST BETS
Best Atmosphere, Food and Luau - South Maui - Maui Inter-Continental Resort, Grand Wailea Resort & Spa
Best Atmosphere, Food and Luau - West Maui - Old Lahaina Luau
Most authentic - Old Lahaina Luau

The following listing is alphabetical.

### GRAND WAILEA RESORT & SPA ★
In Wailea, there is always room for another good luau. The one at the Grand Wailea is the newest to join the many varied luaus around the island, and it is also the most expensive. Luau guests are asked to meet in the front lobby at 5:15 pm where you are greeted by the entertainers who come up to meet you and do a pre-show in the lobby bar. Some hula and even a bit of a fire-knife dance are performed. Not only does this get people in the mood, but it is a good advertisement for those wandering around the resort. This is also a good way to ensure that the guests don't get lost enroute to the luau grounds. Located in an area past their HumuHumu restaurant, the luau grounds are near the ocean, which you can see through the hedges. A fresh flower lei (wow!) is provided along with a drink (Mai Tai or punch) as you set up for your complimentary (yes, that is free!) picture. Entering through a thatched hut, the area is nicely decorated in Hawaiian style with nets and fresh fruit and tables with real chairs. They have a cocktail-only show with a separate seating (if the luau doesn't sell out). A Hawaiian trio entertains and at 6:15 pm they light the torches and the dancers escort the guests to the imu ceremony. This one IS a ceremony, with the pig placed on a tray with

192

long handles surrounded by fruit and leaves and carried from the imu with honors. The pig is served at the table family style. There are two buffet lines which speeds serving. The food was good, the salads were classy and included local style such as lomi lomi, tako, poi along with a fancy mixed green. Hot dishes included pork fried rice, sweet potato with macadamia nuts and coconuts, stir fried vegetables (made in a wok on the luau grounds), teriyaki chicken breasts with a tangy orange peel and hoisin sauce, mahi, fresh papaya salsa (very good), teriyaki steak and a big pan of shellfish steamed in champagne and black bean sauce. Taro rolls and nori (the seaweed stuff used for sushi) were unusual, flavorful and very fresh. The dessert table had haupia (coconut pudding) along with trays of pineapple, melons, and strawberries, assorted miniature cakes and coffee cheesecake. Their Hawaiian sweet bread pudding was topped with fresh thick whipped cream. Very good gourmet food for a luau. The luau show was a cut above too, with no tired lounge show type MC. There were some songs and hula during dinner before the big production which included dances from Samoa, Tahiti, Kahiko hula warriors, and spear dancing with some battle scenes. An explanation of the tatoos on their faces and what they meant was an interesting touch. There were not one, not two, but three fire knife dancers! Most luaus have audience participation of some kind. Often times it is a chance to make the audience members look foolish. The audience did participate at the very end, in a kind of Tahitian finale, which wasn't as bad as some. Just as the show ended, the full moon was beginning to rise behind the stage, and was silhouetted by palm trees. Of course this isn't an every night happening, but it certainly added a special touch to the end of a very enjoyable evening. In summary, the food was a highlight, except for the steaks which were terrible compared to the rest of the food. The MC was a little dull compared to others, but all in all, you pay more, but you get some pleasant extras.

## HOTEL HANA-MAUI AT HANA RANCH
Hamoa Beach Luau is held at Lehoula Beach on Tuesdays at 6 pm. Open to non-hotel guests based on availability for $55.21 including tax. Guests of the hotel are transported via hay wagon or van to the beachfront luau location. A very local and family-oriented production. Many of those involved in the entertainment are folks you might see working in another capacity around the hotel. Phone 248-8211.

## HYATT REGENCY
Hyatt Regency Kaanapali. The "Drums of the Pacific" is more a dinner show than a luau format. It is held on the grounds of the Hyatt, however, there is no ocean view. A 5:30 pm arrival was suggested (times change seasonally), which meant standing in line until 6 pm. Pictures were taken while waiting prior to admission to the grounds, where you were greeted with a lei and taken to a table by your server. The dinner buffet features ono with a nice Hollandaise-type sauce and tropical salsa. The steaks were cooked to order on the grill and were very good. Big slices of Kula potato were unusual and good, as was the kim chee. The desserts were a cut above with the haupia having good texture and favor, the hot bread pudding was baked with a meringue topping and the macadamia nut cream pie didn't have that awful synthetic taste that cream pies sometimes do. They began a new show recently which starts off with a welcome chant by Cliff Ahue who also does the free hula show at the Kapalua Shops. His voice is beautiful and enchanting and his choreography has always been very Hawaiian and very authentic. The kahiko hula followed the chant and had a very effective fog or mist surrounding the dancers. The Imu ceremony was short and nondescript, but did

have the "Pig Procession" carrying his majesty through the center aisle of the audience. A separate side stage for solo dances made things visually interesting. Perhaps the best number was the Maui Waltz, a pretty song with girls in high collared white Victorian blouses and colored skirts. Chief Fa, the fire dancer, continues to be one of the best. A good, professional, fast-paced production, although the Wayne Newton look-alike MC may be to your liking or annoyance. They also offer a cocktail-only show at 7 pm. All in all, it was a show worth seeing. Currently four nights a week. Prices $44 for adults, juniors $36. Cocktail seating $26 adults, $23 for children.

### KAANAPALI BEACH HOTEL (Tiki Terrace)
Auntie Aloha's Breakfast Luau is a bit out of the ordinary. Primarily an orientation breakfast for hotel guests, but anyone can attend. Auntie Aloha has been a vacation briefer for nine years with both American Express and Pleasant Hawaiian Holidays and her goal is to guide visitors toward the most exciting and sometimes unpublicized things to do. Visitors can enjoy Mai Tais, and a breakfast buffet, Mon.-Thurs., $9.95. Not personally reviewed.

### MAUI INTER-CONTINENTAL RESORT ★
The Inter-Continental refers to their luau as "Wailea's Finest Luau" and we'd have to agree. The fabulous outdoor setting in their luau garden is both beautiful and spacious with a sublime ocean view. The stage is set up to offer the ocean and beautiful sunset as backdrop. An open bar is available. Dinner moves swiftly through several buffet lines serving sauteed ono, teriyaki steak and kalua pig (which was the best of the all the luaus with good flavor, solid but juicy texture and chunks of meat). The dessert table remains the best of the luaus, with plenty of varied pies. Kauluwehi is the show MC and he introduced the show after an opening kahiko hula, which was followed by a paniolo number, and then a Hollywood hula with the girls in their brightly colored cellophane skirts. The MC did a Princess Pupule number that was cute and funny. No bad lounge jokes, but instead pleasant narratives. The choreography was done by Kauluwehi and was particularly good. More love songs, Tahitian numbers and finally the fire-knife dancer, Ifi So'o, who proved to be the best of any of the luaus. He did stunts, somersaults across the stage and even seemed to twirl much faster. After a half

dozen luaus, it is pretty hard to be impressed, but this guy was impressive. (Apparently the judges in Honolulu thought so too: he just won the 1994 World Championship Fire-Knife Dancer competition held at the Polynesian Cultural Center.) The music is still provided by the group Paradyse and they did an Over the Rainbow number that was wonderful. The final number was Somewhere Out There, which wasn't at all Hawaiian, but finished the show with a nice touch. This luau continues to rate in our book as the best overall luau, running a close tie with the Grand Wailea. This luau is $6 less, but then the Grand does provide a free flower lei and picture, so it is about the same. The show begins just as the sun is setting with Ka Poe o Hawaii and Paradyse. This show features a good range, quality of entertainment and one of the best outdoor settings. And, an outstanding fire-dancer. For overall food, entertainment and setting, this is a great luau. Tues.-Thur.- Fri., 5:30-8 pm. Adults $52, children 6-10 $26. Phone 879-1922.

## MAUI LU

Maui Lu in Kihei. Twice weekly, the "Legends of Hawaii" bills itself as a dinner show. The show transports you back in time, but not necessarily ancient Polynesia. The whole experience had a very nostalgic '60s feel about it. The Maui Lu Longhouse (which has been doing dinner/luau shows off and on for years) is an old-fashioned dinner showroom, the kind that was around just after statehood when tourism was just beginning in the islands. It is the kind of place and show you'd expect in an old Elvis movie or a teenage surfer movie where a bunch of "guys and gals" are on vacation in equal parable numbers so they can all converge at some big clubhouse to meet and fall in love. Then Elvis or some other amazingly talented member of the group gets up and performs some spontaneous song or drum solo or something. In other words, you wouldn't have felt out of place in a flower shift with a bubble hairdo! It was a simple and basic show and atmosphere and the food the type you would have found at luaus before they became big business. In keeping with that kind of old-fashioned theme, the two best things about the buffet were the homemade soup, a big pot of turkey vegetable, and real cooked chocolate and vanilla pudding served in stemmed glassware for dessert. The buffet also included prime rib, roast pork, mahi, chicken and assorted side dishes and salads. A nice touch was the passion fruit iced tea. No imu ceremony, so the show began with the blowing of the conch shells. The MC duties rotate between Hulu Lindsey and Jesse Nakaooka. Not being a fan of Jesse, we were pleased that our evening we had Hulu. She was pleasant, providing a straight narration, and no bad jokes. The short audience participation number was quick and painless, recognizing honeymoon and anniversary couples in the audience with husbands coming on stage to get a flower lei to present to their wives, followed by the Hawaiian Wedding Song. The standard numbers from Tahiti, Samoa and elsewhere were interspersed with legends of lovers or other pieces of history. Auntie Lani (of Pancake Cottage fame) did her famous "naughty" hula that she used to perform at Auntie Emma's Aloha Mele luncheons years ago. This more casual atmosphere was evidenced by the number of locals in the audience, as well as a kumu hula group from Oahu. We're uncertain if the 60's nostalgic feel of this show was planned or it just happened, but it was a nice and unusual element. At $48.50 (including open bar and gratuity) this is one of Maui's least expensive shows (look for the $40 coupon or call direct to make your reservations). Children are $24.50 and be sure to ask for senior citizen rates or kamaaina prices if appropriate. Again, a good production, but not top of the line. If you're looking for a more local luau, this is the one.

## MAUI MARRIOTT RESORT

Daily except Monday, $50 for adults, children $24. The bar opens at 6:45 pm for drinks while guests can enjoy, and participate in, Hawaiian games and crafts from 5-6 pm. Beginning at 6:45, fruit punch and Mai Tais are available and continue through the show from a self-service table. The imu ceremony is held following the games and crafts and the show begins with Auntie Betsy Hinau. She is both a talented singer and a hostess, and comes through naturally. While guests line up for the buffet, Betsy narrates a fashion show with muu muus, pareaus and the like. The food lines move quickly past the selection of kalua pig, teriyaki beef steak, sweet and sour chicken, mahi mahi, fried rice and more. The show begins with Barry Kim as MC. The presentation is a lively one, with Fiji warriors doing lots of high jumps, a Hollywood hula segment and the Maori men from New Zealand and girls with poi balls doing an effective number. The fire-knife dancer is the finale. Although we think Betsy would have been a wonderful warm MC for the entire show, Barry seemed to keep the crowd well entertained. This is one of those luaus that offered nothing truly exceptional or extraordinary, but it certainly had everything you go to for a luau for, so nothing was lacking or disappointing.

## OLD LAHAINA LUAU ★

The Old Lahaina Luau at 505 Front Street in Lahaina is situated right on the beach and offers the most beautiful luau setting. A celebration of aloha in the traditional Hawaiian style is emphasized with guests greeted by flower leis and offered a choice between table sitting or mats on the ground. The many young Hawaiians that form their helpful and friendly staff dressed in colorful Hawaiian garb. One beautiful young lady demonstrates and sells leis by the water's edge. They provide a souvenir program which they can personalize for each party attending and even add Happy Anniversary or Congratulations salutations too. This luau is one of Maui's smallest, with a maximum of 280 people. Following the imu ceremony it's time to visit the buffet where selections include a pleasing array of half a dozen salads and entrees such as chicken, fish and, of course, kalua pig! They've added new beverage service and now serve tropical drinks which include pina coladas and chichis and have added a taro leaf salad, a seafood salad and BBQ sirloin steaks to their buffet line. There are four buffet lines which speed the guests through smoothly. Get your cameras ready as the show begins with a bit of a surprise. The show changes from time to time, but it is strictly Hawaiian, no fire-knife dancers here. Auntie Eileen and Piilani Jones perform the duties of show hostesses. For food, atmosphere and good Hawaiian entertainment rates this luau the best in West Maui. Make sure you make your reservations in advance, as this has become a popular attraction. They have received top honors receiving the "Keep it Hawaii" Kahili Awards program sponsored by the Hawaii Visitors Bureau. Held Tues.-Sat. at 5:30 pm. Phone 667-1998. Adults $56, children $28, tax not included.

## PIONEER INN

A Polynesian Revue at the Pioneer Inn was recently introduced. Friday afternoon only, from 11:30 am-2 pm. The Aloha Friday Lunch Buffet and Polynesian Review is hosted by Rodney Arias. The buffet show runs $25 for adults $10 for children 12 and under or order from the regular menu and add $10 for the show. The buffet includes one complimentary beverage (coffee, soda or tea) with bar service available. Seating for 150, they can also schedule private functions. The food proved to be good, and Rodney Arias is a great MC.

The Pioneer Inn courtyard atmosphere is pleasant and it is a nice afternoon option. Visitors are kind of geared to evening performances and an afternoon buffet is a little too much food for some. The menu option is a great idea. A good price, and a pleasant alternative. We hope it catches on!

### ROYAL LAHAINA RESORT

In Kaanapali. Nightly at 5:30 or 6 pm (changes seasonally), $47 plus tax for adults, $23.50 or children 5-12 years, children under 5 free. The ready-made Mai Tais, fruit punch, open bar and shell leis were the first order of business, but they have a new twist on the photographs. They take two of them, one with your party and male and female greeters, and the other is a circle inset in a picture of the luau performers on stage, making it an effective souvenir. The luau grounds are near the ocean, but without an ocean view (unless you peek over the hedge). Seating is at padded picnic table benches. The imu ceremony was the shortest and some people hadn't even reached the pit before it was over!

While people were settling in, hostess Makalapua welcomed guests. Dinner began at 6:45 with four tables and eight lines allowing people to flow quickly through. Real "glass" glasses for drinks were a pleasant surprise, although the coffee cups were plastic. Large wooden trays offered plenty of room to pile on the teri beef, kalua pig, pineapple chicken, lomi lomi salmon, poi and salad bar with an interesting selection of pea salad, macaroni, mein noodles and more. The desserts had improved from the last visit and the coconut cream cake was particularly good as was the passion fruit cake (although it tasted more like carrot). Frank Hewitt, a prominent kumuhula and songwriter is the show's choreographer and he wrote all the songs in the show, except the Hawaiian Wedding song. Just the right amount of audience interaction with Makalapua providing a short hula lesson with instructions about moving and wiggling your papayas and bananas, which was sort of cute. A fashion show followed and the production began with the blowing of

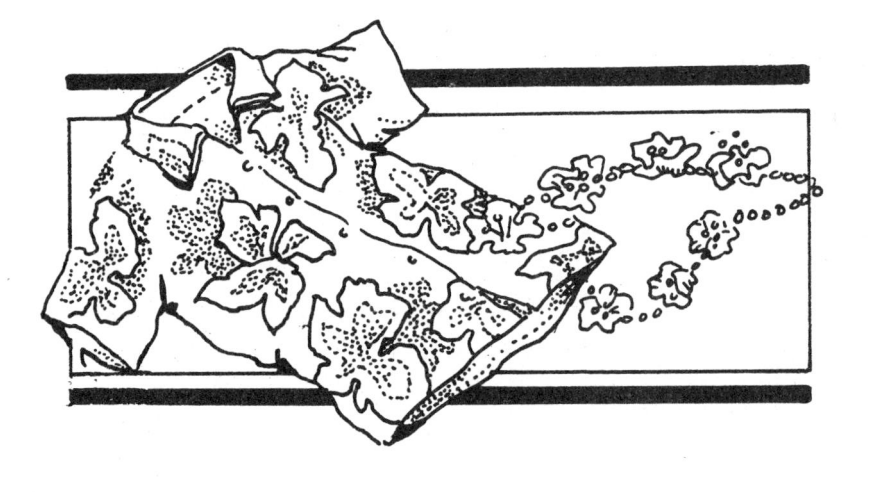

the conch shell and kahiko hula, male dancers, making a nice entrance thru the audience to be joined by the female dancers on stage. Co-MC Warren Molina sang a lively countryish dance which was followed by several very entertaining numbers. The song and hula about the legend of the rain resulted in a very fine water spray reaching the front of the audience. They still have the Hollywood number which is a fun piece, followed by a romantic Hawaiian song. The finale was the fire-knife dance.

Drawbacks at this luau included the gravel covered dirt ground which made annoying crunching sounds as people got up throughout the show to pick up a drink at the bar, which remained open during the show. This is another good, but not great luau. A nice touch is the original music and choreography. They have the advantage of moving their luau into their indoor Alii Room if the weather is uncooperative.

### SHERATON MAUI HOTEL
At Kaanapali. Sheraton is closing for renovation beginning December 1994 and is slated to remain closed for two years.

### HAWAIIAN COUNTRY BARBECUE-TROPICAL PLANTATION
Waikapu. Currently on Tuesday, Wednesday and Thursday 4:45-7:30 pm. The theme is a combination Hawaiiana and cowboy country and it works well musically and visually. The dancers wore muu muus, but they were made out of gingham and bandanna prints. When they wore jeans, they also wore hakuleis or had flowers in their hair. The music was fun with Buddy Fo as the headliner. The food was, in some cases, surprisingly good, with steaks grilled on an outdoor BBQ and an all-American selection on the buffet table. BBQ chicken thighs, cornbread, chips and salsa served with an excellent homemade guacamole. The dessert table was mediocre fare. Mai Tais and sodas were available during the meal. A nice addition was the real silverware and set tables! The audience appeared to have fun and clapped along with the show. Adults $46.95, children 5 - 17 years $19.95, plus tax, under five no charge. For a fee they can supply transportation from your accommodations to the Tropical Plantation. Inquire when making reservations, 244-7643.

## *Here are some facts and figures you may not want to know!*

Luaus are definitely not low-calorie dining options. So eat and enjoy, but just in case you are interested, here is the breakdown! Kalua Pig 1/2 cup 150 calories, Lomi Lomi salmon 1/2 cup 87 calories, Poi 1 cup 161 calories (but who could eat that much!), fried rice 1 cup 200 calories, fish (depending on type served) 150-250 calories, chicken long rice 283 calories, haupia 128 calories, coconut cake 200-350 calories, Mai Tai 302 calories, Pina Colada 252 calories, fruit punch 140 calories, Blue Hawaii 260 calories, Chi Chi 190 calories.

# LAHAINA

## INEXPENSIVE

**AMILIO'S DELICATESSEN**   *American*
840 Wainee St., Lahaina Square, north end of town (661-8551) HOURS: Mon,-Fri. 8 am-8 pm, Sat. 8 am-6 pm, Sun. 8 am-4 pm. COMMENTS: Take out or eat in. Deli sandwiches ($4.75-$4.95/second sandwich $.99), plate lunches ($3.95-$4.95). New owners are Ron and Rosemary "Mom" Boswell.

**ATHENS GREEK RESTAURANT**   *Greek*
Located inside the Lahaina Cannery Mall (661-4300) HOURS: 9:30 am-9 pm daily. A fast food Greek restaurant features Gyros or Souvlaki Shishkabob $5.15, platter special $7.25, Greek salad $5.25. COMMENTS: Limited mall seating.

**B.J.'S CHICAGO PIZZERIA**   *Italian*
730 Front St. (661-0700) HOURS: 11 am-11 pm, same menu all day. SAMPLING: Pizzas for the small, medium or large appetite includes a Lahaina Pie (Portuguese sausage, black beans, cilantro and red onions) $13.95-$21.95, or a cheese and tomato pizza $7.45-$12.56 to add your own toppings. B.J. specialty salads include chopped Italian or sesame chicken $.95-$7.45, pasta dishes $6.95-$10.95, homemade sandwiches on B.J.'s freshly baked rolls $4.95-$6.50. COMMENTS: The landmark Front Street location opened the summer of 1994 and is filled with woodwork, murals and historic photographs, back to the tradition of it's former life as The Blue Max. This is the ninth restaurant in the B.J. chain and they come to Maui with a good reputation. Their deep-dish Chicago-style pizza has a crust that is thick, while surprisingly light and the toppings are fresh and innovative. For dessert try their Pizookie n' Cream, a chocolate chip or white chocolate and macadamia cookie baked in a mini-pizza pan and served warm with vanilla ice cream.

**THE BAKERY ★**   *French/American*
911 Limahana (turn off Honoapiilani Hwy. by Pizza Hut) (667-9062) HOURS: Mon.-Fri. 5:30 am-3 pm, Sat. 5:30 am-2 pm, Sun. 5:30 am-noon. SAMPLING: Whole wheat cream cheese croissants, also ham, or turkey-stuffed croissants, or small sandwiches such as turkey dijon. Huge fresh fruit tortes, fudge, and fresh breads are made here daily. COMMENTS: There is no seating area. Arrive early in the day to insure getting the best selections. It's well worth the stop if you are a lover of pastries. Try their stuffed Tongan bread! The selections are delicious!

**BETWEEN THE BUNS**   *Sandwiches*
888 Wainee Street, (661-5733). HOURS: 11 am-2 pm. SAMPLING: Sandwiches!

**BLUE LAGOON**   *American*
658 Front. St. Located on the lower level of the Wharf Cinema Center (661-8141) HOURS: 11 am-9:30 pm. SAMPLING: Sandwiches include prime rib, turkey or club sandwiches, soup, and assorted steak and seafood entrees $6.95-$16.95. BLT and club sandwiches served until 5 pm, all other menu items available all day. Table seating in the courtyard of the center.

### BURGER KING  *American*
632 Front St., (667-6162) By the Banyan Tree. HOURS: 6:30 am-11 pm, Fri. & Sat. until midnight. SAMPLING: Breakfast sandwiches, salad bar, and theusual burgers at prices slightly higher than the mainland. (Another Burger King located at the Cannery Mall, 661-4395, open 9 am-9 pm daily.)

### CHEESEBURGER IN PARADISE ★  *American*
811 Front St., Lahaina (661-4855) HOURS: Lunch/dinner served 10 am-11 pm SAMPLING: Select from their classic BLT $5.95, calamari rings $6.50, and a number of vegetarian dishes included a tofu, spinach nut or garden burger $6.95. Their famous "Cheeseburger in Paradise" is $6.95. COMMENTS: A casual dining atmosphere with open-air dining and wonderful views of the Lahaina Harbor and Front Street from the upstairs loft. Very good hamburgers, plus a view at no charge! Live music nightly 4-7 pm and 8 - 11 pm. They also have created some new tropical drinks. The Lahaina Sunburn, the Lahainaluna Swirl or how about Trouble in Paradise? It can be crowded at meal times.

### CHUBBY'S HIDEAWAY  *Mexican*
Lahaina Business Plaza, behind the Chevron (661-9113). HOURS: Mon.-Fri. 11 am-7:30 pm, Sat. until 4 pm. SAMPLING: Ala carte items are the usual Mexican fare from enchiladas, to hard or soft shell tacos, tostados, Mexican salad, nachos and burritos $2.25-$4.75 Combination plates include rice and beans $6-$7. COMMENTS: Chubby isn't so chubby, but tucked away in the Lahaina Business Plaza, it is certainly a hideaway.

### CHUN'S KOREAN RESTAURANT  *Korean*
658 Front St., Wharf Cinema Center. (661-9207) HOURS: Lunch and dinner 10 am-10 pm. SAMPLING: Beef bul ko gi $7.50/$12.50 (thinly sliced BBQ marinated meat), Meat Jun (BBQ beef in egg batter), Kook soo (noodles, vegetables and egg in a clear broth) or Yuk ke jang (spicy beef soup with vegetables and rice noodle). The BBQ dishes are cooked on table with grill in the center.

### DENNY'S  *American*
Lahaina Square Shopping Center (667-9878) HOURS: 24 hours a day. SAMPLING: Breakfast served anytime. Burgers and local style dishes. Dinners include steak, seafood and chicken $7 - $12.

KONA COFFEE                                    JBAYOT

**GOLDEN PALACE**   *Chinese*
Lahaina Shopping Center (661-3126) HOURS: Lunch 11 am-2 pm, dinner 5-9 pm. Also take out. SAMPLING: A large variety of selections with Chinese and some Szechuan dishes. Affordably priced from $6 - $12. COMMENTS: Beer, cocktails, and Chinese wine are also available. This place is an institution on Maui, in business now for 29 years.

**HARD ROCK CAFE** ★   *American*
Lahaina Center. (667-7400) HOURS: Daily from 11 am, bar opens 11:30. SAMPLING: Grilled burgers or chicken breast sandwiches $6.95-$8.95, lime BBQ chicken $10.95, HRC famous baby rock watermelon ribs $12.95. Chicken, beef or combination fajitas $10.95. COMMENTS: A lively atmosphere, if the music isn't too loud for you. Fun and interesting memorabilia around the room, such as a Steinberger guitar signed by Ziggy Marley, a bustier worn by Madonna during her 1989 world tour, or an autographed bass drum skin by Fleetwood Mac. And not to worry, they can provide you with a brochure to serve as a self-guided tour of this rock-n-roll memorabilia that covers the restaurant walls AND the bathrooms, too.

A very popular eatery, possibly due to the great prices and good food, so expect it might be crowded or even a waiting line to get in during peak dining hours. This is one of the places the kids will want to be sure visit, if not to eat, then to get a T-shirt!

**HAWAII'S BEST ESPRESSO COMPANY**   *Coffee/pastry*
736-D Front St. (667-2666) HOURS: Mon.-Sat. 7 am-10 pm, Sunday 8 am-10 pm. SAMPLING: Danish, cookies, cinnamon rolls or muffins are the only food fare here, but order an espresso drink, or try one of their Granitas (an icy, thin coffee beverage) while giving the feet a rest from your day in Lahaina. They have a number of chairs and tables in the rear with a reading room offering books, magazines and a daily paper.

### JUICY'S SANDWICH AND JUICE BAR  *Vegetarian*
505 Front St. #142, Lahaina (667-5727) HOURS: 8:30 am-9 pm Mon.-Sat., 11 am-6 pm on Sunday. SAMPLING: Freshly squeezed juices, including wheat grass $3-$4.50. Specialties include hummus wrap, nachos, burrito, garden or tofu burger $2.75-$4.95. Mile high sandwiches include avocado, hummus, egg salad or tempeh. Daily entrees served with a salad and vary from Shepherds pie to veggie lasagna or seitan pepper steak. (Editor's note: Jean Merrick gives Juicy's her vote for the best sandwiches on Maui! And daughter Dona says she's usually right!)

### KIROUAC'S  *Sandwiches*
180 Dickenson St., (661-7299) Located at Dickenson Square, the corner of Wainee and Dickenson. This deli and cafe is open Mon.-Thurs. 7:30 am- 9 pm, Fri. and Sat. 7:30 am-10 pm, Sun. 8 am-8 pm. SAMPLING: Deli sandwiches from $4.75, smoothies $3.59, hot entrees are limited to pasta with marinara $3.95, roast beef or roast turkey $4.95, Italian lasagna $4.29. Sunrise fare includes waffles, omelettes, and bagels. Everything is made fresh. Worth the walk uptown! COMMENTS: Limited seating, a few tables outside and inside.

### LAHAINA BROILER  *Seafood/American*
887 Front St. (661-3111) HOURS: Lunch 11 am-2 pm, late lunch 2-5 pm, dinner 5-11 pm. Sunday brunch 9 am-2 pm. SAMPLING: Sunday brunch is served off the menu, not buffet style, and includes omelettes, egg dishes, hot cakes, burgers and salads $6.95-$11.95. Lunch sandwiches, salads or entrees $4.95 - $9.25. Dinner entrees served with seafood chowder, bean soup or tossed salad. Entrees Hawaiian fish and fries, shrimp Tahitian, seafood brochette, baby back ribs $11.95-$19.95. COMMENTS: A wonderful, open ocean view setting done in hues of grey, green and mauve. While the atmosphere is great the food has not proven to be outstanding. A good meal, but perhaps not a great one. An outstanding location for an evening beverage.

### LAHAINA TREEHOUSE TROPICAL BAR & RESTAURANT
*Seafood-American*
Lahaina Market Place on Front St. (661-3235) HOURS: Lunch & dinner-same menu 11 am-9 pm. After 5 pm dinner specials. SAMPLING: Mahi mahi sandwich, pirate shrimp, NY steak, Philly sandwich, grilled chicken breast sandwich, all served with fries or salad $6.95-$7.97. COMMENTS: Renovation has provided lighter decor and a more open feeling. Food service currently available only on the ground floor.

### LANI'S BY DAY/ALEX'S BY NIGHT ★  *American/Italian*
658 Front St., Wharf Cinema Center, across from the Banyan Tree (661-0955) HOURS: Breakfast 6 am-3 pm, lunch from 11 am. Dinner from 6 pm. SAMPLING: In addition to the popular breakfast fare they offer entrees such as fish and chips or chili burgers $4.50 - $6.50. COMMENTS: Very busy during breakfast hours, offering seating indoors or on the patio. Alex's Hole in the Wall purchased this restaurant from Lani, and has now brought their popular Italian food to this location each evening. They've closed their original Alex's location at the other end of Lahaina.

**MCDONALD'S** *American*
Located at Lahaina Shopping Center (667-2681) HOURS: 6 am-10 pm, Mon.-Thurs., 6 am-11 pm Fri. and Sat. HOURS: Open for breakfast, lunch, and dinner. SAMPLING: The usual for McDonald's with a few added items such as Saimin. COMMENTS: Indoor eating and also a drive-thru.

**MOONDOGGIES** *Italian-American*
666 Front St., Lahaina (661-3966) HOURS: Daily 8 am-10 pm daily. SAMPLING: Breakfast served until noon, omelettes, quiche and fruit, Hawaiian pancakes $4.95-$7.50, lunch fare served noon until 5 pm includes hot dog $5.55, and sandwiches $6.95-$7.95, dinners are under $20. COMMENTS: Owner Koji Takashima's restaurant theme is "surf bistro" in decor making a very light and spacious atmosphere and a good use for this open-air location. The Italian food ($10.95-$12.95 for dinner) is better than average, with good spaghetti and meatballs even! The "Big Curls" is a sort of combination between calzone and cornish pastie, baked dough stuffed with several options. The spinach filling was excellent, using fresh leaves that had been lightly marinated. The sliders are miniburgers. Or how about the apple pizza pie a la mode! You can get a whole "pizza" or just a slice. Basically it is a slice of pizza with apple pie topping and a big scoop of ice cream, served warm ($3.25)!

**ORANGE JULIUS** *American/Sandwiches*
Wharf Cinema Center, lower level. HOURS: Daily 9:30 am-9:30 pm SAMPLING: Owner Kris Krewson has gone beyond the usual OJ, so we feel they merit a listing. A variety of hot dogs include the more unusual pepperoni or Rueben dog $1.82-$2.40, nachos $1.75-$3.25, hamburger or hot dog chili plate lunches $5, and daily specials $4-$6.50. Soups and salads round out the menu. Seasonal Julius flavors include guava-passion, mango, pina colada or Tropical Julius. Yum!

**PIKAKE BAKERY & CAFE** ★ *Sandwiches/Pastries*
505 Front St. (661-5616) HOURS: Mon.-Fri. 7:30 am-6 pm, Sat. until 5 pm. SAMPLING: Their signature cake is an almond cake brushed with Frangelico and filled with chocolate mousse! Breads include red potato with rosemary, Mexican jalapenos, or sundried tomato. Danishes, muffins and scones too. For lunch they offer daily specials along with salads, meatless lasagna, eggplant parmesan, chicken cordon bleu or foccacio pizza $2.95-$6.95. COMMENTS: Their breads are all sugar-free and vegetarian (except for those containing cheese) and are baked fresh daily. They also have a location in Kihei.

**PIZZA HUT** *Italian*
127 Hinau, Lahaina, (661-3696). HOURS: 11 am-10 pm daily, Fri. and Sat. until 11 pm. They now have seven locations on Maui from Honokowai to Kihei, and from Kahului and up to Pukalani. We've heard some good reports on their salad bar. COMMENTS: For years we have driven by, and never stopped. After all, we have Pizza Huts at home, so why eat here? So, we still have never stopped, but we keep getting letters from those of you who do that the pizza is great and so is the salad bar. In fact we probably get more letters about this single restaurant than any other.

**PLANET HOLLYWOOD** *California Cuisine*
744 Front St. (667-7877). HOURS: 10 am-2 am daily. SAMPLING: A selection of smoked and grilled meats and fish $13.95-$19.95, salads include Caesar with grilled chicken or shrimp $6.95-$11.95, pasta dishes $9.95-$10.75, fajitas $12.95-$13.95, burgers including turkey $6.95-$7.25, and pizzas $8.75-$9.75. The pasta selections include a vegetable combination, Oriental with E-fun noodles or a Linguine with fresh garlic and plum tomatoes. Desserts include Arnold Schwarzenegger's mother's renowned Apple Strudel, pina colada bread pudding or caramel crunch pie. COMMENTS: After two years on hold, this project was officially blessed in January 1994 and finally opened in June. Shareholders of this project include Arnold Schwarzengger, Bruce Willis, Sylvester Stallone, Demi Moore, among others. The food was actually better than expected, the chicken crunch (made with Cap'n Crunch cereal) was good, a fun idea and rather sweet tasting. The vegetable pasta was like a good primavera but with pesto. The Ebony and Ivory brownie had lots of rich flavor and texture. Similar to Hard Rock Cafe, they feature a collection of movie memorabilia including Cleo, the man-eating plant from Addams Family Values, the 5-foot whale model from Free Willy, the ship's figurehead from the original Mutiny on the Bounty and the Joker's helicopter from Batman. The downstairs level is colorful and lively, the upstairs submarine room is very effective with dim lighting and cozy booths. And no surprise here, you're also be able to buy T-shirts, watches, designer sunglasses, varsity jackets ($225), beach towels or bags, leather jackets ($325) and even swim suits in their merchandise shop. If we had a category for longest restaurant opening, this would be it!

**REY-CEL FILIPION FAST FOOD** (dba N.R. Fil Variety Store) *Filipino*
Lahaina Business Plaza 888 Wainee St. (667-5486) SAMPLING: Plate lunch selections with two scoops of rice. Three daily specials offered $3.95-$5.95. Take out only. They also operate at the Kahului Store at 230 Hana Hwy (871-6251).

**SAENG'S THAI ★** *Thai*
1312 Front St. (667-0822) HOURS: Lunch Mon.-Fri. 11 - 2; dinner daily 5-9:30 pm. SAMPLING: Entrees $7.50-$9.95, seafood dishes $8.50-$13.95, salads $5.50-$7.95, curries $7.50-$11.95. COMMENTS: Located on the outskirts of Lahaina across from the Cannery. Same menu as the Wailuku location, only here you can enjoy the ocean view and the sunset.

**SANDWICH ISLAND** *Sandwiches*
Lahaina Cannery (661-6128) HOURS: 9:30 am-8:30 pm daily. SAMPLING: Sandwiches served on French baguette, or large white or cracked wheat rolls. Sandwiches and salads $4.95-$4.25. Daily specials are generally pasta made fresh on Maui and include flavored varieties such as basil linguini or cilantro linguini.

**SCAROLES VILLAGE PIZZERIA** *Italian*
At 505 Front St. (661-8112) HOURS: Lunch and dinner daily. SAMPLING: Pizza is available in Neapolitan style (thin crust) or Sicilian (thick crust). A 14" plain pizza starts at $11.50, a combo of 4 items $16.25. Calzones and pasta items $6.50-$11.95. Lunch specials served 11 am-3 pm. COMMENTS: The clam and garlic pizza is a specialty here! There is also a Scaroles Restaurant with a full Italian menu in Lahaina and Scaroles Too restaurant in Wailea.

**SIR WILFRED'S ESPRESSO CAFE**   *Sandwiches/coffee*
Lahaina Cannery Mall, Kaanapali side of Lahaina (667-1941) HOURS: 9 am-9 pm. SAMPLING: Limited menu includes quiche, lasagna, sandwiches $3.95 - $5.95, pastries, cookies, cheesecake and they can be enjoyed with a great cup of coffee or an espresso drink. Also available is 100% Kona coffee by the pound. They also have the only walk-in humidor on Maui, so you cigar and pipe smokers will be delighted! COMMENTS: A very small, pleasant eatery. Gourmet coffees available for purchase.

**SONG'S ORIENTAL KITCHEN**   *Chinese-Hawaiian*
658 Front St. at the Wharf Cinema Center (667-1990) HOURS: Daily for lunch and dinner. SAMPLING: This is okazuya style buffet with chicken adobo, kim chee, stir fry vegetables and more. After viewing the selections in the display case, your plate is dished up for you. Only a single table near the door offers seating, or get yours to go. Saimin, lomi lomi, stuffed cabbage. Chow Fun $1.85, plate lunches $5, side dishes under $1.

**SUNRISE CAFE**   *Sandwiches/pasta*
693A Front St. (661-3326) HOURS: 6 am-10 pm. SAMPLING: All menu items under $7. Homemade soups, salads, plate lunches, salads, quiche, also espresso drinks and bakery items. COMMENTS: This is a very small, quaint eatery with food available to go.

**SUSHIYA**   ★ *Japanese*
117 Prison Street (661-5679). HOURS: Mon.-Fri. 6 am-4 pm, take out available. SAMPLING: Beef teri plate $4.75, chicken teri plate $3.95, hamburger $3.50, a la carte items include saimin $1.65, kim chee, corned beef hash, macaroni salad from $.60-$4.75. Plate lunches and daily specials $3.95-$5. COMMENTS: This place is a real find in West Maui. We've tried for 10 years to try out this hole-in-the-wall restaurant, and they were either closed or on vacation. In operation for 30 years, the daughter-in-law took over the family business about 15 years ago. Visitors are discovering what the locals have known for years. Inside you'll find family style tables and benches. It's a clean, comfortable self-service restaurant with no frills. Some interesting selections too -- how about a side order of eggplant or spam? So escape the hustle and bustle of in-town Lahaina and take a short walk for some local-style dining.

**TAKE HOME MAUI**   *American*
121 Dickenson (661-8067 or 661-6185). From the mainland 1-800-545-MAUI. HOURS: 6 am-5:30 pm, Mon.-Sat., open 8:30 am-5:30 pm on Sunday. SAMPLING: Fresh fruit smoothies $3.25, toffuti, sandwiches $3.85-$5.95, salads $2.95-$4.75, ice cream and sodas in the freezer. Papayas, pineapples, onions and Hawaiian coffee are among the items to be shipped or taken home. They offer free airport or hotel delivery. COMMENTS: Limited seating. Fruit smoothies are delicious and their sandwiches are good, too!

**TOM'S CAFE**   *Vegetarian*
888 Wainee Street, Suite 106 (661-1888). HOURS: 7:30 am-4 pm, Mon.-Fri. SAMPLING: Breakfasts include toasted bagel or breakfast burrito $2.50-$2.75. Luncheon items include hot pasta selections, veggie burger, and pasta, salad, or green salads $4-$5. Most items are vegetarian.

### WIKI WIKI PIZZA AND SPORTS BAR    *Italian*

1285 Front St. (661-5685) HOURS: 11 am-10 pm for food, bar service until 2 am. SAMPLING: In addition to pizza they offer hot and cold sandwiches and salads from $6.95. COMMENTS: They have a full bar liquor license, a big screen TV and a large sun deck and advertise that they are Maui's only outdoor sports bar.

### ZUSHI    *Japanese*

Lahaina Business Plaza at 888 Wainee St., (667-5142). Open 11 am-1:30 pm for lunch $4.25-$5.50, and dinner 5 pm-7:30 pm for $7.80-$12.50. Closed Sundays. COMMENTS: A little expensive for the fare and atmosphere.

## MODERATE

### ALOHA CANTINA    *Mexican*

839 Front St. (661-8788) HOURS: Daily for breakfast 8-11 am, Lunch 11-4 pm, dinner 4-10 pm, pupus until 1 am. Live rock 'n roll music Thurs.-Sat. SAMPLING: Salads include tostados and aloha Caesar. Nachos, quesadillas and ceviche can begin your meal $5.25-$6.95. Dinners include Lahaina Fajitas $13.95, cheese enchiladas, chile rellenos, lobster tacos, chile verde $9.95-$12.95. Carne asada or ono Vera Cruz run $17.95-$18.95. COMMENTS: Stop by and enjoy a plate of nachos with your hurricane. Huh? That's right! At this new Front Street restaurant, diners get a little something extra with their meal. The hurricane winds happen every 90 minutes, but only the sound of heavy winds, thunder, rain pelting down on a tin roof and lightning; no actual gusts will be part of the experience.

### BENIHANA    *Japanese Teppanyaki*

658 Front St. at the Wharf Cinema Center on the upper level (667-2244) HOURS: Lunch 11:30 am - 2 pm, dinner 5-9:30 pm. SAMPLING: Lunches $6.50-$14, dinners $14.50-$29.75 are teppanyaki style, prepared at your table. Full dinners include soup, salad, vegetable. Between 5 and 6:30 pm they feature an early bird special for $9.95. COMMENTS: This well known mainland chain has joined the ever increasing number of teppanyaki style restaurants on Maui. This method of cooking involves a great deal of flourish and preparation by a chef who cooks your meal at the table in front of you. Part of the price of the dinner is for the show!

### BLUE TROPIX RESTAURANT & NIGHTCLUB    ★ *Euro-Pacific*

900 Front St., Lahaina Center (upstairs) (667-5309) HOURS: Dinner nightly 6 pm-1 am, dancing until 2 am. SAMPLING: Tequila lamb is roasted with rosemary and served with blanched string beans and julienne vegetables in a tequila pepper lime sauce, stir fry (the owner's favorite) is a blend of shrimp and scallops with kula greens, snap peas and tomatoes in a plum wine teriyaki sauce, or pan fried lasagna (an excellent and popular selection) $13-$20. Unusual pizzas include a sashimi pizza, grilled vegetable, sweet and sour duck or eggplant $10-$13. COMMENTS: Both the restaurant and nightclub can stand on their own, but together they are great for a full evening out! Most nightclubs have so-so food, but this is good restaurant fare and the nightclub doesn't detract. The music is an eclectic mix. Each night is a different mood, different crowd and different age group. You might enjoy live reggae, groovehouse techno, mixed dance music, or

celebrity look-alikes with modern and house music for dancing in-between sets. A $5 cover charge after 9 pm nightly except for special events. Avoid the cover charge by arriving before 9 pm or get a V.I.P. card. Owner is Mark Dirga, who also owns Dollies in Honokowai.

### CASA DE MATEO ★ *Mexican*
505 Front St. (661-6700) HOURS: Lunch and diner daily 11 am-11 pm. Mariachi entertainment Thurs.-Sun. SAMPLING: Taco de Rez $12.95, burritos Oaxaquenos $12.95, camarones al ajo $15.50, pato con mole verde $14.50. COMMENTS: Not the usual American style Mexican fare here, this is the real thing. When you arrive, you'll probably be greeted by owner Mateo Madoni. Sample one of his excellent appetizers including guacamole prepared at your table, ceviche (also prepared tableside) or cactus gratinado (grated cactus hearts sauteed in garlic butter). You may forget you're in Hawaii and think you ventured South of the Border. A great newcomer to the Maui dining scene.

### CHART HOUSE ★ *American*
1450 Front St. (661-0937). HOURS: Dinner daily 5-10 pm. SAMPLING: Filet Mignon $25.95, Prime Rib $22.95, Grilled Chicken Breast $16.50, shrimp teriyaki $22.95. Entrees include their unlimited fresh garden or Caesar salad, hot squaw bread, sourdough bread, and rice. Children's menu available. COMMENTS: There is a comfortable atmosphere with lots of wood and lava rock. The limited number of oceanview tables are a hot commodity and require that you arrive when they open. Potatoes and rice are available at an extra charge. They provide one of the best keiki menus we've seen. The adult entree portions are large! There is also a Chart House restaurant in Kahului and another in Wailea. Reservations accepted.

### CHRIS' SMOKEHOUSE *American BBQ*
1307 Front St., near The Cannery (667-7005) HOURS: 11 am-11 pm daily. SAMPLING: BBQ ribs, steak, fish, and chicken. Lunch menu served only 11 am-4 pm $4.95-$7.95. Ribs, chicken, steak, fish, dinners available a la carte $8.95-17.95.

### COMPADRES ★ *Mexican*
Lahaina Cannery Mall. (661-7189). HOURS: 11 am-11 pm daily, Sunday brunch served 10 am-2 pm. SAMPLING: They've really improved their menu, which runs continuously for lunch and dinner. Their Quesadillas Internacionales features some tortillas with a new flair! Japonesa is a large flour tortilla with spicy cream cheese, smoked chicken breast, avocado slices, chopped tomato and cucumber cut like sushi and served with watsabi-guacamole. A Baja version highlights a tortilla with Mexican shrimp in a spicy BBQ sauce. A selection of lite entrees, under 400 calories, is a nice feature as well. They still have their popular lobster burrito on the menu too, menu selections run $8.95-$13.95. COMMENTS: Sunday they feature a very good Champagne Brunch 10 am-2 pm. Adults $11.95, kids 11 and under $4.95. This all you can eat buffet includes Santa Fe potatoes, fresh chile rellenos or pork carnitas, a taco bar, and specials of the day such as Mexican style eggs Benedict. Their dessert table is laden with Bunuelos and fruit salad. They earned a star this year for their innovative new menu, quality, authenticity, a great brunch and all-around good dining fare.

**GREEK ZORBA** *Greek and Mediterranean*
Wharf Cinema Center. HOURS: 11 am-10 pm. SAMPLING: Greek dishes are served with rice pilaf and sauteed vegetables $8.95-$14.95 and include falafel, chicken kabobs, baby lamb chops, or dolmades. Appetizers are plentiful from calamarakia to tabouleh and hummas $3.95-$5.95. COMMENTS: Owner George Abdallah operated several restaurants in Greece before relocating to Maui from California. Opened in July 1994 and word is spreading that this is a winner. The blue and white decor is attractive and the murals on the wall provide a pleasant atmosphere.

**HARBORFRONT** *Asian/European*
658 Front St., Wharf Cinema Center, top level (667-5122) HOURS: 10 am-10 pm. SAMPLING: Sandwiches $9-$15. Dinner entrees $12-$19.50.

**KIMO'S** ★ *American/seafood*
845 Front St. (661-4811) HOURS: Lunch 11:30 am-2:30 pm. Dinner daily 5-10:30 pm, bar until 1 am. SAMPLING: Lunches $6.50-$9.95 range from breast of chicken sandwich, to rueben, grilled ham, swiss & turkey sandwich or burgers. Hot & chilled pupus, Hawaiian style, are available downstairs daily. Dinner at the bar available with a limited menu selection 5-11 pm. Dinner entrees include Kimo's Caesar salad, freshly baked carrot muffins and sourdough rolls and steamed herb rice. Fresh fish of the day $17.95-$19.95 prepared in one of five ways, beef, seafood or island favorites such as kushiyaki or Koloa ribs $145.95-$17.95. A Keiki menu for guests 12 and under $4.50-$5.95. COMMENTS: They have a waterfront location and, if you're really lucky, you'll get a table with a view. Opinions vary greatly about Kimo's. Some really like it and others really don't. Our experience has been very good service and well prepared fresh fish. They must be doing something right -- one of a handful of restaurants to continue in Lahaina. They also have a bar on the lower level and an ocean view which provides a pleasant sunset. Hawaiian music Wednesdays thru Sundays during the sunset hour. Aloha Friday features live music and "Phil's Pupu Corner" from 3-6 pm with a $4 pupu plate including cajun chicken, teriyaki chicken, fresh (lightly breaded) ahi, egg roll & baby back ribs w/Kimo's plum sauce.

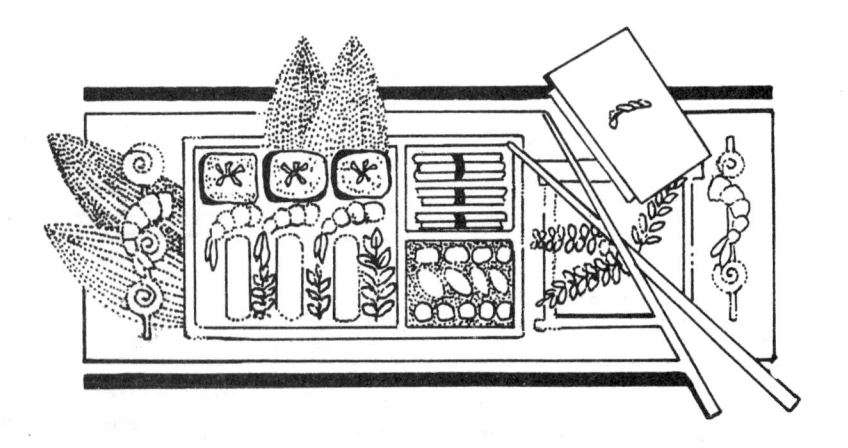

**KOBE JAPANESE STEAK HOUSE ★** *Japanese Teppanyaki-Sushi Bar*
136 Dickenson (667-5555) HOURS: Dinner from 5:30 pm. SAMPLING: Teriyaki
chicken $13.90, hibachi steak $19.50, or sukiyaki steak $16.90. Dinners include
soup, shrimp appetizer, vegetables and rice. COMMENTS: A sister of the Palm
Springs and Honolulu restaurants, they offer teppan cooking (food is prepared on
the grill in front of you) and the show is as good as the meal. Keiki menu offers
either hibachi steak or chicken teriyaki $6.90-$8.90. The sushi bar is very popular
and they'll even make up your favorite sushi item if it is not on their sushi menu.

**LAHAINA COOLERS ★** *American*
180 Dickenson St., Dickenson Square, (661-7082) HOURS: Breakfast, lunch,
dinner 7 am until midnight. SAMPLING: Pasta dishes available in appetizer or
entree portions $5.90 - $13.50 includes chicken Azteca (bacon, tomato, cilantro
and wine), or zebra ravioli in gorgonzola sauce. The evil jungle pasta is their best
seller. Bistro burger $8.75, Thai green curry sauce with chicken $12.50, evil
jungle pizza $10.75, or fresh fish. Enchilada verde is a new item and they make
their own tomatilla sauce out of green tomatoes. Also new is their garden burrito,
served chilled with garbanzo bean spread and rice salad. Their newest dessert, the
Riviera banana split is fried banana with ice cream and carmel sauce, they report
that these are flying out of the kitchen! COMMENTS: They have a great slogan,
"Because Life is Too Short to Eat Boring Food." We found the food items exotic
and unique. Their chocolate taco filled with tropical fruit and berry "salsa" is a
wonderful combination of flavors! The pizzas $9.50 - $11.50, are pretty much a
single serving, ample for lunch, a little small for a hearty dinner eater.

**LAHAINA FISH COMPANY** *Seafood*
831 Front St. (661-3472) HOURS: Dinner served nightly 5-10 pm. SAMPLING:
Fish and shellfish, prime rib, and fresh Hawaiian fish $8.95-$22.95. COM-
MENTS: Pleasant ocean view setting. Check for 50% off the second dinner or buy
one get one free coupons in *This Week, The Maui Drive Guide* and the *Lahaina
Historical Guide.* Early bird dinner specials 5 - 6 p.m.

**MOOSE McGILLYCUDDY'S** *American*
844 Front St., upper level of Mariner's Alley, a small shopping alley at the north
end of town (667-7758) HOURS: Breakfast from 8 am-11 am with early bird
specials 8-9 am, lunch 11-4:30, dinner 4:30-10 pm. Early bird specials 4:30-5:30
pm run $8.95. SAMPLING: Lunch menu consists of burgers, sandwiches, salads
and pupus in the $6-$8 price range. Dinner selections include burgers, fresh fish,
prime rib, fresh fish tacos and salads $9.95-$19.95. COMMENTS: Currently in
phase two of their remodeling which will allow a Front Street entrance and all
seating will be on the Front Street side. This place really gets hopping at night
with lots of young adults and music on the loud side.

**OLD LAHAINA CAFE AND LUAU ★** *Hawaiian*
505 Front St. (661-3303) HOURS: Breakfast 7:30-11:30 am, lunch 12-3:30 pm,
dinner 6-10 pm, Sunday brunch 8 am-3:30 pm. SAMPLING: Breakfast options
include Anahola granola $5.95, Belgian waffle, loco moco, French toast, Portu-
guese omelette $5.95-$8.95. Lunches range from $5.95-$10.95 and range from
island fruits salad, crab & shrimp sandwiches, kalua pig & cabbage plate lunches.

Dinners include local favorites such as shrimp lau lau, lamb chops, papaya ginger mahi, seafood madras, linguine vongole, and coconut prawns $17.95-$21.95. COMMENTS: Early and late specials from 6-7 pm and 9-10 pm include Teri-steak, broiled half chicken or pasta du jour $9.99. They also have a second restaurant, *Aloha Mixed Plate*, located at the Kaahumanu Center Food Court in Kahului.

### PACIFIC 'O ★ *Contemporary Pacific cuisine*
505 Front St. (667-4341) HOURS: Lunch 11 am-3 pm, dinner 5:30-10:30 pm, jazz on the beach Thurs, Fri. & Sat. 9 pm until midnight. Pupus served until midnight. SAMPLING: Lunches include an eclectic assortment of appetizers and salads ranging from steamed clams to potstickers or smoked shrimp with goat cheese and eggplant caviar $6.50-$10. Entrees offered for your mid-day meal include a shiitake mushroom omelette or a diablo chicken sandwich $5.50-$10.95. Dinners range from $14-$22 for Peking duck, Kiawe grilled NY steak, sesame crusted lamb or banana imu style fish and are very artistic and unusual presentations. COMMENTS: A great ocean front location. Recently they were awarded first place in the fish & seafood division of the Taste of Lahaina competition.

### PIRATE'S *American*
608 Front St. (661-8500) HOURS: 7:30 am-midnight, daily. SAMPLING: Most dinners $9-$12, include Cornish game hen, Kailua roast pork loin, vegetarian lasagna and prime rib. Lunches $5 - 9 include club house sandwich, veggie burger, corned beef and swiss. Breakfasts $5 - 9 feature giant Belgian waffles, breakfast quesadilla and omelettes. Owners Steve and Linda operated the Hanalei Shell House on Kauai for ten years. COMMENTS: The only restaurant on Maui where the waiters and waitresses play musical instruments and perform live at your table! Opened summer of 1994, not reviewed before press time.

### PIONEER INN BAR & GRILL *Pacific rim*
Pioneer Inn (661-3636) HOURS: Breakfast, lunch and dinner. SAMPLING: Even though the old atmosphere is gone, they still have their Hawaiian sweet bread French toast $4.50! Other breakfast items include eggs, Portuguese sausage, Belgian waffles, and flavored pancakes $4.50-$7.95. Lunches include salads $5.95-$10.95, sandwiches, and pasta dishes. Dinners include pasta dishes such as pad Thai noodles, chicken and shrimp piccata $9.95-$16.95, seafood entrees from $17.95, and a selection of smoked roast grill items ranging from baby back ribs to roast duck $15.95-$18.95.

### RED LOBSTER ★ *Seafood*
900 Front St. at Lahaina Center (661-9988) SAMPLING: Lunch and dinner include lobster and shrimp appetizer pizza (a kids dinner) $5.99, macadamia mahi $11.99, and shrimp and chicken $12.99. All are complete meals. COMMENTS: The restaurant is one of a seafood chain, but each of their restaurants does have an individual style. This one has two stories with a Fisherman's Wharf/Cannery feel to the inside of the building with wood and brass and tapa print cloths on the booths. Casual enough that you don't need to dress up, but a nice enough atmosphere that you wouldn't be out of place if you did. The prices, even by island standards, are good. The Fisherman's Feast at $21.99 included lobster, fresh fish, mixed seafood scampi over linguini and baked potato or vegetable served with a salad and some very good homemade garlic cheese biscuits served warm.

They offer fresh fish specials and fresh opakakpaka is hard to come by at any price and at $18.99 it is a great value. Their fresh fish can be served more than a half dozen ways. They have tried to add in a couple of more Hawaiian-style dishes, and offer a fresh fish option with macadamia nut crumb topping. The kids menu, as with all their restaurants, are a cut above most others, in the $5 range. The prices are slightly higher than mainland, of course. Good family dining!

### THAI CHEF   *Thai*
Lahaina Shopping Center (667-2814) HOURS: Lunch 11 am-2:30 pm Mon.-Fri., dinner 5-10 pm nightly. SAMPLING: Entrees such as Thai crisp noodles, green papaya salad and garlic squid are $6.95 - $11.95. COMMENTS: A very lengthy menu ranging from noodle dishes to salads, seafoods, vegetarian fare and curry dishes. Entrees available in mild, medium or hot! They have recently opened a second location in the Rainbow Mall in Kihei. My kids LOVED their Thai Tapioca for dessert!

### YAKINIKU TROPICANA   *Japanese/Korean*
843 Wainee St., Lahaina Shopping Center (667-4646) HOURS: Lunch 10 am-4 pm. Dinner after 4 pm. SAMPLING: Lunch specials include fish chun, shrimp tempura, beef plate $7-$9.50. Dinners run $14.95-$18.95. COMMENTS: The menus are printed in English, Korean and Japanese and most of the employees speak Korean as their native language. They also offer a full sushi bar. Yakiniku means table grilled, so you'll be able to enjoy watching your own meal be prepared.

### YUM YUM TREE   *American*
Lahaina Cannery, formerly Marie Callender's (667-PIES) HOURS: Breakfast 7 am-11 am, lunch 11 am-5 pm and dinner 5-10 pm. Bar service late. SAMPLING: Burgers, sandwiches, pot pies, salads $5.45-$7.95 are lunch selections. Dinners up to $11.95. The Yum Yum Tree is a chain of family style restaurants and pies are their specialty.

## EXPENSIVE

### AVALON ★ *Hawaiian Regional Cuisine*
844 Front St., (667-5559) HOURS: Mon.-Sat. 11:30 am-10:30 pm, Sundays 5 pm-10:30 pm. SAMPLING: A number of the dishes may be prepared to your liking: mild, medium or spicy. Their chili seared salmon tiki style at $18.95 is as much a visual as a culinary experience. A layered salad of mashed potatoes, eggplant, salmon, greens, island and tomato salsa served with plum vinaigrette $18.95. Pina colada chicken $14.95, BBQ lamb chops, or Indonesian stir fry $14.95-$27.95. Vegetarian selections include salads, pasta dishes and stir fried vegetables. An interesting array of starters include summer rolls, grilled eggplant salad, fresh clams wok steamed, or our favorite Kona style crab cakes. Carmel Miranda is Avalon's only dessert. COMMENTS: Mark Ellman, as owner/chef, continues in his fine tradition of HRC. The Gado Gado salad $10.95 comes from the island of Bali and is a tasteful blend of romaine lettuce, cucumbers, tofu, steamed vegetables on a bed of brown rice and topped with peanut sauce. Equally delicious is the Chinese tofu salad at $9.95. Both are large portions. The name Avalon, according to Celtic or Gaelic legend, is the West Pacific island paradise where King Arthur and other heroes went following death. The look here is '40's Hawaiian with antique aloha shirts adorning the walls, ceiling fans whirring and wonderful multicolored oversized dishes. This one is a favorite of ours and we don't visit Maui without stopping by at least once.

### CHEZ PAUL ★ *French*
Five miles south of Lahaina at Olowalu (661-3843) HOURS: Two dinner seatings 6:30 and 8:30 pm. Closed Sundays May-Nov. SAMPLING: Dinners run $21 for vegetarian fare, $22 - $33 for other meals. The entrees include fresh fish, scampi, lobster, duck, veal, lamb and beef. Dinners include French bread, soup or salad and two vegetables. Escargot, seafood crepe, and shrimp are available as appetizers. Save room for some very special desserts. COMMENTS: This small restaurant has maintained a high popularity with excellent food and service. It's not surprising they have won numerous dining awards. The wine list is excellent, although expensive. Wines are also available by the glass. Reservations required. Their menu adds, "no pipes or cigar smoking and keep the cry babies at home."

### DAVID PAUL'S LAHAINA GRILL ★ *New American*
127 Lahainaluna at the Lahaina Hotel (667-5117) HOURS: Nightly from 6 pm. SAMPLING: The menu is described as New American Grill Cuisine with a Southwestern flair. The menu changes, but David's popular Tequila shrimp and firecracker rice has become a permanent fixture on his menu. Kona coffee roasted lamb, or kalua duck might be among the other options $15.95-$28.95. COMMENTS: David Paul Johnson was born in Montana, raised in Utah, and began cooking as a teenager. He was formerly with the Black Orchid on Oʻahu and chef at Chez Michelle and the Hyatt Regency on Oʻahu, among others, before opening his Maui location in February 1990. The seating area is attractively furnished with a crisp look to it. Black and white floors are contrasted with a beautifully detailed fresco blue/green ceiling, peach table cloths and French impressionist art. While beautiful, it somehow lacks the cozy ambiance of one of our favorite restaurants just across the street, Gerard's. They recently completed renovations and have doubled their dining area. The food is excellent and David Paul's has a continually changing menu, which keeps your dining options interesting! We sampled their

Caesar salad, which was excellent and an ample portion for two people. The soft shelled crab was very unusual and the pasta was delicately seasoned. The crab is cooked shell and all! Shipped in from the east coast, these crabs are "harvested" when they are in the molting process so that their shell is very soft. The fresh fish, opakapaka, was again a hearty portion served grilled with an accompanying tomato/onion zucchini sauce served finely chopped over eggplant. The tequila shrimp is available in mild, medium or hot. Medium proved to be plenty warm!

### GERARD'S ★ *French*
In the lobby of the Plantation Inn at 174 Lahainaluna Rd. (661-8939) HOURS: Dinner only. SAMPLING: Dinner 1-10 pm, entrees in the $22-$36 range. Selections might include millefeuille of salmon and avocado with vanilla mousseline Sauce, seafood paella with lobster, old-fashioned coq au vin. COMMENTS: We were recently thinking back to the first time we dined at Gerard's, in its old, small, hole-in-the-wall location. It was wonderful then and it still is today! No one on vacation should deny themselves at least one night of special fine dining enjoyment. And if we have to pick among only one, Gerard's might well win out over several of our other favorites. Although partial to Maui's sunset ocean views while dining, sitting beneath a mango tree on the veranda of the Plantation Inn while dining at Gerard's is hard to beat. Just a short walk up Lahainaluna Road off Front Street in Lahaina, you are swiftly moved worlds away to a picturesque atmosphere reminiscent of a "Gone With The Wind" era. Crisply attired in green and peach, the restaurant offers indoor or outdoor seating. A wine list features a range of moderate to expensive selections from California, France and the Pacific Northwest. On a recent evening we began with a wonderful rich crab bisque followed by Ulua, the fresh fish and the evening special, a calamari with pasta dish. Our guidelines for a restaurant review center around the fresh fish. In other words a restaurant is as good as its fish! And Gerard's did not disappoint. The entrees arrived, complimented with miniature vegetables. The calamari was a healthy portion in a wonderfully seasoned sauce. The fish was prepared with a spinach and bernaise sauce and not only was it excellent, but it was the best fish meal in recent memory and a good size filet too! The desserts, wonderful of course, vary nightly. Try the chocolate decadence complimented by a cafe au lait or a cappucino. The perfect evening was rounded out with background guitar music. Entrees include quails, stuffed with basmati rice and baked in a puff pastry with procini sauce with chanterelles and morels $28.50, seafood paella $29.50, or Beef culotte ragout Burgundy style $26.50. Desserts are all priced at $7.50, and the selection numbers more than a dozen, from fresh fruit creations to rich la creme caramel opera.

### LA TASCA NOUVEAU BISTRO *Euro-American Cuisine*
900 Front St., in Lahaina Center (661-5700) HOURS: Lunch Mon.-Fri. 11:30 am-2:30 pm, dinner daily 5:30-10 pm. SAMPLING: Early bird special daily 5:30-7 pm includes a choice of three entrees, meat, fish or pasta served with soup or salad for $13.95. Lunches includes pasta, mahi sandwich, salads, soups $3.95-$8.95. Dinners offer a huge selection of hot and cold tapas so that you could snack your way through dinner. Carpaccio of beef, pate champagne, peppered steak or pan fried oysters $5-$9.95. Dinner entrees include paella, giant prawns, lamb chops or rack of lamb, roast rabbit or osso bucco $17.95-$23.

## LONGHI'S ★ *Continental*

888 Front St. (667-2288) HOURS: 7:30 am - 10 pm, breakfast served until 11:30 am, lunch until 4:45 pm, dessert served until 11 pm. SAMPLING: The menu is given orally by the waiter. A possible selection of a'la carte entrees might include fettucini Alfredo, lobster and chicken canneloni, shrimp Longhi, and prawns amaretto. Seafood $18-$24, meat and poultry $18 - $26, pastas $13 - $22, salads, vegetables, desserts from $4. COMMENTS: This is another of those Maui restaurants that people either love or they hate. In any case, in their 18 years on Maui they have become a near legend in Lahaina. The setting is casual, with lots of windows open to the bustling Lahaina streets. Personally, we have enjoyed our meals here, although the oral menu can sometimes mean you spend a little more than planned! An early breakfast before the visitors arrive in Lahaina is a great way to start the day. They offer espresso and a good wine selection. Valet parking nightly. Entertainment and dancing Friday and Saturday evenings.

## SCAROLES ★ *New York Style Italian*

930 Wainee St., Lahaina (661-4466) HOURS: Dinner 5:30-9 pm daily, lunch weekdays 11:30-2 pm. SAMPLING: Lunch items are light fare pasta, sandwiches and pizza $4.95-$13.95. Dinner $17.95-$24.95. COMMENTS: Scaroles advertises itself as "The New York side of Lahaina" and we'd tend to agree. Located on the Kaanapali side of Lahaina the restaurant is an open air, smallish, but cozy, dining room for 30 inside and a table or two outdoors. A basic Italian black and white color scheme is the decor here. Daily specials are featured and lunch items are similar to dinner selections, just smaller portions. All entrees are served with homemade minestrone soup or a salad that is presented with a bit of tomato and cucumber and fabulous warm-from-the-oven onion rolls. We're told by those who know that it is authentic New York Italian-style food. They also have a pizza restaurant on the other side of town at 505 Front Street. Reservations advised given the limited dining area.

# KAANAPALI

## INEXPENSIVE

### BEACH BAR *American*
Westin Maui (667-2525) Located atop the center island of the pool/deck area. HOURS: 10 am-6 pm. SAMPLING: Services three pools with hot dogs, shave ice cart, and light menu to go.

### GARDEN BAR *American*
Westin Maui, located near the beach (667-2525) HOURS: 9 am until midnight serving a poolside menu 11 am until 6 pm. Cocktails served. SAMPLING: Sandwiches, hot dogs, etc.

### KAANAPALI BEACH HOTEL KOFFEE SHOP ★ *American-Hawaiian*
Kaanapali Beach Hotel (661-0011) SAMPLING: Prime rib dinner buffet 4-9 pm for $11.95, breakfast buffet 6-10:45 am for $6.95, lunch buffet 11 am-2 pm for $6.95, or their afternoon deli buffet 2 pm-4 pm with cheese and cold cuts to create your own sandwich plus soup, salad and desserts for $5.95. COMMENTS: The best value in Kaanapali, especially for the hearty appetite.

### KAANAPALI PIZZA *Italian*
Located at the Lahaina side entrance to Kaanapali. (661-4500) HOURS: noon - 2 am. SAMPLING: Assorted spaghetti pasta dishes $5.99-$9.99, baked lemon basil chicken $6.99, BBQ ribs $9.99-13.99, all-American pizzas from $7.99 for a single serving - $12.99 for a large cheese. Chicago stuffed pizza and calzone.

### KAU KAU GRILL BAR *American*
Poolside at the Maui Marriott. (661-1200) HOURS: Continental breakfast 6 am-7 am, breakfast from the grill 7 am-11 am is limited to eggs with accompaniments. Lunch menu available 11 am-4 pm includes salads, burgers, and sandwiches $4-$7.95. A poolside Pizza Hut kiosk offers personal pan pizza $3.25, as well as larger pizza pies. Bar menu available until 5 pm. Continental breakfast 5:30-7 am, breakfast 7-11 am, lunch and snacks 11-4 pm. SAMPLING: Lunch menu includes cheeseburgers, pizzas by the slice, salads, and sandwiches. The most popular item is their chicken Caesar salad. The connected bar serves cheese sticks, calamari, onion rings.

### MADE IN THE SHADE *American*
Royal Lahaina Resort (661-3611) HOURS: 11 am-5 pm. Grilled items such as burgers or turkey breast sandwich, hibachi salads such as grilled sausage with pasta or cold seafood salad $6.25-$8.50.

### THE MAKAI BAR *American*
Maui Marriott (667-1200) HOURS: 4:30 pm-12:30 am. Located lobby level, Lanai wing. COMMENTS: Open air cocktail lounge with sweeping ocean view of the island of Lana'i. Great gathering place and nice sunset vistas. Their pupu m has proven very popular over the years with mini-roast beef sandwiches, tako poke, sashimi, or ceviche priced affordably $2-$6.75. The Ma Bar has weekly entertainment, currently with Karaoke three ni weekly Comedy Club.

**MAUI YOGURT**   *American*
Whaler's Village (661-8843) SAMPLING: Sandwiches such as cheese and egg salad, turkey or avocado and garden or fruit salads in the $4-$5 range. COMMENTS: No seating in the restaurant, but a few tables outside. Call ahead and order a picnic lunch.

**OHANA BAR AND GRILL**   *American-Italian*
Embassy Suites Resort (661-2000) HOURS: 10 am-10 pm daily, entertainment nightly 6-11 pm, full bar. SAMPLING: If you are a guest of the hotel, this is where you'll find your morning breakfast cooked to order. They also offer poolside lunch and dinner selections. Sandwiches include ohana burger, beef skewers Oriental style, grilled chicken breast, and pizza $5.95-$7.95.

**ROYAL SCOOP**   *American sandwiches/ice cream*
Royal Lahaina Resort. HOURS: 6 am-9 pm. SAMPLING: Limited selection, but a few salad and sandwich items, and of course ice cream!

# MODERATE

**BEACHCOMBERS**   *Pacific Rim*
Royal Lahaina Resort (661-3611) HOURS: Dinner nightly 6-9:30 pm, closed Sunday. Sundowner (early bird) dinner specials Mon.-Sat. from 5-7 pm. SAMPLING: Evening early bird specials range from guava basted BBQ chicken to T-Bone steak $9.95-$13.95 served 5-7 pm (not applicable on holidays). Nightly specials run $19.95-$22.95 and include seafood platter, Maine lobster, fish Trilogy or prime rib. Their main menu offers seafood items or Oriental dishes from the wok such as chop suey, curry, or lo mein $13.50-$19.95.

**CHICO'S**   *California style Mexican/American*
Whaler's Village Shopping Center (667-2777) HOURS: Daily for lunch 11:30 am-2:30 pm, taco bar 11:30 am-midnight, dinner 5-10 pm, cocktails until 1 am. SAMPLING: Dinner combinations from $9.50, fajitas $9.95-13.95 and American fare such as London broil, burgers, salads or mango fettucine with smoked chicken $9.95. Children's menu items include burgers, grilled cheese or hot dogs $3.95-$4.50. COMMENTS: A good variety of Mexican fare with their freshly made flour tortilla shells enticing you as you enter. On the 5th of every month they feature Cinco de Chico with live music, drink and nacho specials.

**COOK'S AT THE BEACH** ★   *American*
Westin Maui ...th side of the swimming pool (667-2525) HOURS: Breakfast 6:30-11... ...ast buffet 7-11 am, lunch 11 am-2 pm and dinner 6-11 pm. SA... ...breakfast buffet is $14.50 adults, children $1.25 per year. ...items are limited, but include egg beater fritatta, Continental ...oast and rolls. Lunch offers cold sandwiches or grilled ...sandwiches $7.75-$11.50. Dinner features their prime ...the day cooked to order. Caesar salad, fresh catch, ...s kobe style baby back pork ribs, or roasted Peking ...and a very nice dessert carte for $22.95 adults, ...ion to their dinner menu, they offer appetizers and ...NTS: A good family restaurant with a varied ...ne and fairly reasonable prices for a resort!

## HULA GRILL  *Hawaiian Regional/Seafood*

Whaler's Village Shopping Center, on the beach (667-6636) HOURS: Lunch 11:30 am-4 pm, dinner 5-10 pm, Barefoot Bar & Cafe 4-11 pm, Cocktails 11:30 am-1 am. SAMPLING: Dinner entrees are served with coconut risotto and include teriyaki ahi steaks with papaya lime salsa $18.95, kiawe grilled mahimahi, shrimp and rice noodles $18.95 or fresh vegetable and tofu lo mein $12.95. COMMENTS: The Hula Grill, formerly the location of El Crab Catcher, features Hawaiian Regional Cuisine focusing on Hawaiian fish and seafood designed by award-winning Chef Peter Merriman. Among the fresh fish entrees are kiawe grilled mahi mahi, herb grilled shutome (broadbill swordfish) and baked opakapaka with coconut curry glaze and fresh mango chutney. The coconut risotto is an interesting acompaniment, a sticky rice that doesn't detract from the entree. The Barefoot Bar Menu features a varied selection of appetizers, pizzas, salads, side dishes and sandwiches priced at under $10. The casual oceanfront restaurant, reminiscent of a 1930's Dickey-style beach house, is surrounded by tropical gardens and ponds. Yet the interior has a homey atmosphere with a cozy library-type room for a waiting area. More than $2 million was spent renovating the restaurant which features an exhibition cooking line with large kiawe grill/BBQ and an imu-style oven for the pizzas. The food is good, but not great or as innovative as some of the other HRC (Hawaiian Regional Cuisine) restaurants.

## KAANAPALI BEACH HOTEL  (Tiki Terrace Restaurant)  *Sunday brunch*

2525 Kaanapali Parkway (661-0011) HOURS: Sundays 9:30 am-1:30 pm. SAMPLING: Start at the stir fry station and select among varied ingredients for your cooked-to-order selection. On the Hawaiian favorites table you'll find a trio of tako poke, ahi poke and lomi salmon along with limu salad, huli huli whole roast pig and more. More ordinary brunch fare includes smoked salmon, omelettes cooked to order, Belgian waffles, KBH's famous bread pudding, and assorted desserts. Price may be slightly higher on holiday weekends. COMMENTS: A great value and a very popular brunch with visitors and residents.

## LEILANI'S ★  *American-Seafood*

Whaler's Village Shopping Center, on the beach (661-4495) HOURS: Lunch 11:30 am-4 pm, dinner 5-10:30 pm, pupu bar 4 pm-midnight. SAMPLING: Fettucine pescatore $15.95, fresh island fish $17.95-19.95, ginger chicken $13.95, baby back pork ribs $15.95. COMMENTS: Known for offering one of the best sunset viewing spots in Kaanapali, the outdoor lounge and terrace dining room overlook the beach. Leilani's specializes in fresh fish, steak, BBQ chicken and ribs prepared on lava rock broilers in koa wood ovens. The Beachside Grill, located on the lower level beachside of the restaurant, features casual menu fare such as smoked chicken pasta, barbequed chicken pizza or seared ahi salad on Kula greens, priced under $10. They also have a children's menu. Reservations are a good idea for dinner.

## LUIGI'S PASTA PIZZARIA  *Italian*

Kaanapali Resort, by the golf course (661-4500) HOURS: Daily 11:30 am-midnight, bar until 2 am. SAMPLING: Lunch selections include pasta or pizza as well as sandwiches such as submarines, French dip or club. Dinner selections include seafood ravioli, seafood pescatore, calamari in marinara or chicken parmesan $12.99-$18.99. How about a roasted garlic bulb served in butter sauce and served with fresh pasta....? Your friends are gonna love you!

## MOANA TERRACE ★ *American-Buffet*

Maui Marriott Hotel (667-1200) HOURS: 6:30 am-10 pm. SAMPLING: Breakfast 6:30-11:30 am, breakfast buffet $13.95 served 6:30 am-11 am, lunch from 11:30-2 pm, dinner from 5-10 pm, soup and salad bar 5 pm-10 pm, dinner buffets on Friday and Saturday evening 5-9 pm. SAMPLING: Friday dinner buffet is prime rib for $9.95 and Saturday they serve up an array of seafood for $19.95. The soup and salad bar is available only on non-buffet nights and is an all you can eat arrangement for $9.95 for adults, kids six and under $5.95. Children twelve years and under have a special menu with a dozen breakfast, lunch or dinner options. Dinner entrees include grilled swordfish, pasta with seafood, fried chicken basket as well as sandwiches $8.95-$15.95. COMMENTS: Their set of menus is as long as a book! They have the most varied and changing assortment of meals, buffets etc. of any restaurant on Maui. The good news is that this is one of the best family values on the island.

## MOZZARELLA TIKI CAFE *Italian*

Hyatt Regency HOURS: 11 am-6 pm, seasonally open at night 6:30-9:30 pm. Poolside snacks feature pasta, pizza and waffle cones.

## PAVILION *Blends Pacifica*

Hyatt Regency Maui, lower level (661-1234) HOURS: Daily for breakfast 6 am-11:30 am and lunch 11:30 am-6 pm. SAMPLING: Both their breakfast and lunch menu feature "cuisine naturelle" which offers some healthy alternatives. Egg white omelet, whole grain cereal with berries or chicken has florentine $4.75-$8.50 are available along with regular egg fare. Lunch provides a selection of salads, pizza, burgers, sandwiches or entrees including grilled chicken breast, vegetable club or grilled salmon $7-$14.50.

## REILLY'S *Irish/American*

2290 Kaanapali Parkway (667-7477) HOURS: Saturday and Sunday champagne and eggs brunch 9:30 am-2:30 pm, lunch and dinner daily. SAMPLING: More than just Irish fare they offer tuna melt, veggie, fried oyster roll or teriyaki chicken breast sandwiches, along with an assorted burger selection $6.75-$7.75. For the heartier appetite they offer fried oysters, fish and chips, NY strip, ribs, and daily specials $8.50-$15.95.

## ROYAL OCEAN TERRACE *American*

Royal Lahaina Hotel (661-3611) HOURS: Breakfast a la carte menu 6 am-11 am, Mon.-Sat. On Sundays 7-10 am. Breakfast buffet 6 am-10 am, Monday thru Saturdays, Sunday 7 am until 10 am. Sunday champagne brunch 10 am-2 pm. Dinner 5 pm-10 pm. Their nightly buffet has a theme, Monday: Oriental, Tuesday: Italian, Wednesday: German, and so on. Their a la carte menu is served nightly with dinner specials available. Dinner entrees include BBQ selections, seafood or items from the grill $14.25-$19.95. COMMENTS: The Royal Ocean Terrace is really aiming to meet the needs of the conservative, budget minded traveler, to give them the most for their vacation dining dollars. This is a very attractive, airy restaurant. The resort also offers a *Tequila Sunset Package*, done out on the beach front looking out to the Pacific Ocean. Served 5:30-7:30 pm, the menu is for two persons and includes torches and a private charcoal hibachi along with a cabana built for two. The chef prepares the food in the kitchens and then it is brought to the cabana for guests to cook themselves. Enjoy the margaritas with your sunset.

### THE RUSTY HARPOON   *American*
Whaler's Village (661-3123) HOURS: Breakfast 8 am-11 am, lunch 11 am-5 pm, dinner 5-10 pm, early bird special 4-6 pm. SAMPLING: Their Belgian waffle bar at $7.50 offers coconut, fudge or maple syrups along with assorted fruit toppings, nuts, coconut, granola and even ice cream $7.50, other breakfast items $2.75-$11.25, burgers sandwiches, soups and salads for lunch begin at $3.50 and range up to $10.95 for shrimp scampi. Dinner entrees are accompanied by soup or salad, rice or potato, vegetable and roll and include chicken piccata, prime rib, or seafood selections $15.95-$21.95. Childrens menu.

### SEN JU SUSHI BAR
Westin Maui at Kaanapali. HOURS: Daily 5-10 pm. COMMENTS: The name Sen is for the owner of the Westin Maui, but it also means "a thousand" and Ju means happy times. The bar has seating for only seven, but there is sushi or bento-style sushi and sashimi trays that can be enjoyed at the tables in the Colonnade. They also offer hot sake, American and Japanese wine and beer.

### SOMEPLACE DIFFERENT   *American*
Poolside at the Sheraton Hotel (661-0031) The Sheraton is scheduled to be closed for major renovations beginning in January 1995 for two years. We suggest a phone call as plans have been known to change!

### TIKI TERRACE   *American-Hawaiian*
Kaanapali Beach Hotel (661-0011) HOURS: Breakfast 7-11 am, Sunday breakfast menu is served 7 am-8:45 am followed by their Sunday champagne brunch 9 am-2 pm. SAMPLING: Dinners include seared yellow fin tuna, steamed onaga, veal piccata or island bouillabaisse $17.95-$24.95. COMMENTS: Complimentary hula show nightly with Hawaiian entertainment throughout the evening while you dine.

### VILLA RESTAURANT AND VILLA TERRACE ★
*American-Seafood/Asian influences*
Westin Maui (667-2525) HOURS: Dinner only 6-10 pm. SAMPLING: Seafood is the specialty! The Villa Restaurant serves dinner 6-9 pm, with special seafood

WILIWILI

festivals that might include "Crustacean Sensation" or "Lobster Maine-IA." Foods have a bit of an Asian influence with their shrimp wok fried soba noodles and appetizer of grilled Asian flatbread. Pupus are an interesting array of primarily seafood selections $5.25-$11. Chef's entrees include prime rib, strip steak, lamb chops or their excellent selection of fresh fish served imu style, wrapped in Won Bok and baked, brushed with macadamia nut butter and grilled, chilled with asparagus and champagne Hollandaise or wok charred with Hawaiian spices. From shutome to ulua, they generally have among the best selection of different types of fresh seafood in West Maui. The adjoining Terrace Villa serves an outstanding seafood buffet, nightly 6-9 pm, $23.95 adults. COMMENTS: One of our best bets for fresh island fish and a beautiful setting. All tables look out onto the lagoon where swans and exotic ducks float along peacefully.

## EXPENSIVE

### DISCOVERY ROOM *Continental-American*
Sheraton Hotel, atop picturesque Black Rock (661-0031). The Sheraton is sched-uled to be closed for major renovations beginning in January 1995 for two years. We suggest a phone call as plans have been known to change! Initial reports say that the Discovery Room will be relocated to below the lobby. Things are still, and probably will be, up in the air.

### LAHAINA PROVISION COMPANY ★ *American*
Hyatt Regency Maui (661-1234) HOURS: Lunch 11:30-2 pm and dinner 6-11 pm. Chocoholic bar 6-11 pm, lounge from 11 am-11 pm. SAMPLING: Luncheon items run $6.50-$9.50 for sandwiches, salads. Dinner selections include Prime rib, beef brochette, or Hawaiian paella $19-$27. COMMENTS: This restaurant is cleverly perched above the pool and on the edge of one of the Hyatt's waterfalls. Dinners here are very pleasant. Warm caraway bread begins the meal and the fettucini that accompanied the meal was outstanding. Ask whether they have a children's Camp Hyatt menu or children can order most entrees on the menu at 1/2 price for 1/2 size. This place may be a favorite if you're a chocolate lover. They have a CHOCOHOLIC BAR that features rich ice cream with an incredible choice of terrific temptations to top it. If you have dinner, it's an additional $3.95, but you can come later for dessert only and indulge for $6.95. We recommended this dessert as a definite Maui Best Bet! For lunch they have a very good Monte Cristo and a fabulous seafood Napoleon with a very flaky pastry crust. One of the best appetizers ever is their coconut shrimp! Reservations are recommended for dinner or dessert. Major credit cards are accepted.

### LOKELANI ★ *American-Seafood*
Maui Marriott Hotel (667-1200) HOURS: Dinner served 6-9 pm. SAMPLING: All of the fish is market priced daily and your selection may be prepared in a variety of ways. Appetizers, soups, salads such as seafood chowder, seafood Caesar salad or mussels. Entrees $18-$20, are by Maui standards fairly inexpensive given the very diverse selection. Sample Maalaea seafood pasta, Hunan barbequed wild boar, filet mignon with seared foie gras, baked ono, seared tiger prawns, rack of lamb. COMMENTS: The Maui Marriott has always been the leader in offering quality early bird dinner specials, and have won several dining awars. They continue offering a complete prix fixe dinner which changes nightly for $19.

**NIKKO JAPANESE STEAK HOUSE**   *Japanese*
Maui Marriott Hotel (667-1200) 6-9 pm for dinner only. Samari Sunset Menu is served only from 6-6:30 pm daily and prices are considerably less, for example chicken $12.95, scallops $17, sukiyaki steak $14.95 are served with steamed rice, teppan-yaki vegetables, Japanese green tea and green tea ice cream. Children's menu for 10 and under $8.95. After that the menu selections increase in price with a sesame chicken dinner $19.95, filet mignon $25.95, shrimp or scallops both $24. Part of the price is the "show." The chef works at your table and is adept at knife throwing and other dazzling cooking techniques. Note: The menu states that a 15% service charge will be added to your check.

**NORTH BEACH GRILLE**   *Pacific Rim cuisine*
Embassy Suites Resort (661-2000) HOURS: Dinner 5:30-10 pm. SAMPLING: Entrees on their recently revised menu include veal medallion, scallops on jade sauce, steamed manila clams, roasted rack of lamb or sesame and ginger crusted shutome $21-$34. COMMENTS: We haven't tried out their new menu, but some of the selections sound wonderful! They also offer one of the island's better salad bars and they have killer bread!

**SOUND OF THE FALLS** ★   *Pacific Bistro*
Westin Maui (667-2525) HOURS: Champagne brunch served Sunday brunch 10-2 pm. Dinner 6:30-9:30 pm, closed Thursdays and Sundays. Call to check, they may be open additional nights, they seem to change frequently. SAMPLING: Begin your dinner with a sesame seared ahi sashimi or layered Dungeness crab and morel mushroom ravioli $7-$11, and follow with a Hawaiian style Caesar salad. Entrees change weekly, but might include grilled shutome swordfish with potato crab cake $23, or ogo battered Pacific abalone $36. The Sunday brunch is outstanding with seafoods including spiced shrimp, kiawe smoked mahi or peppered mussels. Breakfast items such as omelettes, Belgian waffles and eggs Benedict or cheese blintz as well as smoked baby ribs, cajun style mahi and prime rib. Some folks simply fill their plate with items from the sushi bar. The Sound of the Falls merits our Best Bet for one of the best brunches in West Maui. For the sushi lover it is worth the price alone for all you can eat! Desserts are fit for royalty and beautifully presented. Add to all this a very lengthy wine selection. A beautiful setting plus excellent service makes this a highly recommended dining experience.

### SPATS TRATTORIA ★ *Northern Italian*

Hyatt Regency Maui (661-1234) HOURS: Dinner daily 6:30-10 pm. SAMPLING and COMMENTS: They have an all new menu, but their renovated atmosphere remains comfortable and homey, yet very classy. The disco music is gone. A few new and interesting touches include a table at the entrance with small glasses of wine for sampling. A different bottle is offered each night.

The old bar has been converted to an Antipasto Bar and offers a help-yourself mini-buffet of appetizers for $8.75. Sampling might include calamari with pine nuts, assorted meats (i.e. salami, prosciutto), grilled eggplant and squash or marinated mushrooms. The Tuscan flatbread, which accompanies the meal, was topped with cheese and herbs and arrives with a side of fresh pesto along with olive oil and herbs for dipping.

Entrees, mostly priced at under $20, include pan seared shrimp wrapped with pancetta $22, veal piccata $21, baked lasagna $16.25, gnocchi with asparagus $13.50 or Spats original malfidine with lobster, a combination of ribbon pasta with mushrooms, lobster tail and herb cream $19. Entrees include seasonal vegetables.

### SWAN COURT ★ *Continental*

Hyatt Regency Maui (661-1234) HOURS: Open for breakfast buffet 7 am-11:30 a.m Monday-Saturday and until 1 pm on Sunday. Dinner 6-10 pm daily. SAMPLING: Their breakfast buffet is $14.95 and includes fresh-squeezed orange juice, macadamia pancakes with a variety of toppings, French toast, cereals, yogurt, fresh fruits, and a good choice of hot breakfast foods. Breakfast items off the menu also available. Dinner menu includes hot and cold appetizers $10-$14, and featured entrees such as marinated island opakapaka, Hunan marinated rack of lamb or potato crusted venison tenderloin $25-$37.

The atmosphere and the view of the Swan Court are worth it for a special treat! Our "best bet" for a daily breakfast buffet. The dinners are excellent and many unusual preparations are offered. Our only criticism is the proximity of other tables and noise seems to carry. Reservations are advised.

# KAHANA - NAPILI - KAPALUA

## BAR ONLY

### KAPALUA BAY RESORT - BAY LOUNGE ★ and LOBBY TERRACE
Kapalua Bay Resort (669-5656) HOURS: 4:30-8 pm. COMMENTS: Enjoy a fabulous sunset in this elegant setting. Live soft background music is provided. Hotel guests can enjoy complimentary coffee service in the lobby terrace daily 6:30-10:30 am and tea service 3-5 pm daily.

### THE LOBBY LOUNGE AND LIBRARY
The Ritz-Carlton, Kapalua HOURS: Noon until midnight for cocktails, pupus until 9 pm. Afternoon tea served 2:30-4:30 pm upon request, with advance reservations required. Full tea $13.75, light tea $9.25.

### THE SUNSET LOUNGE
The Ritz-Carlton, Kapalua HOURS: Cocktails 5:30 pm- midnight, dessert 8-10:30 pm, Mon.-Sat. Entertainment ranges from solo piano to a jazz duo 6:30-11:30 Mon.-Sat. Located adjacent to The Grill Restaurant.

## INEXPENSIVE

### (THE) COFFEE STORE   *Coffee/pastries*
Napili Plaza (669-4170) HOURS: Daily 6:30 am-8 pm. Coffee drinks, with a few unusual selections including a banana mocha cooler! Also quiche, muffins, scones, veggie lasagna, garden burger, or croissant sandwiches $1.95-$6.50.

### DOLLIES ★ *American-Italian*
4310 Honoapiilani Hwy. at the Kahana Manor (669-0266) HOURS: 10 am-midnight. SAMPLING: A great assortment of sandwiches from tuna salad on pita bread, roast beef and provolone, or BLT $4.95-$7.95. Pasta dishes include linguini with meatballs or lasagna $7.95-$10.95. Salad bar is priced by weight. Dollies scored high marks in several categories of our Paradise Publications pizza contest a few years back! You'll also find one of the best selections on Maui with more than 40 domestic and imported beers. Espresso too! Food to go. Very popular spot with local residents.

### FISH AND GAMES SPORTS GRILL *Seafood*
Kahana Gateway (669-FISH) HOURS: 10 am-12:30 am, 7 am opening on weekends and special sporting events. SAMPLING: Opened in August 1994 for lunch and dinner, may add breakfast. Lunch prices $4.95-$12.95, dinners $9.95-$19.95 include specialty items such as live Dungeness crab priced up to $29.95. A variety of fresh oysters, salmon, and shell fish. COMMENTS: A retail seafood market, sports bar and dining room with exhibition kitchen is the concept of this newcomer to Kahana. The sports bar offers state of the art equipment and satellite system. Not open to review as we go to press, their menu is an ambitious one with all menu items available at the bar. They will feature an oyster bar serving oysters raw, in a Bloody Mary, with cucumber relish or ceviche or freshly shucked and roasted in shell served in a variety of ways. A turn-of-the century

Gentlemen's club motif, this upscale fish market resembles a Harrod's Food Hall of London. A good wine list with many served by the glass. Thomas LaCloche, formerly the GM for the Erik's chain of restaurants and Cary Button, owner of Oyster Seafood Specialty ,are combining talents for this new Dining/Sports Bar/Fish market concept.

## GAZEBO   *American*
5315 Lower Honoapiilani Hwy., the Napili Shores Resort (669-5621) HOURS: 7:30 am-2 pm breakfast and lunch 11 am-2 pm. SAMPLING: Breakfast offers an assortment of egg dishes, but they may be most popular for their macadamia nut pancakes $4.95-$6.50. Lunch selections include burgers, sandwiches and salads $4.95-$7.95. COMMENTS: Popular with Maui residents for the friendly atmosphere with a wonderful ocean view.

## HONOLUA GENERAL STORE   *American*
Above Kapalua as you drive through the golf course. HOURS: 6:30 am-8 pm. SAMPLING: Breakfasts include pancakes, eggs and such. Lunches include four local plate lunches daily which might include stew or teri chicken $4.95-$5.95 or a smaller portion called a hobo which is just a main dish and rice for $3.50. Sandwiches and burgers from their deli, too. The spam masubi, a local favorite, is usually sold out by noon. COMMENTS: The Kapalua Hotel refurbished this once funky and local spot. The front portion displays an assortment of Kapalua clothing and some locally made food products.

## KAFE KAHANA   *American*
Kahana Gateway (669-6699) HOURS: 7 am-9 pm. SAMPLING: Fresh fruit smoothies, espresso drinks (one is called Why Bother? made with lowfat milk and decaf espresso), sandwiches $6.50, and be sure to sample their freshly made cinnamon rolls! COMMENTS: Co-owner Steve Wolff also operates the Cinnamon Roll Fair in Kihei.

## LUDWIGS MAUI   *Appetizers/bar*
Kahana Gateway Mall. (669-3786) HOURS: 4:30 pm-1:30 am daily. SAMPLING: Stuffed mushrooms, drum-o-sticks served in a drum (with a fire extinguisher on request), artichoke alla Saui, chili, ratatouille, Tacos $4-12. COMMENTS: Club owner Bill Ludwig III, is the grandson of William F. Ludwig, founder of Ludwig Drum Co. Combining his love for music and cooking, he opened Ludwig's Maui in summer 1994 featuring live music and a light appetizer menu. The dance floor and stage are fully equipped at all times so, he adds, that you will never know who may show up. Jazz from 4:30-6:30 pm during their Sunset Specials. Later entertainment, who knows!

## MARKET CAFE   *American-Italian*
Kapalua Bay Hotel Shops (669-4888) HOURS: Daily for breakfast served until 11 am, Sundays until 1 pm, lunch and dinner. Open 8 am-10 pm. SAMPLING: Omelettes, tropical pancakes, hot oatmeal with blueberries $5.95-$8.95. Lunch items include burgers, sandwiches, and salads $6.95-$8.95 as well as cafe specials such as lox and bagels, roasted eggplant or fettucine $8.95-$11.95. Dinners run $9.95-$15.95 for pasta, seafood, beef and chicken. Full bar. COMMENTS: This small restaurant has good, affordable fare and is part of a market that carries some unusual imported foods. Wednesday night is 2 for 1 pasta night.

**McDONALD'S OF KAHANA** *Fast food*
Located in the Kahana Gateway shopping center, a large indoor dining area. Breakfast, lunch and dinner served.

**MAUI TACOS** *Mexican*
Napili Plaza (665-0222) Potato enchiladas, hard tacos, quesadillas, or special hand-held burritos $2.75-$6. Their shredded beef is moist and flavorful, not too dried out. The salsa bar offers several choices with jalapenos, onions and more. The guacamole was chunky and fresh. Good values! Operated by Mark Ellman of Avalon. (Opening soon in Lahaina.)

**SUBWAY** *Deli sandwiches* - 5095 Napilihau. (669-0099)

**VILLAGE CAFE** *American*
Village Golf Course at the first hole. (669-1947) HOURS: 6:30 am-6:30 pm. SAMPLING: Breakfasts $2.95- $4.95, lunches $5.95-$9.95. They serve Lappert's Kona Coffee roasted. Sandwiches such as The Village Cheeseburger as well as grilled cheese steak, deli delights, grilled chicken, and salads. COMMENTS: They make a great burger here! Let us know what you think!

# MODERATE

**BANYAN TREE** *Mediterranean*
The Ritz-Carlton, Kapalua HOURS: 11:30 am-4 pm daily for lunch. COMMENTS: Located poolside. SAMPLING: Tropical libations and non-alcohol fruit smoothies. Food items include a prix fixe lunch for $16.50, sandwiches or pizza $9-$13.

**BEACH CLUB** *American*
Kaanapali Shores Resort (667-2211) HOURS: Breakfast 7-11 am, lunch 11:30-3:00 pm the cafe menu includes sandwiches, soups and light fare served 3 - 9:30 pm. and dinner from 5:30-9:30 pm. SAMPLING: Cafe menu includes appetizers and light meals $3.25-$7.50. Lunch menu includes hamburgers, hot and cold sandwiches in the $6.95 range. Breakfast $4.50-$9.95. Dinners range from seafood and chicken to steak, specials each evening runs $9.95-$11.95. Full bar service and specialty coffee drinks available.

**THE BEACH HOUSE** *American*
The Ritz-Carlton, Kapalua HOURS: Lunch served 10:30 am-4:30 pm. Bar service with daily specialty drinks. SAMPLING: Lunch selections range from hot dogs to mahi sandwiches $5.50-$11. COMMENTS: Located adjacent to Fleming Beach, this open-air restaurant utilizes more than 40 fully-grown coco palms to offer a natural roof.

**CHINA BOAT** *Cantonese-Szechuan-Mandarin*
4474 L. Honoapiilani (669-5089) HOURS: Lunch daily 11:30-2 pm, dining nightly 5-10 pm. Karaoke (weekends only) and cocktails 10 pm until 1:30 am. SAMPLING: Shrimp with vegetables, beef with broccoli, and some hot and spicy dishes as well. Entrees from $8.95 for lemon chicken to Peking duck at $32.50.

**ERIK'S SEAFOOD GROTTO**   *American-Seafood*
4242 Lower Honoapiilani Hwy. on the second floor of the Kahana Villa Condo (669-4806) HOURS: Dinner daily 5-10 pm. SAMPLING: Dinners include chowder or salad, potatoes or rice, and bread, with entrees of BBQ shrimp, steaks, seafood brochette $14.95-$19.95. COMMENTS: Check for early bird dinner specials. This is one of those restaurants that we don't hear much good about, but then we don't hear anything bad either! Kind of a non-memorable dining experience. Currently, early bird specials from 5-6 pm for $11.95 - $12.95 includes N.Y. steak, island mahi, lobster stuffed boneless chicken breast or crab stuffed prawns.

**KAHANA KEYES**   *Seafood-American*
Valley Isle Resort in Honokowai (669-8071) HOURS: Dinner only 5-10 pm, live music and dancing until 1:30 am. SAMPLING: Early bird specials 5-7 pm, $10.95, regular menu $9.95-$14.95.

**KAPALUA GRILL AND BAR ★**   *New York style grill with Pacific Rim flavor*
200 Kapalua Drive, just across the road from the Kapalua Hotel and a short drive up Kapalua Drive (669-5653) HOURS: Lunch 11:30-3 pm and dinner 5-10:30 pm, cocktails 11 am-12:30 am. SAMPLING: J.J.'s baked artichoke is an appetizer that has been made famous here $9.95. Burgers and pizzas $7.50-$9.95. Entrees include fresh fish of the day $17.95-19.95, shrimp and scallop linguine, Chinatown duck served with a Szechuan peppercorn sauce, rack of lamb, and several vegetarian dishes $13.95-$22.95. An admirable wine list, one of the better ones on the island, begins at about $16-$18. Guess they must have sold their bottle of '45 Chateau Lafitte Rothschild at $990, because now a Charles Krug cabernet is the most expensive at $200. Tank tops are okay daytime attire, but not appropriate for evening. This is a sister facility to Leilani's and Kimo's, but its menu is a little more gourmet. A golf course and ocean view add to the pluses of this restaurant. Dinner reservations suggested.

**KOHO GRILL AND BAR ★**   *American*
5095 Napilihau St., Napili Plaza (669-5299) HOURS: Daily 11 am-10 pm, bar open until 2 am. SAMPLING: Soups & salads include chicken Caesar, Oriental chicken, taco salad or ahi salad $5.95-$7.25, sandwiches from $4.75, entrees priced $8.45-$14.95 and range from pork chops to a rib plate or fettucini primavera. COMMENTS: A diverse menu and affordable prices which boils down to great family dining. The same restaurant team also operates the other Koho Grill and Bar in Kahului, The Plantation Restaurant at Kapalua and the new SeaWatch restaurant in Wailea. They have a great keiki (kids) menu! A few new salads and dinner entrees have livened up the menu.

**ORIENT EXPRESS**   *Thai-Chinese*
Napili Shores Resort, one mile before Kapalua (669-8077) HOURS: Dinner 5:30-10 pm. SAMPLING: Ginger beef, garlic shrimp, seafood in clay pot, and spinach pork are priced $9.75-$14.95. COMMENTS: This restaurant is run by the same folks who operate Chez Paul. They have an early bird special for $11.95.

**PINEAPPLE HILL**   *Continental*
Up past Napili, turn left for Kapalua and you will see the entrance. (669-6129) HOURS: Dinner 5-10 pm with cocktails beginning at 4:30 pm. SAMPLING: Baked half chicken $11.95, prawns Tahitian $24.95, or BBQ ribs $15.95.

Pineapple Hill was once the home of plantation manager David Fleming. He was one of Maui's early agricultural pioneers who helped establish mango, lichee, pineapple and other exotic plants and trees. Just past Kapalua is the beach park bearing his name. He completed the plantation house in 1915 and planted those beautiful Norfolk pines which line the drive. It opened for dining in the early 1960s. Pineapple Hill has one of the loftiest settings for sunset viewing. We recommend enjoying cocktails out on the front lawn while watching the sun descend. Recent renovations have freshened up the interior. Several recent reports indicate that both service and food have improved, although in the past we have had mixed reviews.

**POOL TERRACE RESTAURANT AND BAR** *International*
Kapalua Bay Hotel, poolside (669-5656) HOURS: Breakfast daily 6:30-10:30 am, lunch 11 am-5:30 pm, a la carte dinner served Sunday, Monday and Tuesday 5:30-9 pm, Saturday night Hawaiian Paniolo BBQ buffet 5:30-9:30 pm, closed for dinner Wednesday, Thursday and Friday. Hawaiian Entertainment Saturday thru Tuesday 5:30-8:30 pm. SAMPLING: The Paniolo Buffet runs $16.95 for adults, $12.95 for children 12 and under and includes BBQ chicken, spicy BBQ sausage, smoked BBQ beef brisket, assorted salads, breads and desserts. Lunch menu runs $7.25-$13 for hamburgers, pizza, pasta, and sandwiches. Dinners $11.25-$14.50 for pastas, pizza, Hawaiian cioppino, stir fired prawns, broiled ono and fish curry. COMMENTS: The beautiful location of this casual poolside setting features an ocean view from every seat. Hawaiian poolside entertainment here is wonderful. Good values.

**SEA HOUSE** *American*
5900 Lower Honoapiilani Rd., beachfront at Napili Kai Beach Club (669-1500) HOURS: Breakfast 8-11 am, lunch 12-2 pm, and dinner 6-9 pm. SAMPLING: Sunset specials nightly $13.95. Dinner entrees are served with chowder or salad, vegetable, rice or potato. Peppered lamb $18, NY steak $20, scampi $19, or herb chicken $14. Several items are offered in a light portion. Keiki menu offers hamburger, mahi or chicken for $7. On Friday evening they offer a Polynesian Dinner Show performed by the children of the Napili Kai Foundation. Price is $25 adults, $20 children. Luncheon fare includes sandwiches and salads $5.25-$7.25. COMMENTS: One reader reports that they sampled the Thursday evening lobster special and found it to be very good! A nice oceanfront location is a plus too! Local entertainment most nights 8-10 pm.

**TERRACE RESTAURANT AND BAR** *American*
4299 L. Honoapiilani Hwy., Sands of Kahana Resort (669-5399 ext. 22) HOURS: Breakfast 7:30-11 am, lunch 11 am until closing and dinner 5:30-9 pm. SAMPLING: Pupu menu at bar. Lunch menu offers sandwiches, salads, hamburgers $5-$8. Complete dinners with entrees of N.Y. steak, Maui ribs, vegetable stir fry, fresh catch of the day, fish and chips, steamed clams $7.95-$14.95. COMMENTS: Very quiet dining, this restaurant seems to be primarily used by the resort guests. A good selection of menu items and lunch items available at dinner too. Check on nightly dinner specials $11.95-$14.95.

## EXPENSIVE

### THE BAY CLUB ★ *French-Seafood*

At Kapalua near the entrance to the resort (669-8008 after 5 pm, 669-5656 before 5 pm) HOURS: Lunch 11:30 am-2 pm, poolside dining 11:30 am-5 pm, dinner nightly 6-9:30 pm, with pianist as entertainment in the adjoining Bay Lounge until 10 pm. SAMPLING: Lunches include seafood, sandwich and salad bar $9-$17, poolside dining has lighter fare with appetizers, sandwiches and salads, $6-9. You can walk up from the beach to have a poolside snack. Dinners include sauteed jumbo prawns, South Pacific bouillabaisse, filet, lamb chops, roast Long Island duckling $23.50-$29.50 a la carte. COMMENTS: Recent renovations and restoration have freshened up this oceanview restaurant. New chairs, tables, carpeting, and even dinnerware have been replaced along with windows, doors, tile, flooring, and artwork. The restaurant is situated on a promontory overlooking the ocean, is an idyllic setting from which to enjoy the scenic panorama along with pupus and cocktails. You might want to indulge in one of their ice cream libations, such as a Bay Lounger (dark rum, fresh pineapple and ice cream) or the Bay Club Delight (Kahlua, Grand Marnier, Amaretto and ice cream) $6 ish. Extensive wine list. The dress code requires swimsuit coverups for lunch and, in the evening, long sleeve dress shirts or jackets for men and no denim. A pianist serenades you adding a romantic touch. With the changes in ownership over the last few years, service has suffered. We hope that the current management can restore the impeccable service and food because, for us, this has always been a very special restaurant. Renovations have brightened up and greatly improved the atmosphere.

### THE GARDEN RESTAURANT ★ *Continental*

Kapalua Bay Resort Hotel (669-5656) HOURS: Sunday brunch buffet 9:30 am-1:30 pm. A la carte dinner served Wednesday, Thursday and Saturday 6-10 pm, Friday night seafood buffett 5:30-9:30 pm. SAMPLING: Menus change seasonally. Dinner menu ranges from $6 for appetizers to $20 for an entree. Their prix fixe dinner runs $38 with two options of a four course meal. Their four course prix fixe menu runs $40. Friday night Vintner seafood buffet is $24.95, but arrive between 5:30 and 6 pm and enjoy the buffet for only $20.95. One of the first to offer a seafood buffet, The Garden is the only one to offer it as a Vintner dinner, too. Each week a different winery is featured with selected wines at special prices to go with the sauteed shrimp, calamari and scallop salad, Caesar and spinach salads tossed to order, smoked fish assortment, fresh fish entree, variety of bread and elaborate smoked fish assortment, fresh fish entree, variety of breads and elaborate dessert display. COMMENTS: Reservations recommended. Adults $24.95, children 12 and under $16.95. Excellent food in a lovely dining room. The early bird Friday night buffet is a seafood lovers dream come true.

### THE GRILL ★ *Hawaiian Regional Cuisine*

The Ritz-Carlton, Kapalua (669-1665) HOURS: Dinner served Mon.-Sat. 6 pm-9:30 pm, closed on Sundays. SAMPLING: Their appetizer menu is seafood oriented featuring dungeness crab cake $14.50, smoked sea scallops $12.50 or a medley of Kona oysters, lomi lomi salmon, onaga poki and sweet water prawn $13.50. Soups and salads provide an interesting and tasty prelude to the meal. The spicy dandelion and mustard greens salad is accompanied by puna goat cheese $9 and proved a wonderful salad. They offer a prefix vegetarian menu for $38.50.

Other entrees include Kiawe smoked chicken breast with sweet Molokai corn polente and grilled vegetables $21, island fish bouillabaisse $36 or charred rack of lamb with mango compote $29.50. The desserts round out a memorable meal. They are unique in texture and flavor, and in fact could be considered objects d'art. Selections might include raspberry creme brulee on almond nougat wafer, Granny Smith apple cobbler tart which is an enclosed muffin with vanilla bean ice cream, a hot dessert is a lumpia with tropical fruit fried with coconut parfait which is cold or a white chocolate cheese cake. COMMENTS: Superb service in an elegant, warm and cozy setting, spacious and comfortable, but "ritzy." Their food is marvelous too!

**NICOLINA** ★ *California/Southwestern*
Kahana Gateway, 4405 Honoapiilani Hwy. (669-5000) HOURS: Dinner only. COMMENTS: Named after Roy and Janne Yamaguchi's daughter, Nicole, this became the fifth addition to the family of Roy's restaurants which originated in Honolulu. The food here ventures away from the Euro-Asian-Pacific style of cuisine and turns to the Mainland US with a flare toward California-Southwestern, with the kitchen headed by Jacqueline Lau.

Prior to the opening of this restaurant, Roy tried a family-style southwestern restaurant called RJ's. We thought the food was wonderful, but a little heavy for Hawaii. This new restaurant opened in December 1993 with a fresher, lighter menu. Fresh island fish is prepared with pineapple avocado salsa and spicy tomatillo sauce, or the striped marlin is accompanied by white bean veggie risotto and balsamic basil butter sauce. Entrees and pastas offer a choice between penne primavera and roast duck alfredo. Again the menu here changes nightly based on what foods are the freshest available.

**THE PLANTATION HOUSE** ★ *Seafood-Continental*
2000 Plantation Club Drive, Kapalua (669-6299) HOURS: Breakfast/lunch 8 am-3 pm, dinner from 5:30 pm. SAMPLING: The breakfast/lunch menu is a combination which offers either fare until 3 pm. Egg dishes, sandwiches, soups and salads $5.95-$9.95. Dinner includes fresh fish, daily quote, prawns nunui, chicken Mediterranean, or lamb chops $18-$23. COMMENTS: The food is great and complimented by what is, no doubt, the best ocean view dining location in West Maui. Located in the clubhouse of the Plantation Golf Course, the management is well experienced with the dining scene on Maui. This restaurant is affiliated with the popular Koho Grill & Bar in Kahului and in Napili and the newest SeaWatch in Wailea. If you have a sweet tooth, don't miss the "Brownie to Da Max." It is sure to become the Hula Pie of the '90s. It is served in a huge dish and it is plenty big for two to enjoy. Plan to come a half hour or so before sunset to experience the view!

**ROY'S KAHANA BAR AND GRILL** ★ *Pacific Rim Cuisine*
4405 Honoapiilani Hwy., Kahana Gateway (669-6999) HOURS: Nightly from 6:30 pm. SAMPLING: Nightly specials change daily, so we really can't tell you what to expect! Surf and turf items range from filet mignon to rack of lamb, lots of fresh fish items, too. Standard menu items include lemon grass chicken $13.95, shrimp and scallop stir fried $15.96, individual imu pizzas $4.95-$7.50, kiawe grilled shrimp linguine $16.95. All entrees are a la carte. New chef Tod Michael Kawachi has some lighter fare items planned for the menu. COMMENTS: The

food is as good as you have heard and Roy's is certainly deserving of it's many varied rave reviews and awards. He is one of the top chef's in the islands that have made Hawaiian Regional Cuisine (HRC) a trend of the 90's. However, the noise from the kitchen combined with the high ceilings make it difficult to carry on a conversation. With its consistently good cuisine, you'll never know who might be dropping by. We dined next to Pierce Brosnan. The neighboring Nicolina Restaurant is operated by Roy's as well.

**THE TERRACE** ★ *Pacific Rim Cuisine*
The Ritz-Carlton, Kapalua HOURS: Breakfast 6:30 am-11:30 am. Dinner 5-10 pm. Italian buffet every Wednesday $24, seafood buffet $26-$32 every Friday, Sunday brunch 10:30 am-2:30 pm. SAMPLING: Breakfast $12-$17, Sunday brunch $24, dinner $25-$33. Entrees at $18.50 for chow mein noodles with clams, shrimp and sea scallops, duck pizza $15, or wok fried snapper $26. The seafood buffet offers a la carte selections $22-$23 or combine them with the buffet for $31-$32. The buffet only is $26. The buffet offers an array of seafood platers featuring smoked seafood, sushi and sashimi, couscous with saffron and calamari, or cured gravlox. Salads range from lomi lomi to scallops with grilled leeks and wild mushrooms. The Italian buffet features Caesar salad, hot Italian entrees which vary weekly, plus platters of marinated shrimp, Italian cheeses and meats and salads such as saffron rice. Sunday brunch includes platter selections of exotic fresh fruit, assorted seasonal berries, couscous salad, chilled asparagas, smoked fish and assorted cheeses as well as a variety of cereals and yogurts. The hot station offers an omeltte and waffle station prepared to order by the chef, eggs Benedict, breakfast meats and potatoes, cheese blintze with mango sauce, fresh fish of the day and a display of coffee cakes and homemade bakery items that may tempt you to start at that table first. COMMENTS: Overlooking the courtyard and pool area. A very pleasant, informal atmosphere with sunset views.

PLANTATION HOUSE RESTAURANT

# KIHEI

## INEXPENSIVE

### ALEXANDERS FISH, CHICKEN AND RIBS   *American*
1913 S. Kihei Rd. (874-0788) HOURS: 11 am-9 pm daily. SAMPLING: Meals $4.95-$9.95. Mahi, oysters, calamari, clams, chicken, ono, and shrimp. Fish available by the piece. A la carte items include zucchini sticks, cornbread, french fries, rice, coleslaw, onion rings or a broiled ono or broiled chicken sandwich. Also broiled shrimp. Dine in with limited seating or take out. We haven't tried them, but Tobi says they're good!

### BERNUNZIO'S BAKERY   *Pastries*
1819 South Kihei Rd. in Kukui Mall (879-0261) HOURS: Daily 7 am - 9 pm. COMMENTS: Assorted breads, cakes, cookies and muffins.

### BOOMERS   *American*
Kihei Gateway Plaza (875-84742) HOURS: 6:30 am-8 pm, Fri./Sat. until 10 pm. SAMPLING: Boomer burgers and Boomer fogs, along with chicken, fish, or rueben sandwiches $2.60-$4.75. Tacos and burritos, deli sandwiches and breakfast specials. Nothing on the menu over $5.25. COMMENTS: Located in an area removed from the tourist traffic, this place probably appeals most to local residents. It is a self-service restaurant with a few tables. Nothing inspired, but if you've a family to feed or a budget, and want something other than McDonald's, stop by.

### CHUMS ★   *Local Style*
2439 S. Kihei Rd., Suite 20-A, (874-9000) HOURS: Daily 6:30 am-11 pm, breakfast served until 11 am. Entertainment nightly. SAMPLING: The menu is exactly the same as the Wailuku location, although the prices are just a little higher on some items. A huge bowl of saimin $3.85, French dip $5.55, hot turkey, roast pork or roast beef sandwich $5.45, island style meals such as pork katsu, roast pork, teri beef from $5.10-$6.75. COMMENTS: Breakfast served 6:30-11 am, menu is the same for lunch and dinner. A great family dining spot and a nice alternative to Denny's! Evening entertainment is Hawaiian music or karaoke.

### (THE) COFFEE STORE   *Coffee/pastries*
Azeka's Place II, 1279 S. Kihei Rd. (875-4244) HOURS: Daily 7 am-10 pm. Coffee drinks, with a few unusual selections including a banana mocha cooler! Also quiche, pizza, salads, quesadillas, calzones, muffins, scones, veggie lasagna, garden burger, or croissant sandwiches $1.95-$6.50.

### DENNY'S   *American*
Kamaole Shopping Center (879-0604) HOURS: 24 hours daily. SAMPLING: Burgers, local style dishes and dinners which include steak, seafood and chicken $7-$11. Breakfast served anytime. COMMENTS: Senior specials available.

### HENRY'S BAR AND GRILL   *American*
Lipoa Shopping Center (879-2849) HOURS: 10 am-2 am. SAMPLING: Limited menu, chicken wings or hamburgers $4.50. COMMENTS: A satellite with four televisions, one a big screen, for sporting events or your favorite soap opera.

**INTERNATIONAL HOUSE OF PANCAKES**   *American*
Azeka's Place Shopping Center on South Kihei Rd. HOURS: Sunday-Thursday
6 am-midnight, Friday and Saturday 6 am-2 am. SAMPLING: Breakfast, lunch,
and dinner choices served anytime. The usual breakfast fare and sandwiches.
"Homestyle" dinners run $5.95-$10.95 and include soup or salad, roll and butter.
COMMENTS: A children's menu is available. Very crowded on weekends.

**JOE'S PLACE**   *Local style*
Kihei Town Center, next to Foodland, 1881 South Kihei Rd. (875-7474). HOURS:
Monday-Friday 9:30 am-8 pm., Saturday until 6 pm, closed Sunday. SAMPLING:
Okazuya style, which basically means buffet, offers their steamtable selections
from 9:30 am-4:30 pm. The Chef's Kitchen menu is available until 8 pm. Daily
lunch specials include salads, fish, Hawaiian plate specials, or salads. Dinner
specials served 5-8 pm. Serving line items are $4.50 for one entree, $5.25 for two,
$5.75 for three and come with rice, macaroni salad and marinated cabbage. Menu
items include beef teriyaki, chicken yaki, hamburgers and saimin $3-$5. COM-
MENTS: We haven't tried it, but a good selection of local style food. No credit
cards, which probably helps keep the prices down! Owner is Joe Talon, former
Food and Beverage Manager at the Maui Prince.

**KAL BI HOUSE**   *Korean*
1215 S. Kihei Rd., near Longs Drugs (874-8484) HOURS: 9 am-9 pm, lunch
served until 2 pm. SAMPLING: Lunch and dinner is the same menu with slightly
lower lunch prices. Order mixed plate combination meals or separate entrees.
BBQ short ribs, fried calamari, Bi Beem Bap (great name), hot spicy chicken,
chicken katsu or fried oysters. Stew and Soups include some more exotic selections including small intestine stew, cuttle fish stew, seaweed soup and rice or
Mandeoo Kook. (Editors note: These weird words just drive my computer spell
check system nuts!)

**KIHEI CAFFE**
1945 S. Kihei Rd. (870-2230) HOURS: Breakfast, lunch and dinner. SAMPLING:
Another one of the newer additions to the Kihei dining scene, they are open 7
days a week. Breakfast served until 11 am, until noon on Sunday, lunch items
available all day, dinner Tues., Wed., Thurs. until 10 pm, Friday and Saturday
until 11 pm. Breakfasts include biscuits with gravy, bagels, French toast, and egg
items $3.95-$5.95. Lunch selections range from couscous and tabouli or Greek
salads to tempeh burger or hot pastrami $3.75-$5.95. Dinner entrees served with
garlic bread and salad with an emphasis on Italian, calamari parmesan, lasagna,
calzones, pizza, and pasta $6.95-$11.95. Desserts are all freshly made and they
serve espresso drinks. COMMENTS: A popular restaurant for locals to hang out
and visitors have begun discovering it as well. They have a full-time baker that
makes all their muffins, pies, breads and pastries on location.

**LA PASTARIA**
41 East Lipoa (879-9001). HOURS: Breakfast, lunch and dinner Mon.-Sat. 10 am-
8:30 pm. SAMPLING: Italian, pizza, pastas, calzone and salads. Pastas $6.75,
sandwiches $5-$6, pizza $10-19. They also deliver! No liquor license, but they
charge a $5 corkage if you'd like to bring your own wine.

**McDONALD'S** *American*
1900 area of South Kihei Rd. at the Kihei Shopping Center. HOURS: Breakfast, lunch, and dinner. Breakfast served only from 6 am-10 am. SAMPLING: There are a few unusual island items added to the menu which make it worth including in our listing. For breakfast, you can have Portuguese sausage with rice, and chase it down with chilled guava juice. COMMENTS: Indoor seating available. Prices slightly higher than mainland.

**NEW YORK DELI** *American*
2395 S. Kihei Rd. (879-1115) HOURS: 8 am-8 pm. SAMPLING: In addition to luncheon meats there is a wide selection of salads and entrees such as lasagna, and tortellini. Bagels available in every variety. Sandwiches run $5-$7. COMMENTS: They tell us that, "The wide variety of fresh deli salads, sold by the pound will soothe the pangs of Manhattan separation anxiety." They also have unique houseware and gift items.

**OASIS POOL BAR** *American*
Maui Coast Hotel, 2250 S. Kihei Rd. (879-6284) HOURS: 11 am-10 pm daily. SAMPLING: Soups, salads, sandwiches and appetizers. Happy Hour Mon-Fri. 4-7 pm. Live music begins 5:30. COMMENTS: They also plan on events such as fashion shows, bikini contests and satellite TV. Full bar service.

**PAIR O' DICE** *Italian*
Kukui Mall, 1819 South Kihei Rd. (874-1968) HOURS: Mon.-Thurs 11 am-9 pm, Fri. & Sat. until 10 pm, Sun. noon - 9 pm. SAMPLING: A hearty array of over 30 toppings can be enjoyed on whole wheat and thin or thick crust. A REALLY nice addition to the topping ingredients will be appreciated by those of you with sensitivity or allergies to dairy products. Those of you with family members that can't tolerate dairy, have to pretty well avoid pizza! Pair O' Dice is the first we've seen that offers soy cheese as a topping alternative! Also available are entrees such as calzone, vegetarian lasagna or chicken parmesan. Pizza available in 12" size, beginning at $8.99, and large, 16", beginning at $11.99. Also available by the slice. Oh yeah, we like the name too!

**PANDA EXPRESS** *Mandarin Chinese*
At Azeka Place II Shopping Center. HOURS: Daily 10:30 am-9 pm. SAMPLING: Combination plates $3.59-$5.79, a la carte items $3.99-$7.99. COMMENTS: A chain of restaurants.

**PEGGY SUE'S** *Burgers and such*
Azeka Place II, 1279 S. Kihei Rd. (875-8944) SAMPLING/COMMENTS: They feature an original 1954 Seeburg juke box which operates from the box or by remote from the dining tables. David and Cathy Tarbox are the owners and with David's background as an authentic 1950's soda jerk. They appear to have had a great time planning and decorating this new restaurant. The pink and blue decor are a suitable "Peggy Sue" look and there are plenty of cool, creamy selections, from banana split dishes, to sodas and sundaes. Their dining menu is the hamburger/hot dog variety and includes a bag of chips, a pickle and a medium soft drink. Select from a Good Golly Miss Molly (teriyaki burger with pineapple), Earth Angel (garden burger), Bee-Bop a Lula (avocado burger), the Funky Chicken, The King (your basic burger), Ain't Nothing but a Hound Dog is priced

$4.25-$5.95 or How Much is the Little Dog in the Window (kid's meal that includes hot dog & free sundae $3.25). Open daily, Monday-Saturday 11 am - 11 pm, Sunday 11 am - 10 pm.

**PIKAKE BAKERY** ★  *Bakery/Italian*
Kihei Commercial Area (879-7295) HOURS: Mon.-Fri. 7:30 am-6 pm, Sat. until 5 pm. SAMPLING: Their signature cake is an Almond cake brushed with Frangelico and filled with chocolate mousse! Breads include red potato with rosemary, Mexican jalapenos, or sundried tomato. Danishes, muffins and scones too. For lunch they offer daily specials along with salads, meatless lasagna, eggplant parmesan, chicken cordon bleu or foccicio pizza $2.95-$6.95. COMMENTS: You're going to have to look a little harder to find their Kihei location, located off the Piialani Hwy you turn on Ohukai Rd. Their breads are all sugar-free and vegetarian (except for those containing cheese) and are baked fresh daily. They also have a location in Lahaina at 505 Front Street.

**PIZZA FRESH**  *Italian*
2395 S. Kihei Rd. in Dolphin Plaza (879-1525) HOURS: Daily 3-9 pm. SAMPLING: White or whole wheat crust pizza that they make and you bake. Available in four sizes, small to X-large and thirty-five toppings from which to choose. Also salad, calzones, pizza rolls and cheesecake. They also deliver!

**ROYAL THAI CUISINE**  *Thai*
1280 S. Kihei Rd. at Azeka's Shopping Center (874-0813) HOURS: Mon.-Fri. 11-3 pm for lunch, daily 5-9 pm for dinner. SAMPLING: Appetizers, soups, salads and entrees such as chicken cashew basil, evil prince chicken or garlic cabbage $4.50-$8.25. COMMENTS: The prices are pretty decent, but the portions are a little small. Food was good, but nothing outstanding.

**THE SAND WITCH**  *American*
145 North Kihei Rd., by Sugar Beach Condos (879-3262) HOURS: Daily Mon.-Sat. 11 am-11 pm. SAMPLING: Sandwiches, burgers, salads $3.95-$5.25.

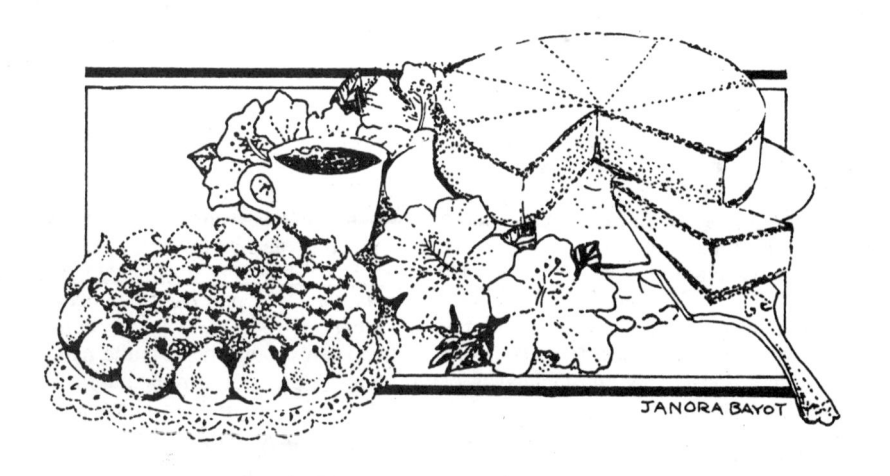

JANORA BAYOT

**SHAKA SANDWICH AND PIZZA** ★  *American-Italian*
Located behind Jack 'n the Box in Paradise Plaza on South Kihei Rd. near Azeka's market (874-0331) HOURS: 10 am-9 pm Monday thru Saturday, closed Sunday. SAMPLING: Hot Philadelphia cheese steak sandwiches served with or without fired onions in small or large portions, cold hoagies $3.75-$7. All sandwiches are served on their homemade Italian bread that has been a recipe past down in the family for years. Pizza available in thin crust or thick square Sicilian pies. COMMENTS: If you like New York subway-style pizza you're in for a real treat. If you have no idea what New York subway-style pizza is, you're also in for a real treat. Their gourmet white cheese pizza with garlic and broccoli was outstanding. Don't miss stopping by for a piece of the pie!

**THE SPORTS PAGE GRILL AND BAR**  *American*
2411 S. Kihei Rd. (879-0602) HOURS: 11:30 am-11:30 pm. SAMPLING: Portland Blazers Reuben, Utah Jazz Ham and Cheese, Robby Naish Tuna Salad, Pete Rose BLT (Bet, Lose..Trial), or Joe Montana Chicken Salad. COMMENTS: You probably already have the idea! This is definitely the spot for the sports aficionado. With confident good humor their menu resembles a newspaper tabloid and reads, "You will be served in 5 minutes...or maybe 10 minutes...or maybe even 15 minutes...relax and enjoy yourself." It may take at least 15 minutes to read over the menu. The front page covers exotic beverages and a hearty selection of imported beers, followed on the inside by dugout dogs, champion burgers, sport fishing sandwiches, bowl games (those are salads), and "game favorite" sandwiches. Not much on the menu over $5.95. A big screen TV with remote monitors and satellite reception should ensure plenty of good conversation for the athletic enthusiast!

**SUBWAY SANDWICHES**  *American/Sandwiches*
Kukui Shopping Center (879-9955) HOURS: 9 am-midnight.

**SUDA SNACK SHOP**  *Local Style*
61 S. Kihei Rd. by the gas station along S. Kihei Rd. (879-2668) HOURS: Pizza served after 3 pm phone (879-7133) HOURS: 5 am-1 pm, pizza after 3 pm. SAMPLING: Plate lunch $4.75, burgers $1.65-$2.40, chow fun $2.40. The pizza portion of the restaurant is only open 3 pm-9 pm, and has a special phone number. Both closed Sunday. COMMENTS: We were disappointed that this little "dive" wasn't one of the island's best kept secrets. The burgers were so-so, the french fries were pricey for the portion and the chow fun wasn't a meal, it was snack size. See you in Wailuku for burgers and chow fun!

**SURFER JOE'S GRILL & BAR**  *American*
61 South Kihei Rd. is located next to Suda's Store in Kihei. (879-8855) HOURS: Bar open 11 am-2 am, food served 11 am-10 pm.SAMPLING: A limited, but interesting selection! A "South Swell Burger" is a mahi filet at $6. "Hookipa Sandwich" is a vegetarian blend of lettuce, tomato, onions, cheese, cream cheese and sprouts $5.50. "Totally Awesome Tostada" $5.50. Also available are "Jalapeno Poppers," "Duke's Fried Zukes," "Major Onion Rings" and "Totally Tubed Calamari." COMMENTS: A funky bar with booths and a patio. Food available to go. No personal checks or credit cards, dude.

**SUMMER PALACE**   *Asian buffet*
Kukui Mall, 1819 S. Kihei Rd. Formerly Perry's Smorgy (875-6188) HOURS: Lunch buffet 11:30 am-2:30 pm, dinner buffet 5-10 pm. SAMPLING and COMMENTS: Both buffets feature similar items, with added entrees featured at dinner. Selections will vary, but might include General's chicken (similar to sweet and sour), spiced salt baked shrimp (good, and spicy!), Cha shui bao (pork buns), assorted sushi, and a good selection of varied salads from oriental noodles or spicy zucchini to macaroni and kim chee. Desserts include mini custard Napoleon, almond cookies and mini fruit turnovers. Attractive family style restaurant with etched glass panels around booths and ceiling fans. This restaurateur, Pang Chu Bai, and his family have 12 years in the restaurant business and still operate three restaurants in Reno. They are bringing a Casino type buffet restaurant to Maui to provide the best food with fair prices and friendly service. Lunch buffet $7.95, dinner buffet $16.95. The assortment proved interesting and diverse and the food was a step above the ordinary all-you-can-eat buffet. They also have a sushi bar, items priced separately. The buffet includes your choice of soft drinks, tea, coffee, milk, or fruit punch. Beer, wine and cocktails available at extra charge. NOTE! A 15% gratuity will automatically be added to your check.

**TOBI'S ICE CREAM AND SHAVE ICE** ★   *American-local*
1913 South Kihei Rd. (879-7294) HOURS: Tues.-Sat. 11 am-9 pm, Sunday and Monday 11 am-6 pm. SAMPLING: They serve Roselani Ice Cream, (made right here on Maui by the happy cows of Haleakala) as well as garden burgers, sandwiches, chili dogs and other original treats created by Tobi and her mom, Puddie. Prices range from $1.50-$5. COMMENTS: They will soon, if not already, become famous for their shave ice served in 27 flavors. Also homemade ice cream pies, smoothies and frozen bananas. Stop by and you'll probably be greeted by either Tobi, her mom or maybe her brother. This is a family operation and the store was built by her father. It features an old woody surfboard that has been made into a table. Along with their great shave ice, you'll get a warm aloha greeting! Say hello from us! Traveler's checks and cash, no credit cards.

**WIKI WIKI PIZZA OF KIHEI** ★   *Italian*
2411 S. Kihei Rd. (874-9454) HOURS: 11 am-10 pm. SAMPLING: Limited table seating outside. Pizzas are baked and available to go. Pizzas from $9.95 for a 12" cheese. A vegetarian delight, 16" is $19.95. Co-winner of our pizza contest in the over all best pizza category a few years back.

## MODERATE

**BUZZ'S WHARF**   *American-Seafood*
Maalaea Harbor (244-5426) HOURS: Everyday 11 am-11 pm. SAMPLING: Lunch includes sandwiches, salads and hot entrees $3.95-$12.95. Dinners include rainbow trout, scallops, BBQ ribs, pesto pasta, and prawns $13.95-$23.95. Entrees are served with salad, vegetables and bread. COMMENTS: Offers a lovely Maalaea harbor view. Their specialty Tahitian shrimp, is very good. Bar/lounge.

**C & R CANTINA**   *Mexican*
2463 South Kihei Rd., Kamaole Shopping Center (875-1111) HOURS: 4 pm-10 pm daily, happy hour 4-6 pm. SAMPLING: Dinner selections the usual Mexican assortment of fajitas, quesadilla, burritos and chimichangas $7.95-$12.95.

**CANTON CHEF**   *Cantonese-Szechuan*
Kamaole Shopping Center (879-1988) HOURS: Lunch 11-2 pm and dinner 5-9:15 pm. SAMPLING: Vegetable, chicken, beef, duck, seafood and pork dishes priced $6-$12.

**CHUCK'S**   *American*
Kihei Town Center (879-4488 or 879-4489) HOURS: Lunch Mon.-Sat. 11 am-2:30 pm, interim menu Mon.-Fri. 2:30-5 pm, dinner 5-10:00 pm daily. SAMPLING: Dinner selections include rice or baked potato or fries and salad bar and bread. T-Bone, prime rib, kalbi ribs, seafood brochette, cajun mahi. COMMENTS: The salad bar only is available for $7.95 and a pretty fare selection. No reservations taken. Children's menu $6-$11. Especially popular for its salad bar.

**ERIK'S SEAFOOD BROILER**   *American-Seafood*
2463 S. Kihei Rd., Kamaole Shopping Center (879-8400) HOURS: Dinner 5-10 pm. SAMPLING: Dinners include soup or salad, potato or rice, vegetable and bread. Entrees include cioppino, seafood curry, BBQ shrimp or chicken breast $13.95-$20.95. COMMENTS: Early bird specials 5-6 pm, $11.95-12.95.

**FIVE PALMS BEACH GRILLE**   *Cross cultural*
Mana Kai Resort, 2960 S. Kihei Rd. (879-2607). HOURS: Breakfast and lunch 7 am-2 pm, dinner served 5-10 pm. Bar hours 10 am-11 pm with bar pupus available 2 pm-10 pm. SAMPLING: They offer their full breakfast and lunch menu from opening until 2 pm, $3-$10, so if you're appetite is on Eastern time when you get up, then by all means order lunch! Menu items include Macadamia nut pancakes, ham & egg pizzas, monkfish with poached eggs and citrus Hollandaise. They aim to specialize in seafood with menu items to include oysters, cherry stone clams in the shell, live Dungeness crab, steamed cockles, fresh Hawaiian ahi sashimi and their signature dish will be sizzling whole catfish. Other "land" fare includes whole roasted chicken, prime rib, crispy mahogany duck with homemade plum sauce. They promise nothing mediocre on the menu, but the best of different cuisines and the freshest of foods...with waves crashing, sun setting, palm trees swaying, great food, great service (owner-mangers), great value ... could this be Shangrila?" COMMENTS: They're touting that they have Maui's best hamburger, but they weren't open in time to review, so you'll have to judge and let us know. What we do know is that their beachfront location is outstanding and it is a location that deserves some quality food. When asked their "type of food" they labeled it as cross cultural. That just about covers it all! Owners Karl and Dave moved to Maui from Colorado in 1992 in search of a location to open a New England-Hawaiian style seafood restaurant. There are five partners in this operation, hence the name "Five Palms." In the kitchen you'll find Paul Wade, formerly executive chef at Haliimaile General Store, Carelli's on the Beach and Seasons Restaurant at Four Seasons. We do know that when the owners have an active hand in the management of a restaurant, their odds of success go up dramatically. We wish this new kid on the block, good luck, and look forward to trying out their cross cultural cuisine in person.

**FRANGIPANI**   *American*
175 E. Lipoa St., at the Maui Sun Hotel (875-9000) HOURS: Breakfast 6:30-11 am, pupus 2:30-9 pm, dinner 5:30-9 pm, lounge open until 11 pm, and on Friday and Saturday until 1 am. No lunch served, a sandwich bar in lobby. SAMPLING:

Daily breakfast buffet. Dinners range from $8.95 for honey dipped chicken or $5 for loco moco to $14.95 for spring ginger chicken or $10 for their seafood grill. Friday and Saturday nights they offer a prime rib buffet and crab leg buffet, $19.95 adults, children 5-10 years $10.95. COMMENTS: Dining room entertainment ranges from talent night, to country western music, to ballroom dancing.

### FRESH ISLAND FISH   *American-Seafood*
Maalaea Harbor (242-5364) HOURS: 10 am-5 pm Mon.-Sat. SAMPLING: Menu changes daily. COMMENTS: This restaurant/seafood market is not inexpensive, but you can pick up some fresh fish to cook at your condo.

### GREEK BISTRO ★   *Greek*
Kai Nani Shopping Center, 2511 South Kihei Rd. (879-9330) HOURS: Dinner served 5-9:30 pm. SAMPLING: Prawns Island style, mousaka, lamb shishkabob or Mediterranean chicken $11-$15. COMMENTS: This little restaurant is a delightful surprise. We tried the Greek Gods Platter which was a combo of Greek specialties for $11.95 and found it excellent. Table seating is limited to a small outdoor area. Check this one out!

### KAMAOLE BAR AND GRILL
Maui Coast Hotel. 2259 S. Kihei Rd. (874-6284) HOURS: Lunch and lite entrees 11 am-5 pm. Dinner served 5-10 pm. Lunch fare is a selection of fish and chips, burgers, sandwiches, fettucini $5.95-$10. Dinners are served with soup or salad, potatoes or rice, vegetable and rolls. Entrees include chicken Adrian (artichoke hearts and sun dried tomatoes with grated parmesan), provencal lamb rack, fresh island fish, fettucini, or scampi $10.95-$22.95.

### LA BAHIA   *Mexican*
2511 S. Kihei Rd., at Kai Nani Village (875-1007) HOURS: Lunch 11:30 am-4 pm, dinner until 10 daily, the lounge is open 11:30 am-1 am. SAMPLING: Same menu served all day and includes sandwiches, burgers as well as entrees with a Mexican flare. A new menu has some interesting selections including pork medallions with fire and spice, pasta New Mexico, Margarita Prawns, or Artichoke and Prawns with cilantro $14.50-$21. They also feature a fresh catch of the day served Creole style, or broiled and served with lime caper beurre blanc or sauteed and glazed with wasabi soy sauce $19.50. A step up from their previous Mexican fare.

### LUIGI'S PASTA PIZZARIA   *Italian*
Azeka's Shopping Center on S. Kihei Rd. (879-4100) HOURS: Daily 11:30 am until 10 pm, pizza until midnight. SAMPLING: Lunch selections include pasta or pizza as well as sandwiches such as submarines or French dip. Dinner selections $12.99-$18.99. Early bird specials served 4-6 pm for $7.99

### MARGARITA'S BEACH CANTINA   *Mexican*
101 N. Kihei Rd., Kealia Village (879-5275) HOURS: Food service from 11:30 am until 10 pm, bar open until midnight. SAMPLING: Lunch menu offers carnitas, quesadillas, tamales, or traditional burgers $6.95-$8.95. Dinners $8.95-$16.95. COMMENTS: Outdoor dining on their oceanview deck. Daily happy hour from 2:30-5:30 pm offer margaritas at $.96.

**MAUI LU LONGHOUSE**  *Polynesian*
Maui Lu Resort, 575 South Kihei Rd. (879-5881) HOURS: Tuesday, Thursday
and Friday 5:30-9 pm, and Sunday 4-8 pm, an all-you-can-eat buffet runs $9.95
for adults, $5.95 for children. Their twice weekly luau, Legends of Hawaii, is
featured on Wednesday and Saturday, adults $48.50, children $24.50. The buffet
menu rotates with the days of the week, each one featuring a meat, poultry and
seafood entree, a soup, a basic salad bar, mashed potatoes, rice, vegetables,
noodles and rolls. Not elaborate, but basic food fare. Fill up those teenagers!

**MEXICO CALIENTE & CANTINA**  *Mexican*
1945 S. Kihei Rd. (875-0404) HOURS: Lunch 11 am-5 pm, dinner 5:30-10 pm.
SAMPLING: Luncheon selections includes taco salads, tostada caliente, flaquitas,
quesadillas $5.95-$8.75. Dinners include carne a la Mexicana, pollo gratinado,
carnitas, camaroes (shrimp) and chile verde $5.95-$14.55. COMMENTS: One of
the business partners, Vianney Rodriquez, tells us that all the ingredients are made
from scratch, from the salsa to the main entrees. He and another partner have both
been in the restaurant business in Mexico and he promises that there is "not better
Mexican food but that cooked by Mexicans." They offer classical guitar
entertainment and on weekends have live band music.

**SILVERSWORD GOLF CLUB RESTAURANT**  *American-French*
Located at the Silversword Golf Course (879-0515) HOURS: 10:30 am-3 pm for
lunch daily. SAMPLING: Sandwiches, hamburgers, soups, salads and lunch
entrees are affordably priced $3.25-$5.75. Located on a lofty setting with a
pleasant view of Kihei and beyond Kaho'olawe and Molokini.

**STELLA BLUES CAFE & DELI**
Longs Center, 1215 S. Kihei Rd. (874-3779) HOURS: Breakfast, 8 am-11 am,
Sunday until 2 pm, lunch 11 am-4 pm, dinner 4-8 pm, later on Wed. and Fri. Live
music Wed., Fri. & Sat. SAMPLING: Breakfasts $6.50-8.50, salads and
sandwiches $7.25, dinner menu $10.95 - $17.95. COMMENTS: We tried it, we
didn't like it. But then it was only once for breakfast. Being served coffee in a
plastic mug, with breakfast fare at these prices, didn't impress us. Let us know
your impressions, and if they've started serving coffee in a real cup!

**THAI CHEF**  *Thai*
Rainbow Mall, 2439 S. Kihei Rd. HOURS: Lunch 11-2:30 Mon.-Fri., dinner 5-10
nightly. SAMPLING: Same menu as their Lahaina location with entrees such as
Thai crisp noodles, green papaya salad and garlic squid are $6.95 - $11.95.
COMMENTS: A very lengthy menu ranging from noodle dishes to salads,
seafoods, vegetarian fare and curry dishes. Entrees available in mild, medium or
hot! They have recently opened a second location in the Rainbow Mall in Kihei.
My kids LOVED their Thai tapioca for dessert!

## EXPENSIVE

**A PACIFIC CAFE-MAUI**  ★ *Hawaiian Regional Cuisine*
1279 S. Kihei Rd., Azeka Shopping Center (822-0013) HOURS: 5:30-10 pm.
SAMPLING and COMMENTS: Jean-Marie Josselin, owner and chef of the highly

*A Pacific Cafe* in Kapaa, Kauai, opened a Maui branch in July of 1994. They plan to change their menu regularly taking advantage of the foods as they come into season. Menu entrees might include Opah (moonfish) with lemongrass Thai curry sauce and roasted banana salsa, Smoked chicken chorizo, or Ahi tournedos with shrimp falafel cake and lemon dressing. Entrees priced $14-$25. They offer two separate dining areas, a wine room which seats up to 25, and an island bar. The tables are trimmed in koa wood with a copper inlay and the blonde rattan chairs are covered in tropical brocade. As with their Kauai restaurant, the ceramic plates on which appetizers are presented are one-of-a-kind in varying sizes and shapes designed and hand-made by Chef Josselin's wife, Sophie. Not open in time to review before going to press, but chances are this will be a great addition to the Kihei dining scene and based on their Kaua'i reputation, we'll give them a star.

## CARELLI'S ON THE BEACH   *Italian*
2980 S. Kihei Rd. at the Wailea Oceanfront Hotel (875-0001) HOURS: Dinner only 6-10 pm nightly, mangia bar menu served until 11 pm. SAMPLING: Pasta selections $18-$26 include linguine, seafood cannelone, fusili pesto or select house specialties included cioppino, shrimp Bob Longhi or island fish $26-$30. They also have wood-fired pizzas $12-$15. COMMENTS: The small print tells us that there is a minimum food charge of $25 per person dining at the dining tables. They may have a wonderful oceanview, but as a traveling family with those kind of minimums, we aren't likely to find out. No minimum at Rocco's Mangia Bar.

## KIHEI PRIME RIB AND SEAFOOD HOUSE ★   *American*
2511 South Kihei Rd., in the Nani Kai Village (879-1954) HOURS: Dinner from 5-10 pm, early bird specials served 4-6 pm. SAMPLING: Prime rib, cajun style chicken breast, chicken macadamia, rack of lamb, shrimp scampi $18.95-$23.95. Early bird specials $11.95-13.95. COMMENTS: Dinners include a salad bar, Caesar salad, or red snapper chowder, and is served either with fettucini noodles or rice. Homemade bread also accompanies your meal. The salad bar was very good, and the choices included sweet Kula onions. The high-beamed ceilings with the hanging plants compliment the gorgeous wood carvings done by Bruce Turnbull and paintings by a German artist, Sigrid. They offer piano entertainment nightly. A long time Kihei favorite.

NIGHTBLOOMING CEREUS

## SUNSETS ON THE BEACH

760 S. Kihei Rd., at the Menehune Shores Condominiums (874-5787) HOURS: Mon.-Sat. Lunch 11 am-2 pm, pupus 2-5 pm, dinner 5-9 pm. Daily drink and pupu specials. Sunday brunch 9 am - 2 pm, pupus 2-5 pm, dinner 5-9 pm. Sushi from 11 am-4 pm, with a more extensive sushi menu available 5-10 pm. SAMPLING: Dinners include catch of the day $22.95 macadamia nut chicken $24.95, lemon chicken $17.95, pasta dishes $17.95-$21.96. Entrees include sauteed vegetables, rice or pasta and a choice of Caesar salad, green salad, rock shrimp salad or their soup and salad bar. Salad bar only $12.95. Lighter entrees are served a la carte $11.95-$13.95. Pupu menu $5.95-$12.95. Sunday brunch is not a buffet, but varied egg, waffle and pancake selections ordered from their menu. COMMENTS: A keiki menu is offered for youth ages 12 and under, with a selection of salad bar, fish, pasta, burgers or hot dog $5.95. One of only a handful of island restaurants located oceanfront, they now have also added a sushi bar. The area in front of this resort complex was an ancient Hawaiian fish pond.

## WATERFRONT ★ *Seafood*

At the Milowai Condo, Maalaea (244-9028) HOURS: Dinner only from 5 pm. SAMPLING: Fresh island fish prepared nine different ways, or select cioppino, baked prawns Wellington, Hawaiian spiced chicken or Oriental Veal Chop $18.95-$26.95. COMMENTS: A family operation, the Smith's have done a consistently excellent job ever since they opened, winning a number of awards and many deserving accolades. The dinner entrees are all served with garden salad with a choice of four homemade dressings, vegetables and rice or potatoes. What a great location to get their fish right off the boat at the Maalaea Harbor. Can't get it much fresher than that!

# WAILEA-MAKENA

## LOUNGES

### BOTERO GALLERY

Grand Wailea. HOURS: noon to midnight. The lobby bar is a beautiful setting and they do offer Hawaiian musical entertainment.

### GROTTO BAR

Grand Wailea. HOURS: 10:30-5 pm. Dress code *required* here is a swim suit. Set in the midst of waterfalls, rock slides and channels, this is the only swim-up bar in Hawaii. Offering a variety of tropical drinks in a volcanic cavern-like setting.

### KEA LANI LOBBY LOUNGE ★

HOURS: 5:30-11 pm, evening contemporary, jazz and Hawaiian music, appetizers include sushi and sashimi. A sushi menu available. The Kea Lani Lounge overlooks the Pacific Ocean and tropical gardens and features a very different atmosphere with couches and overstuffed chairs.

### MOLOKINI LOUNGE ★

Maui Prince Hotel, Makena (874-111) COMMENTS: A wonderful opportunity for a sunset view. Pupu menu 5-9:30 pm daily, $4.50-$6.95. Call to check on entertainment available in the lounge or in their lovely outdoor courtyard.

**SUNSET TERRACE ★**
Stouffer Wailea Beach Resort, on the lobby level (879-4900) HOURS: Open nightly 5-10 pm. Pleasant evening entertainment seven nights a week 5:30-9:30 pm ranges from Hawaiian vocalist to hula, pupu menu $5.50-$10.

**VOLCANO BAR**
Located at the Grand Wailea Resort & Spa (875-1234) HOURS: Lunch served 10 am-6 pm, bar open until 7 pm, no entertainment. Sandwiches and salads served. Features smoothie and tropical fruit drinks.

## INEXPENSIVE

**CAFFE CIAO ★**  *Italian*
Kea Lani (875-4100) HOURS: 6:30 am-8 pm. SAMPLING: Full bakery, capuccinos, deli items, Italian gelatos, homemade sausages, antipasto items. Sandwiches $5.59-$6.50, antipasta available by the pound. Daily dine in or take away entrees $5.50-$6.50. COMMENTS: Black and gold decor with high stools and tables, but it is a deli and seating is limited, no table service. Enjoy indoor and outdoor patio seating along the row of shops. While dining you can relax by reading one of a variety of complimentary newspapers, from the San Francisco Chronicle to the Australian News. The sausages are made in-house and they have several varieties, Italian, Portuguese, French and garlic, or try one of several salami varieties including wild boar! They smoke their own salmon and produce their own private label of products, macadamia nut honey, peppercorn ketchup, Maui poha berry butter or pineapple jam. Other items sold are imported from Italy. Jumbo oatmeal or chocolate chip cookies, freshly made cheese Danish croissants, macadamia nut pies, Italian tiramisu, banana nut bread, are just a few of the items tempting the visitor. But don't forget, they also have deli style sandwiches! Also "gelati" and Italian sodas.

**ED & DON'S**  *American*
Wailea Shopping Village (879-1227) HOURS: 9 am-7 pm Mon. thru Sat. 10 am-6 pm on Sunday. SAMPLING: Sandwiches, ice cream and candies available here.

**ISLAND TERRACE**  *"Nutritional Cuisine"*
Diamond Resort. 555 Kaukahi St., Wailea (874-0500) HOURS: Breakfast 6-10:30 am, lunch 11 am-2:30 pm. SAMPLING: This restaurant is on the upper level of the Diamond Resort. An exclusive resort which makes their restaurants available to the general public. The menu features eating right selections for the health conscious and describes the theme of this restaurant as nutritionally balanced cuisine in harmony with fitness and longevity.

**MAKENA GOLF COURSE RESTAURANT**  *American*
5415 Makena Alanui. At the Golf Course, just beyond Wailea (879-1154) HOURS: Lunch 10:30 am-3:30 pm, pupus 3-6:30 pm. SAMPLING: Fruit, cobb or Caesar salads along with French dip, smoked chicken tostada, island curry or reuben sandwich $5.25-$11. COMMENTS: Furnished in a tan and green theme, this open-air restaurant features an outstanding golf and ocean view.

**MAUI ONION**   *American*
Stouffer Wailea Beach Resort, poolside (879-4900) HOURS: Lunch 11 am-3:30 pm, bar open until 6:30 pm. Take out sandwiches for golfers $4. SAMPLING: Sandwiches, salads, specialties $9-$12.75. COMMENTS: Great onion rings and burgers!

**POLO BEACH GRILLE AND BAR**   *American*
Kea Lani, poolside. (875-4100) HOURS: 11 am-7 pm. SAMPLING: Luncheon menu priced $8-$13 offers local tuna salad, grilled chicken sandwich, smoked turkey sandwich or burgers. Bar service.

## MODERATE

**BISTRO MOLOKINI ★**   *"Light" California-Italian*
Grand Wailea Resort & Spa (875-1234) HOURS: 11:30 am-4 pm, dinner 6-10 pm, bar open until 11 pm. SAMPLING: pasta, pizza and piatto forte run $15-$29. Scalloppine alla sorrentina, fresh fish, chicken with porcini mushrooms or seafood pizza. COMMENTS: An open-air bistro overlooking the activity pool and the Pacific Ocean. Casual shorts and shoes are acceptable. The menu 'is definitely Italian, but very light and innovative. Their children's menu offers alphabet soup, chicken nuggets, or pizza $2-$4.50.

**CABANA CAFE**   *American*
Four Seasons, Wailea (874-8000) HOURS: 11 am-7:30 pm, all day menu. Sunset entertainment in the evenings. COMMENTS: A casual atmosphere serving lunch and an afternoon bar with pupus out of doors. Cabanas line the pool area for in or out of the sun lounging. The iced coffee drinks were fabulous (alcoholic and non) and a wonderful way to spend an afternoon, just sipping by the pool.

**CAFE KIOWAI**   *Polynesian-American*
Maui Prince Hotel, Makena (874-1111) HOURS: Breakfast 6:30-11 am, lunch 11-2 pm, dinner 5-9 pm. SAMPLING: Dinner entrees include "Flavors of the Orient" such as sesame grilled fresh catch of the day or Chinese barbecued boneless lamb loin, "Tastes of the Mediterranean" offer veal picatta, grilled vegetable lasagna or tiger prawns $14.75-$26.50. COMMENTS: Keiki menu available. Kiowai pronounced "Key-oh-wy" means "fresh flowing water." A casual atmosphere.

**CAFE KULA ★**   *Spa Cuisine*
Located at the Grand Wailea (875-1234) HOURS: 7 am-9 pm. SAMPLING: Breakfasts $6-$10, lunch $10-$15, dinners $10-$16. How about starting your day with a gigantic breakfast banana split, heaped with mangos, papayas, local fresh strawberries, blackberries, pineapple passion fruit sorbet, homemade granola and lilikoi yogurt $9.95. Lunch includes sesame chicken couscous salad with mixed Maui field greens, tomatoes, Maui onions, and baby green beans. For dinner select their mahi mahi with papaya cilantro chili salsa $11.50, or housemade pappardelle pasta primavera $10.50. COMMENTS: Cooking classes weekly on Tuesday and Saturday. Interesting dining fare that is creative yet affordable. Kathleen Daelme-man's heads up the kitchen and the bakery goods are from the Piikake Bakery in Kihei.

RESTAURANTS
*Wailea-Makena-Moderate*

**CHART HOUSE**   *American*
100 Wailea Ike Drive, Wailea (879-2875) HOURS: Dinner nightly 5:30-10 pm, lunch served 11 am-2 pm. SAMPLING: Dinner seafood selections include salmon $22.95 or shrimp teriyaki. Other entrees range from steak fare or prime rib to chicken breast grilled or teriyaki style $16.95-$28.95. Entrees include salad, bread and rice. Former location of the Wailea Steak House. Kids menu available!

**FAIRWAY ★**   *American-Continental*
100 Kaukahi St., at Wailea Golf Course Clubhouse (879-4060 or 879-3861) HOURS: Breakfast from 7:30-10:45 am, lunch 11-4:30 pm. No dinner served. SAMPLING: Ginger Stir Fry, assorted Salads, or Club House sandwich $7.25-$9.95. They also offer homemade chili at their chili bar, available with rice and potato salad, with a "dog" or just with crackers $3.75-$5.50. COMMENTS: This restaurant is open-air with outdoor seating available. It offers a beautiful ocean view. Cocktails are available from the adjoining bar, the Waterhole. Their ice cream drinks are richly refreshing any time of day. Here is a sampling to tempt your palate: Fairway Grasshopper - creme de menthe, creme de cocoa, and ice cream all blended together, and topped with chocolate mint liqueur and chocolate sprinkles. Wailea Almond Joy - Amaretto, Kahlua, ice cream, blended and topped with whipped cream and almond slices. Brandy Alexander - Brandy, ice cream, and creme de cocoa blended and sprinkled with nutmeg. These wonderful concoctions run $6-ish.

**HARRY'S SUSHI AND PUPU BAR**   *Japanese*
See Lobster Cove which follows. (879-7677)

**LANAI TERRACE ★**   *International*
Maui Inter-Continental Wailea (879-1922) HOURS: 6-11 am for breakfast. 5-11 pm for dinner, Sunday brunch 9 am-1 pm. SAMPLING: Dinner selections of light suppers such as cheeseburger or saimin $9.75-$12.50. Entrees $25.95-$21.95. Sunday Champagne Brunch $28 is shown as served at the Lana'i Terrace, but another press release reports it is in the Makani Room. Served 9 am-1 pm, check both places! Hawaiian entertainment. Theme night at the Lanai Terrace includes a Tuesday night Asian Buffet $16.95, Wednesday night for pasta $15.95, Thursday night a Sunset Grill $19.96, Friday night a Seafood fare $23.95 and Saturday night a prime rib option $17.95. The seafood buffet has four rotating menus, so you can go for a month of Fridays to enjoy all your favorites and still try new and different choices each week. You can always get the curried shrimp, grilled scallops and Mediterranean tuna, but the hot buffet offers weekly variations on fresh fish, seafood stir fry, seafood pasta and cioppino or bouillabaisse. It also features oysters and clams on the half shell. Breakfast offers individual bakery items, fruits and juices to put together your own Continental breakfast or select from waffles, omelettes, eggs and meats or pancakes $5-$11. Their daily breakfast buffet runs $14.95 or select their continental buffet with pastries, fruits and juices for $10.95.

**SANDCASTLE ★**   *American*
3750 Wailea Alanui, Wailea Shopping Center (879-0606) HOURS: Lunch menu 11:30 am-9 pm and dinner daily from 5 pm. SAMPLING: Lunch selections includes soup, salads, and sandwiches $4.95-$12.95. Dinner choices of fresh fish, shellfish, pasta, meat and fowl $9.95-$14.95. COMMENTS: Their current menu

has changed a great deal from the last edition of our guide. There are a good variety of selections and since they serve from their lunch menu all day, a good affordable dining option for families. The selection of sandwiches is great, and the Monte Cristo is outstanding.

## EXPENSIVE

### GRAND DINING ROOM ★

Grand Wailea (875-1234) HOURS: Breakfast 6:30-11 am, Sunday brunch 9 am-2 pm, dinner 6-10 pm, Entertainment Sundays 10 am-1 pm, nightly 7-9:30 pm. SAMPLING: Their Champagne Sunday brunch at $38 is the island's most expensive, although a lavish display! Select from whole and sliced tropical fruits and fresh berries, an array of pastries, a seafood display on crushed ice laden with smoke salmon, shrimp and crab claws, assorted meats, pates and cheeses and eight stations from which to choose, or sample all of them! The Japanese selection from Kincha features sushi and sashimi made to order by a Kincha Chef, also miso soup and traditional breakfast items. A breakfast station features omelettes, eggs Benedict and similar fare. Pancakes and breakfast meats range from sausage to corned beef hash. A donut station that guests can top with fondue, chocolate, sprinkles and more. The carving station offers two items weekly, perhaps a pork loin with fennel or shabu shabu (assorted island seafood lobster, scallops, shrimp, clams, and mussels with capellini pasta cooked to order by the chef). Stop at the Sate station for chicken, beef, shrimp, mahi sates cooked to order with a variety of sauces. An antipasto station, a Caesar salad station and pasta made to order. Follow this up, if you can believe it, with hot meat items, hot seafood selections, hot starch and hot vegetable dishes. If you've been able to sample all this, you'll have to waddle over to exclaim over the Grand Pastry Chef's incredible tarts, French pastries and island specialty sweets. Hungry now? Their dinner menu offers meats and fowls, seafood and special dining for two options $27-$32, $75-$80 for the double entrees. A rather extensive, albeit expensive wine list. COMMENTS: Dress code requires slacks and a collared shirt for men, ladies evening resort wear. A beautiful dining room, and a wonderful way to pamper yourself.

### HANA GION ★ *Japanese*

Stouffer Wailea Resort (879-4900) HOURS: Open daily, except Thursday, 6-10 pm, reservations are required for teppanyaki seating and recommended for restaurant dining. SAMPLING: The restaurant offers a selection of complete dinners including chicken mizutaki, sukiyaki, yosenabe, shabu shabu, $35-$60. Their Hana Gion dinner is an eleven course meal with 24 hour advance reservations requested for two or more persons, $100 each. A sushi bar is also available. COMMENTS: The decor is as authentic as its cuisine. Woodwork, screens, stone flooring, bamboo trim, and decorative artifacts were all produced in Japan to exacting standards. In fact, parts of the dining area were actually constructed in Japan before dismantling them for shipment to Stouffer Wailea. The name Gion originates from the Gion district of Kyoto Traditional Japanese fare emphasizes freshness, subtle flavors and delicate preparations. Reserved teppanyaki seating is offered three times nightly. The main dining room seats 22, while private dining rooms seat four to six guests each. The sushi bar accommodates only ten. The restaurant is designed to promote the feeling of privacy and intimacy.

### HAKONE ★ *Japanese*

Maui Prince Resort, Makena (874-1111) HOURS: Dinner only, 6-9:30 pm. SAMPLING: Bordering maxi-expensive range, dinners start at $22 for chicken kara age, and range up to Hakone Gozen (a bento style meal) $42, or Nabemono selections which are cooked at your table and require a two person minimum by reservation $33-$35. COMMENTS: Authenticity is the key to this wonderful Japanese restaurant, from its construction (the wood, furnishings and even small nails were imported from Japan) to its food (the rice is flown in as well). The food and atmosphere are both wonderful here, and of course even the presentation of the food is artistic! Their Maui roll is a specialty here, made with smoked salmon, Maui onions and cucumbers. There is also a sushi bar, but with only 11 seats, it is definitely a first come basis.

### HULA MOONS *Seafood-American*

Maui Inter-Continental Resort (879-1922) HOURS: 11 am-5 pm daily for lunch and dinner. SAMPLING: Lunch includes sandwiches, salads, pizza and pasta or burgers $9-13.50. Hula Moons has a wonderful salad bar served during dinner and it comes with your entree, or on its own for $11.50. Dinner entrees yakitora grilled chicken breast $17, mixed grill seafood $28.95, grilled shrimp and scallops $18.95 or surf 'n turf $38. COMMENTS: Hula Moons is dedicated to the spirit of Don Blanding, Hawai'i's well known poet, artist and musician. "Hula Moons" was the title of one of his most popular books. The restaurant is located on the pool level and flickering torches and live Hawaiian music add to the ambiance of this ocean view restaurant. Hula moons provides either indoor or outdoor dining. Early bird specials are 5-6 pm nightly and are $3 off an adult entree. Live entertainment evenings from 5:30-8 pm.

### HUMUHUMUNUKUNUKUA'PUA'A *Seafood*

Grand Wailea (875-1234) HOURS: Dinner only 5:30-10 pm, bar open until 10:30 pm. SAMPLING: Whole sizzling snapper, wok seared scallops, kamameshi, seafood cioppino or roasted baby chicken $28.50-$40 a la carte. Side dishes include broccoli, steamed rice or stir fried vegetables $5-$9.50, desserts $6.50-$8.50. COMMENTS: This restaurant is named for the trigger fish, which is rather a mouthful, so the eatery is more affectionately referred to as humu-humu for short. It is a wonderful dining location. Tucked in the front grounds of the resort it is situated on top of a saltwater pond filled with aquatic life. The huge saltwater tank that divides the bar area is worth stopping by to just admire. The construction of this restaurant over the lagoon is really wonderful and inspires a rather Robinson Crusoe setting. They also offer smaller size portions for children 12 and under. Entrees are a la carte and given the prices of an entree, combined with a side dish or two, makes this a little bit more than just expensive fare. Not very affordable family dining, but definitely a place to take the kids (or grownups) to look around!

### KEA LANI RESTAURANT   *Euro-Pacific Cuisine*
4100 Wailea Alanui, Kea Lani Resort (875-4100) HOURS: Breakfast 6:30-11 am, breakfast buffet 7 am-11 am, lunch,  and dinner 5:30-11 pm. SAMPLING: Breakfast and lunch items $9.50-$15. The dinner menu changes monthly, but runs $6.50-$12 for a lengthy selection of salads, soups and appetizers. Dinner entrees might include Cantonese pepper steak, teppan style scallops or vegetarian stir fry $24-$36. Ohana menus (served for two or more) are family style, served on platters and accompanied by a garden salad. The Ohana menu generally has two selections priced in the $16.95-$19.95 range, but arrive for their ohana sunset special between 5:30 and 6:30 and pay about $3 per dinner less. COMMENTS: The Kea Lani features their own specialty line of gourmet products which they use in the restaurant and also sell at Caffe Ciao. They include garlic peppercorn catsup, guava catsup, banana nut bread and macadamia nut honey. They utilize fresh island ingredients and have their own Kea Lani herb garden. The hotels fine dining restaurant features 40-foot vaulted ceilings designed in a southern Mediterranean style and offers great ocean views. The menu is termed "Euro-Pacific" cuisine which is a combination of classic cooking styles of Europe with the flavors and foods of the Pacific. Once each month, Kea Lani Executive chef Steven Amaral and Maui artist Piero Resta bring together an intriguing blend of culinary, visual and performing arts at their "Arts a la Carte." The evening includes a five-course feast complemented by selected wines, live music, and a featured visual artist of local or international renown. The event is held mid-month and reservations are required. One traveling family told us that their stay at the Kea Lani was a package including daily breakfast buffet, and that with their teenage son it saved them huge amounts of money on the food travel budget and the breakfast selections were diverse enough to keep their palates interested for the entire week.

### LE GUNJI ★   *Japanese*
555 Kaukahi St., located at the Diamond Resort (874-0500) HOURS: Breakfast 7-10 am, lunch 11 am-1:45 pm and two nightly dinner seatings at 6 pm and 7:30 pm. Shorts and sandals not permitted. SAMPLING: A teppan-yaki restaurant the chef's special course runs $80 and includes fresh catch, lobster or filet mignon along with quite a list of side dishes! Other teppanyaki meals run $50-$65. Not quite a mega-expensive restaurant, but with $50 the cheapest entree, it is getting up there. COMMENTS: Note that they are now serving breakfast, but we did not receive breakfast or lunch information, so call to verify. The dining room is small and intimate with a beautiful garden courtyard located behind where the chef cooks. This Teppan-yaki is a bit different in that it is cooked with a French flair since their Chef Gunji Ito, from Osaka, previously cooked French cuisine.

**LOBSTER COVE-HARRY'S SUSHI BAR**   *Seafood-Japanese*
Located next to the Chart House in Wailea (879-7677) HOURS: Dining room
5:30-10 pm, Harry's sushi bar and dining patio open from 5:30 until 1 am.
Harry's Sushi, operated by Harry Okumara is located adjacent to Lobster Cover
and is open until 1 am. Lobster entrees are augmented with Hawaiian ahi, fresh
seafood ravioli, filet mignon, and grilled salmon $19-$25. We didn't stop in to try
Harry's Sushi and Pupu Bar, but the place was busy! The menu includes maki
sushi, nigiri sushi and sashimi $4.75-$10.75.

**PACIFIC GRILL**   *East-West*
Four Seasons Resort in Wailea (874-8000) HOURS: 6 am-11 pm for breakfast,
lunch 11:30 am-2:30 pm, dinner 6-9:30 pm. SAMPLING: A lunch buffet $16.75,
is available during the winter season offering an array of ever-changing island
fruits and vegetables, meats and fish and an array of salads, soups and desserts.
Available year round is their lunch menu with a wonderful lobster salad sandwich
served on sourdough toast or a Yucatan chicken salad accompanied by roasted
corn and black bean salad $9.75-$15.75. The dinner menu continues to be an East-
West theme. The more traditional western influences are accented with a sampling
of distinctive regional accents from the Hawaiian islands. Main courses include
Angus NY Sirloin Steak, Lamb T-Bone steak, spinach fettucini, or seafood stew
$14.75-$26. Also available are lite fare selections such as cobb or lobster salad
or hamburgers $9.75-$15.74. They still have their Pacific Rim specialties which
offer wok fried salmon with spicy peanut sauce, sweet and sour stir fried chicken
and tempura prawns or charred chicken breast with Chinese pancakes and plum
wine sauce. COMMENTS: A pleasant dining environment with indoor or lana'i
seating.

**PALM COURT** ★   *International-Buffet*
Stouffer Wailea Beach Resort (879-4900) HOURS: Breakfast a la carte and buffet
served 6 am-11 am. Sunday Champagne Brunch 10 am-2 pm, with an a la carte
menu available from 6 am-9:30 am. Dinner served 6-10 pm. SAMPLING:
Breakfast buffet is $15.75 for adults, $8 for children 12 and under. Sunday
Champagne Brunch is $26 for adults, half price for children 12 and under. Dinner
buffet prices range $26-$34 on Tuesday, Wednesday and Fridays for Italian, prime
rib or seafood themes. All other nights feature an a la carte menu with prices $5-
$22. This open-air dining hall is festively decorated in reds and greens and offers
evening breezes and an ocean view. Reservations are accepted only for a group
of 5 or more.

**PRINCE COURT** ★   *Hawaiian Regional Cuisine*
Maui Prince Hotel, Makena (874-1111) HOURS: Dinner 6-9:30 pm, closed
Monday and Tuesday, Sunday brunch 10 am-1:30 pm. SAMPLING: Appetizers,
soups, and salads $5.50-$13.50 are the prelude to an outstanding selection of
delicious entrees. Sample three Hawaii fishes prepared in three different styles
$30, fresh whole Kona lobster steamed and shelled and nestled on coconut risotto
$48, sauteed mahi with bay scallops $29 or herb roast chicken with andouille
sausage and kula vegetables $24. Items that might be found on the Sunday buffet
include croissants stuffed with Portuguese sausages or ham, smoked oysters,
octopus or island fish, avocados stuffed with crab, or an unusual and delicious
midora bisque soup. Brunch entrees during our visit ranged from roast lamb or
prime rib to veal piccata. The dessert table is beyond belief! Reservations are

recommended. COMMENTS: Hawaiian Regional Cuisine continues to be the "buzz" word in dining experiences in the islands. It is simply the opportunity to experience the many varied selections of fresh foods grown, raised or caught in the islands. The culinary cuisine of the Prince Court is an incredible blend of flavors which highlight the best and freshest Hawaiian produce, meats and fish. Chef Roger Dikon is perhaps one of the best and most innovative chefs in all of Hawai'i and a main force behind the emergence of H.R.C. (Hawaiian Regional Cuisine). Beautifully situated the dining room offers a splendid view of the ocean and hotel grounds. The Sunday brunch is on our list for a tasteful extravaganza.

**RAFFLES'** ★ *Pacific Rim Cuisine/Hawaiian Regional Cuisine*
Stouffer Wailea Beach Resort (879-4900) HOURS: Tuesday-Saturday 6:30-10 pm. SAMPLING: Entrees range from Pacific seafood paella, pan fried chicken bread, filet of opapakaka with lilikoi ginger butter and roasted rack of lamb with Hunan marinade $24-$34. Hawaiian estate coffees, from either Maui, Kona or Molokai $7 serves 2 persons. COMMENTS: This restaurant has kept us on our toes, first opening, then closing then reopening and changing the menu yet again. It seems the high end (expensive) restaurants in Wailea are having a bit of a time of it, or perhaps there are just too many of them. Nearby Maui-Intercontinental finally closed their fine dining La Perouse restaurant a couple of years back. Stouffer's also moved their Sunday brunch from Raffles to Palm Court, but now that Raffles' is once again open, it appears the brunch is remaining at Palm Court. We're confused. Raffles' is named for Sir Thomas Stamford Raffles (1781 - 1826), the British founder of the city of Singapore where the Raffles' Hotel has become a legend. For over 100 years the Singapore establishment entertained seafaring merchants, literary giants and even royalty, and amid the splendor they sipped the drink crated by Raffles -- the Singapore Sling. This restaurant has a special appeal for us, as it was one of the first we dined at during our first visit to Maui.

'ILIMA

### SATORU RESTAURANT   *Japanese*

Diamond Resort, 555 Kaukahi St., Wailea (874-0500) HOURS: Breakfast 7 am-10 am, lunch (daily except Tuesday) 11 am-1:45 pm, early bird dinner 5:30-6:30 pm, dinner 5-9 pm. SAMPLING: Set menu options run $35-$80 per meal. A La carte items include tempura, teriyaki or udon $3.50-$30. Their lunch menu is considerable less expensive with donburi and udon dishes $8-$12. Their Japanese breakfast menu, again a set option, is not available on Tuesdays. Price is $14. An exclusive property that makes their fine restaurants available to the general public. The dining hall is large with cathedral-like ceilings and lots of attractive rock-work. Very simple, elegant decor. They now have added a Plumeria Counter, 5:30-8 pm, a place to enjoy their menu items individually. A la carte items on the menu include Ono Mono, Otsukuri, Wan Mono $5-$30 (the menu notes that they will explain the items when you order) or tempura, Teriyaki, udon dishes $3-$30. (Oshinko, "a small portion of today's selected pickles" runs $3). I guess it is kind of pickle du jour!

### SCAROLES RISTORANTE TOO   *Italian*

131 Wailea Iki Place (875-7433) HOURS: Lunch 11:30 am-3:30 pm, pupus 3:30-5:30, dinner 5:30-9:30 pm with Italian style steak, chicken, pasta and veal. Dinners run $13.95 for pasta marinara to $23.95 for veal marsala. COMMENTS: Expanding from Lahaina, you can now enjoy their New York style in Wailea.

### SEASONS   *Continental-Californian*

Four Seasons Resort in Wailea (874-8000) HOURS: Dinner only 6:30-9:30 pm. SAMPLING: Main courses vary from lemon crusted veal medallion with a ragout of wild mushroom salsa to grilled tenderloin of beef with fennel and gorgonzola potato fritters or fresh fish $26-$33 a la carte. COMMENTS: Terrace seating with an ocean view combined with background music performed by a jazz trio. The Four Season's Sunset Lounge offers nightly entertainment and dancing 6 pm-1 am. Children's portions are available. An elegant dining atmosphere.

### SEAWATCH   ★ *Island Regional*

100 Wailea Golf Club Drive (875-8080) HOURS: Breakfast/lunch menu served 8 am-3 pm, grill menu 3-10 pm and dinner 5:30-10 pm. SAMPLING: "Scads of Sandwiches," "Oodles of Noodles," "Dishes by the Dozen" are breakfast selections which range from fresh fruit to omelettes, burgers, and pasta $6.25-$10. Breakfast and lunch items both available from opening until 3 pm. Dinners $18-$24 include miso chili glazed tiger prawns, rack of lamb, fresh fish or Szechuan BBQ chicken. COMMENTS: Breakfast and lunch options are relatively inexpensive, for a room with a view, too! A nice option is the choice of lunch for breakfast or breakfast for lunch, which few restaurants offer. The SeaWatch opened in January of 1994 with an interior that has several distinctive dining areas. The lanai dining area offers the best views of Molokini, Kaho'olawe, Makena and Ma'alaea, the grill room is highlighted by giant glass doors and artwork from Arthur Johnson, a Big Island muralist. The lounge has a white baby grand piano as its centerpiece. SeaWatch is led by the capable Maui restaurateurs Roy Dunn and Mike Hook, proprietors of the two Koho Grill and Bar locations and the Plantation House Restaurant in Kapalua. Chef Richard Matsumoto was previously at Raffles'. Their pan-seared filet mignon had a fabulous Japanese pepper/red onion sauce, that was very unique. Sweet, but not overpowering that complimented the meat perfectly. Chef Matsumoto says the recipe for this dish popped into his head while he was

hiking out of Kanaio after spending a long afternoon fishing. Wouldn't you think after a day of fishing, a seafood dish would have popped into his head? Guess he didn't catch anything that day. The liliko'i cheese cake is very European-like, but distinctive and unusual with a not too sweet flavor. Great view and ambiance, and with the tables spread out, and the high ceilings, a wonderful spaciousness.

## MEGA-EXPENSIVE

**KINCHA**  *Japanese*
Grand Wailea (875-1234) Hours: Dinner only, 6-10 pm. COMMENTS: The "mega-expensive" is a new category this year, since just "expensive" really isn't descriptive enough for this new, very authentic Japanese restaurant. It appears the race is on for which Japanese Restaurant in Wailea can charge the most for a meal. The Japanese restaurant at the Grand Wailea Resort, Kaiseki Ryori, appears to be taking the lead with a per dinner per diner price of $500. Yes, that is not a typo, and it is dollars, not yen. This premium dining experience affords the guest to enjoy a Miyabi meal, translated it means elegance. Their menu reads, "Set menu of finest, Authentic Japanese food served on individual selected tableware." The Nishiki (means Golden Embroidery) runs $150 and includes home made fruit wine, sakizuke, appetizer, clear broth soup, sashimi, broiled vegetable, deep fried, vinegar course, rice, miso soup, pickles, seasonal fruit, sweet dessert and finest green tea. Two other set meals are Aya (means coloration) $200, Miyabi (means elegance) and their Tokubetsu Kaiseka which can be served in their private Ozashiki-Tatami Room if you request, $500. Full course dinners include sushi, tempura, lobster, steak or broiled fish, complete with soup, vegetables, rice, dessert, pickles, vinegar course and for $75-$100. Kama'aina Kaiseki, their kincha authentic Japanese full course dinner offers three servings, plus dessert for $58. You choose an appetizer, soup, or sushi, followed by a Japanese style salad and your selection of sushi, tempura or kincha steak as an entree. Sake (per small container) $11-$15. Sushi and tempura counters are also available. The sushi counter has a capacity for only 17 people and the tempura bar 15. Their children's menu is called "Keiki Kincha" and is a set meal with milk or juice, mini salad, deep-fried items of the day, rice miso soup, and a choice of Japanese style steak or chicken teriyaki plus ice cream for $35. While we may find these prices outrageous, the Japanese visitor on Maui, accustomed to paying the high "yen" for a meal in their homeland, may not be in for a shock. We're told that a fine meal in Japan runs several hundred dollars or more.

## *KAHULUI-WAILUKU*

Along Lower Main Street in Wailuku are a number of local restaurants which are not often frequented by tourists and may well be one of the island's best kept secrets! Don't expect to find polished silver or extravagant decor, but do expect to find reasonable prices for large portions of food in a comfortable atmosphere. Note that many of these local restaurants may not accept credit cards. Dairy Queen, Pizza Hut, McDonald's, Burger King, and Jack in the Box are a few of the restaurants in and around Kahului and the Maui Mall. These don't require elaboration. Orange Julius at Kaahumanu Mall offers top your own waffles and seafood and turkey pita sandwiches.

## INEXPENSIVE

While not restaurants, two of our favorite haunts bear mention here. The *Home Made Bakery* at 1005 Lower Main, open 6 am-9 pm daily, is an island institution. Recently remodeled and expanded, they have more than just donuts, you'll find unusual specialties such as empanadas, manju, and bread pudding. They began over 35 years ago on Maui and do not add any preservative to their made from scratch formulas. They are the home of the original Maui Crispy Manju and noted for their Maui Crunch bread. Some items available at island groceries. 244-7015.

Nearby is the *Four Sisters Bakery* on Vineyard and Hinano in Wailuku. It is run by Melen, Mila, Beth and Bobbie who arrived from the Philippines after helping their father run a Spanish Bakery in Manila for fifteen years. Not a large selection, but delicious and different items. One is a sweet bread filled with a cinnamon pudding, a sponge cake "sandwich," as well as cinnamon rolls and butter rolls. The only place you can purchase these delicacies is at their bakery or at the Saturday Swap Meet in Kahului. 244-9333. Hours 5 am-5 pm Saturday and Sunday, 5 am-8 pm Monday thru Friday.

### A TOUCH OF SAIGON ★ *Vietnamese*
1246 Lower Main St., Wailuku (244-7845) HOURS: Mon-Sat. 10 am-9:30 pm continuous service, same menu all day. SAMPLING: Dishes run $6-$16, with most in the $6.50-$8.50 range. They include god noodle dishes, rice plates, Vietnamese fondue dishes, or stir fried dishes. COMMENTS: If you haven't sampled Vietnamese food, you're in for a treat! Very different from Chinese or Japanese, it is a refreshing combination of flavors that sets it apart. Lemon grass, cucumbers, sour garlic sauce, daikon pickles, fresh island basil and mint leaves are among the many distinctive ingredients used for seasoning dishes such as Ga Xao Xa Ot (curried chicken with lemon grass) or Bo Lui (grilled beef sirloin rolls). And, thankfully, you don't have to be able to pronounce the food to enjoy it! Very simple atmosphere, but very good food. It's a best bet!

### AKI'S HAWAIIAN FOOD AND BAR *Hawaiian*
309 N. Market, Wailuku (244-8122) HOURS: Mon.-Sat. 11 am-10 pm, Sunday 5-9 pm. SAMPLING: Chicken hekka, Hawaiian favorites such as kalua pig with cabbage and a wonderful octopus soup. The prices remain in the very affordable $4-$6 range for lunch or dinner. A good stop if you want to try some local Hawaiian food.

### ALOHA MIXED PLATE  See Food Court.

### ARCHIE'S *Japanese*
1440 Lower Main St., Wailuku (244-9401) COMMENTS: We found their food good and their prices reasonable, but when we called for current information they simply replied, "Archie no want to give you nothing." Enough said.

### BACK STREET CAFE *American*
335 Hoohana Blvd., #7A, Kahului (877-4088) HOURS: Mon.-Fri. breakfast 6-9:30 am, lunch 10:30 am-2 pm. SAMPLING: Daily homemade specials, salads and sandwiches. Take-out lunches available as are catering services. Very popular with the local residents. Lunch special $4.75. Free delivery Kahului/Wailuku.

**BAMBOO RESTAURANT**   *Local/Asian*
1032 Lower Main St. (244-1166) HOURS: 9 am-9 pm, Mon.-Sat. SAMPLING: Squid stir fry, chicken katsu, monk fish, Kal bi ribs $5.50-$13.50.

**BANGKOK ROYALTY**   *Thai*
55 Kaahumanu Ave (871-5151) HOURS: Lunch 10:30-2:30 pm, dinner 5-10 pm. SAMPLING: All-you-can-eat Thai buffet $8.50. Entertainment and karaoke.

**CAFE KUP A KUPPA ESPRESSO BAR-CAFE**   *International*
79 Church St. (244-0500) HOURS: Mon.-Fri. 7 am-4:30 pm., Sat. 8 am-3 pm. SAMPLING: Breakfast burrito $5, frittata $5, Belgian waffle $5 or "lunch things" which include four kinds of gourmet pizza fresca $6-$15, healthy sandwiches or quesadilla $5.50. Salads range from Caesar to oriental chicken $5, and desserts are homemade at $2.75. COMMENTS: Bruce Mann and Dennis Mitchell combine for a great team. Bruce Mann says it's his mastery of his prized, twenty year old, Italian Espresso machine and Dennis Mitchell says it's the clean Iao Valley water, either way, this coffee is something to buzz about.

**CHINA EXPRESS**   *Chinese*
At Safeway, 170 E. Kamehameha Ave., Kahului (877-3377) SAMPLING: Items in 1/2 pint, pint, quart, two quart size or pound. Plate lunches $3.99-$5.79.

**CHUM'S**   *Local Style*
1900 Main Street, Wailuku (244-1000) HOURS: 6:30 am-10:30 pm Monday thru Saturday, Sunday 7 am-10 pm. SAMPLING: Homemade soups, stew, local style meals include beef tomato, mahi mahi, roast pork, fried chicken $5.15-$6.60 and chili, priced $2.50-$5.95. Breakfast until 11 am, same menu for lunch and dinner. COMMENTS: A good option for a late evening snack after a movie in Kahului!

**THE CLASS ACT** ★   *Continental*
Maui Community College Campus, Kahului (242-1210) HOURS: Lunch only Wednesday and Friday 11 am-1:30 pm. COMMENTS: This is one of Maui's best kept secrets. Insiders know they are in for a treat when they stop by for a five-course gourmet lunch for $9. The Food Service students of the Maui Community College prepare and wait on the tables as well, with a varied selection of entrees weekly. Two selections are prepared, one is a healthy heart selection which is low in sodium and fat. The program is only offered during the school year, so be sure and call to check on availability and schedule a reservation. They suggest calling for reservations on Wednesday and Friday 8:30-10:30 am, but reservations are taken up to two weeks in advance. The Class Act is located on the MCC campus adjacent to the cafeteria. Evening gourmet dining once a term, cost is about $35.

**THE COFFEE STORE**
Kaahumanu Center (871-6860) HOURS: Mon., Tues. Wed. 7 am-6 pm, Thurs., Fri. 7 am-9 pm. Saturday 8:30 am-6 pm, Sunday 9 am-4 pm. SAMPLING: Muffins $1.85, lasagna, $4.50, cheesecake, assorted pastries $2-$3.50, quiche of the day $3.50. COMMENTS: They also have locations in Kihei and Napili. In addition to freshly roasted coffee, they serve locally made fresh pasta dishes, croissants, salads and sandwiches. Voted as having the best capuccino on Maui in the "Best of Maui" contest conducted by the Maui News.

## CUPIE'S
134 W. Kamehameha Ave. (877-3055 or 871-6488) HOURS: Mon.-Sat. 6 am-9 pm for breakfast, lunch and dinner. SAMPLING: Breakfast served until 10:30, plate lunches, bento, mini bento and full menu served all day. This used to be one of those places where you sat in your car with the trays on your window, now it is a drive up and order "to go" or seating there. Plate lunches $5.25-$6, sandwiches $.99 (grilled cheese) - $2.69 for beef teriyaki. Chow funand broasted chicken.

**EDO JAPAN** (See Food Court)  **ESPLENDIDO** (See Food Court)

## FOOD COURT
Food court at the newly renovated Kaahumanu Center will feature eight restaurants near the main entrance. Edo Japan will feature Japanese food, Yummy Korean BBQ, Aloha Mixed Plate (Hawaiian and local food), Maui Yogurt, Esplendido Restaurant (Mexican), Panda Express (Chinese) and Mama Brava (Italian). Minimum hours in the food court are 11 am-9 pm daily, although some may open earlier for breakfast and remain open later. Yummy Korean, Explendido and Aloha Mixed Plate are all locally owned and operated, Mama Brava is an east coast chain, Panda Express is a chain and Edo Japan is out of Calgary, Canada. There is also an Orange Julius/Arby's. Also part of the mall are Koho Grill & Bar is a sit down restaurant. Prices $4-7 range.

## FUJIYA'S ★ *Japanese*
133 Market Cafe, Wailuku (244-0206) HOURS: Lunch 11-2 Mon.-Fri., dinner 5-9 Mon.-Sat. SAMPLING: Tempura $9.50, teriyaki $6.50, chicken $5.75. Five dinner choices include a combination such as tempura with yakitori, fried ahi, tsukemono, miso soup and rice. Combination plate $9. Beer & sake available. COMMENTS: One of our best bets for Japanese food. Sushi lovers will appreciate their sushi bar where a large variety of selections are available at half the usual resort area price.

## HAMBURGER MARY'S *Mexican*
Corner of Main and Market St., Wailuku (244-7776) HOURS: Open daily, breakfast, lunch and dinner. SAMPLING: They promise the biggest burgers on Maui, and serve vegi burgers as well. Garden delights, meatless selections $3.75-$7.95. The restaurant is packed with antiques from the 30's and 40's. They also feature a full service bar, videos and dancing. The first Hamburger Mary's opened in San Francisco over 23 years ago featuring homestyle cooking that continues here on Maui.

## ICHIBAN THE RESTAURANT *Japanese*
Kahului Shopping Center (871-6977) HOURS: Breakfast 7:30 am-2 pm, Saturday 10:30 am-2 pm. Dinner 5 pm-9 pm, closed Sunday. SAMPLING: Luncheon menu offers chicken katsu, teri chicken, or donburi and noodle meals $4.95-$7.50. Dinner combinations $11.95, stir fry dishes $8.50, special combination plates $14.95, or steak and lobster $21.95. COMMENTS: Located in the older Kahului Center, this restaurant doesn't stand out as memorable for its food or ambiance.

## IMPERIAL TEPPANYAKI *Japanese*
Maui Palms Hotel, Kahului (877-0071) HOURS: Nightly from 5:30-8:30 pm. SAMPLING: A buffet with different items prepared by teppanyaki chefs at the buffet. Entrees might include fried fish, ika tempura, chicken yakitori. From the

salad bar sample miso soup, tofu with ginger sauce, sashimi and other local favorites, $16.95 plus tax.

### INTERNATIONAL HOUSE OF PANCAKES  *American*
Maui Mall, Kahului (871-4000) HOURS: Sun.-Thurs 6 am-midnight, Fri. and Sat. until 2 am. COMMENTS: A very large facility with a menu that is popular with all family members. Something for everyone and at reasonable prices. Basic dinners begin in the $5 range.

### KOHO GRILL AND BAR ★  *American*
Kaahumanu Shopping Center, Kahului (877-5588) HOURS: Daily for breakfast 7-11 am, lunch and dinner until 10 pm, bar service until 1 am. SAMPLING: Soups & salads include chicken Caesar, Oriental chicken, taco salad or ahi salad $5.95-$7.25, sandwiches from $4.75, entrees priced $8.45-$14.95 and range from pork chops to a rib plate or fettucini primavera. COMMENTS: A diverse menu and affordable prices which boils down to great family dining. The same operators run this restaurant and also the Plantation House in Kapalua, another Koho Grill and Bar in Kahului and the new SeaWatch restaurant in Wailea. They also have a great keiki (kids) menu and, knowing how fussy some kids can be, they'll even cut the crusts off the sandwiches! A few new salads and dinner entrees have livened up the menu. One of only a few restaurants in the area open on Sundays! Convenient for a bite enroute to the airport.

### LOPAKA'S BAR AND GRILL  *American*
161 Alambra, Kahului Industrial Area (871-1135) HOURS: 6 am-11 pm, pupus until 1 am. SAMPLING: Same menu for lunch and dinner. Burgers and sandwiches, plate lunches, BBQ beef $5.25-$7.50. COMMENTS: More a bar atmosphere than restaurant, they've added breakfast service.

### LUIGI'S  *Italian*
Maui Mall, Kahului (877-3761) HOURS: 11:30 am-4 pm for lunch, 4-10 pm for dinner. SAMPLING: Lunch offers potato skins, saimin, calamari strips, pasta, pizza and burgers $3.99-$8.99. Dinner offers veal marsala, steamed mussels, more pasta and pizza $10.99-$18.99. COMMENTS: Daily specials.

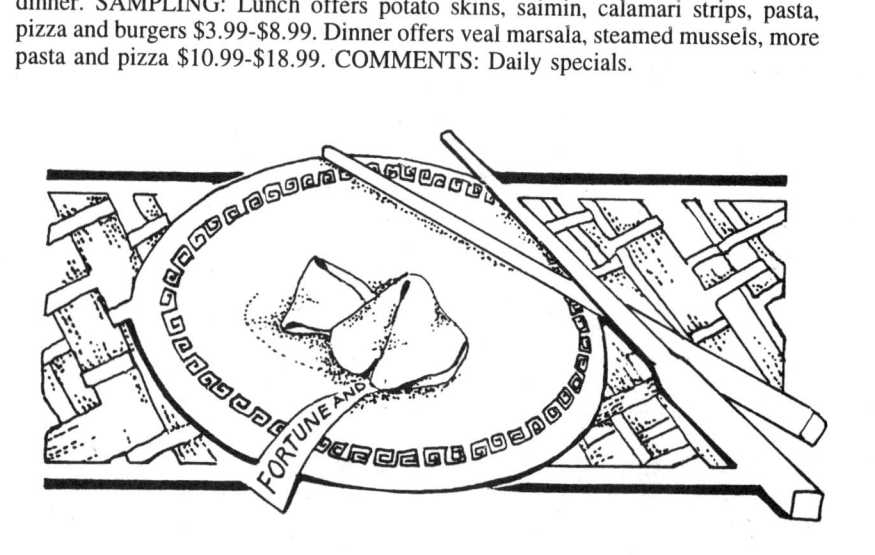

**MAMA BRAVA** (See Food Court)

**MAMA DING'S PASTELES RESTAURANT** ★ *Puerto Rican-Local*
255 E Alamaha St., Kahului (877-5796) HOURS: Breakfast/lunch 6:30 am-1:30
pm Mon.-Fri. You can have lunch at 7 am and breakfast at 1 pm! SAMPLING:
Eggs Bermuda (2 eggs whipped with cream cheese and onion) served with
potatoes or rice and toast $4.50 or a Puerto-Rican plate lunch $5.95 with pastele,
gandule rice, empanadilla, choice of meat, bacalao salad and dessert. Other
lunches run $2.75-$5.75. COMMENTS: Ready for a different breakfast? Skip
IHOP or Denny's and try this cozy restaurant tucked away in the Kahului
Industrial Area. Try a pastele which has an exterior of grated green banana and
a filling of pork, vegetables and spices that is then steamed. Delicious! We've
tried several breakfasts, all were good! No credit cards.

**MAUI BAKE SHOP & DELI** ★ *European Pastries-Deli*
2092 Vineyard St., Wailuku (242-0064) HOURS: Mon.-Fri. 6 am-6:30 pm, Sat.
7 am-5 pm. SAMPLING: They seem to be getting a thumbs up from visitors and
tourists alike. An early morning arrival assures a greater selection from the many
varied goodies. Some items are novelty desserts, shaped like pigs and chickens!
This European style bakery is a combination of efforts between Jose and Claire
Fjuii Krall, a French husband-chef and his Japanese wife. They have pizzas,
quiches and sandwiches on French bread, soups, salads or croissant sandwiches
$1.95-$5.95. The big stone oven is still there, left over from the Yokouchi family
that was in this location in the 1930s. Pastries include cakes, napoleans and other
very fancy pastries. One was a hollowed sweet roll filled with custard, then
topped with marzipan leaves and a bit of round orange marzipan and they called
it a "peach" -- cute and it looked just like a peach, but we were surprised that the
custard flavor was vanilla. At Christmas holiday time check out their stollen
gingerbread and yule logs, at Easter indulge in a marzipan egg. There are a few
ice cream tables and chairs. Jose Krall began cooking in 1976 in France and since
then has trained in Belgium and France before becoming Executive Pastry Chef
at the Maui Prince in Wailea before opening this shop in Wailuku. Yum!

**MAUI BAKERY, BAGELRY AND DELI**
201 Dairy Rd., Kahului (871-4825) HOURS: 6:30 am-5:30 pm. SAMPLING:
Sandwiches on French bread, specialty baked goods like foccacia, and pesto
calzone. Salads include tuna, potato, egg, curry chicken and nine varieties of
cream cheese toppings $3-$5.50. Dessert items such as brownies, coffee cake and
macaroons can round out your meal. COMMENTS: Freshly baked bagels!

**MAUI BOY** *Hawaiian-Local Style*
2102 Vineyard St., Wailuku (244-7243) HOURS: Breakfast 7-11 am, lunch 11
am-5 pm, dinner 5:30-9 pm, Fri and Sat dinner served until 10 pm. SAMPLING:
Hawaiian favorites such as Kalua pig and poi or lau lau. Local style plate lunches
available for lunch and dinner include seafood plate, teri beef, Korean shortribs,
pork katsu $6.35-$6.95 or combination dinners with two entrees for $7.95. Also
burgers and sandwiches.

**MAUI COFFEE ROASTERS (BEAN'S WORLD)**
444 Hana Highway, Kahului (877-CUPS) HOURS: 7:30 am-6 pm. SAMPLING:
Veggie bagel, French toast, veggie burger, basmoto sandwich, Caesar salad, or

turkey sandwich $3.95-$5.95. COMMENTS: Cute little shop, where you can purchase a broad array of freshly roasted coffees and enjoy great prices on food and beverages. Specialty drinks included honey lemonade made with Maui lemons, filtered water and honey, Thai high iced tea, or espresso drinks such as a depth charge (a shot of espresso in their kona coffee).

## MEL'S LUNCH TO YOU
1276 Lower Main St., at the Nagasako Fish Market, Wailuku (242-8271) HOURS: Mon.- Fri. 7 am - 1 pm, and Sat. 9 am - 1 pm. SAMPLING: Select from over 10 dishes on their steam table, some daily entrees remaining the same, others changing weekly. The Hawaiian plate lunch and the Friday special seafood platter are proving very popular. Their bento boxes run $5.50 and you can select the three items to be included. One of the cooks is Filipino, so expect some authentic food from his homeland. COMMENTS: Just as they opened we had some of our readers writing to let us know that this place is a find! The Nagasako Fish Market (242-4073) Store is operated by Jordan Nagasako of the Lahaina Nagasako grocery family. As a fisherman, he can buy and sell fish wholesale, thus offering an amazing variety of fish and shellfish for you to cook in your Maui home. Exotic reef fish include opelu, akule, or oio. Live clams and crabs too!! Looking for something more unusual? Then try some of their poke (marinated raw fish). A very interesting assortment that might include conch-shell poke with flying-fish eggs.

## MUSHROOM
2080 Vineyard, Wailuku (244-7117) HOURS: Lunch only 10 am-2 pm. SAMPLING: Local style lunches include Chinese pasta $5.50, calamari $5.75, vegetable special $4.25, and many noodle and saimin dishes. COMMENTS: Nagato Kato opened his restaurant in early May of 1994. Formerly with Kobe restaurant in Lahaina, he now also works at Humuhumu at the Grand Wailea. Great local fare, one of the best reasons to come to Wailuku is to eat!

### NAZO'S   *Hawaiian-Local Style*
1063 Lower Main St., Wailuku, at Puuone Plaza (244-0529) HOURS: Mon.-Sat. 6 am-9 pm. SAMPLING: Sandwiches include egg salad at $1.75, or grilled ham and cheese $2.25. Entrees include soup or salad, rice or mashed potatoes, coffee, tea or fruit punch. Selections include liver with bacon, shrimp tempura for $5-6. A tossed salad adds 80 cents. Luau stew is featured on Wed., pig feet on Thurs. and Sat. COMMENTS: A small, family-owned restaurant which is very affordable and prides themselves on their home-style cooking. No credit cards.

## NOODLES
3 Baldwin Ave., Paia (579-8383) HOURS: Daily 9 am-9 pm. SAMPLING: Noodles every which way, hot or cold. Korean Seoul, linguine with tofu and clam, chicken log rice or their Saimin $4.25-$5.75.

### NORM'S CAFE   *Local style*
740 Lower Main St. (242-1167) HOURS: Breakfast and lunch Tues.-Sat 5 am-2 pm, Sun. 6 am-2 pm, serves dinner Fri. and Sat. 5-9 pm. SAMPLING: Local foods with okazuya. Local style "grinds" served with rice, macaroni salad, tossed green salad or coleslaw and includes roast pork, mahi, beef stew, beef tomato or roast pork $4.95-$5.30. Norm's sandwiches $2-$7. Also noodles and salads.

**PANDA EXPRESS** (See Food Court)

**PINATA'S** *Mexican*
395 Dairy Rd., Kahului (877-8707) HOURS: Mon. - Sat. 10:30 am-7 pm. SAMPLING: Nachos, tostados, quesadillas, Mexican salads $2.45-$4.95. Combination plates $5.65-$6.95. COMMENTS: Owner Steve Waller reports that everything is made from scratch, from the beans to the salsa (two kinds, blended and smooth or chunky) and they use only 100% cholesterol free oils. A family operation, they wanted to keep the prices affordable, yet maintain a high standard. Transplanted from Southern California, they wanted to bring to Maui the Mexican flavors of food found in the Los Angeles and San Diego area. They offer quite a few vegetarian selections as well. Mexican food is kind of a personal thing, so perhaps that is why the reviews on this place are a bit mixed. A very convenient stop enroute to the airport.

**PUPULE CAFE** *Local/vegetarian*
318 North Market St., Wailuku (Formerly location of Sam Sato's) (242-8449). HOURS: Breakfast 7 am-11 am. Lunch and dinner menu served 11 am-2:30 pm Mon.- Fri. and 5-10 pm Mon.-Sun. SAMPLING: Sandwiches include veggie melt, stuffed spuds, salads, and house specialties such as hoisin marinated baked chicken. They plan on adding pizza soon. Most expensive item on the menu is $5.95. Many menu items are vegetarian. COMMENTS: Owners Janna and Mark Folger also operate Banana Bungalow and have spruced up and redecorated the place with bright colors, curtains and tables with real legs. (Yes, real legs, with feet and brightly colored shoes.) They also have a big screen TV and a dart board. Their specialty is Shepherd's pie and lasagna. Pupule is pronounced like the song, "Princess Pupule got plenty papaya" and it means crazy!, nuts!, have fun!

**RAINBOW DINING ROOM**
Maui Beach Hotel in Kahului. HOURS: Friday night only for dinner. SAMPLING: Prime rib, sauteed fish and pasta buffet runs $16.95 for adults, $8.50 for children.

PUPULE PUB & CAFE

**SAM SATO'S**   *Local Style-Hawaiian*
1750 Wili Pa Loop, Wailuku (244-7124) HOURS: Breakfast and lunch 7 am-2 pm, pastries served until 4 pm. Closed Sun. SAMPLING: Noodles are their specialty. Breakfast includes eggs or pancakes. Lunch options include combination plates $4.50-$5.75 such as teriyaki beef, stew, chop steak or spare ribs. Sandwiches and burgers. Saimin and chow fun are served in small portions for $2.55-$2.75, or large portions for $3.55-$5.25. COMMENTS: The homemade pastries are wonderful. The peach, apple and coconut turnovers were fragrant and fresh. In addition to noodles they specialize in manju, a Japanese tea cake. It may come as a big surprise when you discover that these tasty morsels are actually filled with a mashed version of lima beans! They moved in 1994 to a new, slightly larger location near Wailuku post office in the Millyard.

**SEOUL KAL BI**   *Korean*
Kahului Shopping Center (877-0141) HOURS: Mon.-Sat. 9 am-9 pm, Sunday 11 am-8 pm. Take out and catering available. SAMPLING: They specialize in Korean barbecue short ribs, teriyaki beef and pork, but also augment their menu with a number of Korean vegetable dishes $4.95-$6.95. Most of their menu items are boiled, steamed or barbecue grilled. They serve two types of kim chee, one the hotter Korean version and the other a milder style. They are open for breakfast, lunch and dinner. Serving American style breakfasts but bentos available upon request. Owners You Bun Ji and his wife are from Seoul, Korea.

**SIAM THAI**   *Thai*
123 N. Market St., Wailuku (244-3817) HOURS: Lunch Mon.-Fri. 11 am-2:30 pm, dinner daily 5-9:30. Exotic green papaya salad $4.95, eggplant tofu $6.95, lemon chicken $6.50. COMMENTS: The white table cloths give this restaurant an elegant air. According to our waiter we dined at the same table Robert Redford used when he visited. Very good Thai food although the competition is stiff with Saeng Thai just around the corner. They recently opened a Thai/Lao market offering cooking ingredients and cookware. Store hours Mon.-Sat. 9 am-8 pm.

**SIR WILFRED'S ESPRESSO CAFE**   *American*
Maui Mall, Kahului (877-3711) HOURS: Daily 9-6 pm, Fri. until 9 pm, live jazz entertainment on Sundays. SAMPLING: Continental breakfasts with fresh pastries. Bagels or deli-style sandwiches are available for lunch as well as a variety of salads or quiche $4.75-$5.95. Also gourmet teas, coffees or beer and wine.

**SIZZLER**   *American*
355 E. Kamehameha Hwy, Kahului (871-1120) HOURS: 6 am-10 pm, until midnight on Fri. and Sat. SAMPLING: Sirloin steak, sizzler steak, chicken dishes all in the $8-$15 range. All-you-can-eat salad bar includes soup, salad and tostada bar for only $7.99 lunch, $8.99 dinner. A keiki (children's) menu offers special meals Mon.-Thurs. for $.99 and Fri. and Sat. for $2.29. Available for those guests ages 10 and under. COMMENTS: As Sizzlers go, this is one of the better ones. A good selection of entrees at family prices and a very good salad bar as well!

**SUBWAY SANDWICH**   *Sandwiches*
1955 Lower Main, Wailuku, in the Wailuku Industrial Center, 244-9999. Also at 737 Lower Main, Wailuku, 242-1900 and at 340 Hana Hwy, Kahului, 877-7272.

### TASTY CRUST ★ *Local Style*

1770 Mill St., Wailuku (244-0845) HOURS: Daily 5:30 am-1:30 pm for breakfast and lunch daily, 5-10 pm for dinner except Mon. SAMPLING: Unusual and delicious crusty hotcakes are their specialty, two are a meal for $2.20, or French toast $2. Add an egg for 50 cents. Lunches and dinners a la carte. Spare ribs, fried shrimp, roast beef $4.95-$5.15 are served with rice and a salad. Sandwiches and hamburgers $1.65 and up. COMMENTS: Local atmosphere and no frills, just good food at great prices.

### TIN YING *Chinese*

1088 Lower Main St., Wailuku (242-4371) HOURS: Daily 10 am-9 pm. SAMPLING: Selections include Hong Kong or Szechuan style with prices ranging from $5.75-$9.25. Eat in or take out. COMMENTS: Okasuya style lunches at $2.95 include an entree and fried rice or noodles and are a real good value.

### TOKYO TEI ★ *Japanese*

1063 E. Lower Main St., Wailuku. (242-9630) HOURS: Lunch 11-1:30 pm Mon.-Sat., dinner daily 5-8:30 pm. Sunday dinner served until 8 pm. Lunch runs $3.25-$5.75. SAMPLNG: Teishoku trays include shrimp tempura, sashimi, fried fish, teriyaki pork or steak. Dinner selections such as hakata chicken, seafood platter, and a number of others that are difficult to pronounce run $6-$10.75 and include rice, miso soup, namasu and ko-ko. COMMENTS: Small and cozy atmosphere. Great food! Take out meals also available. Cocktails. Very popular with local residents and tourists and deservedly so. Winner of one of our top three awards for best local restaurants. Great food, great value, don't miss this one!

### YUMMY KOREAN (See Food Court)

## MODERATE

### CHART HOUSE ★ *American-Seafood*

500 N. Puunene Ave., Kahului (877-2476) HOURS: Lunch 11 am-2 pm Mon-Fri, and dinner 5-10 pm nightly. SAMPLING: Lunches run $8-$12. Prime rib is their specialty, also fresh seafood and chicken priced $15-$23. COMMENTS: Large portions, excellent children's menu. You can be sure it will be less crowded on this side of the island. A pleasant ocean view.

### GRAND WAIKAPU GRILL

Golf course at Waikapu, just outside of Wailuku. HOURS: Breakfast 6:30 am-11 am and lunch 11 am-3 pm only. Pupus served 3-6 pm. SAMPLING: Omelettes, lox and bagel, frittata are breakfast options with lunch selections ranging from curry pork stew, vegetable primavera, London broil, or cobb salad $6.95-$11.95. A pupu menu is available.

### MARCOS GRILL & DELI *Italian*

444 Hana Highway (877-4446) HOURS: Breakfast Mon.-Fri 6:30 am-10:45 am, Sat. & Sun 8 am-1 pm. Lunch and dinner daily 10:45 am-10 pm. SAMPLING: Deli sandwiches, grilled sandwiches, such as chicken parmigiana or NY strip steak $7.95-$10.95, salads from $4.95, entrees $10.95-$19.95 include seafood pasta, ravioli, or mushroom chicken. COMMENTS: They recently expanded to include more tables and a cocktail lounge with a big screen TV. Although they have had

good response, our lunch wasn't exceptional. Service was very slow and the menu had very little appropriate on the menu for children. For the money we feel we could have done better elsewhere.

**MING YUEN**   *Chinese*
162 Alamaha, Kahului (871-7787) HOURS: Lunch daily 11:30 am-5 pm, dinner 5-9 pm. COMMENTS: Cantonese and Szechuan style foods, dishes $6 and up. A little off the beaten track, you'll find it tucked behind Safeway off Kamehameha Ave. in the industrial area. Not as inexpensive as some of the other local eateries, but they do a great job. They celebrate the Chinese New Year, in Jan. or Feb. - it varies,  with a very popular ten course meal. In fact the event has become so popular, they have expanded to run it several nights.

**RED DRAGON CHINESE RESTAURANT**   *Chinese*
Maui Beach Hotel, Kahului (877-0051) HOURS: Nightly 5:30-8:30 pm, closed Mon and Tues. SAMPLING: Cantonese buffet dinner with over fifteen selections which change nightly. Entrees may include haposai, clams in hot sauce, sweet and sour pork or roast chicken. Reservations required. Buffet runs $12.95.

**SAENG'S THAI CUISINE ★**   *Thai*
2119 Vineyard St., Wailuku (244-1567) HOURS: Lunch Mon.-Fri. 11 am-2:30 pm, dinner daily 5-9:30 pm. SAMPLING: Appetizers, soups and salads $4.95-$8.50, entrees, noodle dishes, rice dishes, curries, and seafood $6.50-$11.95. Shrimps asparagus, crispy fish curry, Thai broccoli noodles or tofu salad are among the choices. This is one of the most attractive local restaurants in Wailuku. Owners Toh, Tom and Zach Douangphoumy have created a little Eden with lots of plants providing privacy between tables. They also know how to cook Thai. Traveling in India, Laos, Vietnam and Thailand in their youth they had an opportunity to sample a diversity of foods. This is the best of Maui's Thai cuisine. Not only was the service attentive, but the portions generous and every new dish better than the last. We were especially partial to the peanut sauce. In fact it was so good that enroute to the airport and bound for the mainland we picked up some peanut sauce "to go!" Don't miss this one! Also a Lahaina location.

**SANDALWOOD RESTAURANT**
Grand Waikapu Golf Course, Waikapu HOURS: Lunch Thurs-Sat. 11 am-3:30 pm. Dinners served twice weekly: Friday night seafood buffet, Saturday night prime rib buffet. Sunday brunch served 10:30 am-2:30 pm. SAMPLING: Lunch selections include eggplant Napoleon, fish and chips or veggie burgers as well as soup and salad selections $3.50-$9.   Their Sunday brunch begins with a cold buffet of salads and appetizers, kula vegetables with salsa, maki sushi rolls, smoked salmon with capers are among the selections and ends with a dessert selection. Hot items are cooked to order and individually priced a la carte or available with the buffet. Entrees include omelettes, chocolate chip pancakes or pan seared fresh island fish $5.95-$10.95. The cold buffet with one cooked to order entree runs $18.50. Cold buffet only $13.95. The Seafood buffet served on Fridays offers a Fresh Fish Station (the catch of the day is sauteed to order), Steamer Station (featuring clams, mussels and crab legs) and Caesar Salad Station (tossed fresh with your choice of toppings) along with an assortment of seafood salads, corn-on-the-cob and potatoes. A quality over quantity selection of desserts rounds out the buffet - all for $22.50.

**WOLFGANG'S BISTRO GARDEN**   *German-American*
Kahului Bldg., 33 Lono Ave. (871-7555) HOURS: Lunch Monday to Friday 11 am-2:30 pm and dinner nightly 5:30-10 pm. SAMPLING: Lunches run $6.75-$12. Dinners range from $17 for their house specialty, a boneless cornish game hen stuffed with wild rice, braised in grapes and red wine (served in a clay pot that you get to keep) to Wolf's wiener schnitzel $14.50, steak and firecracker shrimp $17.75, half spring chicken $9.50, or Australia rack of lamb $19.50. COMMENTS: Keiki menu for children under 10 years is only $4.99 and includes fresh fish! A split charge of $5 for sharing meals will be applied. On Saturday and Sunday nights from 5-9 pm they offer a prime rib buffet for $15.95, children under 10 years $4.99. You get more for your money in Kahului!

# UPCOUNTRY

## INEXPENSIVE

**COURTYARD DELI**   *Sandwiches/American*
3620 Baldwin Ave. #102A, Makawao (572-3456) SAMPLING: Garden burger, soups and salads or create your own sandwich $3.95-$5.50. Breakfast offers tofu scramble, Belgian waffles or breakfast burritos $3.00-$4.25. Courtyard coolers include honey lemonade, real orange juice and fruit smoothies.

**CROSSROADS CAFFE**   *Continental/Vegetarian*
3682 Baldwin Ave., corner of Baldwin and Makawao in Makawao town (572-1101) HOURS: Breakfast, lunch and dinner. SAMPLING: Boboli sandwiches, stuffed potatoes, turkey melt, veggie dog, soups and salads $2.50-$5.95. Featured presentations offer gourmet vegetarian and vegan dinner specials with an international flair. Monday is Indian, Tuesday travel to France, Wednesday it could be anywhere, Thursday it is off to Asia, Friday to Italy and Saturday night highlights Greek or Russian Cuisine. Saturday evening 6-8 pm they offer live music.

**DAIRY QUEEN - MCDONALD'S** - Pukalani

**FU WAH**   *Chinese-Szechuan*
Pukalani Shopping Center (572-1341) HOURS: 10:30 am-9 pm daily. SAMPLING: Dinner entrees from $5.95 or choose family dinner combinations $12.50-$26.50. Sizzling platters and braised pot courses from $6.50.

**GRANDMA'S COFFEE HOUSE** ★   *Local Style*
Located in Keokea (878-2140) HOURS: Monday thru Saturday 7 am-5 pm., Sunday 7 am-3 pm. COMMENTS: This is a family operation run by Alfred Franco, his wife and their two young children (son Derek is known as "the boss" and a younger sister Alyson). Alfred is encouraging the return of the coffee industry in Upcountry Maui. Born and raised in Upcountry, his grandmother taught him how to roast the coffee beans to perfection. He does this several times a day in his 104 year old coffee roasting machine that was brought from Philadelphia by his great grandmother. The coffee is sold by the pound in a blend known as "Maui coffees." Some of the beans used are grown on Moloka'i which is part

of Maui County. Prices are high, and there is no decaf available. (Grandmother never taught Alfred how to do that.) A few tables are an invitation to visitors to sit down, enjoy a cup of coffee, espresso, capuccino, or fresh fruit juice along with cinnamon rolls (only made on the weekends - get there early!), muffins, and more, all fresh from the oven. A bit more of an appetite might require one of their fresh avocado sandwiches, a bowl of chili and rice or homemade Portuguese bean soup. With the popularity of this place among locals and visitors alike, it is tough for them to keep up with the demand for these goodies. So if you're hungry in Upcountry, be sure to stop in at Grandma's, just five miles before the Tedeschi Winery. Alfred's goal is to put Keoke on the maps and minds of everyone. And he just may do it!

**KITADA'S KAU KAU CORNER**   *Local Style*
3617 Baldwin Avenue, Makawao (572-7241) HOURS: 6 am-1:30 pm daily except Sun. SAMPLING: Small or large portions of pork tofu, chopsteak, served with rice, macaroni salad and salted cabbage $3.50-$4.75. Sandwiches $1.50-$2.50. COMMENTS: Popular local eatery and with these prices, and varied local plate lunches, you can see why.

**MIXED PLATE**   *Local Style*
Pukalani Terrace Center (572-8258) HOURS: Daily 6 am-1 pm for breakfast and lunch, dinner Friday evenings from 4-8 pm. SAMPLING: Any of four breakfast specials $3.95, lunch offers an Okazuya daily menu with selections such as won ton min, tofu patties, mochiko chicken, teriyaki steak and lau lau. Several lunch specials served daily. Dinner specials begin at $4.75 for mixed plates including halemalu chicken mahi, kalua pork or chicken katsu.

**PIZZA FRESH**   *Italian*
1043 Makawao Ave., Unit 103 (572-2000) They make it, you bake it.

**UPCOUNTRY CAFE**   *Local style*
7-2 Aewa Place, Pukalani (572-2395) HOURS: Sunday breakfast only 6:30 am until noon. Monday and Wednesday thru Saturday open 6:30 am-3 pm. Closed Tuesday. SAMPLING: Loco Moo-co includes two eggs, Upcountry hamburger patty smothered with brown sauce and steamed rice $6.25, vegetable fritatta $5.25, or raisin cinnamon French toast $4.95. Lunch selections include boneless teriyaki breast, saimin, beef curry stew or vegetarian lasagna $3.75-$6.50. COMMENTS: The theme here is "cow" and the cow pie dessert is a rich blend of macadamia nuts and chocolate cream cheese filling a chocolate cookie tart, this was created by chef Aaron Heath's wife Tammy. They also make all their own salad dressings, jams and jellies!

## MODERATE

**CASANOVA ITALIAN RESTAURANT AND DELI**   *Italian*
1188 Makawao Ave., Makawao (572-0220) HOURS: Lunch Mon.-Sat. 11 am-2 pm., dinner 5:30-9:30 pm, Mon.-Sat. SAMPLING: The deli offers hot sandwiches, pastries, capuccino and fresh juices. Pizza too! Restaurant entrees include filetto di manzo, petto di pollo valdostana or pizzas cooked in their wood-fired authentic Napoli style oven. The burning kiawe wood reaches and maintains a constant temperature of 700 degrees, creating a crispy crust on their pizza. Pizzas

$8.95-$14.85, pastas, salads and entrees $5.50-$19. COMMENTS: Another one of those restaurants that some people hate and others love. They won the Maui News survey two years running as the best Italian restaurant on Maui. We'll let you decide!

**KULA LODGE**   *Hawaiian Regional Country Cuisine*
Five miles past Pukalani on Haleakala Highway (878-1535) HOURS: Breakfast 6:30-11:30 am, lunch 11:30-5 pm, dinner 5-9:30 pm. SAMPLING: Lunch and dinner menus changing, but include a varied selection of sandwiches and salads, making use of the many varied types of organic produce grown in the Kula area. Dinners $11.75-$17.75. Lunches $6.50-$8.75. Breakfasts include tofu scramble, Kula Lodge corned beef hash, or Malted Belgian Waffle $3.95-$6.50. COMMENTS: An added benefit here is the fireplace, a warming delight after a cold trip to the mountain top, a panoramic view, and cocktails. Children's portions available. They've recently added several vegetarian specials which include stuffed eggplant with spaghetti squash and feta cheese and vegetarian crepes with non-dairy bernaise.

**POLLI'S**   *Mexican*
1202 Makawao Ave., Makawao (572-7808) HOURS: 11:30 am-10 pm daily. SAMPLING: Mexican dinner specials include chile relleno, tamale plate, also burgers, salads, fajitas and Tim Ellison has brought back their popular baby back ribs and barbequed chicken $5.95-$7.50. You might even have seen Polli's on Wheels, a mobile restaurant that brings their food to you. Catering also available!

**PUKALANI COUNTRY CLUB RESTAURANT**   *American-Hawaiian*
360 Pukalani Rd. (572-1325) Turn right just before the shopping center at Pukalani and continue until the road ends. HOURS: Open 10-2 for lunch, 5-9 for dinner. SAMPLING: Lunch offers a Kalua pig Hawaiian plate for $8.10 or tripe stew for $7.25. More regular fare includes a tuna melt, jumbo hot dog, or egg salad sandwich $4.10-$5.95. Dinner menu offers similar selections at slightly higher prices. COMMENTS: Lunch reservations are a must, as this is a popular place with the tour groups. Or eat lunch elsewhere and stop back on the way down from Upcountry for a drink, tropical sunset and a wonderful view. They also have an early bird dinner special $8.95 offered Mon.-Fri. They continue to offer their authentic Hawaiian menu with nightly specials. Laser karaoke on Wednesday and Sunday evenings.

**STOPWATCH SPORTS BAR**   *Italian/American*
1127 Makawao Ave. in Makawao (572-1380) HOURS: Daily 7 am-11 pm. COMMENTS: This is a new building designed and built to accommodate the decor of the area. The architecture is patterned after the old Nashiwa Bakery in Paia that was destroyed by a tidal wave. Outside it has a Southern colonial garden look and inside you'll find lots of brass and windows with a spaciousness resulting from the open beam ceiling. The bar area has several TV screens for sporting events and a giant screen which will be used for special events. Lunch is served on the outside patio which overlooks green pastures and the Pacific Ocean below. The sports bar menu offers pupus, pizza or hamburger, chili and rice, desserts $2.50-$4.95. Dinner specials range from quiche to meat loaf $4.95-$6.95. Opened in August 1994.

# EXPENSIVE

**HALIIMAILE GENERAL STORE ★**  *Continental*
Haliimaile Rd., Haliimaile (572-2666) HOURS: Lunch 11 am-2:30 pm, dinner 6:30 pm-10 pm, Sunday brunch 10 am-3 pm. Sushi served Tues.-Sat. 5:30-9:30 pm. Kaamaina discounts Sunday and Mondays. SAMPLING: The sushi bar in the back room opened up in the fall of 1993 and has proved so popular, they've extended the number of nights. Two sushi chefs, formerly with Isana Shogun, perform the culinary tasks at the sushi bar, with a few tables.

Their brunch menu offers a crab boboli, eggs nova, French toast made with thick Hawaiian sweet bread, or omelettes $6-$9. Lunches offer chicken club, Chinese chicken salad and vegetable torte $8-$10. Dinners range from $13-$24 with interesting entrees such as coconut seafood curry, whole boneless duck breast seared with apricot-ginger-cranberry sauce or lamb Hunan style. Lunches include a creative selection of sandwiches and salads $5-$8 served with unusual salad accompaniments. Sunday brunch offers breakfast brunch and lunch brunch items. Lox and bagel $9, Bev's boboli (pizza topped with crab dip) $6, eggs Blackstone $8, vegetable frittata $7 or chicken club sandwich $8, fresh catch sandwich $9. While the items change, standard items include an entree of Rack of lamb Hunan style $24 or paniolo ribs $16 and the popular blackened sashimi appetizer $10. Other menu items might include paniolo stuffed artichoke $8, Thai coconut fettucini $13, shrimp scorpio $19. Lunches offer Chinese chicken salad $9, Caesar salad $7, vegetable torte $9, sandwiches and weekly specials.

COMMENTS: This restaurant has put Haliimaile on the map since it opened in October, 1988. The original structure dates back to the 1920s when it served as the General Store and hub of this community. The 5,000 square foot restaurant has a main dining room, and their sushi room behind. The high ceiling is the original and the floors are refurbished hardwood. The tables are set with cloths in green and peach and there is a huge beautifully designed bar in the front dining room.

The menu rotates stressing quality in their food preparation and includes the fresh herbs they cultivate in their own garden. The dinner menu features an interesting selection of dishes with unusual and creative preparations. An admirable wine list that includes some nice ports, sherrys and cognacs too. Our only previous complaint was the lack of choices for the traveling toddler in the group. Well, thanks to Bev and Joe Gannon, for adding a Haliimaile style peanut butter and jelly sandwich served on raisin bread of course! This place has style! No complaints now. It's worth the drive across the island.

**MAKAWAO STEAK HOUSE**  *American*
3612 Baldwin, Makawao (572-8711) HOURS: Dinner nightly from 5 pm. SAMPLING: Scampi $22, N.Y. steak $23, pork chop rosemary $17 and fresh fish varies daily. Dinners includes choice Portuguese bean soup, clam chowder or one of four salads. Fresh vegetables, potato or rice and breads complete the entree. COMMENTS: Another one of those restaurants that haven't changed much over the years. The kids menu is limited: pizza, spaghetti or chicken $4.25-$7.25.

# *PAIA*

## INEXPENSIVE to MODERATE

**BANGKOK CUISINE** *Thai*
120 Hana Highway in Paia (579-8979) HOURS: Lunch daily 11 am-3 pm, dinner 5-9:30 pm. SAMPLING/COMMENTS: Mike Kachornscrichol, who owned Siam Thai in Wailuku a couple of years back, is the owner of this new restaurant. A la carte items $7-$14 and include evil prince fish, garlic shrimp, zucchini beef, pork or chicken, available in mild, medium or hot.

**CHARLEY'S** *American-Italian*
142 Hana Highway in Paia (579-9453) HOURS: Breakfast 7 am-2 pm, lunch 11:30 am-2 pm and dinner 5-10 pm daily. SAMPLING: Pizza, calzone, entrees including BBQ ribs, chicken marsala are on the evening menu $9.25-$15.95. Breakfasts $3.75-$6.50 with lunch specials including veggie benedict or huevos rancheros. Lunch fare offers salads, soups, burgers, burritos, pizza $4.95 and up. Breakfast selections available Mon.-Saturday until 2 pm. COMMENTS: Charley's recent renovations have freshened and enlarged the dining area. They have a Big Screen (72 inch) television for sporting events by satellite. Every Sunday 2:30-6:30 pm is "The Sunday Jam" featuring local and mainland musicians. They have added a commercial smoker and are now serving kiawe smoked ribs, chicken and fish. Their popular Woofer burgers are still served daily from 11:30-2 pm and 5-10 pm. Charley's began on Front Street in Lahaina as a granola type restaurant selling avocado sandwiches, carrot juice and the like. Charley was named for the owners black and white great dane who roamed freely around the streets of Lahaina back in the old days. Charley and Charley's moved to Paia in 1971 and finally Charley P. Woofer restaurant and saloon was born. Charley, the dog, was named for the movie *"Goodbye Charley"* in which Debbie Reynolds was reincarnated as a great dane. The original Charley has been replaced by A.C. (after Charley) and Charley II. You'll find the story of Charley in its entirety on their menu!

WINDSURFING

266

**KIHATA RESTAURANT**   *Japanese*
115 Hana Highway, Paia (579-9035) HOURS: Closed all day Monday, hours 11 am-1:30 for lunch Tuesday thru Saturday, open for dinner Tues.-Sun. 5-9 pm. SAMPLING: Lunches include chicken katsu, noodle dishes, beef teriyaki $5-$8. Dinner Teishoku meals include miso soup, rice, shrimp tempura, chicken teriyaki and fish for $14-$17. Bento lunches and sushi also available. COMMENTS: Good food, but prices are slightly higher than similar restaurants in Wailuku.

**PAIA FISH MARKET RESTAURANT**   *American-Seafood*
101 Hana Highway, on the corner of Baldwin Ave. and Hana Highway (579-8030) HOURS: Lunch 11 am-4 pm and dinner 4-9:30 pm. SAMPLING: Lunch and dinner selections similar to lunch plates. Lunches $8.95-$13.95, dinners $10.95-$16.95. A blackboard slate recounts the selections such as fish tacos, fish chowder, shrimp fajitas, ahi burgers. Fresh fish is selected from the case and runs $10-$16.95 for a dinner portion served with rice or home fries and coleslaw. Beer, wine and champagne. COMMENTS: This is the sixth restaurant for owner Warren Roberts from Malibu California. Our trial here was disappointing. Order at the counter and then pick up your meal and seat yourself at a half-dozen over-sized picnic tables. A dark interior at night with interesting and humorous artifacts lining the walls. The fish in the display looks fresh, but filets of such fish as mahi or onaga were dried out when charbroiled. Our fish was accompanied by a pile of fried potatoes that filled up the plate. We were disappointed in the selections for children. They also sell fresh fish $10.95-$13.95 per pound.

**PAUWELA CAFE**
375 W. Kuiaha Rd., Haiku (575-9242) HOURS: 7 am-6 pm Mon.-Sat., Sun. 9 am-3 pm. COMMENTS: The lively artwork of Nancy Hoke dresses the walls of this cannery cafe, located on Highway 37 in the old Libby Pineapple Cannery, about 15 miles from Kahului. Built in 1918, it now houses many famous manufacturers of windsurf and surfing gear. Breakfast is served throughout the day and includes freshly baked goods such as Basque cake, fruit tarts and pineapple or raspberry scones. Lunch selections include kalua turkey sandwich with green chile pesto, pan bogna tuna sandwich with peppers, capers, olives, tomatoes and Maui onions, and varied daily specials $5-$10. Take outs.

**PEACH'S AND CRUMBLE**   *American-Healthy*
On Baldwin Ave. just off Hana Highway (579-8612) HOURS: Mon, Tues, Wed, Sat, Sun 6:30 am-6 pm, Thurs, Fri 6:30 am-7:30 pm. SAMPLING: No meals, just sandwiches and bakery items. Unusual baked items include carrot cake with guava filling, lilikoi cheesecake, "jungle bars" (dried organic bananas, coconut, macadamia nuts and passion fruit). Sandwiches such as salmon with cream cheese or Mexican avocado are made on their own freshly baked bread. A few counter seats. Espresso drinks. The "Peaches and Crumble" is their version of a peach cobbler.

**PICNIC'S**   *American-Healthy*
30 Baldwin Ave, a few blocks off the Hana Highway (579-8021) HOURS: 7:30 am -7 pm, 7 days a week. Closed Thanksgiving and New Years. SAMPLING: The Plantation breakfast includes eggs scrambled with cheddar, coffee and toast $3.75. Their lunch specialty is the spinach nutburger $5.50, mahi mahi supreme $5.26, turkey $4.75, avocado and swiss $4.75. Countryside box lunch at $7.95 for

one, $15.95 for two, $42.50 for 4-6 persons and includes choice of sandwich, drink, cookie, chips and fruit. COMMENTS: A very popular place to pick up some lunch goodies for the road to Hana or Haleakala. Anything on their menu is available to go and everything is ready from 7:30 am. No need to call ahead, just stop by enroute.

**THE VEGAN RESTAURANT**   *American-Vegetarian*
115 Baldwin Ave., a few blocks off the Hana Highway (579-9144) HOURS: 11:30 am-8:30 pm. SAMPLING: Serves only vegetarian foods. Salad platters available in small or side portions $3.50-$4.95, their vegan burger $4.95, Mexican fiesta combo $5.95, or entrees with selections varying daily $8.95. COMMENTS: It is hard to believe with the wealth of restaurants that this is the only strictly vegetarian one. It opened in late 1989 with an aim to create foods with tastes and textures to resemble meat products, but without the use of animal products or cholesterol in any of their food. Vegan is a non-profit organization that has been doing vegetarian nutrition seminars for more than six years before opening this restaurant. Seating for a dozen people. Catering also available.

**WUNDERBAR**   *German*
89 Hana Highway, Paia (579-8808) HOURS: Breakfast 7:30-11 am daily except Monday, and lunch 11 am-2 pm. Dinner served 5-10 pm. Entertainment Thurs.-Sat. begins at 10 pm. SAMPLING: Daily changing menu, with most dinner entrees running $13-$17 and include wiener schnitzel, paella of the day, piccata Milanese, Hungarian goulash, peppersteak, Bavarian hunter steak served with spaetzle and fresh seafood entrees. Desserts run $4-$6 and range from fresh baked apple strudel to a Grand Marnier souffle or chocolate mousse. Cocktails, wine and beer available. Lunches include burgers, salads, fruit boat, pastas, or seafood $6-$10. COMMENTS: It took several years after Benard Weber and Birgit Schaefer first came to Maui and discovered the town of Paia before their dream of opening a European style restaurant was realized. The interior is a cozy, warm and friendly European style atmosphere, decorated with memorabilia such as a black forest clock, an old piano from Vienna, big railway signs and beer ads. In sampling the menu items the pasta proved hearty, basic and homemade. The basil bread was unusual and aromatic but a bit overdone. The sauerkraut with potatoes was a nice blend of flavors. The sauce on the grilled Mediterranean style fish was a bit pungent. Overall, the food was a little different, and would certainly satisfy the meat and potatoes palate. The dishes were generally all good, healthy food in a homemade fashion. The use of Kula vegetables is a nice feature. The desserts are a European style and not overwhelmingly sweet. The Schoggimousse is a chocolate mousse from Switzerland that was not too airy or too pudding-like, but just right. They also serve the only German beer on Maui, but due to popularity, it might not be in stock. It's like an Inn with a very family feel.

# EXPENSIVE

**MAMA'S FISH HOUSE** ★   *Continental-Seafood*
On Highway 36 just 1 1/2 miles past Paia, look for the ship's flagpole and the angel fish sign (579-8488) HOURS: Daily 11 am-9:30 pm. Lunch until 2:30, followed by pupus in the afternoon and dinner beginning at 5 pm. SAMPLING: Lunches run $7.95-$19.95 and includes luncheon salads and sandwiches, Maui

crabcakes, shrimp or chicken. Fresh fish $19.95. Dinner entrees include fresh fish prepared a half-dozen different ways $29.95, fish curry $24.95, chicken with ginger teriyaki $23.95, NY steak $29.95, fresh scallops $26.95, scampi $25.95 or spicy southeast Asian fish $28.95. They still have macadamia cheesecake and banana and mango crisp for dessert, along with Kuau pie, a chocolate mousse with melted carmel in graham cracker and Oreo cookie crust and a new chocolate surprise! Full bar service, reservations suggested.

COMMENTS: They have been doing some renovations which has really freshened up the atmosphere, although they have kept a bit of the funky, Mama's Beachhouse look. They've added a new section and an interesting "Art Gecko" sidewalk. The gecko pattern is etched into the cement with the geckos connecting together like a big puzzle. Mama's opened in 1973 and has become one of the oldest restaurants on the island, and one of the few that consistently has an outstanding variety of excellently prepared foods. Mama's mission was "to serve creative seafood dishes with that elusive taste of Maui island cooking." And it appears she has meet her mission! Expensive, but if you're looking for great Hawaiian seafood, put this one on your must do list.

# HANA

## INEXPENSIVE

### CAFE AT HANA GARDENLAND   *Light and healthy*
Located just before Hana at the Gardenland. (248-7340) HOURS: Daily 9 am-5 pm. SAMPLING: Breakfast and lunch menu served all day. Sample steamed eggs and salsa, granola topped with fresh island fruit, smoked turkey sandwich, lasagna, pesto pasta or Hanamole and chips $4.25-$6.75. Fresh squeezed orange or carrot juice and freshly squeezed lemonade are sure to quench your thirst after that drive from Kahului. Hillary Rodham Clinton and daughter Chelsea visited Maui in 1993 and enjoyed their first meal so much, they came back every day while they vacationed in Hana. So, follow in the foot steps of the White House family. Good food and a relaxing atmosphere.

TUTU'S

**Also in Hana:**
HANA RANCH STORE - Open daily, ready-made sandwiches and hot dogs.
HASEGAWA GENERAL STORE - Open daily, a little bit of everything!!
TUTU'S - Hana Bay, 8:30-4 pm. Sandwiches, plate lunches.

## MODERATE

Nothing in Hana qualifies for this price range.

## EXPENSIVE

**HANA RANCH RESTAURANT** *American*
Downtown Hana. (248-8255) SAMPLING: Plate lunches $5.75-$6.25 include mahi, lasagna, won ton mein, or fried chicken. Burgers and sandwiches $5.25-$5.75. Dinners served only Friday and Saturday 6-8 pm. Entrees include $15.94, BBQ guava smoked 1/2 chicken $17.50, and NY steak $23.95. Hana Ranch Restaurant also offers pizza night menu on Wednesday, large cheese pizza is $13.50 with additional toppings $1 each. Sun-Thurs from 4-8 pm, take out only. Wednesday, Friday and Saturday, lunch take-out available until 4 pm. COMMENTS: Attire is casual. Full bar service. Dinner reservations recommended.

**HOTEL HANA MAUI DINING ROOM ★** *Continental*
(248-8211) HOURS: Breakfast 7:30-10 am, lunch 11:30 am-2 pm, late lunch 1:30-4 pm, dinner 6-9 pm. SAMPLING: Breakfast main selections $6.50-$14.50, side orders $1.95-$3.50. Beverages $1.95. Children under 12 years are half price. Lunch menu offers sandwiches, salads and hot entrees $9.95-$14.95. A lighter later lunch is served in the Paniolo Lounge, just down the steps from the Dining Room between 1:30 and 4 pm and offers soups, salads, sandwiches and appetizers $6.95-$12.50. The dinner menu changes nightly with entrees priced $19-29 and served a la carte. Selections may include Hana Bay cioppino, smoked and roasted pork loin, New Zealand lamb chops or roast Chinese-style duck. COMMENTS: Wonderful food served with unusually, light, delicious sauces. Prices are a little high, but when you're the only fine dining place in town, I guess you're entitled!

POINSETTIA

# SUNSETS AND NIGHTLIFE

Here are a few suggestions as to what to do when and after the sun goes down on Maui. These locations usually offer entertainment, however, call to see what they are offering and which night, as it varies. Check *This Week* or the "Scene" section of the Thursday edition of the *Maui News,* which lists current late night happenings. Another good source for what is happening is "The Maui Bulletin," another free publication found around town.

## SUNSET WATCHING SUGGESTIONS

The Plantation House Restaurant, Kapalua
The new SeaWatch Restaurant in Wailea
On the front lawn of the Pineapple Hill Restaurant, Kapalua
From the lobby bar of the Kapalua Bay Resort with their wonderful pupus
The Kapalua Grill and Bar
On the promontory at the Bay Club, Kapalua
Enroute down from Haleakala, at the Pukalani Country Club
The Fairway at the Wailea Golf Course (try an ice cream drink)
Enjoy the lobby bar at Stouffer Wailea Beach Resort
Sunsets in Kihei

## NIGHT SPOTS & ENTERTAINMENT

Consult "The Scene" section of the *Maui News*, Thursday edition, to see who is playing when and where. The following spots generally offer entertainment, but as everything else, things change quickly!

### LAHAINA - KAANAPALI - KAPALUA AREA

*Lahaina:* Moose McGillycuddy's is always hopping for the young crowd. Lahaina Broiler offers entertainment several nights a week, dance floor. Moon-doggies has musical entertainment. Now popular is the Karaoke Entertainment at a number of restaurant/lounges. Karaoke is where a member of the audience selects a song that has music only, no words. They are given a sheet with the words and they sing along. There is usually a fee to entertain. The Maui Marriott hosts karaoke parties every Thursday, Friday and Saturday in their lobby bar and on Monday evenings have a Comedy Club. Phone 667-1200 for information. Lahaina Broiler has karaoke as well. Kobe Japanese Steakhouse and Lahaina Coolers have entertainment, and the Blue Tropix Nightclub has entertainment which varies nightly and is probably the hottest spot in West Maui. Aloha Cantina has rock and roll Thurs.-Sat.

*Kaanapali:* At the Marriott, the Makai Bar features entertainment and a very small dance floor with karaoke entertainment in their lobby bar. Hula Grill at Whalers Village has live Hawaiian style musical entertainment. The Royal Lahaina resort has a group that performs authentic and traditional Hawaiian music.

*Kahana:* Ludwig's Maui offers jazz 4:30-6:30 pm evenings. Dollies has sports satellite as does the new Fish and Games Sports Grill.

271

## KIHEI - WAILEA - MAKENA AREA NIGHTSPOTS

The Inu Inu Lounge at the Maui Inter-Continental Wailea is a prime spot for evening entertainment in South Maui. In Makena, The Maui Prince has something special planned each evening, for more information see the Makena area listing under Molokini Lounge. The Maui Sun hotel has entertainment which varies from pianists to talent night or dance bands. The Maui Lu frequently has shows that benefit a variety of worthwhile causes. Check "The Scene" in the *Maui News.* Chum's in Kihei has evening entertainment.

Tsunami, the high-tech place to be is at the Grand Wailea. Featuring laser and neon lights, and a 10,000 square foot dance floor. Open 9 pm-1 am Sun.-Wed., Thurs. until 2 am, Friday and Saturday until 4 am. Entertainment is top 40 music with a disc jockey. No beachwear, shoes required. Cover charge on Fridays is $5, and $10 on Saturdays. No charge for in-house guests.

## ELSEWHERE

Check Wunderbar Restaurant in Paia for varied entertainment. Casanova's in Makawao features blues, jazz, western, disco and a bit of anything else. Charley's in Paia for Sunday jam sessions.

# BEACHES

## *INTRODUCTION*

If you are looking for a variety of beautiful, uncrowded tropical beaches, nearly perfect weather year round and sparkling clear waters at enjoyable temperatures, Maui will not disappoint you.

With beaches that range from small to long, white sand to black sand or rock, or more exotic shades of green or salt and pepper. Many are well developed, a few (at least for a little longer) remain remote and unspoiled. There is something for everyone, from the lay-on-the-beach-under-a-palm-tree type, to the explorer-adventurer will not want for the appropriate beach.

The Maui Visitors Bureau reports that there are 81 accessible beaches, 30 with public facilities around an island that spans 120 linear miles.

Maui's beaches are publicly owned and most have right-of-way access, however, the access is sometimes tricky to find and parking may be a problem! Parking areas are provided at most developed beaches, but are generally limited to 30 cars or less, making an early arrival at the more popular beaches a good idea. In the undeveloped areas you will have to wedge along the roadside. It is vital that you leave nothing of importance in your car as theft, especially at some of the remoter locations, is high.

At the larger developed beaches, a variety of facilities are provided. Many have convenient rinse-off showers, drinking water, restrooms, and picnic areas. A few have children's play or swim areas. The beaches near the major resorts often have rental equipment available for snorkeling, sailing, boogie boarding, and even underwater cameras. These beaches are generally clean and well maintained. Above Kapalua and below Wailea, where the beaches are undeveloped, expect to find no signs to mark the location, no facilities, and sometimes less cleanliness.

Since virtually all of Maui's good beaches are located on the leeward side of East and West Maui, you can expect sunny weather most of the time. This is because the mountains trap the moisture in the almost constant trade winds. Truly cloudy or bad weather in these areas is rare but when the weather is poor in one area, a short drive may put you back into the sun again.

Swells from all directions reach Maui's shores. The three basic swell sources are the east and north-east trade winds, the North Pacific lows, and the South Pacific lows. The trades cause easterly swells of relatively low heights of 2-6 feet throughout most of the year. A stormy, persistent trade wind episode may cause swells of 8-12 feet and occasionally 10-15 feet on exposed eastern shores. Since the main resort areas are on leeward West and East Maui, they are protected.

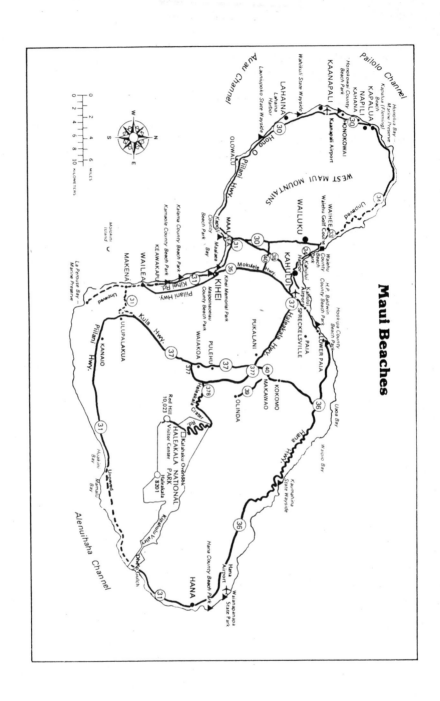

# Maui Beaches

North Maui and Hana are exposed to these conditions however, along with strong ocean currents, therefore very few beaches in these areas are considered safe for casual swimming.

Kona winds generated by southern hemisphere storms cause southerly swells that affect leeward Maui. This usually happens in the summer and will last for several days. Surf heights over eight feet are not common, but many of the resort areas have beaches with fairly steep drop offs causing rather sharp shore breaks. Although it may appear fun to play in these waves, many minor to moderate injuries are recorded at these times. Resorts will post red warning flags along the beach during times of unsafe surf conditions. Most beaches are affected during this time causing water turbidity and poor snorkeling conditions. At a few places, such as Lahaina, Olowalu and Maalaea, these conditions create good surfing.

Northerly swells caused by winter storms northeast of the island are not common, but can cause large surf, particularly on the northern beaches, such as Baldwin, Kanaha and Hookipa Beach Parks.

Winter North Pacific storms generate high surf along the northwestern and northern shores of Maui. This is the source of the winter surf in Mokuleia Bay (Slaughterhouse), renowned for body surfing, and in Honolua Bay which is internationally known for surfing.

Land and sea breezes are local winds blowing from opposite directions at different times depending on the temperature difference between land and sea. The interaction of daytime sea breezes and trade winds, in the Wailea-Makena area particularly, produce almost daily light cloudiness in the afternoon and may bring showers. This is also somewhat true of the Honokowai to Kapalua region.

Oceanic tidal and trade wind currents are not a problem for the swimmer or snorkeler in the main resort areas from Makena to Kapalua except under unusual conditions such as Kona storms. Beaches outside of the resort areas should be treated with due caution since there are very few considered safe for casual swimming and snorkeling except by knowledgeable, experienced persons.

Maui's ocean playgrounds are probably the most benign in the world. There is no fire coral, jelly fish are rare, and sharks are well fed by the abundant marine life and rarely come into shore. However, you should always exercise good judgement and reasonable caution when at the beach.

1. "Never turn your back to the sea" is an old Hawaiian saying. Don't be caught off guard, waves come in sets with spells of calm in between.
2. Use the buddy system, never swim or snorkel alone.
3. If you are unsure of your abilities, use flotation devices attached to your body, such as a life vest or inflatable vest. Never rely on an air mattress or similar device from which you may become separated.
4. Study the ocean before you enter; look for rocks, breakers or currents.
5. Duck or dive beneath breaking waves before they reach you.
6. Never swim against a strong current, swim across it.
7. Know your limits.

8. Small children should be allowed to play near or in the surf ONLY with close supervision and should wear flotation devices.
9. When exploring tidal pools or reefs, always wear protective footwear and keep an eye on the ocean. Also, protect your hands.
10. When swimming around coral, be careful where you put your hands and feet. Urchin stings can be painful and coral cuts can be dangerous.
11. Respect the yellow and red flag warnings when placed on the developed beaches. They are there to advise you of unsafe conditions.

*Paradise Publications has endeavored to provide current and accurate information on Maui's beautiful beaches, however remember, nature is unpredictable and weather, beach and current conditions can change. Enjoy your day at the beach, but utilize good judgement. Paradise Publications cannot be held responsible for accidents or injuries incurred.*

Surface water temperature varies little with a mean temperature of 73.0 in January and 80.2 in August. Minimum and maximum range from 68 to 84 degrees. This is an almost ideal temperature (refreshing, but not cold) for swimming and you will find most resort pools cooler than the ocean.

### BEST BETS
On South Maui our favorite beaches are Makena for its unspoiled beauty, Maluaka for its deep fine sand and beautiful coral, Wailea and Ulua-Mokapu for their great beaches, good snorkeling and beautiful resorts, and Keawakapu and Kamaole II which offer gentler offshore slopes where swimming is excellent. A good place for small children is the park at the end of Hauoli Street in Maalaea, just past the Makani A Kai condos. There are two small, sandy-bottomed pools protected by reefs on either side of the small rock jetty.

On West Maui, Kapalua offers a well protected bay with very good swimming and snorkeling. Hanakaoo Beach has a gentle offshore slope and the park has lots of parking, good facilities, numerous activities, and is next to the Hyatt. Olowalu has easy access and excellent snorkeling. An excellent place for small children to play in the sand and water is at Pu'unoa Beach, which is well protected by a large offshore reef.

# BEACH INDEX

# MAALAEA TO LAHAINA

The beaches are described in order from Maalaea to Lahaina and are easy to spot from Honoapiilani Highway. They are all narrow and usually lined by Kiawe trees, however, they have gentle slopes to deeper water and the ocean is generally calmer and warmer than in other areas. The offshore coral reefs offer excellent snorkeling in calm weather, which is most of the time. These beaches are popular because of their convenient access and facilities as well as good swimming and snorkeling conditions.

### PAPALAUA STATE WAYSIDE PARK
As you descend from the sea cliffs on your way from Maalaea you will see an undeveloped tropical shoreline stretch before you. At the foot of the cliffs at mile marker 11, Papalaua Park is marked by an easily seen sign. There are picnic tables, BBQ grills, and portable restrooms. The beach is long, (about 1/2 mile) and narrow and lined with Kiawe trees that almost reach the water's edge in places. The trees provide plenty of shady areas for this beautiful beach. Good swimming and fair snorkeling, popular picnicking area.

### UKUMEHAME BEACH PARK
The entrance to the park is near mile marker 12, but there is no identifying sign. There is off-street paved parking for about 12 cars. Five concrete picnic tables. This is also a narrow 1/2 mile long sand beach with lots of Kiawe trees providing shade. Good swimming, fair snorkeling.

### OLOWALU BEACH ★
About 2/10 mile before and after mile marker 14 you will see a large, but narrow stand of Kiawe trees between the road and the beach, followed by a few palm trees, then a few more scattered Kiawe trees. Parking is alongside the road. No facilities. This narrow sand beach slopes gently out to water four or five feet deep making it good for swimming and beach playing. There are extensive coral formations starting right offshore and continuing out a quarter mile or more, and a fair amount of fish expecting handouts. The ocean is generally warmer and calmer than elsewhere, making it a popular snorkeling spot.

### AWALUA BEACH
The beach at mile marker 16 may be cobble stone or sand depending on the time of year and the prevailing conditions. No facilities. At times when Kona storms create a good southern swell, this becomes a very popular surfing spot for a few days until the swells subside.

### LAUNIUPOKO STATE WAYSIDE PARK
This well-marked beach park near mile marker 18 offers a large paved parking area, restrooms, many picnic tables, BBQ grills, rinse-off showers, drinking water, pay phone, and a large grassy area with trees, all of which makes for a good picnic spot. There is a large man-made wading pool constructed of large boulders centered in the park. (Sand has accumulated to the extent that even at high tide there is no water in the pool). To the right is a rocky beach and to the left is a 200-yard dark sand beach with fairly gentle slope. It looks nice, but signs posted

warn "Sharks have been seen in the shallow water off this beach. Entry into the water is discouraged." This area is rumored to be a shark breeding ground with shark fishing done here in the past. There is also a no alcohol sign posted. For some reason the beach does not seem to be used for much besides picnicking! However, a couple hundred yards offshore is good snorkeling and you may see snorkel excursions visit this shoreline when the weather prohibits a trip to Lana'i.

### PUAMANA BEACH PARK
Well marked beach park near mile marker 19, just south of the Puamana Resort complex. Parking for 20 cars in paved parking area, with additional parking along the highway. Nice grassy park with seven picnic tables and plenty of shade trees. At the park itself there is no sandy beach, only a large pebble beach. The only beach is a narrow 200 yards long white sand beach just north of the park and fronting Puamana Resort. Fairly gentle slope to shallow water.

## LAHAINA AND KAANAPALI

### LAHAINA BEACH
There is a large public parking lot across from the 505 Front Street shopping center with easy access to the beach through the mall. There is also on-street parking near the Lahaina Shores with public right-of-way to the beach at the south end of the complex. Restrooms and showers are only available at the resort. The Lahaina Sailing Center is located on the beach. This narrow sand beach fronts the Lahaina Shores and 505 Front Street and is protected by a reef 30-50 yards out. The beach is generally sandy offshore with a gentle slope. The water stays fairly shallow out to the reef and contains some interesting coral formations. The area offers fair snorkeling in clear water on calm days. A good place for beginning snorkelers and children, but not good for swimming due to shallow water and abundant coral.

### PUUNOA BEACH ★
The beach is at the north end of Lahaina between Kai Pali Rd. and the old Mala Wharf and can be seen as you leave Lahaina on Front St. Southern access: Take Kai Pali Rd. off Front St. Parking for about 20 cars along the road which is the entrance for the Puunoa Beach Estates. Public Beach access sign with concrete sidewalk to the beach. Mid beach access: Take Puunoa Place off Front St. at the Public Beach access sign. Parking for about four cars at the end of the road which ends at the beach. A rinse off hose here is the only facility for the beach. North access: Take Mala Wharf off Front St. Parking for approximately 20 cars along the road just before the entrance to the Mala boat launching parking area.

This narrow, dense, darker sand beach is about 300 yards long and well protected by a reef approximately 100-150 yards offshore. The beach slopes gently to water only 3-4 feet deep. Unfortunately, rock and coral near the surface make swimming unadvised. There are areas of the beach clear of coral 10 - 15 feet out where children can play safely in the calm, shallow water. At high tide there are more fish to see while snorkeling. This continues to be a favorite with our children because of the calm, warm water.

## WAHIKULI STATE WAYSIDE PARK

There are three paved off-street parking areas between Lahaina and Kaanapali. Many covered picnic tables, restrooms, showers, and BBQ grills are provided. The first and third parking areas are marked but have no beach. The second unmarked area has an excellent, darker sand beach with a gentle slope to deeper water. There is some shelf rock in places but it's rounded and smooth and not a problem. With the handy facilities, trees for shade, and the nice beach, this is a good, and popular, spot for sunning, swimming, and picnicking.

## HANAKAOO BEACH PARK ★

Off Honoapiilani Highway, immediately south of the Hyatt Regency, there is a large, well-marked, off-street parking area. The park has rinse-off showers, restroom, and picnic tables. Wide, darker sand beach with gentle slope to deeper water. This is a popular area because of the easy parking, facilities, good beach, shallow water and good swimming, and you are right next to the Hyatt.

## HANAKAOO BEACH ★ (Kaanapali Beach)

The beach fronts the Hyatt Regency, Marriott, Kaanapali Alii, Westin Maui, Whaler's Shopping Center and condos, Kaanapali Beach Hotel, and the Sheraton, and is known as Kaanapali Beach. Access is through the Kaanapali Resort area. Turn off Honoapiilani Highway at either of the first two entrances. This area was not designed with non-guest use in mind, and parking is definitely a problem.

A) The Hyatt end of the beach is only a short walk from the large parking area of Hanakaoo Beach Park.

B) Public right-of-way with parking for 10 cars at the left of the Hyatt's lower parking lot.

C) Public right-of-way between the Hyatt and Marriott, no parking.

D) Public right-of-way between Marriott and Kaanapali Alii with parking for 11 cars only.

E) Public right-of-way between Kaanapali Alii and Westin Maui, no parking.

F) Public right-of-way between Kaanapali Beach Resort and the Sheraton with parking for 11 cars only.

G) The Whalers Shopping Center has a three-story pay parking lot, but with beach access only through the complex.

H) There is no on-street parking anywhere in the Kaanapali Resort complex.

The Hyatt, Marriott, Westin Maui, and Sheraton all have restrooms, showers, bars, and rental equipment. There is a beautiful, long, wide, white sand beach with an abrupt drop-off to deep water. There are small areas of offshore coral from the Hyatt to the Westin Maui at times, but no true offshore reef. Great swimming and good wave playing with the exception of two or three points along the beach where the waves consistently break fairly hard. In the winter, snorkeling can be fair off the Westin Maui when the coral is exposed underwater. The best snorkeling is at Black Rock, fronting the Sheraton Hotel. The water is almost always clear and fairly calm, with many types of nearly tame fish due to the popularity of hand feeding by snorkelers. (Bread, frozen peas and packaged dry noodles seem popular.) Not much colorful coral. The best entrance to the water is from the beach alongside Black Rock.

## KAANAPALI BEACH (South End)

This beach begins at the north side of Black Rock and runs for over a mile to the north fronting the Royal Lahaina Resort and the Maui Kaanapali Villas. Turn off Honoapiilani Road at the last Kaanapali exit at the stop light by the Maui Kaanapali Villas. There are a few places to park on the side of the road near the Public Access beach sign. With the airport now closed there is more parking available. This area is being prepared for future hotel and condo developement and should eventually have much improved public access, facilities and parking. The only facilities now are those of the nearby hotels. This wide, (usually) white sand beach has a steep drop-off to deep water and is usually calm - a good place to swim. Snorkeling around Black Rock is almost always good.

# *KAHANA - NAPILI - KAPALUA AND BEYOND*

## KAANAPALI BEACH (North End)

This section of beach fronts the Mahana Resort, Maui Kai, Embassy Suites, Kaanapali Shores, Papakea, Maui Sands and Paki Maui from south to north, and ends at the Honokowai Beach Park. Access is generally only through the resorts. Most of the resorts have rinse-off showers convenient to the beach, however, no other facilities are available. This is a long, narrow, white sand beach which is fronted by a close-in reef. All the resorts except the Kaanapali Shores and Embassy Suites have retaining walls along the beach. The Kaanapali Shores has, over the last couple of years, suffered considerable erosion of its once wide beach and has recently completed an expensive new under-the-sand retaining wall in an effort to stabilize and restore it. There is also a cleared area through the coral in front of the resort. This is the only good swimming area on the north section of the beach and is the only good access through the reef for snorkeling.

The reef comes into shore at the south end of Papakea and again at the Hono-kowai Beach Park. At low tide the reef fronting Papakea can be walked on like a wide sidewalk. (See GENERAL INFORMATION - Children, for night walking on the reef.) The reef is generally only 10-20 yards offshore and the area between is very shallow with much coral and rock making it undesirable for swimming and snorkeling. The middle section of beach, fronting the old Kaanapali Airport, is slated for future development.

## HONOKOWAI BEACH PARK

Turn off the Honoapiilani Hwy. on the first side street past the airport (at the Honokowai sign) and get onto Lower Honoapiilani Hwy., which parallels the ocean. The park is across the street from the Honokowai Grocery Store (a pay phone is available there). There is paved off-street parking for 30 cars. There are 11 picnic tables, 5 BBQ pits, restrooms, showers, and a grassy park with shade trees. The white sand beach is lined by a wide shelf of beach rock. Between the shelf rock and reef there is a narrow, shallow pool with a sandy bottom which is a good swimming area for small children. There is a break in the reef at the north end of the beach where you can get snorkeling access to the outside reef. Water sport equipment for rent at the Honokowai Store.

## KAHANA BEACH
In front of the Kahana Beach Condominiums, Sands of Kahana, Royal Kahana, Valley Isle Resort and Hololani from south to north on Lower Honoapiilani Hwy. There is limited off-road parking at the south end of the beach. Other access would be through the condos. The only facilities available are at the condos, usually rinse-off showers. There are several grocery stores, one at the Valley Isle Resort, the other at the Hololani condos. This white sand beach varies from narrow to wide and its offshore area is shallow with rock and sand, semi-protected by reef. Good swimming, fair snorkeling. The beach may be cool and windy in the afternoons.

During the past years, from about 1989, this area has been particularly plagued by the unexplained green algae bloom which tends to concentrate here due to the wind, current and shoreline continues. The beach is frequently unappealing for swimming and beach use due to the amount of slimy green algae on the beach and in the water. One possible cause of this unsightly mess may be the nitrates and other chemicals which are used for agriculture and golf course maintainence, flowing into the ocean. The county is continuing to investigate and may find it necessary to institute some controls.

## KEONENUI BEACH ★
The beach is in front of and surrounded by the Kahana Sunset with no convenient public access. A lovely wide crescent of white sand with a fairly gentle slope to water's edge, then fairly steep slope to deeper water. The beach is set in a small shallow cove, about 150 yards wide, which affords some protection. At times, especially in winter, rough seas come into the beach. When calm (most of the time), this is an excellent swimming and play area with fair snorkeling.

## ALAELOA BEACH ("The Cove")
This miniature, jewel-like cove is surrounded by low sea cliffs. The small, approximately 25-30 yard long, white sand beach has a gentle slope with scattered rocks leading into sparkling clear waters. Pavilion and lounge chair area for use by Alaeloa guests. Good swimming and snorkeling with very clear and calm waters except when storm-generated waves come in. Fortunately, or unfortunately, depending on your point of view, this small cove is surrounded by the Alaeloa residential area which has no on or off-street public parking, therefore, public access to this beach is very difficult.

## NAPILI BAY ★
There are two public accesses to this beautiful beach. There is a small, easily missed, public right-of-way and Napili Beach sign just past the Napili Shores at Napili Place Street. On-street parking at sign for Napili Surf Beach Resort. The public beach right-of-way sign shows the entrance to the beach. Public telephone in parking lot of Napili Surf. The second entrance is at the public beach right-of-way and Napili Sunset, Hale Napili, and Napili Bay signs on Hui Street. On-street parking and pay phone at entrance to beach walk. This is a long, wide crescent of white sand between two rocky points. The offshore slope is moderately steep. Usually very safe for swimming and snorkeling except during winter storms when large waves occasionally come into the bay. At the south end of the beach are a series of shallow, sandy tide pools which make an excellent place for children, but only under close supervision. Coral formations 30 - 40 yards offshore can provide

fair snorkeling on calm days especially at the northern end of the beach and decent boogie boarding with mild swells. No public facilities along the beach. A grocery store is past the second entrance at the Napili Village Hotel.

### KAPALUA BEACH ★
Just past the Napili Kai Beach Club you will see a public beach right-of-way sign. Off-street parking area for about 30 - 40 cars. Showers and restrooms. A beautiful crescent of white sand between two rocky points. The beach has a gentle slope to deeper water, maximum about 15 feet. From the left point, a reef arcs toward the long right point creating a very sheltered bay, probably the nicest and safest swimming beach on Maui. Shade is provided by numerous palm trees lining the back shore area. Above the beach are the lovely grounds of the Kapalua Bay Resort. Swimming is almost always excellent with plenty of play area for children. Snorkeling is usually good with many different kinds of fish and interesting coral. It is no surprise that this beach has been selected as one of the top ten beaches in the world. For many years local knew this beach as "Flemings Beach" and called D.T. Fleming's Beach "Stables." *REMEMBER* parking is limited, so arrive early!

### NAMALU BAY ★
Park at Kapalua Beach and take the concrete path along the beach, up through the hotel's grounds, and out to the point of land separating Kapalua Bay from Namalu Bay. This small bay has a shoreline of large lava boulders, no beaches. On calm days snorkeling is very good and entry and exit over the rocks is easy. This little known spot is definitely worth the short walk down the trail.

### ONELOA BEACH
Enter at the public right-of-way sign just past the Kapalua Bay Resort. Paved off-street parking for 12 - 15 cars only, no other facilities. Long, straight white sand beach with a shallow sand bar that extends to the surfline. The beach is posted with a warning sign "No swimming at time of high surf due to dangerous currents." This area tends to get windy and cloudy in the afternoons, especially in the winter months. We have usually found this beach deserted.

### D. T. FLEMING BEACH PARK
The County maintains a life guard on this beach. The Ritz-Carlton operates The Beach House Restaurant. Off-street parking for 70 cars. Public showers. Private restrooms by the Beach House rstaurant. The long white sand beach is steep with an offshore sand bar which may cause dangerous water conditions when swells hit the beach. This beach was named for David Thomas Fleming (1881-1955), who became manager of the Honolua Ranch in 1912. Under his guidance, the Baldwin cattle ranch was converted to a pineapple plantation. His home is now the Pineapple Hill restaurant at Kapalua. This was once called "Stables Beach" by local residents as the Fleming family kept their horses at this site into the 1950's.

### MOKULEIA BEACH ★ (Slaughterhouse)
On Highway 30, past D. T. Fleming Beach Park, look for cars parked along the roadside and the Mokuleia-Honolua Marine Reserve sign. Park your car and hike down one of the steep dirt and rock trails - they're not difficult. There are no facilities. The wide, white sand beach has a gentle slope to deep water and is bordered by two rocky points and is situated at the foot of steep cliffs. The left

middle part of the beach is usually clear of coral and rocks even in winter when the beach is subject to erosion. During the winter this is *THE* bodysurfing spot, especially when the surf is heavy, however, dangerous water conditions also exist. This area is only for the strong, experienced swimmer. The summer is generally much better for swimming and snorkeling. In the past couple of years, this has become a very popular beach. Snorkeling is fair to good, especially around the left rocky point where there is a reef. Okay in winter when the ocean is calm and visibility good. NOTE: The beach is known as Slaughterhouse because of the once existing slaughterhouse on the cliffs above the beach, not because of what the ocean can do to body surfers in the winter when the big ones are coming in! Remember this is part of the Honolua-Mokuleia Bay Marine Life Conservation District - look but don't disturb or take.

## HONOLUA BAY ★

The next bay past Slaughterhouse is Honolua Bay. Watch for a dirt side road on the left. Park here and walk in along the road. There is no beach, just cobblestone with irregular patches of sand and an old concrete boat ramp in the middle. Excellent snorkeling in summer, spring, and fall especially in the morning, but in winter only on the calmest days. In summer on calm days the bay resembles a large glassy pond and in our opinion, this is the best snorkeling on Maui. Note: After a heavy rainfall, the water may be turbid for several days before it returns to its sparkling clear condition again. You can enter at the boat ramp or over the rocks and follow the reefs either left or right. Remember this is a Marine Life Conservation area, so look but don't disturb.

There is an interesting phenomenon affecting the bay. As fresh water runoff percolates into the bay, a shimmering boundary layer (usually about three feet below the surface) is created between the fresh and salt waters. Depending on the amount of runoff it may be very apparent or disappear entirely. It is less prevalent on the right side of the bay. Honolua Bay is also an internationally known winter surfing spot. Storm generated waves come thundering in around the right point creating perfect waves and tubes. A good vantage point to watch the action is the cliffs at the right point of the bay, accessible by car on a short dirt road off the main highway.

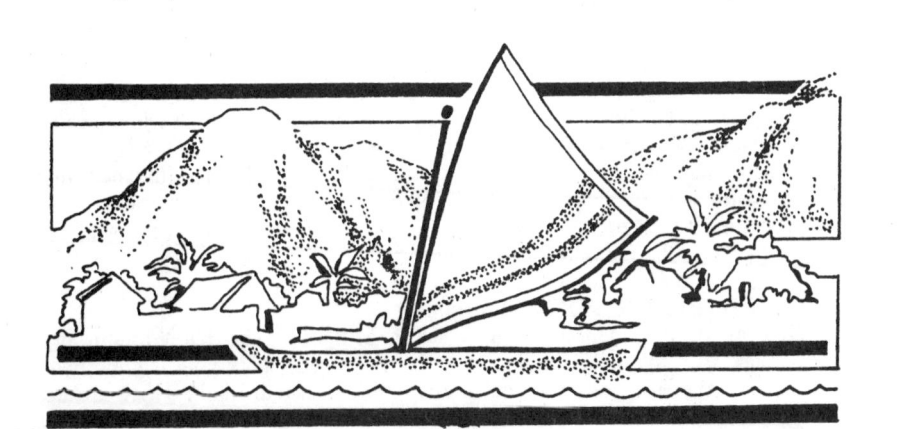

# KIHEI BEACHES

The Kihei beaches aren't quite as beautiful as Wailea's. They don't have the nicely landscaped parking areas, or the large, beautiful resort complexes (this is condo country). They do offer increased facilities such as BBQs, picnic tables, drinking water, and grassy play areas. The Kamaole I, II and III beaches even have lifeguards. The beaches are listed in order from Maalaea Bay to Wailea.

## MAALAEA BAY BEACH
This gently curving white sand beach stretches three miles from the Maalaea boat harbor to Kihei. For the most part, the beach is backed by low sand dunes and large generally wet, sand flats. Public access is from many areas along South Kihei Road. There are no facilities. Casual beach activities are best early in the morning before the strong, mid-morning, prevailing winds begin to sweep across the isthmus. Due to the length of the beach and the hard-packed sand near the water, this has become a popular place to jog. Windsurfing is popular in the afternoons.

The beach begins in front of the last three condominiums in Maalaea, the Kana'I A Nalu, Hono Kai and the Makani A Kai. Just past the Makani A Kai on Hauoli Street is a public park and beach access. There is a good section of beach here with a fairly gentle drop off. Also there are two small, sandy-bottomed pools, protected by the reef on either side of the small man-made rock jetty. These are good play areas for kids. The waves remain fairly calm, except at high tide or high surf conditions. The best snorkeling is out from the beach here, but the conditions are extremely variable, from fairly clear to fairly murky, depending on the time of year and prevailing conditions. Snorkeling is usually better in the winter months. The beach from this point to North Kihei is generally fronted by shelf rock or reef and is not good for swimming, but excellent for a lengthy beach walk! The beach becomes excellent for swimming and other beach activities in front of the North Kihei condos. Snorkeling is fair. A beach activity center is located on the beach at the Kealia Beach Center.

## MAI POINA OE IAU BEACH PARK
On South Kihei Road, fronting Maui Lu Resort. Paved parking for 8 cars at the Pavilion (numerous other areas to park are along the road). 5 picnic tables, restrooms, showers. This is actually part of the previous beach. In-shore bottom generally sandy with patches of rock, fronted by shallow reef. Swimming and snorkeling are best in the morning before the early afternoon winds come up. Popular windsurfing area in the afternoon.

## KAONOULULU BEACH PARK
Located across the street from the Kihei Bay Surf. Off-road parking for 20 cars, restrooms, drinking water, rinse-off showers, picnic tables, and four BBQ grills. Very small beach, well protected by close-in reef.

## KAWILIKI POU PARK
Located at the end of Waipulani Street. Paved off-street parking for 30 cars, restrooms, large grassy area, and public tennis courts. Fronts Laule'a, Luana Kai

and the Maui Sunset Hotel. Tall graceful palms line the shoreline. Narrow sandy beach generally strewn with seaweed and coral rubble. (See GENERAL INFORMATION - Children, for frog hunting information)

## KAWILILIPOA AND WAIMAHAIKAI AREAS

Any of the cross streets off South Kihei Road will take you down toward the beach where public right-of-ways are marked. Limited parking, usually on street. No facilities. The whole shoreline from Kalama Park to Waipulani Street (3 - 4 miles) is an area of uninterrupted beaches lined by residential housing and small condo complexes. Narrow sandy beaches with lots of coral rubble from the fronting reefs.

## KALAMA BEACH PARK

Well-marked, 36-acre park with 12 pavilions, 3 restrooms, showers, picnic tables, BBQ grills, playground apparatus, soccer field, baseball field, tennis courts, volleyball and basketball courts. Lots of grassy area. There is no beach (in winter), only a large boulder breakwater. Good view of the cinder cone in Makena, Molokini, Kahoolawe, Lanai, and West Maui.

## KAMAOLE I

Well-marked beach across from the Kamaole Beach Club. Off-street parking for 30 cars. Facilities include picnic tables, restrooms, rinse-off showers, rental equipment, children's swimming area, and lifeguard. Long, white, sandy beach offering good swimming, poor to fair snorkeling. NOTE: The small pocket of sand between rock outcroppings at the right end of the beach is known as Young's Beach. It is also accessible from Kaiau Street with parking for about 20 cars. Public right-of-way sign at end of Kaiau Street.

## KAMAOLE II

Located across from the Kai Nani shopping and restaurant complex. On-street parking, restrooms, rinse-off showers, rental equipment, and lifeguard. White sand beach between two rocky points with sharp drop-off to overhead depths. Good swimming, poor to fair snorkeling.

## KAMAOLE III ★

Well-marked beach across from the Kamaole Sands Condominiums. Off-street parking, picnic tables, BBQ's, restrooms, rinse-off showers, drinking water, playground equipment, a grassy play area, and a lifeguard. 200-yard long, narrow (in winter) white sand beach with some rocky areas along the beach, and a few submerged rocks. Good swimming, fair snorkeling around rocks at south end of the beach. Kamaole II and III are very popular beaches with locals and tourists because of the nice beaches and easy access.

# WAILEA BEACHES

This area generally has small, lovely, white sand beaches which have marked public access. Parking is off-street in well maintained parking areas, and restrooms as well as rinse-off showers are provided. You won't recognize this area from a few years ago. The new Grand Hyatt Wailea, Kea Lani and Four Seasons Resorts, along with the renovated Stouffer Wailea Beach and Maui Inter-Continental Resorts, have transformed this once under developed area into a world class resort destination riviling Kaanapali, and even surpassing Kaanapali in some ways.

## KEAWAKAPU BEACH ★
There are two convenient public accesses to this very nice but generally under-used beach. There is paved parking for 50 cars across the street from the beach, about 2/10 mile south of Mana Kai Resort. Look for the beach access sign on the left as you travel south. There are two small crescent shaped, white sand beaches separated by a small rocky point. Good swimming, off-shore sandy bottom, fair snorkeling around rocks at far north end. There are rinse-off showers and a restaurant at the Mana Kai which is right on the beach. Access to southern end of beach - go straight at left turn-off to Wailea, road says "Dead End." Parking for about 30 cars. Rinse-off showers. Beautiful, very gently sloping white sand beach with good swimming. Snorkeling off rocks on left. Popular scuba diving spot. Four hundred yards off shore in 80-85 feet of water there is supposed to be an artificial reef of 150 car bodies.

## MOKAPU BEACH ★
A public access sign (Ulua/Mokapu Beaches) is near the Stouffer Wailea Beach Resort. Small parking area, restrooms and showers. Rental equipment at nearby Wailea Resort Activities Center at Stouffer's. Beautiful white sand beach. Excellent swimming. Good snorkeling in mornings around the rocks which divide the two beaches. The best snorkeling is on the Ulua beach side.

## ULUA BEACH ★
A public access sign (Ulua/Mokapu Beaches) is located near the Stouffer Wailea Beach Resort. Small paved parking area with a short walk to beach. Showers and rest rooms. Rental equipment is only a short walk away at the Wailea Ocean Activities Center. Beautiful white sand beach fronting the Elua Resort complex. Ulua and Mokapu Beaches are separated by a narrow point of rocks. The area around the beaches is beautifully landscaped because of the resorts. The beach is semi-protected and has a sandy offshore bottom. Good swimming, usually very good snorkeling in the mornings around the lava flow between the beaches. Come early to get a parking space!

## WAILEA BEACH ★
One half mile south of the Inter-Continental Resort there is a public beach access sign and a paved road down to a landscaped parking area for about 40 cars. Restrooms and rinse-off showers. Rental sailboats and windsurfing boards are available. Beautiful wide crescent of gently sloping white sand. Gentle offshore slope. Good swimming. Snorkeling is only fair to the left (south) around the rocks (moderate currents and not much coral or many fish). The new Kea Lani resort is situated on this beachfront.

### POLO BEACH

Just past the Kea Lani Resot turn right at the Wailea Golf Club-Fairway Restaurant sign and head down to the Polo Beach Resort condominiums. The public access sign is easy to spot. Parking for 40 cars in paved parking area. Showers and restrooms. The beaches are a short walk on a paved sidewalk and down a short flight of stairs. There are actually two beaches, 400 foot long north beach and 200 foot long south beach, separated by 150 feet of large rocks. The beaches slope begins gently, then continues more steeply off-shore and is not well protected. This combination can cause swift beach backwash which is particularly concentrated at two or three points and also a rough shore break, especially in the afternoons. The beach is dotted with large rocks. Fair swimming, generally poor snorkeling.

## MAKENA BEACHES

This area includes the beaches south of Polo Beach, out to La Perouse Bay (past this point, you either hike or need to have a four-wheel drive). The Makena beaches are relatively undeveloped and relatively unspoiled, and not always easy to find. There are few signs, confusing roads, and some beaches are not visible from the road. Generally, no facilities and parking where you can find it. The nearest grocery is at the Wailea Shopping Center. We hope our directions will help you find these sometimes hard-to-find, but very lovely, nearly pristine beaches.

### PALAUEA BEACH

As you leave Wailea, there is a four-corner intersection with a sign on the left for the Wailea Golf Club, and on the right for the Polo Beach Condos. 8/10 mile past here turn onto the second right turnoff at the small "Paipu Beach" sign. At roads end (about 1/10 mile), park under the trees. Poolenalena Beach lies in front of you. Walk several hundred feet back towards Polo Beach over a small hill (Haloa Point) and you will see Palauea Beach stretching out before you. A beautiful beach, largely unkown to tourists. The area above the beach at the south end has been developed with pricey residential homes.

If you drive down to the Polo Beach Condos instead, you can continue on Old Makena Road which will loop back to Makena Alanui Road after about a mile. Palauea Beach lays along this road, but is not visible through the trees. There is a break in the fence .35 miles from Polo Beach with a well worn path to the beach. Although this is all private and posted land, the path and the number of cars parked alongside the road seems to indicate that this beautiful white sand beach is getting much more public use than in the past. Good swimming. No facilities. Both Palauea and Poolenalena beaches have the same conditions as Polo Beach with shallow offshore slope then a steep dropoff which causes fairly strong backwash in places and tends to cause a strong shore break in the afternoon.

### POOLENALENA BEACH

See directions for Palauea Beach. This is a lovely wide, white sand beach with gentle slope offering good swimming. This used to be a popular local camping spot, however no camping signs are now posted.

## UPCOUNTRY ROAD
1.4 miles from Polo Beach. Currently closed in dispute over maintenance.

## PAIPU BEACH (Chang's Beach)
Continue another 2/10 to 3/10 miles on Makena Alanui Rd., past Poolenalena and you will come to the Makena Surf Town Houses (about 1.2 miles from the Wailea Golf Club sign). This development surrounds Chang's Beach, however, there is a public beach access sign and paved parking for about 20 cars. It's a short walk down a concrete path to the beach. A rinse-off shower is provided. This small but sandy beach is used mostly by guests of the Makena Surf.

## ULUPIKUNUI BEACH
Turn right just past the Makena Surf and immediately park off the road. Walk down to the beach at the left end of the complex. The beach is 75-100 feet of rock strewn sand and is not too attractive, but is well protected.

## FIVE GRAVES
From the Makena Surf, continue down Old Makena Road another 2/10 mile to the entrance of Five Graves. There is ample parking. The 19th century graves are visible from Makena Rd. just a couple hundred feet past the entrance. There is no beach, but this is a good scuba and snorkeling site. Follow the trail down to the shore where you'll see a good entrance to the water.

## MAKENA LANDING - PAPIPI BEACH
Continue another 2/10 mile on Old Makena Rd. to Makena Landing on the right. There is off-street parking for 22 cars. The beach is located at the entrance and is about 75-100 feet with gentle slope, sometimes rock strewn. Not very attractive and is used mostly for fishing, but snorkeling can be good if you enter at the beach and follow the shore to the right. Restrooms and showers available.

Instead of turning right onto Old Makena Road at the Makena Surf, continue straight and follow the signs to the Makena Golf Course. About 9/10 mile past the Makena Surf there is another turnoff onto Old Makena Rd. At the stop sign at the bottom of the hill, you can turn right and end up back at Makena Landing or turn left and head for Maluaka Beach. 2/10 mile past the stop sign you will see the old Keawalai Church U.C.C. and cemetery. Sunday services continue to be held here. Along the road is a pay phone.

## MALUAKA BEACH ★ (Naupaka)
3/10 mile past the stop sign there is a turnaround and public entrance to this beach on the right. There are a few parking places near the entrance along the road, however, the main parking lot with restrooms and showers is located a short walk back up the road. The resort above the beach is the Maui Prince. This gorgeous 200-yard beach is set between a couple of rock promontories. The very fine white sand beach is wide with a gentle slope to deeper water. Snorkeling can be good in the morning until about noon when the wind picks up. There are interesting coral formations at the south end with unusual abstract shapes, and large coral heads of different sizes. Coral in shades of pink, blue, green, purple and lavender can be spotted. There are enough fish to make it interesting, but not an abundance. In the afternoon when the wind comes up, so do the swells, providing good boogieboarding and wave playing.

### ONEULI BEACH (Black Sand Beach)
On Old Makena Hwy., past the Maui Prince Resort, just past the intersection of the old road is a dirt road turnoff. A 4-wheel drive or a high ground clearance vehicle is a good idea for the very rutted 3/10 mile to the beach. The beach is coarse black sand and the entire length of the beach is lined by an exposed reef. No facilities.

### ONELOA BEACH ★ (Makena Beach)
The entrance for the north end of the beach is at the second dirt road to the right off Old Makena Hwy. after the intersection of the old road. It is 3/10 mile from the turnoff to the beach and parking area with room for quite a few cars. The old, very rutted dirt road has been replaced by a graded and somewhat graveled road.

This very lovely white sand beach is long (3/4 mile) and wide and is the last major undeveloped beach on the leeward side of the island. Community effort is continuing in their attempt to prevent further development of this beach. The 360-foot cinder cone (Pu'u Olai) at the north end of the beach separates Oneloa from Puuolai Beach. The beach has a quick, sharp drop off and rough shore break particularly in the afternoon. Body surfing is sometimes good. Snorkeling around the rocky point at the cinder cone is only poor to fair with not much to see, and not for beginners due to the usually strong north to south current.

### PUUOLAI BEACH (Little Makena)
Take the first Oneloa Beach entrance, and park at Oneloa Beach. From there, you hike over the cinder cone. There is a flat, white sand beach, with a shallow sandy bottom which is semi-protected by a shallow cove. The shore break is usually gentle and swimming is good. Bodysurfing sometimes. Snorkeling is only poor to fair around the point on the left. Watch for strong currents. Although definitely illegal, beach activities here tend to be au naturel.

### AHIHI-KINAU ★ (NATURAL RESERVE AREA)
About 3/4 mile past Makena Beach, a sign indicates the reserve. There is a small, 6-foot wide, sandy beach alongside the remnants of an old concrete boat ramp. Although it's located in a small cove and is well protected, the beach and cove are very shallow with many urchins. There is also very limited parking here. Up around the curve in the road is a large parking area. It's a short walk to the shore on a crushed lava rock trail. Another couple hundred feet to a very small (3 foot) and partially hidden sand and pebble beach that makes a better entrance to the water than over the rocks. There is excellent snorkeling directly off shore to the right and left. Remember, this is a marine reserve - look, but don't disturb. No facilities.

### LA PEROUSE BAY
2 miles past Ahihi-Kinau, over a road carved through Maui's most recent lava flow, is the end of the road unless you have a 4-wheel drive. The "road" is extremely rough and we would recommend a hike rather than a ride. It's about 3 or 4 miles from road's end at La Perouse Bay to the Kanaio beaches. If you hike, wear good hiking shoes as you'll be walking over stretches of sharp lava rock. There are a series of small beaches, actually only pockets of sand of various compositions, with fairly deep offshore waters and strong currents.

# WAILUKU - KAHULUI BEACHES

Beaches along this whole side of the island are usually poor for swimming and snorkeling. The weather is generally windy or cloudy in winter and very hot in summer. Due to the weather, type of beaches, and distance from the major tourist areas on the other side of the island, these beaches don't attract many tourists (except Hookipa, which is internationally known for wind surfing).

## WAIHEE BEACH PARK
From Wailuku take Kahekili Highway about three miles to Waihee and turn right onto Halewaiu Road, then proceed about one-half mile to the Waihee Municipal Golf Course. From there, a park access road takes you into the park. Paved off-street parking, restrooms, showers, and picnic tables. This is a long, narrow, brown sand beach strewn with coral rubble from Waihee Reef. This is one of the longest and widest reefs on Maui and is about one thousand feet wide. The area between the beach and reef is moderately shallow with good areas for swimming and snorkeling when the ocean is calm. Winter surf or storm conditions can produce strong alongshore currents. Do not swim or snorkel at the left end of the beach as there is a large channel through the reef which usually produces a very strong rip current. This area is generally windy.

## KANAHA BEACH PARK
Just before reaching the Kahului Airport, turn left, then right on reaching Ahahao Street. The far south area of the park has been landscaped and includes BBQs, picnic tables, restrooms, and showers. Paved off-street parking is provided. The beach is long (about one mile) and wide with a shallow offshore bottom composed of sand and rock. Plenty of thorny Kiawe trees in the area make footwear essential. The main attraction of the park is its peaceful setting and view, so picnicking and sunbathing are the primary activities. Swimming would appeal mainly to children. Surfing can be good here.

KIHIKIHI                                                                JBayot

## H. A. BALDWIN PARK

The park is located about 1.5 miles past Spreckelville on the Hana Highway. There is a large off-street parking area, a large pavilion with kitchen facilities, picnic tables, BBQs, and a tent camping area. There are also restrooms, showers, a baseball and a soccer field. The beach is long and wide with a steep slope to overhead depths. This is a very popular park because of the facilities. The very consistent, although usually small, shore break is good for bodysurfing. Swimming is poor. There are two areas where exposed beach rock provides a relatively calm place for children to play.

## HOOKIPA BEACH PARK

Located about two miles past Lower Paia on the Hana Highway. Restrooms, showers, four pavilions with BBQ's and picnic tables, paved off-street parking, and a tent camping area is provided. Small, white sand beach fronted by a wide shelf of beach rock. The offshore bottom is a mixture of reef and patches of sand. Swimming is not advised. The area is popular for the generally good and, at times (during winter), very good surfing. Hookipa is internationally known for its excellent wind surfing conditions. This is also a good place to come and watch both of these water sports.

# *HANA*

## WAIANAPANAPA STATE PARK

About four miles before you reach Hana on the Hana Highway is Waianapanapa State Park. There is a trail from the parking lot down to the ocean. The beach is not of sand, but of millions of small, smooth, black volcanic stones. Ocean activities are generally unsafe. There is a lava tunnel at the end of the beach that runs about 50 feet and opens into the ocean. Other well marked paths in the park lead to more caves and fresh water pools. An abundance of mosquitos breed in the grotto area and bug repellent is strongly advised.

## HANA BEACH PARK

If you make it to Hana, you will have no difficulty finding this beach on the shoreline of Hana Bay. Facilities include a pavilion with picnic tables, restrooms and showers, and also Tutu's snack bar. About a 200-yard beach lies between old concrete pilings on the left and the wharf on the right. Gentle offshore slope and gentle shore break even during heavy outer surf. This is the safest swimming beach on this end of the island. Snorkeling is fair to good on calm days between the pier and the lighthouse. Staying inshore is a must, as beyond the lighthouse the currents are very strong and flow seaward.

## KAIHALULU BEACH (Red Sand Beach)

This reddish sand beach is in a small cove on the other side of Kauiki Hill from Hana Bay and is accessible by trail. At the Hana Bay intersection follow the road up to the school. A dirt path leads past the school and disappears into the jungle, then almost vanishes as it goes through an old cemetery, then continues out onto a scenic promontory. The ground here is covered with marble-sized pine cones which make for slippery footing. As the trail leads to the left and over the edge of the cliff, it changes to a very crumbly rock/dirt mixture that is unstable at best.

You may wonder why you're doing this as the trail becomes two feet wide and slopes to the edge of a 60 foot cliff in one place. The trail down to the beach can be quite hazardous. Visitors and Hana residents alike have been injured seriously. It is definitely not for the squeamish, those with less than good agility or youngsters. And when carrying beach paraphernalia, extra caution is needed. The effort is rewarded as you descend into a lovely cove bordered by high cliffs and almost enclosed by a natural lava barrier seaward. The beach is formed primarily from red volcanic cinder, hence its name. Good swimming, but stay away from the opening at the left end because of rip currents. Although definitely illegal, beach activities here may be au naturel at times. The Hotel Hana Maui has plans to improve the access to this beach sometime in the future.

### KOKI BEACH PARK
This beach is reached by traveling 1.5 miles past the Hasegawa Store toward Ohe'o Gulch. Look for Haneoo Road where the sign will read "Koki Park - Hamoa Beach - Hamoa Village." This beach is unsafe for swimming and the signs posted warn "Dangerous Current."

### HAMOA BEACH ★
This gorgeous beach has been very attractively landscaped and developed by the Hotel Hana Maui in a way that adds to the surrounding lushness. The long white sand beach is in a very tropical setting and surrounded by a low sea cliff. To reach it, travel toward Ohe'o Gulch after passing through Hana. Look for the sign 1.5 miles past Hasegawa store that says "Koki Park - Hamoa Beach - Hamoa Village." There are two entrances down steps from the road. Parking is limited to along the roadside. The left side of the beach is calmer, and offers the best snorkeling. Because it is unprotected from the open ocean, there is good surfing and bodysurfing, but also strong alongshore and rip currents are created at times of heavy seas. The Hana Hotel maintains the grounds and offers restrooms, changing area, and beach paraphernalia for the guests. There is an outdoor rinse-off shower for non-hotel guests. Hay wagons bring the guests to the beach for the hotel's weekly luau.

# RECREATION AND TOURS

## INTRODUCTION

Maui's ideal climate, diverse land environments, and benign leeward ocean has led to an astounding range of land, sea and air activities. With such a variety of things to do during your limited vacation time, we suggest browsing through this chapter and choosing those activities that sound most enjoyable. The following suggestions should get you started.

### BEST BETS

To see and experience the real Maui, take a hike with guide Ken Schmitt.

For spectacular scenery and lots of fresh air, try the 38-mile coast down the world's largest dormant volcano on a bicycle, or one of several other Upcountry bicycle trips.

For great snorkeling try Honolua Bay, Namalu, Ahihi Kinau, or Olowalu.

Take a helicopter tour and get a super spectacular view of Maui.

Golf at one of Maui's excellent courses.

Sail to Lana'i and snorkel Hulopoe Beach with the Trilogy Cruise.

If the whales are in residence, take advantage of a whale watching excursion to view these beautiful mammals a bit more closely. An estimated 1,500 whales winter each year in the waters surrounding Maui.

For an underwater thrill consider an introductory scuba adventure, no experience necessary. Or sample a newer arrival to the Maui aquatic scene, snuba!

For those who like to stay dry in the water, take a submarine trip to view the underwater sights off Lahaina.

For a wet and wild water tour, plus snorkeling, try a raft trip.

If you're really adventurous, consider parasailing (during the summer when the whales have gone back north!), sea kayaking, or try scuba kayaking at Kapalua.

For great scenery at a great price, drive yourself to Hana and visit the pools at Haleakala National Park-Kipahulu at the O'heo stream or to Upcountry and Haleakala.

# OCEAN ACTIVITIES

## SNORKELING

Maui offers exceptionally clear waters, warm ocean temperatures and abundant sea life with safe areas (no adverse water conditions) for snorkeling. If you are a complete novice, most of the resorts and excursion boats offer snorkeling lessons. From the youngest to the oldest, everyone can enjoy this sport that needs little experience and there is no need to dive to see all the splendors of the sea. If you are unsure of your abilities, the use of a floatation device may be of assistance. Be forewarned that the combination of tropical sun and the refreshing coolness of the ocean can deceive those paddling blissfully on the surface, and result in a badly burned backside. Water resistant sunscreens are available locally and are recommended.

Equipment is readily available at resorts and dive shops, and as you can see, much less expensive at the dive shops (even better are the weekly rates). For a listing of dive shops see Scuba Diving. All snorkeling boat trips provide equipment as a part of their package. Some even offer a limited selection of prescription masks.

### TYPICAL RENTAL PRICES - MASK-FINS-SNORKEL FOR 24 HOURS:
*Maui Sun Divers* in Kihei - $5.00
*Fun Rentals* in Lahaina - $2.50-$8 depending on equipment
*Frogman* in Lahaina and Kihei - $2.50-$8 depending on equipment
*Hyatt Regency Resort* at Kaanapali - $15 per hour 8 am-6 pm, no 24 hour rentals

### WEEKLY RATES
*Snorkel Bob's* in Lahaina and Kihei charges $15 per set per week. Silicon set $29 per week, prescription masks $39.
*Aunt Snorkel and Uncle Boogie* in Kihei (Rainbow Mall) and Lahaina (505 Front St.) charge $11.95 per week for regular gear, $14.95 for silicon set.

REEF DWELLERS                                                    J. BAYOT

Most major dive shops can fit you with a prescription mask, as long as your vision impairment is not too severe. (Editors note: As a contact wearer with an strong prescription, I wear my soft lenses with a good fitting mask.)

Good snorkeling spots, if not right in front of your hotel or condo, are only a few minutes' drive away. The following are our favorites, each for a special reason.

## WEST MAUI

*Black Rock* - At the Sheraton in the Kaanapali Resort. Pay for parking at Whalers Village and walk down the beach. Clear water and a variety of tame fish - these fish expect handouts!

*Kapalua Bay* - Public park with off street parking, restrooms and showers. A well protected bay and beautiful beach amid the grounds of the Kapalua Resort. Limited coral and some large coral heads, fair for fish watching. Arrive early as parking is very limited!

*Namalu Bay* - Park at Kapalua Bay, walk over from Kapalua Bay to the bay which fronts the grounds of the resort. Difficult entry, very good on calm days.

*Honolua Bay* - No facilities, park alongside the road and walk a 1/4 mile to the bay, but the best snorkeling on Maui, anytime but winter.

*Olowalu* - At mile marker 14, about 5 miles south of Lahaina. Generally calm and warmer waters with ample parking along the roadside. Very good snorkeling. If you find a pearl earring, let us know, we have the match!

## EAST MAUI

*Ulua-Mokapu Beach* - Well-marked public beach park in Wailea with restrooms and showers. Good snorkeling on the Ulua side of the rocky point separating these two picturesque and beautiful beaches.

*Maluaka Beach* - Located in Makena, no facilities and along the road parking. Good coral formations and a fair amount of fish at the left end of the beach.

*Ahihi Kinau Natural Reserve* - Approximately five miles past Wailea. No facilities. This is not a very crowded spot and you may feel a little alone here, but the snorkeling is great with lots of coral and a good variety of fish.

Generally at all locations the best snorkeling is in the morning until about 1 p.m., when the wind picks up. For more information on each area and other locations, refer to the BEACHES chapter.

A good way to become acquainted with Maui's sea life is a guided snorkeling adventure with *Ann Fielding*, marine biologist and author of *Hawaiian Reefs and Tidepools and Underwater Guide to Hawai'i*. She takes small groups (minimum 2, maximum 6) to the best location, but generally Honolua Bay in summer and Ahihi Kinau in winter. These morning (8:30 am - 12:30 pm) excursions begin with an introductory discussion on Hawaiian marine life, identification and ecology which is followed by snorkeling. Floatation devices, snorkel gear and refreshments are provided for the $40 fee. Call ahead for your reservation at (808) 572-8437.

You may feel the urge to rent an underwater camera to photograph some of the unusual and beautiful fish you've seen, and by all means try it, but remember, underwater fish photography is a real art. The disposable underwater cameras are a fun and inexpensive and available everywhere, but your resulting photos may be disappointing.

There are several video tapes of Maui's marine life available at the island bookstores if you want a permanent record of the fish you've seen. Several of the sea excursions offer video camera rentals.

There are two other great places to snorkel, however, you need a boat to reach them. Fortunately, a large variety of charter services will be happy to assist.

*Molokini Crater* - This small semicircular island is the remnant of a volcano. Located about 8 miles off Maalaea Harbor, it affords good snorkeling in the crater area. These waters are a marine reserve and the island is a bird sanctuary. Molokini is usually a 1/2 day excursion with a continental breakfast and lunch provided. Costs are $40 - $80 for adults, $25 - $42 (plus tax) for children under 12. (You may find rates even lower with current price wars.)

*Hulopoe Beach, Lana'i* - This is our favorite. Located on the island of Lana'i, it's worth the trip for the beautiful beach and the abundant coral and fish. We saw a school of fish here that was so large that from the shore it appeared to be a huge moving reef. After swimming through the school and returning to shore we were informed that large predatory fish like to hang out around these schools! Lana'i is usually a full-day excursion with continental breakfast, BBQ lunch and a optional island tour. $79 - $139 for adults, $35-$44 under 12. Half-day trips are available on the new Navatek.

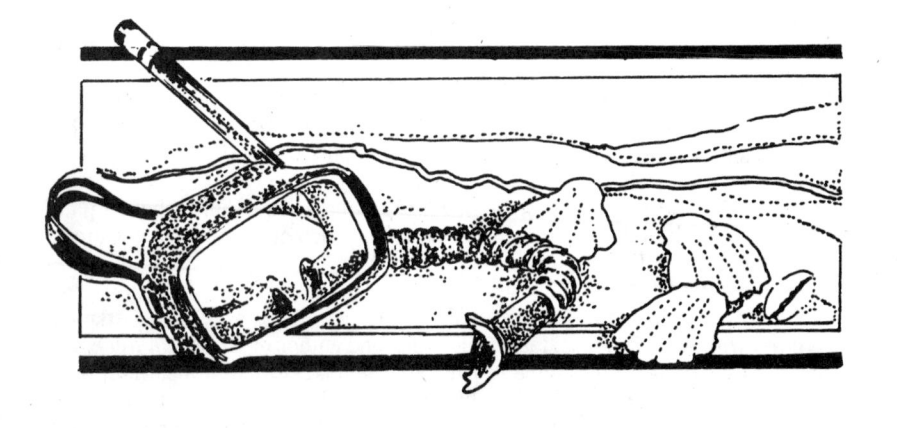

A variety of snorkel/sail/tour options are available for snorkeling along East and West Maui's coastline, Molokini, Moloka'i or Lana'i. Your first decision is choosing between a large or small group tour. Large groups go out in substantial monohull or catamaran motor yachts of 60 - 90 feet in length. They get you there comfortably and fast, but without the intimate sailing experience of a smaller, less crowded boat. There are also many sleek sailboats (monohull, catamaran or trimaran) that you can share with 4 to 8 people or privately charter. Another option for a Maui sea excursions is the Zodiac type rafts that use 20 - 23 foot inflatable rafts powered by two large outboards. These rides can be rough, wet and wild. All tours provide snorkel gear with floatation devices, if needed, and instruction. Food and refreshments are provided to varying degrees. The new Navatek promises a state-of-the-art ride on their half-day Lana'i trip. For a list of outings, see the section on Sea Excursions.

## MOLOKINI... again
Molokini is a 10,000 year old dormant volcano with only one crescent shaped portion of the crater rim now providing a sanctuary for marine and bird life. The crater on the inside of the island offers a water depth of 10 - 50 feet, a 76 degree temperature and visibility sometimes as much as 150 feet on the outer perimeter creating a fish bowl effect. Molokini has been making a slow comeback. Our first trip to the crescent shaped crater was in the days when only two or three boats operated trips. It was truly picture perfect, resembling a huge fish bowl. However, for several years after the detonation of some submerged bombs by the Navy, the aquatic life was sparse. The many tour boats dropping anchors further damaged and destroyed the reef. While it hasn't been restored to the way it was during our first excursions a number of years ago, it is now returning to a much improved condition. Fortunately, concerned boat operators were granted semi-permanent concrete mooring anchors, thereby preventing further reef damage. Most trips are taken in the morning, some do offer afternoon trips, but expect rougher ocean conditions. On occasion even the morning trips are forced to snorkel at an alternative site, usually La Perouse.

We recommend *Blue Water Rafting* ★ for those die-hard snorkelers who would enjoy their early bird arrival to the crater with the opportunity to explore three different Molokini dive locations. They arrive at the crater first and snorkel the best spot before the big boats come in. Then it's a stop at the far crater wall for a second snorkeling opportunity. A third stop takes you to a spot over the underwater crater rim where the water on the crater side is shallow, but drops off out of sight dramatically on the other side. Prices range $39-99 depending on trip length which run 2-5 1/2 hrs. (808) 879-7238

The *Four Winds* departs daily from Maalaea from Molokini. The half-day excursion is 7:30 - 12:30 and priced at $66 per person, under age 12 $35, max. 112 passengers. Book direct and pay $53 for adults. Unfortunately, at capacity the boat can be a little bit crowded. One of several boats operated by Classic Charters, this one has a few unique options. They offer a BBQ as compared to a very similar basic (buffet) deli lunch and the breakfast is a varied selection of fresh bagels and cream cheese with jellies. A nice change from the old Danish! Also fresh pineapple and orange slices. The BBQ lunch is cooked on board on three grills on the back of the boat...lunch selections include Mahi Mahi, Burger or chicken breast. All very good, and nice selections of condiments for the burgers.

Beer, wine and soda included as well. Lay-out of the boat is nice, but it lacks seating except on the top deck. An optional activity is snuba which takes six people at a time with air tanks carried on rafts which float at the surface ($39). You can go down to a depth of twenty feet. They do an afternoon snorkel cruise. (879-8188)

A good option for those preferring a larger, more ferry-type boat is 92' motor yacht *The Prince Kuhio*. (242-8777 or 1-800-468-1287).

*The Pride of Maui* ★ 65' catamaran featuring a large indoor cabin and outdoor sundecks. They offer daily departures at 8 am from the Maalaea Harbor for morning dives at two destinations, Molokini and "Turtle Town" (Pu'u Ola'i). Depending on weather conditions, snorkel location may be Olowalu or Coral Gardens. (875-0955). See Sea excursions for more information.

The Coon family's Trilogy operation also offers a Molokini snorkel aboard their 44' trimaran cutter *Trilogy IV*. Adults $75, Children $37.50, they serve breakfast enroute, a snack and then serve BBQ chicken lunch. 661-4743 or 1-800-874-2666

# SCUBA DIVING

Maui, with nearby Molokini, Kaho'olawe, Lana'i and Moloka'i, offers many excellent diving locations. A large variety of dive operations offer scuba excursions, instruction, certification and rental equipment. If you are a novice, a great way to get hooked is an introductory dive. No experience is necessary. Instruction, equipment and dive, all for $34.95 - $95 with the average about $60. Dives are available from boats, or less expensive from the beach. A beginning beach dive may be advisable for the less confident aquatic explorer. For those who are certified but rusty, refresher dives are available.

The mainstay of Maui diving is the two-tank dive, two dive sites with one tank each. Prices depend on location and include all equipment. A trip runs about $90. If the bug bites and you wish to get certified, the typical course is five days, eight hours each day, at an average cost of $350 plus books. One dive shop suggested that visitors with limited time, do "PADI" dive preparation on the mainland and can then be certified on Maui in just two days. Classes are generally no more than 6 persons, or if you prefer private lessons, they run slightly more. Advanced open water courses are available in deep diving, search and recovery, underwater navigation and night diving (at a few shops). If you wish to rent equipment only, a complete scuba package runs $25 per day, wet suit additional $5.

The larger resorts also offer instruction and some offer certification courses and arrange for excursions. Many of the dive operators utilize boats specifically designed for diving.

Information, equipment, instruction and excursions can be obtained at the following dive shops and charter operators. As you can see by the number of listings, diving is very popular around Maui.

**WEST MAUI**

Aquatic Charters &
Underwater Video
879-0976

American Institute
of Diving, Lahaina
667-5129

Beach Activities
of Maui, 661-5500

Captain Nemo's
150 Dickenson St.
Lahaina, 661-5555
1-800-367-8088

Kapalua Dive Co.
Kapalua Bay Hotel
669-4664

Dive Maui, Inc.
Lahaina, 667-2080

Extended Horizons
P.O. Box 10785
Lahaina, 667-0611

Frogman
278 Wiliko Pl # 20
Lahaina 667-0485
Dolphin Plaza, Kihei

Hawaiian Reef Divers
129 Lahainaluna
Lahaina, 667-7647

Lahaina Divers
710 Front St.
Lahaina, 667-7496
1-800-998-3483

Maui Dive Shop
Ocean Activities
661-5388

Maui Marriott
661-3631/667-1200

**EAST MAUI**

Ed Robinson's
Diving Adventures
Kihei, 879-3584
1-800-635-1273

Maui Dive Shops
Kihei Town Center
Kihei, 879-1919

Makena Coast Charters
Kihei, 874-1273

Maui Dive Shops
Azeka Center, Kihei
879-3388

Maui Sun Divers
Kihei, 879-3631 or
879-3337

Mike Severns
Kihei, 879-6596

Ocean Activities
1847 S. Kihei Rd.
#203, Kihei
879-4485

Molokini Divers
1993 S. Kihei Rd
879-0055

The Dive Shop of
Kihei, 879-5172

Underwater Habitat
Groups of 6
Lana'i and Molokini
879-3483

Scuba Shack
Valley Isle Divers
Kihei, 879-3483

SCUBA DIVING

Kapalua Dive Company is featuring a Kayak Scuba Dive that was developed out of necessity in the summer of 1990. The Kapalua area coastline offers some of the finest diving on the West Coast of Maui, however, entry over lava rock was not feasible. "The Scrambler" offers the means to reach terrific dive spots while not creating the noise or potential anchor damage of a full size dive vessel. "The Scrambler" kayak was designed by Tim Niemier, Olympic Kayak coach. It weighs 35 lbs., is approximately 11 feet long, made of recyclable polyurethane and is described as a sit on top, self scupping kayak. The paddler is not tied, strapped or sealed inside the kayak, therefore, if it should roll the paddler is free to swim to the side, roll the kayak back upright and climb aboard. The term self scupping refers to the design which allows water to drain free of the topside without any procedures on the part of the paddler. This makes the kayak unsinkable. Departing from Kapalua Bay, each diver paddles his or her own kayak (although a double kayak is available for tight knit buddy teams) along the rugged and scenic Kapalua coastline for 15 to 20 minutes prior to reaching one of two different dive sites. Trips are limited to a maximum of four divers, price is $89 per person. Also available are Underwater Scooter Dives, Night Dives, snorkeling, sailing and windsurfing. Call direct to the Kapalua Activity Center at 669-4664.

Books of interest available at dive shops or area bookstores:
*Diving and Snorkeling Guide to the Hawaiian Islands* by Doug Wallin, 106 pp., $11.95
*Diving Hawaii* by Steve Rosenberg, 128 pages, $18.95
*The Diver's Guide to Maui* by Chuck Thorne. $7.95
*Skin Diver's Guide to Hawaii* by Gordon Feund. 72 pages, $2.50.
*Hawaii Diver's Manual*, 162 pages, $3.00.
*Underwater Videographer's Handbook*, 128 pages, by Lynn Laymon $19.95

# SNUBA

One of the newer water recreations available is Snuba which is a combination of snorkeling and scuba diving, allowing the freedom of underwater exploration without the heavy equipment of scuba diving. In brief, the snuba diver has a mask and an airhose that is connected to the surface. Two vessels currently offer Snuba excursions, The Pride of Maui 875-0955 and The Four Winds 879-8188. Cost is $40 in addition to the cruise fee.

# SEA EXCURSIONS

Maui offers a bountiful choice for those desiring to spend some time in and on the ocean. Boats available for sea expeditions range from a three-masted schooner, to spacious trimarans and large motor yachts, to the zodiac type rafts for the more adventurous. Your choice is a large group trip or a more pampered small group excursion with a maximum of six people. Two of the most popular snorkeling excursions are to Molokini and Lana'i. Most sailboats motor to these islands and, depending on wind conditions, sail at least part of the return trip. All provide snorkel equipment. Food and beverage service varies and is reflected in the price. Many sailboats are available for hourly, full day or longer private charters.

Note: Due to weather conditions, your trip to Molokini may, at the last minute, be altered to another location, usually along the Southern shore of Maui.

One of the nicest new additions to a number of boats is the option of a freshwater shower! Some of them even have solar heated their water which provides a refreshing rinse off after your saltwater snorkel/swim.

Excursion boats seem to have a way of sailing off into the sunset. The number of new ones is as startling as the number of operations that have disappeared since our last edition.

As mentioned previously, competition to Molokini has become fierce. Twenty to thirty boats a day now arrive to snorkel in this area. Many more boats now take trips to Lanaʻi as well.

Currently there is only Princess Cruises offers inter-island transportation to Molokaʻi.

In the following list, phone numbers of the excursion companies are included in case personal booking is desired, however, most activity desks can also book your reservation. The best deal with an activity operator is *Tom's Cashback Tours* who can book most boats and offers a 10% refund. They are located in Lahaina at 834 Front St. and can be reached at 661-8889.

PRICES PER PERSON WILL RUN YOU ACCORDINGLY
TAX NOT INCLUDED:

    Full day trip to Lanaʻi $79 - $140
    Club Lanaʻi $79
    1/2 day trip to Molokini (3 - 6 hours) $35 - $99
    1/2 day Maui coastline (3 - 4 hours) $40- $65
    Full day Maui coastline $80 - $90
    Sunset sails (1 1/2 - 2 hrs.) $30 - $50
    Whale watching (3 hrs./seasonal) $30- $50
    Private charters $75 per hour and up, $400 per day and up
    Dinner cruise $50 - $80

LAHAINA HARBOR

# EXCURSION -

## CHARTER LISTING

**ADVENTURE ONE** - Powerboat - 25 people Molokini snorkel with food $49.95 plus tax, whale watch seasonal. Departs Maalaea. 242-7683, 1-800-356-8989.

**ALIHILANI YACHT CHARTERS** ★ - *First Class*, a 65' sailboat, takes 24 passengers on morning snorkel sails, departs Kaanapali beach or Lahaina Harbor, includes continental breakfast as well as beer & wine. Departs 8 am returns 11:30. $65 adult, $55 child. Afternoon tradewind sail is a 1 1/2 hours of *true* sailing, beverages only served. Departs 2 pm and 3:30 pm. $35 adult, $25 child. Whale watches seasonal. 667-7733, FAX (808) 667-0314.

Private charters and overnight charters can include catered meals. This cruise is a real find, but will appeal to a very specific kind of traveler. It's nothing like any of the other visitor boats, this is a yacht! It should appeal to people who REALLY like to sail, and for the more adventurous types. If you enjoy sailing, don't miss this one. It is reportedly the fastest charter yacht in the islands.

**BLUE WATER RAFTING** ★ - 3 1/2 hr. Molokini snorkel, 3 different sites in the crater, 2 hr. Molokini, snorkel 1 site, $39 - $99. Departs Kihei Launch ramp in their zodiac rafts. Max. 6 people. 879-7238. See review in "Snorkeling" and following excursion listings.

**CAPT. NEMO'S** - is a vendor for activities as well as a dive shop. They no longer operate their own boat. They can book your trip for a morning snorkel, sunset sail, whale watch, introductory or certified scuba dive. Scuba dive prices $85-$112. 661-5555, 1-800-367-8088.

**CINDERELLA YACHT CHARTERS** - *Cinderella*, 50' Columbia Sloop. 3/4 day sail/snorkel, max. 6 people. Departs Maalaea harbor, 242-2779.

**CLUB LANA'I** - See description following excursion listings. Day trip to private beach on Lana'i. $79 price for adults is all inclusive. Children 13-20 years $59, child under age 13 $29. 871-1144

**EXPEDITIONS** ★ - Ferry service from Lahaina to Lana'i four times daily, five trips on Fridays. $50 round trip adult, $40 child. 661-3756. If you'd like to explore Lana'i on your own, you can take the early morning ferry boat over and return on the late afternoon trip.

From the dock it is a moderate, but easy walk to Manele Bay and the adjacent Manele Bay Resort. There is a shuttle that runs between the dock and the Manele Resort and the Koele Lodge, which is restricted to golf and resort guests. From the dock to Lana'i City is a shuttle service that charges $10 round trip. A rental car $59, or Jeep $109, for more in-depth explorations can be obtained from (808) 565-7227.

**FROGMAN -** Frogman began operations in 1986 and now has two sailing catamarans, *Frogman* and *Seabird*, which leave Maalaea Harbor each morning for a Molokini Snorkel and Scuba Adventure. the trips include breakfast, lunch, beverages, equipment and instruction. During season, they also offer afternoon whale watch. They also have rental equipment of everything from boogie boards, to surfboards or Hana tape tours at their Boss Frog's Snorkel Shop at 888 Wainee across from McDonalds in Lahaina or at 2396 S. Kihei Rd., behind Pizza Hut in Dolphin Plaza in Kihei.

*Frogman II* is a 55' sailing catamaran with a 66 passenger capacity. It features a waterslide, fresh water shower and gear. $49.95 per adult for morning Molokini snorkel, children under 12 $29.95, one tank certified or intro $69.95, two tank certified $99.95. Departs 7 am and returns 1 pm. *Seabird* is a 44' sailing catamaran with 40 passenger capacity. Adults $39.95, Children $24.95, one tank scuba $69.95 for their morning Molokini trip. Seasonal two hours whale watch $20 adults, $15 youth 4-12 years.

**FRIENDLY CHARTERS** - *Maalaea Kai II*, 44' trimaran, takes a max. of 36 people on a Molokini snorkel/cruise. Seasonal whale watching. Private charters available. Maalaea Harbor. 871-0985.

**GEMINI CHARTERS** - 64' glass bottom catamaran. Offers a Picnic Snorkel Sail $65 adults, under 12 $40. This 4 hour trip includes a hot buffet lunch. The Gemini Adventure Sail includes a continental breakfast, hot buffet lunch, and two or three snorkel locations. $95 adults, under 12 $55, 9am-3pm. This trip becomes a whale watching adventure during whale season. Once a week they offer a 9 hour special sail which circumnavigates the island of Lana'i, stopping for snorkeling, swimming and sightseeing. The cost is $125 for adults and $75 for children. The offer a Sunset sail for adults as well as the Gemini's Kaanapali Teen Sail, an interesting concept. An exclusive Friday Night for teens includes two hours of sailing, swimming, music and hot pizza. Departs about 5 pm. $30. They also have a keiki snorkel as a part of their Kamp Kaanapali program at the Maui Westin. Departs Kaanapali Beach. Reservation phone 661-2591 after 8 am, PO Box 10846, Lahaina, HI 96761. FAX (808) 669-1700.

**HAWAIIAN RAFTING ADVENTURES**
**DESTINATION PACIFIC** - 1223 Front St., Lahaina. 661-7333.
Trips range from $80 - $110 for a 1 tank introductory dive or a 2 tank dive at Lana'i to PADI certification $325 or private charter $600. *Zodiac* - 23' zodiac rafts, max. 16. Seasonal whale watching $45 adult, $35 child. 1/2 snorkel/whale watch $59 adult, $45 child. Equipment, snacks and beverages included. Departs Mala Wharf. *Gina Marie* - a 36' dive boat departs Mala.

**KAMEHAMEHA SAILS, INC.** - *Kamehameha*, 40' catamaran. Snorkel/sail, sunset sail, whale watching, private charter, max. 15 people. Departs Lahaina harbor, 661-4522.

**KAULANA** - 65' power catamaran, departs Lahaina Harbor, 871-1144. Whale watching/sunset cocktail cruise. This vessel ferries visitors to Club Lana'i.

**KIELE V** - 55' catamaran, 4 hr. snorkel/sail $65 adult, $39 kids under 12 (plus tax). Afternoon sail $39 adults, $19 kids. Contact Hyatt Regency, Kaanapali (808) 661-1234 ext. 3104.

**MAKENA BOAT PARTNERS** - *Kai Kanani*, 46' catamaran, departs at Maui Prince Hotel for Molokini, 879-7218.

**MAUI CLASSIC CHARTERS** - *Lavengro*, a 60' gast rigged Schooner built in 1926, does Molokini sail, $56 adult, $39 child. *Four Winds*, a 53' double deck glass bottom catamaran, has BBQ grills, waterslide, daily learning snorkel, afternoon whale watch. Adults $39, child $29. Departs Maalaea harbor, 879-8177 or 879-8188.

**MAUI DIVE SHOP** - Books boating activities at Kihei Town Center 879-1919, Azeka's 879-3388, and Lahaina 661-5388.

**MAUI-MOLOKAI SEA CRUISES** - *Prince Kuhio*, 92' motor yacht. Whale watching, private charters, 1/2 day Molokini, departs Maalaea. 242-8777 or 1-800-468-1287. This boat has the benefits of a larger vessel with more comforts, but with a bigger capacity, there are alot more people!

**NAVATEK** - Described in their brochure as "travel beyond the usual" is a new part of the Maalaea Harbor activities. This new $3 million cruise vessel will definitely catch your eye. The technology of this new vessel offers a revolutionary smooth ride as a result of a SWATH design (Small Water Plane Twin Hull) which is the result of 13 years of research focussed on minimizing ship motions. The ship rides above the water rather than on it. The main cabin is air conditioned, offers a full service bar and special viewing area with amphitheater seating.

The Navatek system was designed by Steven Loui, a Honolulu shipbuilder. The Navatek I is based in Honolulu, and version II was built in 1994 in the Honolulu shipyard as well. The cruise ship is 82 feet long and 36 feet wide, can carry 149 passengers plus crew and has a cruising speed of 22 knots. There are two full decks offering 3,250 square feet of space including an enclosed main deck and an open observation deck with amphitheater bow seating, tanning areas, lounge chairs, restrooms, a hot shower, a service bar and full commercial kitchen.

They offer two excursions for island visitors and residents. "Lana'i Voyage of Discovery" is a half-day adventure to Lana'i to visit scenic points around the island including Shipwreck beach, Pu'u Pehe Rock and Shark Fin Rock. If you'd like to sample a cruise ship, then the *Navatek II* comes close.

A naturalist from Earthrust is on board giving a talk and offering displays, pamphlets and charts about dolphins, whales, fish, coral and a "stuffed" sea turtle registered and officially designated for educational use. (The green sea turtle isn't actually green, they are called that because their inside body fat is green!) Your day begins early (before 7 am) when a tender shuttles you out from the Lahaina Harbor to the Navatek where a waffle bar breakfast is being prepared. The hot Belgian waffles with fruit toppings (peaches, blueberries and strawberries), syrups (guava, passion strawberry and cane) whipped cream, nuts, and assorted fruits are breakfast fare.

After circumnavigating Lana'i, the boat anchors at Nanahoa (also called Five Needles) about 9 am. The snorkeling was good, but not great, but it is a spot seldom seen by visitors. Lunch was served about 10:30 am and included BBQ pineapple sausage or hot dogs, grilled herbed chicken, marinated roasted vegetables (shitake mushrooms, eggplant and squash), corn on the cob, a lettuce salad, chips and dips, fruit and cookies for dessert. Following lunch the Cruise Director sang and played easy listening music on his guitar. Return to Lahaina about 1:30 pm. They also offer a Sunset Odyssey Dinner Cruise (see Sunset and Dinner Cruise section).

For you land-lubbers with dreams of the sea, but a stomach for the earth beneath your feet, this may be the one for you! The Lana'i Voyage is offered Monday through Saturday $120 for adults, $60 for children 5-12 years, plus tax and harbor fee. For information and reservations phone (808) 661-8787.

**OCEAN ACTIVITIES** - Departures from Maalaea and Lahaina Harbor for scuba diving aboard the 37' Trolleycraft *No Ka Oi IV*, sunset champagne cruises aboard the 65'catamaran *Wailea Kai*, deep sea fishing aboard the Trolleycraft *No Ka Oi III*, Molokini trips on the 65' power cat *Maka Kai*, dinner sail aboard the *Manute'a*, half-day snorkel trips to Lana'i and Molokini picnic snorkel cruises. Whale season and party boat fishing are seasonal. 879-4485 or 1-800-798-0652.

**OCEAN ENTERPRISES** - 6 passenger cabin cruisers, snorkeling, scuba, sportfishing. 879-7067 or 874-9303

**OCEAN RIDERS** - "Adventure Rafting" on one of two rafts, 15 - 18 people max. 3 unusual destinations (depends on daily weather conditions). Reefs of Kaho'olawe, Moloka'i's cliffs or Lana'i. 661-3586

**PACIFIC WHALE FOUNDATION CRUISES** ★ - *Whale One*, 53' motor vessel, Maalaea. *Whale Two*, 50' sailing ketch, Lahaina. Whale watching, Molokini snorkel, sunset cruise. A portion of each ticket is donated to Pacific Whale Foundation. 879-8811.

SPINNER DOLPHINS

**PARAGON SAILING CHARTERS** -The *Paragon* is a 47' Catamaran. A new sailing enterprise on Maui, they tell us their ship was built in California and is presently the only one of its kind featuring new construction techniques and a hull designed paired with a state-of-the-art rotating carbon fiber mast.

The Cabin House offers sunshade and shelter and trampolines offer outside lounging. They sail from Maalaea Harbor offering a morning snorkel-sail that begins with a 7:30 am departure and a light breakfast as you head toward Molokini. Snorkel gear is provided and they also have small size gear for children. A fresh hot/cold water shower is located on top of the swim ladder for refreshment after your swim and before a buffet lunch.

The 5 hour trip is $59, special rates for children under 12. The afternoon 3 hour trip includes snorkeling followed by a speed run in excess of 20 knots. Write RR2, Box 43, Kula, HI 96790. Reservations (808) 244-2087. Fax (808) 878-3933.

**THE PRIDE OF MAUI ★** - 65' catamaran featuring a large indoor cabin and outdoor sundecks. They offer daily departures at 8 am from the Maalaea Harbor for morning dives at two destinations, an option not offered by most other companies. They stop at Molokini and "Turtle Town" (Pu'u Ola'i). Depending on weather conditions, snorkel location may be Olowalu or Coral Gardens. Whale watching available.

Handicap access, freshwater showers, glass bottom viewing, slide, underwater video cameras available for rent. Built with a 149 passenger maximum, they limit their trips to 110 guests. The morning snorkel includes breakfast, lunch, beverages, equipment. Adults are $65, Juniors (13-18 years) $45, Children 4-12 years $30. Scuba certified $25 for one tank, $45 for two tanks. Snuba available for an additional $40.

They also offer an afternoon snorkel trip 2:30-6:30 to Molokini or Coral Gardens. Adults $32, children 5-12 $16. Lunch is optional. A third option is their two hour evening sunset sail and whale watching during that season as well. $54 couple, $28 adult, $18 Junior, $12 child. Includes sunset cocktails, appetizers, soda and prize giveaways. Additional beer, wine, Mai Tais and Margaritas available for small fee. (808) 875-0955.

**PRINCESS CRUISES** - *Lahaina Princess* (whale watching and dinner cruises) and the *Maui Princess,* a 150 passenger 118' excursion ferry which provides service between Maui and Moloka'i daily. $25 adults one way. $50 round trip. Children half price. 1-800-833-5800, (808) 661-8397

**RAINBOW CHASER** - A 46 x 26 foot catamaran with 24 passenger maximum per trip. Snorkel locations are chosen daily by the captain and crew depending o weather conditions. Destinations for snorkeling might include Honolua Bay and rainbow Bay, Coral Gardnes & Olowalu, and on the island of Lana'i, Shark Fin Rock and Manele Bay. Adult only sunset celebration is a 2 1/2 hour sale $69. 677-2270

**SAIL HAWAII** - *Fiesta* and *Mele Kai*, 37' and 40' sailing yachts. 6 people max. 5 hr. Molokini snorkel or sunset sail. Trip destinations flexible. Departs from Kihei Cove Park, 879-2201.

**SEA ESCAPE** - You-drive zodiac raft and boat rentals, 879-3721.

**SCOTCH MIST CHARTERS** - *Scotch Mist II* is a Santa Cruz 50' sailboat, which takes 23 people max on West Maui 1/2 day snorkel/sail, or champagne sunset sail, or private charters. Whale watching seasonal. Departs Lahaina harbor. 661-0386

**SENTINEL YACHT CHARTERS** - 42' sloop, max. 6 passengers for snorkeling, whale watching, overnight inter-island charters. Two night minimum $850. Food is $30 per day per person or bring your own. 661-8110.

*SILENT LADY* - Handsome 64' custom built whaling schooner. Previously only available as private charter, but now offer public five hour snorkel sail to Molokini, seasonal whale watching. 242-6499 or 661-1118

**SPIRIT OF WINDJAMMER** - *Spirit of Windjammer*, 70' 3-masted schooner offers 2-hour Maui coastline dinner cruise ($65), seasonal whale watching ($36.50), (Lunch cruise offered during non-whale season $36.50) takes large groups. Children under 12 years are half price. Departs Lahaina. 667-8600.

**TERALANI** - A 53 foot, catamaran, recently redesigned and refurbished. They offer daily excursions that include picnic/snorkel sails and sunset cruises. They also have a monthly Vintner Sail. Seasonal whale watches. Picnic snorkel sail $65, Sunset sail $39, Champagne Dinner Cruise includes a champagne toast to the days end, then return to the beach for a relaxing dining experience at an ocean-side Kaanapali Restaurant. (This is the way to do a dinner cruise!) Monthly Vintner Sail $39-$59 features wines from Northern California, Oregon and Washington. Vintner Representatives accompany the sail. 970 Limahana Place, Suite 204, Lahaina, HI 96761. 661-0011 ext. 134. (Formerly Anuenue.)

**TRILOGY EXCURSIONS** ★ - *Trilogy I*, 64' trimaran, *Trilogy II*, catamaran, and *Trilogy III*, a 51' catamaran, do full-day snorkel/picnic/sightseeing tours to Lana'i. A definite best bet. *Trilogy IV*, a 44' trimaran, does 1/2-day sail/snorkel to Molokini. Departs Lahaina Harbor. $139 all day Lana'i, $75 half day to Molokini. 661-4743 or 1-800-874-2666. See review following excursion listings.

*WHALE MIST* - 36' monohull sailboat. Whale watch/sunset cruise, snorkeling trip goes to area off shore from Launiupoko Beach. Also has parasail/snorkel combo for $68. Departs from Lahaina Harbor. 667-2833, 1-800-366-6478.

**WHITE WING CHARTERS** - *White Wing*, 35' trimaran, 6-hr. sail, snorkel, and fishing. Available for overnight and inter-island excursions, max. 6. Departs Kihei Boat Ramp. 579-8705.

*ZIP-PURR* - 47' catamaran, departs Kaanapali Beach. Built by owner/captain Mike Turkington. Morning snorkel sail along Maui's coastline. Sunset cocktail sail, seasonal whale watch, private charters. 667-2299

## BLUE WATER ADVENTURES!

While Molokini continues to be a much touted snorkeling spot, those seeking something a little different should check with *Blue Water Rafting* ★ about their *South Coast of Maui* trip. The area past Makena is geologically one of Maui's youngest and the coastline is only accessible by foot. However, a trip on the zodiac raft will get you up close to see the beautiful and unusual scenic wonders of Mother Nature. Natural lava arches, pinnacles and caves are explored with the picturesque slopes of Haleakala providing a magnificent backdrop. Our chosen day for the expedition proved to be an exhilarating wet one! The ocean conditions were somewhat rougher than desired, but our hearty group agreed to push forward. With spray from the ocean drenching us, one of the more witty members of our group donned his snorkel and mask which worked admirably at keeping the water out of his eyes! The scenic vistas were fabulous and the boat was able to maneuver through one of the arches and up close to the cliffs which appeared to have been sculpted by a fine artisan. A brief stop for some mid-morning nourishment and a snorkel at La Perouse before returning to Kihei. This is a trip that can be best experienced only in this manner. To the best of our knowledge, only Blue Water Rafting is offering this trip. The 5 1/2 hour trip includes snorkeling with sea turtles. So, for an unusual and exciting Maui adventure, check this one out! Cost is $99, children 5 years 10% discount. Phone 879-7238.

## A TRIP TO LANA'I

It appears that the Coon family knows not to mess with a good thing. The morning boat trip over to Lana'i still starts earlier than most would like, but once underway with warm (yes, still homemade by the Coons) cinnamon rolls and a mug (the ceramic kind, no styrofoam here!) of hot chocolate or coffee, it seems all worth the effort. Don't forget to bring the camera! Two boats bring about 60 guests to the island each day for snorkeling, sun and fun at Manele Bay. With the additional number of people on the trip, they have now divided the snorkeling and Lana'i island tour in two. One boat load walks to the beach and snorkels, tours the island and eats. The beginning snorkelers are carefully instructed in a tide pool before entering the ocean. The other group tours the island, snorkels and then eats at a second "sitting." If you would prefer, you can also skip the tour of Lana'i City and snorkel even longer. The chicken is cooked on the grill by the ship's captain and served on china-type plates. Accompanied by a delicious stir-fry, fresh rolls and Mrs. Coon still isn't giving out the secret ingredients for her salad dressing to anyone. The eating area is a series of picnic tables covered with heavy naugahyde cloth and shaded by an awning. Plans are for a new BBQ and pavilion during the next couple of years. The meal is followed up by some sweet Lana'i pineapple, but save room for homemade ice cream on the sail back home. Leftovers from the meal are deposited nearby and you might catch a glimpse of the "wild" cats dining side by side with the "wild" turkeys! Unfortunately the Coon brothers don't get out of the office much any more to skipper the boats, but our Captain was energetic and really seemed to enjoy the trip as much as the rest of us. This is a very special outing and well worth considering as a part of your island holiday. Phone (808) 661-4743 or 1-800-874-2666. $125 - $139 for this all day trip (7 a.m. to 4 p.m.). Includes continental breakfast, lunch and snorkel gear. Trilogy now also offers a video of a sample day on their cruise to Lana'i and Molokini. Although it shows probably a little more aquatic life than you'd actually see on a given day, it certainly is a good way to sample before you buy.

**CLUB LANA'I**

This is a one-of-a-kind operation on Maui and the closest thing the visitor will find to Gilligan's Island. It began operating in 1987, closed and then reopened in the spring of 1992. Things have changed little since they opened originally. The current going rate is $79 for a trip that departs the Lahaina Harbor at 7:30 a.m. and returns at 3:30 p.m. Enroute there is a continental breakfast of donuts and coffee and, once you arrive, it is a full day of choosing whatever you want to do. There is biking and kayaking and plenty of time to do nothing at all but enjoy a hammock. The craftmaking in the little huts is gone, apparently they have a more casual theme where they demonstrate coconut cutting or the like along the beach for guests to watch. Lunch is a very heavy meal which includes mahi, beef and chicken, served with macaroni salad, coleslaw, green salad, bean salad and marinated vegetables. They serve iced tea and punch and they still serve their special Lana'i Tais at the bar. Most of the guests take advantage of the coastline snorkeling, which leaves plenty of room for the remaining guests to pick out the perfect hammock. Keep an eye out for Mary Ann and the professor! (871-1144)

# SUNSET - DINNER CRUISES

Sunset cruises are quite popular on Maui with their free flowing Mai Tai's, congenial passengers, tropical nights, and Hawaiian music which entertains while the boat cruises along the coastline. Dinner aboard one of these catamarans or other vessels is most definitely not haute cuisine, but usually quite satisfactory, especially after a few Mai Tai's. The live entertainment varies from amateur to very good to none at all. (We have a personal dislike for those cruises that get the slightly intoxicated guests up to don Hawaiian attire and perform the hula.) Dinner cruises typically last about two hours and prices run $70 and up. Samples of dinners listed may vary. All in all, don't expect the kind of food quality you'd experience at one of the islands land-locked restaurants. The sunset cruises have replaced most of the dinner cruises and are a pleasant way to enjoy a Maui evening and run in the $40 range.

The *Lahaina Princess*, with its table seating and formally dressed crew, is probably what most would envision a dinner cruise to be. But many are an evening of precariously balancing a paper plate on your lap.

The *Manutea* would be a good dinner cruise one to do if you've been to Maui before, it's more like the Old Lahaina Luau of Dinner Cruises - more subtle, peaceful and relaxing and more romantic, while still being more casual.

The *Navatek II* offers the smoothest ride and with an on board kitchen, the most freshly prepared food.

The true sailing enthusiast should investigate the *First Class*. *Sea Sails* was fun and the *Kaulana* pleasant and comfortable. It's a really tough choice, but there is a quality trip for any visitor.

*First Class* ★- (Sunset cruise) Alihilani Yacht Charters offers an evening sailing cruise aboard the yacht *First Class*, operated by Ross Scott, Jr., of the Sunshine Helicopter family. This is a quality operation with a brand new, very sleek yacht. The boat is a 65' MacGregor with a beautiful, plush interior! Beverages only served, mai tai's, soft drinks and beer. Departs 2 pm, $35 adult/$25 child. This cruise is a real find to a very specific kind of traveler. It's nothing like any of the other visitor boats, this is a yacht! It should appeal to people who REALLY like to sail and for the more adventurous types. The boat glides through the water making a very fast, but smooth ride! If you enjoy sailing, don't miss this one. 667-7733, FAX (808) 667-0314.

*Gemini* - (Sunset Cruise) This 64' glass bottom catamaran, used by the Westin and departs from Kaanapali Beach. They offer a sunset sail nightly from 5-6:30 pm which includes pupus, beer and wine and non-alcoholic beverages. The tradewinds cruise costs $30 for adults and $15 for children. This is a glass bottom catamaran with long tables and padded seats inside which are accessible for dining. The wide passage area is all around, accessible steps and ample headroom make it a comfortable boat. There are viewports on each side (glass bottom windows) and big side windows. No music or entertainment, just a good chance to wind down on a pleasant sail. The Gemini also does snorkel sails. (661-2591)

*Kaulana* - (Sunset cruise) Departing from the Lahaina Harbor this vessel offers good seating areas on benches on top and on the sides. Musical entertainment included Hawaiian and contemporary music, and there was room to dance. Pupus included fresh vegetables and dip, cheese cubes served with crackers and bread sticks, fruit platter, chicken wings and drumsticks (spicy!) and onion rings with dip. Open bar. The cruise went up past Kaanapali. Daily 5 - 7 p.m. (times change with the seasons). $36 adults, $19 kids ages 4-16 years. An enjoyable, comfortable trip aboard this 65' power catamaran. Operated by the folks that run Club Lana'i. (871-1144)

ORCHIDS

***King Kamehameha*** - (Sunset cruise) A small catamaran, maximum 15 people, with limited padded seating around the wheel area and a big net out front. You may have recognized it by the big picture of King Kamehameha on the sail! Owner Tom Warren has been sailing on various charter boats since 1969 and purchased the *Kamehameha* in 1977. This is the most inexpensive of all the sunset cruises, only $24, and again is one of those BYOB. Snacks include Maui Chips. A good option if you're seeking a smaller boat. Unfortunately, we were not able to do a personal review of this one. (661-4522)

***Lahaina Princess*** - (Dinner cruise) This boat is operated by the same company as the *Maui Princess*, which runs a Maui to Moloka'i shuttle. This cruise begins a little later than the others. The tables below are set up for dinner and this reviewer found it a bit confining. It can be compared with a dining car on a train, tables on both sides and nice big windows to look out. The live music below proved a bit too loud for the small area. On the top deck there was an open air cocktail lounge which was pleasant, but the space filled quickly and if you didn't arrive first, there was only standing room. Their aim seems to be to take the place of the Stardancer, but, on a much smaller boat this is extremely difficult to do. The burgundy of the crew's bow ties and cummerbunds matched the burgundy linen napkins on pink linen tablecloths add a bit of elegance. The food was served with silverware and china, although the drinks were in plastic cups. While guests were up above, salads were set out along with a tray of baked potato toppings. Dinner was a choice of prime rib or teriyaki chicken and both were very good. They were accompanied by a baked potato and carrots. Cheesecake with raspberry puree made for a tasty dessert. The dancing area could accommodate about three couples maximum. They certainly get an "E" for effort in elegance, but its pretty hard to compete with its predecessor. We can recommend it, but not very enthusiastically. Adults $59, children $35. Departs Lahaina Harbor. From O'ahu toll free 1-800-533-6899, from Mainland toll free 1-800-833-5800, local reservations and information 661-8397.

*Manutea* - (Dinner cruise) A 50' catamaran, which appears to be very casual and sporty, actually transforms into a rather romantic dining atmosphere. Dinner is served on wooden "table for two" trays which are brought out and placed on plastic bench-type seats. So each couple has a private table in-between. The boat cuts the engine to make for a very quiet and peaceful dining experience. The music is mellow/easy listening guitar and no dancing, polynesian revue or hula show here. The food was exceptionally good for a dinner cruise - catered by the Maui Marriott and served with china and linen napkins. Very like an airplane dinner in First Class - a cut above coach and passable in a good restaurant, but still a bit like "airline" (boat) food. A choice of entrees includes New York Strip with Madeira Sauce, boneless breast of chicken teriyaki, Mahi Mahi or a vegetarian Pasta Primavera. Accompanying the meal was rice pilaf, sauteed vegetables and dessert was cherry pie. Wine and champagne are included for dinner. Seating is a maximum of 30 which also adds to the romantic ambience. Price is $59 per person. Children are not encouraged as evidenced by the single price. Currently operating four days per week. (879-4485)

*Navatek II* This is a new state-of-the art vessel offers contemporary live music to entertain guests while they dine on a full course dinner. Since this vessel has a full commercial kitchen, chances are your evening meal will be served hot! Maui has been lacking a quality ocean dining experience and a good meal in a first class setting, and this is as good as it gets. The dinner cruise is a rather expensive $78 adult, $39 for children 5-12 years plus harbor fee and tax, but you're paying for the uniqueness of this particular vessel. Departure is 5:30 (times may change seasonally) and returns at 7:30 pm. They serve a glass of non-alcoholic bunch as you board and then alcoholic drinks are served after you are out of the harbor. The dining area is nice with tall, wide windows on both sides making it easy to see out either side even across other people and tables. The brass backed chairs have a deco-ish design. The glasses were plastic, but looked like real glass and the duraline china had a quality look and feel about it as did the linen napkins. There was a plate of veggies and potato chips as you were seated and a side dish of dip and salsa. The Caesar salad topped with crab was, in fact, excellent. Three entrees include chicken breast with macadamia nut sauce, catch of the day, or sirloin beef au jus with accompaniments of a pasta selection, rice pilaf, and steamed vegetables. Dessert is a simple and refreshing macadamia nut ice cream with fresh fruit. The service was good, subtle and subdued and very efficient. This boat even has a Cruise Director which adds to the feel that you are on a small ship rather than a big boat. The experience was first class, with good food, but again not quite up to restaurant standards. The technology of this new vessel promises an incredibly smooth ride, another wonderful benefit. If you can live with the price and figure you are paying the price of new technology, it is a pleasant evening out. (808) 661-8787. See additional description under SEA EXCURSIONS.

*Scotch Mist* - (Sunset Cruise) 23 passenger max. Trips daily. Beer, wine, soft drinks, no pupus, just chips. $35 adults, $25 for kids under age 12. Departs Lahaina Harbor. (661-0386)

*Silent Lady* - (Sunset cruise) 64' custom built whaling schooner available for sunset cruises only by private charter. R. R. Box 379, Suite 410, Wailuku, HI 96793. (242-6499 or 661-1118)

*Spirit of Windjammer* - (Dinner cruise) A 70' three masted schooner with table seating, open bar. Hawaiian music provided by Ernie Paiva and his brother Damian with a couple of hula dancers (who also serve as your waitresses) finishing the evening with a hula. The crew was nice and the seating up top was comfortable. The food was very good, as dinner cruises go, with an all you can eat, but not a buffet. You simply ask for seconds or thirds and it will be served to you. Dinner began with a basket of rolls followed by a salad topped with mandarin oranges and almonds. The prime rib was surprisingly tender and the chicken breast cooked on the barbecue grill proved very good with lemon butter sauce, accompanied by rice, fresh fruit and a dessert of cheesecake topped with a flavored fruit sauce. Two complimentary drinks are included. An open bar is available as well. The lunch cruise is an all-you-can-eat lighter fare with chicken as the only entree and brownies for dessert, and served with a glass of champagne. They also plan a continental breakfast cruise during whale season. The food is prepared in the on-board galley, which makes the food a step above. The dinner cruise at $65, children 3-12 years half price, is a little higher than most, and we could recommend it a little more heartily if the price were more in line. It rates a marginal thumbs up. The lunch cruise runs $36.50 adults, and again half price for kids 3-12 years. (661-8600).

*Teralani* -- A 53', catamaran, recently redesigned and refurbished offers sunset sail $39, champagne dinner cruise ($65) includes a champagne toast to the days end, then returns to the beach for a relaxing dining experience at an ocean-side Kaanapali Restaurant. (This is the way to do a dinner cruise!) Monthly Vintner Sail $39-$59 features wines from Northern California, Oregon and Washington. Vintner Representatives accompany the sail. 970 Limahana Place, Suite 204, Lahaina, HI 96761. 661-5500.

*Wailea Kai* - (Dinner cruise) Departs Maalaea Harbor four nights a week 5 - 7 p.m. This 75 passenger, 65' catamaran which is nice, but seems better suited for an afternoon swimming/snorkeling excursion rather than a dinner cruise. Only one section is somewhat "inside" with a few seats and the buffet and bar along with the two musicians can be found there. There is a semblance of a very small dance floor. This cruise was a bit less expensive than the others. The buffet is an all you can eat, but the food was, at best, mediocre and served on sectional trays which didn't add to the enjoyment. This reviewer would have preferred quality over quantity. A hula dancer entertained and following dinner the same dancer preformed a Tahitian number. Then the guests decked out in hula finery to perform a dance number (they loose a few points from us for this!). A very basic, typical dinner cruise with nothing in particular to recommend. (879-4485) $50 adults and children.

*Whale Mist* - (Sunset cruise) 36' monohull sailboat, max. 18, whale watch/sunset cruise, $35 adults/$25 children. Sunset cruise. Depart Lahaina, slip #6. Combo trip includes sunset or three hour snorkel and a parasail during non-whale season. (667-2833)

*Whale II* - (Sunset cruise) Operated by Pacific Whale Foundation the trip is two hours, with departure time varying seasonally. No entertainment, but a naturalist/researcher is on board to provide information on whales and other marine life. They serve veggie and meat platters with deli meats, cheese and crackers. Guests were provided with paper "trays" which worked well for holding the pupus. The drinks included coke, beer, wine or mai tais. Price is $30 adults, $24.50 children. Departs Lahaina Harbor. (879-8811)

***Zip-purr*** - (Sunset Cocktail Cruise) Owned by Julie and Mike "Turk" Turkington. He built this 47' sailboat and is its captain. While it can carry a maximum of 49 passengers, they prefer to book no more than 35 - 40. They do their cruise daily and ALWAYS sail, even though it can be a bit rough, which should appeal to the sporty types. There is no entertainment. The buffet is more snack foods offering Maui chips, pretzels, peanuts along with cheese and crackers, manapua and sliced chicken $35. A nice padded seating area inside and benches at various spots. They pick up at three different areas, depending on the weather. At Hula Grill at Whalers Village, the Sheraton and in front of the Maui Eldorado's Beach Club at Kaanapali Beach. They put out a line to troll and while on board a fish was hooked, which was exciting. Earlier in the day they had caught a large fish and cut it up right there and everyone sampled very fresh sashimi. The crew was pleasant, but didn't spend any time getting to know the guests. (667-2299)

# SUBMARINES

The ***Atlantis Submarine*** has a two hour tour that runs $79 for the deluxe trip (which includes photos, guidebook, a diver that shows sea creatures and a lecture by Earth Trust, an environmental organization). The regular version runs $59 adults for their regular trip. Children $29-$39. The fully submersible submarine is an 80 ton, 65 foot touring vessel that accommodates 46 passengers. They operate eight dives daily beginning at their Pioneer Inn shop, which also affords you plenty of time to shop for logo items from polo shirts, to visors, beach bottles, jelly beans or beach towels. There is a short boat ride to reach the submarine and quite surprisingly it suddenly emerges out of the middle of the depths of the Pacific. Then you step across from the tender and load onto the submarine. The seats are lined up on both sides in front of 1/2 a porthole. The submarine submerges about 100 feet. The area is a little close, but the temperature is kept cool and comfortable. There are plenty of fish, and fish cards at each station help you identify them.

HUMUHUMUNUKUNUKUAPUAA

Rocks and coral formations resemble an environ that is somehow extra-terrestrial. Upon completion of the trip you have one more chance to do a little shopping! 667-2224.

The *Nautilus* is a semi-submersible, meaning it only partially submerges, so at any time you can go up on deck for some fresh air, or if you feel a bit claustrophobic. It departs at least 5 times a day, times change seasonally. The bottom is six feet below the surface and they cruise around about 5 feet from the ocean floor off of Puamana. The total trip is an hour, but once you are underway, you begin viewing, while the Atlantis does require some coordinating to get from the dock to the submarine. The Nautilus seats are more comfortable, allowing for a bit more room to walk around. One of the crew scuba dives out to hold up interesting items for the guests to view. $45 adults, $22.50 children 5 - 12 years, children 5 and under are free. 667-7647. (Special note: They are always running specials so check the prices and the local papers!)

The *Atlantis* does have clearer viewing since they are down so deep and have infra-red lights. The *Nautilus* makes use of sunlight, which at times can be bright, other times cause the water to be hazy. In brief, the *Nautilus* is more like dry snorkeling and the *Atlantis* more like dry scuba diving. The *Atlantis* has a smoother, plane-like motion, while the *Nautilus* is more like a helicopter, bobbing and rocking as it maneuvers. The *Atlantis* does provide the submarine experience, but you pay the price. The *Nautilus* is $45, quite a bit less expensive than the *Atlantis*. If you are a snorkeler, you won't see much on the *Nautilus* than you would if you were swimming. But if you are unable or unwilling to get wet, then one of these trips may be an option to consider.

## WHALE WATCHING

Every year beginning November 15 and continuing until April 15 (official whale season), the humpback whales arrive in the warm waters off the Hawaiian Islands for breeding, and their own sort of vacation! The sighting of a whale can be an awesome and memorable experience with the humpbacks, small as whales go, measuring some 40 - 50 feet and weighing in at 30 tons.

The panoramic vistas as you drive over the Pali and down the beachfront road to Lahaina afford some excellent opportunities to catch sight of one of these splendid marine mammals. However, PLEASE pull off the road and enjoy the view. Many accidents are caused by distracted drivers.

For an even closer view, there are plenty of boat trips. Although most every boat operator does whale watching tours in season, you may want to check into the one sponsored by Pacific Whale Foundation 879-8811. As they are a research group, they are very well informed and knowledgeable about the whales. You can report your sightings by calling Whale Watch Hotline at 879-8811.

## DEEP SEA FISHING

Deep sea fishing off Maui is among the finest in the world and no licenses are required for either trolling or bottom fishing. All gear is provided. Fish that might be lured to your bait include the Pacific Blue, Black or Striped Marlin (Au) weighing up to 2,000 lbs., Yellow Fin Tuna (Ahi) up to 300 lbs., Jack Crevalle (Ulua) to 100 lbs., Bonita-Skipjack (Aku) to 40 lbs., Dolphin Fish (Mahi) to 90 lbs., Waho (Ono) to 90 lbs., Mackerel (Opelu), Amerjack (Kahala), Grey Snapper (Uku), Red Snapper (Onaga), and Pink Snapper (Opakapaka).

Boats generally offer half or full-day fishing trips on a share or private basis with prices running from $60 - $110 shared or $325 - $550 private for a half day (4 hr.), and $85 - $135 shared or $500 - $800 private for a full-day (8 hr). Some are willing to take non-fishing passengers along at half price. Most boats take 4 - 6 on a shared basis, however several can handle larger groups.

*FINDING A CHARTER:* Your local activity center may be able to direct you to a particular boat that they favor, or you could go down to the docks at the Lahaina or Maalaea Harbor in the afternoon and browse around. There are also a number of activity booths at both harbors that can be consulted. When reserving a spot, be aware that some boats will give full refunds only if 48-hour notice is given for cancellation.

If you want to take children fishing, many have restrictions for those under age 12. If you are a serious fisherman, you might consider entering one of the numerous tournaments. Some charters offer tournament packages. Following are a list of just some of the charter fishing boats. While not a scientific study, Finest Kind and Exact (both operated by Finest Kind, Inc.) have managed to be consistently mentioned in the local newspaper for regular catches of very large fish.

*A WORD OF ADVICE:* The young man had a grin that reached from ear to ear as he stood on the pier in Maalaea, holding up his small ahi for a snapshot of his big catch. The surprise came when the deck hand returned it to the ice chest and continued on with his work. The family all stood, unsure what to do. It appeared that the fish was to remain on board, while the family had envisioned a nice fresh fish dinner. Finally one family member spoke up and a very unhappy crew member sliced a small filet, tossed it into a sack and handed it to the young man.

Unlike sportsfishing charters in some parts of the country, the fish caught on board generally remain the property of the boat. The pay to captain and crew is minimal and it is the selling of the boat's catch that subsidizes their income. Many vacationers booking a fishing excursion are unaware of this fact. There seems to be no written law for how fishing charters in Hawaii handle this, at least everyone we talked to had different answers. Many of the brochures lead one to believe that you keep your fish, and they neglect to mention that it may be only a filet of fish. Occasionally you may find a head boat which operates under a different sort of guideline. In this situation, you pay for your bait, gear, and boat time and then keep the fish. In any case, be sure you check when you book your trip about just what and how much fish will be yours to keep. If the person at the activity desk assures you that you keep your catch, don't leave it there, also check with the captain when you board. Communication is the key word and have a mahi mahi day!

## LAHAINA HARBOR

ABSOLUTE SPORTSFISHING
*Absolute*, 31' Bertram sportfisher
8 hour charter, $625
Direct 669-1449
Westin Maui 661-2591

AERIAL SPORTSFISHING
CHARTERS
PO Box 831, Lahaina, HI 96761
667-9089
Aeril II and III

FINEST KIND, INC.
*Exact*, 31' Bertram
*Finest Kind*, 37' Merritt
Reel Hooker, 35' Bertram
PO Box 10481, Lahaina, HI 96761
Maximum 6 people, 661-0338

HINATEA SPORTFISHING
*Hinatea*, 41' Hatteras
PO Box 5375, Lahaina, HI 96761
Full day only 667-7548
Slip #27-Lahaina Harbor

ISLANDER II SPORTSFISHING
36' Uniflite, 667-6625

LAHAINA CHARTERS
*Broadbill*, 36' Harcraft (max 6)
*Judy Ann II*, 43' Delta (max 8)
*Alohilani*, 28' Topaz (max 6)
PO Box 12, Lahaina, HI 96761
maximum 6 people, 667-6672

LUCKEY STRIKE CHARTERS
*Luckey Strike II*, 45' Delta
*Kanoa*, 31' Uniflite, max. 6
Full sunshade that can
accommodate up to 27 people.
Also does bottom fishing.
PO Box 1502, Lahaina, HI 96767
661-4606

## MAALAEA HARBOR

CAROL ANN CHARTERS
33' Bertram, max. 6
877-2181

OCEAN ACTIVITIES CENTER
Departs Maalaea, 879-4485

RASCAL
SPORTFISHING CHARTERS
*Rascal*, Bertram 31', 874-8633
Slip #13 Maalaea

# *SMALL BOAT SAILING*

Small boat sailing is available at a number of locations with rentals, usually the 14', sometimes 16' and 18', Hobie Cat. Lasers are also available. Typical rental prices are $35 - $50 per hour, and lessons are available. Most of the resorts have sailing centers with rental facilities on the beaches. There is also one at the Kealia Center in Kihei.

**FOR MORE INFORMATION ON RENTALS CONTACT:**

*West Maui Sailing School.* Also windsurfing, kayak and snorkel equipment. (667-5545)

*Sea Sails* - Located at the Kaanapali Beach Hotel Beach Shack. (661-5222)

*Maui Sailing Center* - Kealia Beach Plaza (879-5935)

*Ocean Activities Center* - Stouffer Wailea Beach Resort. (Direct: 879-9969, Resort: 879-4900)

# *WINDSURFING*

Windsurfing is a sport that is increasing in popularity astronomically. *Hookipa Beach Park* on Maui is one of the best windsurfing sites in the world. This is due to the consistently ideal wind and surf conditions, however, this is definitely NOT the spot for beginners. For the novice, boardsailing beginner group lessons run $40 - 60 an hour, which generally involves instruction on a dry land simulator before you get wet with easy to use beginners equipment. Equipment and/or lessons are available from the following:

*Hawaiian Island Windsurfing* - Pro shop, sales, service, rentals and instruction. Three hour group (only 3 students) beginner lessons or advanced water start $59. Private instruction $48 for 75 minutes or three lessons $124. Toll free 1-800-231-6958 or 871-4981.

*Hawaiian Sailboarding Techniques* - 444 Hana Hwy., Kahului. Alan Cadiz and his staff of professional instructors offer a full range of small group and private lessons for beginner or expert. They specialize in one-on-one instruction tailored to each person's ability, travel schedule, budget and goals. 871-5423.

*Hi-Tech Surf Equipment* - Sales and Rentals. Kahului 877-2111, Paia 579-9293.

*Kaanapali Windsurfing School* - Beginner lesson 1 1/2 hour $45, 1 1/2 hour plus 1 hour supervised practice $55. Rental equipment per hour $20, $45 for three hours, $110 for 10 hours. Three locations: Whalers Village, Sheraton Black Rock (may be closed during Sheraton renovation), Royal Lahaina. 667-1964

*Maui Magic Windsurfing School* - Group & private lessons for all levels. Beginning group 2 1/2 hours $59; private 1 1/4 hours $69; three day lesson package $165, also rental equipment via their Maui Windsurf Co. 520 Keolani Place, Kahului (877-4816), 1-800-872-0999 U.S. and Canada.

*Maui Sailing Center* - Two hour class begins first on land and then proceeds into the water. Lesson reservations necessary. Rental equipment available. Kealia Beach Center, 101 N. Kihei Rd. (879-5935).

*Ocean Activities Center* - At Stouffer Wailea Beach Resort (879-9969)

*Second Wind* - Has exclusive rights on Maui for sales of Angulo custom boards, clothing and Angulo rentals. Proshop rental, used and new sales. Private lessons $45 per hour, $49 for two hour class. Also exclusive sales for GEM and LOGO SZ. (808-877-7467).

*Wind Surfari* - Offers packages which include accommodations, rental car, windsurfing equipment and excursions with Alan Cadiz's Hawaiian Sailboarding. 1-800-736-6284 or (808-871-7766).

*Windsurfing West Maui* - Provides windsurfing lessons and equipment. 397 Dairy Rd. in Kahului. (808-871-8733) or 1-800-358-2377.

Some resorts offer their guests free clinics. Rental by the hour can get expensive at $20 per hour and $40 - $65 per four hours. A better rate is $45 for all day. If you are interested in renting equipment for longer periods or desire more advanced equipment try:

*Hawaiian Island Windsurfing* - (871-4981), 460 Dairy Road, Kahului.

*Sailboards Maui* - (871-7954) 397 Dairy Road, Kahului. Typical costs are $45 for full day, $250 for 7 days. Deposit may be required. Rental includes board, universal mast, boom, sail and soft car rack. Credit card deposit required. You pay for broken, lost or stolen equipment.

# SURFING

Honolua Bay is one of the best surfing spots in Hawaii, and undoubtedly the best on Maui, with waves up to 15 feet on a good winter day and perfect tubes. A spectacular vantage point is on the cliffs above the bay. In the summer this bay is calm and, as it is a Marine Reserve, offers excellent snorkeling.

Also in this area is Punalau Beach (just past Honolua) and Honokeana Bay off Ka'eleki'i Point (just north of the Alaeloa residential area). In the Lahaina area there are breaks north and south of the harbor and periodically good waves at Awalua Beach (mile marker 16).

On the north shore Hookipa Beach Park, Kanaha Beach, and Baldwin all have good surfing at times. In the Hana area there is Hamoa Beach. There are a couple of good spots in Maalaea Bay and at Kalama Beach Park.

Conditions change daily, and even from morning to afternoon around the island. Check with local board rental outlets for current daily conditions.

***Hawaiian Sailboarding Techniques*** - (871-5423) 444 Hana Hwy., Kahului. HST goes "surf-surfari" to wherever the best place for learning happens to be that particular day. Small groups and private instruction available for beginners wanting to cruise the waves their first time out, also intermediate and advanced lessons. Current rates for longboard surfing class is $60 each two hours, three people per class maximum, includes surfboard.

***Indian Summer Surf Shop*** - Lahaina. Surfboard rentals. Can recommend instructors. Also have kayak rentals. 661-3053 and 661-3794.

***Maui Surfing School*** - (875-0625) Andrea Thomas originated the "Learn to Surf in One Lesson" and has taught thousands of people between the ages of 3 and 70. She's been teaching on Maui since 1980 and offers private and group lessons specializing in the beginner and coward. Board rentals available. Lahaina Harbor.

Books of interest available at local bookstores: *Surfing Hawaii* by Bank Wright, 96 pages softcover $5.95. *Surfer's Guide to Hawaii* (Hawaii Gets all the Breaks!) by Greg Ambrose. 156 pp, $10.95. *Essential Surfing Guide* by George Orbelian $9.95. *Surfing Huge Waves with Ease* by Fred Van Dyle, 5 pp., $7.95.

## BODY SURFING

Mokuleia (Slaughterhouse) Beach has the best body surfing especially in the winter. This is not a place for weak swimmers or the inexperienced when the surf is up, it can be downright dangerous. The high surf after a Kona storm brings fair body surfing conditions, better boogieboarding, to some beaches on leeward Maui.

## JET SKIIS

Thrillcraft activities, which include parasailing and jetskiing have been banned during whale season. Currently the "open season" for participating in jet skiing recreation is May 16th until December 14th.

Currently the only jet ski operation, ***Pacific Jet Ski Rental***, is at the south end of Kaanapali Beach at Hanakaoo Beach Park. They have two and three passenger wave runners. Rental prices are per jet ski, not per person. 1/2 hr. $47, 1 hr. $67, two people max. 1/2 hr. $57, 1 hr. $78, three people max. (667-2066)

# PARASAILING

The parasail "season" on Maui is May 16 - December 14th due to the restrictions during whale season. For those that aren't familiar with this aquatic adventure, parasailing is a skyward adventure where you are hooked to a parachute and attached to a tow line behind a boat and soon are floating high in the air with a bird's eye view of Maui. The flight lasts 8 to 10 minutes which may be either too long or too short for some! Prices $32.50-$50. Some charge for an "observer" (friend) to go along, others allow them free.

*Lahaina Para-sail* - 1 and 2 seaters. Observers welcome. 661-4887.
*Parasail Kaanapali* - Departs from Mala Wharf. $50 for 10 minute ride. (669-6555).
*UFO Parasail* - Observers can go for $15. Departs in front of Whalers Village. They use a new wrinkle, a self-contained "winch" boat. You get started standing on the boat and as your parachute fills, you are simply reeled out 200 - 400 feet. When it comes time to descend, you're simply reeled back in. $32.50 early bird, $37.50 standard, $48 deluxe.
*West Maui Para-sail* - Lahaina Harbor, Slip #15. Uses "Skyrider," a three passenger aerial recliner as well as harness flights. Dry take-off and landing. Boat departs every 30 minutes with six passengers. They use a 700 ft. line so passengers are 400 feet above the water. Call for reservations. (661-4060).

# WATERSKIING - Currently there are no water skiing operators on Maui.

# KAYAKS

*Indian Summer Surf Shop* - Lahaina. Has kayak rentals, per 24 hours, $20 single, $30 double. (661-3053 or 661-3794)
*Kaanapali Windsurfing School* - Kayak Rentals 1 hour $10 one person, $25 two persons. Kayak tour 9 am-noon, $65 includes snorkel, lunch, pickup in Kaanapali or Lahaina. 667-1964.
*Kayak Rentals and Tours* - Has guided 1 1/2 to 5 hour trips $39-$85. All day tours $125. Kayak rentals $20-$60 per day includes car rack, paddles, life vests. Weekly rates available. They also rent chairs, coolers, snorkel gear and boogie boards. Located at the Kihei Rainbow Mall, 2439 Kihei Rd. 875-4848 and also at 505 Front Street in Lahaina 661-8400.
*Maui Kayaks* - The novice or experienced paddler can join a half or full day guided trip along the Kihei coast. Hourly rentals also available. Contact: Bill Pray, Maui Kayaks, 50 Waiohuli St., Kihei, Maui 96753. (874-3536)
*Maui Sailing School* - Has kayaks. Kealia Beach Center. (879-5935)
*South Pacific Kayaks* - Has two locations, Rainbow Mall at 2439 S. Kihei Rd. (875-4848) and Lahaina at 505 Front Street (661-8400) They offer introductory paddle and snorkel excursions with short paddling distances combined with offshore snorkeling 2 1/2-3 hrs. $55, departures from both West and South Maui. Their Explorer Kayak Snorkel Tour travels a greater distance with more paddling, and includes sandwiches, snacks and beverages, $79 for the 5 hour trip. Also available are single and double kayaks as well as car racks, life vests, snorkel bear, boogie boards and more.

# LAND ACTIVITIES

## *LAND TOURS*

Land excursions on Maui are centered upon two major attractions, Hana and the O'heo Valley, and Haleakala Crater. Lesser attractions are trips to the Iao Valley or around West Maui. You can do all of this by car (refer to the WHERE TO STAY - WHAT TO SEE chapter), however, with a tour you can sit back and enjoy the scenery while a professional guide discourses on the history, flora, fauna and geography of the area. The single most important item on any tour is a good guide/driver and, unfortunately, the luck of the draw prevails here.

Another, somewhat expensive option, is a personalized custom tour. A local resident will join you in your car for a tour of whatever or wherever you choose. You can do the driving or sign on your guide with your rental car company to do the driving. This may allow you the opportunity to linger at those places you enjoy the most, without following the pace of a group. Your guide may also be able to take you to locations the tour vans don't include. *Local Guides of Maui* recommends a 24 hour advance reservation, 877-4042 or from the mainland 1-800-228-6284.

Driving to Hana and back requires a full day and can be very grueling, so this is one trip we recommend you consider taking a tour. A Haleakala Crater tour spans 5-6 hours and can be enjoyed at sunrise (3 am departure), mid day or sunset. The West Maui and Iao Valley trips are half-day ventures. Only vans travel the road to Hana, however, large buses as well as vans are available for other trips. (Be aware that some vans are not air conditioned.) Prices are competitive and those listed here are correct at time of publication. Some trips include the cost of meals, others do not.

Also available are one day tours to the outer islands. The day begins with an early morning departure to the Big Island, O'ahu or Kaua'i. Some excursions provide a guided ground tour, others offer a rental car to explore the island on your own.

*Arthur's Limo Service* - They provide tours to Haleakala and Hana in their luxury limousine or their new super stretch van. $69.50 per hour (2 hour minimum) plus tax and tip. (871-5555 or 1-800-345-4667 inter-island or from Mainland.)

*Ekahi Tours* - Tours of Hana $75 adult, $55 child, Sunrise Haleakala $55 adult, $45 child via van. Other areas charter for $65 per hour. (877-9775)

*Grayline* - Provides a variety of large bus and small van tours Haleakala, Hana and other scenic and visitor areas. Hana trip is $75.50 and includes lunch at Hana Ranch. Prices depend on pick up and length of trip. (877-5507)

*Local Guides of Maui* - Discover Maui in your car with an island resident as your guide. Explore the destinations of your choice. $174 for two people, 6 hours, (plus gas) or $210 for 2 people, 8 hours, including lunch (plus gas). (877-4042) (1-800-228-6284).

*Maui Art Tours* - See listing under Art Tours

*Polynesian Adventure* - Haleakala Sunrise $51.04 adult, $35.46 child, includes tax. Haleakala Day trip $54.17 adults, $36.46 child. Hana $67.71 adult, $44.27 child. They also offer one day trips to Kaua'i, The Big Island of Hawaii, or O'ahu. These one day, one island trips run $165.63 adults, $160.42 child. (877-4242 or 1-800-622-3011 from Mainland U.S.)

*Roberts-Hawaii Tours* - Offers land tours in their big air conditioned buses or vans. They depart to all scenic areas from Kahului, Kihei, Wailea, and the West Maui Hotels. Prices vary depending on tour. (871-6226 or 1-800-767-7551 U.S. Mainland)

*Sugar Cane Train* - The Sugar Cane Train makes six round trips daily with one way fares for adults $8, two way is $13. Children 3-12 years are $4 one way, $6 round trip. Their main depot is located just outside of Lahaina, turn at the Pizza Hut sign. The Kaanapali Station is located across the highway from the resort area. The free Kaanapali trolley picks up at the Whalers Village and drops off at this station. The Puukolii boarding platform and parking lot is located on the Kapalua side of Kaanapali. They offer several package options which includes a self-guided tour of historic landmarks and admission into the Baldwin Home, Wo Hing Temple, the Chinese Museum and the Carthaginian II for $13.50 adults or combine the train ride with the Omni Experience Theater $16.50 adults $8.25 children. If you plan on a full day round trip excursion, buy your return tickets early as they often sell out quickly. (661-0089 has recorded information. Reservations are needed for 12 or more person phone 661-0080.)

*Temptation Tours* ★ - If you'd really like to pamper yourself, then enjoy the luxury of a tour by these folks. Working in conjunction with Blue Hawaiian Helicopter they provide a unique option to either Hana or Upcountry Maui. The "Hana Sky-trek" is their ultimate package that begins with a helicopter trip to Hana, a tour of the town and Waianapanapa in a luxury van, an elegant lunch and then drive back to Kahului. Or the reverse trip where you drive to Hana and fly back $199. The Hana picnic is a round trip in their 6-8 passenger limo van for $110, or have substitute lunch at the Hotel Hana Maui for $139. One upcountry tour begins with an ascent up Haleakala in their luxury limo-van, to the eucalyptus forests an pastureland of the Thompson Ranch. An hour and a half to enjoy the view on horseback is followed by elegant lunch at the Silver Cloud Ranch. There is also time to enjoy the jacuzzi with a view. Price is $159 plus tax for the all day excursion. Another upcountry adventure offers a trip to the summit of Haleakala, a tour through the Kula area with lunch at Makawao with a chance to visit the galleries there. A trip to the Hawaii Protea Cooperative, the major supplier of fresh cut proteas and other tropical exotic flowers to the US mainland before returning to Kahului area. This 8 hour trip runs $115 plus tax. Also available is a Haleakala Sunrise Tour. (877-8888)

*Trans Hawaiian* - A day trip to Hana $77.10 adult, $71.19 senior, $57.80 children under 12 tax included, departs 7 am and returns about 5:30, lunch at Hana Ranch included. Haleakala sunrise or morning tour $46.90 adult, $41.65 senior, $33.05 child under 12. Japanese language phone number 871-7940, or 877-7308 from the U.S. Mainland phone 1-800-533-8765.

# ART CLASSES AND ART TOURS

**Maui Art Tours** offers visitors an opportunity to visit the homes and studios of three or four of Maui's fine artists, meet them and watch them work. This unique day-long adventure is provided in a luxury air-conditioned car and includes a gourmet lunch. Cost is $200 per person. P.O. Box 1058, Makawao, HI 96768. (808-572-3453)

**Hui Noeau Arts Center** near Makawao offers art classes (808-572-6560) and the soon-to-open **Art School of Kapalua** (808-665-0007) will also offer art education.

# THEATER AND THE ARTS

With the opening of the new **Maui Arts and Cultural Center** in May 1994, new doors of opportunity have opened for theater on Maui. However, clearly Maui has a history of strong community support and involvement of many long-time performing arts organizations. The individual theater groups will now be performing at the cultural center as well as their individual locations. The center's ticket office is (808) 242-SHOW. Check the local paper for listings of performances of the **Maui Symphony**. They periodically have 40-minute concerts for children as a part of their Youth Education Performances. There are also performances by the **Valley Isle Symphony Orchestra**.

**Maui Onstage** produces dramatic performances at the Historic Iao Theatre in Wailuku. This is another non-profit organization which has been in existence in varying forms since the 1920's. Then, it was two different theatre groups, the Maui Players and Little Theatre of Maui. In 1931, these two organizations joined forces to create the Maui Community Theatre. The Maui Onstage's production schedule continued through the 1930's but was interrupted during the war years and not rekindled until 1971 when a group of Maui citizens reactivated the organization. In 1972, Maui OnStage took up residency in the Maui County Fair Grounds' Territorial Building, until the fall of 1984 when it, along with all the props, costumes, light and sound equipment, was destroyed by fire. They reorganized and moved to their present home in the historic Iao Theatre on Market Street. Phone 242-6969.

The **Baldwin Theatre Guild** offers five shows yearly. Generally they do a musical, a children's show, a dramatic presentation, a summer musical and an annual revue. The group was formed in 1964 when interested students expressed a desire to organize and perform theatrical productions. Over the years, hundreds of students have been a part of this organization. Workshops are held at various times during the month and in addition to the performances, the guild also offers its members involvement in other social activities, such as dances or picnics. For information on performances phone 242-5821 or check the local paper.

**Theatre Theatre Maui** (TTM) is a nonprofit organization founded in 1991 whose mission is to offer all West Side residents the opportunity to experience a full spectrum of live, hands-on theatre. During the first three years they offered one adult and three children productions. TTM offers summer workshops which culminate in an annual production, usually held in July. They are partially funded through grants from the County of Maui and private foundations. 244-8760.

The *Maui Academy of Performing Arts* clearly has it all when it comes to entertainment. An educational and performing arts organization for youth and adults, the Academy is located in its own building on the grounds of the Maui Arts and Cultural Center. They offer community theatre performances, special events, dance, drama and voice classes, and special drama and dance workshops for youth and adults. Open to the public. For more information on any of the current programs or daily schedule, call the Academy offices at 244-8760.

# BIKE TOURS

The Hawaiian Islands offer an endless array of spectacular air, sea and land tours, but only on Maui is there an experience quite like the bicycle ride down from the 10,000 foot summit of the world's largest dormant volcano. Bob Kiger, better known as Cruiser Bob, was the originator of the Haleakala downhill. (Cruiser Bob is reported to have made 96 individual bike runs himself to thoroughly test all aspects of the route before the first paying customers attempted the trip).

Each tour company differs slightly in its adaptation of the trip, but the principal is the same, to provide the ultimate in biking experiences. For the very early riser (3 am) you can see the sunrise from the crater before biking down. Later morning expeditions are available as well. Your day will begin with a van pickup at your hotel for a narrated trip to the Haleakala summit along with safety information for the trip down. The temperature at the summit can be as much as 30 degrees cooler than sea level, so appropriate wear would include a sweater or sweatshirt. General requirements are for riders to wear closed-toe rubber soled shoes, sun glasses or prescription lenses (not all helmets have visors), a height requirement of 5 feet is requested by some and no pregnant women are allowed on the trip. Bikers must also sign an acknowledgement of risk and safety consideration form. For the descent, riders are equipped with windbreaker jackets, gloves, helmets and specially designed bicycles with heavy duty brakes.

A leader will escort you down the mountain curves with the van providing a rear escort. Somewhere along the way will be a meal break. Some tours provide picnics, others include a sit-down meal at the lodge in Kula or elsewhere. Actual biking time will run about 3 hours for the 38-mile downhill trip. The additional time, about 5 hours for the entire trip, is spent commuting to the summit, meals, and the trip from the volcano's base back to your hotel. Prices for the various tours are competitive and reservations should be made in advance.

We biked down with Maui Downhill and opted for the "late" 7 am trip. We found them to be very careful, courteous and professional. Unfortunately they don't have control over the weather and the day we chose was clear on the drive up, fogged in and misty at the summit and a torrential downpour for more than half of the 38 miles down. Due to the weather, we couldn't enjoy much of the scenery going down, but probably wouldn't have had much time to gander as it is important to keep your eyes on the road! The leader set a fairly slow pace, not much of a thrill for the biking speedster, but safe and comfortable for most. At any time we were invited to hop in the van, but ours was a hearty group and after a stop to gear up in rain slickers, we all continued on. Our leader also advised that if the weather posed any kind of risk, he would load us on the van. The weather broke just long enough for us to enjoy sandwiches or salads at the Sunrise Market and to bask in the sun's momentary warmth. In radio contact with the group just ahead of us we were advised that the rain promised to await us just a little farther down the volcanic slope. As predicted, the drizzle continued as we biked down through the cowboy town of Makawao. We arrived in Paia only a little wetter for the experience.

***Chris's Bike Adventures*** - (871-2453) They offer some unusual bike expeditions and interesting options. These bike rides take riders around upcountry, not just down it. They use 21 speed mountain bikes and provide helmets, gloves and weather gear. Bike at your own pace. The Haleakala Wine Trek travels to the Tedeschi Winery and beyond to the remote lava fields above La Perouse. Includes crater viewing and short hike, a continental breakfast and picnic lunch. Sunrise, full day and half day trips available. $95 full day, $69 half day. The Wilder Side of Haleakala is the above trip plus some biking along the wilder, remote backside of Haleakala. Forty miles, all day $110. The Coastal Challenge is a trip along the remote northwest coastal (Kahakuloa) side of Maui. Includes off-road biking, half $55 or full day $89. Or combine a boat trip with a bike exploration of either Lana'i or Moloka'i $160 for the full day adventures. Chris hopes to soon offer three day and one week "inn to inn" trips - bike, hike and kayak with bed and breakfast overnights.

***Cruiser Bob's*** - (579-8444) (1-800-654-7717 U.S. Mainland or inter-island.) This is the original Haleakala downhill trip. You can choose between an early (3 am) sunrise trek or the regular excursion for $120 includes tax. Both include continental breakfast and sit down lunch at Kula Lodge.

***Maui Downhill*** - (871-2155 or 1-800-535-2453 in U.S.) Transportation from your hotel/condo. The sunrise trek includes a brunch after the ride. The day trip begins with a continental breakfast at the base yard before departure up the mountain and a picnic lunch at the Sunrise Market (and protea gardens) on the way down. Sunrise is $110 including tax. Must be over 12 years. Continental breakfast/brunch in Kula.

***Maui Mountain Cruisers*** - (572-0195 or 1-800-232-MAUI in U.S.) Pickup provided from Kaanapali, Lahaina, Kahului and Kihei. Sunrise cruise includes a continental breakfast and brunch in Kula. Midday trip includes a continental breakfast and later lunch in Kula. $110 plus tax.

***Mountain Riders*** - (242-9739) Offer sunrise Haleakala $105, winery tour with crater view $89.

# *BIKE RENTALS*

Bikes and mopeds are an ambitious and fun way to get around the resort areas, although you can rent a car for less than a moped. Available by the hour, day or week, they can be rented at several convenient locations.

*A & B Rentals* - 3481 Honoapiilani Hwy. at the ABC store in Honokowai. They have mopeds, bicycles, beach equipment, surfing and boogie boards, snorkel gear, fishing poles and underwater cameras. Mopeds run $28 for 24 hours, bikes $10 day or $50 week. (669-0027)

*Fun Bike Rentals* - 193 Lahainaluna Rd., Lahaina. In addition to bikes they have boogie boards, beach chairs and even baby strollers! 24 hours $15-50 depends on the type of bike. Weekly rate $45-$300. Delivery available. (661-3053 or 661-3794)

*Kukui Activity Center* - Kukui Activity Center (875-1151 or 874-6798) 1819 S. Kihei Rd. Bicycles $12 day, $65 week. Mopeds $27.50 - 24 hours.

*Maui Mountain Bike Adventures* - Honokowai. Pick-up and delivery included in price. Bicycles Day $19, 3-6 days $15 per day. Week $69.

*South Maui Bicycles* - (874-0068) 1913 S. Kihei Rd.

*South Pacific Kayaks* - Located at 505 Front Street offers 4 hours FREE bike rentals or $5 additional 4 hours or $55 per week. No gimmick! The bicycle has a canvas basket that carries a promotional for 505 shops. What a deal!!

# GOLF

Maui's golf courses have set for themselves a high standard of excellence. Not only do they provide some very challenging play, but they also offer distractingly beautiful scenery. Most of the major resorts offer golf packages and for the avid player, this may be an economical plan.

For more golf information see the ORDERING section at the back of the book for *The Hawaii Golf Guide*.

*Sunseeker Golf Schools* at Kaanapali offers golf instruction for the beginner or the advanced. Each Saturday at 10 am they conduct a free golf clinic. They offer private lessons ($35 for 45 minutes; couple $50), playing lessons (one person $100, couple $150) and special one day classes by arrangement ($175). Phone 667-7111.

## KAANAPALI

The Kaanapali Resort offers two championship courses. Green fees are $100 for 18 holes, cart included for resort guests. Green fee for non-guests $110. Twilight rate $60. Residents $50. Located at the Southern entrance to the Kaanapali resort area is the Royal Kaanapali driving range. (661-3691). Discounts during low season May 1 - November 30.

*The North Course* has been attracting celebrities since its inaugural when Bing Crosby played in the opening of the first nine holes. Designed by Robert Trent Jones, this 6,305 yard course places heavy emphasis on putting skills. At par 72, it is rated 70 for men and 71.4 for women.

**The South Course** first opened in 1970 as an executive course and was reopened in 1977 as a regular championship course after revisions by golf architect Arthur Snyder. At 6,205 yards and par 72 it requires accuracy as opposed to distance, with narrower fairways and more small, hilly greens than the North Course. As an added distraction, the Sugar Cane Train passes by along the 4th hole.

## KAPALUA

The Kapalua Resort features the Bay Course, Village Course and Plantation Course. Green fee for the Bay and Village Course: $110 includes cart; registered guests of Kapalua Bay Hotel & Villas, The Kapalua Villas and The Ritz-Carlton, Kapalua $70; Maui resident $45; Twilight play 2 p.m. - 6 p.m. $60. Green Fee for the Planation Course: Standard $120, registered guests of Kapalua Bay Hotel & Villas, The Kapalua Villas and The Ritz-Carlton, Kapalua $75. Twilight play $65. Replay on any of the courses, the same day is $25. Club and shoe rentals available. Practice range is open 8 am - 4:30 pm, $5 per bucket. Guests may reserve tee-off times up to 7 days in advance. Non-guest reservations 2 days in advance. Special golf events include the GTE Hawaiian Tel Hall of Fame Championship (May), Kapalua Clambake (June), Lincoln-Mercury Kapalua International (Nov.) In 1992 Golf Digest ranked The Plantation Course #4 among resort courses in the U.S. and all three courses are listed in Hawaii's top 7. One day golf school includes instruction and lunch at the Kapalua Grill and Bar $200. Also available are video golf lessons, to analyze your swing, and playing lessons are offered. Daily clinics are available Mon.-Fri. 4-5 pm and each day work on a specific aspect of your golf game. Clinic fee is $20. (669-8044)

**The Bay Course**, under the design of Arnold Palmer, opened in late 1975, sprawls from sea level to the mountain's edge. This beautiful and scenic par 72, 6,600 yard course has a distinctly Hawaiian flavor. With its picturesque signature hole extending onto an ocean-framed black lava peninsula, The Bay Course is an excellent example of a premier resort golf course.

**The Village Course** opened in 1981 and sweeps inland along the pineapple fields and statuesque pine trees. At par 71 and 6,632 yards designer Arnold Palmer and course architect Ed Seay are reported to have given this course a European flavor. Resembling the mountainous countryside of Scotland, this course is reputed to be the most difficult and demanding in Hawaii and one of the most challenging in the world.

**The Plantation Course** opened in May 1991, designed by Coore and Crenshaw of Austin, Texas and home of the Lincoln-Mercury Kapalua International held each November. The 18-hole championship is situated on 240 acres north of the Village Course. The 7,263 yard course has a par 73. The course features expansive greens, deep valleys and expansive fairways.

## KIHEI

**The Silversword Golf Course**, a non-resort course, offers a 6,800 yard par 71, 18-hole course located off Piilani Highway near Lipoa Street. Green fees, which are currently $67, includes shared cart. Rider (non-golfer) $15. Golf Special April thru December 18 $55. Twi-lite (no guarantee on 18 holes, after 1 pm; must be in barn by 6 pm) $42, Twi-light April thru December 18 $40. Rental clubs $22, rental shoes $10. Driving range offers a bucket of balls for $3, open 8 am-9 pm, except Sat. and Sunday nights, Thursdays noon - 9 pm. (874-0777)

## MAKENA

Makena offers two courses. The original 18-hole course opened at the same time as the Maui Prince resort in 1991-1992. The second 18 holes opened November 1993. It is a bit confusing, but what they have done is taken the original 18 holes, divided it in two, and added an additional 9 holes to each course. Both courses were designed by Robert Trent Jones. Resort guests $80; twilight $60 (after 2 pm). All others $110; twilight $70. Fees include cart. (879-3344)

*The South Course* is a more classic open style course that leads to the ocean. The large cactus which abound in this area were imported to feed the cattle which were once ranched in this area. This course is 6168 yards with a par 72.

*The North Course* is a narrower course that travels along the slopes of Haleakala offering some spectacular panoramic views. The North Course has a par 72 and is 6151 yards.

## WAILEA

The Wailea resort offers the challenging Orange, Blue and Gold Courses. Current green fees for the Blue or Gold course is $125; for resort guests $80. Carts included. The Orange Course is closed through the end of 1994 for extensive reconfiguration. Maui residents receive kamaaina rates at the Wailea courses. Golf Pro Don Pasquariello offers morning clinics $25, afternoon golf school 2-4 hrs. $100-200, or private lessons at $40 per half hour. (875-5111, fax 875-5114)

**The Orange Course** originally opened in 1978, designed by Arthur Jack Snyder. It is scheduled to re-open the end of 1994 after being transformed into a tropical paradise by Robert Trent Jones Jr. Designed to be enjoyable for golfers of all caliber, the course will also boast spectacular scenery. Definitely worth packing a camera along with your clubs. Call for current prices and information.

**The Blue Course** is par 72 and 6,758 yards from the championship tees. A creation of Arthur Jack Snyder, it opened in 1972. Four lakes and 74 bunkers provided added hazards along with the exceptional scenery. The 16th hole is especially lovely with numerous people stopping to snap a picture from this magnificent vantage point.

**The Gold Course**, is par 72, stretching 7,070 yards across the lower slopes of Haleakala, affording exquisite views of the Pacific Ocean. Designed by golf course architect Robert Trent Jones Jr., it opened January 1, 1994. Jones design concept was to create a classical, rugged style of golf - that takes advantage of the natural sloping terrain.

## WAIKAPU

**Waikapu Sandalwood Golf Course** is a par 72, 5,162-6,469 yard course, depending on your choice of the blue, white or red tee-offs. Mandatory cart fee is included. Non-player is extra charge. Regular $75, Rental clubs $30, rental shoes $5, Hawaii resident $35. (242-4653 or fax 242-8089)

**The Grand Waikapu Resort Country** offers a special Golf and Spa package. A $200 all inclusive package offers a round of 18-holes plus use of the golf course spa facilities. The ladies facilities includ jacuzzi, sauna, showers, TV, lounge and juice bar. The men's feature a furo (Japanese bath) sauna, showers, lounge area. What a way to finish your day of golf! Guests of the Grand Wailea or Four Seasons receive additional discounts. Spa hours daily from 11 am - 7:30 pm.

In 1949 Frank Lloyd Wright designed a luxury home for the Windfohr family in Fort Worth, Texas which was never built. In 1952, Raul Bailleres, a Cabinet Member of the Mexican Government, had the Windfohr design modified for a site on an Acapulco cliffside. Unfortunately, the Dailleres' suffered the loss of their son, and the project was abandoned. In 1957, Marilyn Monroe and her husband Arthur Miller, requested Mr. Wright design a country home for them in Connecticut. Mr. Wright, being fond of this particular design, again modified the original for Monroe and Miller. However, once again the project was abandoned. The design was ultimately purchased for Taliesen West by the Grand Waikapu Country Club owners and has been constructed as the Grand Waikapu Country Club. The Grand Waikapu Country Club clubhouse is tri-level with two thirds of the building underground, and measuring a total of 74,788 square feet. 244-7888.

## SPRECKELSVILLE

**The Maui Country Club** is a private course which invites visitors to play on Mondays. Call on Sunday after 9 am to schedule Monday tee times. It originally opened in 1925. The front 9 holes have a par 37 as do the back nine. Greens fees are $45 cart included for 9 or 18 holes. (877-0616)

## PUKALANI

*Pukalani Country Club and Golf Course* is nestled on 160 acres along the slopes of Haleakala and affords a tremendous panoramic view of Central Maui and the ocean from every hole. Designed by Bob Baldock, the first 9 holes opened in 1980. Nine additional holes have been added making a par 72, 6,692 yard course. Greens fees are $55 for 18 holes, $30 for nine holes, cart included. (572-1314)

## WAILUKU

*The Waiehu Municipal Course*, which is north of Wailuku, opened with nine holes in 1929 and an additional 9 holes were added later. The mens course is 5330 yards par 72, women's course is 5511 yards par 71. Green fees are $25 weekdays and $30 weekends and holidays. A cart is optional. $7.50 per person for 9 holes, $15 per person for 18 holes. Phone 243-7400 or pro shop 244-5934.

## MINIATURE GOLF

The only course is the 18-holes on the roof of the *Embassy Suites Resort* at Kaanapali from 9 am-9 pm daily. Adults $5; $3 ages 12 & under. 661-2000.

## THE ISLAND OF LANA'I

Two 18-hole courses are offered on Lana'i, *The Challenge at Manele* and *The Experience at Koele* courses. Non-guests are charged $150 for either course. A day package which includes round-trip transportation via the Expeditions out of Lahaina, green fees and Lana'i island transfers are available, 808-565-7227. Trilogy Excursions 1-800-874-2666 or 808-661-4743 also offers a golf surf & turf package at the Challenge at Manele course. See the Lana'i section of this guide for course descriptions.

# TENNIS

Tennis facilities abound on Maui. Many condos and major hotels offer tennis facilities, also, there are quite a few very well kept public courts. They are, of course, most popular during early morning and early evening hours.

## PUBLIC COURTS

*Hana* - Hana Ball Park, one double lighted court.
*Kahului* - Maui Community College (Kaahumanu and Wakea Ave.) has 2 unlighted courts. Kahului Community Center (Onehee and Uhu St.) has two lighted courts. The Kahului War Memorial Complex has four lighted courts, located at Kaahumanu and Kanaloa Ave. 243-7389.
*Wailuku* - Wellspark has 7 lighted courts, S. Market St. and Wells St. 243-7389.
*Kihei* - Kalama Park has four lighted courts. Six unlighted courts in park fronting Maui Sunset condos. 879-4364.
*Lahaina* - Lahaina Civic Center has five lighted courts and there are four lighted courts at Malu-ulu-olele Park. 661-4685.
*Makawao* - Eddie Tam Memorial Center has two lighted courts. 572-8122.
*Pukalani* - Pukalani Community Center has two lighted courts, located across from the Pukalani Shopping Center. 572-8122.

## PRIVATE COURTS WITH FACILITIES OPEN TO PUBLIC

*Hyatt Regency*, Kaanapali. Six unlighted courts. 7 am-6 pm. (661-1234 ext. 3174). Fee charged for guests or non-guests.
*Kapalua Bay Hotel*, Kapalua. Offers the Tennis Garden with 10 courts, 4 are lighted. Tennis attire required at all times. Guests $10 per day, non-guest $12. They also have a Village Tennis Center with 10 courts, 5 are lighted. Charge is $10 per day for resort guests, non-guests $12. Phone 665-0112. (669-5677)
*Makena Tennis Club*, 5415 Makena Alanui, Makena Resort. Two lighted courts. Resort guests $14 per hour, non-guests $18. (879-8777)
*Maui Marriott Resort*, Kaanapali. Guests $6 pr hour and non-guests $7.50 per hour can play on five courts, three are lighted. 7 am-6 pm. (667-1200)
*Royal Lahaina*, Kaanapali. Has the 2nd largest facility on the island with 11 courts, 6 lighted and 1 stadium court. Guests are free, non-guest $$6.50 all day. They have complete facilities including private lessons, ball machine, clinics, pro shop. (661-3611).
*Sheraton Maui Hotel*, Kaanapali. Renovating beginning January 1995.
*Wailea Tennis Club*, Wailea. Has fourteen courts, 3 lighted, 3 grass. Grass for Wailea Resort Guests $20 per hour, non-guests $25 per hour. Regular courts same price for one hour, ore time if space is available at no extra charge. They offer summer workshops for kids. (879-1958)


## RESORT COURTS RESTRICTED TO GUESTS

Hale Kamaole, Hotel Hana Maui, Kaanapali Alii, Kaanapali Plantation, Kaanapali Shores, Kaanapali Royal, Kahana Villa, Kamaole Sands, Kihei Akahi, Kihei Alii Kai, Kihei Bay Surf, Kuleana, Maalaea Surf, Mahana, Makena Surf, Maui Hill, Maui Islander, Maui Lu Resort, Maui Vista, Papakea, Puamana, Royal Kahana, Sands of Kahana, Shores of Maui, The Whaler.

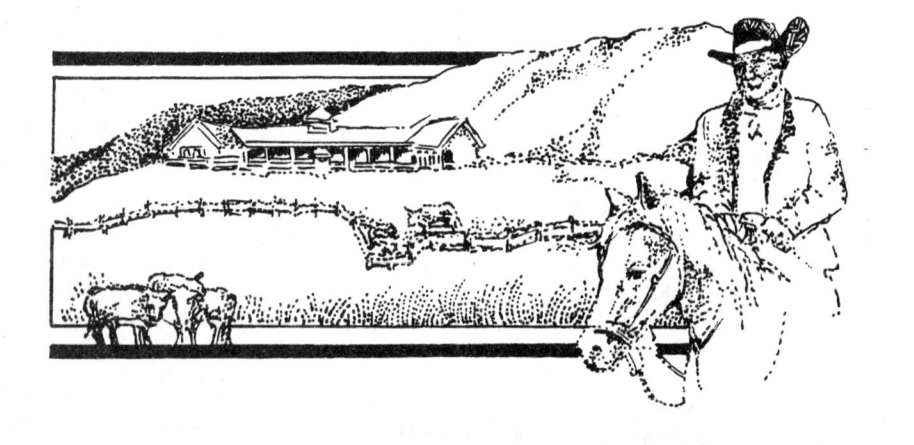

# HORSEBACK RIDING

Historically, the first six horses arrived on the islands in 1803 from Baja California. These wild mustangs were named "Lio" by the Hawaiians, which means "open eyes wide in terror." They roamed and multiplied along the volcanic slopes of Maui and the Big Island until they numbered 11,000. They adjusted quickly to the rough terrain and had a reputation for terrific stamina. Today these ponies, also known as Kanaka ponies or Mauna Loa ponies, are all but extinct with fewer than a dozen purebreds still in existence.

Lush waterfalls, pineapple fields stretching up the mountain's flanks, cane fields, kukui nut forests and Haleakala's huge crater are all environments that can be enjoyed on horseback. Beginner, intermediate or experienced rides lasting from 1-2 hours or up to three days. Most stables have age restrictions.

***Adventures on Horseback*** - A 5 hour waterfall ride outside Haiku is $170 per person and includes lunch and gear. Enjoy the cliffs of North Maui, the slopes of Haleakala, the old Hana Hwy, rainforest streams and secluded waterfalls. breakfast, picnic lunch, and swimming. Maximum 6 riders. (242-7445) Office phone (572-6211).

***Charley's Trailride and Pack Trips*** - Features overnight trips to Haleakala with guide arranging cabin and supplies. Rates for 4 - 6 people are $250 per person, food provided; $225 per person if you bring your own. Rates for 2 - 3 people are $300 each with food provided. $75 non-refundable deposit unless rain cancels trip. Write Charles Aki, c/o Kaupo Store, Hana, Maui, HI 96713. (248-8209)

***Hotel Hana Maui*** - Guided trail rides around the 4,500 acre working cattle ranch on open range, shoreline, rain forest and mountains. $50, private 2 hour ride. $27.50 for one hour guest ride. Maximum 10 riders. (248-8211)

***Holo Lio Stables*** - Located near the Makena Beach. Shoreline, sunset or moonlight rides $20 - $35. All day trips $65, bring your own food as none is provided. George, the owner and your guide, so his prices are lower. (879-1085)

***Makena Stables*** - 7299 South Makena Rd., rides are along the King's Hwy. and La Perouse Bay. Guided tours $95 for three hour, $135 for six hour. They also go to Ulupalakua Ranch and the Tedeschi Winery. The 3 hour ride has a 2000 ft. elevation, the 6 hour ride has a 3500 ft. elevation climb. (879-0244)

***Ohe'o Stables*** - 3 hour ride with snacks and soda $85. 6-8 people Ride is in Haleakala National Park. 667-2222.

***Pony Express Tours*** - Has trips into Haleakala Crater, weather permitting, Mon. - Fri. The Kapalaoa Cabin Tour is 12 miles and 8 hours starting at the craters rim for $140 plus tax per person and includes lunch. Half day trips $120. One hour rides $35, two hour $60. (667-2202 and 667-2200)

*Rainbow Ranch* - Follow Honoapiilani Hwy. 11 miles north of Lahaina, entrance near exit for Napili. They tour the mountain area. Trips are available for beginning, intermediate or advanced riders in either English or Western style. $75-$150. (669-4991)

*Seahorse Ranch* - 8 persons or less, 3 hour with lunch $95, Highway 340 Waiehu at 10 mile marker. 244-9852.

*Thompson Riding Stables* - Located on Thompson Rd. in Kula, the Thompson Ranch was established in 1902. Located at the 3,700 foot elevation they offer trail and crater tours, sunset and picnic rides. 1 1/2 hours $35. Child can ride with adult. 2 hour picnic $50, 2 hour sunset without food $45. (878-1910 or 244-7412.)

# *POLO*

You'll find Polo events every Sunday in Makawao with the Maui Polo Club at 377 Haleakala Highway. Gates open at noon, game starts at 1 pm, Tickets are $3 for adults, under age 12 are free. Call Emiliano at 572-4915 for more information. Weekly activities may include a practice, a club game or events such as the Oskie Rice Memorial Polo Cup or the Annual Rocking Kapalaia Ranch Cup.

# *HIKING*

Maui offers many excellent hiking opportunities for the experienced hiker, or for a family outing. Comprehensive hiking information is available from several excellent references (see ORDERING INFORMATION). Craig Chisholm and his wife Eila were the pioneers in the field of Hawaiian hiking information with the 1975 release of *Hawaiian Hiking Trails*, and it has been continually updated. They recently began work on separate island hiking guides and have added *Kaua'i Hiking Trails* with *Maui Hiking Trails* and *Big Island Hiking Trails* still underway. The Chisholm's books are attractively done with beautiful color illustrations in the frontpiece, and easy to follow U.S. Geological maps for each of the hikes. Throughout the text are black and white photos. These books are thoroughly researched by the authors and very accurate. The *Hawaiian Hiking Trails* book has six trails described for Maui.

The first edition of Robert Smith's *Hiking Maui* was published in September 1977. He continues to update his book every couple of years. He also has books for the other islands. The books are compact in size with a color cover and a scattering of black and white photographs. The Maui edition covers 27 trails.

Kathy Morey writes *Maui Trails* which is published by Wilderness Press. There are over 50 trails listed in the hiking table of contents, however, some are really more walks than hikes. It has plenty of easy-to-use maps. Also guides for Oahu, Kauai and The Big Island.

We're not going to even attempt to cover the many hiking trails available on Maui, but would like to share with you several guided hiking experiences which we have enjoyed.

Among the most incredible adventures to be experienced on Maui is one, or more, of the fifty hikes your personal guide ***Ken Schmitt*** has available. These hikes, for 2 - 6 people only, can encompass waterfalls and pools, ridges with panoramic views, rock formations, spectacular redwood forests (yes, there are!), the incomparable Haleakala Crater or ancient structures found in East Maui.

Arriving on Maui in 1979, Ken has spent much of that time living, exploring and subsisting out-of-doors and experiencing the "Natural Energy" of this island. This soft spoken man offers a wealth of detailed knowledge on the legends, flora, fauna and geography of Maui's many diverse areas. Ken has traversed the island nearly 400 times and established his fifty day hikes after considerable exploration. His favorites are the 8 and 12 mile crater hikes which he says offer a unique, incredible beauty and magic, unlike anywhere else in the world. The early Hawaiians considered Haleakala to be the vortex of one of the strongest natural power points on earth.

The hikes are tailored to the desires and capabilities of the individual or group and run 1/2 or full day (5 - 12 hours). They range from very easy for the inexperienced to fairly rugged. Included in the $60 - $90 fee (children are less) are waterproof day packs, picnic lunch, specially designed Japanese fishing slippers, wild fruit and, of course, the incredible knowledge of Ken. Also available are overnight or longer hikes by special arrangement. Ken can be reached at 879-5270, or by writing ***Ken Schmitt***, P.O. Box 330969, Kahului, Maui, HI 96733.

Here is a sample of the excursions you might be able to enjoy!

## CENTRAL MAUI
A wonderful hike for the family is to the ***Twin Falls*** area on Maui's windward side. This easy trail passes through cattle pastures and then woodlands to three beautiful and tantalizingly cool fresh water pools formed by cascading falls. It is a popular hike enjoyed by many visitors and island residents over an easy to follow trail described in many hiking books. However, it is Ken that makes the trip special. The average hiker would pass right over the fallen kukui nuts while Ken stops, opens several and passes them around for a taste test, warning that they have a strong laxative quality! A small purple blossom, an herbal blood purifier, is sampled, a juicy guava and liliokoi are tasted and the base of one of the pandanus blossoms with a caramel-like flavor can be chewed on. Passing over a canal, Ken explains the history of the early cane industry when this series of amazing water channels was built one day short of a two year deadline.

## UPCOUNTRY MAUI
Polipoli is ideally situated on the leeward slopes of Haleakala. Cool crisp mountain air provides a temperate climate for hiking and the trails are suitable for the entire family. Since the weather can be cool, warm attire and rain apparel should be included in your day or night pack, however, the clouds often clear and treat visitors to a sunny and very mild afternoon. To get to the turn off, go just past the Kula Botanical Gardens and turn on Waipoli Rd., or go 3/10 mile past the junction of Hwy 37 and Hwy 277. Follow the paved, steep and windy road approximately 3.9 miles (about 26 minutes), then continue another 5.8 miles or about 20 minutes on gravel road. The last 1/4 mile is downhill and especially rutted and can be very muddy and too slippery for anything but a four wheel drive

when wet. *WARNING: Rental car agencies are not responsible for damage done to cars that travel this road.* We have found it passable in a car with high clearance if the road has been recently graded and is dry. Once you reach the park there is a graveled parking area and a grassy camping area. Two BBQ's and the luxury of a flush toilet in a small outhouse. Drinking water is available. Trail options include a .8 mile trek to the Redwood Forest, a 6 mile Haleakala Trail, 4.8 mile loop trail, 1.0 mile to the cave shelter and 1.5 miles to the Plum trail.

The 4.8 mile loop is a very easy trail and with frequent snack stops, even our three year old was able to make it the entire distance. There is an array of lush foliage and plums may be ripe if you arrive during June and July. The clouds can roll quickly in, causing it to be pleasant and warm one minute and cool the next, as well as creating some interesting lighting effects amongst the trees. The cave shelter, is a bit of a disappointment. It is a shallow cavern and reaching it meant a descent down a steep incline of loose gravel that was too difficult for our young ones. The Eucalyptus was especially fragrant as the fallen leaves crunched underneath our tennis shoes. An area along the trail that had been freshly rutted by wild boars demonstrated the incredible power of these animals. On one trip we heard a rustling in the bushes nearby followed by grunting sounds. We have been told that while you definitely want to avoid the wild boars, they are accustomed to being hunted and will also choose to avoid you. Apparently we were down wind of them and since they have poor eyesight we passed by quietly without them noticing us and without seeing them.

## HALEAKALA

A hike, once again with Ken Schmitt, is a thrill for all the senses. Not only does he pack a great lunch and yummy snacks, but the hike provides beauty for the eyes, cool, fresh air for the lungs, tantalizing scents for the nose, peace and serenity for the ears, and an opportunity to touch and get in touch with Maui's natural beauty. We chose a trip to Haleakala to see the awesome crater up close. The trip was an 8-mile hike down Switchback (Halemauu) Trail to the Holua cabin and back. The first mile of the trek was over somewhat rocky, but fairly level, terrain. The next mile seemed like three as we descended seemingly endless hairpin twists down the side of the crater with changing panoramic vistas at each turn. Sometimes fog would eerily sweep in, hovering around and obscuring the view completely, only to soon move away. The vegetation (following a period of heavy rains) was exceptionally lush. All the greenery seemed quite out of place in the usually rather desolate crater.

We continued along the crater floor and past the Holua cabin to reach the Holua lava tube. The small opening was not marked and could be easily overlooked. A small sign advised the use of lights inside the cave. We prepared our flashlights and bundled up for the cooler temperatures to be encountered below. A ladder set by the park service provides access. Once at the base of the ladder, the cavern was large, cool and dark. While there were several directions that lead quickly to dead ends, Ken took us further down the main tube. The cavern was so large that seldom did we have to do more than occasionally duck. Once inside we turned out the lights to enjoy a few moments of the quiet darkness. The tube travels about 100 yards with a gradual ascent to daylight. As daylight peeks down through the dark shaft, it appears the end is in sight. Another turn in the tunnel reveals not the end, but a natural altar like flat rock piled with assorted stones. Light cascading through a hole in the ceiling casts an almost supernatural glow to eyes now accustomed to the darkness. The effect is to create a luminescence on the stones making them appear to be statues set in a natural cathedral. A very awesome experience. Returning to the cabin, we picnicked on the grounds while very friendly nene geese begged for handouts. Ken advised against feeding them as the park rangers would prefer the geese not become dependent on human handouts. After a rest in the warm sun, we retraced our path back up Switchback Trail to the van and continued on to enjoy the summit before heading back to town.

Other more strenuous and lengthy crater ventures include the Sliding Sands Trail and one that traverses down the side of the volcano through the Kaupo Gap.

Available through Paradise Publications are two excellent photo-filled books from K.C. Publications. *Haleakala* and *Hawai'i Volcanos.* Order information is available at the end of the book.

Sierra Club Maui Group of the Hawaii Chapter invites the public to join their guided hikes. This is a wonderful and affordable way to enjoy Maui with a knowledgeable group of people. There are weekend outings twice a month, donations are accepted. At the Sierra Club contact Mary Evanson (572-9724). The main office Sierra Club, Hawaii Chapter is in Honolulu (538-6616).

*The Hawaii Nature Center*, 875 Iao Valley Road, Wailuku, Maui, HI 96793. (244-6500) This is a field site on Maui of the Hawaii Nature Center, a non-profit environmental education group. The main center is on Makiki on Oahu. They offer a limited number of hikes, cost is $5.

*The Waikamoi Preserve*, Box 1716, Makawao, Maui, HI 96768. (For reservations call 572-7849 or fax 572-1375) On the second Saturday of every month hikes are conducted on this 5,230 acre Nature Conservancy preserve located on the northeast slope of Haleakala. The preserve was established in 1983 in cooperation with Haleakala Ranch Company and protects vital habitat for 14 native Hawaiian birds, eight of which are endangered. Vegetation types range from dense rain forests to open shrub and grasslands to introduced pine tree plantations. The area is remote and very rugged with many steep gulches. The area is named after a stream that runs through the property. Along with a waiver and release form, they will provide you with an information sheet on hiking dates, work party dates as well as background on the native and introduced birds of the area and a brochure on the many island areas throughout the islands that are under their protection. Elevation in the Waikamoi Preserve ranges from 4400-9000 feet and annual rainfall varies from 50-200 inches per year. Temperature ranges are 35-70 degrees. The hike begins at Hosmer's Grove in Haleakala National Park at 9 am and finishes around noon at the same location. The recommend binoculars, cameras as well as warm raingear and non-canvas shoes.

The Nature Conservancy is a non-profit Environmental Awareness Group which has under its protection 13,000 acres of habitat critical to the survival of many of Hawaii's native plants and animals. A donation is appreciated. Reservations are required. On Moloka'i the Nature Conservancy also runs monthly tours at the Kamakoau Preserve (a rain forest preserve). The Moloka'i address is PO Box 220, Kualapuu, Moloka'i, HI 96757. (553-5236)

*Haleakala National Park* offers guided hikes to two different areas on Tuesday and Friday mornings, 9 am. The hikes are free of charge, but admission to the National Park is $4 per car. Call to verify days and times with the range office at 572-9306 or recording for basic information 572-7749.

Hiking off established trails without a knowledgeable guide is *definitely* not advised, however, the following sources will help you find and enjoy the many established hikes. *Hawaiian Hiking Trails* by Craig Chisholm, 128 pages, $15.95, has nearly 50 hiking trails throughout the islands, seven of these are on Maui. Robert Smith's book *Hiking Maui* 160 pages, $9.95, will guide you on 27 fairly accessible trails throughout Maui. Both of these publications are available from Paradise Publications. See ordering information at the back of the book.

*Hawaii, Naturally* is an environmentally oriented guide to the wonders and pleasures of the Islands by David Zurick, 206 pp, $12.95.

# CAMPING

## MAUI COUNTY PARKS
County permits for the two county parks, H.A. Baldwin and Rainbow Park, can be obtained by writing the Dept. of Parks and Recreation, County of Maui, 1580 Kaahumanu Ave., Wailuku, Maui, HI 96793. (243-7389). Maximum length of stay is three consecutive nights per campsite. Fee per night is currently $3 per adult and 50 cents per child below age 18.

*H.A. Baldwin Beach Park* - This county park is a grassy fenced area near the roadside. It is located near Lower Paia on the Hana Hwy. and has tent camping space, restrooms and outdoor showers.

*Rainbow Park* - Located in Paia. Facilities: Restrooms.

## STATE PARKS
There are only two State Parks on Maui where camping is allowed. A permit is required from the Division of State Parks at 54 South High Street, Wailuku, HI 96793. (243-4345) There is currently no charge for tent camping, but a permit is required. The two campsites on Maui are Polipoli and Wainapanapa. Permits are issued between 8 am and 4:15 pm on weekdays only. The maximum length of stay is five consecutive nights and they do have a limit on the number of campers per campsite. You will need to provide names and ID numbers of those camping. ID numbers consist of Social Security Number, Driver's License, State ID or Passport.

*Polipoli Springs Recreational Area* - Located in Upcountry, this state park has one cabin and offers tent camping. This is a wooded, two-acre area at the 6,200 foot elevation on Haleakala's west slope and requires four wheel drives to reach. Extensive hiking trails offer sweeping views of Maui and the other islands in clear weather. Seasonal bird and pig hunting. Nights are cold, in winter below freezing. No showers. Toilets, picnic tables. The single cabin sleeps 10 and has bunk beds, water, cold shower, kitchenware. Sheets and towels can be picked up along with the key. See additional description in the hiking section which precedes.

*Wainapanapa State Park* - Located near Hana. Tent camping, 12 cabins. More information on this location can be found under WHERE TO STAY - HANA. Restrooms, picnic tables, outdoor showers. This is a remote volcanic coastline covering 120 acres. Shore fishing, hiking, marine study, forests, caves, blow holes, black sand beach and heiau. The park covers 7.8 acres. BRING MOSQUITO REPELLENT!

Other day use state park camps, see beaches.

## NATIONAL PARKS
The most recent information we have received states that a permit is not currently required to camp at either Hosmer's Grove or O'heo. A maximum stay of three nights is allowed. For information on camping within the Haleakala Crater, contact them at PO Box 369, Makawao, HI 96768 or phone (808) 572-9306 for the latest data. For information on use of one of the three cabins located in the Haleakala Crater, please refer to the Upcountry accommodations section of this book. 572-9177 for a recording with camping information.

*Hosmer Grove* - Haleakala National Park. Tent camping. No permit required. Located at the 7,000 foot elevation on the slope of Haleakala. Cooking area with grill, pit toilets, water, picnic tables.

*Ohe'o Gulch* - Haleakala National Park, just outside of Hana. Tent camping. No permit required. Chemical toilets, picnic tables, BBQ grills, bring your own water.

Currently there are no rental companies offering camping vehicles. Car rental agencies prohibit use of cars or vans for camping.

Camping, hiking and activity package tours are offered from *Pacific Quest Outdoor Adventures* on Kaua'i, Moloka'i, The Big Island and Maui. Eight day (two islands) to fourteen day (four island) trips are offered year round and include inns, camping, meals, local air and ground transportation, natural and cultural history tours. Trips begin at $1,400. PO Box 205 Haleiawa, HI 96712. (808) 638-

BREADFRUIT

8338, FAX (808) 638-8255. Toll Free 1-800-367-8047 ext. 523. (They also offer New Zealand packages).

***Charley's Trail Rides*** offers guided overnight horseback trail excursions from Kaupo up the Haleakala slopes to the crater. Parties of 4 - 6 persons $250 each includes meals, cabin or campsite equipment, parties of 2 - 3 are $300 each. Advance notice and deposit required. Write c/o Kaupo Store, HI 96713. See Horseback riding information for Hana. (248-8209)

# HUNTING

Contact Bob Caires, owner/guide of ***Hunting Adventures of Maui, Inc.***, 1745 Kapakalua Rd., Haiku, Maui, HI 96708 (808-572-8214). Year round hunting season. Game includes (Kao) Spanish Goat and (Pua'a) Wild Boar. Hunting on 100,000 acres of privately owned ranches with all equipment provided. Rates: Goat $450 one person, $375 second and third person each. Boar $500 one person, $400 second and third person each. Non-hunters $100. Three persons maximum. Includes sunrise-sunset hunt, food, beverages, four wheel drive transportation, clothing, boots, packs, meat storage and packing for home shipment, Kahului airport pick up. Rifle rentals and taxidermy available. Also available are sightseeing safaris.

# ARCHERY

Valley Isle Archers holds weekly meetings in Kahului at the National Guard Armory each Wednesday, visitors are welcome. An annual competitive shoot is held each year in June on Kamehameha Day - actually a three day weekend event. Call John at Maui Sporting Goods in Wailuku or 244-3880 or 877-5555.

# SHOOTING

Papaka Sporting Clays offers over 30 shooting stands scattered within 12 acres, each offering a moving clay target as a challenge for varied abilities. Each guest is fitted with eye and hearing protection. They promise that if you have never fired a shotgun before, they'll have you hitting targets in no time. They also have a new computerized game for more accomplished marksman. Pick up is arranged from one of several Wailea area hotels. A maximum of fourteen people per group. Reservations must be made with a credit card and there is a 24 hour cancellation policy. Allow two and three and one half hours. Morning or afternoon pickups available seven days a week. Write or Phone, 1295 South Kihei Rd., Suite 3006, Kihei, HI 96753. (808) 879-5649.

# BOWLING

Maui Lanes in Kahului, is the island's only alley. 243-9511.

# RUNNING

Maui is a scenic delight for runners. ***Valley Isle Road Runners*** can provide you with up-to-date information on island running events. For an answering machine for messages and event schedules call 871-6441.

# FITNESS CENTERS AND HEALTH RETREATS

If you are interested in keeping in shape while you are on Maui and you have no fitness center at your resort, there are several fitness centers that welcome drop in Guests. Several fitness retreats are listed below with the following facilities which welcome drop in guests.

***Nautilus World Fitness Center***, Dickenson Square, Lahaina (667-6100)
***Valley Isle Fitness Center***, Wailuku Industrial Park, (242-6851)
***Valley Isle Fitness Center***, Lipoa Shopping Center in Kihei (874-2844)
***World Gym Lahaina, Inc.***, at Lahaina Shopping Center, 845 Wainee (667-0422)
***Powerhouse Gym***, Kihei Commercial Center, 300 Ohukai Rd., C-112 in Kihei (879-1326)

***Grand Wailea Resort and Spa*** invites non-guests to their luxurious spa. Price is $35 admission, $100 per day to use facilities with various added fees for massage and extras. (875-1234).

If you'd like a sneak peak at what to expect at this grand of grand spas, here is Dona Early's first-hand report from the land of Ahhhs: "As soon as you arrive at the magical, underground autonomous "city" of the Grand Wailea Resort Spa, you'll know you're not in Kansas anymore. Spa Grande - designed with Italian marble, original artwork, Venetian chandeliers, mahogany millwork and inlaid gold - offers two full floors of invigorating fitness, rich luxury, soothing relaxation and stimulating rejuvenation. Whether you need your rusty joints oiled and massaged, your body freshened and reshaped, or you just want to come out with your mane washed and conditioned with yummy essences of coconut and mango, Spa Grande is the place to point your ruby slippers. This magic "city" takes you around the globe with a blend of European, Japanese and America spa philosophies and treatments, but it's the "Hawaiian Regional Regime" that makes this spa unique. Cleanse with the Hawaiian Salt Glo Scrub, heal and cleanse with a Ti

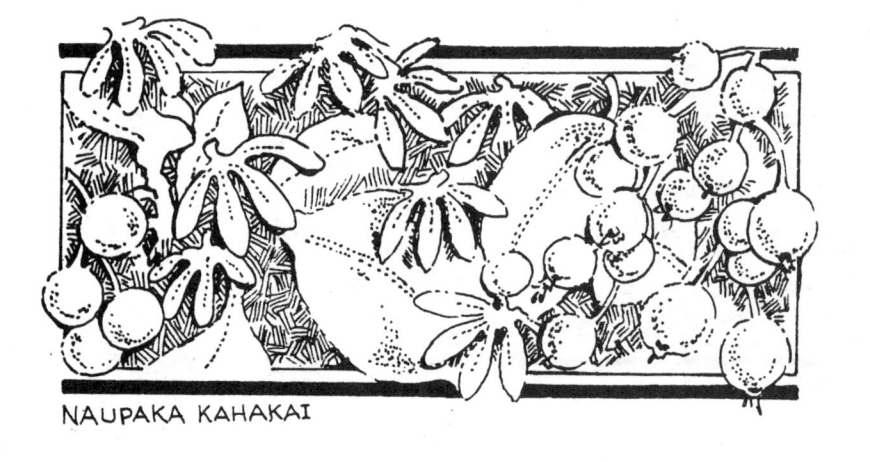

NAUPAKA KAHAKAI

Leaf or Alii Honey Steam Wrap and relax with the healing Lomi Lomi massage or Hawaiian Limu Rejuvenator body masque. Then soak in a soothing bath of seaweed or fragrant tropical enzymes, sit under an indoor waterfall to massage and relieve tired back muscles or refresh under an "ordinary" shower with extraordinary mango shower gel. And what's the password to enter this jewel-like kingdom and enjoy such a multi-faceted experience? Why - "Pamper me" - of course!" --

*The Strong, Stretched and Centered Fitness Body/Mind Institute* is offered by Gloria Keeling. The six week health and fitness retreats are designed for personal wellness as well as fitness instruction certification. Gloria explains that this is a program where people learn completely new lifestyles and learn how to teach those lifestyles to others. The $5,036 cost includes 240 hours of training, workbooks, T-shirt, 30 minute massage weekly, shared housing and meals, including taxes and gratuities. Airfare, shuttles, and spa service gratuities not included. For a single room at $450. P.O. Box 758, Paia, HI 96779. (808) 575-2178.

The exquisite setting of the *Hotel Hana-Maui* combined with the Wellness Center program offers opportunities for exhilarating hiking excursions to treasured spots along the Hana Coast, energizing and strengthening activities, a variety of exercise classes and a relaxing massage. The Wellness Package price includes your choice of all exercise classes, nature walks, excursions and massage treatments and available upon request is gourmet cuisine with the emphasis on fresh island fruits, vegetables, fresh fish, soups, and salads. The Wellness Plan include five active days and four relaxing nights at one of the Sea Ranch Cottages and are available per person or per couple. Additional nights may be added. Current rates are $1,403 per person or $1,640. per couple. The direct number to the Wellness Center at the Hana-Maui is (808) 248-8211 #190, or call the hotel toll free number for reservations at 1-800-321-HANA. Guests of the Hotel Hana-Maui can participate in the Wellness Center and their facilities on a per-use basis. Exercise classes, personal training, nature walks, hiking excursions, snorkeling less and excursion, massages and facials are offered.

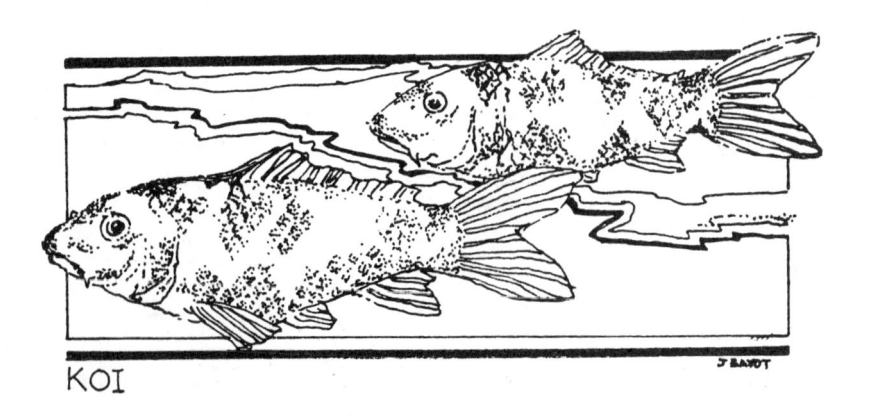

KOI

# AIR TOURS

## SMALL PLANE FLIGHTSEEING

Flightseeing trips are available via small plane. American Pacific Air and Paragon Air are charter companies, no scheduled flightseeing tours are offered. Trips are arranged by customer request and could include Hana and Haleakala as well as island flights to Mauna Loa on the Big Island, O'ahu, Kaho'olawe, Lana'i or Moloka'i. Small plane trips are less expensive, but you won't get as close to the scenery.

*American Pacific Air* - Len Cooper, owner has a 4-passenger aircraft available at $88 per hour. (871-8115 or 808 878-6366)

*Paragon Air* - Charter service to all islands, five and nine passenger planes. Prices are $390 for one hour 5 passenger plane, $490 for one hour in the 9 passenger plane. Trips can include a Kalaupapa-Molokai tour which includes a visit to the remote peninsula and a ground tour given by a former patient. The Big Island Volcano Tour includes a flight to Hilo where you then board a helicopter for a close up view of Madam Pele's spectacle, the Kilauea Volcano. A Jungle Express is an air safari to Hana with ground tour to the Seven Pools. The golf enthusiast will want to check out a package which includes a visit to another island (such as Lana'i) for a round of golf. PO Box 575 Kahului, HI 96732. (244-3356 or 1-800-428-1231, FAX 871-8300)

## BIPLANE

*Biplane Barnstormers* - open-cockpit scenic tours for one or two people in their bright red reproduction of a 1935 Waco biplane. It's just as you'd imagine - you soar high above the island, but not so high you can't tip your wing or wave a friendly "shaka" (Hang Loose!) to the beachgoers, picnickers or snorkelers below. There you are ... "Flying Down to Ohe'o" ... the wind in your face, goggles pressed against your nose, leather helmet jauntily strapped under your chin - all you need is a long flowing scarf trailing behind the plane! Per person prices range from $150 for a 30 minute introduction to $450 for a 90 minute circumnavigation around the island. Another option is an aerobatics ride that takes passengers through loops, spins, rolls - even hammerhead stalls! $175 for 30 minutes. Whether adventurous, nostalgic of just curious, you can say, "Hello, Good Biplane," by calling Cora at 878-2860.

## HELICOPTER TOURS

The price of an hour helicopter excursion may make you think twice. After all it could be a week's worth of groceries at home. We had visited Maui for 7 years before we finally decided to see what everyone else was raving about. It proved to be the ultimate island excursion. When choosing a special activity for your Maui holiday, we'd suggest putting a helicopter flight at the top of the list. (When you get home you can eat beans for a week!) Adjectives cannot describe the thrill of a helicopter flight above majestic Maui. Among the most popular tour is the Haleakala Crater/Hana trip which contrasts the desolate volcanic crater with the lush vegetation of the Hana area. Maui's innermost secrets unfold as the camera's shutter works frantically to capture the memories (one roll is simply not enough). and pilots narrate as you pass by waterfalls cascading into cool mountain pools. Truly an outstanding experience. Keeping up with the prices is impossible. Listed are standard fares, and we hope you'll be delighted to learn of some special discount rates when you call for reservations. Currently all helicopters depart from the Kahului heliport. Most companies include a video of your trip or T-shirt.

*Alexair* - Four passenger. Hughes 500. Hana/Haleakala 45 minute special $119. Other flights range from 20 minute West Maui for $59 to circle of Maui with ground stop for $220. (871-0792) (1-800-462-2281)

*Aris* - Owners Steven and Penni Eggi relocated to Maui after Hurricane Iniki, and currently offer flights ranging from 30-60 minutes. Six passenger AStar aircraft. Steve has been flying 25 years and has logged 20,000 hours flying in a helicopter. A family operation, the office staff and crew range from brothers and mothers to best friends. 877-7005.

*Blue Hawaiian* - Six passenger AStar. (871-8844 or 1-800-745-2583) Hana/Haleakala (45 minutes, $115), Hana/Haleakala Deluxe (60 minute $150), Complete island $2000 (1 hour 45 minutes). One hour sunset package $175, offer Mon.-Fri. includes ground viewing at Ulupalakua.

*Cardinal Helicopters* - (877-2400) 45 minute flight $109, 60 minute flight with two hour Hana land tour $179.

*Hawaii Helicopters Inc.* - (877-3900) 6-passenger AStar jet turbine helicopters. Trips include 30 minutes rainforest and Hookipa beach flight, sunset or sunrise trips, West Maui/Moloka'i, a 2 1/2 hour air and ground excursion which includes a champagne picnic at Wainapanapa Park in Hana.

*Papillon* - (877-0022, FAX 871-2728, 1-800-367-7095) PO Box 1478, Kahului, HI 96732) Recently sold to Georgia based company. They plan to continue operations on Maui, but no announcement if they will keep or change the Hawaii name. They operate 6 AStar helicopters. Tours include a 60 minute Circle Island flight with viewing of Haleakala, the valleys of Hana and West Maui for $129, Circle Island Deluxe $159, West Maui and Molokai $159.

*Sunshine Helicopters Inc.* ★ - (871-0722) (1-800-544-2520) Maui's most experienced pilots fly you with comfort in their "Black Beauties" -- Sunshine's 1993-1994 AStar helicopters featuring state-of-the-art audio and video systems. Three external cameras and one cockpit camera capture live video of your actual flight including passenger reactions. air conditioned comfort and recordable CD players on board make for a ride into our nations largest rainforest "above the rest." West Maui tour with champagne stop ($89); Hana Rainforest Discovery Tour ($99); Circle Island Special ($179); Lanai Trek which includes a West Maui Molokai flight, van tour of Lanai with beach snorkel, BBQ lunch and sail back across the Au Au Channel $269; a Paniolo Horseback Combination with a 30 min. flight and a 3 1/2 hour ranch horseback ride $219. We've flown with Sunshine on a number of occasions and can recommend their courteous ground crew and engaging and informative pilots.

# THE ISLAND
# OF LANA'I - COUNTY OF MAUI

## *INTRODUCTION*

The meaning of Lana'i seems to be steeped in mystery, at least this was our experience. Several guidebooks report that the name means "swelling" or "hump." In discussions with local residents we were told it meant the obvious interpretation of "porch" or "balcony," perhaps because Lana'i is, in a rather nebulous fashion, the balcony of Maui. So, with no definitive answer we will continue the search, but, in the meantime, come enjoy this little piece of Paradise.

Just before and just following the turn of the century, Lana'i was a bustling sheep and cattle ranch. Beginning in the 1920s Dole transformed Lana'i into the largest single pineapple plantation in the world. The 1990s have brought Lana'i into the tourist industry with the opening of two new elegant and classy resorts, the country-style Lodge at Koele in Lana'i City and the seashore resort at Manele Bay. Under the helm of David Murdock, the metamorphosis has been a positive one with young people returning to the island to work in the new tourism industry.

PINEAPPLE

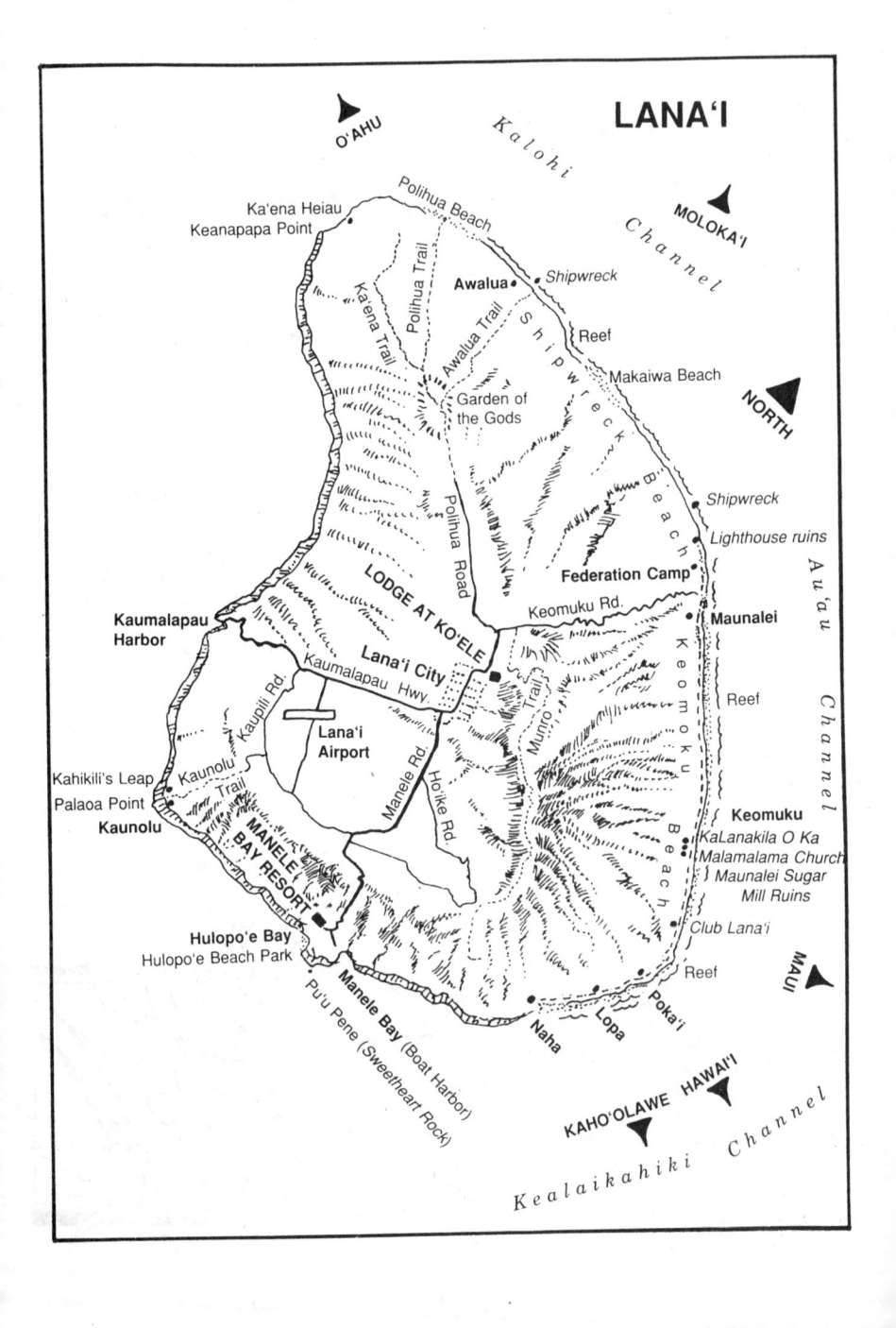

LANA'I

O'AHU

Kalohi Channel

MOLOKA'I

NORTH

Ka'ena Heiau
Keanapapa Point

Polihua Beach

Awalua
Shipwreck

Reef

Makaiwa Beach

Garden of
the Gods

Ka'ena Trail

Polihua Trail

Awalua Trail

Shipwreck Beach

Shipwreck

Lighthouse ruins

Au'au Channel

Polihua Road

Federation Camp

Keomuku Rd.

Maunalei

LODGE AT KO'ELE

Kaumalapau
Harbor

Lana'i City

Kaumalapau Hwy.

Reef

Keomuku Beach

Kaupili Rd.

Lana'i
Airport

Munro Trail

Kahikili's Leap
Palaoa Point

Kaunolu

Kaunolu Trail

Manele Rd.

Ho'ike Rd.

Keomuku
KaLanakila O Ka
Malamalama Church
Maunalei Sugar
Mill Ruins

MANELE
BAY RESORT

Club Lana'i

Reef

MAUI

Hulopo'e Bay
Hulopo'e Beach Park

Manele Bay (Boat Harbor)

Pu'u Pene (Sweetheart Rock)

Naha

Lopa

Poka'i

KAHO'OLAWE HAWAI'I

Kealaikahiki Channel

Cattle are again dotting the landscape and a new piggery has been developed as the silver-blue fields of pineapple rapidly fade into extinction.

While each isle has its own nickname, it appears that Lana‘i has outgrown hers. "The Pineapple Isle" no longer bears much symbolism for an island which has transformed from an agricultural setting to an oasis within an oasis for the lucky tourist. While in the past it had been a wonderful retreat, much of what was good about Lana‘i has not changed. The slow pace of the isle has not been as significantly altered by the arrival of the mega-resort as one might imagine. What new term of endearment will be vested upon the isle? The Isle of Relaxation, Pine Isle, Isle of Enchantment? Time will tell, or perhaps the tourist bureau will!

The rich and famous will very shortly (if not already) be anteing up to purchase a vacation home on Lana‘i with the recent ground-breaking for construction of luxury homes in the Koele district on 68 acres.

As with each Hawaiian Island, Lana‘i is unique. The price for a stay at the two resorts may be steep, but if you want to really indulge, read on! A truly luxurious and relaxing island get-away that is only eight miles, but in many ways, 30 years removed from Maui, Lana‘i will simply enchant you.

## GEOGRAPHY AND CLIMATE

Lana‘i is 140 square miles, making it the sixth largest of the eight major Hawaiian islands. It is situated eight miles to the west of Maui and seven miles south of Moloka‘i.

It is likely that millions of years ago, when the glaciers were larger and the seas much lower, that Maui, Lana‘i, Moloka‘i and Kaho‘olawe comprised one enormous island. This is further substantiated by the fact that the channels between the islands are more shallow and the slopes of the islands visibly more gradual than on the outer coastlines of the islands.

The island of Lana‘i was formed by a single shield volcano. A ridge runs along the eastern half of the island and forms its most notable feature. This large, raised hump is dotted with majestic Norfolk pines. The summit of the island is Lanaihale, located at an elevation of 3,370 feet. A rather strenuous hike along the Munro Trail provides access to this summit where you will be treated to the only location in Hawai‘i where you can view (on a clear day) five other Hawaiian islands. Maunalei and Hauola are Lana‘i's two deepest gulches. Today the Maunalei Gulch continues to supply the island with its water. The center of the island, once a caldera, is now the Palawai Basin and has been used as both farm and ranch land.

Lana‘i has one city, cleverly dubbed Lana‘i City. Located at an elevation of about 1,700 feet, it can be much cooler, and wetter, than the coastline. It is the hub of the island, or what hub there is, and visitors will soon learn that all roads lead to Lana‘i City. The island population in 1994 was about 2,600, with almost everyone a resident of Lana‘i City. The houses are generally small, mostly roofed with tin and the yards are abloom with fruits and flowers.

Rainfall along the coastline is limited, only 4 or 5 inches a year. The heart of the island and Lana'i City, however, may have rainfall of 20 inches or more, and the higher slopes receive 45 to 60 inches annually. The weather in Lana'i City might range from 80 degree days in September with lows in the mid-sixties, to cooler January temperatures in the low 70s, dropping an additional 10 degrees at night. The coastline can be warmer by 10 degrees or more. Pineapples and pines, not palms, were the predominant vegetation on the island. At its peak in the 1970s, there were 15,000 acres of pineapple in cultivation. Castle & Cook made the decision in the 1980's to diversify the island and enter the tourist industry in a big way. The pineapple fields have been reduced to only about 100 - 120 acres, simply enough for local consumption. The production of hay and alfalfa is well underway, and some fields are spotted with black angus cattle. Other acreage has been converted to an organic garden for use by the Manele and Koele restaurants. A piggery and a chicken house have also been established with an aim of making Lana'i more self-sufficient.

The island flower is very unusual. The Kaunaoa is more a vine in appearance than a flower and there are two varieties. One grows in the uplands and the other near the ocean. The ocean species have a softer vine with more vivid hues of yellow and orange than the mountainous counterparts. Strands of the vine are twisted and adorned with local greens and flowers to make beautiful and unusual leis. The mountain vines make a stiffer lei and, we were told, are used for leis for decorating animals. One of the best places to spot this plant is along the drive down to Keomuku and Shipwreck Beach or along the shoreline.

Driving around Lana'i you will note that it is a very arid island. Water supply has always been a problem and most of the greenery is supplied by the Norfolk pines which dot the island.

## HISTORY OF LANA'I

The historical tales of the island of Lana'i are intriguing, filled with darkness and evil. As legend has it, in ancient times the island of Lana'i was uninhabited except for evil spirits. It is said that in the olden days, those who went to Lana'i never returned and that the island was tabu. Hawaiians banished wrong-doers to Lana'i as punishment for their crimes. The story continues that around the 16th century on West Maui there was a chief named Kaka'alanaeo. He had a son named Kaulula'au who was willful and spoiled. The people became furious with his many misdeeds and finally rebelled and demanded that Kaulula'au be put on trial by the ancient laws. The verdict was guilty and, according to the ancient laws, his punishment was death. His father begged for his life and it was agreed that Kaulula'au would be banished to the island of Lana'i. He was set ashore near the Maunalei Gulch, the only source of potable water on the island. His father promised him that if he could banish the evil spirits from Lana'i, he could then set a bonfire as a signal and his father and the warriors would return for him. And, as luck would have it, Kaulula'au managed to trick the evil spirits and send them over to Kaho'olawe. He signaled his father and returned to Maui, heralded now as a hero. (Be sure you take time to view the beautiful, large murals on either side of the entrance at the Manele Bay Hotel. One depicts the fallen son being taken by canoe to Lana'i. The other shows Kaulula'au, head held high in victory, standing over his signal bonfire.) At this time in history, Maui was reaching its population zenith and Hawaiians relocated to Lana'i with settlements near Keomuku and inland as well.

The first archeological studies were done in 1921 by Kenneth Emory from the anthropology department of the Bishop Museum and he published his work in 1923. (Hardcover reprints of the book are available at Walden bookstores on Maui.) Kenneth Emory found many ancient villages and artifacts which had been, for the most part, undisturbed for hundreds of years. He found the area of Kaunolu to be Lana'i's richest archaeological region filled with house sites and remnants of a successful fishing village. He also ventured to the eastern coastline and explored Naha and Keomuku. He noted eleven heiaus, found relics including old stone game boards and discovered a network of trails and petroglyphs. Before the construction on the two new resorts began, the first archeological team since 1921 arrived. Villages were studied and ashes from old fires were analyzed. The findings showed that the ashes dated from 900 A.D., much later than the other islands which were inhabited as early as 40 or 50 B.C. One of the earliest heiaus, The Halulu Heiau, is in the Kaunolu area, and it is thought that this region may have been one of the earliest Hawaiian settlements.

While the Hawaiian population increased throughout the archipelago, Lana'i was left largely uninhabited until the 1500s. Two of Captain Cook's ships, the Discovery and The Resolution, reported a visit to Lana'i. They found the Hawaiians friendly along the windward coastal area where they replenished their supplies of food and water. In talking with the islanders they estimated that the population was approximately 10,000. They observed and noted that the island was a dry dustbowl and that the people fished and grew some taro. About this same time, chiefs of Maui became worried that the people on Lana'i might become too powerful. So they divided Lana'i into 13 ohanas (ohana means family, but this refers more to regions) and put a konahiki in charge of each -- this way insuring that no one chief would be too powerful. These district names are still used today. They are Kaa Paomai, Mahana, Maunalei, Kamoku, Kaunolu, Kalulu, Kealiakapu, Kealiaaupuni, Palawai, Kamao, Pawili and Kaohai.

Six months after the island was visited by Cook's vessels, a tragic event happened that would change life on Lana'i forever. Inter-island battles among the island chiefs were not uncommon, but until this time Lana'i had remained unaffected. In 1778 Kalaniopu'u, the chief on the Big Island, launched an unsuccessful attack on Lahaina, Maui. He retreated, then turned and attacked central Maui. Here again his warriors were overcome. As they returned to the Big Island in great anger, he passed the island of Kaho'olawe, which was loyal to the Maui chieftains. In retaliation, Kalaniopu'u's warriors massacred the entire population on Kaho'olawe. Bolstered by his victory, Kalaniopu'u turned once again to assault Lahaina and again was defeated. Now enraged, Kalaniopu'u and his warriors chose to strike the leeward coastal villages of Lana'i. Lana'i's warriors were unprepared and retreated to the Ho'okia Ridge to have a better location from which to launch their counterattack. However, without access to food and water, the Lana'i warriors soon weakened and Kalanaiopu'u moved quickly to crush them. The Big Island warriors continued around Lana'i and systematically destroyed all the villages. Kalaniopu'u returned to the Big Island of Hawai'i and there, seven months later, he died and his lieutenant, Kamehameha came to rule.

During the rule of Kamehameha the population increased. The king and his warriors would visit Kaunolu Bay on Lana'i's southwestern coastline. Here Kahekili is said to have leaped from a cliff above the sea into the Pacific waters, proving his loyalty to the king. Other warriors were then challenged to follow his example and the area continues to be referred to as Kahekili's Leap.

The elders from the Church of Jesus Christ of Latter Day Saints acquired land on Lana'i from one of the chiefs in 1855. In 1860 Walter Murray Gibson came to Lana'i with the intent of establishing a Mormon colony called the City of Joseph in the Palawai Basin. Gibson had been instrumental in assisting Kamehameha. He served on his cabinet and was among the advisors for the construction of the Iolani Palace. He purchased 20,000 acres of land on Lana'i and obtained leases on more. By 1863 there were about 600 Mormons living on Lana'i. In 1864, when the church elders arrived to visit, they discovered that Walter had purchased additional lands with the church money, but had listed ownership under his own name, and he wasn't willing to release them. He was quickly expelled from the church and the Mormons went on to develop their church on O'ahu. As owner of 26,000 acres Gibson first established the Lana'i Sheep Ranch which later became the Lana'i Ranch. In 1867 the population was 394 people (the 600 Mormons had departed earlier), 18,000 goats and 10,000 sheep. In 1870 Gibson attempted a cooperative farm, but this operation soon proved unsuccessful. By 1875 Gibson was controlling 90 percent of the island for ranch or farming operations. In 1874, Gibson's daughter, Talula, married Frederick Harrison Hayselden, formerly of England and Australia, and by the early 1880s Frederick was managing the ranch. Walter Gibson died in San Francisco in 1888 and ownership of the land transferred to his daughter, Talula Hayselden, and his son-in-law Frederick.

By 1894 the Lana'i Ranch now ran 40,000 sheep, 200 horses, 600 head of cattle in addition to large herds of goats, hogs and wild turkeys. However, by 1898 the ranch was in debt, but the sugar industry looked promising. The Hayseldens established the Maunalei Sugar Company on the island's windward coast. They begin by building three wells and a wharf at Kahalepalaoa for shipment of the cane to Olowalu on Maui for grinding. A railroad was also built between the wharf and Keomuku along with a two-story building, a store, boarding house, camp houses and barracks.

In 1802 a Chinese entrepreneur spent only one season attempting sugar cultivation in Naha from wild sugar cane. The Maunalei Sugar Company in nearby Keomuku did little better, lasting only a little more than two years. The Hayseldens constructed a six mile train track for transporting their sugar cane. However, they failed to respect the local culture and custom. Stones from an ancient heiau (temple) were used to build part of the railroad bed and then the disasters began. Their Japanese workers fell sick and many died. The ever important supply of drinking water went brackish and rain did not fall. Company records show the closure was due to lack of labor and water. The local population knew otherwise. Fred and Talula Hayselden soon left Lana'i.

On Lana'i we heard a report that the Maunalei Plantation House was transported to Maui and became Pioneer Inn, but this was not accurate. Apparently some years ago the Honolulu Star-Bulletin printed an article to this effect. G. Alan Freeland, son of Pioneer Inn's founder George Freeland, spoke with Lawrence

Gay, the owner of most of Lana'i at the turn of the century, and was told that when the construction of the Pioneer Hotel was completed, the similar-designed building on the island of Lana'i was still standing.

In 1902 Charles Gay (a member of the Robinson family from Ni'ihau) and George Munro visited the island of Lana'i and Gay acquired the island at public auction for $108,000. He enlarged his holdings further through various land leases. Gay began making major improvements and bringing cattle from Kaua'i and Ni'ihau to his new ranch on Lana'i. In 1903 Gay purchased the remaining holdings from the Hayseldens and through land leases and other avenues became the sole owner of the entire island. By 1909 financial difficulties forced Charles Gay to loose all but 600 acres of his farmland. On the remaining acres he planted pineapples and operated a piggery while moving his family from Koele to Keomuku.

In 1909 a group of businessmen that included Robert Shingle, Cecil Brown, Frank Thompson and others, purchased most of the island from Charles Gay for $375,000 and formed the Lana'i Ranch Company. At that time there were 22,500 sheep, 250 head of cattle, and 150 horses. They changed the emphasis from sheep to cattle and spent $200,000 on ranch improvements. However, because the large herds were allowed to graze the entire island, destroying what vegetation was available, the cattle industry was soon floundering. The island population had dwindled to only 102 at the turn of the twentieth century with fifty people living in Koele (means farming) and the rest along the windward coastline in Keomuku. There were only thirteen men to work the entire cattle ranch, which was an insufficient number to manage the 40,000 head of beef on land that was over-grazed by the cattle, pigs and goats that roamed freely.

George Munro, a New Zealander by birth and who had visited the island in 1902, and was asked to return by the new owners to manage the ranch. Soon after arrival he began instituting much needed changes. He ordered sections of the range fenced and restricted the cattle to certain areas while allowing other areas to regrow. He also ordered the wild pigs and goats to be rounded up and de-stroyed. In 1911 the large three million gallon storm water reservoir, now the beautiful reflecting pond, was built. In 1912 an effort to destroy the goat popula-tion began in earnest. The first year 5,000 goats were killed and an additional 3,300 more were destroyed by 1916. (It wasn't until the 1940s that the last pigs and goats were captured.) Sheep dogs were introduced to assist the cowboys.

Water continued to be a major concern. An amateur naturalist, Munro noted that the Cook Island pine tree outside his home seemed to capture the mist that traveled past the island. Today, as in the days of Munro, there is only one Cook Island pine tree on the island. The tree planted in 1875 by Frederick Hayselden is the same one that stood outside of Munro's home and has become a noted Lana'i landmark. It remains a stately sight right outside the Koele Lodge. From that pine an idea was born, and Munro ordered the paniolos (Hawaiian cowboys) to carry a bag of Norfolk Pine seeds. They poked a small hole in the sack and, as they traveled the island on horseback, they left a trail of pines. The result is an island of more pine than palm. In 1914 the automobile age arrived on Lana'i in the form of a single 1910 Model T owned by George Munro.

By 1917 there were 4,000 head of cattle and 2,600 sheep, but profits were slim and the Lana'i Ranch Company sold its land to the Baldwin family for $588,000 and George Munro remained as foreman. The ranch slowly became more profitable. In 1920 axis deer were introduced on Lana'i from Moloka'i and a pipeline was constructed from Maunalei Gulch to provide additional sources of fresh water.

In 1920 James Dole came to Lana'i, liked what he saw, and purchased the island in 1922 for $1.1 million from Alexander & Baldwin. George Munro was retained as manager. Castle & Cooke acquired one third ownership in the Hawaiian Pineapple Company soon after. The Kaumalapua harbor was dredged and a breakwater constructed in preparation for shipment of pineapple to O'ahu for processing. Lana'i developed into the single largest pineapple plantation in the world, which produced 90% of the United States' total pineapples. The company was called Hawaiian Pineapple Company until 1960 when the name was changed to Dole Corporation. In 1986 David Murdock became the major stockholder of Castle and Cooke and the chairman of the board. Today the company is called Dole Company Foods.

Also in the 1920s the community of Lana'i City began. The houses were very small, only large enough for the workers, as families were discouraged. The workers arrived from Japan, Korea and the Philippines. The last residents left the Palawai Valley and moved to Lana'i City between 1917 and 1929.

The population of Lana'i soared to 3,000 by 1930. In the 1950s larger homes, located below Fraser Ave., were built to accommodate the workers and their families and in the 1950s employees were given the option of purchasing their homes fee simple. In 1923 Dole realized the need to provide a center for entertaining island guests and had "The Clubhouse" constructed. Today it is known as Hotel Lana'i. The dining room provided meals for guests as well as for the nurses and patients from the plantation hospital. Also constructed in the center of town was Dole Park. The building in the middle was once a bowling alley, pool hall and restaurant until the late 1970s when it was made into a meeting hall. As a part of the development of Lana'i, David Murdock had a large new community center built, complete with swimming pool. It's located a block away from the park. Today less than 100 Lana'ians are part- or full-blooded Hawaiian.

The word Manele means low area. The Manele boat harbor was once a small black sand beach and a fishing shrine found here indicates it was used by the early Hawaiians. You can spot the old pepe (cattle) ramp that Charles Gay used for loading his steers onto freighters.

In the 1970s E.E. Black was contracted to build the breakwater. It is traditional for any new project in Hawai'i to be blessed at the onset, but E.E. Black chose to forego the blessing. After only 20 feet of breakwater were constructed, the huge crane fell in the ocean and the people then refused to work. After great effort, another crane was brought over to lift the first from the ocean, but by the time it was recovered, the saltwater had taken its toll and it was worthless. Before resuming construction E.E. Black held a blessing ceremony, the people returned to work, and the breakwater was completed without further incident.

# GETTING THERE

To reach Lana'i you may travel by air or sea. The Lana'i airport is serviced by Aloha Airlines, IslandAir, Hawaiian Air, and Air Molokai (See Transportation under General Information Chapter.) Airfare is about $60 one way from Lana'i to O'ahu. By boat you can travel a cool and comfortable 45 minutes from the Lahaina harbor aboard Expeditions. For a $25 one-way ticket, children $20, you can have a scenic tour, spotting dolphins, flying fish, and whales during the winter season. It is a pleasant way to travel, and much more affordable for a family than air transportation. The boat travels round trip four times daily (with an extra round trip on Fridays) to Manele Harbor where a shuttle van will pick you up for transport to the Manele Bay Hotel and from there up to Koele Lodge. Reservations are advised as space is limited. They can also arrange an overnight or golf package. Phone: 661-3756.

# GETTING AROUND

A complimentary shuttle runs every hour between the Lodge at Koele and Manele Bay Hotel. Beginning on Friday afternoon at 3 p.m. the schedule increases to every half hour until Sunday afternoon. Depending on how busy they are, they run mini-vans or larger size school type buses. We found no trouble in asking for a van to run us into Lana'i City from the Lodge at Koele. Bikes are available at Koele for guests to use or enjoy a brisk 15 - 20 minute walk to downtown Lana'i City. For further independent exploration there are several rental car companies. Since many of the island's roads are unimproved and even a small rainshower can render dirt roads impassable, most guests are advised to rent one of the 4-wheel drive Jeeps. Jeeps run about $100 per day, cars about $50 and arrangements can be made through the concierge or contact Lanai City Service (808) 244-9538 or (808) 565-7227).

# ACCOMMODATIONS

There are currently three choices for hotel accommodations. Lana'i's original Hotel Lana'i and the two luxury hotels, Manele Bay Hotel and the Lodge at Koele. More on these three accommodations in the following sections.

## CAMPING

Tent camping is available at Hulopoe Bay. Permits are issued by Castle and Cooke, at PO Box L, Lana'i City, Lana'i, HI 96762. Phone (808) 565-6661.

## HOMES

Lana'i Realty never returned our calls and often had no answering machine on, so we are unclear if they still handle home rentals. If you want to try, here's the phone number: (808) 565-6597.

## BED & BREAKFAST

Lucille Graham operates the island's only registered bed and breakfast facility, Lana'i Bed & Breakfast. She rents out two rooms of her three bedroom plantation style home. One room offers a queen size bed and the other a double plus a single bed. The two guest rooms share a half bath, although she tells us that seldom are both rooms rented at the same time. The shower room is also shared. Room rates are $50 for a single person, $60 for double occupancy, 3 adults are $75, and discounts are available for a family of three. Prices do not include the 9% room tax. Lucille might start your day off with her popular buttermilk oatmeal pancakes and then set you on your way with beach towels, snorkeling equipment and a jug of water. We've heard wonderful things about her hospitality and personal touches! Contact Lana'i Bed & Breakfast, Box 956, Lana'i City, HI  96763. Phone (808) 565-6378. Her residence is at 312 Mahana Place in Lana'i City.

Another couple, Michael and Susan Hunter operate "Dreams Come True" offering three rooms in their home/art studio at 547 - 12th St. They also have a separate fully furnished home (2 bedroom plus separate cottage) with outside tubs and showers, enclosed fenced yard, for $190 for six, includes tax. The second home can be rented as a bed and breakfast for a larger group. Continental breakfast provided. Single rate $55, double $75, triple (adults) $95, children $10 per night. Airport pick up and drop off. A truck and a jeepster are available for rent. PO Box 525, Lana'i City, HI  96763. Phone (808) 565-6961.

For other information you might wish to contact the local visitor information center and speak with Vera Chandler, at Destination Lana'i, PO Box 700, Lana'i City, 96763  (808) 565-7600, FAX (808) 565-9316.

## HOTELS

### HOTEL LANA'I
Hotel Lana'i, built in 1923, is also run by Castle and Cooke. Before the opening of the new resorts, this ten room hotel had the only accommodations on the island. You'll still find it a quiet and comfortable accommodation with very basic rooms. Rooms run $95, $135 for cottages. Children ages eight and under are free in room with parents. You'll want to book as far in advance as possible. For information or reservations write: Hotel Lana'i, PO Box A-199, Lana'i, HI 96763. (808) 565-4700, FAX (808) 565-4713 or toll free 1-800-321-4666.

The restaurant at the Hotel Lana'i is a popular place for island residents and it offers the only bar in town. Hours are 7:30 a.m. - 10 a.m. for breakfast, lunch is served 11:30 a.m. - 1:30 p.m. and dinner 5:30 p.m. - 9 p.m. The bar closes at 9 p.m. Breakfast fare runs $6.25 for a pan fried fritata or $5.25 for biscuits and gravy to $8 for "The Warehouseman's Breakfast."

Lunches include an assortment of sandwiches or plate lunches $6-$8. A pleasant addition to their dinner menu is the option of several sandwiches for the less hearty appetite or children in your group. Sandwiches $7.50-$9, dinner entrees include shrimp or chicken stir fry $16/$17, pork chops $19, Prime Rib $19 or Lana'i Venison (seasonal).

## THE MANELE BAY HOTEL

The resort is spread across the cliffside of Hulopo'e Beach like an enormous Mediterranean Villa. It is a strikingly beautiful building with a pale blue tile roof. There are four buildings in the East wing and five in the West wing, and each is slightly different. The rooms line sprawling walkways which meander through five lush courtyard gardens, each with a unique theme. The gardens include The Hawaiian, The Bromelaid, The Chinese, the Japanese and The Kaamaina Gardens. The original resort plan called for a 450 room hotel directly on the beach, but was revised to the current structure with 250 rooms on the cliff alongside the beach. Behind the resort is the newest 18 hole golf course, The Challenge of Manele, which encompasses 138 acres along the ocean.

The *Hulopo'e Court* is the more casual of the two dining rooms and serves breakfast and dinner, with a children's menu available. Breakfasts include entrees $12-$22 such as smoked salmon on toasted bagel, catch of the day, poached egg with paprika Hollandaise or homemade corned beef hash and poached eggs. Side orders such as rice, sausage or potatoes $2.50-3.50. Pancakes, waffles or French toast run $9.50. Their dinner menu features Contemporary Hawaiian Regional Cuisine and features the culinary talents of Executive Chef Philippe Padovani assisted by JoAn Kosowski. Appetizers run $9.50 and up and include pan fried crab cake, seared ahi with spicy crust or Chinese spring rolls. Soups or salads $6.50-$9. Fresh pasta is available in appetizer or entree size portions $14-$20. Appetizers, soups and salads are considered "First Courses" and run $11 and up. Main courses include Pan fried Lana'i venison with Moloka'i sweet potato puree $42, poached pali kali with julienne cucumbers $35, pan fried onaga $33, sauteed Moana duck liver terrine $36, roasted squab breast with marmalade of onions $34. Adding a beverage, soup or salad and dessert will make this elegant dining experience an expensive one.

The *Ihalani*, is the formal dining room at the Manele Bay Hotel. They feature French Mediterranean selections with Executive Chef Philippe Padovani heading the kitchen. They have two menus each evening that run from soup to dessert.

MANELE BAY RESORT

A sample dinner might be as follows: Vine ripe tomato petals, summer vegetable salad, Pan Fried Onaga with sugar snap peas in creamy curry sauce, followed by sauteed veal rib eye served with woodland mushroom sauce and a ragout of vegetables. A selection of gourmet cheese and walnut bread is followed by the dessert of the evening. Price per person is in the range of $75-95. We haven't had the opportunity to dine here, so let us know if you do!

Hale Aheahe, which means House of Gentle Breezes, is located off the upper main lobby. There is an indoor lounge and outdoor veranda from which to enjoy nightly entertainment. Afternoon and evening entertainment is also provided in the Kailani Terrace, the lower lobby area. The Pool Grill opens at 11 a.m. and serves sandwiches and salads and a children's menu is also available here. Sandwiches, salads and "Hawaiian Favorites" run $10-$17.

In many of the areas the ceilings have been given very special attention. In the main dining room are huge floral paintings, in the Hale Aheahe lounge you'll see fish and starfish. The resort took advantage of the undiscovered talent of the island residents and much of the artwork was done by local residents.

If you're thinking that maybe too much lying in the sun and fine food will affect your waistline, then hurry into the fitness studio. Open 6 a.m. - 6 p.m. there is plenty of equipment, then treat yourself to a steam room, massage, pedicure or facial.

This place is truly an island get-away. If our stay was any indication, then celebrities have quickly found Lana'i to be a convenient and luxurious retreat. Both Kevin Costner and Billy Crystal were guests during our brief stay.

We enjoyed the proximity to the beachfront, but the pool seemed the place to be and lounges were filled by mid-afternoon. It seems here on Lana'i, there is no reason to hurry. The pool water is slightly warm, yet delightfully refreshing and, if the Hawaiian sun becomes too hot, pool staff are on hand to provide chilled towels or atomizers of spring water facial spritzers. Attendants from the adjoining restaurant circulate, taking drink and sandwich orders. The poolside restaurant was a little pricey, but the portions large and even the fish sandwich featured the fresh catch. We noted with appreciation that they provided a more economical children's menu here as well as in their main dining rooms.

The rooms are spacious, a bit larger than the standard rooms at Koele and each wing differs slightly in decorating style. Our wing had bright, bold yellow wall coverings and bedspreads accented with very traditional furniture. The bathroom amenities thoughtfully included suntan lotion and moisturizer in a little net bag to take along to the pool or beach. Rooms have a private butler mini-refrigerator. Reservation information is available from Rock Resorts, Inc., PO Box 774, Lana'i City, HI 96763. Phone 565-7300. *Room rates are as follows: Terrace Room $225, Garden Room $295, Ocean View $350, Ocean Front $395, Ocean Mini-Suite $595, Ocean Front Suite $695, Butler Floor Suites $595-$2000. Full American Plan (Breakfast, lunch and dinner) or Modified American Plan (Breakfast, Dinner) are available. Prices through the end of 1994 for FAP are $115 adult, $30 child 8 years and under. MAP $90 adults, $25 child 8 and under.*

## LODGE AT KOELE

The Lodge at Koele is not what a visitor might expect to find in Hawai'i. Guests arrive via a stately drive lined with Norfolk pine to this Victorian era resort that typifies turn of the century elegance. The inscription on the ceiling of the entry was painted by artist John Wullbrandt and translates "In the center of the Pacific is Hawai'i. In the center of Hawai'i is Lana'i, In the heart of Lana'i is Koele" and Lana'i may quickly find its way into your heart as well.

The rug in the entry is circa 1880, made of Tibetan wool. The Great Hall features enormous natural stone fireplaces that hint at the cooler evening temperatures here in upcountry Lana'i. The twin fireplaces on either side of the lobby are the largest in the state of Hawaii and the Lodge itself sets the record for being Hawai'i's biggest wooden structure. The high beamed ceilings give the room a spacious character, yet the atmosphere is welcoming and the comfortable furnishings invite you to sit and linger. Designer Joszi Meskan of San Francisco spent more than two years securing the many beautiful artifacts from around the world. A descriptive list is available from the concierge. The Great Hall's rug was handmade in Thailand for the resort and utilizes 75 different colors. Some of the furniture are replicas, but many pieces are antiques, including the huge altar desk where steaming morning coffee awaits the guests. Be sure to notice the two exotic chandeliers, with playful carved monkeys amid the leaves, designed for the great hall by Joszi Meskan. The large portrait on one end of the Great Hall is of Madame Yerken, painted by Belgian artist Jan Van Boern in 1852. An intricately stenciled border runs around the perimeter of the ceiling with antelope, deer and wild turkeys. Another more subtle stenciling is done around the floors. The skylights are beautiful, etched glass. The furnishings are covered in lush brocade tapestries and suede upholstery in hues of burgundy, blues and greens. The room is accented with fresh flowers, many of them orchids grown in the greenhouse located beyond the reflecting pool. The woodwork is finely carved, with pineapples often featured. At the end of an exhausting day of vacationing, there is

KOELE LODGE

nothing like curling up in the big overstuffed armchair next to a crackling fire with an after dinner drink to enjoy the evening entertainment, play a game of checkers or visit with local women as they demonstrate Hawaiian quilting. Green is the color theme throughout the resort with the bellman, concierge and front desk staff crisply attired in pine green suits.

Surrounding the main building is a wonderful veranda with comfortable rattan furniture accented by Hawaiian quilted pillows. (Similar pillows, by the way, are for sale through the concierge, $100 each.) Huge trees hug the building and the view of the horses and fields beyond has a tranquilizing effect. The setting is truly picture perfect.

Several public rooms surround the Great Hall. The library overlooks spacious lawns and offers newspapers from around the world as well as books, backgammon and chess. A large screen television shows movies in the evenings with popcorn. The trophy room also has an assortment of board games and an interesting, but very uncomfortable, English horn chair. Both of these rooms have fireplaces which can be lit at the request of the guests. A music room and tea room on the other side of the lobby host afternoon tea served daily between 3 - 5 p.m. and pupus (appetizers) from 5 - 7 p.m. A slide show depicting the history of Lana‘i is offered several times a week.

Adjoining the Great Hall is the Terrace Dining Room, open for breakfast, lunch and dinner. The food is excellent and the service outstanding. In fact, the restaurants at the Lodge at Koele could very possibly be the best in all of Hawai‘i. We were also very pleased that they provided a children's menu which offered a varied dinner selection priced $5 - $7. The formal dining room, open for dinner only, is tucked away in the corner of the resort and requires a jacket and tie for the gentlemen. Restaurant Executive chef, Edwin Goto, makes excellent use of the five acre organic farm to ensure the freshest ingredients in his meal preparations. Herbs, white eggplant, purple turnips, and yellow teardrop tomatoes are among the interesting and varied crops. Simple foods with unusual ingredients and elegant presentations are the key here.

Breakfast at the Terrace Dining Room might include Lana‘i axis deer sausage, Kaunolu bananas on coconut cream, zucchini omelette of Lana‘i farm fresh eggs with basil and Gruyere cheese, or sweet rice waffle $4.75-$12.25. Lunch is another dining experience extraordinaire. Sample a toasted sandwich of lobster, avocado and Gruyere cheese $13.75, Ko‘ele cobb salad $11.50, or cilantro pasta salad with grilled scallops $14.50. Dinner (served 6-9:30 pm) entrees offer special daily features such as veal osso bucco or select from their standard menu between a grilled chuck burger with cheddar cheese $9.50, or grilled lamb and Japanese eggplant sandwich $15.25. The Golf Clubhouse at Koele also serves lunch and has proven popular with the local residents and visitors alike, with their selection of quality meals at prices more reasonable than the lodge. Samples include a grilled fresh fish sandwich $8, grilled sandwich of three cheeses with vine ripe tomatoes $5.25, saimin with char sui $4.50 or Chinese chicken salad $7.

This was once the site of the farming community known as Koele and the pine lined driveway was planted in the 1920s and led to the 20 or 30 homes in this area. Only two remain on the property and are owned by the Richardson family, descendants of the early Lana‘i paniolos. The church was moved to the front grounds of the Lodge and a small schoolhouse is being restored and converted into a museum. The grounds of this country manor are sprawling and exquisitely landscaped. More than a mile of lush garden pathways and an orchid house can be enjoyed while strolling the grounds. The large reflecting pond was once the reservoir for the town of Koele. There are plenty of activities to be enjoyed from strolling the grounds to swimming or just relaxing in the jacuzzis. (See WHAT TO DO for more information.) In fact, it is so relaxing and so lovely that we didn't even miss the beach. But if you're hankering for some sand and sun, it is only a 25 minute shuttle trip to the shore.

Maids in starched black and white add to the elegance and the uniformed staff are very friendly and courteous. We were impressed with the quality of service at the Lodge. It is also pleasing to know that the development of the tourist industry on Lana‘i has meant a return of many of the island's young people.

There are 102 guests rooms at the Lodge and they are artistically decorated in three different fresh, bright color schemes. The artwork that lines the corridors was done by some of the many talented Lana‘i residents and each floor has a different theme. The beds feature a pineapple motif and were custom made in Italy, then handpainted by Lana‘i artisans. The floral pictures on each door were painted by the postmaster's wife! The bathrooms have Italian tile floors and vivid blue marble counter tops. Room amenities are thoughtfully packaged and include an array of fine toiletries. There are in-room televisions with video recorders and a couple of beautifully carved walking sticks in the closet tempt the guest to enjoy one of those leisurely walks around the grounds.

*Choose Garden Rooms ($350) which are located on the ground floor and the Koele Rooms ($295), which are the same size, are on the second floor. The Plantation Rooms ($395) are slightly larger. Plantation Suites ($775) have a wrap*

KOELE LODGE GROUNDS

*around lanai and a separate living and sleeping area with a murphy bed in the living room. The Plantation Room and Plantation Suite can be combined into one large living area. The Norfolk, Terrace Junior or Plantation Suites $550-$775 provide separate living room and sleeping areas, an oversized lanai plus the added luxury of private butler service. These rooms are located along the balcony above the Great Hall and are the only guest rooms that are air conditioned. The Kapuahi or Fireplace Suite runs $875-975. They are slightly larger than the regular rooms and just as beautifully decorated. Whether your luggage needs packing, a bath needs to be drawn, a dinner reservation is required or a suit needs pressing, the butler is ready to assist. The butlers are schooled for a year and must pass rigorous testing before being licensed. Full American Plan (Breakfast, lunch and dinner) or Modified American Plan (Breakfast - Dinner) are available. Prices through the end of 1993 for FAP are $115 adult, $30 child 8 years and under. MAP $90 adults, $25 child 8 and under. Reservation information is available from Rock Resorts, Inc., PO Box 774, Lana'i City, HI 96763. Phone 565-7300.*

As much as we enjoyed the Manele Bay Hotel, we found something very appealing about this Lodge in upcountry. Perhaps it was because the service was so superb, perhaps it was because the air was so fresh, perhaps it was the comfortable and homey quality of the great hall, or perhaps it was because we truly were in the heart of Lana'i. This resort had a special quality, and both kids and adults in our group were enchanted. Our visit will long be a fond memory... that is until we visit once again!

## *SHOPPING - LOCAL EATING*

There are two grocery stores from which to choose. **Richard's**, which has the honor of being on Lana'i since 1946, and the small **Pine Isle Market**. Since everything must be brought in by barge, prices are steep. Don't be surprised if they are closed for noontime siesta and shut for the day by 6 p.m. You won't find any fresh pineapple in the stores here. After working long hours in the field, the residents have little craving for this fruit. Visitors, however, can arrange through the concierge to order pineapples by the dozen to take home.

The building called **S.T. Properties** had us under the impression that inside would be a real estate office. We were pleasantly surprised to discover this was one of two local fast food restaurants and is locally known as **Tanegawa's**. Open for breakfast and lunch and closed for the day at 12:30, you can select a sandwich or burger $1.50-$3, plate lunches $4-$5 and breakfasts $4 - $5. The fare is filling and the atmosphere charmingly rustic. Next door is the only other casual dining spot in Lana'i City.

The **Blue Ginger** serves up the best, freshly made pastries in town. (They also happen to be the only bakery!) Open at 5:30 a.m. for breakfasts which are surprisingly diverse for such an early hour! They offer eggs, pancakes or waffles with blueberries, strawberries or macadamia nuts. Lunch include sandwiches, local style plate lunches and saimin, dinners include steak, seafood and pizza. Prices are moderate. There are now two restaurants on Lana'i open for three meals a day, and Blue Ginger serves in-between meal hours too! HOURS: 5:30 a.m. - 9 p.m. Phone: (808) 565-6363. The *Hotel Lana'i* has a restaurant, see description listed under the Hotel Lana'i section. The Lodge at Koele and the Manele Bay Hotel both have small sundry gift shops. There are also shopping excursions available to Lahaina. Leaving the Manele Harbor aboard *Expeditions*, you can arrange for a day of shopping in Lahaina town. Cost is $25 per person one way.

Across the park is an art gallery called *Island Collections* operated by Dean and Suzanne Crimmins. This is the beginning of Lana'i's cultural center. Work by Lana'i artists and other island artists are on display. Just another building down is the workshop where island residents can come to pursue their artistic abilities.

# RECREATION

## GOLF

There are a number of selections for the golfer on Lana'i. At Koele there is the 18-hole *Experience at Koele* course, another, older 9-hole course and one stupendous 18-hole putting course is also adjacent the Lodge. The *Challenge at Manele* is the newest 18 hole course.

Golfers and non-golfers of all ages will delight in the executive 18-hole putting green at Koele, beautifully manicured course with assorted sand traps and pools lined with tropical flowers and sculptures. Putt-putt will never be the same again! No charge. Course rates for the 18-hole Challenge of Manele or Koele Experience is $150 for non-guests and $99 for hotel guests.

The *Challenge of Manele*, designed by Jack Nicklaus and Greg Norman, is the island's newest course and opened on December 25, 1993. Built on several hundred acres of lava out-croppings among natural kiawe and ilima trees, this links-style golf course features 3 holes constructed on the cliffs of Hulopo'e Bay using the Pacific Ocean as a dramatic water hazard.

The 18-hole *Experience at Koele* was designed by Greg Norman and Ted Robinson. From a golfer's standpoint, Greg Norman assures the golfing guest that this course will require both skill and strategy and adds that it is the only course in Hawaii with Bent grass greens. The beauty of the course, he continues, with its lush natural terrain -- marked by thick stands of Norfolk pines -- and panoramic views will make concentrating on the game difficult for even the most expert golfer. The signature 8th hole of the Experience at Koele has a truly inspired setting. This is a 390 yard par 4 with a dramatic 200 foot drop in elevation from tee to green. The course is laid out on a multi-tiered plan. The upper seven holes meet the lower eleven at this sublime tee. From the top of the bluff at the eighth tee is a view so stunning that our first thought was that this could be right out of Shangri-la. The mist floats by this enchanted valley, filled with lush vegetation and with a lovely lagoon. The lagoon at one time had served as a back up reservoir for the old cattle ranch. Now, while we are not golf aficionados, this single hole was enough to at least consider taking up the sport! Charges for either the Experience at Koele or the Challenge of Manele is $75 for resort guests, $130 for non-resort guests. A restaurant at the Golf Clubhouse offers some good luncheon selections.

**The Cavendish**, a 9 hole, 36 par, 3071 yard course, (complimentary for guests of either resort) is located at the front of the Koele Lodge and was the island's first.

## TENNIS

There are plexipave courts at both Koele and Manele Bay. These are complimentary for use by hotel guests. Lessons are available at an extra charge. There is also a public court at Lana'i School in Lana'i City.

## THEATER

In February 1993 the Lanai Playhouse refurbishment was complete and it opened as Lana'i's movie theater.

## HORSEBACK RIDING

The Lodge at Koele has an impressive stable. A variety of rides are available, beginning with 15-minute pony rides $10. Other rides include one, two or three hour excursions in the hills surrounding Koele. The two-hour Paniolo Trail ride ($65) travels up through guava groves and patches of Ironwood tree. Here the rider will enjoy the spectacular views of Maui and Molokai and have the opportunity to glimpse Axis deer, quail, wild turkeys and cattle and pass through the dryland forest of Kanepu'u. Also available are the one-hour Plantation Trail Ride ($35) and the Paniolo Lunch Ride which is a three hour trip ($90). Private trail rides can also be scheduled ($95 per two hours). Riders must wear long pants and sport shoes and children must be at least 9 years of age and four feet in height to ride. Riders must be 12 years or older to sign up for the Paniolo rides. Maximum weight of riders is 225 lbs. Safety helmets are provided for all riders. The horse drawn buggy is another equine activity. Stable phone numbers are (808) 565-4421 or 565-4424.

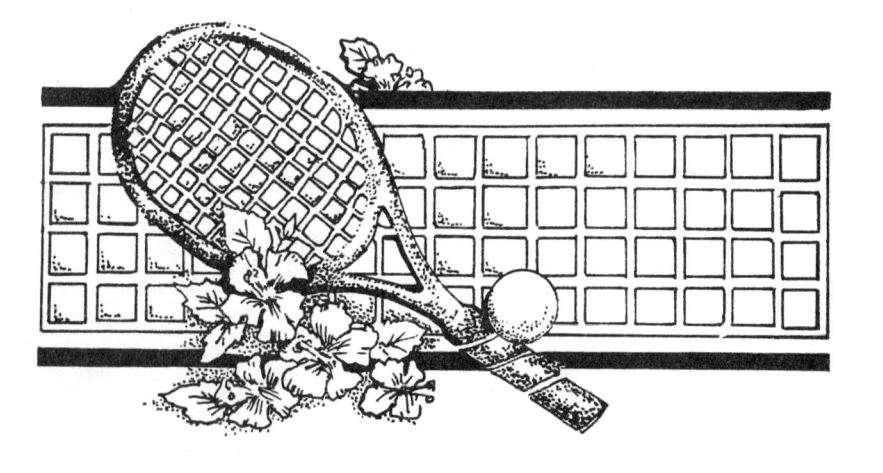

# HIKING

Walking sticks are provided in all the rooms at the Lodge at Koele for guest usage. It's almost impossible to resist strolling around the pastoral grounds. Near the Koele Lodge are two small houses. These were originally located where the orchid house is now. The Richardson families live here; their ancestors were among the early Lana'i paniolos. You can stroll around the front grounds to view the enormous Cook Island pine or enjoy watching guests try their hand at lawn bowling, croquet or miniature golf. Walk down to the horse stables or peek inside the old church. The stables are new, but the church was relocated due to the construction of the Lodge. A small school was also moved and it is currently being restored and perhaps will one day house Lana'i's first museum.

The Munro Trail is a 20 mile loop trek along the ridge of Lana'i. The view from the 3,370 ft. summit of Lanaihale can be spectacular on a clear day. This route can be tackled by four-wheel drive vehicles, but only during very dry conditions. For the adventurous, there is also the High Pasture Loop, the Old Cowboy Trail, Eucalyptus Ladder or Beyond the Blue Screen. A light to moderate weight raincoat might be a good idea to take along if you're planning on hiking. The concierge can provide you with a map showing the various routes. Picnics can be provided by the hotel.

# MISCELLANEOUS

Lawn bowling and both English and American croquet fields surround the Lodge at Koele. Guests can also borrow a mountain bike and ride into town, around the resort paths, or in the early morning or early evening they are allowed to ride along the golf course paths. One evening we followed one of the garden paths behind the putting green that led to a very steep golf cart track from the lower nine holes to the upper nine. It was so steep, in fact, that it proved quite a challenge to just walk the bikes up. After the journey up, we were delighted to find an ample supply of water and cups that reappeared every couple of holes on the golf course. Once on top we traveled around a few holes of the golf course which were fairly level. We were pleasantly surprised to find ourselves at the tee off for the 8th hole of the golf course, and as previously described, it was an inspired location. We then attempted to ride down from the tee to the green. The path down was so steep that it required brakes on full force to go slow enough to maintain control! Beyond is another picturesque lagoon and more golf cart trails to follow, again, on flat ground. The walk into town takes about 15 minutes at a fairly brisk pace, but only about 5 minutes by bike. Biking is a good option for seeing Lana'i City or if you want to sample some of Lana'i's local eateries.

Both resorts have wonderful swimming pools. The Koele pool, flanked by two bubbling jacuzzis was seldom busy. The Manele pool is slightly larger and, at a lower elevation than Koele, became quite hot during the afternoon. The adjacent poolside restaurant provided refreshing drinks and light food fare, while pool attendants would circulate with chilled towels and spring water spritzer for a quick facial spray. Guests at the resorts have pool privileges at both facilities.

Scuba diving, fishing expeditions, raft trips and other ocean excursions can be arranged through the concierge at either resort. Half day raft trips (2 1/2 hr.) run $40 - $60. Half day (3 1/2 hr.) sailing and snorkeling trips depart three times daily and run about $80.

At both resorts, a sheet describing the activities for the next day are left in the room with the evening maid service.

LODGE AT KOELE -- Daily activities greet the guest to the lodge. One day might be a pineapple cutting demonstration, another a display of ancient Hawaiian weapons or there may be an evening opportunity to visit with local women as they sew Hawaiian quilts. Each morning guests are invited to enjoy a complimentary hot beverage and just sit in the Great Hall and relax.

Tea is served in the tea room each afternoon and in the evening there are complimentary pupus, also available in the tea room. The music room has an array of interesting musical instruments lining the walls and the grand piano may be used by the guests. In the trophy rooms are board games; the library has books and evening movies with popcorn. Complimentary video tapes are available at the concierge for guests to view in their rooms. At night there is varied musical entertainment in the Great Hall. The twin fireplaces are ablaze and the overstuffed chairs invite you to slow down and relax. The fireplaces are lit, upon request, in the library, music or trophy room. This may be as close to heaven on earth as you can get.

MANELE BAY HOTEL - Manele also has varied daily activities. A tour of the resort is available and there is afternoon and evening entertainment in the lower lobby and the bar. Complimentary video tapes are available for guest use in their rooms and complimentary morning coffee is a pleasurable experience in Orchid Lounge or Coral Lounge.

## ART

If you're a resident or a visitor and interested in pursuing your artistic talents, you can register for the *Lana'i Art Program.* Classes are taught by local and visiting artists and might include a variety of paint medias or even craft classes such as bead making. For registration or other information phone (808) 565-7503.

## TOURS

Both Manele and Koele offer complimentary tours daily of their resorts. Just sign up at the concierge. The tour of Koele is especially informative and discusses the many unique pieces of art gracing the lobby, making it a worthwhile 30 minutes.

There is also a 1 1/2 - 2 hour guided island tour. It leaves from the Lodge at Koele and there is a $10 charge. Guests board a mini-van for a mini-tour of the island. Our guide was Joe, who had worked in the pineapple industry for many years before joining the resort staff. You'll learn a great deal about the island's history and see its more scenic points.

You can also take a historical tour without leaving the comfort of the Koele's music room. Several times a week guests are invited to a slide presentation depicting the early history of Lana'i.

## WHAT TO SEE

There are only three paved roads on Lana'i outside of Lana'i City, no stop lights, and very few street signs once you leave town. After driving around on even a dry day, we assure you that they aren't kidding when they recommend a four-wheel drive. On rainy days, you can be fairly certain you'll get stuck in the mud and muck! You can fairly well see all of Lana'i in a long day, but if you want to slow down, do some hiking, or simply sit in the sun on a quiet beach, there is plenty to occupy you for days. Either of the resorts can provide you with a map and advice. We were pleased that Pete Agliamo forfeited a day of fishing to act as a tour guide. Born in the Philippines, he has lived for 43 years on the island and worked for Dole driving pineapple trucks. Besides being an active fisherman he has hunted around the island for years and was a most knowledgeable guide. Leaving the driving to him was a delight as we cruised along the dirt roads and "talked story." Along the road to the Garden of the Gods we asked him if he was taking a short cut. Judging by the fact that we were zooming between pastures with cattle and abandoned pineapple fields with no street signs at all, we were certain we'd taken the back way, but he assured us we were on the main road. It seemed to us that it wouldn't be all that hard to get lost on Lana'i! Since there are no local quick marts, be sure you pack plenty of water and bring along a picnic, because we're sure you'll find the perfect spot to enjoy it.

We headed east and were pleasantly surprised to find the road to the *Garden of the Gods* was smooth, packed dirt that was free of ruts. (However this may not always be the case.) A 20 minute ride took us through a stand of ironwoods before we reached the large carved stone announcing our arrival in the Garden of the Gods, which was named in 1935. (It happened that the stone had been carved by Pete's daughter!) We arrived during mid-day, but the best time to see this lunar-like and rather mystical place is early morning or late evening. In the early

GARDEN OF THE GODS

morning, on a clear day, you can see the faint outline of Honolulu's skyscrapers and a sharp eye can observe axis deer out foraging. The rays of the sun in the early evening cast strange shadows on the amber baked earth and huge monolithic rocks and your imagination can do the rest. Interestingly enough, here, in what seems to be the middle of nowhere, with no one in sight, and a peaceful stillness, (except for the occasional call of a bird or the wind brushing against your cheek) are street signs! One indicates Awailua Rd. which is a very rugged and steep dirt path down to the ocean. Most of these roads are used by the local residents for fishing or hunting. Be advised, if you attempt to start down, there may be no place to turn around should you change your mind. Follow Polihua Road and you'll arrive at a stretch of white sandy beach with rolling sand dunes. According to Lawrence Kainoahou Gay, in his account entitled "True Stories of the Island of Lana'i," the word Polihua means Poli (cover or bay) and hua (eggs). He reports that in this area turtles would visit to lay their eggs above the high water mark. He had seen turtles, in days gone by, that were large enough to carry three people! This beach is not recommended for safe swimming or other water activities. The Kaena Road winds down to a very isolated area called Kaena Iki Point, which is the site of one of Lana'i's largest Heiaus.

*Shipwreck Beach*, or Kaiolohia, on Lana'i's northeast coast, is about a half hour drive along a paved road from the Lodge at Koele. Enroute down you'll note that there are many little rock piles. At first glance they appear to be of some relic of the distant past, however, they began to appear in the 1960's, a product of tourists and/or residents and have no historical or other significance. The road is lined with scrub brush, and as you begin the descent to the shoreline you catch a glimpse of the World War II liberty ship. Be sure to keep an eye out for pheasant, deer, turkeys and the small Franklin partridges.

At the bottom of the road you can choose to go left to Shipwreck Beach or continue straight and follow the coastline on the unpaved, dusty and very rugged Awalua Road to Club Lana'i. Club Lana'i is a day resort that shuttles visitors from Lahaina, Maui to the leeward shores of Lana'i for a day of relaxation and recreation--sort of a Hawaiian version of Gilligan's Island. It's a bit of a drive and slow going. Four wheel drive vehicles are advised. It is about five miles down the road to Keomuku. There are still remnants of the failed Maunalei Sugar Company near Keomuku, and a Japanese cemetery, also a memento of the failed sugar company. The beaches are wonderful for sunbathing or picnicking, but not advisable for swimming. Beyond are Naha and Lopa, two uninhabited old villages. The old Kalanakila a ka Malamalama church located near Keomuku, was recently renovated. There are also some ancient Hawaiian trails at Naha. The road ends at Naha and you will have to drive back by the same route.

If you're headed for Shipwreck Beach, go left where the sign says "Federation Camp." This is Lapahiki Road, and while dry and bumpy during our drive, we understand a little precipitation can make it impassible except in a four-wheel drive.

The dirt road is lined by Kiawe trees and deserted little houses. This is a getaway spot for the local residents, although there is no fresh water. The reef along Kaiolohia Beach is very wide, but the surf can be high and treacherous. During a storm, waves come crashing down over the liberty ship that now sits on the reef.

This was one of three Navy L.C.M.'s ships that were not shipwrecked, but purposely grounded in 1941-1942. The other two have disappeared after losing their battle to the ocean. Barges are also towed over, anchored and left to rot as well. The channel between here and Moloka'i is called Kolohi, which means mischievous and unpredictable. The channel between Lana'i and Maui is the 'Au'au channel which means to bathe. There were several ships that were wrecked here or on other parts of the island. In the 1820s the British ship *Alderman Wood* went aground; in 1826 the American ship *London* was wrecked off Lana'i. In 1931 George A. Crozier's *Charlotte C.* foundered somewhere along the beach. The 34 foot yawl called *Tradewind* was wrecked off the mouth of the Maunalei Valley on August 6, 1834 while cruising from Honolulu to Lahaina. There is a remnant of an old lighthouse and also some old petroglyph sites nearby. The concierge desk can give you a list of petroglyphs around the island. Please respect these sights. The beach is unsafe for swimming, but you might see some people shorefishing. Sometimes after storms, interesting shells, old bottles and assorted artifacts are washed up along the shoreline.

One area you probably won't visit is Pohaku "O" which roughly translates to mean rock. This is in the Mahana region of Lana'i on the island's leeward side. The rocks here resemble tombstones and were avoided by the early Hawaiians as a place of evil. In the evenings, and sometimes during the day if the breezes are favorable, the wind blowing by the rock creates an "O" sound that changes with the wind, which is the reason this rock received its evil connotations.

For another adventure, leave Lana'i City and follow Kaumalapau Hwy. past the small airport and continue on another five minutes toward Kaumalapau Harbor. It's paved all the way! The harbor isn't much to see, but the drive down to the water shows the dramatically different landscape of Lana'i's windward coastline. Here you can see the sharply cut rocky shoreline that drops steeply into the ocean, in some places more than 1,500 feet. The Kaunolu Bay can be accessed from the Kaumalapau Hwy. along a very, very rugged road. Follow the road just a bit further and you'll reach the harbor. The bulk of the island's materials come in by barge and barges were the route used to take the thousands of tons of pineapples to O'ahu for processing. Each pineapple crate weighed seven tons and a barge could haul 170 crates at a time. Today, pineapple production has become too expensive on Lana'i. Hawai'i is finding it hard to compete with countries such as the Philippines, where people are willing to work at a much lower daily wage and the fruit can be grown and processed for much less. In the past, freight was brought to Lana'i aboard the barges returning from Honolulu after delivering the pineapple. Today the Young Brothers have the contract for freight delivery.

*Hulopo'e Beach* is a splendid marine reserve. Along a crescent of white sandy beach is Hulopo'e Beach which fronts Manele Bay Hotel. It is also Lanai's best swimming beach. As with all beaches, be aware of surf conditions. There are attendants at the beach kiosk who can provide beach safety information. Although netting and spearfishing are not allowed, shorefishing is permitted.

The best snorkeling is in the mornings before the surf picks up. Across the bay from the Manele Hotel are a series of tidal pools. When the tide drifts down, sea creatures emerge, making this a great spot for exploration. The Lodge and Manele Bay Hotel both offer a handy "Tide Pool Guide" prepared by Kathleen Kapalka.

It notes that the Hulopo'e Bay and tide pool areas are both part of a marine life conservation district which was set up in 1976. Also included in the conservation district are Manele Bay and Pu'upehe Cove and as such, all animals and plants (dead or alive) are protected from collection or harm. The color brochure is an easy to follow guide to your personal tour of these wonderful tidal areas. Mollusks, arthropods, marine vertebrates, annelids, echinoderms, marine invertebrates and marine plants are described and illustrated. Safety tips and conservation tips include the fact that suntanning oils are detrimental and should be cleansed from the hands before reaching into the pools. This is an excellent brochure which will make your tidal pool adventure a valuable learning experience. Note: Reef shoes are available at the hotel's beach kiosk for resort guests, a recommended protection when prowling around the rocky shoreline.

Climb up the bluff and you will be rewarded with a great view of Maui and Kaho'olawe. A large monolithic rock sits off the bluff. This is Pu'upehe (often referred to as Sweetheart Rock) that carries a poignant local legend. As with most oral history, legends tend to take on the special character of the storyteller. Such is the story of Pu'upehe. We asked three people about the legend and heard three different versions. One made the hero into a jealous lover, the other a thoughtful one. So here is our interpretation. There was a strong handsome young Hawaiian man whose true love was a beautiful Hawaiian woman. They made a sea cave near Pu'upehe rock their lover's retreat. One day the man journeyed inland to replenish their supplies, leaving his love in the sea cave. He had gone some distance when he sensed an impending storm. He hurriedly returned to the sea cave, but the storm preceded him and his love had drowned in the cave. He was devastated. Using superhuman strength he carried her to the top of the monolithic rock called Pu'upehe and buried her there before jumping to his death. Whether there is truth to this legend is uncertain, but some years back a scientist did scale the top of the peak, which was no easy task, to investigate. No bones or other evidence was found. However, we were told that in ancient times, the bones were removed and hidden separately away. And so ends this sad tale of lost love.

Manele is a quaint boat port which offers excellent snorkeling just beyond the breakwater. When the surf at Hulopo'e is too strong, Lana'i tour boats often anchor here for snorkeling.

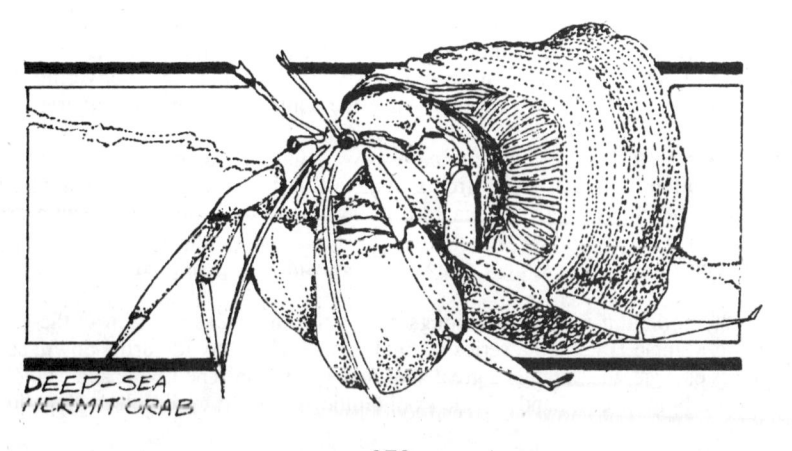

DEEP-SEA
HERMIT CRAB

# WILDLIFE

You'll notice very quickly that there are many, many birds on Lana‘i, a far greater number than on Maui. Fortunately for the birds, Lana‘i does not have the mongoose as a predator. Wild turkeys, the last non-native animal to be introduced to Lana‘i, are hunted in early November for about two weeks. They are easily spotted, but we understand as soon as November 1st appears (the turkeys must have calendars) they disappear until promptly after Thanksgiving. These wild birds look very lean and don't appear to make a very succulent Thanksgiving dinner. The easiest place to spot them is down near the Manele boat harbor where a group of turkeys and a pack of wild cats together enjoy the leftovers from the Trilogy boat's daily picnics. Pheasant are also hunted seasonally. Wild pigs and goats were rounded up and captured years ago, so the only island pigs are now in the piggery where they are raised for island consumption. Pronghorn antelope, introduced in 1959, have now been hunted to extinction. Twelve axis deer were introduced by George Munro and have adapted well to Lana‘i. It is estimated that there are some 3,000 - 6,000 animals and, given the fact that they produce offspring twice yearly, the numbers are ever growing. In fact deer far outnumber Lana‘i's human population. The deer run a mere 110 - 160 pounds and are hunted almost year round. It is easiest to spot these lean, quick deer in the early mornings or late evenings bounding across fields, but during the day they seek sheltered, shaded areas. There are still a few remaining mouflon sheep, a crossbreed between a goat and deer, which have distinctive and beautiful curved horns. You'll note many of the houses in Lana‘i City are decorated with arrays of horns and antlers across their porch or on a garage wall.

# BEACHES IN BRIEF

Along Lana‘i's Northern Shore is Polihua. There is an interesting stretch of long sand dunes. This coast is often very windy, and some days the blowing sand is intense. The surf conditions are dangerous and swimming should not be attempted, ever. Also along the Northern Shore is the area from Awalua to Naha. The beaches are narrow and the offshore waters are shallow with a wide reef. However, the water is often murky. Swimming and snorkeling are not recommended.

Surf conditions can be dangerous. Lopa on the Eastern shore is a narrow white sand beach that can be enjoyed for picnicking and sunbathing.

Along the Western coastline is Kaunola, a rocky shore with no sandy beach and no safe entry or exit. Conditions can be dangerous. Swimming is not advised at any time. Also on the Western shore is Kaumalapau Harbor, the deep water harbor used for shipping. Water activities are not recommended at any time.

The southern coastline affords the safest ocean conditions. Manele Bay is the small boat harbor, but water activity is not recommended due to heavy boat traffic. Hulopoe Bay is the island's best and most beautiful white sand beach. It is located in front of the Manele Bay Hotel. It is popular for swimming, surfing, boogie-boarding and snorkeling. The tidepools make for fun exploration and, although a marine preserve, shore fishing is permitted. On summer weekends the camping area is often filled with local residents. However, large swells, and high surf conditions can exist. During times of high surf, undertows become very strong. Entry is hazardous during these conditions. During these times it is not safe to stand or play even in the shore break, as severe injury can occur. Be aware of water safety signs. There are no lifeguards on duty. However, there are attendants at the resort's beach kiosk who might be able to answer questions you have. Never swim alone and always exercise good water safety judgement.

## CHILDCARE

The Manele Bay Hotel has daytime childcare which can be used by Lodge guests as well. At the time of our visit it was complimentary and not in much demand. It may be that they will charge for it in the future. The 9 a.m. - 3 p.m. program is run by the pool staff and is a very casual affair where the children can play games or swim in the pool. Private babysitting is also available through the concierge for about $10 an hour.

## RECOMMENDED READING

An excellent account of the history of the island is *"True Stories of the Island of Lana'i"* by Lawrence Kainoahou Gay, the son of Charles Gay. First published in 1965 and reprinted in 1981 it is available for $12 at the resort gift shops on Lana'i and probably could be obtained through bookstores on the neighboring islands as well.

MANELE BAY RESORT

# RECOMMENDED READING

Ashdown, Inez. *Ke Alaloa O Maui. Authentic History and Legends of the Valley Isle.* Hawaii: Kama'aina Historians. 1971.

Ashdown, Inez. *Stories of Old Lahaina.* Honolulu: Hawaiian Service. 1976.

Barrow, Terence. *Incredible Hawaii.* Vermont: Charles Tuttle Co. 1974.

Begley, Bryan. *Taro in Hawaii.* Honolulu: The Oriental Publishing Co. 1979.

Bird, Isabella. *Six Months in the Sandwich Islands.* Tokyo: Tuttle. 1988

Boom, Bob and Christensen, Chris. *Important Hawaiian Place Names.* Hawaii: Bob Boom Books. 1978.

Chisholm, Craig. *Hawaiian Hiking Trails.* Oregon: Fernglen Press. 1994.

Christensen, Jack Shields. *Instant Hawaiian.* Hawaii: The Robert Boom Co. 1971.

Clark, John. *Beaches of Maui County.* Honolulu: University Press of Hawaii. 1980.

Daws, Gavan. *The Illustrated Atlas of Hawaii.* Australia: Island Heritage. 1980.

*Echos of Our Song.* Honolulu: University of Hawaii Press.

Fielding, Ann. *Hawaiian Reefs and Tidepools.* Hawaii: Oriental Pub. Co.

Haraguchi, Paul. *Weather in Hawaiian Waters.* 1983.

*Hawaii Island Paradise.* California: Wide World Publishing. 1987.

Hazama, Dorothy. *The Ancient Hawaiians.* Honolulu: Hogarth Press.

Judd, Gerrit. *Hawaii, an Informal History.* New York: Collier Books. 1961.

Kaye, Glen. *Hawaiian Volcanos.* Nevada: K.C. Publications, 1987.

Kepler, Angela. *Maui's Hana Highway.* Honolulu: Mutual Publishing. 1987

Kepler, Cameron B. and Angela Kay. *Haleakala, A Guide to the Mountain.* Honolulu: Mutual Publishing. 1988.

Kyselka, Will and Lanterman, Ray. *Maui, How it Came to Be.* Honolulu: The University Press of Hawaii. 1980.

*Lahaina Historical Guide.* Tokyo: Maui Historical Society. 1971.

Lahaina Restoration Foundation, *Story of Lahaina.* Lahaina: 1980.

London, Jack. *Stories of Hawaii.* Honolulu: Mutual Publishing. 1965.

Mack, Jim. *Haleakala and The Story Behind the Scenery*. Nevada: K.C. Publications, 1984.

Mrantz, Maxine. *Whaling Days in Old Hawaii*. Honolulu: Aloha Graphics. 1976.

*Na Mele O Hawai'i Nei*. Honolulu: University of Hawaii Press. 1970

Nickerson, Roy. *Lahaina, Royal Capital of Hawaii*. Hawaii: Hawaiian Service. 1980.

*On The Hana Coast*. Hong Kong: Emphasis Int'l Ltd. and Carl Lundquist. 1987.

Pukui, Mary K. et al. *The Pocket Hawaiian Dictionary*. Honolulu: The University of Hawaii Press. 1975.

Randall, John. *Underwater Guide to Hawaiian Reef Fishes*. Hawaii: Treasures of Time. 1981.

Smith, Robert. *Hiking Maui*. California. 1990.

Stevenson, Robert Louis. *Travels in Hawaii*. Honolulu: University of Hawaii Press. 1973.

Tabrah, Ruth. *Maui The Romantic Island*. Nevada: KC Publications. 1985.

Thorne, Chuck. *50 Locations for Scuba & Snorkeling*. 1983.

Titcomb, M. *Native Use of Fish in Hawaii*. Honolulu: University of Hawaii Press. 1952.

Twain, Mark. *Letters from Mark Twain*. Hawaii: University of Hawaii Press. 1966.

Twain, Mark. *Mark Twain in Hawaii*. Colorado: Outdoor Books. 1986.

Wallin, Doug. *Exotic Fishes and Coral of Hawaii and the Pacific*. 1974.

Westervelt, H. *Myths and Legends of Hawaii*. Honolulu: Mutual Publishing. 1987.

Wisniewski, Richard A.. *The Rise and Fall of the Hawaiian Kingdom*. Honolulu: Pacific Basin Enterprises. 1979.

*"One cannot determine in advance to love a particular woman,*

*nor can one so determine to love Hawaii.*

*One sees, and one loves or does not love.*

*With Hawaii it seems always to be love at first sight.*

*Those for whom the islands were made,*

*or who were made for the islands,*

*are swept off their feet in the first moments of meeting,*

*embrace and are embraced."*

Jack London

# INDEX

# ENJOY ALL THREE

## OF OUR PARADISE FAMILY GUIDES TO HAWAII

*Finally, Hawaiian guides for every budget and every member of the family. Designed for travelers who want to set their own pace with complete vacation control. These are THE guides to have. Complemented by quarterly newsletters which update the changes in the islands between guidebook revisions. Plenty of "insider" information from authors who really know the islands! These and other Hawaiian titles and videos may be ordered direct from Paradise Publications.*

### MAUI, A PARADISE FAMILY GUIDE
**(Including the Island of Lana'i)** by Greg & Christie Stilson
The island of Maui is one of Hawai'i's most popular. This guide is packed with information on over 150 condos & hotels, 200 restaurants, 50 great beaches, sights to see and travel tips for the valley island. All new! The island of Lana'i, as a part of the County of Maui, has been added to this popular guide. Lana'i recently joined the tourist industry with the opening of two fabulous new resorts. There is fine dining, local eateries, remote beaches, wonderful hikes and an enchantment unlike any other island. *"A down-to-earth, nuts-and-bolts companion with answers to most any question."* L.A Times. 360 pp, multi-indexed, maps, illustrations, $12.95. 6th ed.

### KAUA'I, A PARADISE FAMILY GUIDE, by Don & Bea Donohugh
Island accommodations, restaurants, secluded beaches, recreation and tour options, remote historical sites, an unusual and unique island tour, this guide covers it all. "If you need a 'how to do it' book to guide your next to Kaua'i, here's the one."..."*this guide may be the best available for the island. It has that personal touch of authors who have spent many happy hours digging up facts.*" Hawaii Magazine. 290 pp, maps, $14.95. 4th ed.

### HAWAI'I: THE BIG ISLAND, A PARADISE FAMILY GUIDE,
by John Penisten. Outstanding for its completeness, this well-organized guide provides useful information for people of every budget and lifestyle. Each chapter features the author's personal recommendations and "best bets." Comprehensive information on more than 70 island accommodations and 150 restaurants. Sights to see, recreational activities, beaches, and helpful travel tips. 284 pages. Maps and illustrations. $14.00. 4th ed.

**UPDATE NEWSLETTERS!** *THE MAUI UPDATE, THE KAUA'I UPDATE,* and *HAWAI'I: THE BIG ISLAND UPDATE* are quarterly newsletters published by Paradise Publications that highlight the most current island events. Each features late breaking tips on the newest restaurants, island activities or special, not-to-be missed events. Each newsletter is available at the single issue price of $2.50 or a yearly subscription (four issues) rate of $10. Orders to Canada $12 per year.

*We know you have a wonderful visit to Maui. Since this book expresses primarily our own opinions on accommodations, restaurants, and recreation, we would sincerely appreciate hearing of your experiences. Any updates or changes would also be welcomed. Please address all correspondence to Paradise Publications.*

# ORDERING INFORMATION

*Available from Paradise Publications are books and videos to enhance your travel library and assist with your travel plans, or provide a special gift for someone who is planning a trip! For a full listing of current titles send request to Paradise Publications. Prices are subject to change without notice.*

## BOOKS

*MAUI, THE ROMANTIC ISLAND*, and *KAUA'I, THE UNCONQUERABLE* by K.C. Publications. These two books present full color photographs depicting the most magnificent sights on each island. Brief descriptive text adds perspective. Highly recommended. 9 x 12, 48 pages, $6.95 each, paperback. Also available from K.C. Publications: *HALEAKALA* and *HAWAII VOLCANOES* Each fascinating and informative book is filled with vivid photographs depicting these natural volcanic wonders. A great gift or memento. 9 x 12, $6.95 each.

*DIVERS GUIDE TO MAUI* by Chuck Thorne. This easy-to-use guide will give you all the information you need to choose the perfect dive site. $9.95.

*HAWAII GOLF GUIDE*, published by TeeBox, features every island course. Information is comprehensive covering the basics, such as course location, number of holes and phone number, as well as in-depth information on golf course features aqnd course strategy. 165 pages, published in 1994. $12.95.

*HAWAIIAN HIKING TRAILS*
by Craig Chisholm. This very attractive and accurate guide details 49 of Hawaii's best hiking trails. Includes photography, topographical maps, and detailed directions. An excellent book for the outdoorsperson! 152 pgs., $15.95. 1994.

*KAUAI HIKING TRAILS*
by Craig Chisholm. New from Fernglen Press this 160 page book features color photographs, topographical maps and detailed directions to Kaua'i's best hiking trails. A quality publication. $12.95.

*HIKING MAUI*
by Robert Smith. Discover 27 hiking areas all around Maui. 5 x 8 paperback, 160 pages. $9.95. Also by Robert Smith. *HIKING KAUA'I*, over 40 hiking trails throughout Kaua'i. 116 pages, $9.95. *HIKING HAWAII (The Big Island)*, 157 pages, $9.95. Black & white photographs and maps.

*COOKING WITH ALOHA*
by Elvira Monroe and Irish Margah. Discover the flavors and smells of the Hawaiian islands in your own kitchen with this easy-to-follow cookbook. appetizers to desserts are covered. 9 x 12, paperback, 184 pages, $9.95.

## MAPS!

By popular request, we now carry the excellent series of full-color topographical maps by cartographer James A. Bier. Maps are available for $2.95 each for the islands of O'ahu, Maui, Kaua'i and the Big Island of Hawai'i.

# VIDEOS    (All Videos are VHS format)

**FOREVER HAWAII** -- This 60 minute, video portrait features all six major Hawaiian islands. (Note: Does not include coverage of the new resorts on Lana'i.) It includes breathtaking views from the snowcapped peaks of Mauna Kea to the bustling city of Waikiki, from the magnificent Waimea Canyon to the spectacular Halakeala Crater. A lasting memento. $24.95

**FOREVER MAUI** -- An in-depth visit to Maui with scenic shots and interesting stories about the Valley Isle. An excellent video for the first time, or even the returning Maui visitor. 30 minutes. $19.95

**FLIGHT OF THE CANYON BIRD** -- An inspired view of the Garden Island of Kaua'i from a bird's eye perspective; an outstanding 30 minute piece of cineamatagraphy. This short feature presentation explores the lush tropical rainforests surrounding Waialeale (the wettest spot on earth), the awesome Waimea Canyon and the Napili Coastline. The narration explores the geologic beginnings of the island and its historical beginnings as well. A lasting memento or a gift! $19.95.

**EXPLORE HAWAII: A TRAVEL GUIDE** -- The scenes are similar to that of Forever Hawai'i, but this is a very fast paced 30-minute tour of all six islands. One helpful feature of this tape is the way place names of the areas being viewed are displayed on the screen. $14.95.

**KUMU HULUA: KEEPERS OF A CULTURE** -- This 85-minute tape was funded by the Hawaii State Foundation on Culture and Arts. This beautifully filmed work includes hulas from various troupes on various islands, attired in their brilliantly colored costumes and explores the unique qualities of hula as well as explaining the history. $29.95.

**HULA - LESSONS ONE AND TWO** -- "Lovely Hula Hands" and "Little Brown Gal" are the two featured hulas taught by Carol "Kalola" Lorenzo who explains the basic steps of the hula. A fun and interesting video for the whole family. 30 minutes. $29.95.

*FREE!* A complimentary copy of Paradise Publication's quarterly newsletter, *THE MAUI UPDATE*, is available (at no charge) by writing Paradise Publications (Attention: Newsletter Dept.) 8110 S.W. Wareham, Suite 304, Portland, OR 97223, and enclosing a self-addressed, stamped, #10 size envelope.

**SHIPPING**: In the Continental U.S.-- Please add $4 for 1 to 4 items (books or videos). Each additional item over 4, please add $1. Orders shipped promptly by UPS (United Parcel Service). Addresses which are Post Office boxes will be shipped U.S. Mail, first class. If you'd prefer items shipped bookrate mail, we'll be happy to quote you shipping costs. Hawai'i and Alaska -- Please add $3.50 for the first book/tape, $1 each additional book/tape when shipped to the same address. Orders shipped U.S. first class mail. Canadian Orders -- Please add $4 for the first book and $1 each additional book/tape. Orders shipped U.S. airmail. UPS overnight or 2-day mail service available.

Include your check or money order/Visa or Mastercard information:
**PARADISE PUBLICATIONS, 8110 S.W. Wareham, Suite 304,**
**Portland, Oregon 97223          Phone (503) 246-1555**

# Hawai'i: The Big Island, 4th Edition
## Making the Most of Your Family Vacation

### by John Penisten

This Paradise Family Guide by John Penisten contains all the information you need to ensure that your stay on the Big Island is a most enjoyable one. Included in this essential guidebook for families are detailed descriptions of:

- lodging—the best locations, the best deals
- restaurants—prices, menus, children's meals
- beaches and beach activities—where to snorkel, directions to little-known hideaways
- recreation—golf, tennis, horseback riding
- tours—land, air, and water

**Available now from Prima**